Lecture Notes in Computer Science 1777

Edited by G. Goos, J. Hartmanis and J. van Leeuwen

Springer
Berlin
Heidelberg
New York
Barcelona
Hong Kong
London
Milan
Paris
Singapore
Tokyo

Carlo Zaniolo   Peter C. Lockemann
Marc H. Scholl   Torsten Grust (Eds.)

Advances in Database Technology – EDBT 2000

7th International Conference
on Extending Database Technology
Konstanz, Germany, March 27-31, 2000
Proceedings

Springer

Series Editors

Gerhard Goos, Karlsruhe University, Germany
Juris Hartmanis, Cornell University, NY, USA
Jan van Leeuwen, Utrecht University, The Netherlands

Volume Editors

Carlo Zaniolo
University of California
Computer Science Department
Los Angeles, CA 90095, USA
E-mail: zaniolo@cs.ucla.edu

Peter C. Lockemann
University of Karlsruhe
Computer Science Department
P.O. Box 6980, 76128 Karlsruhe, Germany
E-mail: lockeman@ira.uka.de

Marc H. Scholl
Torsten Grust
University of Konstanz
P.O. Box D188, 78457 Konstanz, Germany
E-mail: {Marc.Scholl,Torsten.Grust}@uni-konstanz.de

Cataloging-in-Publication Data applied for

Die Deutsche Bibliothek - CIP-Einheitsaufnahme

Advances in database technology : proceedings / EDBT 2000, 7th
International Conference on Extending Database Technology, Konstanz,
Germany, March 27 - 31, 2000. Carlo Zaniolo ... (ed.). - Berlin ;
Heidelberg ; New York ; Barcelona ; Hong Kong ; London ; Milan ; Paris ;
Singapore ; Tokyo : Springer, 2000
    (Lecture notes in computer science ; Vol. 1777)
    ISBN 3-540-67227-3

CR Subject Classification (1998): H.2, H.4, H.3

ISSN 0302-9743
ISBN 3-540-67227-3 Springer-Verlag Berlin Heidelberg New York

Typesetting: Camera-ready by author, data conversion by Steingraeber Satztechnik GmbH, Heidelberg
Printed on acid-free paper   SPIN: 10719855   06/3142   5 4 3 2 1 0

Foreword

EDBT 2000 is the seventh conference in a series dedicated to the advancement of database technology. This year's conference special theme, "Connect Millions of Users and Data Sources," underscores the importance of databases for the information age that is dawning with the new millennium. The importance derives not just from the observation that the information age essentially rests on the convergence of communications, computing, and storage. Equally important, many of the concepts and techniques underlying the success of database systems have independent meaning and impact for today's distributed information systems. The papers in the volume should also be seen in this light.

The EDBT 2000 conference program includes 30 research papers selected by the program committee out of 187 submissions, covering advances in research, development, and applications of databases. The conference program also includes six industry and applications papers, a panel discussion, six tutorials, and several software demonstrations. The conference features three distinguished invited speakers: Ashish Gupta discusses database issues in electronic commerce, Stefano Ceri addresses the impact and challenges of XML on databases, and Andreas Reuter shares his views on new perspectives on database technology. The technical contributions presented at the EDBT 2000 conference are collected and preserved in this volume that we are pleased to present to you with the expectation that it will serve as a valuable research and reference tool in your professional life.

The conference would not have been possible without the efforts of many dedicated people. In particular we would like to thank the organization committee, Jay Grieves for supporting the Microsoft Conference Management Toolkit, the program committee members, and the reviewers whose names are also listed in the proceedings.

March 2000   Carlo Zaniolo, Peter C. Lockemann,
                                                  Marc H. Scholl, Torsten Grust

Sponsorship

Promoted by the EDBT Endowment in cooperation with the VLDB Endowment.

Sponsored by: Software AG
Rentenanstalt/SwissLife
Credit Suisse
IBM Deutschland
Sun Microsystems
ORACLE
Dornier GmbH
Swiss Informatics Society (SI) DBTA
German Informatics Society (GI) FG Datenbanksysteme
Universitätsgesellschaft Konstanz e.V.

Conference Organization

General Chair	Peter C. Lockemann	(U Karlsruhe, Germany)
Program Chair	Carlo Zaniolo	(UC Los Angeles, USA)
Executive Chair	Marc H. Scholl	(U Konstanz, Germany)
EDBT Endowment Liaison	Joachim W. Schmidt	(U Hamburg, Germany)
Industrial Program Chair	Peter Dadam	(U Ulm, Germany)
Panel & Tutorial Chair	Klaus R. Dittrich	(U Zürich, Switzerland)
Software Demonstrations	Torsten Grust	(U Konstanz, Germany)

EDBT Endowment Executive Board

Paolo Atzeni	(Italy)	Michele Missikoff	(Italy)
Stefano Ceri	(Italy)	Joachim W. Schmidt	(Germany)
Keith G. Jeffery	(UK)		

Program Committee

Karl Aberer	(Germany)	Yannis Manolopoulos	(Greece)
Gustavo Alonso	(Switzerland)	Yossi Matias	(Israel)
Ricardo Baeza-Yates	(Chile)	Giansalvatore Mecca	(Italy)
Roberto Bayardo	(USA)	Tova Milo	(Israel)
Michael Böhlen	(Denmark)	Shinichi Morishita	(Japan)
Klemens Böhm	(Switzerland)	Maria Orlowska	(Australia)
Surajit Chauduri	(USA)	Gultekin Öszoyoglu	(USA)
Peter Dadam	(Germany)	Ernest Teniente	(Spain)
Klaus R. Dittrich	(Switzerland)	Anthony Tomasic	(USA)
Asuman Dogac	(Turkey)	Peter Triantafillou	(Greece)
Piero Fraternali	(Italy)	Vassilis Tsotras	(USA)
Fosca Giannotti	(Italy)	Shalom Tsur	(USA)
Leana Golubchik	(USA)	Rajeev Rastogi	(USA)
Peter M.D. Gray	(UK)	Tore Risch	(Sweden)
Sergio Greco	(Italy)	Pierangela Samarati	(Italy)
Ralf Hartmut Güting	(Germany)	Praveen Seshadri	(USA)
Marc Gyssens	(Belgium)	Eric Simon	(France)
Jiawei Han	(Canada)	Nicolas Spyratos	(France)
Theo Härder	(Germany)	Nandit Soparkar	(USA)
Daniel A. Keim	(Germany)	V.S. Subrahmanian	(USA)
Martin Kersten	(The Netherlands)	Dan Suciu	(USA)
Donald Kossmann	(Germany)	A Min Tjoa	(Austria)
Laks Lakshmanan	(India)	Ling Tok Wang	(Singapore)
Jorge Lobo	(USA)	Peter Wood	(UK)
Bertram Ludäscher	(USA)	Pavel Zezula	(Czech Republic)

Additional Referees

Acharya, Swarup
Adya, Atual
Akinde, Michael O.
Amer-Yahia, Sihem
Atluri, Vijay
Barros, Alistair
Baru, Chaitan
Bauer, Thomas
Bex, Geert Jan
Bhatia, Randeep
Bonatti, Piero
Bonchi, Francesco
Braumandl, Reinhard
Breitbart, Yuri
Casati, Fabio
Chakrabarti, Kaushik
Che, Dunren
Chou, Cheng-Fu
Ciaccia, Paolo
Comai, Sara
Dawson, Steven
De Capitani d.Vimercati, S.
Dekhtyar, Alex
Dix, Jürgen
Eiter, Thomas
Enderle, Jost
Erwig, Martin
Eyal, Anat
Ezbiderli, Murat
Fayzullin, Marat
Ferrari, Elena
Flesca, Sergio
Frankel, Micky
Friedrich, Matthias
Jensen, Christian S.
Jensen, Ole G.
Jensen, Viviane C.
Josifovski, Vanja
Garofalakis, Minos
Geerts, Floris
Geppert, Andreas
Giacometti, Arnaud
Gupta, Amarnath
Gyles, Stefan
Haas, Peter
Halfeld Ferrari Alves, M.

Heflin, Jeff
Helmer, Sven
Hinneburg, Alexander
Icdem, Cengiz
Johnson, Theodore
Kappel, Gerti
Kesim, Nihan
Kim, Eddie
Kohli, Madhur
Kollios, George
Korth, Hank
Laurent, Dominique
Lechtenbörger, Jens
Lee, Mong Li
Liang, Weifa
Loyer, Yann
Macherius, Ingo
Manco, Giuseppe
Mangisengi, Oscar
Marjanovic, Olivera
Massink, Mieke
Merialdo, Paolo
Mortazavi-Asl, Behzad
Nanni, Mirco
Nanopoulos, Alex
Narasayya, Vivek
Navarro, Gonzalo
Neven, Frank
Ng, Raymond
Nierman, Andrew
Oguz, Deniz
Olivé, Antoni
Orlowski, Marian
Ozcan, Fatma
Ozsoyoglu, Z. Meral
Palopoli, Luigi
Papadopoulos, Apostolos
Papakonstantinou, Yannis
Paraboschi, Stefano
Patel, Jignesh
Pedreschi, Dino
Pei, Jian
Preece, Alun
Psaila, Giuseppe
Qiu, Shiguang
Rauber, Andreas

Reichert, Manfred
Richter, Yossi
van de Riet, Reind
Ritter, Norbert
Ross, Robert
Rouveirol, Celine
Ruggieri, Salvatore
Saccà, Domenico
Sadiq, Shazia
Sadri, Fereidoon
Sander, Jörg
Schiefer, Josef
Schneider, Markus
da Silva, Ilmerio
Souah, Rachid
Srikant, Ramakrishnan
Stamate, Daniel
Stocker, Konrad
Strzeletz, Thomas
Stumptner, Markus
Subrahmanian, V.S.
Subramanian, Subbu N.
Sze, Eng Koon
Teo, Pit Koon
Tesch, Thomas
Thanh, Huynh Ngoc
Thanh Binh, Nguyen
Theodoridis, Yannis
Toroslu, Hakki
Trajcevski, Goce
Tsoukatos, Ilias
Tumer, Arif
Tung, Anthony K.H.
Turini, Franco
Tzouramanis, Theodoros
Ulosoy, Uzgur
Vassalos, Vasilis
Venkatesh, G.
Vianu, Victor
Wang, Ke
Westmann, Till
Zadorozhny, Vladimir
Zhang, Donghui
Zhou, Xiaofang

Table of Contents

Invited Paper

Indexing & Searching

Mediators & Semantic Integration

Cooperation & Security

Performance

Industrial & Applications Track: Performance

Data Warehousing

Semistructured Data

Data Mining

Industrial & Applications Track: XML

Spatial & Temporal Information

Systems & Applications

Query Systems

Author Index

Invited Paper

XML: Current Developments and Future Challenges for the Database Community

Stefano Ceri, Piero Fraternali, and Stefano Paraboschi

Dipartimento di Elettronica e Informazione
Politecnico di Milano
Piazza Leonardo da Vinci, 32
Milano, Italy I-20133
{ceri/fraterna/parabosc}@elet.polimi.it

Abstract While we can take as a fact "the Web changes everything", we argue that "XML is the means" for such a change to make a significant step forward. We therefore regard XML-related research as the most promising and challenging direction for the community of database researchers. In this paper, we approach XML-related research by taking three progressive perspectives. We first consider XML as a data representation standard (in the small), then as a data interchange standard (in the large), and finally as a basis for building a new repository technology. After a broad and necessarily coarse-grain analysis, we turn our focus to three specific research projects which are currently ongoing at the Politecnico di Milano, concerned with XML query languages, with active document management, and with XML-based specifications of Web sites.

1 Introduction

XML is currently in the process of replacing HTML as standard document markup language for the Web; it was developed as an evolution and simplification of SGML, another document markup language which had been available for more than a decade without really influencing the development of Web applications. Database researchers had very little impact on XML design, yet XML improves over HTML along two of the main directions of interest of our research community, i.e., providing data semantics and data independence.

- **Data semantics** is introduced within XML documents by means of *semantic tags* which annotate XML documents; we say that XML documents are self-describing, as the semantic annotations that each document carries along provide information about the document's content. In addition, XML documents may comply with a *document type definition* (DTD), a specification that is given separately from the document, a sort of document schema, that indicates the generic structure of one or more XML documents.
- **Data independence** is achieved because XML documents are specified independently from their presentation. Document presentation is the subject of a companion standard (XSL) which dictates how a *style sheet* can be

C. Zaniolo et al. (Eds.): EDBT 2000, LNCS 1777, pp. 3–17, 2000.
© Springer-Verlag Berlin Heidelberg 2000

associated with an XML document in order to present it on a Web browser. Therefore, issues such as the choice of character sets used to represent a given portion of XML document, the size of these characters, or the various ways of emphasizing character strings are all omitted from the document specification in XML.

The strengths of XML in the domains of data semantics and data independence have slowly been understood and fully appreciated in all their positive implications; they are causing a progressive shift in the emphasis given to the XML standard. XML is turning from a pure document markup language into being considered as an extremely powerful data interchange format, i.e., an instrument for enabling data publication by various applications which need to co-operate. In essence, XML is now being considered as the key enabling concept for achieving data interoperability, a long-term objective of database research.

This shift in the emphasis on XML is becoming evident also within the W3C Consortium. In the "XML Initiative Web page" at http://w3c.org/XML we find the following description of XML goals. XML will:

- *Enable internationalized media-independent electronic publishing.*
- *Allow industries to define platform-independent protocols for the exchange of data, especially the data of electronic commerce.*
- *Deliver information to user agents in a form that allows automatic processing after receipt.*
- *Make it easy for people to process data using inexpensive software.*
- *Allow people to display information the way they want it.*
- *Provide metadata – data about information – that will help people find information and help information producers and consumers find each other.*

The above goals clearly position XML as vehicle for data exchange; they also emphasize the central role that is still played by data and data repositories in the deployment of applications, most notably for e-commerce, and the increasing importance of metadata in future Web applications. The database research community is thus strategically positioned "in the middle" of this evolution stream, and should not miss the many opportunities that are currently offered for driving the stream. In this paper, we analyze XML from three main perspectives, by looking at it first as a data representation standard (in the small), then as a data interchange standard (in the large) and finally as a basis for building a new repository technology. We next describe the recent research that has been carried out at our institute (Politecnico di Milano) on XML.

2   XML As a Data Representation Standard

We approach our survey of research directions on XML by first taking the viewpoint of XML as a data representation standard. In this context, we need abstractions for modeling, querying, viewing, updating, constraining, and mining a collection of XML documents. This viewpoint emphasizes the need for managing XML data as a single collection "in the small" (although such small world can be very large), disregarding for the time being data interchange and interoperability.

2.1   Data Modeling with XML

The notion of DTD, which can be associated with XML documents, introduces data modeling in the XML world. By means of DTDs, it is possible to specify a hierarchy of concepts (or elements) that constitute the XML document; each element may contain PCDATA (i.e., text strings that can be suitably parsed and encoded), attributes (i.e., properties given in the format of pairs <attribute_name, attribute_value>), and then recursively other elements, with arbitrary cardinality (at most one, exactly one, zero or more, one or more). One element may contain another element chosen among a list of several alternative elements. XML documents are lacking the notion of elementary types (such as integer or floating point numbers), as the only supported type in a document is that of PCDATA. For their ability of precisely describing recursive structures (with iterations, optionalities, alternatives, and so on), DTDs correspond to a grammar; an XML document is *valid* relative to its DTD if it can be produced by that grammar.

DTDs have several analogies with object-oriented data models. Every XML element can be considered as equivalent to an object, whereas the corresponding DTD element can be considered as equivalent to an object class. Each object can explicitly be associated with its object identifier (ID attribute), and objects can refer to other objects (IDREF and IDREFS attributes); however, IDREFs are not typed, hence references from one DTD element are not constrained to refer to instances of a given DTD element. The use of alternatives corresponds to union types, a feature that is rarely found in object-oriented models. The missing features with respect to object-oriented data models include class hierarchies, typed object references, and certain integrity constraints; these are the subject of an extension of XML, called XML Schema, which is currently under definition by the W3C (and addressed later on in the paper).

Due to this analogy, we could consider DTD design an instance of the generic problem of database design; indeed, we expect that this will sooner or later be recognized, and that therefore DTD design will be driven by data design abstractions and methods. There is a strong analogy between designing the DTD and conceptually designing a Web application modeled in XML, and Web modeling is in turn becoming a popular subject [7]. So far, however, this was rarely recognized, mainly because there are few instances of XML data and even fewer instances of top-down-designed XML data. Certain data design aspects cause conceptual difficulties and non-obvious trade-offs, such as:

- The alternative use of either attributes or element containment for modeling the same reality.
- How to deal with the substructuring of PCDATA contained by a given element (a typical feature of XML seen as a markup language but not obviously modeled and managed by XML repositories).
- How to deal with element ordering.
- In general, how to deal with all the missing integrity constraints.

Another interesting problem is that of **inferring a DTD** for XML data when this is not natively provided with a DTD. The inference of a DTD should be driven by well-defined requirements, leading to the identification of synthetic DTD structures capturing most of the structure of the XML document, so as to further infer properties that may be useful for its efficient data storage and retrieval. A similar problem is inferring a common DTD for two distinct documents which are merged into a single one. Work in this direction was done at Stanford University in the context of Lorel by defining the notion of *data guides* [12].

2.2 Querying XML

Many efforts of the XML research community are focused on designing a standard XML query language. The first initiative in the field occurred when Dan Suciu and colleagues from AT&T and INRIA deposited a proposed XML query language, called XML-QL [9,11], as a request for standardization to the W3C, thus fueling the debate on query languages for XML. Even before, the language Lorel had been defined at Stanford by Serge Abiteboul, Jennifer Widom and colleagues in the context of semi-structured databases and then found fully adequate for supporting XML queries [1]. The W3C has then taken the lead in driving the efforts towards a standard XML query language, first by organizing a well-attended workshop [17], next by starting a working group focused on the problem, which is expected to produce a standard recommendation by the end of the year 2000 (and hopefully sooner).

In a recent article [4] we carefully compared five XML query languages which are currently proposed. Besides the already mentioned XML-QL and Lorel, we reviewed also the query language facilities already present in XSL [19] and then XQL [15], a simple query language for selecting and filtering XML documents. Finally, we considered XML-GL, a language proposed within Politecnico offering a nice graph-based graphical interface [5]. In that article, we listed several features that should be possessed by an XQL query language, and then analyzed the available documentation (and in certain cases the prototypes) of the languages to check whether those features were supported.

The result of the analysis is represented in Fig. 1, borrowed from [4]. The figure shows that languages can be broadly classified into two classes, the one of *expressive, multi-document query languages* and the one of *single-document query languages*; the main distinction between the two classes is the ability of joining two documents from arbitrary data sources. Between the two classes, XML-GL offers an easy-to-use paradigm, based on the fact that DTDs can be described as hierarchical structures (interconnected by references) and similarly queries can be represented as selections and annotations of those interconnected hierarchies. Although Lorel and XML-QL appear to be comparable in their expressive power (modulo some extensions required to XML-QL), the two languages present quite a different syntactic style; Lorel is deliberately very similar to OQL, while XML-QL is based on an XML-like hierarchical organization of tags, and thus appears much more verbose than Lorel. This can be best appreciated by looking at comparative query examples in [4].

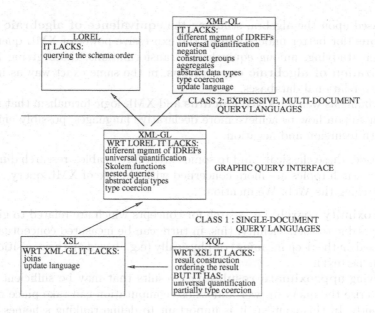

Fig. 1. Classification of query languages for XML (from [4])

In general, Fig. 1 shows the need for:

- A powerful query language, covering all the aspects that are available in a typical SQL- or OQL-like language, normally used from within a suitable API.
- A sublanguage of the above, implementing simple selections and projections of XML documents, possibly compatible with XPath, the path expression language designed by the W3C XSL working group and already defined within the XSL standard.
- A graphic, QBE-like language allowing users to express a subset of the query language identified above in a simple, user-friendly way. Such graphic language should be offered within an interface capable of alternating between the visual and textual expression of queries, as it is customary in many database products.

The field of query language design appears to be frozen until the W3C Working Group will present its results, but a lot of language-independent research can still take place along several dimensions, including classical ones such as:

- Defining an **XML algebra**, i.e., defining a suite of orthogonal and minimal algebraic operators that procedurally define a strategy for expressing a given query. Requirements of the query language on the algebra can be abstracted by looking at the expressive power of Lorel, the most expressive query language, or else by looking to the collection of orthogonal features listed in [4]. Preliminary definitions of XML algebras are given in [10,2].

- Based upon the algebra, studying the **equivalence of algebraic expressions** (for better understanding the expressive power of XML queries) and then studying, among equivalence transformations, those giving an **optimization of algebraic expressions**, in the same exact way as it is done with relational databases.
- Defining as well an **XML calculus** and XML logic formalism that may give hints upon how to achieve more declarative languages, possibly empowered with recursion and negation.

Besides these classical - and to some extent foreseeable - research dimensions, other research topics are more concerned with the use of XML query languages for searching the Web. We mention:

- **Proximity search**, i.e., search for concepts which are related to given concepts due to their vicinity; this, in turn, can be measured conceptually (e.g., based on the deep meaning) or physically (e.g., based on their position within a hypertext).
- Giving **approximate results**, i.e., results that may be sufficient to characterize the query answer and whose computation can take place more efficiently. In this context, it is important to define ranking schemes and also usage patterns for progressively refining query results based on the ranking.
- Combining a full-fledged XML query with **keyword-based search**, which has proven to be enormously efficient when employed from within the Web search engines.

2.3   Beyond the XML Query Language

An XML query language is an essential ingredient at this stage of XML development, but its definition will open up new problems and issues. We survey some of them.

- A query language immediately brings about the notion of **view**. XML views will be particularly relevant as one can envision that XML-based sites could be views of other XML-based sites, thereby building hierarchies of derived XML data. Such an architecture is already very popular in the context of data warehousing. Views bring with them the issues of their materialization and incremental maintenance, which are classical problems of replication management.
- It is essential to define **semantic constraints** (e.g., referential integrity and more general path constraints) and then make use of them in order to filter illegal XML documents or to optimize query processing.
- Similarly, it is essential to extend the query language with an **update language**, capable of systematically applying changes to selected portions of XML documents.
- Along this direction, once updates become supported, then it becomes possible to support active rules or **triggers**, capable of performing reactive processing upon XML documents. Later on, in Section 5.2, we briefly describe the features of Active XML-GL, a trigger language which extends XML-GL.

- Finally, we expect that XML-based data collections will be ideal for supporting novel approaches to **data mining**, where the existence of semantic tagging may help in structuring the knowledge discovery process.

3   XML As a Data Interchange Standard

Data interchange standards are based on the use of SQL, called "intergalactic dataspeak" by Mike Stonebraker, and typically embedded within standard APIs, such as ODBC and JDBC. In the object-oriented world, CORBA and DCOM provide location-transparent method invocation. All of these standards, however, operate by invoking functions on (or shipping functions to) remote data stores; instead, XML promises to enable data interchange, thereby rising the level of interoperability.

The success of XML as a data interchange standard depends largely from the fact that XML is self-describing, due to semantic tags. Therefore, the publisher of XML data provides also the relative meta-information, thereby enabling the correct interpretation of the XML data by the client. When XML data is extracted from relational databases, metadata is simply a well-defined DTD derived from the relational schema, to which the XML data must rigidly comply. However, XML data may also be extracted from arbitrary legacy systems by a wrapper (which should add to XML data suitable meta-information) or may describe arbitrary semi-structured documents.

Assuming that each data provider publishes XML content, it then becomes possible to pursue three of the W3C goals as defined in the introduction section: define platform-independent protocols for the exchange of data, especially the data of electronic commerce; deliver information to user agents in a form that allows automatic processing after receipt; and provide metadata that will help people find information and help information producers and consumers find each other. The above goals open up a number of research problems, including:

- The development of **wrapping technology** helping in the semi-automatic publishing of legacy data in XML.
- The establishing of well-understood **E-commerce protocols** enabling negotiation and bidding in the context of many-to-many buyers and sellers.
- The use of **agent technology** for automatic discovery of information and negotiation in behalf of clients (e.g., searching for the best offer in the Web shops).
- The development of a new generation of XML-based **search engines** capable of extracting from the Web those specific portions of XML documents dealing with given semantic properties.

The skeptical observer may note that "XML is just syntax", and therefore it does not solve the problems of semantic interoperability. However, a variety of XML-based semantic descriptions are being defined for specific domains. The site http://www.xml.org currently lists several proposals for different applicative domains (e.g., for genetic data [16], mathematical data [20], chemical data [8]).

By adopting a domain-specific tag encoding, data providers are guaranteed to share a data interpretation consistent with their customers.

We expect that every scientific community will understand the importance of data interchange through XML and then develop its own XML-based ontology. Specifically, the community of computer scientists and engineers will specialize in the **modeling of computer systems specifications**; these are typically developed within co-operative and distributed contexts and require to be stored in common repositories, hence will take strong advantage from being collected in a format that warrants effective data interchange. The XMI standard [14] is already pursuing this direction; we will describe in Section 5.3 a new specification language for Web applications, called WebML, which is based on XML.

3.1   Beyond XML

DTDs of XML provide a rich collection of structuring primitives, but are clearly incomplete with respect to the data definition primitives available for database schemas, and therefore carry less semantics. This issue is being covered by a W3C working group defining XML Schema, which aims at extending DTDs in the following dimensions:

- Support of (basic) **data types**, thereby adding classical types (such as integers, floating point numbers, or dates) to text (PCDATA) currently supported in XML. Data types in XML Schema are extensible, in the sense that they are autonomously defined and as such can be redefined or augmented without requiring the redefinition of the standard.
- Support of **typed links**, i.e., of links connecting instances of a given element to instances of another, given element.
- Support of **integrity constraints**, including multi-attribute primary and foreign keys, minimum and maximum cardinality constraints, domain and range constraints.

A full description of XML Schema is outside of the scope of this paper and can be found in [22,23]. We observe that XML Schema is very much complete and coherent with respect to the canonical approach to data design and as such it may be too demanding to become really widespread; however, it may serve the need of integrating, within an XML-compliant formalism, the information which is normally available in the data dictionary of many DBMSs.

4   Repository Technology for XML

XML would not be so popular if it were not already backed by a first generation of XML repository systems, generically denoted as **XML servers**.The success of these systems is due in great part to the *Document Object Model* [18], which offers to applications a portable interface for access and management of XML objects. XML servers provide to researchers concrete evidence that XML technology has all the potential to be well supported, and actually to scale to very large sizes.

Several ongoing projects are focused on building repositories for hosting native XML data, as opposed to hosting data in a different format and then wrapping tags "around" it.

Current XML server technology aims at offering services for inserting and retrieving XML objects, normally stored as flat files, using a more efficient format, e.g., pure or interconnected trees. The big debate currently ongoing among database researchers is focused on whether the representation of XML data should be flat and DTD-independent or instead should be more complex and influenced by the DTD (or by the XML Schema) of the stored document. The former solution is clearly indicated when XML data is unstructured, because the mapping of each element to a table would lead to sparse and inefficient databases; the latter solution could be beneficial with structured XML data, and in perspective could guarantee better query processing performance (i.e., better support of the standard XML query language).

Although mapping each element to a table seems too inefficient, we expect that in the long run the winning solution will be found by adapting relational storage servers to the need of XML data, in the same way as many relational storage servers currently support object-oriented and multi-media data management. We also expect that the flat vs structured modeling dilemma will be best solved by hybrid storage structures, and that this will lead to **flexible storage technology**, i.e., one where the physical data representation will be tailored to the kind of XML data to be stored. This will introduce the need not only of providing the underlying storage technology, but also of providing suitable **data storage methods**, that should infer the best physical mapping based on the features of XML data and then be able to reorganize such mapping dynamically, for instance in order to support complex queries.

We also believe that XML storage technology will naturally be distributed, in the sense that documents conceptually belonging to the same document class (and possibly described by the same DTD) will be hosted on several interconnected storage systems; therefore, we anticipate work in the direction of building **distributed XML storage systems**, possibly with data fragmentation and replication. The current efforts on the standardization of XML fragments (see [21]) may provide useful concepts for supporting a logical view of a document collection, irrespective of its physical fragmentation across many sites.

Optimizing the database engine is the current main focus of the database research community; this was considered as short-sighted by the VLDB Endowment, which recently issued a message to DBWorld asking for a redirection of research, emphasizing the need to reach out from the core database technology. We basically agree with such message, but we also note that query optimization for XML data will give to core database research a lot of challenges. Among them, we list new indexing techniques (e.g., supporting queries across links and along containment paths); how to exploit DTD knowledge or semantic constraints in order to speed up the query evaluation; how to deal with replicas and order; and so on. Going outside of a single repository, distributed query processing will be exacerbated by the fact that data sources are potentially very many and not

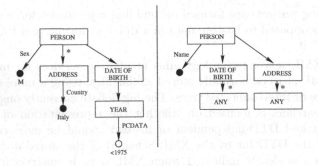

Fig. 2. An XML-GL query

known in advance; therefore, query processing strategies will probably be adaptive. Finally, performances will be achieved by means of parallelism, which may be either at the strategy level (by spawning multiple concurrent searches over distributed XML data) or at the physical level (by XML repositories hosted on multi-processor platforms).

We agree with Alon Levy [13] that we need to reconsider the measuring of performance, and that the new measures should take into account, among other factors, the irregularity of data and the number and heterogeneity of sources from which data are fetched.

5   Research Directions at Politecnico di Milano

After a broad and necessarily coarse-grain inspection of the very many directions of research for XML, we turn our focus to three specific research projects which are currently ongoing at the Politecnico di Milano.

5.1   XML-GL: Graphic Query Language for XML

An XML-GL query can be applied to an arbitrary XML document and produces a new XML document as result. The input document may or may not have a DTD: in the former case, the graphical representation of the DTD is the startpoint for the graphical expression of the query.

A basic XML-GL query is composed by a pair of graphs, called LHS and RHS graphs (see Fig. 2, extracting all male residents of Milano born before 1975). Each graph is composed of labeled nodes (represented by rectangles or small circles) and by directed arcs connecting them. The rectangles correspond to elements, the circles to attributes and to terminal elements (i.e., elements which do not contain other elements). Unlabeled arcs represent element containment; labeled arcs represent references among elements, (IDREF attributes). The * (star) operator on arcs represents an arbitrary navigation along the arcs, and the **any** node matches any element in the document.

The LHS graph identifies the information of interest in the document, specifying where the information must be found and which are the conditions on the data that must be satisfied. In the query in Fig. 2, the LHS searches in the document the PERSON elements which contain: (1) an attribute Sex with value "M"; (2) an ADDRESS element, at an arbitrary level of containment below PERSON, containing an attribute Country with value "Italy"; and (3) a DATE OF BIRTH element containing a YEAR element before 1975. The evaluation of the LHS produces a set of subgraphs, composed by the fragments of the XML document that can be successfully substituted to the graph in the LHS.

The RHS graph is responsible of the construction of the query result; each subgraph produced by the evaluation of the LHS of the query on the input document is elaborated according to the nodes in the RHS to generate a subgraph of the result. Nodes of the RHS and LHS are put in correspondence either by using the same node name, or (in presence of ambiguity) by means of unlabeled non-directed edges connecting one node in the LHS to exactly one node in the RHS. From a document processing point of view, the semantics of the RHS of XML-GL queries is similar to that of a *transformation program* that converts a tagged document into another one by means of pattern matching and rewriting, as proposed for instance in the XSL language [19]. In the example, the result of the query contains the PERSON elements that have been selected in the LHS, complete with attribute Name and their complete subelements DATE OF BIRTH and ADDRESS.

XML-GL offers a rich set of additional features, like unnesting and nesting of XML objects, element ordering, data sorting, arithmetic functions, and aggregate functions. The RHS graph may include nodes that permit a complete restructuring of the document, possibly obtained by combining several distinct documents. Overall, this research effort demonstrates that a graph-based approach is quite natural for XML documents and can offer an intuitive way to represent operations on them.

We are currently working on a tool for query expression which is capable of mapping XML-GL into a well-defined subset of Lorel and vice-versa, linked to the Lorel prototype [1] to support query execution. The objective of this effort is to prove the effectiveness of graphic formalisms for querying XML documents.

5.2   Active XML-GL: Active Rule Language for XML

As a follow-up of our effort on XML-GL, we defined an active rule language, called Active XML-GL. Rules are managed by an **active rule engine**, which operates in the context of an XML document server and may perform several tasks, such as the automatic synthesis of documents, or the checking and repair of integrity constraints, or the incremental maintenance and refresh of views and of related documents, or the implementation of push technology (i.e., the notification of document changes to selected users).

An example of an Active XML-GL rule is in Fig. 3. The rule inserts into a personal address book the list of persons born in Italy before 1975. Each Active XML-GL rule follows the ECA (event-condition-action) paradigm, where:

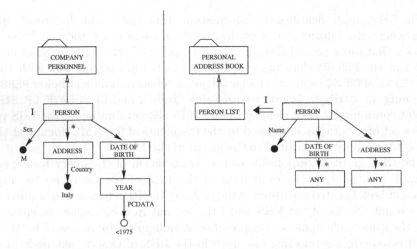

Fig. 3. An Active XML-GL rule

- **Events** are changes to a document. Events may be detected continuously or they can be perceived when the document returns to the repository after having been processed by an application.
- **Conditions** are queries on the document base, expressed using the XML-GL query language; the query normally inspects the content of the changed document and possibly compares it with the content of a document base.
- **Actions** consist of building new documents and/or modifying existing documents in the document base, and then placing them into suitable folders, publishing them on the Web, or sending them by e-mail.

In order to express the above components, we extended the expressive power of XML-GL by adding:

- The representation of **atomic events** applicable to an XML document chosen as the *target* of the rule, with a clear semantics that enables to identify, when an event has occurred, which elements of a target document are affected by (bound to) the event. Events are specified as suitable labelings of the XML-GL graphs; the rule in Fig. 3 reacts to insertions of PERSON elements. We also indicate the activity (i.e., document editing, document publishing in the Web, or message exchange) which causes the event occurrence; the event of the rule in the example occurs when a new element is inserted into the COMPANY PERSONNEL folder.
- The representation of **updates to XML documents**, enabling the declarative specification of the changes of content of XML documents, typically based upon the modified elements of the target document. Updates are defined graphically in the style of XML-GL. Also in this case, the graphical definition of the updates is easy to understand and offers a considerable simplification with respect to a textual description. In the example in Fig. 3, the new PERSON element is added as a subelement to the PERSON LIST element in the PERSONAL ADDRESS BOOK folder.

Two alternatives set-oriented and instance-oriented semantics are supported; they correspond to the alternatives that are offered in relational systems (as introduced by `for each row` and `for each statement` clauses). In order to guarantee portability and independence of the rule engine, we do not assume that change detection should necessarily be performed by specific, low-level changes on XML servers. Rather, we assume that documents can be arbitrarily checked-out for editing and then checked-in; similarly, they can be arbitrarily published on the Web, or received within an arbitrary message. Specific algorithms, called **XML-diff**, compute the difference between the initial and final XML document, expressed as a sequence of elementary changes (called *edit script*). The XML-diff algorithms use cost functions to identify, among all the possible edit scripts, those that minimize the editing costs. We are currently studying an important property of active rules, called *edit-script independence*, that holds when the rule semantics is not affected by the particular choice of edit script performed by an XML-diff algorithm. We are also studying the properties of rule sets execution in the presence of cascading rules and conflicts, as well as the properties of termination, confluence, and observable determinism.

5.3   WebML: XML-Based Web Site Specification Language

Web Modeling Language (WebML) is a specification language for Web applications that enables designers to express the core features of a site at a high level, without committing to implementation-specific details. WebML is based on an XML syntax, which can be processed by software generators for automatically producing the implementation of a Web site in specific mark-up and server side scripting languages (e.g., HTML and Visual Basic Script). WebML concepts are also associated with an intuitive graphic representation, which can be supported by CASE tools and effectively communicated to non-technical site developers (see http://webml.org). WebML concepts are organized in four orthogonal models, called structural, hypertext, presentation, and personalization models.

The **structural model** expresses the data content of the site, in terms of the relevant entities and relationships; it is compatible with the E/R model, the ODMG object-oriented model, and UML class diagrams.

The **hypertext model** describes one or more hypertexts, which can be defined to publish the information of the structure schema in the site. The hypertext model is based on the following abstractions:

- A collection of six **unit types** (data, multidata, index, filter, scroller, and direct), which represent alternative ways of "publishing" objects or sets of objects defined in the structure schema.
- A **composition model**, which permits one to put units into pages and includes structuring mechanisms enabling to recursively compose pages into pages so as to define loadable content packages (e.g., frames in HTML).
- A **navigation model** for interconnecting pages into a hypertext. Links are either non-contextual, when they connect pages, or contextual, when they connect units.

The **presentation model** expresses the layout and graphic appearance of pages, independently of the output device and of the rendition language, by means of an abstract XML syntax. Presentation specifications are either page-specific or generic; in the latter case, they are based on predefined models independent of the specific content of the page.

The **personalization model** is used to describe the delivery of personalized content, navigation, and presentation. Users and user groups are explicitly modeled in the structure schema in the form of predefined entities called User and Group. Then, OQL-like declarative expressions and ECA business rules can be added, which define derived content based on the profile data stored in the User and Group entities or reactions to events for updating user profile data [6].

By combining the WebML concepts of pages, units and links in different ways, it is possible to model arbitrarily complex Web sites. WebML specifications are the input of a novel Web design tool suite (called ToriiSoft, see *http://www.toriisoft.com*), which transforms high-level specifications into multiple output languages (such as HTML and WML), thus supporting multi-device output generation, and then provides the binding of templates to data using multiple server-side script languages (such as Microsoft's Active Server Pages and JavaSoft's Java Server Pages). WebML specifications are stored in an XML repository available to all the tools. The use of XML is fundamental to guarantee portability of the specifications and independence from output languages and template generators.

6   Conclusions

In this paper, we have given a broad overview of the research directions related to the XML standard. After the theorem that "the Web changes everything" [3] we believe in the corollary that "XML is the means" for such a change to make a big step forward. However, the future is always unpredictable, and so the forthcoming years will tell whether this corollary is true (the theorem is obviously true). We have traced a number of research directions, and we believe that the database research community should actively pursue all of them. Most of this research is short-to-medium term, but also XML penetration will either occur in the next few years or else be dropped in view of other priorities.

This road contains a number of new and challenging, "fully original" research topics; but it also contains a number of suggestions for consolidation, i.e., for bringing to the XML world a body of knowledge that the database research community has established over decades, working on relational and object-oriented technology. We believe that such a consolidation is important, as it will give a field-tested proof that a solid transfer of concepts can take place.

References

1. S. Abiteboul, D. Quass, J. McHugh, J. Widom, and J. Wiener. The Lorel query language for semistructured data. *Int. J. on Digital Libraries*, 1(1), Apr. 1997.

2. D. Beech, A. Malhotra, and M. Rys. A formal data model and algebra for XML, 1999. Unpublished report.

3. P. Bernstein, M. Brodie, S. Ceri, D. DeWitt, M. Franklin, H. Garcia-Molina, J. Gray, J. Held, J. Hellerstein, H. V. Jagadish, M. Lesk, D. Maier, J. Naughton, H. Pirahesh, M. Stonebraker, and J. Ullman. The Asilomar report on database research. *ACM SIGMOD Record*, 27(4):74–80, Dec. 1998.

4. A. Bonifati and S. Ceri. Comparative analysis of five XML query languages. *ACM SIGMOD Record*, 2000. to appear.

5. S. Ceri, S. Comai, E. Damiani, P. Fraternali, S. Paraboschi, and L. Tanca. XML-GL: A graphical language for querying and restructuring XML documents. In *Proc. of the 8th Int. World Wide Web Conf.*, Toronto, Canada, May 1999.

6. S. Ceri, P. Fraternali, and S. Paraboschi. Data-driven, one-to-one web site generation for data-intensive applications. In *Proc. of 25th Conf. on Very Large Data Bases*, pages 615–626, Edinburgh, Scotland, Sept. 1999.

7. P. P. Chen, D. W. Embley, and S. W. Liddle, editors. *Workshop on the World-Wide Web and Conceptual Modeling (WWWCM'99)*, Paris, France, Nov. 1999.

8. Chemical Markup Language (CML), 1999. http://www.xml-cml.org/.

9. A. Deutsch, M. Fernandez, D. Florescu, A. Levy, and D. Suciu. XML-QL: A query language for XML. In *QL'98 - W3C Workshop on Query Languages* [17].

10. P. Fankhauser, M. Friedrich, G. Huck, I. Macherius, and J. Robie. Querying XML with locator semantics. Submitted for publication, 1999.

11. M. Fernandez, D. Suciu, and A. Deutsch. XML-QL demo site, 1999. http://www.research.att.com/~mff/xmlql-demo/html/.

12. R. Goldman and J. Widom. DataGuides: Enabling query formulation and optimization in semistructured databases. In *Proc. of the 23rd Int. Conf. on Very Large Data Bases*, pages 436–445, Athens, Greece, Aug. 1997.

13. A. Levy. http://www.cs.washington.edu/homes/alon/widom-response.html. More on data management for XML, 1999.

14. Object Management Group. XML Metadata Interchange (XMI), 1998. http://www.omg.org/.

15. J. Robie, J. Lapp, and D. Schach. XML Query Language (XQL). In *Query Languages 98* [17].

16. Visual Genomics, Inc. Bioinformatic Sequence Markup Language (BSML), 1999. http://visualgenomics.com/bsml/index.html.

17. World Wide Web Consortium. *QL'98 - W3C Workshop on Query Languages*, Cambridge, Mass., Dec. 1998. http://www.w3.org/TandS/QL/QL98.

18. World Wide Web Consortium. The Document Object Model (DOM) Level 1 Specification, October 1998. http://www.w3.org/TR/REC-DOM-Level-1/.

19. World Wide Web Consortium. Extensible Stylesheet Language (XSL) Specification, 1999. http://www.w3.org/TR/WD-xsl.

20. World Wide Web Consortium. Mathematical Markup Language (MathML) 1.01 specification, July 1999. http://www.w3.org/TR/REC-MathML.

21. World Wide Web Consortium. XML Fragment Interchange, June 1999. http://www.w3.org/TR/WD-xml-fragment.

22. World Wide Web Consortium. XML Schema part 1: Structures, Dec. 1999. http://www.w3.org/TR/xmlschema-1.

23. World Wide Web Consortium. XML Schema part 2: Datatypes, Dec. 1999. http://www.w3.org/TR/xmlschema-2.

Indexing & Searching

Trading Quality for Time
with Nearest-Neighbor Search

Roger Weber and Klemens Böhm

Institute of Information Systems
ETH Zentrum, 8092 Zurich, Switzerland
{weber,boehm}@inf.ethz.ch

Abstract In many situations, users would readily accept an approximate query result if evaluation of the query becomes faster. In this article, we investigate approximate evaluation techniques based on the VA-File for Nearest-Neighbor Search (NN-Search). The VA-File contains approximations of feature points. These approximations frequently suffice to eliminate the vast majority of points in a first phase. Then, a second phase identifies the NN by computing exact distances of all remaining points. To develop approximate query-evaluation techniques, we proceed in two steps: first, we derive an analytic model for VA-File based NN-search. This is to investigate the relationship between approximation granularity, effectiveness of the filtering step and search performance. In more detail, we develop formulae for the distribution of the error of the bounds and the duration of the different phases of query evaluation. Based on these results, we develop different approximate query evaluation techniques. The first one adapts the bounds to have a more rigid filtering, the second one skips computation of the exact distances. Experiments show that these techniques have the desired effect: for instance, when allowing for a small but specific reduction of result quality, we observed a speedup of 7 in 50-NN search.

1 Introduction

In the presence of large collections of multimedia objects, notably images or videos, similarity search is an issue of outmost importance. Nearest-neighbor search (NN-search) in high-dimensional spaces is a common implementation of similarity search. The problem with NN-search is its performance, in particular in high-dimensional vector spaces. In such spaces, the complexity of NN-search is linear in the number N of objects to be searched. A number of experiments, whose original intention was to achieve a better performance with trees as index structures, show this [5,4,14]. [15,6] come to the same conclusion using a more formal line of argumentation. Thus, we for our part have developed a data structure for NN-search, the so-called *VA-File* [15], which is not based on trees. Its efficiency is due to its use of approximations. A so-called *approximation file* contains an approximation of each vector. VA-File based NN-search consists of two steps, subsequently referred to as *phases*: the first phase computes an upper

C. Zaniolo et al. (Eds.): EDBT 2000, LNCS 1777, pp. 21–35, 2000.
© Springer-Verlag Berlin Heidelberg 2000

and a lower bound on the distance of each vector. This phase returns the vectors with the smallest bounds, the so-called *candidates*. The second phase retrieves the exact position of the candidates to identify the nearest neighbor. Obviously, the duration of both phases depends on the quality of the approximations.

The objective of this article is to achieve a significant performance gain by resorting to approximate results to NN-queries. Trading result quality for reduced query execution time is completely natural in the context of interactive similarity search: this kind of search typically consists of several steps. Frequently, the result of the initial query does not cover the information need of the user because the query is not *well-posed*. The subsequent steps work with refined queries, e.g. by exploiting feedback information given by the user. To support this interaction, it is crucial to have fast results that may be approximate, rather than long evaluation times.

As a main contribution of this article, we present new approximate evaluation techniques for NN-queries and investigate their performance gain as well as their loss of quality. We do so for one specific data structure, the VA-File. To this end, we proceed as follows:

As a first step, we develop an analytic model for VA-File based search. The motivation is to investigate the relation between the granularity of approximations, i.e. the number of bits used, the effectiveness of the filtering step, and the search performance. We do so by deriving the distribution of the error of the bounds. An important insight is that the bounds noticeably deviate from the distance in the vast majority of cases, i.e., there are hardly any bounds that are 'very close' to the distance. Another relationship derived in this step is the one between the physical structure of the approximation file, i.e., the number of bits per dimension, and the duration of the two phases.

As a second step, we describe two orthogonal approaches to trade result quality for query execution time with the VA-File. The approaches are as follows:

(1) As the bounds significantly deviate from the real distance in almost all cases, we can compute new bounds that are closer to each other. With these new bounds, there are hardly any 'false drops'. This facilitates a coarser approximation file that accelerates the first phase, but that leaves the number of candidates unchanged.
(2) We completely omit the second phase and estimate the distances from the lower and upper bounds.

In the following, Section 2 introduces our notation, and reviews the VA-File. In Section 3, we derive measures for the quality of approximation and the cost of VA-File based search. The findings in this section lead to approximate query evaluation techniques described in Section 4. Section 5 defines different measures for the loss of result quality. We use these measures in Section 6 to evaluate the different techniques. Section 7 discusses related work, and Section 8 concludes.

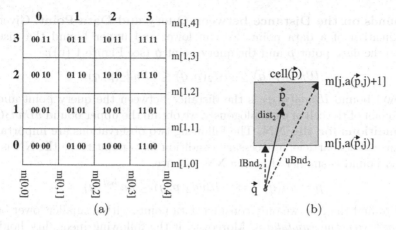

Fig. 1. Illustration of the VA-File

2   Preliminaries

To ease presentation, we explicitly consider only the L_2 distance metric (Euclidean distance). However, it is straightforward to establish the formulae in this paper for other metrics such as L_1 or L_∞ as well.

2.1   On the Relationship Between Similarity Search and NN-Search

Nearest-neighbor search (NN-search) in high-dimensional spaces is a common implementation of similarity search. This implementation assumes that a set of features describes each object. A vector represents the features of each object, and each feature type corresponds to a certain range of vector dimensions. E.g., Dimensions 1–16 describe the shape of the objects, Dimensions 17–32 describe the color etc. A NN-query also has such a vector representation. In our terminology, the *distance* of a vector is its distance to the query vector. NN-search (k-NN search) then means finding the (k) vector(s) with the smallest distance.

2.2   NN-Query Evaluation with the VA-File

Structure. The VA-File consists of a vector file and a file containing approximations of all vectors. The approximations are based on a grid that partitions the data space. The grid has 2^{b_j} intervals along dimension j. The intervals of this grid have numbers from 0 to $2^{b_j} - 1$ (cf. Figure 1 (a)), and the partition points $m[j, 0], \ldots, m[j, 2^{b_j}]$ bound them. These points are determined such that each interval contains the same number of vectors. Given a point p, $a(p, j)$ denotes the interval in dimension j into which p falls. A *bit-string* of length $b = \sum_{j=0}^{d-1} b_j$ represents each cell. Finally, the approximation of p is the bit-string of the cell that contains p.

Bounds on the Distance between Query and Data Point. Given the approximation of a data point, we can lower and upper bound the distance between the data point p and the query point q (see Figure 1 (b)):

$$lBnd_2(p, q) \leq dist_2(p, q) \leq uBnd_2(p, q) \tag{1}$$

The lower bound $lBnd_2(p, q)$ is the distance between the query point and the closest point of the cell of p. Analogously, we obtain the upper bound $uBnd_2(p, q)$.

Conditions for the NN. The following two observations are important in the course of this article: a necessary condition for a point to be the NN is that its lower bound is smaller than the NN-distance.

$$p = nn(q) \quad \Rightarrow \quad lBnd_2(p, q) \leq nn^{dist}(q) \tag{2}$$

Hence, to find the NN, we only consider data points with a smaller lower bound than $nn^{dist}(q)$, the *candidates*. Moreover, if the following inequality holds for two points p and p', p' cannot be the NN.

$$uBnd_2(p, q) < lBnd_2(p', q) \quad \Rightarrow \quad p' \neq nn(q) \tag{3}$$

NN-Search. The search algorithm has two phases: the first phase (filtering step) scans the approximations of the vectors to determine lower and upper bounds on the distance between the current vector and q. Using Equation (3), we can prune vectors: if the lower bound of a vector is larger than the smallest upper bound seen so far, the vector cannot be the NN. In the second phase (refinement step), we visit the remaining vectors sorted by the lower bounds in increasing order. Due to Equation (2), this phase ends if a lower bound is encountered that is larger than the smallest distance seen so far. Hence, the algorithm visits exactly those points whose lower bound is smaller than the NN-distance. It is straightforward to extend the algorithm in order to find the k NN for $k > 1$.

3   Approximation Quality and Cost of NN-Search

In this section, we define two measures for the quality of approximations, namely (1) the mean error of bounds, and (2) the number of vectors visited in the second phase. The objective is to quantify the relation between the granularity of the approximations and approximation quality, as well as the one between the granularity and the search performance. An interesting side issue of the first measure is that the number of bits per dimension of the approximation file grows only logarithmically with d in order to always have the same approximation quality. The second measure, the number of vectors visited in the second phase, allows to predict the response time of VA-File based search given the approximation granularity of the VA-File of an arbitrary data set.

In the following, we characterize a data set by its distance distribution. Let $f(\rho)$ be the distance frequency function, i.e. $f(\rho)$ denotes how frequently there is the distance ρ between two points. The distance distribution $P[dist \leq \rho]$ is the probability that the distance between two points is less than ρ. We further use $f^{lBnd}(\rho)$ to denote the lower bound frequency. Analogously, $P[lBnd \leq \rho]$ denotes the probability that the lower bound is smaller than ρ.

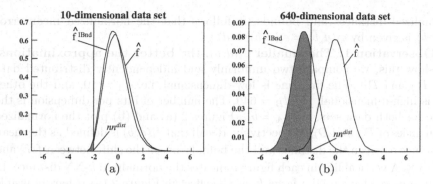

Fig. 2. Frequencies of normalized distances and bounds.

3.1   Deriving the Distribution of the Mean Error of the Bounds

For simplicity, we assume that data points are uniformly and independently distributed in the data space $\Omega = [0,1]^d$, and that each dimension has the same number of bits $\bar{b}$, i.e. $\forall j : b_j = \bar{b}$. Since data is uniformly distributed, the intervals in each dimension are of equal size. Thus, the partition points are $m[j,i] = m[i] = i/2^b$.

The VA-File uses Equations (2) and (3) to prune the data set. These equations are also valid if we use squared bounds and distances[1]. Therefore, if the squared bounds are close to the squared distances, the real bounds also approximate the distance well. Hence, we define the mean error of the bounds as follows (definition for upper bound is analogous):

$$\varepsilon_l(d, \bar{b}) = \int_{p \in \Omega} \int_{q \in \Omega} \left(dist_2(\boldsymbol{p}, \boldsymbol{q})^2 - lBnd_2(\boldsymbol{p}, \boldsymbol{q})^2 \right) \overrightarrow{dq} \overrightarrow{dp} \qquad (4)$$

After a number of transformation steps (cf. [16]), we obtain:

$$\varepsilon_l(d, \bar{b}) = d\frac{2^{1+\bar{b}} - 1}{6 \cdot 2^{2\bar{b}}} \approx \frac{d}{3 \cdot 2^{\bar{b}}} \qquad \varepsilon_u(d, \bar{b}) = d\frac{2^{2+\bar{b}} + 2^{1+\bar{b}} - 1}{12 \cdot 2^{3\bar{b}}} \approx \frac{d}{3 \cdot 2^{\bar{b}}} \qquad (5)$$

Further, the mean squared distance $E(d)$ between points and the standard deviation $\sigma(d)$ in a uniformly distributed data set in the space $[0,1]^d$ are given by: $E(d) = d/6$, $\sigma(d) = \sqrt{7 \cdot d/180}$.

To show what this result means, we introduce the notion of a *normalized lower bound distribution*. Let r be a distance. Then, the normalized distance $\hat{r}$ is defined as $\hat{r} = (r - E(d))/\sigma(d)$. In the same way we can normalize the bounds. Let $\hat{f}(\hat{r})$ denote the normalized distance distribution, defined as $\hat{f}(\hat{r}) = f(\hat{r} \cdot \sigma(d) + E(d))$. Analogously, let $\hat{f}^{lBnd}(\hat{r})$ be the normalized lower bound distribution. Using

---

[1] It is considerably faster to consider only squared distances and bounds to avoid applying the sqrt-function.

normalized distances and bounds, it follows that the normalized mean error $\hat{\varepsilon}_l(d, \bar{b})$ is given by $\hat{\varepsilon}_l(d, \bar{b}) = \varepsilon_l(d, \bar{b})/\sigma(d)$.

Observation 1: The smaller $\hat{\varepsilon}_l(d, \bar{b})$, the better the approximations. To show this, we compare two uniformly and independently distributed data sets $\mathcal{D}_A$ and $\mathcal{D}_B$. The first one is low-dimensional, i.e. $d_A = 10$, and the other one is high-dimensional, i.e. $d_B = 640$. The number of bits per dimension is the same for both data sets, i.e. $\bar{b}_A = \bar{b}_B$. Figures 2 (a) and (b) plot the normalized frequencies of $\mathcal{D}_A$ and $\mathcal{D}_B$, respectively. Recall that $\hat{\varepsilon}_l(d, \bar{b})$ is defined as the mean difference between the distance and the bounds, i.e. as the shift between $\hat{f}(\hat{r})$ and $\hat{f}^{lBnd}(\hat{r})$. A vertical line in each figure indicates the normalized k-NN distance. In the figures, we have used a large k, as the effect in Figure 2 (a) is hardly visible when $k = 1$. According to Equation (2), the shaded area corresponds to the relative size of the candidate set. We see that there are much more candidates in the high-dimensional case, and approximation quality is thus much lower. The reason is that the shift $\hat{\varepsilon}_l(d, \bar{b})$ is much larger: from the equations derived above, we see that it grows with $\sqrt{d}$. Consequently, this shift directly reflects the approximation quality. The smaller the shift, the better is the pruning in the first phase and the less candidates are visited in the second phase.

Observation 2: $\bar{b}$ grows logarithmically with d to yield the same approximation quality. To establish an approximation for $\mathcal{D}_B$ with the same quality as one for $\mathcal{D}_A$, $\hat{\varepsilon}_l(d, \bar{b})$ must be equal for both data sets. From that, it follows that the number $\bar{b}_B$ of data set B depends on the one of A as follows:

$$\bar{b}_B = \bar{b}_A + \frac{1}{2} \cdot \log_2 \left(\frac{d_B}{d_A} \right) \tag{6}$$

In our example, i.e. $d_A = 10$ and $d_B = 640$, we have to use 3 additional bits per dimension for $\mathcal{D}_B$ to obtain the same approximation quality. Experiments have shown that a good approximation for $d = 10$ needs 5 bits per dimension. Using approximations with $\bar{b} = 12$, the quality of the bounds of a $163,840$-dimensional data set is as good as the one of the 10-dimensional data set. We conclude that the VA-File does not degenerate for very high-dimensional data sets.

Observation 3: The error of bounds concentrates around $\varepsilon_l(d, \bar{b})$. Analogously to the mean error of the bounds, one can derive the standard deviations σ_l and σ_u for the error of the lower and the upper bound, respectively:[2]

$$\sigma_l(d, \bar{b}) \approx \frac{\sqrt{d}}{3 \cdot 2^{\bar{b}}}, \qquad \sigma_u(d, \bar{b}) \approx \frac{\sqrt{d}}{3 \cdot 2^{\bar{b}}} \tag{7}$$

Figure 3 (a) shows the frequency of $\varepsilon_l(\boldsymbol{p}, \boldsymbol{q})$ for two different numbers of bits per dimension: $\bar{b} = 4$ and $\bar{b} = 6$. The data set was uniformly and independently distributed with $d = 100$ and $N = 100,000$. For $\bar{b} = 4$, Equations (5) and (7) yield a mean error of 2.08 and a standard deviation of 0.21. Thus, most errors of the bounds lie around 2. In the case of $\bar{b} = 6$, the bounds are 4 times closer to the real distance on average. A further interesting observation is that for

---

[2] The derivation is analogously to $\varepsilon(d, \bar{b})$, but is omitted here for lack of space.

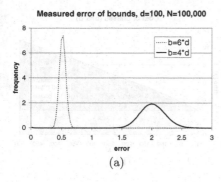

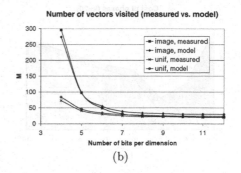

(a)   (b)

Fig. 3. (a) Frequency of $\varepsilon_l(p, q)$ for $\bar{b} = 4$ and $\bar{b} = 6$. (b) Number of visited vectors in a uniform and a real data sets ($d = 10$, $N = 100,000$).

$\bar{b} = 4$, $\varepsilon_l(p, q)$ is larger than 1.5 in the vast majority of cases. Hence, it is highly probable that $\mathbf{lBnd_2}(p, q)^2 + \mathbf{1.5}$ is also a lower bound on the distance between p and q. We will use this observation subsequently to reduce the number of bits per dimension without noticeably losing on result quality.

3.2   Number of Vectors Visited

In the previous subsection, we have shown that $\hat{\varepsilon}_l(d, \bar{b})$ reflects the quality of the approximation. However, a measure based on $\hat{\varepsilon}_l(d, \bar{b})$ would not directly tell us the cost of VA-File based search. In this subsection, we determine the number M of vectors visited in the second phase for a given data set and a given k. Note that M is related to $\hat{\varepsilon}_l(d, \bar{b})$: the smaller $\hat{\varepsilon}_l(d, \bar{b})$, the smaller is M. Thus, M also measures the quality of approximation. We derive a formula for M under the assumption that the distance distribution is the same from each point of the data space (*homogeneity assumption* [8]). Note that this assumption is more general than the uniformity assumption in the previous subsection. Thus, our estimation of M applies to real data sets as well.

Expected Nearest Neighbor Distance. A good estimation of the NN-distance of a query is the expected NN-distance of the data set over all possible queries. The probability that the k-NN-distance ρ of an arbitrary query is at most r is:

$$P_k[\rho \leq r] = 1 - \sum_{i=0}^{k-1} \binom{N}{i} \left(P[dist \leq r]^i (1 - P[dist \leq r])^{N-i} \right) \qquad (8)$$

We obtain the expected k-NN-distance $\nu(k)$ by integrating over all distances r:

$$\nu(k) = \int_0^\infty r \frac{\partial P_k[\rho \leq r]}{\partial r} dr \qquad (9)$$

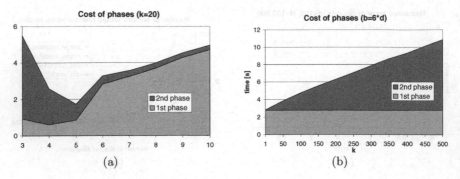

Fig. 4. The costs of the phases of VA-File based NN-search.

Number of Vectors Visited. The VA-File algorithm visits a point if its lower bound is smaller than the NN-distance. To estimate M, we use the expected NN-distance $\nu(k)$ given by Equation (9):

$$M = N \cdot P[lBnd \leq \nu(k)] = N \cdot \int_0^{\nu(k)} f^{lBnd}(x)dx \qquad (10)$$

From Equations (9) and (10), it follows that M grows with increasing k. Finally, Figure 3 (b) compares the estimated number for M with the measured one for two data sets and different numbers of bits. The data sets chosen were a 10-dimensional uniformly distributed data set, and a 9-dimensional feature data set of our image database, both with $N = 100,000$. For both cases, one can see that the estimates obtained with Equation (10) are of sufficient quality.

3.3 Cost of VA-File-Based NN-Search

Given the number of bits per dimension, we now are able to determine the size of the approximation file, and the number M of vectors to visit in the second phase of the search algorithm. Given these two measures, we easily can establish a cost model for VA-File based search. The details are omitted here for lack of space, but are contained in the longer version of this article [16].

Figure 4 depicts the costs of the two phases, obtained experimentally. Figure 4 (a) shows these costs as a function of $\bar{b}$ with $k = 20$, Figure 4 (b) as a function of k with $\bar{b} = 6$. For these figures, we have used a 320-dimensional set of image features with $N = 100,000$. The buffer size was around 25 MB. Consequently, only the approximation files with $\bar{b} < 6$ has fit into main memory. According to the figure, the cost of the first phase varies with $\bar{b}$. But the dependency is not linear due to the limited buffer size and due to the different costs of bit-operations. The second phase depends on both b and k. While the cost of the second phase grows linearly with k, it decreases with growing $\bar{b}$. Figure 4 (a) reveals the optimal setting for $k = 20$: performance is best if $\bar{b} = 5$.

4 Approximating NN-Query Results

In this section, we describe techniques to trade quality for response time for VA-File based search.

4.1 Adapting the Bounds in the First Phase

The evaluation from Subsection 3.1 tells us that $\varepsilon_l(\boldsymbol{p}, \boldsymbol{q})$ is larger than a threshold value α in the vast majority of cases. E.g., for $\bar{b} = 4$, $\alpha = 1.5$, as Figure 3 shows. In other words, $lBnd_2(\boldsymbol{p}, \boldsymbol{q})^2 + 1.5$ is very likely to lower bound the distance, and $uBnd_2(\boldsymbol{p}, \boldsymbol{q})^2 - 1.5$ upper bounds the distance with high probability. Thus we define new bounds as follows:

$$lBnd_2'(\boldsymbol{p}, \boldsymbol{q})^2 = lBnd_2(\boldsymbol{p}, \boldsymbol{q})^2 + \alpha, \qquad uBnd_2'(\boldsymbol{p}, \boldsymbol{q})^2 = uBnd_2(\boldsymbol{p}, \boldsymbol{q})^2 - \alpha \quad (11)$$

Subsequently, we refer to α as *adaptation value*. Given the distance frequency $f^{\varepsilon_l}(\rho)$ for the error of the lower bound, we can determine the probability $P(\alpha)$ that the new bound $lBnd_2'$ is wrong:

$$P(\alpha) \quad = \quad \int_0^\alpha f^{\varepsilon_l}(\rho) d\rho \qquad (12)$$

On average, out of the k vectors that are the result of an accurate k-NN search, the adapted bounds of $P(\alpha) \cdot k$ vectors are wrong. In the worst case, these vectors are not in the approximate result. Thus, an upper bound on the average number of false dismissals is given by: $P(\alpha) \cdot k$. Subsequently, we call this approximate query evaluation technique VA-BND.

4.2 Avoiding Vector Visits in the Second Phase

The approximate query evaluation techniques now described reduce the number of vectors visited in the second phase. This is especially important if k is large, as Figure 4 (b) shows. One alternative is to completely omit the second phase, i.e. the vectors with the k smallest lower bounds are the approximate result. We refer to this approximate query evaluation technique as VA-LOW.

In many situations, distances to the query object are meaningless to the user. Rather, a retrieval system assigns scores to the result objects based on a scoring function. With the bounds computed in the first phase and the scoring function, we can approximate these scores. If approximate scores are not sufficient, we have to access the k vectors in the approximate result to determine the exact distances and to compute the scores. With the experiments to follow, VA-LOW-k denotes an approximate query evaluation technique that works like VA-LOW but accesses the k members of the result to determine the exact distance. Note that the results of VA-LOW and VA-LOW-k for a given query contain the same vectors but possibly with a different ranking.

With the above approximate techniques, we may have false dismissals. An upper bound on the number of false dismissals is $M - k$, where M denotes the number of candidates of an accurate search. This is because each of the M candidates may be in the accurate result, but VA-LOW and VA-LOW-k consider only the first k candidates. Consequently, $min(k, M - k)$ upper bounds the number of false dismissals. Since M is typically very small, e.g. $M = 14$ for $k = 10$, the number of false dismissals is also small (4 in the example).

Recall that the VA-File uses the upper bound to reduce the number of candidates according to Equation (3). However, with VA-LOW(-k), the result consists of the k vectors with the smallest lower bound. Thus, computing the upper bounds is not necessary. Finally, note that it does not make sense to combine VA-BND and VA-LOW(-k): VA-BND increases all bounds by α. This does not alter the order of the lower bounds. Since VA-LOW(-k) returns the k vectors with the smallest lower bounds, the result is the same as if we use only VA-LOW(-k).

5   Measuring the Result Quality

In order to quantify the loss of result quality, we introduce two measures: the *ratio of false dismissals over* k and the *normalized rank sum*. Notice that the notion of result quality is different from approximation quality, as introduced in Section 3. While the *approximation quality* describes how good an approximation bounds the real distance to the vector, the *result quality* tells us how close the approximate result is to the accurate result.

Ratio of false dismissals over k. Let r_i be the i-th vector in the accurate result, and x_i be the i-th vector in the approximate result. Further, let $rank(x_i)$ be the rank of x_i in the accurate result with $k = N$. Obviously, an approximate result is good if it contains most vectors of the accurate result, i.e. if there are few false dismissals. Our first measure is the ratio of false dismissals rfd:

$$rfd \quad = \quad \frac{1}{k} \cdot \sum_{i=1}^{k} \begin{cases} 1 & rank(x_i) > k \\ 0 & otherwise \end{cases} \tag{13}$$

Values of rfd close to 0 indicate a high quality of the result.

Normalized rank sum. To illustrate the idea behind our second measure, consider an approximation technique for $k = 10$ which is almost exact. But instead of the 10th best vector, its result contains the 11th best vector, i.e. $r_i = x_i$ for $i < 10$, $r_{10} \neq x_{10}$, and $rank(x_{10}) = 11$. Note that the rfd-value does not take into account that the rank of the 10th vector in the approximate result is close to 10. However, it makes a difference whether $rank(x_{10}) = 11$, as in the example, or if $rank(x_{10}) = 20$. In both cases, the rfd is the same, but the later result is of lower quality. This consideration leads to a second measure, the so-called *normalized rank sum* (cf. [9]):

$$nrs \quad = \quad \frac{k(k+1)}{2 \cdot \sum_{i=1}^{k} rank(x_i)} \tag{14}$$

Values of nrs close to 1 indicate a high quality of the result. In the above example, nrs is 0.98 with $rank(x_{10}) = 11$, and 0.85 with $rank(x_{10}) = 20$.

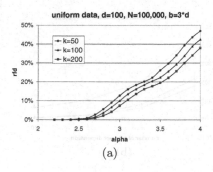
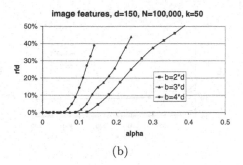

(a)   (b)

Fig. 5. Result quality *rfd* of VA-BND for (a) a uniformly distributed data set, and for (b) an image feature data set.

6 Evaluation

The evaluation consists of two parts: the first part investigates the result quality, and the second part shows how much we can gain in terms of response time if we allow for a certain ratio of false dismissals. For lack of space, we only consider experiments with quality measure *rfd*. Further experiments are described in [16].

6.1 Result Quality When Approximating the First Phase

In the first experiment, we determined the result quality of VA-BND as a function of k and α (" 'alpha' " in the figures). The data set used in Figure 5 (a) consists of 100,000 100-dimensional uniformly distributed points. It depicts the *rfd*-value of an approximate search with $k = 50$, $k = 100$ and $k = 200$ as a function of α. In all experiments, we set $\bar{b} = 3$, i.e. the approximations had a length of $3 \cdot d = 300$ bits. The figure tells us that the number of false dismissals is sufficiently small, i.e. *rfd* < 15%, for $k > 50$ as long as $\alpha < 3$. An interesting observation is that result quality is better the larger k is. In addition, we can use this figure to determine α based on the quality constraint of the user. For example, if the user specifies the constraint that *rfd* < 10% for a 50-NN search with $\bar{b} = 3$, it follows from the figure that α should be smaller than 2.95.

The second experiment shows that VA-BND is also of advantage with real data sets. For Figure 5 (b), we used a feature data set of our image database with $d = 150$ and $N = 100,000$. As with the uniform data set, we can determine α for a given quality constraint based on *rfd*. E.g., for a 50-NN search with $\bar{b} = 2$ and *rfd* < 10%, we obtain $\alpha = 0.18$.

6.2 Result Quality When Approximating the Second Phase

With the next experiments, we have measured the loss of quality of VA-LOW and VA-LOW-k as a function of k and $\bar{b}$. First, we have used a uniformly distributed data set with $d = 300$ and $N = 100,000$. Figure 6 (a) shows the *rfd*-values of

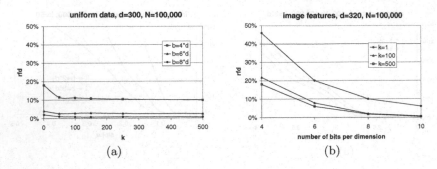

Fig. 6. Result quality *rfd* of VA-LOW and VA-LOW-k for (a) a uniformly distributed data set, and for (b) an image feature data set.

VA-LOW as a function of k for $\bar{b} = 4$, $\bar{b} = 6$, and $\bar{b} = 8$. From this figure, we draw that even for a small number of bits per dimension, the result quality is good. For $\bar{b} = 4$, we see that if k is large, the percentage of false dismissals is around 10%. Only in the case of $k = 1$, one should use more bits per dimension in order to keep *rfd* small. Similarly to determining α, we can use Figure 6 (a) to determine the necessary number of bits to keep result quality above a given value. For example, if the quality constraint is *rfd* < 10% for a 50-NN search, $\bar{b} = 4$ yields sufficient results. In case of a 1-NN search with the same constraint, we have to use $\bar{b} = 6$ to meet the quality requirement.

Figure 6 (b) shows the *rfd*-values of approximate results with VA-LOW for a set of image features ($d = 320$, $N = 100,000$). The x-axis is the number of bits per dimension. k varies with the different graphs, i.e. $k = 1$, $k = 100$, and $k = 500$. As with uniform data, the more bits we use, the higher the result quality. However, to meet the quality constraint *rfd* < 10%, we need $\bar{b} = 8$ for a 1-NN search, and $\bar{b} = 6$ for $k > 100$.

6.3   Trading Quality for Response Time

With the last set of experiments, we want to find out how much we can gain in terms of response time with the approximate search methods compared to accurate search. We have used a data set from our image collections with $d = 320$ and $N = 100,000$. We have varied k and the quality constraint and have measured the response time for each method with its optimal setting $(\bar{b}, \alpha)$. The buffer was 25 MB in all experiments. This means that the approximation file has fit into memory if $\bar{b} < 6$. Figure 7 compares the response times of the approximate methods with the ones of an accurate VA-File search (denoted as VA-File) for $k = 50$, and $k = 500$. On the left side of each figure, the quality constraint is *rfd* < 10%, on the right side it is *rfd* < 20%. Note that a simple sequential scan through all vectors would last 13 seconds in all settings.

In the case of $k = 50$, VA-LOW and VA-LOW-k are 7 times faster than an accurate search if *rfd* < 20%, and 50% slower if *rfd* < 10% (cf. Figure 7 (a)).

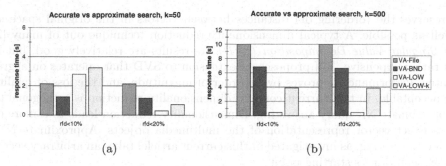

Fig. 7. Performance gain of approximate search methods with a quality constraint of $rfd < 10\%$, and $rfd < 20\%$ for (a) $k = 50$, and (b) $k = 500$.

The performance gain in the first case is basically due to lower costs in both phases: in the first phase, no upper bounds are computed, and in the second phase less (or no) vectors are read. Approximate search with VA-BND is 2 times faster than accurate search, and lasts equally long with both quality constraints. Hence, with a rigid quality constraint, VA-BND yields best results, otherwise, VA-LOW is the best choice.

For $k = 500$, we obtain best search performance with VA-LOW and VA-LOW-k: response times are about 20 times smaller than the ones of an accurate search for both quality constraints (cf. Figure 7 (b)). Even for VA-LOW-k, we obtain a performance gain of 60%. In this case, VA-BND yields only a performance gain of 30%.

An interesting observation is that query evaluation times of VA-LOW are smaller for large k than for small k. In our experiments, the search time for $k = 1$ was 2.76 seconds for $rfd < 10\%$, and for $k = 500$ it was 0.44 seconds. The main reason for this is the buffer limitation: VA-LOW needs more bits for $k = 1$ than for $k = 500$ to meet the quality constraint. As a consequence, for $k = 1$, the approximations do not fit into main memory, and, search is considerably slowed down due to IO-operations.

7 Related Work

NN-query evaluation. The vast majority of techniques for exact NN-query evaluation uses trees as underlying index structure [12,3,5,14,7]. But as the introduction has pointed out, their complexity is linear for large d.

Approximative NN-Search. There are other approaches for approximative NN-search with sublinear complexity even for large d [1,11], but they come without an evaluation of absolute search times. Furthermore, that complexity typically is the one of the main-memory version of the algorithm, and it is close to the linear one for reasonable approximation errors.

Dimensionality reduction. The principle is as follows: one tries to find a mapping of the vectors to vectors in a space with lower dimensionality that preserves the (ordering of) distances between vectors in the original space as well as possible. A typical dimensionality reduction technique out of many [2] is *Singular Value Decomposition (SVD)*. Its results are relatively good, but it is rather expensive. [13] proposes an extension to SVD that operates on aggregates. Performance improves by an order of magnitude, and the loss of quality is acceptable. In this current context, dimensionality reduction is orthogonal to approximate NN-query answering. Dimensionality reduction leads to a more or less exact vector representation of the multimedia objects. Approximate NN-query answering, as investigated in this current article, takes an arbitrary vector representation as starting point.

8   Conclusion

The main contribution of this article are two approximate query-evaluation techniques for the VA-File, a data structure allowing for efficient evaluation of NN-queries in high-dimensional data spaces. To better understand VA-File based query-evaluation techniques, we have derived the distribution of the errors of those bounds. The observation that this distribution is somewhat peculiar has lead to the first approximate evaluation technique. The second technique refers to the second phase of VA-File based search. We have then quantified the loss of quality with these techniques. A 20%-loss of quality, to give an example, typically yields a speedup of 7 (with k=50). For large k, the speedup is even much bigger. Large values of k typically occur with the A0 algorithm that combines ranked results from different subsystems [10].

As 'by-products' from those investigations, this article has contributed the following further results: the approximation quality stays the same if the number of bits per dimension of the approximation file grows logarithmically with the dimensionality of the data space. This means that, from a technical perspective, VA-File based NN-search is feasible for very high dimensional spaces. Furthermore, we have developed a cost model for VA-File based NN-search. Our cost model is useful in many situations, notably for cost-based query optimization.

Acknowledgements. We thank Hans-J. Schek and Martin Breunig for helpful comments.

References

1. Sunil Arya et al. An Optimal Algorithm for Approximate Nearest Neighbor Searching in Fixed Dimensions. Technical report, 1998.
2. D. Barbara, W. DuMouchel, C. Faloutsos, P. J. Haas, J.M. Hellerstein, Y. Ioannidis, H.V. Jagadish, T. Johnson, R. Ng, V. Poosala, K.A. Ross, and K. C. Sevcik. The New Jersey data reduction report. *Data Engineering*, 20(4):3–45, 1997.
3. N. Beckmann, H.-P. Kriegel, R. Schneider, and B. Seeger. The R*-tree: An efficient and robust access method for points and rectangles. In *Proceedings of the 1990 ACM SIGMOD International Conference on Management of Data*, pages 322–331, Atlantic City, NJ, 23–25 May 1990.

4. S. Berchtold, C. Böhm, B. Braunmüller, D.A. Keim, and H.-P. Kriegel. Fast parallel similarity search in multimedia databases. In *Proceedings of the ACM SIGMOD International Conference on Management of Data*, pages 1–12, Tucson, USA, 1997.
5. S. Berchtold, D.A. Keim, and H.-P. Kriegel. The X-tree: An index structure for high-dimensional data. In *Proceedings of the International Conference on Very Large Databases (VLDB)*, pages 28–39, 1996.
6. K. Beyer, J. Goldstein, R. Ramakrishnan, and U. Shaft. When is "nearest neighbour" meaningful? In Catriel Beeri and Peter Buneman, editors, *Proc. 7th Int. Conf. Data Theory, ICDT*, number 1540 in Lecture Notes in Computer Science, LNCS, pages 217–235. Springer-Verlag, 10–12 January 1999.
7. P. Ciaccia, M. Patella, and P. Zezula. M-tree: An efficient access method for similarity search in metric spaces. In *Proceedings of the International Conference on Very Large Databases (VLDB)*, Greece, 1997.
8. Paolo Ciaccia, Marco Patella, and Pavel Zezula. A cost model for similarity queries in metric spaces. In *Proceedings of the ACM Symposium on Principles of Database Systems (PODS)*, 1998.
9. A. Dimai. Spatial encoding using differences of global features. In *Storage and Retrieval for Image and Video Databases IV*, volume 3022 of *SPIE Proceedings Series*, pages 352–360, Feb. 1997.
10. Ronald Fagin. Combining fuzzy information from multiple systems. In *Procedings of the ACM SIGACT-SIGMOD-SIGART Symposium on Principles of Database Systems*, volume PODS, pages 216–226, Montreal, Canada, June 1996.
11. Aristides Gionis, Piotr Indyk, and Rajeev Motwani. Similarity Search in High Dimensions via Hasing. In *Proceedings of the 25th International Conference on Very Large Data Bases*. Morgan Kaufmann, 1999. Edinburgh, Scotland.
12. A. Guttman. R-trees: A dynamic index structure for spatial searching. In *Proceedings of the ACM SIGMOD International Conference on Management of Data*, pages 47–57, Boston, MA, June 1984.
13. K. V. R. Kanth, D. Agrawal, and A. Singh. Dimensionality reduction for similarity searching in dynamic databases. *SIGMOD Record (ACM Special Interest Group on Management of Data)*, 27(2):166–176, 1998.
14. N. Katayama and S. Satoh. The SR-tree: An index structure for high-dimensional nearest neighbor queries. In *Proceedings of the ACM SIGMOD International Conference on Management of Data*, pages 369–380, Tucson, Arizon USA, 1997.
15. R. Weber, H.-J. Schek, and S. Blott. A quantitative analysis and performance study for similarity-search methods in high-dimensional spaces. In *Proceedings of the International Conference on Very Large Databases (VLDB)*, volume 24, New York, USA, August 1998.
16. Roger Weber and Klemens Böhm. Trading quality for time with nearest-neighbor search. Technical report, Dept. of Computer Science, 1999. Available at http://www-dbs.ethz.ch/~weber/paper/EDBT00Long.ps.

Dynamically Optimizing
High-Dimensional Index Structures

Christian Böhm and Hans-Peter Kriegel

University of Munich, Oettingenstr. 67, 80538 München, Germany
{boehm,kriegel}@dbs.informatik.uni-muenchen.de

Abstract. In high-dimensional query processing, the optimization of the logical page-size of index structures is an important research issue. Even very simple query processing techniques such as the sequential scan are able to outperform indexes which are not suitably optimized. Page-size optimization based on a cost model faces the problem, that the optimum not only depends on static schema information such as the dimension of the data space but also on dynamically changing parameters such as the number of objects stored in the database and the degree of clustering and correlation in the current data set. Therefore, we propose a method for adapting the page size of an index dynamically during insert processing. Our solution, called DABS-tree, uses a flat directory whose entries consist of an MBR, a pointer to the data page and the size of the data page. Before splitting pages in insert operations, a cost model is consulted to estimate whether the split operation is beneficial. Otherwise, the split is avoided and the logical page-size is adapted instead. A similar rule applies for merging when performing delete operations. We present an algorithm for the management of data pages with varying page-sizes in an index and show that all restructuring operations are locally restricted. We show in our experimental evaluation that the DABS tree outperforms the X-tree by a factor up to 4.6 and the sequential scan by a factor up to 6.6.

1. Motivation

Query processing in high-dimensional data spaces is an emerging research domain which gains increasing importance by the need to support modern applications by powerful search tools. In the so-called non-standard applications of database systems such as multimedia [16, 33, 34], CAD [11, 13, 21, 25], molecular biology [26, 29], medical imaging [27], time series analysis [1, 2, 18], and many others, similarity search in large data sets is required as a basic functionality.

A technique widely applied for similarity search is the so-called feature transformation, where important properties of the objects in the database are mapped into points of a multidimensional vector space, the so-called feature vectors. Thus, similarity queries are naturally translated into neighborhood queries in the feature space.

In order to achieve a high performance in query processing, multidimensional index structures [20] are applied for the management of the feature vectors. Even a number of specialized index structures for high-dimensional data spaces have been proposed [6,

C. Zaniolo et al. (Eds.): EDBT 2000, LNCS 1777, pp. 36-50, 2000.

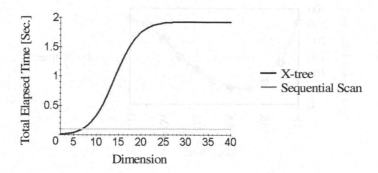

Fig. 1: Performance of query processing with varying dimension.

12, 22, 28, 30, 36]. In spite of these efforts, there are still high-dimensional indexing problems under which even specialized index structures deteriorate in performance. To understand the effects leading to this so-called 'curse of dimensionality', a variety of methods for estimating the performance of query processing has been developed [3, 4, 9, 10, 14, 15, 17, 19, 31, 32, 35]. These cost models can be used for optimization. High-dimensional query processing techniques offer various parameters for optimization such as dimension reduction [8, 16, 30, 34] or the accuracy of the representation of the features [6, 37].

In recent years, a general criticism on high-dimensional indexing has come up. Most multidimensional index structures have an exponential dependency (with respect to the time for processing range queries and nearest neighbor queries) on the number of dimensions. To illustrate this, fig. 1 shows our model prediction of the processing time of the X-tree for a uniform and independent data distribution (constant database size 400 KBytes). With increasing dimension d, the processing time grows exponentially until saturation comes into effect, i.e. a substantial ratio of all index pages is accessed. In very high dimensions $d \geq 25$, virtually all pages are accessed, and the processing time approaches thus an upper bound.

In recognition of this fact, an alternative approach is simply to perform a sequential scan over the entire data set. The sequential scan causes substantially fewer effort than processing all pages of an index, because the reading operations in the index cause random seek operations whereas the scan reads sequentially. The sequential scan rarely causes disk arm movements or rotational delays which are negligible under these circumstances. Assuming a logical block size of 4 KBytes, contiguous reading of a large file is by a factor >12 faster than reading the same amount of data from random positions (cf. [14, 37]).

A second advantage of the sequential scan over index-based query processing is its storage utilization of 100%. In contrast, index pages have a storage utilization between 60% and 70% which causes a further performance advantage of about 50% for the sequential scan when reading the same amount of data. The constant cost of the sequential scan is also depicted in fig. 1. The third advantage of the sequential scan is the lacking

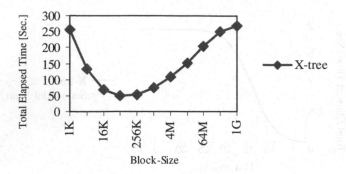

Fig. 2: Block size optimization.

overhead of processing the directory. We can summarize that the index may not access more than 5% of the pages in order to remain competitive with the sequential scan.

In fig. 1, the break-even point of the two techniques is reached at $d = 7$. The trade-off between the two techniques, however, is not simply expressed in terms of the number of dimensions. For instance when data sets are highly skewed (as real data sets often are), index techniques remain more efficient than a scan up to a fairly high dimension. Similarly, when there are correlations between dimensions, index techniques tend to benefit compared to scanning. Obviously, the number of data objects currently stored in the database plays an important role since the sequential scan is linear in the number of objects whereas query processing based on indexes is sub-linear.

Fig. 2 shows the model predictions of the X-tree for 10,000,000 points uniformly and independently chosen from a 20-dimensional data space with varying block size from 1 KByte to 1 GByte. In this setting, the performance is relatively bad for usual block sizes between 1 KBytes and 4 KBytes, quickly improving when increasing the block size. A broad and stable optimum is reached between 64 KBytes and 256 KBytes. Beyond this optimum, the performance deteriorates again. This result shows that block size optimization is the most important advice to improve high-dimensional indexes.

The rest of this paper is organized as follows: Section 2 explains the general idea and an overview of our technique. Section 3 shows the architectural structure of the DABS-tree. The following sections show how operations such as insert, delete and search are handled. In section 6, we show how our model developed in [9, 14] can be applied for a dynamic and independent optimization of the logical block size. Finally, we present an experimental evaluation of our technique.

2. Basic Idea

As we pointed out in section 1, there are three disadvantages for query processing based on index structures compared to the sequential scan:
- data is read in too small portions
- index structures have a substantially lower storage utilization
- processing of the directory causes overhead

In this paper, we will present the DABS-tree (Dynamic Adaptation of the Block Size) which tackles all three problems. We propose a new index structure claiming to outperform the sequential scan in virtually every case. In dimensions where index-based techniques are superior to the sequential scan, the efficiency of these techniques is retained unchanged. In an area of moderate dimensionality, both approaches, conventional indexes as well as the scan, are outperformed.

The first problem is solved by a suitable page-size optimization. As we face the problem that the actual optimum of the logical block size is dependent on the number of objects currently stored in the database and on the data distribution (which may also change over time), the block size has to be adapted dynamically. After a page has been affected by a certain number of inserts or deletions, the page is checked whether the number of points currently stored in the page is close enough to the optimum. Otherwise, the page is split or a suitable partner is sought for balancing or merging.

This means that pages with different logical block size are at the same time stored in the index. Although a constant block size facilitates management, no principal problem arises when sacrificing this facilitation. To solve the second problem, storage utilization, we propose to allow continuously growing block sizes, i.e. we also give up the requirement that the logical block size is a multiple of some physical block size or a power of two or the demand that the block size is only changed by doubling or division by two. Instead, every page has exactly the size which is needed to store its current entries. When an entry is inserted to a page, the block size increases, and the page must usually be stored to a new position in the index file. To avoid fragmentation of the file, we propose garbage collection.

The third problem, directory overhead, cannot be completely avoided by our technique since we do not want to cancel the directory. The directory overhead, however, is weakened, because we simplify the directory. Instead of a hierarchical directory, we only maintain a linear single-level directory which is sequentially scanned. The block size optimization also helps to reduce the directory overhead, because this overhead is taken into account by the optimization.

3. Structure of the DABS-Tree

The structure of the DABS-tree is depicted in fig. 3. Each directory entry contains the following information: The page region in form of a minimum bounding rectangle, the reference (i.e. the background storage address) to the page and additionally the number of entries currently stored in the page. The number of entries is also used to determine the corresponding block size of a data page before loading.

The directory consists simply of a linear array of directory entries. We intentionally cancel the hierarchically organized directory, because the efficiency of query processing is not increased by hierarchies but rather decreased. We confirm this effect by the following consideration:

In our experiment presented in section 1 (cf. fig. 2), we determined an optimum block size of 64 KBytes. For 10,000,000 data points in a 20-dimensional space, we need 20,000 data pages to store the points. Using a hierarchical directory, we need 78 index

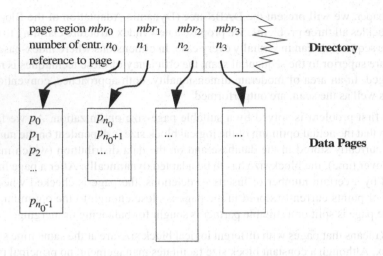

Fig. 3: Structure of the DABS-tree.

pages at the first directory level and the root-page. Even if we assume no overlap among the directory pages, query processing requires an average of 44 directory page accesses. The cost for these accesses are 1.14 seconds of I/O time. A sequential scan of a linear directory, however, requires 0.71 seconds. Both kinds of directory cost are negligible compared to 49 seconds of cost for accessing the data pages. Even though, the sequential scan of a linear directory causes fewer effort than a hierarchical directory. This observation even holds for fairly low dimensions.

The data pages contain only data-specific information. Besides the point data and eventually some additional application-specific information, no management information is required. The data pages are stored in random order in the index file. Conventional index structures usually do not utilize the space in the data pages to 100% in order to leave empty space for future insert operations. In contrast, the DABS-tree stores the data pages generally without any empty position inside a data page and without any gap between different pages. Whenever a new entry is inserted to a data page, the page is stored at a new position. The empty space in the file where the data page formerly used to be is passed to a free memory management. A garbage collection strategy is applied to build larger blocks of free memory, and, thus to avoid fragmentation (cf. section 5). Temporarily, the free blocks decrease the storage utilization of the index structure below 100%. The free blocks, however, are never subject to a reading operation during insert processing. Therefore, the performance of query processing cannot be negatively affected.

In order to guarantee overlap-free page regions, we hold additionally to the linear directory a kd-tree [5]. A kd-tree partitions the data space in a disjoint and overlap-free way. The page regions of the DABS-tree are always located inside a single kd-tree region. The kd-tree facilitates insert processing, because it offers unambiguously a data page for the insert operation. In contrast, the heuristics for choosing a suitable page in the X-tree cannot guarantee that no overlap occurs. The kd-tree is also used for the

```
Point DABS_nearest_neighbor_query (Point q) {
       typedef struct {float distance, int pageno, int num_objects} AplEntry ;
       AplEntry apl [number_of_pages]
       int i, j;
       Point cpc ;
       float pruning_dist = +infinity ;

       // First Phase
       DIRECTORY dir = read_directory () ;
       for (i = 0 ; i < number_of_pages ; i ++) {
               apl [i] . distance = mindist (q, dir [i] . mbr) ;
               apl [i] . pageno = dir [i] . pageno ;
               apl [i] . num_objects = dir [i] . num_objects ;
       }
       qsort (apl, number_of_pages, sizeof (AplEntry), cmp_float) ;

       // Second Phase
       for (i = 0 ; i < number_of_pages && apl [i] . distance < pruning_dist ; i ++) {
               Page p = LoadData (apl [i] . pageno, apl [i] .num_objects) ;
               for (j = 0 ; j < apl [i] . num_objects ; j ++)
                      if (dist (q, p . object [j] . point) < pruning_dist) {
                             cpc = p . object [j] . point ;
                             pruning_dist = dist (q, p . object [j] . point) ;
                      }
       }
       return cpc ;
}
```

Fig. 4: Algorithm for nearest neighbor queries.

merging operation which may be necessary due to delete operations, or because the optimal page size has increased on the basis of a changed data distribution. The kd-tree is not used for search.

4. Search in the DABS-Tree

Point queries and *range queries* are handled in a straightforward way. First, the directory is sequentially scanned. All data pages qualifying for the query (i.e. containing the query point or intersecting with the query range, respectively) are determined, loaded and processed.

Nearest neighbor queries and *k-nearest neighbor queries* are processed by a variant of the HS algorithm [24]. As the directory is flat, the algorithm can even be simplified, because the *active page list* (*APL*) is static in absence of a hierarchy. For hierarchically organized directories, query processing requires permanent insert operations to the APL, because in each processing step the pivot page is replaced by its child pages. Therefore, the APL must be re-sorted after processing a page.

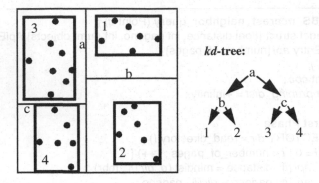

Fig. 5: The additional *kd*-tree.

In our case, the nearest neighbor algorithm works in two phases: The first phase scans the directory sequentially. During the scan, the distance between the query point and each page region is determined and stored in an array. Finally the distances in the array are sorted by the Quicksort algorithm, for instance [23]. In the second phase, the data pages are loaded and processed in the order of increasing distances. The closest point candidate determines the pruning distance. Query processing stops when the current page region is farther away from the query point than the closest point candidate. Fig. 4 depicts the algorithm for nearest neighbor queries. The *k-nearest neighbor* algorithm works analogously with the only difference that a *closest point candidate list* consisting of *k* entries is maintained and that the last entry in this list determines the pruning distance.

5. Handling Insert Operations

5.1 Searching the Data Page

To handle an insert operation, we search in the kd-tree, which is held in addition to the linear directory, for a suitable data page. The kd-tree has the advantage to partition the data space in a complete and disjoint fashion which makes the choice of the corresponding page unambiguous. Eventually, the MBR in the linear directory which is always located inside the corresponding kd-tree region (cf. fig. 5) must be slightly enlarged.

The page is loaded to the main memory, and the point is inserted. Usually, the page cannot be stored at its old position since we enforce a 100% storage utilization of pages. Therefore, it is appended to the end of the index file. The empty block at the former position of the page is passed to a free storage manager which performs garbage collections if the overall storage utilization of the index file decreases below a certain threshold value (e.g. 90%).

Note that in contrast to conventional index structures, the overall storage utilization can never decrease the efficiency of query processing, because empty parts of the index file are not subject to reading operations. By a low storage utilization, we only waste storage memory, but not processing time.

5.2 Free Storage Management

The free storage manager currently observes the storage utilization of the index file. When the storage utilization reaches some threshold value su_{min}, the next new page is not appended to the end of the index file. Instead, a local garbage collection is raised which performs local restructuring of the file to collect empty pages as follows:

Let the size of the next page to be stored be s. The storage manager searches for the shortest interval of subsequent pages in the index file covering s Bytes of empty space. With a suitable data structure to organize the empty space, this search can be performed efficiently. Once the shortest interval with s Bytes of empty space is found, we load all pages in this interval to the main memory and restore them densely, thus creating a contiguous empty space of at least s Bytes. We store the new page to this space.

Now we will claim an important property of the restructuring action: Locality. We show that the size of the interval in the file which is to be restructured is bounded by the size s of the new page multiplied with some factor depending on the storage utilization su_{min}.

Lemma 1. Locality of Restructuring

In an index file with a storage utilization $su \leq su_{min}$, there exists an interval with the length

$$l = \frac{s}{1 - su_{min}}$$

containing at least s Bytes of free storage.

Proof (Lemma 1)

Assume that all intervals of the length l have less than s Bytes of free storage. Then, the number e of free Bytes in the file with length f is bounded by:

$$e < \frac{f}{l} \cdot s$$

By the definition of the storage utilization, we get the following inequation

$$su = 1 - \frac{e}{f} > 1 - \frac{s}{l} = su_{min}$$

which contradicts the initial condition $su \leq su_{min}$.

❑

If we choose, for instance, a storage utilization of $su_{min} = 50\%$, Lemma 1 tells us that restructuring is bounded to an interval twice as large as the size s of the page we want to store. For a storage utilization of $su_{min} = 90\%$, the interval is at most ten times as large as the new page. As there are no specific overflow conditions in our index structure, the pages are periodically checked by using a cost estimation whether they must be split. For the details, cf. section 6.

Deleting in the DABS-tree is straightforward. The point is deleted from the corresponding page and a small block is passed to the free storage manager. If the storage utilization falls below the threshold su_{min}, a local restructuring action is raised for the last data page in the file. Since there is no clear underflow condition in the DABS-tree, the pages are periodically tested by using a cost model whether they are to merge.

6. Dynamic Adaptation of the Block Size

In this section, we will first show the dynamic adaptation from an algorithmic point of view. Then, we will show how the cost model developed in [9, 14] is modified and applied to take split and merging decisions, respectively.

6.1 Split and Merge Management

Basically, it is possible to evaluate the cost model after every insert or delete operation and to determine whether a page must be split or merged with some neighbor. This is, however, not very economic, because the optimum is generally broad. Therefore, we have to check rather seldom if the current page size still is close to the optimum.

We choose the following strategy: For each page, we have an update counter variable which is increased in each insert or delete operation the page is subject to. We perform our model evaluations when the value of the update counter reaches some user defined threshold which may be defined as a fixed number (e.g. 20 operations) or as a ratio of the current page capacity (e.g. 25% of the points in the page).

Note that it is theoretically possible (although not very likely) that pages must be merged after performing insert operations or that pages must be split after performing delete operations. This is not intuitive, as conventional index structures with a fixed block size know to split only after inserts and to merge after deletions. In our dynamic optimization, however, any of these operations can change the distribution of the data points and thus change the page size optimum into each direction.

Whenever the threshold of update operations is reached, a cost estimate for the current page with respect to query processing is determined. Then, some split algorithm is run tentatively. The page regions of the created pages are determined, and the query processing cost for the new pages is estimated. If the performance has decreased, the split is undone, and merging is tested in the same way.

A merging operation can only be performed if a suitable partner is available. In order to maintain overlap-free page regions, only two leaf pages with a common parent node in the kd-tree are eligible for merging. If the current page does not have such a counterpart, merging is not considered. Otherwise, the cost estimates for the two single pages and for the resulting page are determined and compared. If the performance estimate improves, the merge is performed. Finally, the relevant update counters are reset to 0.

6.2 Model Based Local Cost Estimation

For our local cost optimization, we must estimate how cost of query processing changes when performing some split or merge operation. Generally, we assume as reference query the nearest neighbor query with the maximum metric, because this assumption causes the lowest effort in the model computation. Practically, the difference in the page size optimum is low when changing the reference query to the Euclidean metric or to some k-nearest neighbor query.

In both cases, when taking a split or a merge decision, we compare the cost caused by one page with the cost caused by two pages with the half capacity. At the one hand, this action changes the accessing cost, because the transfer cost decreases with decreasing capacity. The access probability is also decreased by splitting. At the other hand, it is unpredictable whether the sum of the costs caused by the two smaller pages is really lower than the cost of the larger page.

Therefore, it is reasonable, to draw the following balance for the split decision:

$$\Delta_T = (t_{Seek} + C_1 \cdot t_{Point}) \cdot X_1 + (t_{Seek} + C_2 \cdot t_{Point}) \cdot X_2 - (t_{Seek} + C_0 \cdot t_{Point}) \cdot X_0,$$

where C_0 and X_0 are the capacity and the access probability of the larger page, and C_1 and C_2 (X_1 and X_2) the capacities (access probabilities) of the two smaller pages. The time t_{Point} is the transfer time for a point, i.e. $t_{Point} = t_{transfer} \cdot$ sizeof (Point). The time t_{Seek} denotes the delay time for a random access operation, subsuming the times for disk head movement and rotational delay. These times are hardware dependent. If the cost balance Δ_T is positive, the larger page causes fewer cost than the two smaller pages. In this case, a split should be avoided and a merge should be performed.

It is possible to estimate the access probability according to the cost estimates provided in [9, 14]. This approach, however, assumes no knowledge about the regions of the pages currently stored in the index. In our local cost optimization, the exact coordinates of the relevant page regions are known. Therefore, we can achieve higher accuracy if this information is considered. Additionally, it is possible to take into account the local exceptions in the data distribution.

First, we determine the fractal local point density according to the volume and the capacity of the larger page:

$$\rho_F = \frac{C_0}{V(MBR_0)^{D_F/d}}$$

Hereby, D_F denotes the fractal dimension of the data set [10]. From the local point density, we can derive an estimation of the nearest neighbor distance:

$$r = \frac{1}{2} \cdot D_F \sqrt{\frac{1}{\rho_F}}$$

Now, we are able to determine the Minkowski sum of the nearest neighbor query and the page region. If MBR_0 is given by a vector of lower bounds ($lb_0, \dots lb_{d-1}$) and upper bounds ($ub_0, \dots ub_{d-1}$), the Minkowski sum is determined by:

$$V_{R \oplus C}(MBR_0, 2r) = \prod_{0 \le i < d} (ub_i - lb_i + 2r)$$

This Minkowski sum can be explicitly clipped at the data space boundary (here for simplicity assumed to be the unit hypercube):

$$V_{(R \oplus C) \cap DS}(MBR_0, 2r) = \prod_{0 \le i < d} (\min\{ub_i + r, 1\} - \max\{lb_i - r, 0\})$$

We assume that the query distribution follows the data distribution. Therefore, the access probability X_0 corresponds to the ratio of points in the Minkowski sum with respect to all points in the database:

$$X_0 = \frac{\rho_F}{N} \cdot V_{(R \oplus C) \cap DS}(\text{MBR}_0, 2r)^{D_F/d}$$

Analogously, the access probabilities for the smaller pages X_1 and X_2 are determined by their page regions MBR_1 and MBR_2. The access probabilities are used in the cost balance for taking split or merge decisions.

6.3 Monotonicity Properties of Splitting and Merging

The most important precondition for the correctness of a local optimization is the monotonicity of the first derivative of the cost function with respect to the page capacity. If the first derivative is not monotonically increasing, the cost function may have various local optima where the optimization easily could get caught in.

As depicted in fig. 2, the cost function indeed forms a single local optimum which is also the global optimum. Cost are very high for block sizes which are either too small or too large. Minimum cost arise in a relatively broad area between these extremes.

Under several simplifying assumptions, it is also possible to prove that the derivative of the cost function is monotonically increasing. From this monotonicity, we can conclude that there is at most one local minimum. The assumptions required for this proof are uniformity and independence as well as neglecting boundary effects. For this simplified model

$$T(C) = \left(d\sqrt[d]{\frac{1}{C}} + 1\right)^d \cdot \left(t_{\text{Seek}} + \frac{C}{\text{sizeof(point)}} \cdot t_{\text{transfer}}\right),$$

it is possible to show that the second derivative of the cost function is positive:

$$\frac{\partial^2}{\partial C^2} T(C) \geq 0.$$

The intermediate results in this proof, however, are very complex and thus not presented here.

7. Experimental Evaluation

To demonstrate the applicability and the practical relevance of our technique, we performed an experimental evaluation on both, synthetic and real data. The improvement potential was already shown in fig. 2 where a clear optimum for page sizes was found at 64 KBytes outperforming the X-tree with a standard page of 4K by a factor of 2.7 and the sequential scan by a factor of 3.6.

The intention of our next experiment is to show that the optimum is not merely a hardware constant but to a large extent dependent on the data to be indexed. For this purpose, we constructed a DABS-tree on several data files containing uniformly and independently distributed points of varying dimension. The number of objects was fixed in this experiment to 12,000. We observed the block size which was generated by the

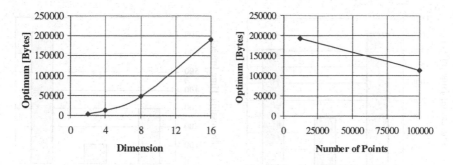

Fig. 6: Optimal block size for uniform data.

local optimization. The results are depicted on the left side of fig. 6. In the two-dimensional case, quite a usual block size of 3,000 Bytes was found to be optimal. In the high-dimensional case, however, the optimum block size reaches values up to 192 KBytes with even increasing tendency.

In our next experiment, depicted on the right side of fig. 6, we show the usefulness of dynamic optimization. We used the 16-dimensional index of the preceding experiments and increased the number of objects to 100,000. Hereby, the optimum page size decreased from 192 KBytes to 112 KBytes.

In our next experiment, depicted in fig. 7, we compared the DABS-tree with the X-tree and the sequential scan. As expected, the performance in low-dimensional cases is similar to the X-tree; in high-dimensional cases it is similar to the sequential scan. In any case, both approaches are clearly outperformed. In the 4-dimensional example, the DABS-tree is 43% faster than the X-tree and 157% faster than the sequential scan. In the 16-dimensional example, the DABS-tree outperforms the sequential scan by 17% and the X-tree by 462%.

In case of a moderate dimensionality, and provided that the number of points stored in the database is high, both techniques, the X-tree as well as the sequential scan, are

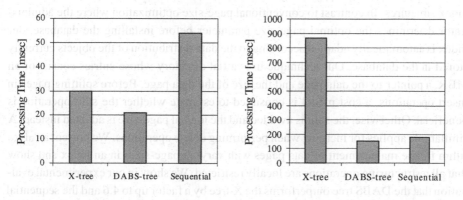

Fig. 7: Performance for 4-dimensional (left) and 16-dimensional (right) data.

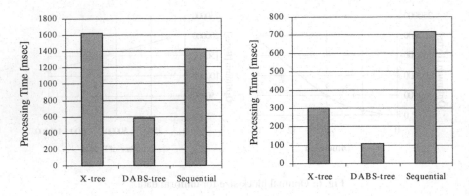

Fig. 8: Query processing on uniform (l.) and real data (r.).

clearly outperformed. This is demonstrated in the example of our 16-dimensional database with 100,000 points (fig. 8, left side). Here, the improvement factor over the X-tree is 2.78. The improvement over the sequential scan is with 2.44 in the same order of magnitude.

The intention of our last experiment (fig. 8, right side) is to confirm that our optimization technique is also applicable to real data and that high performance gains are reachable. For this purpose, we constructed a DABS-tree with 50,000 points from our CAD application. We measured again the performance of nearest neighbor queries. As query points, we also used points from the same application which were not stored in the database. The data space dimension was 16 in this example. We outperformed the X-tree by a factor of 2.8 and the sequential scan by 6.6.

8. Conclusion

In this paper, we have proposed a dynamic optimization technique for multidimensional index structures. In contrast to conventional page-size optimization where the administrator determines the optimal page-size parameter before installing the database, our index is automatically adapted according to the data distribution of the objects currently stored in the database. Our technique uses a flat directory whose entries consist of an MBR, a pointer to the data page and the size of the data page. Before splitting pages in insert operations, a cost model is consulted to estimate whether the split operation is beneficial. Otherwise, the split is avoided and the logical page-size is adapted instead. A similar rule applies for merging when performing delete operations. We present an algorithm for the management of data pages with varying page-sizes in an index and show that all restructuring operations are locally restricted. We show in our experimental evaluation that the DABS tree outperforms the X-tree by a factor up to 4.6 and the sequential scan by a factor up to 6.6.

References

1. Agrawal R., Faloutsos C., Swami A.: *'Efficient similarity search in sequence databases'*, Proc. 4th Int. Conf. on Foundations of Data Organization and Algorithms, 1993, LNCS 730, pp. 69-84

2. Agrawal R., Lin K., Shawney H., Shim K.: *'Fast Similarity Search in the Presence of Noise, Scaling, and Translation in Time-Series Databases'*, Proc. of the 21st Conf. on Very Large Databases, 1995, pp. 490-501.

3. Arya S., Mount D.M., Narayan O.: *'Accounting for Boundary Effects in Nearest Neighbor Searching'*, Proc. 11th Symp. on Computational Geometry, Vancouver, Canada, pp. 336-344, 1995.

4. Aref W. G., Samet H.: *'Optimization Strategies for Spatial Query Processing'*, Proc. 17th Int. Conf. on Very Large Databases (VLDB'91), Barcelona, Catalonia, 1991, pp. 81-90.

5. Bentley J.L.: *'Multidimensional Search Trees Used for Associative Searching'*, Communications of the ACM, Vol. 18, No. 9, pp. 509-517, 1975.

6. Berchtold S., Böhm C., Jagadish H. V., Kriegel H.-P., Sander J.: *'Independent Quantization: An Index Compression Technique for High-Dimensional Data Spaces'*, Proc. Int. Conf. on Data Engineering, Konstanz, Germany, 2000.

7. Berchtold S., Böhm C., Kriegel H.-P.: *'The Pyramid-Technique: Towards indexing beyond the Curse of Dimensionality'*, Proc. ACM SIGMOD Int. Conf. on Management of Data, Seattle, pp. 142-153,1998.

8. Berchtold S., Böhm C., Keim D., Kriegel H.-P., Xu X.: *'Optimal Multidimensional Query Processing Using Tree Striping'*, submitted.

9. Berchtold S., Böhm C., Keim D., Kriegel H.-P.: *'A Cost Model For Nearest Neighbor Search in High-Dimensional Data Space'*, ACM PODS Symposium on Principles of Database Systems, 1997, Tucson, Arizona.

10. Belussi A., Faloutsos C.: *'Estimating the Selectivity of Spatial Queries Using the `Correlation' Fractal Dimension'*. Proceedings of 21th International Conference on Very Large Data Bases, VLDB'95, Zurich, Switzerland, 1995, pp. 299-310.

11. Berchtold S., Kriegel H.-P.: *'S3: Similarity Search in CAD Database Systems'*, Proc. ACM SIGMOD Int. Conf. on Management of Data, 1997, Tucson, Arizona, pp. 564-567.

12. Berchtold S., Keim D., Kriegel H.-P.: *'The X-Tree: An Index Structure for High-Dimensional Data'*, 22nd Conf. on Very Large Databases, 1996, Bombay, India, pp. 28-39.

13. Berchtold S., Keim D., Kriegel H.-P.: *'Using Extended Feature Objects for Partial Similarity Retrieval'*, VLDB Journal Vol. 6, No. 4, pp. 333-348, 1997.

14. Böhm C.: *'Efficiently Indexing High-Dimensional Data Spaces'*, Ph.D. Thesis, Faculty for Mathematics and Computer Science, University of Munich, Utz-Verlag München, 1998.

15. Friedman J. H., Bentley J. L., Finkel R. A.: *'An Algorithm for Finding Best Matches in Logarithmic Expected Time'*, ACM Transactions on Mathematical Software, Vol. 3, No. 3, September 1977, pp. 209-226.

16. Faloutsos C., Barber R., Flickner M., Hafner J., et al.: *'Efficient and Effective Querying by Image Content'*, Journal of Intelligent Information Systems, 1994, Vol. 3, pp. 231-262.

17. Faloutsos C., Kamel I.: *'Beyond Uniformity and Independence: Analysis of R-trees Using the Concept of Fractal Dimension'*, Proceedings of the Thirteenth ACM SIGACT-SIGMOD-SIGART Symposium on Principles of Database Systems, Minneapolis, Minnesota, 1994, pp. 4-13.

18. Faloutsos C., Ranganathan M., Manolopoulos Y.: *'Fast Subsequence Matching in Time-Series Databases'*, Proc. ACM SIGMOD Int. Conf. on Management of Data, 1994, pp. 419-429.

19. Faloutsos C., Sellis T., Roussopoulos N.: *'Analysis of Object-Oriented Spatial Access Methods'*, Proc. ACM SIGMOD Int. Conf. on Management of Data, 1987.

20. Gaede V., Günther O.: *'Survey on Multidimensional Access Methods'*, Technical Report ISS-16, Humbold-Universität Berlin, 1995.

21. Gary J. E., Mehrotra R.: *'Similar Shape Retrieval using a Structural Feature Index'*, Information Systems, Vol. 18, No. 7, 1993, pp. 525-537.

22. Henrich, A.: *'The LSD^h-tree: An Access Structure for Feature Vectors'*, Proc. 14th Int. Conf. on Data Engineering, Orlando, 1998.

23. C.A.R. Hoare, *'Quicksort'*, Computer Journal, Vol. 5, No. 1, 1962.

24. Hjaltason G. R., Samet H.: *'Ranking in Spatial Databases'*, Proc. 4th Int. Symp. on Large Spatial Databases, Portland, ME, 1995, pp. 83-95.

25. Jagadish H. V.: *'A Retrieval Technique for Similar Shapes'*, Proc. ACM SIGMOD Int. Conf. on Management of Data, 1991, pp. 208-217.

26. Kastenmüller G., Kriegel H.-P., Seidl T.: *'Similarity Search in 3D Protein Databases'*, Proc. German Conference on Bioinformatics (GCB`98), Köln (Cologne), 1998.

27. Korn F., Sidiropoulos N., Faloutsos C., Siegel E., Protopapas Z.: *'Fast Nearest Neighbor Search in Medical Image Databases'*, Proc. 22nd VLDB Conference, Mumbai (Bombay), India, 1996, pp. 215-226.

28. Katayama N., Satoh S.: *'The SR-tree: An Index Structure for High-Dimensional Nearest Neighbor Queries'*, Proc. ACM SIGMOD Int. Conf. on Management of Data, 1997, pp. 369-380.

29. Kriegel H.-P., Seidl T.: *'Approximation-Based Similarity Search for 3-D Surface Segments'*, GeoInformatica Journal, Kluwer Academic Publishers, 1998, to appear.

30. Lin K., Jagadish H. V., Faloutsos C.: *'The TV-Tree: An Index Structure for High-Dimensional Data'*, VLDB Journal, Vol. 3, pp. 517-542, 1995.

31. Papadopoulos A., Manolopoulos Y.: *'Performance of Nearest Neighbor Queries in R-Trees'*, Proc. 6th Int. Conf. on Database Theory, Delphi, Greece, in: Lecture Notes in Computer Science, Vol. 1186, Springer, pp. 394-408, 1997.

32. Pagel B.-U., Six H.-W., Toben H., Widmayer P.: *'Towards an Analysis of Range Query Performance in Spatial Data Structures'*, Proceedings of the Twelfth ACM SIGACT-SIGMOD-SIGART Symposium on Principles of Database Systems, PODS'93, Washington, D.C., 1993, pp.214-221.

33. Shawney H., Hafner J.: *'Efficient Color Histogram Indexing'*, Proc. Int. Conf. on Image Processing, 1994, pp. 66-70.

34. Seidl T., Kriegel H.-P.: *'Efficient User-Adaptable Similarity Search in Large Multimedia Databases'*, Proc. 23rd Int. Conf. on Very Large Databases (VLDB'97), Athens, Greece, 1997, pp. 506-515.

35. Yannis Theodoridis, Timos K. Sellis: *'A Model for the Prediction of R-tree Performance'*. Proceedings of the Fifteenth ACM SIGACT-SIGMOD-SIGART Symposium on Principles of Database Systems, June 3-5, 1996, Montreal, Canada. ACM Press, 1996, ISBN 0-89791-781-2 pp. 161-171.

36. White D.A., Jain R.: *'Similarity indexing with the SS-tree'*, Proc. 12th Int. Conf on Data Engineering, New Orleans, LA, 1996.

37. Weber R., Schek H.-J., Blott S.: *'A Quantitative Analysis and Performance Study for Similarity-Search Methods in High-Dimensional Spaces'*, Proc. Int. Conf. on Very Large Databases, New York, 1998.

Slim-Trees: High Performance Metric Trees Minimizing Overlap between Nodes

Caetano Traina Jr.[1],   Agma Traina[2],   Bernhard Seeger[3],   Christos Faloutsos[4]

[1,2] Department of Computer Science, University of São Paulo at São Carlos - Brazil
[3] Fachbereich Mathematik und Informatik, Universität Marburg - Germany
[4] Department of Computer Science, Carnegie Mellon University - USA
[Caetano|Agma|Seeger+|Christos@cs.cmu.edu]

Abstract. In this paper we present the Slim-tree, a dynamic tree for organizing metric datasets in pages of fixed size. The Slim-tree uses the "fat-factor" which provides a simple way to quantify the degree of overlap between the nodes in a metric tree. It is well-known that the degree of overlap directly affects the query performance of index structures. There are many suggestions to reduce overlap in multi-dimensional index structures, but the Slim-tree is the first metric structure explicitly designed to reduce the degree of overlap.

Moreover, we present new algorithms for inserting objects and splitting nodes. The new insertion algorithm leads to a tree with high storage utilization and improved query performance, whereas the new split algorithm runs considerably faster than previous ones, generally without sacrificing search performance. Results obtained from experiments with real-world data sets show that the new algorithms of the Slim-tree consistently lead to performance improvements. After performing the Slim-down algorithm, we observed improvements up to a factor of 35% for range queries.

1. Introduction

With the increasing availability of multimedia data in various forms, advanced query

---

[1] On leave at Carnegie Mellon University. His research has been funded by FAPESP (São Paulo State Foundation for Research Support - Brazil, under Grants 98/05556-5).

[2] On leave at Carnegie Mellon University. Her research has been funded by FAPESP (São Paulo State Foundation for Research Support - Brazil, under Grants 98/0559-7).

[3] His work has been supported by Grant No. SE 553/2-1 from DFG (Deutsche Forschungsgemeinschaft).

[4] This material is based upon work supported by the National Science Foundation under Grants No. IRI-9625428, DMS-9873442, IIS-9817496, and IIS-9910606, and by the Defense Advanced Research Projects Agency under Contract No. N66001-97-C-8517. Additional funding was provided by donations from NEC and Intel. Any opinions, findings, and conclusions or recommendations expressed in this material are those of the author(s) and do not necessarily reflect the views of the National Science Foundation, DARPA, or other funding parties.

C. Zaniolo et al. (Eds.): EDBT 2000, LNCS 1777, pp. 51-65, 2000.
© Springer-Verlag Berlin Heidelberg 2000

processing techniques are required in future database management systems (DBMS) to cope with large and complex databases. Of utmost importance is the design of new access methods which support queries like similarity queries in a multimedia database. While there has been a large number of proposals for multidimensional access methods [1], almost all of them are not applicable to multimedia databases since they assume that data belong to a multidimensional vector space. However, data of multimedia databases often are not in vector spaces, but in metric spaces.

In this paper we address the problem of designing efficient metric access methods (MAM). An MAM should organize a large set of objects in a dynamic environment assuming only the availability of a distance function d which satisfies the three rules of a metric space (symmetry, non-negativity and triangle inequality). Consequently, an MAM is not permitted to employ primitive operations like addition, subtraction or any type of geometric operation. While insertions of new records should be supported efficiently, we are mainly interested in MAMs supporting range queries and similarity queries (nearest neighbor queries). Efficiency of an MAM is determined by several factors. First, since the data set is generally too large to be kept in main memory, one major factor for efficiency is the number of disk accesses required for processing queries and insertions. We assume here that an MAM organizes data in pages of fixed size on disk and that disk access refers to read (write) one page from disk into main memory. Second, the computational cost of the distance function can be very high such that the number of distance calculations has a major impact on efficiency. We expect, however, that there is a strong relationship between the number of disk accesses and the number of distance calculations. Third, storage utilization is another important factor although it has rarely been considered in this context previously. The reason we are concerned about storage utilization is not because of the storage cost, but primarily because of the number of disk accesses required to answer "large" range queries. For those queries, the number of accesses is only low when the storage utilization is sufficiently high. In other words, an MAM can perform less efficiently than a simple sequential scan for such cases.

We present in this paper the Slim-tree, a new dynamic MAM.The Slim-tree shares the basic data structure with other metric trees like the M-tree [2] where data is stored in the leaves and an appropriate cluster hierarchy is built on top. The Slim-tree differs from previous MAMs in the following ways. First, a new split algorithm based on the Minimal Spanning Tree (MST) is presented which performs faster than other split algorithms without sacrificing search performance of the MAM. Second, a new algorithm is presented to guide an insertion of an object at an internal node to an appropriate subtree. In particular, our new algorithm leads to considerably higher storage utilization. Third, and probably most important, the Slim-down algorithm is presented to make the metric tree tighter and faster in a post-processing step. This algorithm was derived from our findings that high overlap in a metric tree is largely responsible for its inefficiency. Unfortunately, the well-known techniques to measure overlap of a pair of intersecting nodes (e.g. circles in a two-dimensional space) cannot be used for metric data. Instead, we present the "fat-factor" and the "bloat-factor" to measure the degree of overlap where a value close to zero indicates low overlap. We show that the Slim-down algorithm reduces the bloat-factor and hence, improves the query performance of the metric tree.

The remainder of the paper is structured as follows. In the next section, we first give a brief history of MAMs, including a concise description of the datasets we used in our experiments. Section 3 introduces the Slim-tree, and Section 4 presents its new splitting algorithm based on minimal spanning trees. Section 5 introduces the fat-factor and the bloat-factor. The Slim-down algorithm is described in Section 6, while Section 7 gives a performance evaluation of the Slim-tree. Section 8 presents the conclusion of this paper.

2. Survey

The design of efficient access methods has interested researchers for more than three decades. However, most of these access methods require that data be ordered in a one- or multi-dimensional vector space.

The problem of supporting nearest neighbor and range queries in metric spaces has recently attracted the attention of researchers. The work of Burkhard and Keller [3] provided different interesting techniques for partitioning a metric data set in a recursive fashion where the recursive process is materialized as a tree. The metric tree of Uhlmann [4] and the vantage-point tree (vp-tree) of Yanilos [5] are somehow similar to a technique of [3] as they partition the elements into two groups according to a representative, called a vantage point. In [5] the vp-tree has also been generalized to a multi-way tree. In order to reduce the number of distance calculations, Baeza-Yates et al [6] suggested to use the same vantage point in all nodes that belong to the same level. Then, a binary tree degenerates into a simple list of vantage points. Another method of Uhlmann [4] is the generalized hyper-plane tree (gh-tree). The gh-tree partitions the data set into two by picking two points as representatives and assigning the remaining to the closest representative. Bozkaya and Ozsoyoglu [7] proposed an extension of the vp-tree called multi-vantage-point tree (mvp-tree) which chooses in a clever way m vantage points for a node which has a fanout of m^2. The Geometric Near Access Tree (GNAT) of Brin [8] can be viewed as a refinement of another technique presented in [3].

All methods presented above are static, in the sense that the data structure is built once and new insertions are not supported. The M-tree [2] of Ciaccia, Patella and Zezulla overcomes this deficiency. The M-tree is a height-balanced tree where the data elements are stored in the leaves, and the M-tree supports insertions similar to R-trees [9].

3. The Slim-Tree: An Improved Performance Metric Tree

The Slim-tree is a balanced and dynamic tree that grows bottom-up from the leaves to the root. Like other metric trees, the objects of the dataset are grouped into fixed size disk pages, each page corresponding to a tree node. The objects are stored in the leaves. The main intent is to organize the objects in a hierarchical structure using a representative as the center of each minimum bounding region which covers the objects in a sub-tree. The Slim-tree has two kinds of nodes, data nodes (or leaves) and index nodes. As the size of a page is fixed, each type of node holds a predefined maximum number of objects C. For simplicity, we assume that the capacity C of the leaves is equal to the capacity of the index nodes.

Analogous to other metric trees, the distance to a representative can be used in combination with the triangle inequality to prune an entry without any extra distance calculation. The regions that corresponds to each node of the Slim-tree can overlap each other. The increasing of overlaps also enlarges the number of paths to be traversed when a query is issued, so it also increases the number of distance calculations to answer queries. The Slim-tree was developed to reduce the overlapping between regions in each level.

3.1 Building the Slim-Tree

The objects are inserted in a Slim-tree in the following way. Starting from the root node, the algorithm tries to locate a node that can cover the new object. If none qualifies, select the node whose center is nearest to the new object. If more than one node qualifies, execute the *ChooseSubtree* algorithm to select one of them. This process is recursively applied for all levels of the tree. When a node m overflows, a new node m' is allocated at the same level and the objects are distributed among the nodes. When the root node splits, a new root is allocated and the tree grows one level.

The Slim-tree has three options for the *ChooseSubtree* algorithm: *random* (randomly choose one of the qualifying nodes), *mindist* (choose the node that has the minimum distance from the new object and the center of the node), *minoccup* (choose the node that has the minimum occupancy among the qualifying ones).

The splitting algorithms for the Slim-tree are:

Random - The two new center objects are randomly selected, and the existing objects are distributed among them. Each object is stored in a new node that has its center nearest this object, with respect to a minimum utilization of each node.

minMax - All possible pairs of objects are considered as potential representatives. For each pair, a linear algorithm assigns the objects to one of the representatives. The pair which minimizes the covering radius is chosen. The complexity of the algorithm is $\Theta(C^3)$, using $\Theta(C^2)$ distance calculations. This algorithm has already been used for the M-tree, and it was found to be the most promising splitting algorithm regarding query performance [10].

MST - The minimal spanning tree [11] of the objects is generated, and one of the longest arcs of the tree is dropped.This algorithm is one of the contributions of this paper, and it is presented next. This algorithm produces Slim-trees almost as good as the minMax algorithm, in a fraction of the time.

4. The Splitting Algorithm Based on Minimal Spanning Tree

In this section we address the following problem. Given a set of C objects in a node to be split, quickly divide them in two groups, so that the resulting Slim-tree leads to low search times. We propose an algorithm based on the minimal spanning tree [11], which has been successful used in clustering. We consider the full graph consisting of C objects and $C(C-1)$ edges, where the weight of the edges refers to the distance between the connecting objects. Therefore, we proceed with to the next steps.

1. Build the MST on the C objects.
2. Delete the longest edge.
3. Report the connected components as two groups.
4. Choose the representative of each group, i.e., the object whose maximum distance to all other objects of the group is the shortest.

Unfortunately, this algorithm does not guarantee that each group will receive a minimum percentage of objects. To obtain more even distribution, we choose from among the longest arcs the most appropriate one. If none exists (as in a star-shaped set), we accept the uneven split and remove the largest edge. The execution time of this algorithm is $O(C^2.\log((C))$ on the number of node objects.

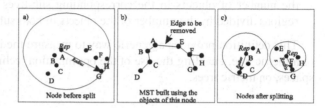

Fig. 1. Exemplifying a node split using the MST algorithm.

Figure 1 illustrates our approach applied to a vector space. After building the MST, the edge between objects A and E will be deleted, and one node will keep the objects A, B, C, D, having B as the representative. The other node will have the objects E, F, G and H, having F as the representative.

5. Overlap Optimization

In this section we present the theoretical underpinnings behind the Slim-down algorithm. The Slim-down algorithm is an easy-to-use approach to reduce overlaps in an existing Slim-tree. Before presenting the algorithm, we have to define the meaning of overlap in a metric space. It should be noted that the notion of overlap in vector space cannot be applied to a metric space [12].

A typical assumption when someone is estimating the number of distance calculations or disk accesses from a tree, is that the tree is 'good' [13][14]. That is, the nodes are tight and the overlaps over the nodes are minimal. The present work directly tackles this subject. That is, the major motivation behind this work was to solve the following problem: *"Given N objects organized in a metric tree, how can we express its 'goodness'/'fitness', with a single number ?"*

We also show that our approach to measuring overlap in a metric space leads to the fat-factor and to the bloat-factor. Both of these factors are suitable to measure the goodness of the Slim-tree and other metric trees. After discussing the properties of these factors, we will present the Slim-down algorithm.

5.1. Computing Overlap in a Metric Access Method

Let us consider two index entries stored in a node of the Slim-tree. In vector spaces, the overlap of two entries refers to the amount of the common space which is covered by both of the bounding regions. When the data is in a vector space, we simply compute the overlap as the volume of the intersection. Since the notion of volume is not available in a metric space we pursue a different approach. Instead of measuring the amount of space, we suggest counting the number of objects in the corresponding sub-trees which are covered by both regions.

Definition 1 - Let I1 and I2 be two index entries. The overlap of I1 and I2 is defined as the number of objects in the corresponding sub-trees which are covered by both regions divided by the number of the objects in both sub-trees.

This definition provides a generic way to measure the intersection between regions of a metric tree, enabling the use of the optimization techniques, developed for vector spaces, on metric trees.

5.2. The Fat-Factor

Analogous to Definition 1 of overlap in a metric space, in this section we present a method to measure the goodness of a metric tree. The basic idea of the following definition of the fat-factor is that a good tree has very little or ideally no overlap between its index entries. Such an approach is compatible with the design goals of index structures like the R+-tree [15] and the R*-tree [16], which were designed with the goal of overlap minimization.

Our definition of the fat-factor makes two reasonable assumptions. First, we take into account only range queries to estimate the goodness of a tree. This assumption is not restrictive since nearest neighbor queries can be viewed as special cases of range queries [17]. Second, we assume that the distribution of the centers of range queries follows the distribution of data objects. This seems to be reasonable since we expect the queries are more likely issued in regions of space where the density of objects is high.

Assuming the above, it is easy to state how an ideal metric-tree should behave. For a point query (a range query with radius zero), the ideal metric-tree requires that one node be retrieved from each level. Thus, the fat-factor should be zero. The worst possible tree is the one which requires the retrieval of all nodes to answer a point query. In this situation the fat-factor should be one. From this discussion we suggest the following definition of fat-factor.

Definition 2 - Let T be a metric tree with height H and M nodes, $M \geq 1$. Let N be the number of objects. Then, the *fat-factor* of a metric tree T is

$$fat(T) = \frac{I_c - H*N}{N} \cdot \frac{1}{(M-H)} \tag{1}$$

where I_C denotes the total number of node accesses required to answer a point query for each of the N objects stored in the metric tree.

Lemma 1 - Let T be a metric tree. Then, *fat(T)* returns a value in the range [0,1]. The worst possible tree returns one, whereas an ideal tree returns zero.

Proof: Let us consider a point query for an object stored in the tree. Such a query has to retrieve at least one node from each level of the tree. In particular, the nodes on the insertion path of the object qualify and are required to be read from disk into memory. A lower limit for I_C (the total number of disk accesses for all point queries) is then $H*N$ resulting in a fat-factor of zero. The worst case occurs when each node has to be read for each of the queries. An upper limit of I_C is then $M*N$ resulting in a fat-factor of one. Since the fat-factor is a linear function in I_c and $H*N \leq I_c \leq M*N$, it follows that the fat-factor has to be in the range [0,1].

QED

Figure 2 shows two trees and their fat-factor. In order to illustrate the relationships between the representative and its associated objects, we have drawn a connection line. Calculating the fat-factor for these trees is straightforward, e.g., for the tree in Figure 2a we have $I_C =12$, $H=2$, $N=6$ and $M=4$, leading to a fat-factor=0. For the tree in Figure 2b we have $I_C =14$, $H=2$, $N=6$ and $M=3$, leading to a fat-factor=1/3.

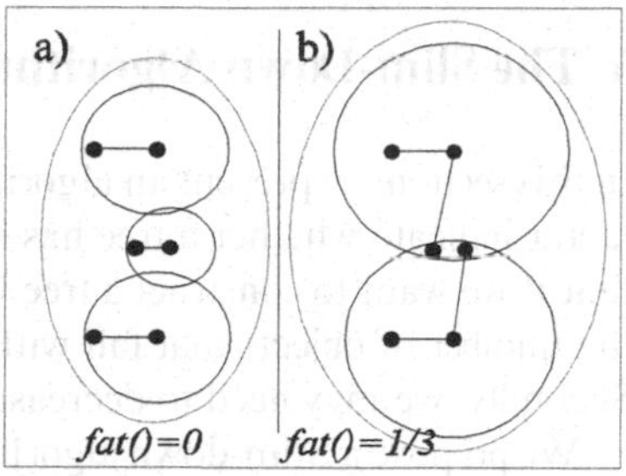

Fig. 2. Two trees storing the same dataset with different number of nodes and fat-factors. Root nodes are shown in broken line.

5.3. Comparing Different Trees for the Same Dataset : The Bloat-Factor

The fat-factor is a measure of the amount of objects that lie inside intersection of regions defined by nodes at the same level of a metric tree. In order to enable the comparison of two trees that store the same dataset (but that use different splitting and/or different promotion algorithms leading to different trees), we need to "penalize" trees that use more than the minimum required number of nodes (and so disk pages). This can be done by defining a new measure, called the "bloat-factor". In a similar way to the fat-factor, the bloat-factor considers not the height and number of nodes in the real tree, but that of the minimum tree. Among all possible trees, the minimum tree is the one with minimum possible height H_{min} and minimum number of nodes M_{min}. Thus, this leads to the following definition.

Definition 3 - The *bloat-factor* of a metric tree T with more than one node is expressed as

$$bl(T) = \frac{I_C - H_{min} * N}{N} \cdot \frac{1}{(M_{min} - H_{min})} \tag{2}$$

This factor will vary from zero to a positive number that can be greater than one.

Although not limited to one, this factor enables the direct comparison of two trees with different bloat-factors, as the tree with the smaller factor always will lead to a lesser number of disk accesses.

The minimum height of the tree organizing N objects is $H_{min} = \lceil \log_C N \rceil$ and the minimum number of nodes for a given dataset can be calculated as $M_{min} = \sum_{i=1}^{H_{min}} \lceil N / C^i \rceil$ where, C is the capacity of the nodes.

It is worth emphasizing that both the fat-factor and the bloat-factor are directly related to the average amount of overlap between regions in the same level of the tree, represented by I_c. The fat-factor measures how good a given tree is with respect to this amount of overlaps, regardless of a possible waste of disk space due to a lower occupation of its nodes. The bloat-factor enables us to compare two trees, considering both the amount of overlaps *and* the efficient occupation of the nodes.

6. The Slim-Down Algorithm

In this section we present an algorithm that produces a 'tighter' tree. The fat and bloat-factor indicate whether a tree has room for improvement. It is clear from Definition 3 that if we want to construct a tree with a smaller bloat-factor, we need first to diminish the number of objects that fall within the intersection of two regions in the same level. Secondly, we may need to decrease the number of nodes in the tree.

We propose a Slim-down algorithm to post-process a tree, aiming to reduce these two numbers in an already constructed tree. This algorithm can be described in the following steps (see Figure 3).

1. For each node i in a given level of the tree, find the farthest object c from the representative b.
2. Find a sibling node j of i, that also covers object c. If such a node j exists and it is not full, remove c from node i and insert it into node j. Correct the radius of node i.
3. Steps 1 and 2 must be applied sequentially over all nodes of a given level of the tree. If after a full round of these two steps, an object moves from one node to another, another full round of step 1 and 2 must be re-applied.

In this way, if object c was moved from node i to node j in step 2, and it is the only object in node i at this distance from the original center, then the correction of the radius of node i will

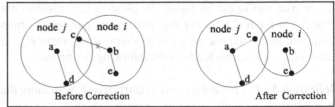

Fig. 3. How the Slim-down algorithm works.

reduce the radius of this node without increasing any other radii. As Figure 3 illustrates, we can assume that object e is the next farthest object from the representative of node i.

Thus, after the reduction, the new radius of node i will be that shown with solid line. With this reduction, at least object c will go out of the region of this node which intersects with the region of node j, reducing I_c counting. Moreover, when this algorithm is applied, we do not guarantee a minimum occupancy in the nodes of the tree, so eventually some nodes can become empty, further reducing the number of nodes in the tree. It must be noted that step 2 can take advantage of the triangle inequality to prune part of the needed distance calculations.

This algorithm can be executed at different phases of the evolution of the tree. The following variations immediately come to mind.

a) A similar algorithm could be applied to the higher levels of the tree.

b) The algorithm could be dynamically applied to slim-down the sub-tree stored in a node just after one of its direct descendants has been split.

c) When a new object must be inserted in a node which is full, a single relocation of the farthest object of one node could be tried instead of splitting.

Besides the algorithm being applied over the leaf nodes after the completion of the tree, we also have implemented variation (b), and we found that it indeed leads to a better tree. Moreover, both variations can be applied isolated or together, and either way, each provides an increase in performance. However, this last variation slows down the building of the tree and does not give results as good as those obtained by working on the completed tree. So, due to lack of space, we are not showing these results here.

7. Experimental Evaluation of the Slim-Tree

In this section we provide experimental results of the performance of the Slim tree. We run experiments comparing the Slim-tree with the M-tree and demonstrating the impact of the MST-splitting method and the slim-down algorithm. The Slim-tree was implemented in C++ under Windows NT. The experiments were performed on a Pentium II 450MHz PC with 128 MB of main memory. Our implementation is based on a simple disk simulator which provides a counter for the number of disk accesses.

Since the performance of insertions is largely determined by the CPU-time (because of the required distance computations and the complexity of split operations), we report in the following only the total runtime for creating metric trees. For queries, however, we report the number of disk accesses which is a good indicator for the query performance. We found that the number of distance calculations is highly correlated with the number of disk accesses.

In order to illustrate the performance of the new MAM proposed, the Slim-tree, we use six synthetic and real datasets throughout the paper. Table 1 reports the most important characteristics of our datasets. Among them there are vector datasets (2- and 16-dimensional) and metric datasets. Specifically note that for the FaceIT dataset we have used a distance function from a commercial software product. In general, we have used the L_2 metric for the vector datasets, but for the EnglishWords dataset, Levenshtein or string edit distance (L_{Edit}) was used. L_{Edit} (x,y) is a metric which counts the minimal number of symbols that have to be inserted, deleted, or substituted, to transform x into y (e.g. L_{edit} ("head", "hobby") = 4 - three substitutions and one insertion).

Let us mention here that the domain of the vector sets is the unit cube. The experiments were performed in the way that we first build up a metric tree by inserting tuples one by one. Thereafter, we run 13 sets of 500 range queries where the size of the range queries was fixed for each set. In the following graphs we report the average number of disk accesses obtained from a set of queries as the function of the query size. All the graphs are given in log-log scale.

Table 1. Datasets used in the experiments.

Datasets	# Objects - N	Dimension - D	Metric	Description
Uniform2D	10,000	2	L_2	Uniformly distributed data
Sierpinsky	9,841	2	L_2	Fractal dataset
MGCounty	15,559	2	L_2	Intersection points of roads from Montgomery County - Maryland
EigenFaces	11,900	16	L_2	Face vectors of the Informedia project [18].
FaceIT	1,056	unknown	FaceIt ™	A dataset constructed by a distance matrix obtained from FaceIt™ software, version 2.51 [19].
EnglishWords	25,143	none	L_{edit}	Words from an English language dictionary.

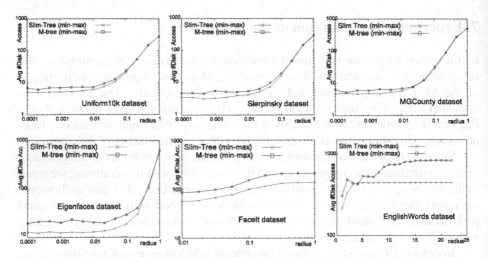

Fig. 4. The query performance (given by average number of disk accesses) for the M-tree and the Slim-tree as a function of the query radius where each of the plots refers to one of our datasets.

7.1 Comparing the Slim-Tree and the M-Tree

Since the M-tree is the only dynamic metric tree available, we compared its alleged best performance to the corresponding one of our Slim-tree. Figure 4 shows the query performance of the Slim-tree and the M-tree for the six datasets. Both trees were built using the minMax-splitting algorithm, which was found to be the most promising for the M-tree [12]. The corresponding capacities of the nodes used in these experiments are reported in Table 3. Note that for both trees we used the same settings of the parameters, leading to a fair comparison.

From the plots in Figure 4 we can see that the Slim-tree constantly outperforms M-tree. One of the reasons is that the occupation of the nodes is higher for the Slim-tree and therefore, the total number of nodes is smaller. This effect is visible for the FaceIt and EnglishWords datasets, where a large number of the pages are required for large range queries. For the vector data sets, however, both trees perform similarly for large query radii. This is because the overlap of the entries is low and therefore, the different insertion strategies of the M-tree and the Slim-tree perform similarly. Note also that for large query radii it might be more effective to read the entire file into memory (using sequential I/Os). However it is common to expect that the majority of queries radii are rather small so that it is beneficial to use a metric tree.

7.2   Comparing minMax and MST Splitting Algorithms

Figure 5 compares the query performance of two Slim-trees where the one uses the minMax-splitting algorithm and the other uses the MST-splitting algorithm. The left and right plot shows the results for Sierpinsky and FaceIt, respectively. The plot shows that both Slim-trees perform similarly. Table 2 give more details about the comparison of the different splitting strategies. Here, the columns "range queries" refer to the CPU time (in seconds) required to perform all the queries of the 13 sets. We point out here that the MST-splitting strategy suffers slightly when the number of objects per node (the capacity) is small. The columns "build" show the time (in seconds) to create the Slim-trees. The MST-algorithm is clearly superior to the minMax-splitting algorithm. For example, the MST-algorithm is faster by a factor of 60 for the two-dimensional datasets. Overall, the MST-splitting algorithm gives considerable savings when a Slim-tree is created and provides almost the same performance as the minMax-splitting algorithm for range queries.

The experiments on the splitting algorithms show that the runtime of the MST-

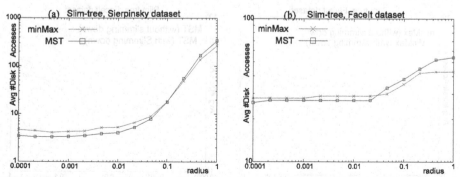

Fig. 5. The query performance of two Slim-trees using the minMax-splitting algorithm and the MST-splitting algorithm. (a). Sierpinsky dataset, (b) FaceIt dataset.

splitting algorithm is increasingly better than the minMax-splitting algorithm as the number of entries increases. From the results of our experiments we can give the following rule of thumb for choosing a split algorithm: when C (the capacity of the nodes) is lower than 20, it is beneficial to use the minMax- splitting strategy. For trees with bigger C, the MST-splitting algorithm is a better choice. It is also important to say that the *ChooseSubtree* algorithm also has an influence on the splitting algorithms.

Table 2 - A comparison of the Slim-trees using the minMax-splitting algorithm and the MST-splitting algorithm. The numbers are wall-clock times in seconds.

Datasets	Slim-tree using the minMax-splitting algorithm (time in sec.)				Slim-tree using the MST-splitting algorithm (time in sec.)			
	build	range queries	slim-down	fat-factor	build	range queries	slim-down	fat-factor
Uniform2D	94.62	17.23	0.23	1.54	1.58	16.62	0.33	1.91
Sierpinsky	103.88	11.86	0.41	0.83	1.68	11.96	0.23	0.99
MgCounty	195.16	20.67	0.38	2.31	3.08	20.78	0.40	2.16
Eigenfaces	61.60	62.33	1.20	0.13	6.46	68.67	0.89	71.10
EnglishWords	1704.44	504.17	82.59	173.36	33.96	513.03	210.41	204.78
FaceIt	0.45	0.13	0.08	0.06	0.15	0.16	0.01	0.16

7.3 Experiments with the Slim-Down Algorithm

The Slim-down algorithm improves the number of disk accesses for range queries in average between 10 to 20% for vector datasets. As these datasets already have a low bloat-factor, this gives small room for improvement through the Slim-down algorithm. For datasets with bigger bloat-factors (as the metric datasets FaceIt and EnglishWords), the average improvement goes to between 25 and 35%.

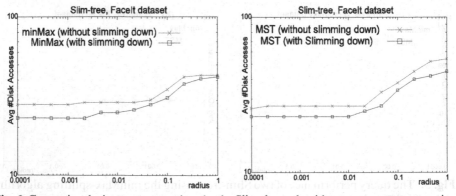

Fig. 6. Comparing the improvements given by the Slim-down algorithm to answer range queries.

Figure 6 compares the query performance of the Slim-trees where the one uses the slim-down algorithm and the other does not. Note that on the left-hand side of Figure 6 we show the results when the minMax-splitting algorithm is used, whereas the results of the MST-splitting algorithm are presented on the right-hand side. Both graphs show that the slim-down algorithm improves the Slim-trees. In Table 2 (column "slim-down") we also show the time to perform the slim-down on the tree. In general, only a small fraction of the build time is required to perform a slim-down on a Slim-tree.

Although the measurement of I_C takes some computing time, the alternative way to obtain some values that represent the performance of a metric tree is to issue several queries for each given radius, keep the average number of disk accesses (or distance calculations) and their standard deviations and then generate the corresponding plots. We measured the times spent to calculate both the fat-factor and the average of disk accesses using 500 randomly generated queries. These measurements are shown in Table 2, and from there we can see that the calculation of the fat-factor is faster than the other alternative.

The last two columns of Table 3 show the fat-factor and the bloat-factor calculated for the Slim-trees using the MST-splitting algorithm. Moreover, we also present the number of nodes and the height of the tree. Note that parameter M refers to the actual number of nodes and parameter M_{min} gives the minimum number of nodes. Analogously, the parameters H and H_{min} refer to the height of the Slim-tree. The number of objects per node (C) varies because of the size of the data objects.

Table 3 - Parameters of the Slim-trees using the MST-splitting algorithm

Dataset	Num. of objects N	Objects per node C	Number of nodes		Height of the tree		Fat factor $Ff()$	Bloat factor $Bl()$
			M	M_{min}	H	H_{min}		
Uniform2D	10,000	52	307	198	3	3	0.03	0.05
Sierpinsky	9,841	52	374	195	3	3	0.01	0.01
MGCounty	15,559	52	568	307	3	3	0.01	0.01
Eigenfaces	11,900	24	930	518	4	3	0.32	0.58
FaceIt	1,056	11	226	106	4	3	0.23	0.51
EnglishWords	25,143	60	476	428	3	3	0.48	0.53

In general, the results of our experiments confirmed that the fat-factor is suitable to measure the quality of a Slim-tree. As a rule of thumb, we believe that a metric tree with a fat-factor between 0 and 0.1 can be considered as a good tree, with a fat-factor between 0.1 and 0.3 as an acceptable tree, and with a fat-factor greater than 0.3 a bad tree. From Table 3 we can see that the Slim-trees for Uniform2D, Sierpinsky and MGCounty are very good trees, but the trees for Eigenfaces, FaceIt and EnglishWords are considered to be barely acceptable.

8. Conclusions

We have presented the Slim-tree, a dynamic metric access method which uses new approaches to efficiently index metric datasets. Our main contributions consist of the Slim-down algorithm and a new splitting algorithm based on the minimal spanning tree (MST). Additionally, we suggest a new *ChooseSubtree* algorithm for the Slim-tree which directs the insertion of an object from a given node to the child node with the lowest occupation when more than one child node qualifies. This leads to tighter trees and fewer disk pages, which also results in a more efficient processing of queries.

The new MST-splitting method is considerably faster than the minMax-splitting method, which has been considered the best for the M-tree [2] [10], while query performance is almost not affected. For a node with capacity C, the runtime of the minMax-splitting method is $O(C^3)$ whereas the runtime of the MST-splitting method is $O(C^2 \log C)$. Their performance difference is reflected in our experiments where the time to build a Slim-tree using the MST-splitting method, is by a factor of up two orders of magnitude lower than using the minMax-splitting method. Both splitting methods result in Slim-trees with almost the same query performance. We observed that query performance suffered a little by using the MST-splitting method, but only for small node capacities (less than 20).

The Slim-down algorithm is designed to be applied to a poorly constructed metric tree in order to improve its query performance. The theoretical underpinning of the Slim-down algorithm is our approach for computing overlap in a metric tree. Although overlap is identified as an important tuning parameter for improving query performance for spatial access methods, it has not been previously used for metric trees due to the inability to compute the volume of intersecting regions. In order to overcome this deficiency, we propose using the relative number of objects covered by two (or more) regions to estimate their overlap. This concept is used in the design of the Slim-down algorithm. In this paper, we used the Slim-down algorithm in a post-processing step, just after the insertion of all objects. This approach does not impedes subsequent insertions since it could also be used when objects have yet to be inserted. In our experiments, the Slim-down algorithm improves query performance of 35% in average.

Our concept of overlap also leads to the introduction of two factors each of them expresses the quality of a Slim-tree for a given dataset using only a single number. The fat-factor measures the quality of a tree with a fixed number of nodes, whereas the bloat factor enables a comparison of trees where the number of nodes is different. Moreover, we foresee that the proposed method of treating overlaps in metric spaces allows us to apply to metric access methods many well-known fine-tuning techniques developed for spatial access methods.

In our future work, we are primarily interested in the following subjects. First, we plan to apply the Slim-down algorithm to the nodes of the upper levels of a metric tree. So far, we have used the algorithm only for the internal nodes on the lowest level (the first level above the leaves). Second, we are interested in a comparison of the Slim-down algorithm with the re-insertion technique of the R*-tree. Third, we will study whether the bloat-factor can be used to develop a cost model for predicting the cost of a range query in the Slim-tree. Fourth, we will investigate whether the definition of the bloat-factor can be generalized when we explicitly distinguish between a set of query objects and a set of data objects.

Acknowledgments

We are grateful to Pavel Zezula, Paolo Ciaccia and Marco Patella for giving us the code of the M-tree.

References

1. Gaede,V., Gunther, O.: Multidimensional Access Methods. ACM Computing Surveys, 30(2) (1998) 170-231.
2. Ciaccia, P., Patella,M., Zezula, P.: M-tree: An Efficient Access Method for Similarity Search in Metric Spaces, VLDB (1997) 426-435.
3. Burkhard,W.A., Keller R.M.: Some Approaches to Best-Match File Searching. CACM 16(4) (1973) 230-236.
4. Uhlmann, J.K.: Satisfying General Proximity/Similarity Queries with Metric Trees. IPL 40(4) (1991) 175-179.
5. Yianilos, P. N.: Data Structures and Algorithms for Nearest Neighbor Search in General Metric Spaces. ACM SODA (1993) 311-321.
6. Baeza-Yates,R.A., Cunto,W., Manber,U., Wu S.: Proximity Matching Using Fixed-Queries Trees. CPM, (1994) 198-212.
7. Bozkaya,T., Özsoyoglu, Z.M. Distance-Based Indexing for High-Dimensional Metric Spaces, ACM-SIGMOD (1997) 357-368.
8. Brin S.: Near Neighbor Search in Large Metric Spaces, VLDB (1995) 574-584.
9. Guttman A.: R-Tree: Adynamic Index Structure for Spatial Searching. ACM-SIGMOD (1984) 47-57.
10. Ciaccia, P., Patella, M.: Bulk Loading the M-tree. ADC'98 (1998) 15-26.
11. Kruskal Jr.,J.B.: On the Shortest Spanning Subtree of a Graph and the Traveling Salesman Problem. Proc. Amer. Math. Soc. (7) (1956) 48-50.
12. Ciaccia, P., Patella,M.,Rabitti, F. , Zezula, P.: Indexing Metric Spaces with M-tree. Proc. Quinto convegno Nazionale SEBD (1997).
13. Faloutsos,C., Kamel, L.: Beyond Uniformity and Independence: Analysis of R-tree Using the Concept of Fractal Dimension. ACM-PODS (1994) 4-13.
14 Traina Jr., C., Traina, A., Faloutsos, C.: Distance Exponent: A New Concept for Selectivity Estimation in Metric Trees. CMU-CS-99-110 Technical Report (1999).
15. Sellis,T., Roussopoulos,N., Faloutsos, C.: The R+-tree: A Dynamic Index for Multi-dimensional Objects. VLDB (1987) 507-518.
16. Beckmann, N., Kriegel,H.-P., Schneider R., Seeger, B.: The R*-tree: An Efficient and Robust Access Method for Points and Rectangles. ACM-SIGMOD (1990) 322-331.
17. Berchtold,S., Böhm,C., Keim, D.A., Kriegel, H.-P.: A Cost Model For Nearest Neighbor Search in High-Dimensional Data Space. ACM-PODS (1997) 78-86.
18. Wactlar, H.D., Kanade, T., Smith, M.A., Stevens, S.M.: Intelligent Access to Digital Video: Informedia Project. IEEE Computer, 29 (3) (1996) 46-52.
19. Visionics Corp. - Available at http://www.visionics.com/live/frameset.html (12-Feb-1999).

Mediators & Semantic Integration

Automatic Deployment of Application-Specific Metadata and Code in MOCHA*

Manuel Rodríguez-Martínez and Nick Roussopoulos

Institute for Advanced Computer Studies
Department of Computer Science
University of Maryland, College Park, MD 20742
{manuel,nick}@cs.umd.edu

Abstract. Database middleware systems require the deployment of application-specific data types and query operators to the servers and clients in the system. Existing middleware solutions rely on developers and system administrators to port and manually install all this application-specific functionality to all sites in the system. This approach cannot scale to an environment in which there are hundreds of data sources, such as those accessed by the Web and even more custom-tailored applications, since the complexity and the cost involved in maintaining a code base system-wide are enormous. This paper describes a novel metadata-driven framework designed to automate the deployment of all application-specific functionality used by a middleware system. We used Java and XML to implement this framework in MOCHA, a middleware system developed at the University of Maryland. We first present the kind of services, metadata elements and software tools used in MOCHA to automate code deployment. Then, we describe how the features of MOCHA simplify the administration and reduce the management cost of a middleware system in a large scale environment.

1 Introduction

Database middleware systems [7], such as database gateways and mediator systems, are used to integrate heterogeneous data sources dispersed over a computer network. To achieve data integration, the middleware layer imposes a global data schema on top of the individual schemas used by each source. With this mechanism, client applications serviced by the middleware system are provided with a uniform view and access interface to the data sets stored by each data source. The translation of the data items to the global schema is performed by either a wrapper or database gateway. Wrappers are used when integration is achieved through a mediator system, such as TSIMMIS [1], DISCO [13] or Garlic [11]. On the other hand, gateways are used when integration is realized by importing the data into a commercial DBMS, such as Oracle [6] or Informix [5].

A problem with the use of middleware systems is the deployment of the application-specific data types and operators necessary to implement the global

---

* This work was supported by the DOD Lucite Contract CG9815.

C. Zaniolo et al. (Eds.): EDBT 2000, LNCS 1777, pp. 69–85, 2000.
© Springer-Verlag Berlin Heidelberg 2000

schema used by the system. Since new applications and data sources are added to the system as time progresses, the global schema must be changed to reflect these new additions. And since the data in each source must be translated from its native format into the middleware-level format, new data types must be custom-built to represent these data in the latter format. Notice that these data types will be used by the middleware to hold the values been processed, and by the client application to present the result values to the user. Moreover, all query operators that cannot be evaluated by the data sources will have to be implemented at and evaluated by the middleware system. Therefore, the scalability of the middleware system depends on how efficiently it can ingest and deploy all this new application-specific functionality to the clients and servers which are part of the system.

In our view, existing middleware solutions fail to provide adequate mechanisms to deploy new or updated functionality to the existing middleware infrastructure. Most systems use either C or C++ as the implementation language for middleware data types and operators. With this approach, the functionality has to be ported to several different hardware and operating system platforms, which can be a very slow and expensive process. In addition, the new code has to be **manually** installed into every machine in which a client, mediator, wrapper or gateway application can be expected to be run. Clearly, as the system grows with new applications, data sources and users, it becomes increasingly difficult and expensive to maintain the software base used throughout the system.

The objective of this paper is to present a novel metadata-driven framework used to automate the deployment of application-specific functionality in a middleware system. We have implemented this framework in MOCHA[1], a prototype database middleware system developed at the University of Maryland. MOCHA is based on the philosophy that all application-specific code should be automatically deployed by the middleware system itself. In MOCHA, this is realized by implementing the new functionality in Java classes, which are then shipped to the client applications and remote servers from which data will be extracted. With this feature of *automatic code deployment*, administrators are freed from having to perform system-wide installations of software. Instead, all the Java classes are stored into one or more *code repositories* from which MOCHA later retrieves and deploys them on a "need-to-do" basis.

MOCHA not only simplifies the administration effort needed to maintain the middleware software, but also provides efficient query services. In [9] we showed how MOCHA leverages its ability to ship Java classes implementing query operators to execute them near the data source or near the client in an effort to reduce data movement over the network. Data "reducing" operators which filter the data and produce smaller values are computed near the data source, while data "inflating" operators which expand their arguments are evaluated near the client. Using this query optimization framework, MOCHA provides substantial performance gains on both single-site and multi-site queries containing complex aggregates, predicates and projections.

---

[1] MOCHA stands for **M**iddleware Based **O**n a **C**ode **SH**ipping **A**rchitecture.

In this paper, we describe the components in the architecture of MOCHA, and the main services, metadata elements and software tools necessary to support automatic code deployment. Since metadata and control must be exchanged between the components of MOCHA, we also present the exchange formats used for this purpose. These formats are based on the well-accepted XML standard for content exchange between networked applications. The remaining of this paper is organized as follows. Sect. 2 presents a brief description of XML and RDF, Internet standards used for metadata and control exchange in MOCHA. The architecture of MOCHA is described in Sect. 3. In Sect. 4 we describe the metadata necessary to support automatic code deployment. Sect. 5 presents the code deployment process used by MOCHA. The implementation status and benefits of our approach are presented in Sect. 6. Finally, our conclusions are given in Sect. 8.

2   Overview of XML and RDF

In this section we briefly review XML and RDF, two technologies we used to build the framework for automatic deployment of application-specific code.

2.1   XML

The Extensible Markup Language (XML) [2], is a standard for data exchange over the Internet. XML is a markup language derived from SGML, but with a much simpler structure, and it is designed to *encode* the content in a document, and make it "machine-readable". In this regard, XML is very different from HTML, which is designed to *present* the content in a document on a Web browser. Figure 1 depicts XML data encoding a personalized phone book. As we can observe from the figure, XML data is organized as a series of *elements* delimited by tags. In this example the tags are **PhoneBook**, **Address**, **Name** and **Phone**. Each XML element either encloses another XML element or a datum encoded as a string. Thus, in XML the schema information and the data are all integrated in the same document. This arrangement makes XML documents machine-readable, or *self-describing*, because applications can parse the XML document and find the tags enclosing the data they need to process. XML is also a fully extensible language, and the ability for programmers to add new tags to XML is one of its most important assets. XML can be customized with new tags that express the schema for many applications, and then provide a mechanism for data exchange specific to these applications. The structure of an XML document can be validated by the applications by using a *Document Type Definition* (DTD). These are grammars which describe the valid structure of a particular XML document. All of the above features in XML have caught the attention of major software vendors, which are now targeting XML as the standard for data interchange used by their products.

```
<PhoneBook>
  <Address>
    <Name>John Smith</Name>
    <Phone>(301)-403-0500</Phone>
  </Address>
  <Address>
    <Name>Adams Morgan</Name>
    <Phone>(999)-201-8931</Phone>
  </Address>
</PhoneBook>
```

Fig. 1. XML Phone Data

2.2 RDF

The Resource Description Framework (RDF) [4] is an extension of XML designed to provide metadata interoperability between applications. RDF provides a standard mechanism to encode and exchange metadata about any entity of interest to any given application. Each object been described by the metadata is termed a *resource* and is uniquely identified by a *Uniform Resource Identifier* (URI) [8]. RDF metadata is organized as a set of properties types and values encoded in XML. Figure 2 shows an example in which a report with URI http://www.umd.edu/report.html is been described. The rdf and Description tags are introduced by RDF to identify the XML elements that contain metadata. The attributes xmlns and xmlns:DC are used to identify the *namespaces* for the tags used in the document. XML supports a *namespace* feature [3] which is used to give a specific context to the tags contained in XML documents. Each namespace used in an XML document is uniquely identified by a URI. In Fig. 2, xmlns gives the namespace for the RDF tags (rdf and Description), and xmlns:DC gives the namespace for the Dublin Core tags, which are those that begin with the DC: prefix. The Dublin Core is a standard set of metadata identifiers used to describe electronic documents, such as those stored in digital libraries. The metadata shown in Fig. 2 indicates the title, author, creation date and general description of the annual report on the status of the University of Maryland. Clearly, RDF-encoded metadata can be readily used by an application to discover the information necessary to find documents of interest to the users, and such documents might reside on the Web, a database server or in the file system of a particular workstation.

3 MOCHA Architecture

In this section, we describe the principal components in the architecture of MOCHA. We have implemented a prototype system for MOCHA using Java, and we have built the system around two fundamental principles. First, all the code which implements data types and query operators is automatically and seamlessly deployed by MOCHA to the clients and servers in the system. Second,

```
<?xml version=''1.0'' ?>
<rdf xmlns = ''http://w3.org/TR/1999/PR-rdf-syntax-199901105#''
      xmlns:DC = ''http://purl.org/DC#''>
    <Description about = ''http://www.umd.edu/report.html'' >
        <DC:Title>Annual Report</DC:Title>
        <DC:Creator>John Mote</DC:Creator>
        <DC:Date>05-01-99</DC:Date>
        <DC:Subject>UMCP, University, Government</DC:Subject>
    </Description>
</rdf>
```

Fig. 2. An RDF example

all query operators that are evaluated by the middleware layer are scheduled for execution at the site that results in minimum data movement over the network.

The components in the architecture of MOCHA [9] are depicted in Fig. 3. At the top of the architecture is the **Client Application**, which provides the user with the Graphical User Interface (GUI) to pose queries to the system and visualize their results. In most cases, we expect the client to be an applet loaded into a Web browser, but it is also possible to use a Java stand-alone application. The client connects to the **Query Processing Coordinator** (QPC) by means of an *Uniform Resource Locator* (URL), and sends to QPC all queries posed by the user. The QPC is an extensible server application which provides the basic query processing services in the system: a) query parsing, b) metadata management, c) query optimization, d) query execution and d) error management. QPC is designed to execute those query operators that produce results larger than their arguments. In addition, QPC is in charge of deploying all the application-specific code to the rest of the system. All the application-specific code is stored in one or more *code repositories*, and the QPC accesses these repositories to fetch the necessary code. The QPC also manages a *catalog*, which contains all the descriptions (encoded as XML documents) of the data sources, data types and query operators available in the system.

In order to access the wealth of information stored in a particular data source, the QPC connects to the **Data Access Provider** (DAP) associated with the data source by means of an URL. The DAP is an extensible server application which extracts data from a source on behalf of the QPC. There are two essential services provided by a DAP: a) data translation, and b) query execution. The DAP extracts requested items from the data source, and translates them from the local schema used by the source into the global schema used by QPC. Also, the DAP is capable of executing query operators that generate new abstractions from the data. In particular, the DAP is designed to execute those operators that filter out the data sets (e.g. a predicate) to produce smaller values. For this reason, the DAP should be run at the data source site or in close proximity to it (e.g. on another host in the same LAN). The QPC delivers all the code for the data types and operators used by each DAP. Similarly, all results produced by

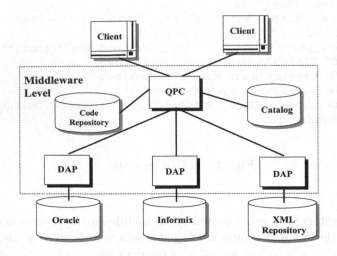

Fig. 3. MOCHA Architecture

each DAP are sent to QPC for further processing until the final answer to the query is fabricated and sent to the user.

The final component in the MOCHA architecture is the **Data Server**, which is the server application that provides storage for the data sets stored and manipulated by each data source. Each DAP in the system must be configured to run on top of a particular Data Server. MOCHA can support a wide variety of data servers, including database servers, XML repositories, Web servers and file servers. Clearly, the architecture of MOCHA provides the foundation for a very flexible, scalable and well-organized middleware solution to integrate a wide range of data sources.

4   Publishing Resources

In this section we use an example application to illustrate the capabilities incorporated in MOCHA to publish resources such as tables, query operators and data types. For simplicity, we assume that the system follows the relational model. The capabilities for publishing resources are built on top of RDF and therefore, each resource is identified by a URI. The exact structure of such URI must be chosen by the system administrator, and should follow the conventions specified in [8]. In this paper we will use two simple conventions. First, the URI for a relation will be of the form:

mocha : // < host > / < database > / < table >

The keyword mocha specifies that the resource been published will be used by MOCHA. The host component specifies the domain name or IP address of the machine hosting the data source. Similarly, the database part gives the name

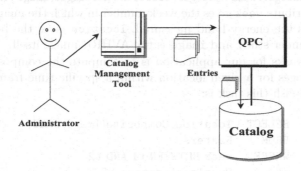

Fig. 4. Catalog Management

of the targeted database space, and `table` gives the name of the table been published. The second convention is for data types and operators. For these resources, the URI is of the form :

$$\text{mocha} : // < \text{host} > / < \text{repository} > / < \text{object} >$$

In this instance, `host` is the domain name or IP address of the machine hosting the code repository containing the Java class for a type or operator. The `repository` component indicates what code repository must be accessed to find the Java class associated with the resource. Finally, the `object` part gives the user-specified name of the type or operator being published.

MOCHA uses the URI for a resource as search key into the catalog to find the metadata for that resource. The metadata is contained in a RDF text document, with a schema specific to MOCHA. In this schema, all tags contain the prefix `mocha :` , which identifies the MOCHA namespace[2]. To register each resource, the administrator uses an utility application program to add a metadata entry, in the form $(URI, RDF\ File)$, into the catalog table specific to the type of resource (e.g. a data type). Each entry is sent to the QPC and then added to the catalog, as illustrated in Fig. 4.

4.1 Motivating Application

Consider an Earth Science application used to manipulate satellite images from different regions of the United States. The data sets accessed by this application are maintained in separate data sources located across the United States. One of the data sources is an Informix database server hosted by a workstation in the Computer Science Department at the University of Maryland. This data source contains a relation named `Rasters`, and it stores satellite AVHRR images containing weekly energy readings from the surface of the State of Maryland. The schema for this relation is a follows:

---

[2] The URI for this namespace is `http : //www.cs.umd.edu/users/manuel/MOCHA/`.

Rasters(week : integer, band : integer, location : Rectangle, image : Raster);
In this case, attribute week gives the week number in which the image was made,
band represents the energy band measured, location gives the bounding box
for the region under study and image is the AVHRR image itself.

One of the tasks for our application is to compute the composite image of
all AVHRR images for a given location within a specific time frame. The SQL
query to accomplish this task is:

```
SELECT    location, Composite(image, band)
FROM      Rasters
WHERE     week BETWEEN t1 AND t2
AND       Overlap(location, RECT)
GROUP BY location
```

We will identify this query throughout the rest of this paper as $Q1$. Function
Composite() used in $Q1$ is an user-defined aggregate, which generates an image
that is the composite of a set of AVHRR images. Similarly, function Overlap()
is an user-defined predicate which determines if two rectangles overlap. Given
this scenario, we now discuss how to configure MOCHA to provide support for
our Earth Science application.

4.2   Tables

The first resources that must be made available to MOCHA are the tables to
be used by the applications. For each table, metadata indicating its name, the
database in which it is stored, the columns names and the middleware types
needed to represent each of its columns must be added to the catalog. This
information will enable MOCHA to access each table, retrieve its tuples, project
one or more of its columns and translate each column value into a middleware
data type.

Figure 5 shows the RDF metadata for table Rasters of our example application. The URI for this table is specified by the about attribute in the RDF
Description tag. Property mocha : Table gives the name of the relation, and
property mocha : Owner gives the e-mail address of its owner. Connectivity information is provided by property mocha : Database. This element specifies the
URL of the DAP associated with the data source (i.e. the Informix Server) and
the name of the database space in which relation Rasters is stored. In this case,
the DAP is located at URL cs1.umd.edu : 8000, and table Rasters is contained
in the EarthSciDB database. Each of the columns in Rasters is described in the
mocha : Columns property, which contains a sequence (specified by tag Seq) of
column descriptions, each one delimited by the li tag. For each column, property mocha : Column indicates the column name, mocha : Type gives the name of
the middleware type used to represent its values and the URI for this data type
is specified by the mocha : URI property. Once this information is added to the
catalog, table Rasters is ready to be used in the queries posed to the QPC.

```
<Description about =                            </mocha:URI>
   ''mocha://cs1.umd.edu/EarthSciDB/Rasters'' >  </li>
<mocha:Table> Rasters </mocha:Table>           <li parseType = ''resource'' >
<mocha:Owner> manuel@cs1.umd.edu </mocha:Owner>   <mocha:Column> location </mocha:Column>
<mocha:Database> cs1.umd.edu:8000/EarthSciDB      <mocha:Type>Rectangle</mocha:Type>
</mocha:Database>                                 <mocha:URI>
<mocha:Columns>                                   mocha:cs1.umd.edu/EarthScience/Rectangle
   <Seq>                                          </mocha:URI>
      <li parseType = ''resource'' >           </li>
         <mocha:Column> week </mocha:Column>    <li parseType = ''resource'' >
         <mocha:Type> MWInteger </mocha:Type>      <mocha:Column>image</mocha:Column>
         <mocha:URI>                               <mocha:Type>Raster</mocha:Type>
         mocha:cs1.umd.edu/BaseTypes/MWInteger     <mocha:URI>
         </mocha:URI>                              mocha:cs1.umd.edu/EarthScience/Raster
      </li>                                        </mocha:URI>
      <li parseType = ''resource'' >           </li>
         <mocha:Column> band </mocha:Column>   </Seq>
         <mocha:Type> MWInteger </mocha:Type>  </mocha:Columns>
         <mocha:URI>                           </Description>
         mocha:cs1.umd.edu/BaseTypes/MWInteger
```

Fig. 5. Metadata for table `Rasters`

4.3   User-Defined Operators

As mentioned in Sect. 3, query operators can be executed by the QPC or the
DAP, and each of these two components contains a dynamically extensible query
execution engine with an iterator-based machinery for data processing. Since
each operator is dynamically imported into the execution engine, the metadata
must provide enough information to instantiate the operator. In particular, the
kind of operator, the number and type of arguments, and the expected result
type must be thoroughly described for the execution engine module. In MOCHA,
query operators are divided into two categories: complex functions and aggregates.

Complex Functions In MOCHA, complex functions are used in complex predicates and projections contained in queries, and these are implemented as static
methods in Java classes. We will not discuss here the specifics of the implementation of these operators due to lack of space. It suffices to say, however, that
the execution engine in a QPC or DAP uses the name of the static method and
the name of the Java class in which the method is contained in order to create a
Java object that executes the body of the particular query operator. The interested reader is referred to the full version of this paper [10] in order to get more
implementation details.

Figure 6 shows the metadata required for function `Overlap()`, which is used in
query $Q1$ of our example application (see section 4.1). Property `mocha:Function`

```
<Description about =
 ''mocha://cs1.umd.edu/EarthScience/Overlap'' >
 <mocha:Function> Overlap </mocha:Function>
 <mocha:Class> Geometry.class </mocha:Class>
 <mocha:Method> Overlap </mocha:Method>
 <mocha:Repository> cs1.umd.edu/EarthScience
 </mocha:Repository>
 <mocha:Arguments>
   <Seq>
     <li parseType = ''resource'' >
       <mocha:Type> Rectangle </mocha:Type>
       <mocha:URI>
       mocha:cs1.umd.edu/EarthScience/Rectangle
       </mocha:URI>
     </li>
     <li parseType = ''resource'' >
       <mocha:Type> Rectangle </mocha:Type>
       <mocha:URI>
       mocha:cs1.umd.edu/EarthScience/Rectangle
       </mocha:URI>
     </li>
   </Seq>
 </mocha:Arguments>
 <mocha:Result>
   <mocha:Type> MWBoolean </mocha:Type>
   <mocha:URI>
   mocha:cs1.umd.edu/BaseTypes/MWBoolean
   </mocha:URI>
 </mocha:Result>
 <mocha:Creator> manuel@cs1.umd.edu </mocha:Creator>
</Description>
```

Fig. 6. Metadata for function `Overlap()`

gives the name of the function and also identifies the metadata block as one for a complex function. Function `Overlap()` is defined in class `Geometry.class` and implemented by the static method `Overlap`, as indicated by the `mocha : Class` and `mocha : Method` properties, respectively. Property `mocha : Repository` contains the URL for the code repository containing class `Geometry.class`. This repository is named `EarthScience` and resides on host `cs1.umd.edu`. The arguments to function `Overlap()` are the two rectangles to be tested for overlap. The metadata for these arguments are contained in a `mocha : Arguments` property. Like in the case for the columns in a table, the arguments are specified using the sequence (`Seq`) construct. For each argument, the name of its type is given in property `mocha : Type`, and the `mocha : URI` property gives the corresponding URI for this type. In similar fashion, property `mocha : Result` is used to describe the return type of the function. In this case, the result is a boolean value, whose type name and type URI are described by properties `mocha : Type` and `mocha : URI`, respectively. Finally, the person who implemented this function is identified with his/her e-mail address in `mocha : Creator`.

Aggregates In MOCHA, an aggregate operator is implemented as an instance of a Java class. Such class must implement the `Aggregate` standard Java interface provided by MOCHA. This interface defines three methods which are used by the execution engine to evaluate the aggregate operator: `Reset()`, `Update()` and `Summarize()`. The execution engine will create an aggregate object for each of the different groups formed during the aggregation process, and each object is first initialized through a call to method `Reset()`. As tuples are read from the source, method `Update()` is repeatedly called to update the internal state in the aggregate. This update is done based on the existing internal state in the aggregate object and the argument attributes from the next tuple read. Once all tuples have been ingested, the result in the aggregate object is extracted by calling method `Summarize()`. The interested reader is referred to [9,10] for more details.

The structure of the metadata for aggregate operators is essentially the same as that for the complex functions, with only two minor differences. First, the name of the aggregate is given by the property `mocha : Aggregate` instead of property `mocha : Function`. Secondly, property `mocha : Method` is not needed, since the aggregate will be manipulated through the three well-known methods defined in the `Aggregate` interface. We will not show here an example of RDF metadata for aggregates due to lack of space, but the interested reader is referred to [10] for an example using aggregate `Composite()` in query $Q1$.

4.4   User-Defined Data Types

From the previous sections, we have seen that most resources depend heavily on data types. In MOCHA, data types are implemented in Java classes, and are organized in a hierarchy of interfaces and base classes, as discussed in [9,10]. Each of the interfaces specifies the methods that define the semantics of the data types, for example, whether a particular type is a BLOB (e.g. an image) or a simpler object like a real number or a rectangle.

Our example application handles AVHRR images, and Fig. 7 presents the metadata for the data type `Raster` used to represent them. The RDF property `mocha : Type` indicates that `Raster` is the name of the type for the images. This type is implemented in class `Raster.class`, as indicated by property `mocha : Class`. As in our previous examples, the information about the code repository, in this case `EarthScience`, is specified by the property `mocha : Repo−sitory`, and the developer by property `mocha : Creator`. Since QPC needs to optimize the queries posed by the user, the size (or at least an approximation) of the attributes accessed by the query must be available to the optimizer to estimate the cost of transferring such attributes over the network. This is provided with property `mocha : Size`, which indicates that the AVHRR images are 1MB in size. Clearly, the QPC will have enough information to use and deploy the Java class for a given data type.

5   Automatic Code Deployment

In this section we describe how MOCHA automatically deploys application-specific code. A more detailed description of automatic code deployment in MOCHA can be found in [10]. When the QPC receives a query from an user, it first parses the query and generates a list with the names of the user-defined data types and operators that are needed. For query $Q1$, this list will contain the `Rectangle` and `Raster` types, and the `Composite()` and `Overlap()` operators.

```
<Description about =
  ''mocha://cs1.umd.edu/EarthScience/Raster'' >
  <mocha:Type> Raster </mocha:Type>
  <mocha:Class> Raster.class </mocha:Class>
  <mocha:Repository> cs1.umd.edu/EarthScience
  </mocha:Repository>
  <mocha:Size> 1MB </mocha:Size>
  <mocha:Creator> manuel@cs1.umd.edu </mocha:Creator>
</Description>
```

Fig. 7. Metadata for data type `Raster`

QPC then maps each name to the URI for each of these resources and accesses the catalog to extract the RDF metadata for each one of them, along with the metadata for the target table(s), which would be `Rasters` for query $Q1$. Then, the QPC determines the best plan P, to solve the query at hand. For query $Q1$, the query plan will specify that the entire query should be executed by the DAP associated with the Informix server, and the QPC should simply gather the results and forward them to the client application. The QPC will send this query plan P to the DAP, and it will be encode in XML. Due to lack of space we cannot show an example of this XML encoding, but the interested reader can find one in the full version of this paper [10]. Once the query plan is determined, QPC's next task is the automatic deployment of all the classes that implement each of the user-defined data types and operators used in the query. In MOCHA, this process is called the *code deployment phase*. As shown in Fig. 8, QPC retrieves each Java class from its code repository and ships it to the other components in the system that require it. The client application and the DAPs will receive only those classes that each one requires, as specified in the operator schedule contained in the query plan P.

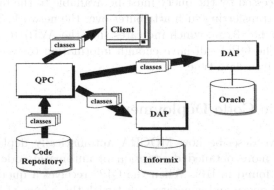

Fig. 8. Automatic Code Deployment

Figure 9 presents the algorithm used by QPC to deploy all the Java classes. The algorithm receives three input parameters: 1) R - a list with the URIs for the operators and data types used in the query, 2) M - a structure containing all the metadata for the query, and 3) P - the execution plan for the query. The algorithm iterates over the list of resources R as follows. First, the entry with the metadata for the current URI i is fetched from M. Next, the name of the repository containing the Java class implementing resource i is found. In step (4), the name of the Java class for resource i is determined. With this information the algorithm uses step (5) to retrieve the Java class file for resource i from the code repository. Then, the set S of all sites which require the Java class for resource i is determined from the query plan P by calling function $getTargetSites()$ in step (6). Having found the target sites, the algorithm iterates over S, and ships the metadata and Java class file for resource i to each site. Notice that in step (8) the metadata is converted to RDF format and then transmitted to the target site. Once the site receives the class file, it loads it into the Java Virtual Machine, and the resource becomes available for use. Notice that this entire process has been completely done by the QPC, and totally driven by the metadata retrieved from the catalog and the operator schedule in the query plan P. There is no human involvement of any kind, and therefore the functionality has been automatically deployed by MOCHA. To the best of our knowledge no other system uses this novel approach.

procedure MOCHA_DeployCode:
/* deploys classes for resources R */

1) **for each** $i \in R$ **do**
2) $entry = findEntry(i, M)$
3) $repository = getRepository(entry)$
4) $name = getClassName(entry)$
5) $class = getClassFile(name, repository)$
6) $S = getTargetSites(i, P)$
7)   **for each** $j \in S$ **do**
8) $shipRDF(entry, j)$
9) $shipClass(class, j)$

Fig. 9. Code Deployment Algorithm.

For query $Q1$, the code deployment phase unfolds as follows. The Java classes for the user-defined data types used in columns `location` (type `Rectangle`) and `image` (type `Raster`) are shipped to the DAP for the Informix server. QPC also ships to it the classes for functions `Overlap()` and `Composite()`. Finally, QPC ships the classes for the columns projected in the query result to the client application, in this case class `Rectangle` for column `location`. Notice that since QPC has found all the functionality for the query, it can simply load all the Java classes it needs into its run time system. In the case of $Q1$, it needs the class for the column `location`. Once each component has extended its query execution capabilities, the query is ready to be solved according to the strategy in plan P. All results are gathered by the QPC and send back to the client application for visualization purposes.

6 Discussion

In this section we describe many of the benefits of MOCHA and the status of the current implementation of the system. For a more detailed treatment refer to [10].

6.1 Benefits of MOCHA

In the MOCHA architecture there is a clear specification of the services to be provided by each component in the system. The most important benefits provided by MOCHA are:

1. **Middle-tier Solution** - In MOCHA, the client application does not connect to the data sources directly. Instead, the client leverages the services provided by the middle-tier software layer composed of the QPC and the DAPs. With this approach, clients can be kept as simple as possible, since there is no need to integrate into them the routines necessary to access each data source. This also makes clients easier and inexpensive to set up and maintain.

2. **Extensibility** - New application-specific software implementing additional features, such as complex types, search operators and numeric aggregates, can be added to MOCHA after it has been deployed. The system is not static, rather it can be extended with additional functionality that is required to support the needs of new applications. Thus, the system can evolve to accommodate the changing requirements of users.

3. **Code Re-usability** - MOCHA is implemented in the Java programming language and, as result, all software used in MOCHA is independent of the computer platform being used at any particular data center or client site. MOCHA can support a vast array of hardware platforms, ranging from desktop PCs to multi-processor workstations. Thus, there is no need to perform expensive and time-consuming ports of the software to different platforms. Instead, the software is written once, and then used anywhere in the system. Also, the cost of software maintenance can be significantly reduced since only one port of the software is needed.

4. **Automatic, "Plug-&-Play" Code Deployment** - MOCHA automatically and seamlessly deploys all the code implementing the application-specific functionality used to process the queries posed to the system. There is no need for the end-users or administrators to make system-wide installations of application-specific software, since MOCHA extracts all code from the code repositories and deploys it as needed and where it is needed.

5. **Efficient Query Evaluation** - MOCHA leverages automatic code deployment in order to provide an efficient query processing service based on data movement reduction. The code and the computation for each of the operators in a query are shipped to and performed at the site which results in minimum data movement over the computer network. This approach not only reduces the time it takes to solve a query, but also increases the query throughput of the system.

6. **XML-based Metadata** - Instead of creating yet another language to represent metadata, MOCHA utilizes the well-accepted XML and RDF standards and leverages the availability of their tools. A schema with the appropriate tags is provided by MOCHA to encode and exchange metadata between the components in the system.

7. **XML-based Control** - Rather than inventing a new control protocol and forcing developers to learn the data structures, formats and APIs needed to implement it, MOCHA encodes all control information as an XML document [10]. A DTD is provided to specify the structure of the plans that must be followed by each DAP during query processing. The developer of a DAP is free to use whatever mechanism he/she prefers to implement the query plan inside the DAP.

In summary, this framework provides the foundation for a scalable, robust, extensible and efficient middle-tier solution for the data integration and interoperability problems faced by many enterprises.

6.2   Implementation Status

We have implemented MOCHA using Sun's Java Developers Kit, version 1.2. We used Oracle's Java XML parser to manipulate all the XML documents accessed by the QPC and DAP. The current version of MOCHA includes a DAP for the Informix Universal Server, a DAP for the Oracle 8 Universal Server and one DAP for an XML repository. We have loaded the Informix Universal Server with data from the Sequoia 2000 Benchmark [12]. This benchmark contains data sets with polygons, points, rectangles and AVHRR raster images, all of which were obtained from the US Geological Survey. The Oracle 8 Server was loaded with data sets describing weather forecast images for the Washington Metropolitan Area, which are stored in a Web server. Finally, the XML repository contains forecast temperatures for several of the major cities in the United States. All three of these data sources are hosted at the Department of Computer Science, University of Maryland, College Park. We have also performed extensive measurements on the performance of MOCHA, using the Informix Server and the Sequoia 2000 Benchmark. The results of these measurements can be found in [9].

7   Related Work

Middleware systems have been used as the software layer that attempts to overcome the heterogeneity problem faced when data is dispersed across different data sources. The goal is to shield the applications from the differences in the data models, services and access mechanisms provided by each data source. Typically, middleware comes in two flavors: database gateways and mediator systems. Database gateways are used to import data from a particular data source into a production DBMS made by a different vendor. The gateway provides a data channel between both systems, and therefore, a different gateway is need for each of the different data sources accessed by the DBMS. Some examples of commercial database gateway products are Oracle Transparent Gateways [6] and the Informix's Virtual Table API [5]. The other kind of middleware system is the mediator system. Here a mediator application is used as the integration server and the data sources are accessed through wrappers. The mediator provides very sophisticated services to query multiple data sources and integrate their data sets. Typically, an object-oriented schema is imposed on top of the schemas used by the individual data sources. Examples of mediator systems are TSIMMIS [1], DISCO [13] and Garlic [11]. The work in [7] considered some of the issues and tradeoffs between the use of gateways or mediator systems. All these middleware solutions require the administrators to manually install all the necessary functionality for query processing into every site where it is needed. In addition, these systems use ad-hoc or proprietary metadata and control exchange protocols, which make it difficult for third-party developers to create compatible and interoperable software modules for these systems.

8   Conclusions

We have presented a novel metadata-driven framework implemented in MOCHA to automatically and seamlessly deploy all application-specific code used during query processing. We have identified the major drawbacks of existing middleware schemes, namely the cost and complexity of porting, manually installing and maintaining middleware software system-wide, and the inability to scale to a large population of clients and servers. In contrast, MOCHA leverages Java, XML and RDF technologies to provide a robust, efficient and scalable solution in which the functionality is automatically deployed. All the code for data types and query operators is implemented in Java classes, which are stored in code repositories. For each query, MOCHA finds and retrieves all the necessary classes from the code repositories, and ships these classes to the sites that require them. Metadata is used not only to understand the behavior of each type or operator, but also to guide the entire code deployment process. The metadata and control exchange between the components in MOCHA is realized through the well-accepted XML and RDF standards. Future work includes the development of XML-based descriptions of data source capabilities and query plans for non-traditional data sources such as semi-structured databases.

References

1. Sudarshan Chawathe, Hector Garcia-Molina, Joachim Hammer, Kelly Ireland, Yannis Papakonstantinou, Jeffrey Ullman, and Jennifer Widom. The TSIMMIS Project: Integration of Heterogeneous Information Sources. In *Proc. of IPSJ Conference*, Tokyo, Japan, 1994.
2. World Wide Web Consortium. Extensible Markup Language (XML) 1.0, February 1998. URL:http://www.w3.org/TR/1998/REC-xml-19980210.
3. World Wide Web Consortium. Namespaces in XML, January 1999. URL:http://www.w3.org/TR/1999/REC-xml-names-19990114/.
4. World Wide Web Consortium. Resource Description Framework (RDF) Model and Syntax, February 1999. URL:http://www.w3.org/TR/REC-rdf-syntax/.
5. Informix Corporation. Virtual Table Interface Programmer's Guide, September 1997.
6. Oracle Corporation. Oracle Transparent Gateways, 1999. URL:http://www.oracle.com/gateways/html/transparent.html.
7. Fernando de Ferreira Rezende and Klaudia Hergula. The Heterogeneity Problem and Middleware Technology: Experiments with and Performance of Database Gateways. In *Proc. VLDB Conference*, pages 146–157, New York, NY, USA, 1998.
8. Internet Engineering Task Force. Uniform Resource Identifiers (URI): Generic Syntax, August 1998. RFC2396.
9. Manuel Rodríguez-Martínez and Nick Roussopoulos. MOCHA: A Self-Extensible Middleware Substrate For Distributed Data Sources. Technical Report UMIACS-TR 98-67, CS-TR 3955, University of Maryland, October 1998.
10. Manuel Rodríguez-Martínez and Nick Roussopoulos. Automatic Deployment of Application-Specific Metadata and Code in MOCHA. Technical Report UMIACS-TR 99-61, CS-TR 4067, University of Maryland, November 1999.
11. Mary Tork Roth and Peter Schwarz. Don't Scrap It, Wrap It! A Wrapper Architecture for Legacy Data Sources. In *23rd VLDB Conference*, Athens, Greece, 1997.
12. Michael Stonebraker. The SEQUOIA 2000 Storage Benchmark. In *Proc. ACM SIGMOD Conference*, Washington, D.C., 1993.
13. Anthony Tomasic, Louiqa Rashid, and Patrick Valduriez. Scaling Heterogeneous Databases and the Design of DISCO. In *Proc. 16th ICDCS Conference*, Hong Kong, 1996.

A Graph-Oriented Model for Articulation of Ontology Interdependencies*

Prasenjit Mitra[1], Gio Wiederhold[1], and Martin Kersten[2]

[1] Stanford University, Stanford, CA, 94305, U.S.A.
[2] INS, CWI, Kruislaan 413, 109 GB Amsterdam, The Netherlands
{mitra,gio}@db.stanford.edu mk@cwi.nl

Abstract *Ontologies* explicate the contents, essential properties, and relationships between terms in a knowledge base. Many sources are now accessible with associated ontologies. Most prior work on the use of ontologies relies on the construction of a single global ontology covering all sources. Such an approach is not scalable and maintainable especially when the sources change frequently. We propose a scalable and easily maintainable approach based on the interoperation of ontologies. To handle user queries crossing the boundaries of the underlying information systems, the interoperation between the ontologies should be precisely defined. Our approach is to use rules that cross the semantic gap by creating an *articulation* or linkage between the systems. The rules are generated using a semi-automatic articulation tool with the help of a domain expert. To make the ontologies amenable for automatic composition, based on the accumulated knowledge rules, we represent them using a graph-oriented model extended with a small algebraic operator set. ONION, a user-friendly toolkit, aids the experts in bridging the semantic gap in real-life settings. Our framework provides a sound foundation to simplify the work of domain experts, enables integration with public semantic dictionaries, like Wordnet, and will derive ODMG-compliant mediators automatically.

Keywords: semantic interoperation, ontology algebra, graph-based model

1 Introduction

Bridging the semantic gap between heterogenous sources to answer end-user queries is a prerequisite and key challenge to support global information systems. The basis for this bridge is found in an *ontology* for the knowledge sources involved. An ontology, in this context, is defined as a knowledge structure to enable sharing and reuse of knowledge by specifying the *terms* and the *relationships* among them. Ontologies relate to knowledge sources like dictionaries relate to

---

* This work was partially supported by a grant from the Air Force Office of Scientific Research (AFOSR).

C. Zaniolo et al. (Eds.): EDBT 2000, LNCS 1777, pp. 86–100, 2000.

literary works. Like the dictionary, the ontology collects and organizes the terms of reference. By analogy, definitions in a dictionary give us the relationships between words while ontologies give us the relationships between terms.

The ontologies considered in this paper are *consistent*, that is, a term in a ontology does not refer to different concepts within one knowledge base. A consistent vocabulary is needed for unambiguous querying and unifying information from multiple sources.

Automation of access to broad information resources, as on the world-wide web, requires more precision than is now achieved. Today, XML [7] is used as a carrier of semantic information, but by itself an XML representation is not sufficient. An XML document can only represent a single domain ontology but can do little to resolve errors introduced by semantic mismatches. We focus on such structured worlds as a starting point, establish how to build *semantic bridges*, i.e, logical rules that bridge the semantic gap between sources and use reasoning based on this semantic information to compose knowledge from multiple knowledge sources.

Bridging the gap between multiple information sources is an active area of research. Previous work on information integration [12] and on schema integration [9] has been based on the construction of a unified database schema. However, unification of schemas does not scale well since broad schema integration leads to huge and difficult-to-maintain schemas. Since the meaning and scope of the database concepts is not made explicit and is likely to differ it very quickly, calls for identification of 'sub-domains' and 'namespaces' [8] to help make the semantic context of distinct sources explicit. Instead, we propose to utilize semantic bridges between such contexts as a starting point so that the source ontologies can remain independent. In most real-life situations, it suffices to just use semantic bridges wherever interaction among information sources is required.

Recent progress in automated support for mediated systems, using views, has been described by [3], [4], [13], and [6]. We share the underlying assumption that a view is a syntactic representation of a semantic context of an information source. Defining such views, however, requires manual specification. Views need to be updated or reconstructed even for small changes to the individual sources. Instead of manually creating and materializing such views, we provide a semi-automatic rule-based framework for interoperation based on articulations of ontologies. Our contention is that, in many cases, an application domain-specific ontology articulation rule set will simplify the work involved. Such rule sets are implicitly found in the standardization efforts encountered in business chains to enable electronic interaction.

Semantic interoperatibility has been studied in work on heterogenous databases [17],[18] and multidatabase systems [19], [1]. One of the strategies used is to merge all system schemas into a global reference schema. Such a strategy suffers the same drawbacks as the information integration approach. Furthermore, relying on the end-user to bridge the semantic gap between information obtained from multiple databases imposes the implicit assumption that all end-users are domain experts. Instead, we envision a system to propose and resolve the semantic gaps only in the intersection among the knowledge sources that is relevant to the application. Such a system is driven by a rule set supplied by the domain interoperation expert, who focuses on creating an articulation. The tedious task of creating an articulation is greatly simplified by using a tool that uses external knowledge sources to propose relevant semantic bridges. It also allows the domain expert to provide immediate feedback on potentially ambiguous constructs.

Ontologies have been represented using various text-based models [2,5]. While a text-based model is easy to construct, its structural relationships is often hard to visualize. This becomes especially crucial if the ontologies have to be presented to a human expert or end-user.

We adopt a graph-based model to represent ontologies. A graph-based model conveys the structural relationships in an ontology in a simple, clean, elegant and more usable format. The graphical scheme deployed is a refinement of the GOOD [10] model, which has been developed to model an object-oriented DBMS using a graph-based framework.

In this paper, we show how ontologies of individual knowledge sources can be articulated into a unified ontology using a graphical representation, where semantic bridges are modeled using both logical rules (e.g., semantic implication between terms across ontologies) and functional rules (e.g. dealing with conversion functions between terms across ontologies).

The novelty of ONION (ONtology compositION) system is an architecture based on a sound formalism to support a scalable framework for ontology integration. The architecture provides a balance between an automated (and perhaps unreliable system), and a manual system specified totally by a domain expert. Its modular framework allows for a clean separation of the several knowledge processing components. The model is simple, yet rich enough, to provide a basis for the logical inference necessary for knowledge composition and for the detection of errors in the articulation rules. An ontology algebra is defined, which is the machinery to support the composition of ontologies via the articulation. The implementation of the ONION system is based on the ontology algebra.

This paper is further organized as follows. In Section 2 we give an architectural overview of ONION. In Section 3 we outline the graphical representation of ontologies. Section 4 deals with the generation of the articulation. In Section 5 we introduce an ontology algebra. Finally, in section 6 we summarize the contributions of the paper.

2   Overview of ONION

Notational Conventions

In the rest of the paper we will use the following terms. The individual ontologies will be referred to as *source ontologies*. *Articulation rules* indicate which terms, individually or in conjunction, are related in the source ontologies. An *articulation ontology* contains these terms and the relationships between them.

The term *articulation* will refer to the articulation ontology and the the rules that relate terms between the articulation ontology and the source ontologies. The source ontologies along with the articulation is referred to as the *unified ontology*.

It is important to note that the unified ontology is not a physical entity but is merely a term coined to facilitate the current discourse. The source ontologies are independently maintained and the articulation is the only thing that is physically stored. As shown in Fig. 1, the unified ontology $Ont5$ contains to the source ontologies $Ont3$ and $Ont4$ and the articulation ontology $Art2$. The articulation of the source ontologies $Ont4$ and $Ont3$ consists of the articulation ontology $Art2$ and the semantic bridges linking it to the source ontologies.

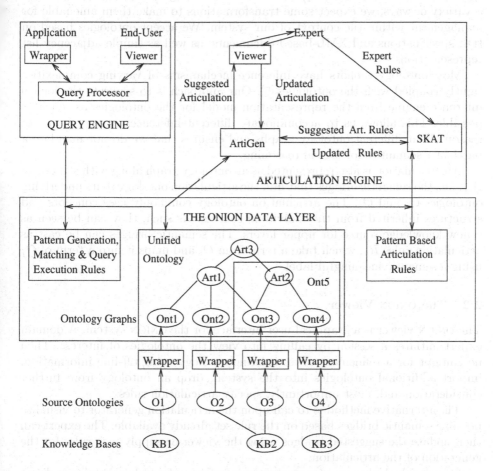

Fig. 1. The ONION system

We now present an overview of the system architecture and introduce a running example. The ONION architecture, shown in Fig. 1, has been designed with strong modularity in mind. It recognizes the need for several underlying knowledge source representations, supporting different kinds of semantic reasoning components, and integration with query processing engines. By keeping the model simple and the architecture modular, we hope to achieve greater scalability and incur less problems in maintenance.

2.1 The ONION Data Layer

The ONION data layer is the primary focus of this paper. It manages the ontology representations, the articulations and the rule sets involved and the rules required for query processing. Each ontology, O_i, represented as a graph, reflects (part of) an external knowledge source. Since ontologies may be represented in a variety of ways, we expect some transformations to make them amenable for management within the context of our system. We accept ontologies based on IDL specifications and XML-based documents, as well as simple adjacency list representations.

Most ontology toolkits have inference mechanisms of varying complexities tightly coupled with the ontologies [5]. Our approach is to separate the logical inference engine from the representation model for the ontologies as much as possible. This allows us to accommodate different inferences engines that can reason about different ontology graphs and ensures that we do not mandate a particular semantics for logical reasoning.

An articulation is also represented as an ontology graph along with structures A_{ij}, i.e., the semantic bridges that link the articulation ontology to its underlying ontologies O_i and O_j. The articulation ontology commonly uses concepts and structures inherited from the individual sources. As such, they can be seen as a new knowledge source for upper layers. The semantic bridges can be cast as articulation rules R_k, which take a term from O_i and maps it into a term of O_j using a semantic meaningful label.

2.2 The ONION Viewer

The ONION viewer is a graphical user interface for the ONION system. A domain expert initiates a session by calling into view the ontologies of interest. Then he can opt for a refinement of an existing ontology using off-line information, import additional ontologies into the system, drop an ontology from further consideration and, most importantly, specify articulation rules.

The alternative method is to call upon the articulation generator to visualize possible semantic bridges based on the rule set already available. The expert can then update the suggested bridges using the viewer or supply new rules for the generation of the articulation.

Once finished, the expert may use the interface to formulate queries or direct the system to generate wrappers for inclusion in concrete applications using the ONION query engine.

2.3 The ONION Query System

Interoperation of ontologies forms the basis for querying their semantically meaningful intersection or for exchanging information between the underlying sources.

The former calls for a traditional query engine, which takes a query phrased in terms of an articulation ontology and derives an execution plan against the sources involved. Given the semantic bridges, however, query reformulation is often required.

The query system has a graphical user interface, wrappers for applications and a query processor which uses the query execution rules to reformulate the query [14] and generate its solution.

2.4 The Articulation Engine

The articulation engine is responsible for creating the articulation ontology and the semantic bridges betwen it and the the source ontologies based on the articulation rules. ONION is based on the SKAT (Semantic Knowledge Articulation Tool) system developed in recent years at Stanford [15]. Articulation rules are proposed by SKAT using expert rules and other external knowledge sources or semantic lexicons (e.g., Wordnet) and verified by the expert. The inference engine uses the articulation rules generated by SKAT and the rules from the individual source ontologies to derive more rules if possible.

The articulation generator takes the articulation rules and generates the articulation, i.e., the articulation ontology graph and the semantic bridges, which is then forwarded to the expert for confirmation. The expert has the final word on the articulation generation and is responsible to correct inconsistencies in the suggested articulation. If the expert suggests modifications or new rules, they are forwarded to SKAT for further generation of new articulation rules. This process is iteratively repeated until the expert is satisfied with the generated articulation.

2.5 Motivating Example

To illustrate our graph model of ontologies and articulation, we use selected portions of two ontologies. The portions of the ontologies *carrier* and *factory* related to a transportation application have been selected (and greatly simplified) (Fig. 2). These ontologies model the semantic relationships 'SubclassOf', 'AttributeOf', 'InstanceOf' and 'Semantic Implication' that are represented as edge labels 'S','A','I','SI' respectively. For the sake of clarity a few of the most obvious edges have been omitted. Apart from the above mentioned relationships, the individual ontologies also contain other binary relationships between terms. The ontologies are expected to have rules that define the properties of each realtionship, e.g., we will have rules that indicate the transitive nature of the 'SubclassOf' relationship. These rules are used by the articulation generator and the inference engine while generating the articulation and also while answering end-user queries.

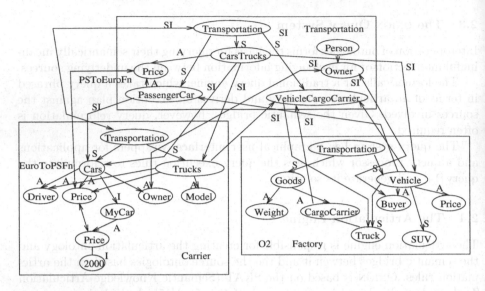

Fig. 2. Articulation of Ontologies

3   Graphical Representation of Ontologies

The ONION system has been anchored in the seminal work on graph-based databases in [10]. In this section we introduce its formal setting and the associated graph operations.

The Graph-Oriented Model. Formally, an ontology O is represented by a directed labeled graph $G = (N, E)$ where N is a finite set of labeled nodes and E is a finite set of labeled edges. An edge e is written as (n_1, α, n_2) where n_1 and n_2 are members of N and α is the label of the edge. The label of a node n is given by a function $\lambda(n)$ that maps the node to non-null string. In the context of ontologies, the label often maps to a noun-phrase that represents a concept. The label α of an edge $e = (n1, \alpha, n2)$ is a string given by $\alpha = \delta(e)$. The string attached to an edge relates to either a verb in natural language or a pre-defined semantic relationship. The domain of the functions λ and δ is the universal set of all nodes (from all graphs) and the range is the set of strings (from all lexicons). *Example* Our running example already elicits the graphical structure envisioned. It is a composition of three independent graphs, each of which provides an ontological context. The semantic model for the sources is built around the relationships { 'InstanceOf', 'SubclassOf', 'AttributeOf' }, which are commonly found in literature.

The Graph Patterns. To manipulate the ontology graphs we need to identify portions of the graphs that are of interest in a concise manner. Graph patterns can be used for this purpose. We define a pattern P to be a graph $P = (N', E')$, which matches a subgraph if, apart from a structural match, the labels of the corresponding nodes and the edges are identical.

Formally, graph $G_1 = (N_1, E_1)$ is said to *match* into $G_2 = (N_2, E_2)$ if there exists a total *mapping function* $f : N_1 \rightarrow N_2$ such that

1. $\forall n_1 \in N_1, \lambda_1(n_1) = \lambda_2(f(n_1))$.
2. $\forall e_1 = (n_1, \alpha, n_2) \in E_1, \exists e_2 = (f(n_1), \alpha, f(n_2)) \in E_2$.

In practice, apart from the strict match described above, the domain inter-operation expert can define versions of fuzzy matching. For example, the expert can indicate a set of synonyms and provide a rule that would relax the first condition and enable nodes to match not only if they have the exact same label but also if they are synonyms as defined by the expert. Alternatively, the second condition that requires edges to have the same label may not be strictly enforced.

In the ONION toolkit, the patterns are mostly identified by direct manipulation of the graph representation. For the textual interface we use a simple notation with (curly) brackets to denote hierarchical objects. Variables are indicated with bounded terms.

Example Possible patterns over our transportation world are *carrier.car.driver*, and *truck(O : owner, model)*. The former partially specifies a pattern in the *carrier* ontology that consists of a node *car* which has an outgoing edge to the node *driver*. The latter refers to a a node labelled *truck* that has attributes *owner* and *model* and the variable O binds with the truck owner object. Space limitations prohibit a further expose of the query facilities using patterns. We refer interested readers to papers on semi-structured query languages [16,7].

Graph Transformation Primitives. In order to transform the ontology graphs we define four primitive operations: addition of nodes, deletion of nodes, addition of edges and deletion of edges. Addition of nodes and edges is used while generating the articulation. Deletion is required while updating the articulation in response to changes in the underlying ontologies. The context of the operations is a graph $G = (M, E)$ where M is the set of nodes $m_1, m_2, \cdots, m_n$ and subscripts $i, j, k \in \{1 \cdots n\}$. The operations are shortly defined as follows:

- *Node addition*
  Given the graph G, a node N and its adjacent edges $\{(N, alpha_i, m_j)\}$ to add, the NA operation results in a graph $G' = (M', E')$ where $M' = M \cup N$ and $E' = E \cup \{(N, alpha_i, m_j)\}$
- *Node deletion*
  Let $N \epsilon M$ be the node to be deleted and $Z = \{(N, \alpha_i, m_j) \cup \{m_j, \alpha_i, N)\}$ the edges incident with N, then the node deletion operation ND, on the graph G, results in a graph $G' = (M', E')$ where $M' = M - N$ and $E' = E - Z$.
- *Edge Addition* Given a graph and a set of edges $SE = \{(m_i, \alpha_j, m_k)\}$ to add the edge addition operation $EA[G, SE]$ results in a graph $G' = (M, E')$ where $E' = E \cup SE$.

– *Edge Deletion* Given a graph and a set of edges $SE = \{(m_i, \alpha_j, m_k)\}$ to remove the edge deletion operation $ED[G, SE]$ results in a graph $G' = (M, E')$
  where $E' = E - SE$.

For the sake of clarity, in the rest of the discussion, we will use a node's label in
place of the node, while referring to an edge from(or to) that node, i.e., instead of
saying edge $e = (n_1, \alpha, n_2)$ where $\lambda(n_1) = A$ and $\lambda(n_2) = B$ we will refer to it as
the edge $e = (A, \alpha, B)$. This is, typically, not a problem for consistent ontologies
where a term (representing a concept) is depicted by one node in the ontology
graph. Thus we use the term(label) interchangeably with the node related to it.

4   Articulation of Ontologies

The ontologies in our running example represent three sections of the real world.
The *carrier* and *factory* ontologies represent two autonomous knowledge
sources, while the *transport* ontology models an articulation of the individual source ontologies and provides the necessary semantic interface to relate the
sources. It does not stand on its own, but captures the semantic objects that
help bridge the semantic gap between *carrier* and *factory*.

This observation has some far-reaching consequences. It reduces the articulation problem to two tasks that are performed by the articulation generator
with advice from the domain expert who is knowledgeable about the semantics
of the two ontologies being articulated. The first task is to identify semantically
relevant classes to include in the articulation ontology. The second task is to generate and maintain the semantic bridges, i.e., the subset-relationships between
articulation classes and the related classes in the underlying source ontologies.
Since the generation of the articulation is semi-automatic, the developers and
users of the ontologies do not have to keep track of the semantic differences between the different ontologies. The focus of this section is to build mechanisms
to carve out portions of an ontology, required by the articulation, using graph
patterns. To complete the model, we introduce functional abstractions to convert
information as required by the articulation process.

4.1   Ontology Terms and Patterns

An articulation graph OA is built from structures taken from the underlying
sources and maintains information regarding the relationships that exist between
them. OA is constructed using both interactive guidance from the domain expert
and deployment of general articulation rules drawn from a knowledge base using
SKAT. Such articulation rules take the form of $P \Rightarrow Q$ where P, Q are complex
graph patterns.

The construct $P \Rightarrow Q$ is read as "the object Q semantically belongs to the
class P", or "P semantically implies Q". In a pure object-oriented setting, this
amounts to restricting the semantic bridges considered to be a "directed subset"
relationship. We shortly discuss the kind of articulation rules encountered and
the method to represent them in ONION.

Semantic Implication Bridges

The rule $O_1.A \Rightarrow O_2.B$ where A and B are simple node identifiers is cast into the single edge $(A, 'SIBridge', B)$ between the ontology structures. It models the case that an A object is a semantic specialization of B and is the simpliest semantic bridge considered.

Prefixing the terms with their respective ontologies is a consequence of a linear syntax adhered to in this paper. In ONION a simple click and drag approach resolves this naming problem.

Example. The articulation rule $(carrier.Car \Rightarrow factory.Vehicle)$ is translated to an edge addition operation, i.e.

$EA[OU, \{(carrier.Car, 'SIBridge', transport.Vehicle),$
     $(factory.Vehicle, 'SIBridge', transport.Vehicle),$
     $(transport.Vehicle, 'SIBridge', factory.Vehicle)\}].$

The first edge indicates that $carrier.Car$ is a specialization of $transport.Vehicle$. The other two edges establish the equivalence of $factory.Vehicle$ and $transport.Vehicle$

In spite of the term $Vehicle$ not occurring in $carrier$, modeling of such an articulation enables us to use information regarding cars in $carrier$ and to integrate knowledge about all vehicles from $carrier$ and $factory$ (at least as far as this is semantically valid).

Example. Alternatively, new terms can be added to the articulation graph using the cascaded short hand $(carrier.Car \Rightarrow transport.PassengerCar \Rightarrow factory.Vehicle)$. To model this rule, the articulation generator adds a node $PassengerCar$ to the $transport$ ontology. It then adds the edges $(carrier.Car, 'SIBridge', transport.PassengerCar)$ and $(transport.PassengerCar, 'SIBridge', factory.Vehicle)$.

Rules are not confined to describing bridging ontologies but are also used to structure the individual source ontologies or the articulation ontology graph itself. Likewise, the notational convenience of multi-term implication is broken down by the inference engine into multiple atomic implicative rules.

Example. The rule $(transport.Owner \Rightarrow transport.Person)$ results in the addition of an edge, to the articulation ontology graph, $transport$, indicating that the class $Owner$ is a subclass of the class $Person$.

Conjunction and Disjunction. The operands for the semantic implication can be generalized to encompass graph pattern predicates. Their translation into the ONION data layer amounts to introducing a node to represent the subclass derived and taking this as the target for the semantic implication. A few examples suffice to illustrate the approach taken.

Example The compound rule $((factory.CargoCarrier \wedge factory.Vehicle) \Rightarrow carrier.Trucks)$ is modeled by adding a node, N, to represents all vehicles that can carry cargo, to the articulation ontology. The default label for N is the predicate text, which can be overruled by the user using a more concise and appropriate name for the semantic class involved. In our example, we introduce a node labeled $CargoCarrierVehicle$ and edges to indicate that this is a subclass of the classes $Vehicle$, $CargoCarrier$ and $Trucks$. Furthermore, all subclasses of $Vehicle$ that are also subclasses of $CargoCarrier$, e.g, $Truck$, are made subclasses of $CargoCarrierVehicle$. This is intuitive since a $CargoCarrierVehicle$ is indeed a vehicle, it carries cargo and is therefore also a goods vehicle.

Articulation rules that involve disjunction of terms, like, ($factory.Vehicle \Rightarrow$ ($carrier.Cars \vee carrier.Trucks$)) are modeled by adding a new node, to the articulation ontology, labelled $CarsTrucks$ and edges that indicate that the classes $carrier.Cars$, $carrier.Trucks$ and $factory.Vehicle$ are subclasses of $transport.CarsTrucks$. Intuitively, we have introduced a term $CarsOrTrucks$ which is a class of vehicles that are either cars or trucks and the term $Vehicle$ implies (is a subclass of) $CarsOrTrucks$.

Since inference engines for full first-order systems tend not to scale up to large knowledge bases, for performance reasons, we envisage that for a lot of applications, we will use simple Horn Clauses to represent articulation rules. The modular design of the ONION system implies that we can then plug in a much lighter (and faster) inference engine.

Functional Rules

Different ontologies often contain terms that represent the same concept, but are expressed in a different metric space. Normalization functions, that take in a set of input paramters and perform the desired conversion are written in a standard programming language and provided by the expert. There is scope for the generation of such functions semi-automatically in the future.

Example. The price of cars expressed in terms of Dutch Guilders and Pound Sterling might need to be normalized with respect to, say the Euro, before they can be integrated. The choice of the Euro - the normalized currency - is made by the expert (or politician!). We expect the expert to also supply the functions to perform the conversions both ways i.e. from Dutch Guilders to Euro and back.

Given the ontology graphs, and rules like ($DGToEuroFn()$: $carrier.DutchGuilders \Rightarrow transport.Euro$), we create an edge ($carrier.DutchGuilders$, '$DGToEuro$', $transport.Euro$) to the articulation ontology from $carrier$. The query processor will utilize these normalizations functions to transform terms to and from the articulation ontology in order to answer queries involving the prices of vehicles.

4.2   Structure of the Articulation Ontology

The construction of the articulation ontology, as detailed above, mainly involved introducing nodes to the articulation ontology and edges between these nodes and nodes in the source ontologies. There are very few edges between the nodes in the articulation ontology, unless explicit articulation rules were supplied to create the edges. Such implication rules are especially essential if the articulation expert envisages a new structure for the articulation ontology. The expert can select portions of O_i and indicate that the structure of OA is similar to these portions using either the graphical interface or pattern-based rules. The articulation generator, then generates the edges between the nodes in the articulation ontology based primarily on the edges in the selected portion of O_i, the transitive closure of the edges in it and other inference using the articulation rules although all transitive semantic implications are not displayed by the viewer unless requested by the expert.

It is important to note that the articulation ontology of two ontologies can be composed with another source ontology to create a second articulation that spans over all three source ontologies. This implies that with the addition of new sources, we do not need to restructure existing ontologies or articulations but can reuse them and create a new articulation with minimal effort.

5   An Ontology Algebra

We define an algebra to enable interoperation between ontologies using the articulation ontology, The input to the *operators* in the algebra are the ontology graphs. *Unary* operators like *filter* and *extract* work on a single ontology [11]. They are analogous to the *select* and *project* operations in relational algebra. They help us define the interesting areas of the ontology that we want to further explore. Given an ontology and a graph pattern an unary operation matches the pattern and returns selected portions of the ontology graph.

Binary operators include *union*, *intersection* and *difference*. Each operation is defined on two ontologies (and the articulation rules) and results in an ontology that can be further composed with other ontologies.

5.1   Union

If the query-plan generated while answering user queries indicates that more than one knowledge base needs to be consulted, queries are directed to the union of the ontologies. The union operator takes two ontology graphs, a set of articulation rules and generates a unified ontology graph where the resulting unified ontology comprises of the two original ontology graphs connected by the articulation. The articulation is generated using the articulation rules as outlined in the previous section.

The ontology union OU of source ontologies $O1$ and $O2$ is defined as $O1 \cup_{rules} O2 = OU$ where *rules* refers to the set of articulation rules either generated automatically or supplied by the expert. Let $O1 = (N1, E1), O2 = (N2, E2)$ be the graphs representing the source ontologies. Let $OA = (NA, EA)$ represent the articulation ontology and BridgeEdges be the set of edges connecting nodes between OA and either $O1$ or $O2$, as computed by the articulation generator to using the articulation rules. Let OU be the graph representing the unified ontology. $OU = (N, E,)$ is such that $N = N1 \cup N2 \cup NA$ and $E = E1 \cup E2 \cup EA \cup BridgeEdges$.

The union of the *carrier* and *factory* ontologies is the *carrier* and *factory* ontologies themselves along with the articulation ontology *transportation* and the edges connecting the *transportation* ontology to the source ontologies.

5.2   Intersection

The Intersection operator takes two ontology graphs, a set of articulation rules and produces the articulation ontology graph. The articulation ontology graph consists of the nodes added by the articulation generator using the articulation rules and the edges between these nodes. In order to ensure that the edges in the articulation ontology connect nodes that are in the articulation ontology graph, the edges that are between nodes in the articulation ontology graph and nodes in the source ontology graphs are not included in the articulation ontology if the nodes in the source ontology graphs are not part of the articulation ontology graph. The intersection, therefore, produces an ontology that can be further composed with other ontologies. This operation is central to our scalable articulation concepts.

The ontology intersection OI of source ontologies $O1$ and $O2$ is defined as $O1 \cap_{rules} O2 = OI$ where $OI = OA$ as generated by the articulation generator.

The intersection of the *carrier* and *factory* ontologies is the *transportation* ontology.

5.3   Difference

The Difference of two ontologies $(O1 - O2)$ is defined as the terms and relationships of the first ontology that have not been determined to exist in the second. This operation allows a local ontology maintainer to determine the extent of one's ontology that remains independent of the articulation with other domain ontologies. If a change to a source ontology, say $O1$, occurs in the difference of $O1$ with other ontologies, no change needs to occur in any of the articulation ontologies. If on the other hand a node occurs in $O1$ but not in $O1 - O2$ then any change related to the node or any edges connecting it to other nodes must also be reflected in the articulation ontologies.

Example. Assume the only articulation rule that exists is $(carrier.Car \Rightarrow factory.Vehicle)$, i.e, a *Car* is a *Vehicle*. It is intuitively clear that to obtain the difference between the ontologies *carrier* and *factory*, we should subtract all vehicles from *carrier*. Since a *Car* is a *Vehicle*, *carrier* should not contain *Car*. Therefore, to obtain the difference between *carrier* and *factory*, the articulation generator deletes the node *Car* from *carrier* and all nodes that can be reached by a path from *Car*, but not by a path from any other node. All edges incident with any deleted node is also deleted. Like the Union, the Difference is computed dynamically and is not physically stored.

Now the difference $(factory - carrier)$ will contain the node 'Vehicle' (provided no other rule indicates that an equivalent class or superclass of vehicle exists in *carrier*.) Although, the first source contains knowledge about cars, which are vehicles, the expert rule does not identify which vehicles in the second source are cars. To compute the difference, only cars need to be deleted from the second source and not any other type of vehicle. Since, with the given rules, there is no way to distinguish the cars from the other vehicles in the second knowledge source, the articulation generator takes the more conservative option of retaining all vehicles in the second ontology. Therefore, the node $Vehicle$ is not deleted.

Let $O1 = (N1, E1), O2 = (N2, E2)$ be the graphs representing the source ontologies, $OA = (NA, EA)$ is the graph representing the articulation ontology. The difference, $OD = O1 - O2$ is a represented by a graph (N, E) such that $n \in N$ only if

1. $n \in N1$ and $n \notin N2$.
2. and there exists no path from n to any n' in $N2$.

and $e \in E$ only if

1. $e \in E1$
2. and if $e = (n1, \alpha, n2)$, $n1 \in N$ and $n2 \in N$.

The algebra forms the basis for the ONION system. The intersection determines the portions of knowledge bases that deal with similar concepts. The union of knowledge bases presents a coherent, connected and semantically sound unified knowledge base that is computed dynamically in response to queries. The difference provides us the portions of the knowledge bases that can be independently manipulated without having to update any articulation.

6   Conclusion

We have outlined a scalable framework for a system that enables interoperation between knowledge sources to reliably answer user queries. The main innovation in ONION is that it uses articulations of ontologies to interoperate among ontologies. A semi-automatic approach ensures that most of the work involved in interoperation is automated, yet an easy-to-use graphical interface is provided to assist the expert in making sure that the system is reliable.

The approach ensures minimal coupling between the sources, so that the sources can be developed and maintained independently. Changes to portions of an ontology that are not articulated with portions of another ontology can be made without effecting the rest of the system. This approach greatly reduces the cost of maintenaning applications that compose knowledge from a large number of sources that are frequently updated like those in the world-wide web.

This paper highlights a formalism used to represent ontologies graphically. This clean representation helps in separating the data layer with the inference engine. Resolution of semantic heterogeneity is addressed using expert rules. Semantic relationships are first represented using first-order logic based articulation rules. These rules are then modeled using the same graphical representation. This representation is simple, easy to visualize and provides the basis for a tool that generates the articulation semi-automatically.

The system architecture provides the ability to plug in different semantic reasoning components and inference engines which can make the task of the expert easier. How such components can use external knowledge sources and lexicons to suggest a better articulation is being currently investigated as part of completing the implementation of the ONION toolkit.

7   Acknowledgements

Thanks are due to Jan Jannink for his help in developing some of the basic ideas.

References

1. The context interchange project, http://context.mit.edu/ coin/.
2. Cyc knowledge base, http://www.cyc.com/.
3. Information integration using infomaster, http://infomaster.stanford.edu/ infomaster-info.html.
4. The information manifold, http://portal.research.bell-labs.com/orgs/ssr/people/ levy/paper-abstracts.html#iga.
5. Ontolingua, http://www-ksl-svc.stanford.edu:5915/doc/project-papers.html.
6. The stanford-ibm manager of multiple information sources, http://www-db.stanford.edu/tsimmis/.
7. Extensible markup language (xml) 1.0 http://www.w3.org/tr/rec-xml, Feb 1999.
8. Resource description framework (rdf) model and syntax specification, http://www.w3.org/tr/rec-rdf-syntax/, February 1999.
9. P. Buneman, S. Davidson, and A. Kosky. Theoretical aspects of schema merging. In *Proc. of EDBT '92*, pages 152–167. EDBT, Springer Verlag, Mar. 1992.
10. M. Gyssens, J. Paredaens, and D. Van Gucht. A graph-oriented object database model. In *Proc. PODS*, pages 417–424, 1990.
11. J. Jannink. *Resolution of Semantic Differences in Ontologies*. PhD thesis, Stanford University.
12. C.A. Knoblock, S. Minton, J.L. Ambite, N. Ashish, P.J. Modi, Ion Muslea, A.G. Philpot, and S. Tejada. Modeling web sources for information integration. In *Proc. of the Fifteenth National Conf. on Artificial Intelligence, Madison, WI*, 1998.
13. A.T. McCray, A.M. Razi, A.K. Bangalore, A.C. Browne, and P.Z. Stavri. The umls knowledge source server: A versatile internet-based research tool. In *Proc. AMIA Fall Symp*, pages 164–168, 1996.
14. P. Mitra. Algorithms for answering queries efficiently using views, http://www-db.stanford.edu/ prasen9/qralgo.pdf. Technical report, Infolab, Stanford University, September 1999.
15. P. Mitra, G. Wiederhold, and J. Jannink. Semi-automatic integration of knowledge sources. In *Proc. of the 2nd Int. Conf. On Information FUSION'99*, 1999.
16. Y. Papakonstantinou, H. Garcia-Molina, and Widom J. Object exchange across heterogeneous information sources, March 1995.
17. P. Scheuermann, C. Yu, A. Elmagarmid, H. Garcia-Molina, F. Manola, D. McLeod, A. Rosenthal, and M. Templeton. Report on the workshop on heterogenous database systems. In *ACM SIGMOD RECORD 19,4*, pages 23–31, 1989.
18. A.P. Sheth and J.A. Larson. Federated database systems for managing distributed, heterogenous, and autonomous databases. In *ACM Computing Surveys*, pages 183–236, 1994.
19. M. Siegel and S. Madnick. A metadata approach to solving semantic conflicts. In *Proc. of the 17th Int. Conf. on Very Large Data Bases*, pages 133–145, 1991.

An Approach to the Semi-automatic Generation of Mediator Specifications

Birgitta König-Ries*

Center for Advanced Computer Studies
University of Louisiana at Lafayette
koenig-ries@acm.org

Abstract Mediator architectures have become popular for systems that aim at providing transparent access to heterogeneous information sources. Similar to a view on a database, a mediator answers queries posed against the common domain schema by executing one or more queries against its underlying information sources and mapping the results back into the common schema. The mapping is usually specified declaratively by a set of rules, where the rule heads define queries against a common domain schema and the rule bodies define their implementations in terms of queries against one or more source schemas. In this paper a mechanism is presented that supports finding these mappings, a task that requires a fair amount of knowledge about the underlying schemas and that involves a lot of effort, thus becoming a major obstacle to scalability.

1 Introduction

Over the last few years, the desire to obtain transparent, integrated access to heterogeneous, distributed information systems has grown tremendously. Mediator-based systems have evolved as the main solution to this need. Mediators [24] are software components that homogenize and integrate data stemming from different sources by mapping the data from their respective source schemas[1] into a common domain schema. The major drawback of these systems is the fact that the creation of mediators is a highly labor-intensive task. Since most potential applications use a large number of information sources and new sources are frequently added to the system, a large number of mediators is needed – some of which have to be generated at run-time. This is a serious obstacle to scalability. Early approaches [6,25] to ease this task unburden the user from the routine work that needs to be done to build a mediator. However, they need mediator specifications as their input. Such a specification is a set of rules where the heads define queries against the common domain schema and the bodies define their implementation in terms of queries against one or more source schemas. Given real-life

---

* The work described in this paper was done at the IPD, University of Karlsruhe, Germany

[1] We use the term schema rather loosely here. Not all the sources will have schemas in the database meaning of the term.

C. Zaniolo et al. (Eds.): EDBT 2000, LNCS 1777, pp. 101–117, 2000.
© Springer-Verlag Berlin Heidelberg 2000

information sources, finding these specifications is hard and labor-intensive. To ensure scalability of mediator architectures, mechanisms are needed to support the user in this crucial step. In this paper, we present such a mechanism.

We will concentrate on *homogenization mediators* [25] in the remainder of this paper. We assume that information sources are attached to the system by wrappers, which handle technical and data model heterogeneities. Each wrapper is then assigned a homogenization mediator, which transforms user queries posed against a common domain schema into equivalent queries expressed in terms of the wrapper, thus overcoming schematic heterogeneity. The approach described is, however, also suited to generating specifications for other types of mediators.

A mediator specification consists of a set of rules and functions, which describe declaratively how queries against the domain schema can be mapped onto equivalent queries against the underlying wrapper. Each rule consists of a query against the domain schema as the rule head and an equivalent query against the wrapper as the rule body[2]. In this paper, we describe a method to find the rule body appropriate to a given rule head semi-automatically.

Imagine we know which entities exist in the two models and which correspondences exist between the entities in the two models. If the description of the correspondences is precise enough, it is quite trivial to find a rule body for a rule head by simply replacing the entities used in the rule head by their correspondents in the other schema. The first subproblem is thus to find formalisms to describe both the schemas and the correspondences between them. We introduce *information models* and *mappings* between information models for this task.

However, this solves only part of the problem. We also need a mechanism to discover the correct mapping between two information models. We address this problem by introducing a *quality function*, which allows to determine how good a proposed mapping is. With this function, we can compare possible mappings and determine the best one. However, since the number of possible mappings is huge, we cannot compute the quality of each of these mappings. Instead, we introduce a *heuristic* that computes good mappings between models based on the quality function. In the remainder of this paper we take a closer look at the two parts of our solution, the description of models and their correspondences, and the discovery of correspondences.

2   Information Models and Mappings Between Them

Homogenization mediators transform queries posed against the domain schema into queries that are expressed in the terms used by the underlying wrapper. Both wrappers and the domain schema are based on the same common data model. Since we want to be able to include non-database sources into our system, we need a data model able to deal with semi-structured data. We use the Object Exchange Model (OEM) [1], a self-describing graph-based model. However, to gain sufficient knowledge about the entities represented in a wrapper

---

[2] To be more precise, rule heads and bodies are abstractions of queries, *query templates*.

and their relationships, self-description is not sufficient. Rather, we need a more detailed schema for the information available through a wrapper. On the one hand, this "schema" has to be less strict than classical schemas to accommodate for the semi-structuredness of the data. On the other hand, we need to capture as much information as possible in the schema to be able to find correspondences between schemas. We thus introduce *information models* as our notion of schema. Information models capture structural information together with meta information about the data provided.

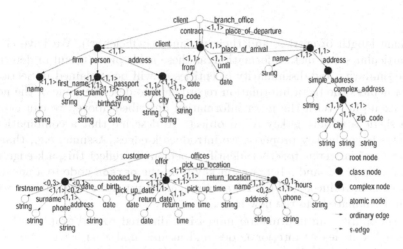

Fig. 1. Example WIM (top) and IIM (bottom)

Information models can be represented by labeled, directed graphs – cf. the top half of Fig. 1 for an example. This information model represents the information provided by a car rental company. It consists of a *root node* from which all other nodes are reachable. The children of the root node are *class nodes* representing entities in the universe of discourse. In our example these are client, contract and branch_office. Person and firm are subclasses of client; this relationship is represented by dashed s-edges. Each of the class nodes has a number of outgoing edges. These lead to atomic or complex subobjects or represent relationships with other classes. Again, s-edges denote the existence of different subtypes of certain objects, for example, the addresses of branch offices can be captured either as strings or as structured subobjects consisting of street, city and zip-code. Edge cardinalities describe how many subobjects with this label a certain object can have. In addition to the information represented in Fig. 1, meta information is kept about the atomic nodes. This meta information is partly on the schema level (e.g. defined length, whether NULL-values are allowed, and whether attribute values are unique, that is, whether the attribute is a key to the object) and is partly gained from a statistical analysis of the underlying information source (e.g. information about average, minimum and

Table 1. Example meta information records in the WIM

field	branch_office.address.street	person.first_name	person.last_name
domain	string	string	string
defined length	30	25	30
unique	FALSE	FALSE	FALSE
NULL permitted	TRUE	FALSE	FALSE
% numbers	10.64	0.00	0.00
% characters	82.98	100.00	100.00
% symbols	6.38	0.00	0.00
max. length	27	8	8
min. length	14	4	5
avg. length	18.80	6.00	6.50
var. coeff.	0.282	0.192	0.131

maximum length of entries, and their variance coefficients[3]). We have chosen this particular set of meta information, as these fields prove useful in determining the similarity and dissimilarity of entities as will be explained in Section 3. Table 1 depicts the meta information record kept to describe some of the nodes in the example[4]. With the meta information described above, we can capture that a single attribute is key to an object. To describe that a combination of attributes have the key property, we introduce k-edges. Assume, e.g., that the firstname and lastname together identify a person. To reflect this, a k-edge with cardinality $< 1, 1 >$ and label person_key from the person node to a new complex node is introduced and the first_name, and last_name edges are moved so that they emanate from the new node.

To summarize, an information model is a directed rooted graph with class and complex nodes as interior nodes and atomic nodes as leaves. Nodes are connected by labeled edges annotated by a cardinality, where the label describes the role the end node has with respect to the start node and the cardinality describes how many outgoing edges with that label the start node may have. Special edges, called s-edges and k-edges, are used to represent specialization relationships and key properties, respectively. Atomic nodes have a domain and a meta information record associated with them.

Since homogenization mediators need to translate queries from the domain schema into the wrapper's schema, we need to describe both these schemas using information models. Assuming that a wrapper possesses some kind of formal specification describing which information it provides, a simple wrapper information model (WIM) can be generated automatically by parsing the wrapper specification and querying the underlying information source to obtain the meta information needed for the WIM. This WIM can be further enhanced if the person building the wrapper provides additional information.We need a similar description for the common domain schema against which user queries are posed.

---

[3] The variance coefficient is defined as the standard deviation divided by the mean value. It reflects how values are distributed.

[4] Slightly different meta information records are kept for nodes with domains that are not strings. For numeric nodes, e.g., avg., min. and max. values and the variance coefficient thereof are held.

We call this extended domain schema *internal information model (IIM)*. It stems
from a thorough modeling of the domain by a human expert. This modeling is
done independently of the information sources. This approach provides stability
of the user interface and the mediators as long as no dramatic changes to the
domain occur.

Since the task of a homogenization mediator is to translate queries and query
results between the IIM and a WIM, our next step is to find a formalism to
describe how entities in the IIM and a given WIM are related. More precisely,
we are interested in how a query posed against the IIM can be transformed into
a query against the WIM delivering the results the user is interested in. We thus
need a formalism allowing this transformation. To find such a formalism, we
define queries first. We use a formalized subset of LOREL [1] as query language.
In this language queries are build out of path constraints and conditions, which
are connected via AND and OR operators. A *path constraint* is a list of labels
from the information model that describes a path from the root node with a
variable added after each label. Usage of the same variable in different path
constraints in one query enforces instantiation to the same object in the result.
Output variables are used to describe which information the user is interested
in[5]. Consider the information models in Fig. 1. The top half of the picture shows
the WIM introduced above, the bottom half depicts the relevant part of our IIM.
An example query against the IIM is:

offer[A].booked_by[B].surname[C] AND
offer[A].pick_up_date[X] AND
C = ''Smith''

This query asks (using output variable X) for the pick-up-dates of all cars rented
by Customer "Smith". The usage of variable A in both path constraints ensures
that the same offer was booked by Mr. Smith and has pick_up_date X.

Mediator specifications do not contain single queries but are based on query
templates describing a whole class of queries. Query templates can be instantiated to queries by adding conditions and replacing variable placeholders by
variables. The following query template describes the query from the previous
example:

offer[V1].booked_by[V2].surname[V3] AND
offer[V1].pick_up_date[V4]

Since the aim of our mappings is to be able to translate queries and path constraints and thus paths in the IIM are the main construct of queries, we choose
paths in the IIM as the domain of our mappings. As an IIM may contain cycles
and thus possess infinitely many paths, we have to restrict the domain of our
mapping to a subset of these paths. We have to make sure that this subset is big
enough to map every query. We therefore restrict the domain to paths originating
in the root and traversing no more than one class node (not counting class nodes
at the beginning of s-edges). This suffices, as path constraints containing more
than one class can be rewritten as a conjunction of path constraints containing
one class each. Consider as an example the query given above. Without changing

---

[5] In contrast to LOREL we do not allow generalized path expressions.

the semantics, it can be rewritten as follows:
```
offer[A].booked_by[B] AND
customer[B].surname[C] AND
offer[A].pick_up_date[X] AND
C = ''Smith''
```

We now have to think about possible images of a path from the IIM under the mapping to a WIM. In the simplest case, a path is mapped to exactly one other path, e.g., `offices.name` → `branch_office.name` (→ depicts *is mapped onto*). However, there are more complicated cases to consider:

- Information that is kept in one entity in the IIM may be spread across several entities in the WIM, e.g. the `address` of a customer in the IIM should be mapped to `street`, `city` and `zip_code` subobjects of `client` in the WIM. Thus, the image of a path can also be a conjunctive combination of paths. In this case, a combination function must also be specified, which describes how the values at the end points of the conjuncts are to be combined into a single value at the end point of the original path.
- There may be only one way to hold certain information in the IIM but several possibilities in the WIM, e.g., a `customer` in the IIM can be either a `person` or a `firm` in the WIM. We thus need disjunctive combinations of paths in the range of values.
- The direction of edges between class nodes is often rather arbitrary. Consider the path `offer.booked_by`. It would be quite possible to express the same relationship between the two classes by a path `customer.booked`. We call a path allowing reversed edges an extended path (eP).
- The same information may be kept using different data types, units of measurement etc. in the different models. In this case, a transformation relation[6] has to be added to the mapping.
- The IIM may contain constructs for which no equivalent in the WIM exists. These paths should be mapped to a special NULL object.

Based on these requirements, we define:

Definition 1 (Mapping). *A mapping* M:IM$_1$ → IM$_2$ *maps each rooted path of* IM$_1$ *that traverses at most one class node (not counting class nodes at the beginning of s-edges) to a rooted path expression in* PE(IM$_2$) *where the set of path expressions* PE(IM$_2$) *of* IM$_2$ *is defined by the following grammar (where* [] *denotes optional elements):*

$$PE \rightarrow \quad (eP[,t])$$
$$| \ (AND(PE,\ldots,PE)[,f])$$
$$| \ (OR(PE,\ldots,PE))$$
$$| \ oemnil$$

---

[6] We use a transformation *relation* rather than a function because there isn't necessarily an inverse in the mathematical sense to every transformation.

where
eP *is an extended path in* IM$_2$,
t is an (optional) transformation relation,
f is an (optional) combination function,
oemnil is the NULL object.

For a mapping M to be *valid*, we demand that for each path p in *domain(M)* ending in an atomic node, all the paths that are part of the image of p under the mapping end in atomic nodes, too. We call this property *cotermination*. The following is a valid mapping of two paths in the IIM to path expressions in the WIM.

```
offices → branch_office
offices.address →
    (OR ( branch_office.address.simple_address,
        (AND (branch_office.address.complex_address.street,
            branch_office.address.complex_address.city,
            branch_office.address.complex_address.zip_code),
            compose_address)))
```

This mapping describes that `address` subobjects of `offices` correspond to either `simple_address` or `complex_address` subobjects of `branch_office`. In the latter case, the image consists of an appropriate combination of `street`, `city` and `zip_code` subobjects, where `compose_address` describes how the combination is to be performed (in this case by concatenating values). In the following, we will consider valid mappings only.

Given an IIM and a WIM and the appropriate mapping between them, it is possible to automatically find the query against the WIM that is the image of a given query against the IIM. In order to do so, each path constraint in the original query is replaced by the image of the respective path where a place for a variable is inserted after each label. Then, the variables that should be put in these places are determined. Basically, a variable occurring after a prefix p_1 of a path p_2 should appear at the terminal nodes of p_1's image (if those nodes appear in the image of p_2). If p_1's image is not a single path but a conjunction (disjunction) of paths, the variable has to be split up (replicated) accordingly. During query execution, results have to be put together reflecting the split/replication. Thus, given the correct mapping, mediator specifications can be generated automatically.

3   Finding Good Mappings

Up to now, we have not addressed the question of how the correct mapping between two information models is found. Obviously, this is no easy task. Therefore, we introduce a method for finding good mappings. The approach is based on a quality function which, based on different factors, computes how well a proposed mapping reflects the semantics of the information models. A heuristic uses this quality function to determine good mappings.

To determine which factors influence the quality of a mapping, we analyzed approaches to solving similar problems, most notably schema integration. We discovered that these approaches (c.f. Section 4) are based on three indicators: resemblance of names, matching of meta information, and preservation of structure.

Definition 2 (Quality function). *We define the quality function* $Q(M)$ *of a mapping* M *as* $Q(M) = w_N{}^*Q_N(M) + w_M{}^*Q_M(M) + w_S{}^*Q_S(M)$, *where* $Q_N(M)$ *is the quality of the mapping with respect to resemblance of names,* $Q_M(M)$ *is the quality of the mapping with respect to matching of meta information,* $Q_S(M)$ *is the quality of the mapping with respect to structure preservation, and* $w_N + w_M + w_S = 1$.

We have determined experimentally that weights $w_N = 0.2$ and $w_M = w_S = 0.4$ work well. The value of the quality function (and of each of the subfunctions) ranges over the interval $[-1, +1]$ with $+1$ being the highest quality. Each subfunction computes for each element in its domain the degree of similarity *sim* and dissimilarity *dissim*. The quality is then determined as *sim* – *dissim*. In the following paragraphs we take a closer look at the three subfunctions.

Resemblance of names: $Q_N(M)$ is computed as the average of $q_N(p)$ for all paths p in the domain of M. Here $q_N(p)$ is the result of the comparison of how well the labels along p match with the labels along p's image pe. In order to do so, we first determine for each label l on p which part of the image pe stems from the mapping of l. Since pe is a path expression this *contribution* $c(l)$ may be a single label, a path (which doesn't need to be rooted), or even a conjunctive/disjunctive combination of such paths. Then, the label l is compared with the labels in $c(l)$. The tool used is WordNet [16], a semantic network which arranges terms in a net of relationships (hypernym, meronym, etc.). If $c(l)$ is a single label, the distance d of l and $c(l)$ in the hypernym hierarchy is computed and the similarity *sim* of the two labels defined as $1/1.5^d$, their dissimilarity *dissim* as *1–sim*.[7] If $c(l)$ is a path, the quality is determined by adding the values of the single comparisons. If $c(l)$ is a disjunction, the value is determined by computing the average of the values. If $c(l)$ is a conjunction, the labels are compared using the meronym hierarchy. S-edges and k-edges along the paths require special treatment, which we are not able to explain here in detail due to space limitations. Basically, the labels of k-edges are ignored and for s-edges either their label or the one of their parent edge is considered. Consider as an example the value for the comparison of `customer.surname` with `client.person.last_name`. WordNet considers `customer` and `client` to be synonyms, the same is true for `surname` and `last_name`, whereas the distance from `customer` to `person` is 2. Due to the special treatment of s-edges this results in a quality of $+1$. Similarly, the comparison of `customer.surname` with `client.person.first_name` and `client.firm.name` results in quality values of -0.11 and 0.33 respectively.

---

[7] This base value was determined experimentally. Obviously, the value should depend on the depth of the hypernym hierarchy in the tool used. WordNet's hierarchy has depth 8.

Matching of meta information: $Q_M(M)$ is computed as the average of $q_M(n)$ for all atomic nodes n that occur as terminal nodes of paths p in *domain(M)*. For each such node, $q_M(n)$ ranges over the interval $[-1, +1]$ and is computed by comparing n's meta information record with those of the terminal nodes of p's image under M. Since we require mappings to *coterminate*, these terminal nodes in the image will be atomic nodes, too, and will thus possess meta information records. In order to be able to compare the records, we first have to transform all meta information records of terminal nodes in the image which have a domain different from the one of n, into meta information records for nodes of n's domain[8]. Then, the meta information records of the end nodes of the image path expression have to be condensed to an aggregated record reflecting the combined meta information. Depending on the domains of the nodes and whether there respective paths are connected conjunctively or disjunctively, weighted averages or sums are computed. Consider as an example the meta information about `street`, `city` and `zip_code` depicted in Table 5. In order to compare this meta information with the meta information record of the `address` node in the IIM, an aggregated meta information record (called `agg` in the table) has to be created. Now, the values for each field of the two meta information records are compared. Based on [15] and own experiments, we have determined for each field in the meta information records how strongly similar (dissimilar) values for this field in two different records suggest similarity (dissimilarity) of the entities that are being described by the records. We thus assign weights reflecting the importance in determining similarity (dissimilarity) to each field. For fields with non-numerical values, these weights *sim* and *dissim* are explicitly defined – c.f. Table 2 for an example

Table 2. Similarity and Dissimilarity of non-numerical meta information

$$\text{sim}_{NULL} = \begin{cases} 0.12, & \text{if both attributes do not allow NULL-values} \\ 0.03, & \text{if both attributes allow NULL-values} \\ 0, & \text{else} \end{cases}$$

$$\text{dissim}_{NULL} = \begin{cases} 0.16, & \text{if just one attribute allows NULL-values} \\ 0, & \text{else} \end{cases}$$

For numerical fields, we first define bounds *simmax* and *dismax* as possible maximum values for *sim* respectively *dissim*. The more important a field, the higher *simmax* and *dismax*. If the values of the two fields differ by less than a predefined threshold value *diff_low*, they are considered similar. *sim* is set to the maximum similarity value *simmax* and *dissim* is set to zero. If, on the other hand, the two values differ by more than a predefined threshold value *diff_high*, *sim* is set to zero and *dissim* to *dismax*. For differences between *diff_low* and *diff_high*, similarity and dissimilarity values progress linearly. Table 3 summarizes the parameters for meta information with numerical values.

---

[8] If the domains of the nodes are incompatible, $q_M(n)$ is set to *-1* and no further comparison of meta information for that particular node is necessary.

Table 3. Parameters for similarity and dissimilarity of numerical meta information-
tion

field	simmax	dismax	diff_low	diff_high
def.length	0.18	0.2	0.2*max	0.3*max
avg. value/length	0.25	0.4	0.15*max	0.3*max
max./min. value/length	0.15	0.25	0.2*max	0.4*max
variance coeff.	0.2	0.4	0.15 +0.15*avg.	0.3 +0.3*avg.

where max (avg) is the maximum (average) of the two values being compared.

The formula is slightly more complicated for the comparison of the fields
% characters (numbers, symbols). Consider two meta information records. The
first has a value of *50* in the field *% characters*, the other a value of *53*. Clearly,
this difference is less significant, than a difference between *0* and *3* in the same
field. This property has to be taken into consideration when calculating *sim*
and *dissim* for these fields. For each field, the field quality is computed as *sim -
dissim*. $q_M(n)$ is then computed as the sum over all the field qualities. Table 4
shows some of the comparisons for our example models.

Table 4. Some example comparisons of meta information

field	surname	person.first_name value	quality	person.last_name value	quality	firm.name value	quality
Def. length	50	25	-0.05	30	-0.02	50	0.18
% numbers	0	0	0.10	0	0.10	0	0.10
% characters	92.54	100	-0.03	100	-0.03	94.74	0.01
% symbols	7.46	0	-0.03	0	-0.03	5.26	-0.02
Max. length	16	8	-0.06	8	-0.06	11	0.00
Min. length	11	4	-0.12	5	-0.09	3	-0.15
Avg. length	13.4	6	-0.14	6.9	-0.12	7.6	-0.01
Var. coeff.	0.107	0.19	0.01	0.13	0.17	0.33	0.00
Unique	F	F	0.03	F	0.03	F	0.03
Null	F	F	0.12	F	0.12	F	0.12
q_M			-0.17		-0.07		0.26

Maintenance of the structure: $Q_S(M)$ is computed from four factors.
The first (and least important one) is how close the overall number of vertices
and edges in the IIM and its image are. This factor gives a rough idea of how
good a mapping might be and can be used to discard unlikely mappings. This
factor has a weight of 0.1 assigned. The other factors have each assigned a weight
of 0.3. They are:

The preservation of the cardinalities of edges: Consider a path *p* in *do-
main(M)* and its image *pe*. For each edge *l* in *p*, the part of *pe*, $c(l)$, that stems
from its mapping can be determined (see above). Similar to condensing several
meta information records into an aggregated record, the cardinalities of the edges
in $c(l)$ have to be combined to a single cardinality if $c(l)$ is not a single edge. In
order to do so, the cardinalities of the edges in $c(l)$ are multiplied if $c(l)$ is a path
or a conjunction of paths and the average of the cardinalities is computed it $c(l)$
is a disjunction. This new cardinality is then compared with the cardinality of
l, resulting in a value between +1 for the same cardinalities and −1 for cardinalities that are completely dissimilar (like $< 1, 1 >$ and $< m, n >$). The quality
value is the average of these values for all edges in all paths in *domain(M)*.

The splitting of classes: A mapping is good, if it reflects the structure of the original model. This factor can be quantified by computing the length of the shortest extended path that has to be traversed to reach each edge that is part of the image of a single path in the domain. Thus, for each path in $domain(M)$, the length of this shortest extended path is determined. The closer this length is to the length of the original path, the better the mapping.

The preservation of relationships between classes: Paths that end in an edge from one class vertex to another, reflect relationships between classes. These relationships should be preserved under the mapping. Consider two paths p_1 and p_2 in the IIM that lead from the root node to two class nodes n_1 and n_2 and a third path p_3 from the root over n_1 to n_2. A good mapping should preserve the relationship between the classes represented by n_1 and n_2. That means: If p_1 is mapped to $pe_1{}'$ and p_2 is mapped to $pe_2{}'$, then the image of p_3 needs to contain a path from each end node in $pe_1{}'$ to one (or all) of the end nodes in $pe_2{}'$ depending on whether $pe_1{}'$ and $pe_2{}'$ contain disjunctions or conjunctions. Again, it can be quantified how well a given mapping complies with this condition and an overall quality value can be determined.

Given two information models and the quality function, the naive approach to finding the best mapping between the models would be to compare the quality values of all possible mappings. Unfortunately, this straightforward approach is not feasible, as the problem of finding the best mapping is NP-hard[9]. Therefore, we introduce a heuristic to find good mappings with reasonable effort.

A heuristic that has been used with good success in similar optimization problems is *Iterative Improvement (II)* [18]. The basic idea of II is to start with an arbitrary state, compute neighboring states and check whether they are better until a better state is found. Then neighboring states of this state are visited etc. until a local optimum is found. By starting several runs of II with different start states, a number of local optimums are found and the best of those is chosen as the result. Prior work (e.g. [22]) has shown that the results of II improve considerably if the runs are not started with arbitrarily determined states but if a certain amount of effort is put into finding good states to start with.

We use a variant of II as our heuristic. Its parameters are chosen as follows:
State space: The set of possible mappings between two models.
Evaluation function: Our quality function.
Neighborhood of a state: Those states that result from changing the mapping of just one edge. The new mapping of this edge may be obtained either by combining the original mapping and a new one disjunctively or conjunctively or by discarding the old mapping and replacing it with a new one. We prioritize the neighboring states as described below, thus visiting the most promising ones first.
Start state: We put considerable effort into computing good starting points for II. Basically, we first try to map class edges[10] in the IIM to class edges in the

---

[9] This property can be proven by reducing the subgraph isomorphism problem to our problem.

[10] A class edge is the path of length one from the root to a class vertex.

WIM based on their names. Since it is possible that more than one mapping per class edge is found, we then compute the quality of all possible permutations of mappings based on labels and preservation of relationships and discard permutations with low quality. Then, paths in the domain that start with a class edge for which an image was determined and that end in atomic or complex nodes are considered. These are mapped to paths in the WIM that start with the image of the respective class edge and that end in atomic or complex children of the image class node. This mapping is based on labels and meta information. If we can not find a mapping for a class edge in the IIM based on its label, we try to find a class edge in the WIM the class vertex of which has similar edges to and from other class nodes as the vertex at the end of the current class edge. If several promising alternatives for the mapping of one path are found, we choose one of them and store the others as alternatives. These are considered first when evaluating neighboring states.

Prioritizing: In contrast to classical II algorithms, our variant uses prioritizing instead of a random choice in two situations: in picking an edge to remap and in selecting the new image of the edge. Edges are chosen in the following order: First, class edges for which alternative mappings exist, second, attribute edges with alternative mappings, third, edges which are mapped to oemniland, fourth, arbitrary other edges are considered. The neighboring states are visited in the following order: For paths leading to class nodes, alternative mappings from the list of alternatives and disjunctive/conjunctive combinations of these are considered. For attribute edges, alternative mappings and their combinations are considered first. Then, mappings are taken into consideration, where the new image of the edge is a child of the image of the edge's father edge, then mappings where the mapping is a "grandchild" of the image of the father edge and so on.

The start state for our example information models can be determined as follows: First, we try to find mappings for all the class edges in the IIM to class edges in the WIM based on the resemblance of names. We consider mappings where the quality is bigger than *-0.3* as possibilities[11]. Using this criterion, we find the following mappings (the number in parentheses is the quality based on the semantic comparison using WordNet):

    customer → client (1) ∥ person (-0.11)
    offices → branch_offices (0.3)
    offer → oemnil (0.0)

In the next step, we determine which combination(s) of these class mappings have an overall quality of more than *0.25*. This calculation leaves only the first mapping of customer to be considered. Now, we try to find mappings for the subobjects of the classes in the domain. At first, we restrict our search to the atomic subobjects of the images of the classes. For these, we compare resemblance of names and the matching of the meta information. We have computed these values for the surname attribute of customer previously (see above). Calculating the average of the two quality values, results in the mapping to

---

[11] This, and other threshold values were determined experimentally.

client.person.last_name being the best with an overall value of 0.46 , with the mapping to client.firm.name being an alternative (0.29), whereas the mapping to client.person.first_name has a value of −0.14. Similarly, mappings for the other attributes can be determined. For customer.address we couldn't find a mapping looking at atomic attributes only, however, when expanding the search space to allow paths through complex vertices, the mapping to client.address and its three subobjects turns out to be satisfactory: the label quality is 1, to determine meta information quality, the meta information of the three subobjects are first combined as described above and then compared to the meta information about customer.address as depicted in Table 5.

Table 5. Example of combined meta information

field	street	city	zip_code	agg	address	quality
Def. length	50	30	20	100	73	0
% numbers	11.67	0.00	100	22.95	20.81	0.04
% characters	82.02	100	0	73.70	68.63	0.00
% symbols	6.31	0.00	0	3.35	10.56	0.00
Max. length	19	9	5	33	34	0.13
Min. length	13	9	5	27	29	0.10
avg. length	15.85	9	5	29.85	32.20	0.13
Var. coeff.	0.09	0	0	0.05	0.05	0.2
Unique	F	F	F	F	F	0.03
Null	F	F	F	F	F	0.12
Q_M						0.75
Q_L						1.00
$(Q_M + Q_L)/2$						0.88

Finally, we try to find a mapping for the offer class edge which we could not map in the beginning. We look at the relationships to other classes this class has and try to find a class with similar relationships in the IIM. This comparison results in a mapping of offer to contract. Now, initial mappings of the attributes of offer are determined. Whereas no mapping (other than the one to oemnil can be found for offer.time, the mappings found for all the other attributes are the intuitively correct ones, e.g. offer.booked_by is being mapped to contract.client, offer.pick_up_date and offer.return_date to contract.from and contract.until, respectively. In our simple example, this state is already the intuitively correct mapping. When running II, no better mapping is found. With this heuristic it is possible to find good mappings between two information models. The weights have been set in such a way that the method behaves conservatively, e.g. it tends to assign oemnil as the image of an edge rather than assigning a wrong value. These mappings can then be presented to the person building the mediator (e.g. the administrator of the underlying source) for correction. Correcting a good mapping is much easier than finding a mapping without any support from the system, thus the human effort needed to build a mediator is reduced considerably.

4   Related Work

We are not aware of any work that addresses the problem described in this paper in its entirety. However, work from numerous areas has dealt with the different parts of the problem. In this section, we give an overview of these approaches.

We have introduced *information models* as a way to describe OEM databases. In recent years, a number of approaches introducing schemas for graph-based data models have been developed: There exist a couple of approaches that try to extract schemas from given extensions. In [13] the graph representing the extension is transformed to a schema-like graph by a method comparable to the transformation of a nondeterministic finite automaton to a deterministic one. [20] base their schema on the extraction of type hierarchies using common subsets of attributes among objects. Both approaches are not able to capture all the information needed by our approach. The same holds for the schema model introduced in [5]. In this approach a schema is a rooted graph labeled with regular expressions. This definition allows for numerous possible schemas describing a given data source. Many of these are very imprecise (e.g. the graph consisting of the root node and a cyclic edge with the label *true* is a correct schema for every database.). The schema proposed by [17,4] consists of labeled nodes and edges. In this approach the label of a node contains the name of the object and some meta information about the children of the node. Although this schema is in some respects quite similar to ours, it would need some extensions to capture all the information about the sources that we hold in the information models. In particular, no meta information about the instance level is captured. Finally, the schema model in [7] treats meta information as first class objects. The disadvantages are that the connection between data and meta information is lost to a certain degree and that the approach does not deal with semi-structured data. Recently, XML has become popular as a data model [12,2]. XML DTDs provide a schema-like description of XML information sources. However, they capture less information than our information models.

We have introduced *mappings* as a way to capture which correspondences exist between entities in different information models. The database community has long dealt with similar tasks in the context of schema integration [3]. Examples for work in this area are [19], which describes a theory of attribute equivalence, or the classification of potential conflicts in [14]. However, as these approaches do not aim at the automatic translation of queries, they often are too imprecise to solve our problem of describing mappings precisely. Another area of interest are mappings between information sources with graph-based data models. The work closest to ours is [17]. However, they provide equivalence rules only and, which is even more restricting, allow a class to be mapped to another class only (not to an attribute). Similarly, [23] contains equivalence rules only. If the domain model is too imprecise to find an entity that is equivalent to an entity in a source, the domain model can be adapted during the mapping. In contrast, our domain model is fixed. [7] does not deal with semi-structured data and does not answer a number of important questions, e.g. how to combine attribute values to a new value other than by concatenation. [8] aims at finding relational schemas for semi-structured data. A mapping language allows to translate semi-structured data into instances of the relational schema and thus provides the basis for query rewriting. Since in this approach, the relational schema attempts to reflect the structure of the original semi-structured source, it is not necessary to allow, e.g., objects of the original source to be split across several objects (or in this case relations) in the target model. Since in our scenario the two models between which the mapping is defined are developed independently, we need a more complex mapping.

Our *quality function* is based on factors that we identified to be important from a number of other approaches: The first approaches to find relationships between entities at least semi-automatically stem from the schema integration community. Whereas earlier work on schema integration [3] relied almost exclusively on the user to find correspondences between schemas, more recent approaches try to give at least hints on which entities might be related. These hints are determined by taking into account one or more of the following indicators: Resemblance of names, resemblance of meta information (like similar key properties), resemblance of structure. See [11] for an overview, and e.g. [15,10,9] for individual approaches. TranScm [17] is an approach to semi-automatically map graph-based information sources, however, the decision on how to map is based on purely structural information.

5   Conclusions and Future Work

In this paper, we have presented an approach to facilitate the generation of mediators by supporting the finding of the mediator specification. The four building blocks of our solution are:

- *Information models* to describe the participating schemas,
- *Mappings between information models* to capture precisely the correspondences between models,
- A *quality function* allowing to evaluate how good a given mapping is, and
- A *heuristic* to find good mappings with limited effort.

Although we could only describe the generation of homogenization mediators in this paper, the generation of other types of mediators is supported as well, requiring only some minor changes, e.g. a means to address different information sources.

The results we have obtained when applying our method to sample information sources are very promising. We intend to do further testing against various real-world information sources to further evaluate the method.

Additionally, we are currently looking at adapting our method to generating mediators for XML-based information sources. These sources are typically described by a DTD, however (as observed e.g. in [21]) this description is not very precise. We are currently developing a schema model for XML information sources based on DTDs and are adapting the quality function to taking some XML specifics, e.g. the lack of data types and the ordering of subelements, into account. Overall, the adaptations are minor.

Acknowledgements

I would like to thank Peter Lockemann and Gerd Hillebrand for their guidance during the work described in this paper. I am also grateful to Niki Pissinou and the anonymous reviewers for their comments and suggestions.

References

1. S. Abiteboul, D. Quass, J. McHugh, J. Widom, and J. Wiener. The Lorel Query Language for Semistructured Data. *Digital Libraries*, 1997.
2. C. Baru, A. Gupta, B. Ludäscher, R. Marciano, Y. Papakonstantinou, P. Velikhov, and V. Chu. XML-based Information Mediation with MIX. In *Exhibitions Prog. of ACM Sigmod*, Philadelphia, USA, 1999.
3. C. Batini, M. Lenzerini, and S. B. Navathe. A Comparative Analysis of Methodologies for Database Schema Integration. *ACM Computing Surveys*, 18(4):323–364, December 1986.
4. C. Beeri and T. Milo. Schemas for Integration and Translation of Structured and Semi-structured Data. In *Proc. of ICDT*, Jerusalem, Israel, 1999.
5. P. Buneman, S. Davidson, M. Fernandez, and D. Suciu. Adding Structure to Unstructured Data. In *Proc. of ICDT*, Delphi, Greece, 1997.
6. S. Chawathe, H. Garcia-Molina, J. Hammer, K. Ireland, Y. Papakonstantinou, J. Ullman, and J. Widom. The Tsimmis Project: Integration of Heterogeneous Information Sources. In *Proc. of IPSJ*, Tokyo, Japan, 1994.
7. K.-H. Cheung and D.-G. Shin. A Framework Designed to Represent Both Data and Meta-Data to Enhance Database Interoperability. In *Proc. of the 3rd Biennial World Conf. on Integrated Design and Process Technologies – Issues and Applications of Database Technology*, Berlin, Germany, 1998.
8. A. Deutsch, M. Fernandez, and D. Suciu. Storing Semistructured Data with STORED. In *Proc. of ACM SIGMOD*, Phildadelphia, USA, 1999.
9. P. Fankhauser and E. J. Neuhold. Knowledge Based Integration of Heterogeneous Databases. In D.K. Hsiao, E. J. Neuhold, and R. Sacks-Davis, eds., *Interoperable Database Systems(DS-5)*, 1993.
10. M. Garcia-Solaco, M. Castellanos, and F. Saltor. Discovering Interdatabase Resemblance of Classes for Interoperable Databases. In *Proc. of RIDE-IMS*, 1993.
11. M. Garcia-Solaco, F. Saltor, and M. Castellanos. *Object-Oriented Multidatabase-Systems (ed. Omran Bukhres and Ahmed Elmagarmid)*, chapter: Semantic Heterogeneity in Multidatabase Systems. Prentice Hall, 1996.
12. R. Goldman, J. McHugh, and J. Widom. From Semistructured Data to XML: Migrating the Lore Data Model and Query Language. In *Proc. of the 2nd Intl.WebDB Workshop*, Philadelphia, USA, 1999.
13. R. Goldman and J. Widom. Dataguides: Enabling Query Formulation and Optimization in Semistructured Databases. In *Proc. of 23rd VLDB Conf.*, Athens, Greece, 1997.
14. W. Kim, I. Choi, S. Gala, and M. Scheevel. *Modern Database Systems*, chapter: On Resolving Schematic Heterogeneity in Multidatabase Systems, Addison Wesley, 1995.
15. W. Li and C. Clifton. Semantic Integration in Heterogeneous Databases Using Neural Networks. In *Proc. of 20th VLDB Conf., Santiago, Chile*, 1994.

16. G. Miller, R. Beckwith, C. Fellbaum, D. Gross, and K. Miller. Introduction to Wordnet: an On-Line Lexical Database. *Intl. Journal of Lexicography*, 3(4):235–244, 1990.
17. T. Milo and S. Zohar. Using Schema Matching to Simplify Heterogeneous Data Translation. In *Proc. of 24th VLDB*, New York City, USA, 1998.
18. S. Nahar, S. Sahni, and E. Shragowitz. Simulated Annealing and Combinatorial Optimization Alternatives. In *Proc. of the 23rd Design Automation Conf.*, 1986.
19. S. Navathe, J. Larson and R. Elmasri. A Theory of Attribute Equivalence in Databases with Application to Schema Integration. *IEEE Trans. on Software Engineering*, 14(4), 1989.
20. S. Nestorov, S. Abiteboul, and R. Motwani. Inferring Structure in Semistructured Data. In *Ws. on Management of Semistructured Data*, Tucson, 1997.
21. Y. Papakonstantinou and P. Velikhov. Enhancing Semistructured Data Mediators with Document Type Definitions. In *Proc. of ICDE*, Sydney, Australia, 1999.
22. A. Swami. Optimization of Large Join Queries. In *Proc. of the 1989 ACM-SIGMOD Conf.*, Portland, OR, 1989.
23. H. Wache. Towards Rule-Based Context Transformation in Mediators. In *Proc. of EFIS*, Kuehlungsborn, Germany, 1999.
24. G. Wiederhold. Mediators in the Architecture of Future Information Systems. *IEEE Computer*, p. 38–48, March 1992.
25. L. Yan, M. Özsu, and L. Liu. Accessing Heterogeneous Data Through Homogenization and Integration Mediators. In *Proc. of CoopIS 97*, Kiawah Island, USA, 1997.

Cooperation & Security

Securing XML Documents*

Ernesto Damiani[1], Sabrina De Capitani di Vimercati[1], Stefano Paraboschi[2],
and Pierangela Samarati[1]

[1] Università di Milano, Dip. Scienze Informazione, 20135 Milano - Italy
edamiani@crema.unimi.it, {decapita,samarati}@dsi.unimi.it
[2] Politecnico di Milano, Dip. Elettronica e Informazione, 20133 Milano - Italy
parabosc@elet.polimi.it

Abstract Web-based applications greatly increase information availability and ease of access, which is optimal for public information. The
distribution and sharing by the Web of information that must be accessed
in a selective way requires the definition and enforcement of security
controls, ensuring that information will be accessible only to authorized
entities. Approaches proposed to this end level, independently from the
semantics of the data to be protected and for this reason result limited.
The eXtensible Markup Language (XML), a markup language promoted
by the World Wide Web Consortium (W3C), represents an important
opportunity to solve this problem. We present an access control model
to protect information distributed on the Web that, by exploiting XML's
own capabilities, allows the definition and enforcement of access restrictions directly on the structure and content of XML documents. We also
present a language for the specification of access restrictions that uses
standard notations and concepts and briefly describe a system architecture for access control enforcement based on existing technology.

1 Introduction

An ever-increasing amount of information, both on corporate Intranets and the
global Internet, is being made available in unstructured and semi-structured
form. Semi-structured data sources include collections of textual documents (e.g.,
e-mail messages) and HTML pages managed by Web sites. While these sites are
currently implemented using ad-hoc techniques, it is widely recognized that, in
due time, they will have to be accessible in an integrated and uniform way to
both end users and software application layers. Nevertheless, current techniques
for Web information processing turn out to be rather awkward, due to HTML's
inherent limitations. HTML provides no clean separation between the structure
and the layout of a document. Moreover, site designers often prepare HTML
pages according to the needs of a particular browser. Therefore, HTML markup
has generally little to do with data semantics.

---

* This work was supported in part by the INTERDATA and DATA-X - MURST 40%
projects and by the Fifth (EC) Framework Programme under the FASTER project.

C. Zaniolo et al. (Eds.): EDBT 2000, LNCS 1777, pp. 121–135, 2000.
© Springer-Verlag Berlin Heidelberg 2000

To overcome this problem, a great effort was put in place to provide *semantics-aware* markup techniques without losing the formatting and rendering capabilities of HTML. The main result of this standardization effort is the *eXtensible Markup Language (XML)* [3], a markup meta-language recently standardized by the World Wide Web Consortium (W3C). While HTML was defined using only a small and basic part of SGML (Standard Generalized Markup Language: ISO 8879), XML is a sophisticated subset of SGML, designed to describe data using arbitrary tags. One of the main goals of XML is to be suitable for the use on the Web, thus providing a general mechanism for enriching HTML. As its name implies, extensibility is a key feature of XML; users or applications are free to declare and use their own tags and attributes. XML focuses on the description of information structure and content as opposed to its presentation. Presentation issues are addressed by separate languages: XSL (XML Style Language) [19], which is also a W3C standard for expressing how XML-based data should be rendered; and XLink (XML Linking Language) [7], which is a specification language to define anchors and links within XML documents. For its advantages, XML is now accepted in the Web community, and available applications exploiting this standard include OFX (Open Financial Exchange) [6] to describe financial transactions, CDF (Channel Data Format) [8] for push technologies, and OSD (Open Software Distribution) [17] for software distribution on the Net.

Security is among the main concerns arising in this context. Internet is a public network, and traditionally there has been little protection against unauthorized access to sensitive information and attacks such as intrusion, eavesdropping, and forgery. Fortunately, the advancement of public-key cryptography has remedied most of the security problems in communication; in the XML area commercial products are becoming available (such as AlphaWorks' XML Security Suite [1]) providing security features such as digital signatures and element-wise encryption to transactions involving XML data. However, the design of a sophisticated access control mechanism to XML information still remains an open issue, and the need for addressing it is well recognized [15].

The objective of our work is to define and implement an authorization model for regulating access to XML documents. The rationale for our approach is to exploit XML's own capabilities, defining an XML markup for a set of *security elements* describing the protection requirements of XML documents. This security markup can be used to provide both *instance level* and *schema level* authorizations with the granularity of XML elements. Taken together with a user's identification and its associated group memberships, as well as with the support for both permissions and denials of access, our security markup allows to easily express different protection requirements with support of exceptions. The enforcement of the requirements stated by the authorizations produces a view on the documents for each requester; the view includes only the information that the requester is entitled to see. A recursive propagation algorithm is also presented, which ensures fast on-line computation of such a view on XML documents requested via an HTTP connection or a query. The proposed approach, while powerful enough to define sophisticated access to XML data, makes the design of a server-side *security processor* for XML rather straightforward; guidelines for design are also provided.

1.1   Related Work

Although several projects for supporting authorization-based access control in the Web have recently been carried out, authorizations and access control mechanisms available today are at a preliminary stage [15]. For instance, the Apache server (`www.apache.org`) allows the specification of access control lists via a configuration file (access.conf) containing the list of users, hosts (IP addresses), or host/user pairs, which must be allowed/forbidden connection to the server. Users are identified by user- and group-names and passwords, to be specified via Unix-style password files. By specifying a different configuration file for each directory, it is possible to define authorizations on a directory basis. The specification of authorizations at the level of single file (i.e., web pages) results awkward, while it is not possible to specify authorizations on portions of files. The proposal in [16] specifies authorizations at a fine granularity by considering a Dexter-like model for referencing portions of a file. However, again, no semantic context similar to that provided by XML can be supported and the model remains limited. Other approaches, such as the EIT SHTTP scheme, explicitly represent authorizations within the documents by using security-related HTML tagging. While this seems to be the right direction towards the construction of a more powerful access control mechanism, due to HTML fundamental limitations these proposals cannot take into full consideration the information structure and semantics. The development of XML represents an important opportunity to solve this problem. Proposals are under development by both industry and academia, and commercial products are becoming available which provide security features around XML. However, these approaches focus on lower level features, such as encryption and digital signatures [1], or on privacy restrictions on the dissemination of information collected by the server [14]. At the same time, the security community is proceeding towards the development of sophisticated access control models and mechanisms able to support different security requirements and multiple policies [10]. These proposals have not been conceived for semi-structured data with their flexible and volatile organization. They are often based on the use of logic languages, which are not immediately suited to the Internet context, where simplicity and easy integration with existing technology must be ensured. Our approach expresses security requirements in syntax, rather than in logic, leading to a simpler and more efficient evaluation engine that can be smoothly integrated in an environment for XML information processing. The use of authorization priorities with propagation and overriding, which is an important aspect of our proposal, may recall approaches made in the context of object-oriented databases, like [9,13]. However, the XML data model is not object-oriented [3] and the hierarchies it considers represent part-of relationships and textual containment, which require specific techniques different from those applicable to ISA hierarchies in the object-oriented context.

```
<!ELEMENT laboratory (project)*>
<!ELEMENT project (fund,manager*,paper*)>
<!ELEMENT fund (organization,amount)>
<!ELEMENT organization (#PCDATA)>
<!ELEMENT amount (#PCDATA)>
<!ELEMENT manager (flname,address)>
<!ELEMENT flname (#PCDATA)>
<!ELEMENT address (#PCDATA)*>
<!ELEMENT paper (title,author+)>
<!ELEMENT title (#PCDATA)>
<!ELEMENT author (flname,address,e-mail?)>
<!ELEMENT e-mail(#PCDATA)>
<!ATTLIST project   name CDATA #REQUIRED
        type CDATA #REQUIRED>
<!ATTLIST paper   category (public|private) #REQUIRED
        pid ID #REQUIRED>
        (a)
```

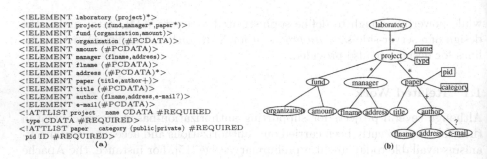

(b)

Fig. 1. An example of DTD (a) and the corresponding tree representation (b)

1.2   Outline of the Paper

The paper is organized as follows. Section 2 illustrates the basic characteristics of the XML proposal. Section 3 and 4 discuss the subjects and the objects, respectively. Section 5 presents the authorization model. Section 6 introduces the document view produced by the access control system for each requester and presents an algorithm for efficiently computing such a view. Section 7 addresses design and implementation issues and sketches the architecture of the security system. Section 8 gives concluding remarks.

2   Preliminary Concepts

XML [3] is a markup language for describing semi-structured information. The XML document is composed of a sequence of nested elements, each delimited by a pair of start and end tags (e.g., `<project>` and `</project>`) or by an empty tag. XML documents can be classified into two categories: *well-formed* and *valid*. An XML document is well-formed if it obeys the syntax of XML (e.g., non-empty tags must be properly nested, each non-empty start tag must correspond to an end tag). A well-formed document is valid if it conforms to a proper *Document Type Definition* (DTD). A DTD is a file (external or included directly in the XML document) which contains a formal definition of a particular type of XML document. A DTD may include declarations for elements, attributes, entities, and notations. Elements are the most important components of an XML document. Element declarations in the DTD specify the names of elements and their content. They also describe sub-elements and their cardinality; with a notation inspired by extended BNF grammars, "*" indicates zero or more occurrences, "+" indicates one or more occurrences, "?" indicates zero or one occurrence, and no label indicates exactly one occurrence. Attributes represent properties of elements. Attribute declarations specify the attributes of each element, indicating their name, type, and, possibly, default value. Attributes can be marked as `required`, `implied`, or `fixed`. Attributes marked as `required` must have an explicit value for each occurrence of the elements to which they are associated. Attributes marked as `implied` are optional. Attributes marked as `fixed` have a fixed value indicated at the time of their definition. Entities are used to include text and/or binary data into a document. Notation declarations specify how to manage entities including binary data. Entities and notations are important in the description of the physical structure of an XML document, but are not considered in this paper, where we concentrate the analysis on the XML logical description. Our authorization model can be easily extended to cover these components. Figure 1(a) illustrates an example of DTD for XML documents describing projects of a laboratory.

XML documents valid according to a DTD obey the structure defined by the DTD. Intuitively, each DTD is a *schema* and XML documents valid according to that DTD are *instances* of that schema. However, the structure specified by the DTD is not rigid; two distinct documents of the same schema may widely differ in the number and structure of elements.

DTDs and XML documents can be modeled graphically as follows. A DTD is represented as a labeled tree containing a node for each attribute and element in the DTD. There is an arc between elements and each element/attribute belonging to them, labeled with the cardinality of the relationship. Elements are represented as circles and attributes as squares. Each XML document is described by a tree with a node for each element, attribute, and value in the document, and with an arc between each element and each of its sub-elements/attributes/values and between each attribute and each of its value(s). Figure 1(b) illustrates the tree for the DTD in Figure 1(a).

In the remainder of this paper we will use the terms *tree* and *object* to denote either a DTD or an XML document. We will explicitly distinguish them when necessary.

3   Authorization Subjects

The development of an access control system requires the definition of the *subjects* and *objects* against which authorizations must be specified and access control must be enforced. In this section we present the subjects; in Section 4 we describe the objects.

Usually, subjects can be referred to on the basis of their *identities* or on the *location* from which requests originate. Locations can be expressed with reference to either their numeric IP address (e.g., 150.100.30.8) or their symbolic name (e.g., tweety.lab.com). Our model combines these features. Subjects requesting access are thus characterized by a triple ⟨user-id,IP-address,sym-address⟩, where user-id is the identity [1] with which the user connected to the server, and IP-address (sym-address, resp.) is the numeric (symbolic, resp.) identifier of the machine from which the user connected.

---

[1] We assume user identities to be local, that is, established and authenticated by the server, because this is a solution relatively easy to implement securely. Obviously, in a context where remote identities cannot be forged and can therefore be trusted by the server (using a Certification Authority, a trusted third party, or any other secure infrastructure), remote identities could be considered as well.

To allow the specification of authorizations applicable to sets of users and/or to sets of machines, the model also supports user *groups* and *location patterns*. A group is a set of users defined at the server. Groups do not need to be disjoint and can be nested. A location pattern is an expression identifying a set of physical locations, with reference to either their symbolic or numerical identifiers. Patterns are specified by using the wild card character * instead of a specific name or number (or sequence of them). For instance, 151.100.*.*, or equivalently 151.100.*, denotes all the machines belonging to network 151.100. Similarly, *.mil, *.com, and *.it denote all the machines in the Military, Company, and Italy domains, respectively. If multiple wild card characters appear in a pattern, their occurrence must be continuous (not interleaved by numbers or names). Also, consistently with the fact that specificity is left to right in IP addresses and right to left in symbolic names, wild card characters must appear always as right-most elements in IP patterns and as left-most elements in symbolic patterns. Intuitively, location patterns are to location addresses what groups are to users. Given a pair p_1 and p_2 of IP patterns (symbolic patterns, resp.), $p_1 \leq_{\mathsf{ip}} p_2$ ($p_1 \leq_{\mathsf{sn}} p_2$, resp.) only if each component of p_1 is either the wild card character or is equal to the corresponding, position wise from left to right (right to left, resp.), component of p_2.

Instead of specifying authorizations with respect to only one of either the user/group identifier or location identifier, and having the problem of how different authorizations can be combined at access request time, we allow the specification of authorizations with reference to both user/group and location. This choice provides more expressiveness (it allows to express the same requirements as the alternative and more) and provides a natural treatment for different authorizations applicable to the same request. We will elaborate on this in Section 5. Let UG be a set of user and group identifiers, IP a set of IP patterns, and SN a set of symbolic name patterns. We define the *authorization subject hierarchy* as follows.

Definition 1 (Authorization subject hierarchy). *The* authorization subject hierarchy *is a hierarchy* $\mathsf{ASH} = (\mathsf{AS}, \leq)$, *where* $\mathsf{AS} = \langle \mathsf{UG} \times \mathsf{IP} \times \mathsf{SN} \rangle$ *and* $\leq$ *is a partial order over* AS *such that* $\forall \langle ug_i, ip_i, sn_i \rangle, \langle ug_j, ip_j, sn_j \rangle \in \mathsf{AS}$, $\langle ug_i, ip_i, sn_i \rangle \leq \langle ug_j, ip_j, sn_j \rangle$, *if and only if* ug_i *is a member of* ug_j, $ip_i \leq_{\mathsf{ip}} ip_j$, *and* $sn_i \leq_{\mathsf{sn}} sn_j$.

According to the fact that requests are always submitted by a specific user (anonymous can also be interpreted as such) from a specific location, subjects requesting access are always minimal elements of the ASH hierarchy. Authorizations can instead be specified with reference to any of the elements of ASH. In particular, authorizations can be specified for users/groups regardless of the physical location (e.g., $\langle \mathtt{Alice}, *, * \rangle$), for physical locations regardless of the user identity (e.g., $\langle \mathtt{Public}, \mathtt{150.100.30.8}, * \rangle$), or for both (e.g., $\langle \mathtt{Sam}, *, \mathtt{*.lab.com} \rangle$). Intuitively, authorizations specified for subject $s_j \in \mathsf{AS}$ are applicable to all subjects s_i such that $s_i \leq s_j$.

4 Authorization Objects

A set Obj of Uniform Resource Identifiers (URI) [2] denotes the resources to be protected. For XML documents, URI's can be extended with *path expressions*, which are used to identify the elements and attributes within a document. In particular, we adopt the XPath language [20] proposed by the W3C. There are considerable advantages deriving from the adoption of a standard language. First, the syntax and semantics of the language are known by potential users and well-studied. Second, several tools are already available which can be easily reused to produce a functioning system. We keep at a simplified level the description of the constructs to express patterns in XPath, and refer to the W3C proposal [20] for the complete specification of the language.

Definition 2 (Path expression). *A path expression on a document tree is a sequence of element names or predefined functions separated by the character / (slash): $l_1/l_2/\ldots/l_n$. Path expressions may terminate with an attribute name as the last term of the sequence. Attribute names are syntactically distinguished preceding them with the special character @.*

A path expression $l_1/l_2/\ldots/l_n$ on a document tree represents all the attributes or elements named l_n that can be reached by descending the document tree along the sequence of nodes named $l_1, l_2, \ldots, l_{n-1}$. For instance, path expression /laboratory/project denotes the project elements which are children of laboratory element. Path expressions may start from the root of the document (if the path expression starts with a slash, it is called *absolute*) or from a predefined starting point in the document (if the path expression starts with an element name, it is called *relative*). The path expression may also contain the operators *dot*, which represents the current node; *double dot*, which represents the parent node; and *double slash*, which represents an arbitrary descending path. For instance, path expression /laboratory//flname retrieves all the elements flname descendants of the document's root laboratory.

Path expressions may also include functions. These functions serve various needs, like the extraction of the text contained in an element and the navigation in the document structure. The language provides a number of predefined functions, among which: child, that permits to extract the children of a node; descendant, that returns the descendants of a node; and ancestor, that returns the ancestors of a node. The name of a function and its arguments are separated by the character ':: '.

For instance, expression fund/ancestor::project returns the project node which appears as an ancestor of the fund element. The syntax for XPath patterns also permits to associate conditions with the nodes of a path. The path expression identifies the nodes that satisfy all the conditions. Conditions greatly enrich the power of the language, and are a fundamental component in the construction of a sophisticated authorization mechanism. The *conditional expressions* used to represent conditions may operate on the "text" of elements (i.e., the character data in the elements) or on names and values of attributes. Conditions are distinguished from navigation specification by enclosing them within square brackets.

Given a path expression $l_1/ \ldots /l_n$ on the tree of an XML document, a condition may be defined on any label l_i, enclosing in square brackets a separate evaluation context. The evaluation context contains a predicate that compares the result of the evaluation of the relative path expression with a constant or another expression. Conditional expressions may be combined with predefined operators and and or to build boolean expressions. Multiple conditional expressions appearing in a given path expression are considered to be anded (i.e., all the conditions must be satisfied). For instance, expression /laboratory/project[1] selects the first project child of the laboratory. Expression /laboratory/project[./@name = "Access Models"]/paper[./@type = "internal"] identifies internal papers related to the project "Access Models".

5   Access Authorizations

At each server, a set Auth of access authorizations specifies the actions that subjects are allowed (or forbidden) to exercise on the objects stored at the server site. The object granularity for which authorizations can be specified is the whole object for unstructured files, and the single element/attribute for XML documents. Authorizations can be either positive (permissions) or negative (denials). The reason for having both positive and negative authorizations is to provide a simple and effective way to specify authorizations applicable to sets of subjects/objects with support for exceptions [11,12].

Authorizations specified on an element can be defined as applicable to the element's attributes only (*local* authorizations) or, in a recursive approach, to its sub-elements and their attributes (*recursive* authorizations). Local authorizations on an element apply to the direct attributes of the element but not to those of its sub-elements. As a complement, recursive authorizations, by propagating permissions/denials from nodes to their descendants in the tree, represent an easy way to specify authorizations holding for the whole structured content of an element (on the whole document if the element is the root). To support exceptions (e.g., the whole content *but* a specific element can be read), recursive propagation from a node applies until stopped by an explicit conflicting (i.e., of different sign) authorization on the descendants. Intuitively, authorizations propagate until overridden by an authorization on a *more specific object* [10].

Authorizations can be specified on single XML documents (*document* or *instance* level authorizations) or on DTDs (*DTD* or *schema* level authorizations). Authorizations specified on a DTD are applicable (through propagated) to all XML documents that are instances of the DTD. Authorizations at the DTD level, together with path expressions with conditions, provide an effective way for specifying authorizations on elements of different documents, possibly in a content-dependent way. Again, according to the "most specific object takes precedence" principle, a schema level authorization being propagated to an instance is overridden by possible authorizations specified for the instance. To address situations where this precedence criteria should not be applied (e.g., cases where an authorization on a document should be applicable unless otherwise stated at the DTD level), we allow users to specify authorizations, either local or recursive, as *weak*. Nonweak authorizations have the behavior sketched above and have priority over authorizations specified for the DTD. Weak authorizations obey the most specific principle within the XML document, but can be overridden by authorizations at the schema level. Access authorizations can be defined as follows.

Definition 3 (Access authorization). *An access authorization a ∈* Auth *is a 5-tuple of the form:* ⟨subject, object, action, sign, type⟩, *where:*

- subject ∈ AS *is the subject to whom the authorization is granted;*
- object *is either a URI in* Obj *or is of the form URI:PE, where URI ∈* Obj *and PE is a path expression on the tree of URI;*
- action = **read** *is the action on which the authorization is defined;*[2]
- sign ∈ {+, −} *is the sign of the authorization;*
- type ∈ {L, R, LW, RW} *is the type of the authorization (*L*ocal,* R*ecursive,* L*ocal* W*eak, and* R*ecursive* W*eak, respectively).*

Example 1. Consider the XML document http://www.lab.com/CSlab.xml instance of the DTD in Figure 1(a) with URI http://www.lab.com/laboratory.xml. The following are examples of protection requirements that can be expressed in our model. For simplicity, in the authorizations we report only the relative URI (http://www.lab.com/ is the base URI).

Access to private papers is explicitly forbidden to members of the group Foreign.
⟨⟨Foreign,*,*⟩,laboratory.xml:/laboratory//paper[./@category="private"],read, −,R⟩

Information about public papers of CSlab is publicly accessible, unless otherwise specified by authorizations at the DTD-level.
⟨⟨Public,*,*⟩,CSlab.xml:/laboratory//paper[./@category="public"],read,+,RW⟩

Information about internal projects of CSlab can be accessed by users connected from host 130.89.56.8 who are members of the group Admin.
⟨⟨Admin,130.89.56.8,*⟩,CSlab.xml:project[./@type="internal"],read,+,R⟩

Users connected from hosts in the it domain can access information about managers of CSlab public projects.
⟨⟨Public,*,*.it⟩,CSlab.xml:project[./@type="public"]/manager,read,+,W⟩

The type associated with each authorization on a given object, at the instance or schema level, determines the "behavior" of the authorization with respect to the object structure, that is, whether it propagates down the tree, it is overridden, or it overrides. The enforcement of the authorizations on the document according to the principles discussed above essentially requires the indication of whether, for an element/attribute in a document, a positive authorization (+),

---

[2] We limit our consideration to read authorizations. The support of other actions, like write, update, etc., does not complicate the authorization model. However, full support for such actions in the framework of XML has yet to be defined.

a negative authorization ($-$), or no authorization applies. Since only part of the authorizations defined on a document may be applicable to all requesters, the set of authorizations on the elements of a document and the authorization behavior along the tree can vary for different requesters. Thus, a first step in access control is the evaluation of the authorizations applicable to the requester. This may entail the evaluation of the conditions associated with authorizations, but it does not introduce any complication, since each element/attribute will either satisfy or not such condition. As a complicating factor, however, several (possibly conflicting) authorizations on a given element/attribute may be applicable to a given requester. Different approaches can be used to solve these conflicts [10,12]. One solution is to consider the authorization with the most specific subject (*"most specific subject takes precedence"* principle), where specificity is dictated by the partial order defined over ASH; other solutions can consider the negative authorization (*"denials take precedence"*), or the positive authorization (*"permissions take precedence"*), or no authorizations (*"nothing takes precedence"*). Other approaches could also be envisioned, such as, for example, considering the sign of the authorizations that are in larger number. For simplicity, in our model we refer to a specific policy and solve conflicts with respect to the "most specific subject takes precedence" principle and, in cases where conflicts remain unsolved (the conflicting authorizations have uncomparable subjects), we stay on the safe side and apply the "denials take precedence" principle. The reason for this specific choice is that the two principles so combined naturally cover the intuitive interpretation that one would expect by the specifications [12]. It is important to note, however, that this specific choice does not restrict in any way our model, which can support any of the policies discussed. Also, different policies could be applied to the same server. The only restriction we impose is that a single policy applies to each specific document. This capability goes towards the definition of multiple policy systems [11].

6   Requester's View on Documents

The view of a subject on a document depends on the access permissions and denials specified by the authorizations and their priorities. Such a view can be computed through a tree labeling process, described next. We will use the term node (of a document tree) to refer to either an element or an attribute in the document indiscriminately.

6.1   Document Tree Labeling

The access authorizations state whether the subject can, or cannot, access an element/attribute (or set of them). Intuitively, the analysis of all the authorizations for a subject produces a sign (plus or minus) on each element and attribute of a document to which some authorization applies. This unique sign is sufficient to represent the final outcome of the tree labeling. However, in the process itself it is convenient to associate to each node more than one sign corresponding

Algorithm 61 *Compute-view algorithm*
Input: A requester rq and an XML document *URI*
Output: The view of the requester rq on the document *URI*
Method: /* L is local, R is recursive, LW is local weak, RW is
        recursive weak, LD is local DTD-level, RD is recursive
        DTD-level */
1. $Axml := \{a \in Auth \mid rq \leq subject(a), uri(object(a)) = URI\}$
2. $Adtd := \{a \in Auth \mid rq \leq subject(a), uri(object(a)) = dtd(URI)\}$
3. Let r be the root of the tree T corresponding to the
   document *URI*
4. initial_label(r)
5. $L_r := \text{first\_def}([L_r, R_r, LD_r, RD_r, LW_r, RW_r])$
6. For each $c \in children(r)$ do label(c, r)
7. For each $c \in children(r)$ do prune(T, c)

Procedure initial_label(n)
   /* It initializes $\langle L_n, R_n, LD_n, RD_n, LW_n, RW_n \rangle$. */
   /* Variable t_n spaces over those elements according
      the value of variable t */
1. For t in {L, R, LW, RW} do
   1a. $A := \{a \in Axml \mid type(a) = t, n \in object(a)\}$
   1b. $A := A - \{a \in A \mid \exists a' \in A, subject(a') \leq subject(a)\}$
   1c. If $A = \emptyset$ then $t_n := `\varepsilon'$
       elsif $\exists a \in A$ s.t. $sign(a) = `-'$ then $t_n := `-'$
       else $t_n := `+'$
2. For t in {LD, RD} do
   2a. $A := \{a \in Adtd \mid type(a) = t, n \in object(a)\}$
   2b. $A := A - \{a \in A \mid \exists a' \in A, subject(a') \leq subject(a)\}$
   2c. If $A = \emptyset$ then $t_n := `\varepsilon'$
       elsif $\exists a \in A$ s.t. $sign(a) = `-'$ then $t_n := `-'$
       else $t_n := `+'$

Procedure label(n, p)
   /* Determines the final label of node n basing on
      the label of n and that of its parent p */
   /* It uses first_def, which returns the first non null
      (different from 'ε') element in a sequence */
1. initial_label(n)
2. **Case of**
   2a. n is an attribute **do**
       $LD_n := \text{first\_def}([LD_n, LD_p])$
       if $LW_n = `\varepsilon'$ then $L_n := \text{first\_def}([L_n, L_p, LD_n])$
           else $L_n := \text{first\_def}([L_n, LD_n, RD_p, LW_n])$
   2b. n is an element **do**
       if $RW_n = `\varepsilon'$ then $R_n := \text{first\_def}([R_n, R_p])$
       $RW_n := \text{first\_def}([RW_n, RW_p])$
       $RD_n := \text{first\_def}([RD_n, RD_p])$
       $L_n := \text{first\_def}([L_n, R_n, LD_n, RD_n, LW_n, RW_n])$
       For each $c \in children(n)$ do label(c, n)

Procedure prune(T, n)
   /* Determines if n has to be removed from T */
1. For each $c \in children(n)$ do prune(T, c)
2. if $children(n) = \emptyset$ and $L_n \neq `+'$
   then remove n from T

Fig. 2. Compute-view algorithm

to authorizations of different types. For instance, with respect to a given element, a negative Local authorization and a positive Recursive authorization can exist; the semantics for this would be that the whole element's structured content (with exception of its direct attributes) can be accessed. Such semantics must be taken care of in the context of authorization propagation. In principle, therefore, each element can have associated a different sign with respect to the local and recursive permissions/denials, at the instance as well as at the schema level. For this reason, our tree labeling process associates to each node n a 6-tuple $\langle L_n, R_n, LD_n, RD_n, LW_n, RW_n \rangle$, whose content initially reflects the authorizations specified on the node. Each of the elements in the tuple can assume one of three values: '$+$' for permission, '$-$' for denial, and 'ε' for no authorization. The different elements reflect the sign of the authorization of type Local, Recursive, Local for the DTD and Recursive for the DTD, Local Weak, and Recursive Weak, holding for node n. (Note that both Local Weak and Recursive Weak for the DTD is missing, since the strength of the authorization is only used to invert the priority between instance and schema authorizations.) The interpretation of authorizations with respect to propagation and overriding (see Section 5) determines the final sign ($+$ or $-$) that should be considered to hold for each element and authorization type. Authorizations of each node are propagated to its attributes and, if recursive, to its sub-elements, possibly overridden according to the "most specific object takes precedence" principle, by which: (1) authorizations on a node take precedence over those on its ancestors, and (2) authorizations at the instance level, unless declared as weak, take precedence over authorizations at the schema level. Hence, the labeling of the complete document can be obtained by starting from the root and, proceeding downwards with a preorder visit, updating the 6-tuple of a node n depending on its values and the values of the 6-tuple of node p parent of n in the tree. In particular, the value of R_n (RW_n

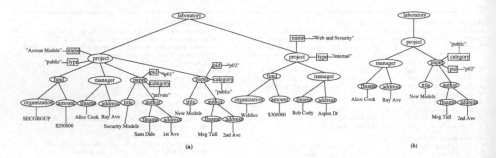

Fig. 3. Tree representation of a valid XML document (a) conforming to the DTD in Figure 1(a) and the view of user Tom (b)

resp.) is set to its current value, if either R_n or RW_n is not null (most specific overrides), and to the value of R_p (RW_p resp.) propagated down by the parent, otherwise. Schema level authorizations propagate in a similar way and the sign RD_n reflecting schema authorizations is set to the current value of RD_n, if not null, and to the value RD_p propagated down by the parent, otherwise. Given this first propagation step, according to the defined priorities, the sign $(+/-)$ that must hold for the specific element n is the sign expressed by the first not null value (if any) among: L_n, R_n, LD_n, RD_n, LW_n, and RW_n. L_n is updated to such value so that, at the end of the tree visit, L_n contains the "winning" sign for n. The 6-tuples assigned to attributes are updated in a similar way with some minor changes due to the fact that: (1) R_n, RW_n, and RD_n are always null for an attribute (being a terminal element of the tree, no propagation is possible), and (2) authorizations specified as Local on the node p parent of the attribute must propagate to the attribute.

Figure 2 illustrates an algorithm, **compute-view**, enforcing the labeling procedure described. The algorithm uses function `first_def` which, given a sequence of values on the domain $\{-, +, \varepsilon\}$, returns the first value in the sequence different from 'ε'. Given a requester rq and an XML document URI, the algorithm starts by determining the set of authorizations defined for the document at the instance level (set $Axml$ in step 1) and at the schema level (set $Adtd$ in step 2). The initial label of the root r is determined and (since the root has no parent) its final L_r can easily be determined by taking the sign with the highest priority that is not null, that is, the one coming first (`first_def`) in the sequence $L_r, R_r, LD_r, RD_r, LW_r, RW_r$. Procedure **label**($c,r$) is then called for each of the children (element or attribute) c of the root to determine the label of c. Procedure **label**(n,p) first computes the initial labeling of n by calling procedure **initial_label**. Step 1 of **initial_label** computes the initial value of L_n, R_n, LW_n, and RW_n. For each authorization type $t \in \{L, R, LW, RW\}$, the set A of authorizations of type t is determined (Step 1a). Set A is then updated by discarding authorizations overridden by other authorizations with more specific subjects (Step 1b). If the resulting set is empty, t_n (i.e., L_n, R_n, LW_n, or RW_n, depending on the value of t) is set to 'ε'. Otherwise, it is set to '$-$' or '$+$', according to whether a negative authorization exists ("denials take precedence") or does not exist in A (Step 1c). In a similar way, Step 2 determines the sign of LD_n and RD_n, respectively. Procedure **label**(n,p) updates the initial label so produced on the basis of the label of n's parent p as previously discussed. If n is an element, the procedure is recursively called for each sub-elements of n.

6.2   Transformation Process

As a result of the labeling process, the value of L_n for each node n will contain the sign, if any, reflecting whether the node can be accessed ('+') or not ('−'). The value of L_n is equal to 'ε' in the case where no authorizations have been specified nor can be derived for n. Value 'ε' can be interpreted either as a negation or as a permission, corresponding to the enforcement of the *closed* and the *open* policy, respectively [11]. In the following, we assume the closed policy. Accordingly, the requester is allowed to access all the elements and attributes whose label is positive. To preserve the structure of the document, the portion of the document visible to the requester will also include start and end tags of elements with a negative or undefined label, which have a descendant with a positive label. The view on the document can be obtained by pruning from the original document tree all the subtrees containing only nodes labeled negative or undefined. Figure 2 illustrates a procedure, **prune**, enforcing the pruning process described.

The pruned document may not be valid with respect to the DTD referenced by the original XML document. This may happen, for instance, when required attributes are deleted. To avoid this problem, a *loosening* transformation is applied to the DTD. Loosening a DTD simply means to define as *optional* all the elements and attributes marked as *required* in the original DTD. The DTD loosening prevents users from detecting whether information was hidden by the security enforcement or simply missing in the original document.

Example 2. Consider the XML document http://www.lab.com/CSlab.xml in Figure 3(a) and the set Auth of authorizations in Example 1. Consider now a request to read this document submitted by user Tom, member of group Foreign, when connected from infosys.bld1.it (130.100.50.8). Figure 3(b) shows the view of Tom resulting after the labeling and transformation process.

7   Implementation of the Security Processor

We are currently implementing a *security processor* for XML documents based on the security model described in this paper. The main usage scenario for our system involves a user requesting a set of XML documents from a remote site, either through an HTTP request or as the result of a query [4]. Our processor takes as input a valid XML document requested by the user, together with its *XML Access Control List* (XACL) listing the associated access authorizations at instance level. The processor operation also involves the document's DTD and the associated XACL specifying schema level authorizations. The processor output is a valid XML document including only the information the user is allowed to access. In our system, documents and DTDs are internally represented as object trees, according to the Document Object Model (DOM) Level One (Core) specification [18]. Our security processor computes an *on line transformation* on XML documents. Its execution cycle consists of four basic steps.

1. The *parsing* step consists in the syntax check of the requested document with respect to the associated DTD and its compilation to obtain an *object-oriented document graph* according to the DOM format.
2. The *tree labeling* step involves the recursive labeling of the DOM tree according to the authorizations listed in the XACLs associated to the document and its DTD (see Section 6.1).
3. The *transformation* step is a pruning of the DOM tree according to its labeling (see Section 6.2). Such a pruning is computed by means of a standard postorder visit to the labeled DOM tree. This pruning preserves the validity of the document with respect to the *loosened version* of its original DTD.
4. The *unparsing* step consists in generating a valid XML document in text format, simply by unparsing the pruned DOM tree computed by the previous step.

The resulting XML document, together with the loosened DTD, can then be transmitted to the user who requested access to the document.

Two main architectural patterns are currently used for XML documents browsing and querying: *server side* and *client side* processing, the former being more common in association with translation to HTML.

Our access control enforcement is performed on the server side, regardless of whether other operations (e.g., translation to HTML) are performed by the server site or by the client module. The XML document computed by the security processor execution is transferred to the client as the result of its original request. In our current design, the security processor is a *service component* in the framework of a complete architecture [5]. The reason for this architectural choice are twofold: first, server-side execution prevents the accidental transfer to the client of information it is not allowed to see or process; second, it ensures the operation and even the presence of security checking to be completely transparent to remote clients.

8   Conclusions

We have defined an access control model for restricting access to Web documents that takes into consideration the semi-structured organization of data and their semantics. The result is an access control system that, while powerful and able to easily represent different protection requirements, proves simple and of easy integration with existing applications. Our proposal leaves space for further work. Issues to be investigated include: the consideration of requests in form of generic queries, the support for write and update operations on the documents, and the enforcement of credentials and history- and time-based restrictions on access. Finally, we intend to prepare in a short time a Web site to demonstrate the characteristics of our proposal.

References

1. AlphaWorks. *XML Security Suite*, April 1999. http://www.alphaWorks.com/-tech/xmlsecuritysuite.
2. T. Berners-Lee, R. Fielding, and L. Masinter. *Uniform Resource Identifiers (URI): Generic Syntax*, 1998. http://www.isi.edu/in-notes/rfc2396.txt.
3. T. Bray et.al. (ed.). *Extensible Markup Language (XML) 1.0*. World Wide Web Consortium (W3C), February 1998. http://www.w3.org/TR/REC-xml.
4. S. Ceri, S. Comai, E. Damiani, P. Fraternali, S. Paraboschi, and L. Tanca. XML-GL: A Graphical Language for Querying and Restructuring XML Documents. In *Proc. of the Eighth Int. Conference on the World Wide Web*, Toronto, May 1999.
5. S. Ceri, P. Fraternali, and S. Paraboschi. Data-Driven, One-To-One Web Site Generation for Data-Intensive Applications. In *Proc. of the 25th Int. Conference on VLDB*, Edinburgh, September 1999.
6. CheckFree Corp. *Open Financial Exchange Specification 1.0.2*, 1998. http://www.ofx.net/.
7. S. DeRose, D. Orchard, and B. Trafford. *XML Linking Language (XLINK)*, July 1999. http://www.w3.org/TR/xlink.
8. C. Ellerman. *Channel Definition Format (CDF)*, March 1997. http://www.w3.org/TR/NOTE-CDFsubmit.html.
9. E.B. Fernandez, E. Gudes, and H. Song. A Model of Evaluation and Administration of Security in Object-Oriented Databases. *IEEE TKDE*, 6(2):275–292, April 1994.
10. S. Jajodia, P. Samarati, and V.S. Subrahmanian. A Logical Language for Expressing Authorizations. In *Proc. of the IEEE Symposium on Security and Privacy*, pages 31–42, Oakland, CA, May 1997.
11. S. Jajodia, P. Samarati, V.S. Subramanian, and E. Bertino. A Unified Framework for Enforcing Multiple Access Control Policies. In *Proc. of the 1997 ACM International SIGMOD Conference on Management of Data*, Tucson, AZ, May 1997.
12. T.F. Lunt. Access Control Policies for Database Systems. In C.E. Landwehr, editor, *Database Security, II: Status and Prospects*, pages 41–52. North-Holland, Amsterdam, 1989.
13. F. Rabitti, E. Bertino, W. Kim, and D. Woelk. A Model of Authorization for Next-Generation Database Systems. *ACM TODS*, 16(1):89–131, March 1991.
14. J. Reagle and L.F. Cranor. The Platform for Privacy Preferences. *Communications of the ACM*, 42(2):48–55, February 1999.
15. Rutgers Security Team. *WWW Security. A Survey*, 1999. http://www-ns.rutgers.edu/www-security/.
16. P. Samarati, E. Bertino, and S. Jajodia. An Authorization Model for a Distributed Hypertext System. *IEEE TKDE*, 8(4):555–562, August 1996.
17. A. van Hoff, H. Partovi, and T. Thai. *The Open Software Description Format (OSD)*, August 1997. http://www.w3.org/TR/NOTE-OSD.html.
18. L. Wood. *Document Object Model Level 1 Specification*, October 1998. http://www.w3.org/pub/WWW/REC-DOM-Level-1/.
19. World Wide Web Consortium (W3C). *Extensible Stylesheet Language (XSL) Specification*, April 1999. http://www.w3.org/TR/WD-xsl.
20. World Wide Web Consortium (W3C). *XML Path Language (XPath) Version 1.0*, October 1999. http://www.w3.org/TR/PR-xpath19991008.

Using Checksums to Detect Data Corruption

Daniel Barbará, Rajni Goel, and Sushil Jajodia

Center for Secure Information Systems *
George Mason University
Fairfax, VA 22030
{dbarbara,rgoel,jajodia}@gmu.edu

Abstract In this paper, we consider the problem of malicious and intended corruption of data in a database, acting outside of the scope of the database management system. Although detecting an attacker who changes a set of database values at the disk level is a simple task (achievable by attaching signatures to each block of data), a more sophisticated attacker may corrupt the data by replacing the current data with copies of old block images, compromising the integrity of the data. To prevent successful completion of this attack, we provide a defense mechanism that enormously increases the intruders workload, yet maintains a low system cost during an authorized update. Our algorithm calculates and maintains two levels of signatures (checksum values) on blocks of data. The signatures are grouped in a manner that forces an extended series of block copying for any unauthorized update. Using the available information on block sizes, block reference patterns and amount of concurrently active transactions in the database, we calculate the length of this chain of copying, proving that the intruder has to perform a lot of work in order to go undetected. Therefore, our technique makes this type of attack very unlikely. Previous work has not addressed protection methods against this knowledgeable and equipped intruder who is operating outside the database management system.

1 Introduction

The vulnerability of crucial information stored in computer systems makes the need for tools to detect malicious intentional attacks crucial. Lately, a large number of incidents into sensitive data have been reported [5]. Some of these attacks aim to modify the data for personal gain or simply to degrade or interrupt applications, which heavily depend on the correctness of the data. In this paper, we investigate a novel approach to detecting an intruder who is replacing data in a stored database with incorrect values. We assume that this intruder acts at the disk level, bypassing the database management system. The granularity of the targeted data may vary from a tuples in a relation to an entire disk block. Currently, a database system may use available integrity checking tools to protect its objects. Known mechanisms are powerful in preventing unauthorized

---

* This work has been supported by Rome Laboratories grant F30602-98-C-0264.

C. Zaniolo et al. (Eds.): EDBT 2000, LNCS 1777, pp. 136–149, 2000.

(illegitimate) users, whereas, our detection technique also achieves detection of the insider threat. A legitimate user misusing the system within his or her access domain, or attackers having sniffed passwords thus appearing as authorized users could pose the inside threat. Access controls or encryption technologies do not stop this kind of data corruption. Detecting intrusion at the disk level is a complex issue. It requires the system to establish whether the item updated or inserted is incorrect or not, and, if the change is malicious. Our algorithm provides an internal tracing mechanism that protects the items of a database by associating checksums (signatures) to them at two levels. With this algorithm, the intruder attempting to tamper with the current state of a database and remain undetected has to perform a significantly large amount of work, relative to the amount of work that needs to be done when processing an authorized update. Our technique forces an attacker to implement a lengthy iterative chain of changes in order to successfully complete the update.

To illustrate, consider a system user who is unauthorized to perform transactions on this simplified bank account balance database with six customers, $C_1, C_2, C_3, C_4, C_5, C_6$ and two banks B_1, B_2, as shown in Figure 1. Each column, i, represents a stored block of information on a disk, with its signature value, Ck_i^1, stored on the same block.

	C_1	C_2	C_3	C_4	C_5	C_6
B_1	40	30	45	10	24	30
B_2	10	20	25	15	18	98
	Ck_1^1	Ck_2^1	Ck_3^1	Ck_4^1	Ck_5^1	Ck_6^1

Fig. 1. Example database showing the checksums of each block of data. The C_i are customers, the Ck_j^1 is a checksum taken over the column j.

For security, the database utilizes a one way hashing function, f, to compute a checksum value [9] involving all item values on a block: E.g., for the first column, $f(10, 40) = Ck_1^1$. This function uses a secret key, securely kept by the system. When changing the value(s) stored in a block, the system, with the block in main memory, computes and validates the checksum for each transaction involving an item of the block; then, the block is stored back on the disk according to the buffer manager of the system. When an unauthorized user corrupts an item, it is highly probable that the computed signature will no longer be valid, thus indicating intrusive behavior. That is, if the intruder does not have access to old copies of the blocks, it becomes trivial to detect the intrusion, since the checksums will not match and the intruder does not have access to the secret key.

Unfortunately, there is a way to circumvent this protection: an internal legitimate system user (or an intruder who, using previously acquired knowledge of passwords, has broken into the system), operating outside of the DBMS, may have extensive knowledge of the layout of the disk structure and information storage. If this user has collected previous copies of numerous combinations of the valid database blocks with the valid checksum associated to them, he or she can compromise the integrity of the data as follows. This equipped intruder can replace current value(s) on a page by copying over it an entire old valid block of data. If the system performs a checksum validation on this block, it will not discover any anomaly in the data. In our example above, an intruder has copies of the blocks of the database as shown in Figure 1. The state of the database after several updates take place is shown in Figure 2.

	C_1	C_2	C_3	C_4	C_5	C_6
B_1	40	15	45	50	34	60
B_2	10	70	20	15	10	58
	$Ck_1^{1'}$	$Ck_2^{1'}$	$Ck_3^{1'}$	$Ck_4^{1'}$	$Ck_5^{1'}$	$Ck_6^{1'}$

Fig. 2. The state of the database of Figure 1 after updates.

To maliciously modify tuple value for customer C_2, bank B_2 (70) back to the original value (20), the attacker replaces the current disk block, column 2 in Figure 2, with a block copy of the previous values, column 2 in Figure 1. Data corruption has been successfully completed. Moreover, discovering the corrupted data at this point becomes extremely difficult. McDermott and Goldschlag discuss this type of corruption in more general terms as 'storage jamming,' [7,8] However, their work does not specifically cover the case of intrusions at the disk level. In order to prevent the attack we described above, we formulate a technique that combines a set of data blocks checksums to compute a second checksum. The motivation is to link objects in the database, so that one change causes another automatic modification elsewhere in the system. An intruder must account for all the changes in the first-level and second-level checksums (signatures) when making one corrupted copy. The consequence of adding this new level of checksums is that even the most well equipped inside intruder who is fully aware of the system architecture will be required to perform a very lengthy chain of precise data changes in order to remain undetected. Moreover, this design is flexible and scalable with the database size.

This paper is organized as follows. In Section 2 we present our technique including its analysis. We utilize research on block reference patterns indicating which blocks have a high transaction rate [4,10], as well as the average number of concurrently active transactions on these blocks. In section 3, we show numerical results and identify critical issues that significantly influence the outcome of our procedure including the rate and location of authorized transactions, block size, the attacker extent of knowledge and information about the targeted database, and the architecture of the system being targeted. Different scenarios of database transactions are presented to display the cost of the work the attacker must perform in order to successfully corrupt just one record. In section 4, we conclude by comparing and relating the technique to prior work. Finally, in Section 5 we present the conclusions as well as the future direction of research in this area.

2   Our Technique

Our technique formulates a second set of checksums to detect the kind of attack introduced in Section 1. The technique protects the database in the worst case scenario in which the intruder has done extensive 'intelligence gathering.' He or she has knowledge about the system's internal structure and architecture: data layout, checksum model being used, and the algorithm to calculate the combinations of the second-level checksum, but not the trusted key of the hashing function. This intruder also may have accumulated a very large set, or stock, of prior valid copies of database blocks and various generations of second-level checksum blocks. We indicate how an intruder may attempt to bypass this security system from two unique avenues of attack, and calculate the theoretical costs associated with each type of attempt. The goal of the model is to have the system incur a minimal cost (few block accesses) yet force this equipped attacker to face significantly larger number of block accesses to succeed.

2.1   Design

We view the database as a set of m disk blocks, each with blocking factor n. Any new pages added to the database have a common blocking factor, n. The first-level checksum, Ck^1, generated for each block by a function f using a secret key, operates over all n data values on that page, i.e., $Ck^1 = f(t_1, t_2, \cdots, t_n, TK)$, where TK is the secret key, unavailable to the intruder. (Hence, f can not be computed without TK.) Here, t_i represents the key of the data item i in the block and Ck^1 is the checksum for that block. The size of the checksum is s bytes. Each block stores data and a signature, Ck^1; the block has enough capacity to store n items plus one s byte checksum. Every transaction that changes the value of an item stored in a block, b_j, needs to recompute Ck_j^1. A second checksum function, g, uses a set of checksums, Ck_j^1, $1 < j < m$, to compute another signature, Ck^2 as $Ck_j^2 = g(Ck_1^1, Ck_2^1, Ck_3^1, \cdots, Ck_m^1, TK)$. Ck_j^2 is the second-level checksum. To enhance concurrency, copies of the Ck_l^1 needed for computing Ck_l^2 are replicated onto a signature block containing Ck_l^2. Later we discuss why this replication is beneficial. The system computes the second-level signature using combinations of these replicated values and stores the result on the second-level checksum block. We assume that the key is secret and protected from attacks (something in the system has to be secure in order to build upon it.) If any parameter value of the function is altered, the signature value must change. This prevents the attacker from simply changing data values on the block. Notice that a simple attack where a value is changed by the intruder without making the corresponding change to the checksums can be readily detected. That is why we focus on attacks where the intruder knows previous values of both the item keys and checksums, as explained in Section 1.

Schemes for computing these signatures for multiple objects are well-establi-shed. The actual calculation of the checksum is not the focus of this paper: any algorithm satisfying the criteria discussed above is appropriate. Since updates are managed by the DBMS in the context of transaction, one is guaranteed that the change to both blocks (or to all the blocks involved in the transactions) is to be done preserving the ACID properties.

To form an effective second-level checksum, the database blocks are grouped into two groups: hot and warm blocks. Hot blocks are the portion of the database which are highly updated relative to the remaining warm blocks. The system first establishes the block transaction patterns to determine the blocks involved in high number of transactions. Then, the algorithm includes exactly one highly updated block checksum in the combination that is the parameter of function g, resulting in each second-level signature. Later, when the necessity of having each combination change is presented, the need for the highly updated blocks will be evident.

The percentage of blocks (p_1) with a high update rate determines the number of checksums in each second signature combination. The m block database has mp_1 hot (highly updated) blocks and $m(1 - p_1)$ warm blocks. The warm blocks are distributed among the hot so that each second-level combination contains ex-actly one hot block. Hence, the number of warm blocks per combination,($m(1 - p_1))/(m(p_1))$, plus one hot block results in k first-level checksums in each com-bination, with k as shown in Equation 1

$$k = \lceil (1 - p_1)/p_1 + 1 \rceil = \lceil 1/p_1 \rceil \qquad (1)$$

Each second-level signature occupies $s(k + 1)$ bytes (k first- level signatures per combination plus the second signature value itself). We refer to the number of second-level signatures per block as the combination-blocking factor (CBF). Considering a block size of B, the CBF for each second-level block is the block size divided by the size of each Ck^2, as shown in Equation 2.

$$CBF = \lceil B/(s(k+1)) \rceil \qquad (2)$$

CBF represents not only the number of second-level signatures per block, but it also equals the number of hot data blocks per second-level block. The intruder needs to track all possible values of these second signatures, where each signature is computed by using k first-level signatures. As each data block is updated, exactly one second-level signature automatically changes.

We are also interested in the total replicated first-level checksums per second-level block ($TRCB$). This provides the number of data block signatures (Ck^1s) replicated onto each second-level block in order to compute the second-level sig-natures. With k values per combination, $CBF \times k$ replicated copies are necessary. The $TRCB$ is defined in Equation 3.

$$TRCB = k[B/(s(k+1))] = B/(s(1+p1)) \qquad (3)$$

The $TRCB$ will affect the 'stock' of replicated blocks the intruder must keep in storage. One type of intruder collects exactly one valid set of copies that appeared simultaneously together at some prior time. This set includes one snapshot copy of one second-level block and the appropriate data block copies with corresponding checksums to match the replicated checksum values on the second-level block copy. This intruder completes a malicious update by copying his snapshot onto the second-level checksum block, as well as replacing any of the replicated first-level checksums ($TRCB$) with snapshot copies of data blocks with checksums that match those on the second-level block. In the analysis and results, we discuss this type of intruder's numerical cost (block accesses) as a percentage of the database size. A second type of intruder attempts corruption by copying exactly two blocks: one corrupted data block, with Ck^1, and the one second-level block on which Ck^1 is replicated. This intruder's cost now includes the expense in accumulating an enormous library, stock, of all possible second-level block snapshots. This stock must include all prior combinations of values occurring within the $TRCB$. If the first-level signature function, f, has produced c different values for each signature, then the total different possible combinations of the $TRCB$ replications is $c \times TRCB$. The system automatically recalculates the combinations of checksums involved in the second-level checksum as blocks are added or deleted from the database. Figure 3 shows the basic system structure.

Figure 3 shows the structure of the second-level checksums for a database of m blocks, assuming that each combination includes an arbitrary number of k signatures. Applying this to the banking example, when the second tuple on block C_2 changes, the system expects a valid block checksum Ck_2^1, as well as a correctly calculated second-level checksum, Ck^2, involving Ck_2^1. Having copied the data block with a corrupted tuple value and correct matching Ck_2^1, the attacker needs to replace the block containing the corresponding Ck^2 with a value consistent with the Ck_2^1 change. This assumes the intruder's existing extensive knowledge of the data base and disk layout, as well as a large stock of previously existing blocks.

2.2   Model Analysis

During authentic item updates, the system calculates f and g of the block and combination, respectively, which includes the target tuple t_k. Only when a valid value is computed will the system write the update to the database. The system's cost to implement the algorithm is always two block accesses. However, the intruder's expense is proportional to the quantity and location of updates throughout the database. The average number of transactions per second dictates the cost for the intruder, (measured by the number of blocks the intruder must access to change).

Incorporating each block checksum in a second checksum makes necessary a long chain of block substitution from the part of the attacker. During an authorized update, the system automatically calculates and validates the first and second-level checksums. That makes the system I/O requirements for an authorized user to be exactly two blocks per update. (One block contains the

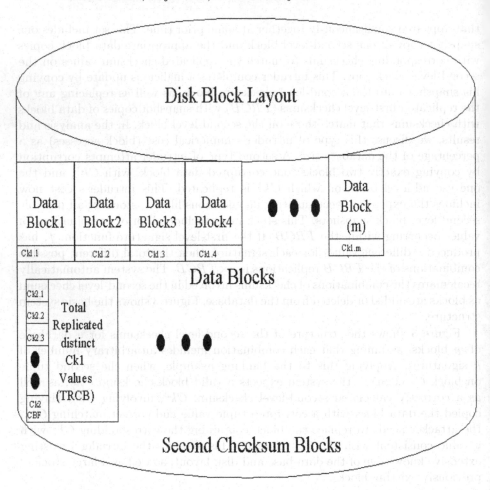

Fig. 3. Blocks on a disk; data blocks and second-level checksum blocks.

value to be changed and the other contains the second signature in which the first block checksum is involved.) This is guaranteed by the following reasons:

- The replication of each first-level signature (Ck_j^1) on the same block as the second-level signature for which it serves as a parameter. This guarantees that during authorized second signature calculation, the system will not need to access each block involved in the combination.
- The fact that each Ck_j^1 appears exactly once in the calculation of a second-level checksum.

The contention for the hot block first-level checksums is minimized by distributing them among the combinations (only one hot checksum per second-level checksum). Transactions only need to access the corresponding second-level blocks after all the updates are performed, therefore the time for which these blocks are locked is not too large.

On the other hand, the intruder's cost includes is usually larger. This cost is directly proportional to the $TRCB$. When the intruder corrupts a tuple value by replacing the page with a valid prior copy, the block checksum matches. But the corresponding second-level checksum, on block b_2, must also be copied to match the corrupted checksum of the data block. Since the remaining $TRCB - 1$ checksums on block b_2 are validated against the first-level checksums, if any of these data blocks that have had simultaneous transactions, they need to be replaced with a block copy having a checksum coinciding with the replicated value on b_2. Though the attacker has knowledge of the algorithm and disk block structure, he or she has no control of where and when the other concurrently active authorized updates are occurring throughout the database. Since these updates generate changes in the first and second-level checksums, the intruder is forced to continue replacing enough data blocks so the copied checksum values consistently match with the simultaneously changing computed signature values. Not only does the intruder need access to all other changes occurring in the database, the copying of the initial second checksum triggers a chain of copying for the attacker. As the percentage of concurrently active authorized updates increases, so does the intruder's need of replacing more blocks. We explain later why this chain is proportional to the number of concurrently active transactions involving a change in the first-level checksum. This mechanism thus covers a broader spectrum than McDermott and Goldschlag's notion of detection by bogus values, which successfully works if the intruder chooses to replace an element of the act bogus values [7,8]. If all the records of the database are being modified, all blocks will need to be copied at one time by the intruder. We show that even under lighter loads, the intruder still has to do a considerable amount of work.

Factors directly affecting the attacker's cost include: size of the disk block (B), database size (m), size of signature (s), number of different values for each first-level signature (c) and the percentage of updates concurrently occurring in the database. From Equation 3, we know that $TRCB$ is directly proportional to the disk size, and inversely proportional to signature size. As $TRCB$ increases, the possible blocks the intruder may need to copy increase. The actual numerical portion that the attacker must copy is proportional to the percentage of authorized updates changing $TRCB$. As the percentage of updates increases, more $TRCB$ values change, so the intruder's work of copying to match the checksums increases. Having the CBF hot blocks on each second-level block guarantees that portion of the database will change, meaning increased work for the attacker. The higher the probability that at least one update occurs on each hot block the greater the guarantee. The greater the probability that other concurrently active transaction are occurring throughout a large percentage of $TRCB$, the larger the number of blocks the intruder needs to replace.

The technique also creates a large workload for the intruder collecting the library of second-level block snapshots. It requires the intruder to accumulate an exponentially large number of replicated block copies, the 'stock.' After copying (corrupting) the initial data block, the intruder, lacking time to copy many more data blocks, may attempt to complete the corruption by copying one and only one more block : a second-level block that accounts for all changes in the first-level signatures due to the concurrently active transactions. Then, any first-level checksum $(TRCB-1)$ on this block, which simultaneously changed values, will need to be accounted for in that one copy. Recall that stock $(c \times TRCB)$ accounted for the changes possibly occurring on the $TRCB - 1$ data blocks. As the $TRCB$ increases, the necessary amount of stock increases exponentially. This aspect of our defense mechanism only adds cost to the intruder's workload, and none to the system's.

3   Results

In our study, we use a signature size of 4 bytes, and assume that the block reference pattern follows the commonly known 80-20 rule. As discussed above, the size of the attacker's stock measures the level of protection against the one type of intruder attempting to defeat our algorithm. Figure 4 displays the increase in the replicated copies as the block size increases. In this example, we assumed only the naive case that each data block has only 2 valid checksum values $(c = 2)$. We show the results when assuming only any 2 or 3 or 4 of the $TRCB$ values to have changed. Note that as c would also increase, the 'stock' value grows enormously. (Due to the exponential increase, we have shown the log of the actual values.) The technique forces the tedious task of collecting all such possible combinations.

The number of data blocks the intruder copies depends on the distribution of the concurrently active transactions, C, across the database; especially on the t database blocks involved in signatures on second-level block including the initial corrupted data block signature. Assuming the attacker accessibility to view all on going transactions, we considered several scenarios with possible values of C at various locations.

- Case 1 **One Update per block** : One implementation of the algorithm assumes that one tuple on each block of the database is updated at the time of intrusion. We consider the most optimistic scenario for the intruder, that while he or she is replacing the data blocks no block's signature changes more than once. Considering the worst case, the attacker's replacement of one page corrupts only one tuple value t_k. At some time, the intruder replaces the block containing the second-level combination (Ck_1^2), containing t_k, with the corresponding valid value, Ck_2^2. Any authorized transactions (occurring before that time) which change the remaining replicated blocks involved on this second-level signature block will need to be accounted for by the attacker. Assuming one update per block in the database, Figure 5 shows the percentage of the database of size m that needs to be copied by the intruder relative to the block size. Note that with a block size of 65, 536 and a million blocks in the database, the intruder must copy over 1.5 percent of the one

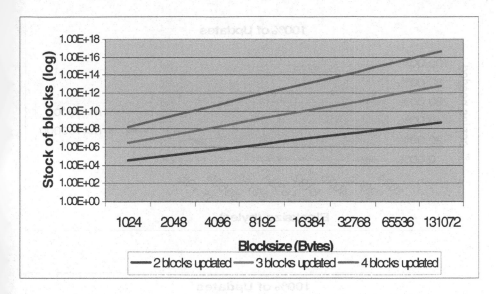

Fig. 4. Increase in the number of replicated copies ('stock') required by intruder to accommodate updates in 2, 3, or 4 of the replicated checksums on b_2

million blocks. This cost is very large in comparison to the two-block access of an authorized transaction. In actuality, once a data block is replaced, it may happen that during the chain of copying, the same replaced block has another authorized update. That block again needs to be replaced, adding to the cost indicated above. Hence, the intruder's minimum cost is $t + 1$ block accesses: the number of data blocks replaced plus one second-signature block itself. The limit to the maximum cost is infinite if blocks undergo recurring authorized updates during the intruder's chain of copying.

– Case 2 **Hot Block Updates:** The rate and location of the updates is a primary factor in this model; it determines the chain of data blocks the intruder must replace to match the checksums he or she copied onto the second-level block. Incorporating the CBF "hot" blocks on each block will guarantee the length of this chain. Assuming that each "hot" block has at least one concurrently active transaction guarantees that CBF checksums have changed on the second-level block since the being of the intrusion. The workload is a minimum of $(CBF + 1)$ blocks. If any block checksum is modified during the replacement of the CBF blocks, the cost increases by the number of changes. Also, any authorized updates in the remaining $(TRCB - CBF)$ checksums increase the intruders cost by the exact number of simultaneous transactions. In essence, a high quantity of updates guaranteed in the CBF with a uniform percentage of updates in the remaining $(TRCB - CBF)$ blocks, is directly proportional to the assurance of the amount of copies the intruder implements. Much research indicates existence of patterns and non-uniformity in block accessing and updating [4,10]. Figure 6 displays the

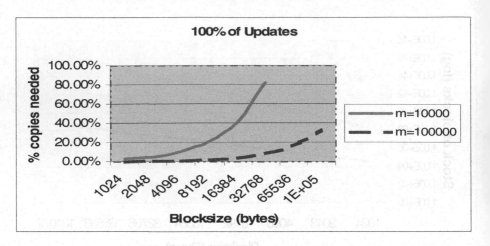

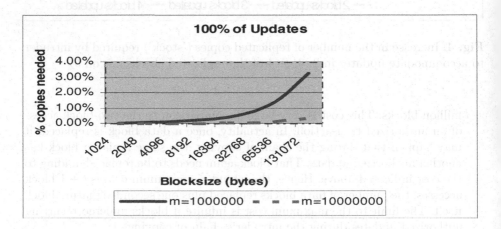

Fig. 5. Increase in the minimum percentage of database blocks that the intruder needs to replace vs. block size (assuming one tuple per block is concurrently updated).

percentage of the database (m) that the intruder must access if the algorithm assumes updates only in 20% of the blocks. It indicates the situation if only one first-level checksum in each second signature combination is changed. Hence, with one million blocks, if only 20% of the data blocks (known to be the hot blocks) are concurrently updated, then the algorithm guarantees the intruder must still access over 1/2 percent of the one million blocks. This makes the work for the attacker very difficult. This is assuming no updates on the warm blocks. If a high percentage of C (average number of concurrently active transactions) happen in each of the hot blocks, then the algorithm guarantees a minimum cost of $(CBF + 1)$ blocks.

From the previous discussion, we conclude that if at least one blocks checksum in each second-level combination is guaranteed modification, then the intruder's cost of block accesses is proportional the number of updates occurring in CBF blocks of database.

4   Related Work

Much of the research has studied intrusion detection at the OS level, with little work addressing the need to prevent an intruder from changing data at a DBMS level. Prior work regarding data corruption involves protecting data corruption due to special purpose application code being integrated with database system codes [2]. Techniques to protect data from "addressing errors" caused by copy overruns and "wild writes" include hardware memory protection and codewords associated with regions of data [2]. Also related work includes ways to detect changes in hierarchically structured information [3] as well as detecting corrupted pages in replicated files [1]. But, to our knowledge, no prior research specifically addresses stored data corruption due to malicious replication at the disk level. Tripwire integrity checking tool [6] uses the signature idea to protect files but it also does not address the intruder who has ability to copy valid checksums in the database storing the signatures. Storage jamming is a broader topic; it includes the malicious modification of data done in a variety of avenues, whereas we discuss one specific type of intrusion where the "jammer" performs a form of "repeat-back jamming" [7,8].

5   Conclusions and Future Directions

The data corruption addressed by our model involves copying of blocks by intruders who bypass the database management system and act at the disk level. Our technique forces the intruder who wishes corrupt a data item while remaining undetected to either engage in a long chain of updates or to keep a large stock of block combinations. The system's cost is exactly two block accesses for an authorized update in the database, ensured by replication of signatures. Results display that when the intruder wishes to corrupt one data item, the technique guarantees that he or she has to incur in a number of block accesses that is prohibitive (given that the database has minimum percentage of updates in its blocks). Intruders who want to avoid this long chain of changes need to keep a sizable stock of block combinations around.

We have largely ignored in this paper the issue of recovery after the attack has been discovered, because, for reasons of space it falls out of the scope of this paper. The issue can be easily addressed by replaying the transactions that have been committed since the last checkpoint that falls before the attack. However, using the structure of the checksum distribution, we believe that we can cut the recovery work by identifying the possible set of items that may have been corrupted and replaying only transactions that have modified those items. At this point, we are trying to experimentally quantify the overhead that our technique

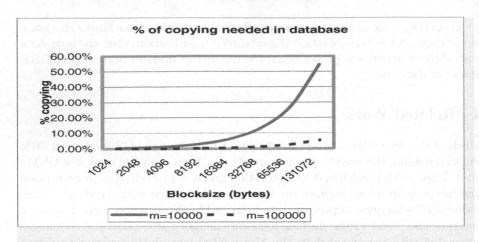

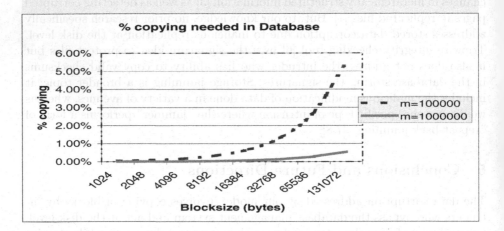

Fig. 6. Percentage of m total database intruder needs to copy assuming 20% of database blocks are updated.

imposes over the transaction processing system. We are also trying to extend our ideas to non-database environments, such as sets of files (e.g., binary executables, or WWW pages) to protect other objects from similar attacks.

References

1. Barbará, D., Lipton, R.J.: A Class of Randomized Strategies for Low-Cost Comparison of File Copies. IEEE Transactions on Parallel and Distributed Systems, **2:2** April 1991.
2. Bohannon, P., Rastogi R., Seshadri S., Silberschatz A., Sudarshan S.: Using Codewords to Protect Database Data from a Class of Software Errors. Proceedings of the International Conference on Data Engineering, 1999.

3. Chawathe, S., Rajaraman, A., Garcia-Molina, H., Widom, J.: Change Detection in Hierarchically Structured Information. Proceedings of the International ACM-SIGMOD Conference on Management of Data. (1995).

4. Choi, J., Noh S., Min, S.L., Cho, Y.: An Adaptive Block Management Scheme Using On-Line Detection of Block Reference Patterns. Proceedings of the Int'l Workshop on Multimedia Database Management Systems, 1998.

5. Durst, R., Champion, T, Witten, B., Miller E., Spagnuolo L.: Testing and Evaluating Computer Intrusion Detection Systems. Communications of the ACM, July 1999, 53–61.

6. Kim, G., Spafford, E.H.: The Design and Implementation of Tripwire: A File System Integrity Checker. Proceedings of the 2nd ACM Conference on Computer and Communications Security. (1994).

7. McDermott, J., Goldschlag, D.: Storage Jamming. Database Security IX: Status and Prospects, Chapman & Hall, London (1996) 365–381.

8. McDermott, J., Goldschlag, D.: Towards a Model of Storage Jamming. Proceedings of the IEEE Computer Security Foundations Workshop, June 1996, 176–185.

9. Merkle, R. C.: A Fast Software One-way Hash Function. Journal of Cryptology, 3(1): 43–58 (1990).

10. Salem, K., Barbará, D., Lipton, R.J.: Probabilistic Diagnosis of Hot Spots. Proceedings of the Eight International Conference on Data Engineering, 1992.

Navigation-Driven Evaluation
of Virtual Mediated Views

Bertram Ludäscher, Yannis Papakonstantinou, and Pavel Velikhov

ludaesch@sdsc.edu, {yannis,pvelikho}@cs.ucsd.edu

Abstract. The MIX mediator systems incorporates a novel framework for navigation-driven evaluation of virtual mediated views. Its architecture allows the *on-demand* computation of views and query results as the user navigates them. The evaluation scheme minimizes superfluous source access through the use of *lazy mediators* that translate incoming client navigations on virtual XML views into navigations on lower level mediators or wrapped sources. The proposed demand-driven approach is inevitable for handling up-to-date mediated views of large Web sources or query results. The non-materialization of the query answer is transparent to the client application since clients can navigate the query answer using a subset of the standard DOM API for XML documents. We elaborate on query evaluation in such a framework and show how algebraic plans can be implemented as trees of lazy mediators. Finally, we present a new buffering technique that can mediate between the fine granularity of DOM navigations and the coarse granularity of real world sources. This drastically reduces communication overhead and also simplifies wrapper development. An implementation of the system is available on the Web.

1 Introduction and Overview

Mediated views integrate information from heterogeneous sources. There are two main paradigms for evaluating queries against integrated views: In the *warehousing* approach, data is collected and integrated in a materialized view *prior* to the execution of user queries against the view. However, when the user is interested in the most recent data available or very large views, then a *virtual, demand-driven* approach has to be employed. Most notably such requirements are encountered when integrating Web sources. For example, consider a mediator that creates an integrated view, called `allbooks`, of data on books available from `amazon.com` and `barnesandnoble.com`. A warehousing approach is not viable: First, one cannot obtain the complete dataset of the booksellers. Second, the data will have to reflect the ever-changing availability of books. In contrast, in a demand-driven approach, the user query is composed with the view definition of `allbooks` and corresponding subqueries against the sources are evaluated only then (i.e., at query evaluation time and not a priori).

Current mediator systems, even those based on the virtual approach, compute and return the results of the user query *completely*. Thus, although they do not materialize the integrated view, they materialize the result of the user query. This

C. Zaniolo et al. (Eds.): EDBT 2000, LNCS 1777, pp. 150–165, 2000.
© Springer-Verlag Berlin Heidelberg 2000

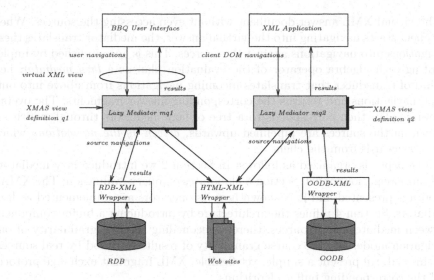

Fig. 1. Virtual XML Document (VXD) mediation architecture

approach is unsuitable in Web mediation scenarios where the users typically do not specify their queries precisely enough to obtain small results. Instead, they often issue relatively broad queries, navigate the first few results and then stop either because the results seem irrelevant or because the desired data was found. In the context of such interactions, materializing the full answer on the client side is not an option. Instead, it is preferable to produce results as the user navigates into the virtual answer view, thereby reducing the response time.

In this paper, we present a novel mediator framework and query evaluation mechanism that can efficiently handle such cases. We use XML, the emerging standard for data exchange, as the data model of our mediator architecture (Fig. 1). User queries and view definitions are expressed in XMAS[1], a declarative XML query language borrowing from and similar to other query languages for semistructured data like XML-QL [17] and Lorel [1].

The key idea of the framework is simple and does not complicate the client's code: In response to a query, the client receives a *virtual* answer document. This document is not computed or transfered into the client memory until the user starts navigating it. The virtuality of the document is transparent to the client who accesses it using a subset of the DOM[2] API, i.e., in exactly the same way as main memory resident XML documents.

Query evaluation is navigation-driven in our architecture: The client application first sends a query to the mediator which then composes the query with the view definition and translates the result into an algebraic evaluation plan. After the preprocessing phase, the mediator returns a "handle" to the root element

---

[1] **XML M**atching **A**nd **S**tructuring Language [16]
[2] **D**ocument **O**bject **M**odel [6]

of the virtual XML answer document without even accessing the sources. When the client starts navigating into the virtual answer, the mediator translates these navigations into navigations against the sources. This is accomplished by implementing each algebra operator of the evaluation plan as a *lazy mediator*, i.e., a kind of transducer that translates incoming navigations from above into outgoing navigations and returns the corresponding answer fragments. The overall algebraic plan then corresponds to a tree of lazy mediators through which results from the sources are pipelined upwards, *driven by the navigations* which flow downwards from the client.

The paper is organized as follows: In Section 2 we introduce lazy mediators and our navigation model. Section 3 elaborates on query evaluation: The XMAS algebra is presented and it is shown how its operators are implemented as lazy mediators. Section 4 refines the architecture by introducing a buffer component between mediators and sources, thereby reconciling the fine granularity of our navigation model and the coarse granularity of results returned by real sources. To this end, we present a simple, yet flexible, XML fragment exchange protocol and the corresponding buffer algorithms.

The complete presentation of XMAS, its algebra, the algorithms, and the software architecture is found in [16]. A preliminary abstract on the architecture appeared in [11]. The implementation is available at [14].

Related Work. Our navigation-driven architecture extends the virtual view mediator approach as used, e.g., in TSIMMIS, YAT, Garlic, and Hermes [15,4], [5,10]. The idea of on-demand evaluation is related to pipelined plan execution in relational [8] and object-relational [12] databases where child operators proceed just as much as to be able to satisfy their parent operator's requests. However, in the case of (XML) *trees* the client may proceed from multiple nodes whose descendants or siblings have not been visited yet. In contrast, in relational databases a client may only proceed from the current cursor position. Also the presence of order has an impact on the complexity wrt. navigations and the implementation of lazy mediators.

Note that we use the terms *lazy* and *demand-driven* synonymously, whereas in the context of functional languages, *lazy evaluation* refers to a specific and different on-demand implementation technique for non-strict languages [2,9].

Our XML query language XMAS borrows from similar languages such as XML-QL, MSL, FLORID, Lorel, and YAT [17,15,7,1,4]. However, most of the above rely on Skolem functions for grouping, while XMAS uses explicit group-by operators thereby facilitating a direct translation of the queries into an algebra. In that sense our implementation is closer to implementations of the nested relational and complex values models.

2   Navigations in the VXD Framework

We employ XML as the data model [18]. Note that the techniques presented here are not specific to XML and are applicable to other semistructured data models and query languages. The paper uses the following abstraction of XML where, for simplicity, we have excluded attributes: XML documents are viewed as *labeled ordered trees* (from now on referred to simply as *trees*) over a suitable underlying domain $\mathbf{D}$.[3] The set of all trees over $\mathbf{D}$ is denoted by $\mathbf{T}$.

A tree $t \in \mathbf{T}$ is either a *leaf*, i.e., a single atomic piece of data $t = d \in \mathbf{D}$, or it is $t = d[t_1, \ldots, t_n]$, where $d \in \mathbf{D}$ and $t_1, \ldots, t_n \in \mathbf{T}$. We call d the *label* and $[t_1, \ldots, t_n]$ the *ordered list of subtrees* (also called *children*) of t.

In XML parlance, t is an *element*, a non-leaf label d is the *element type* ("tag name"), $t_1, \ldots, t_n$ are *child elements* (or *subelements*) of t, and a leaf label d is an atomic object such as character content or an empty element. Thus, the set $\mathbf{T}$ of labeled ordered trees can be described by the signature $\mathbf{T} = \mathbf{D} \mid \mathbf{D}[\mathbf{T}^*]$.

DOM-VXD Navigation Commands. XML documents (both source and answer documents) are accessible via navigation commands. We present the navigational interface DOM-VXD (DOM for *V*irtual *X*ML *D*ocuments) that is an abstraction of a subset of the DOM API for XML. More precisely, we consider the following set $\mathbf{NC}$ of *navigation commands*, where p and p' are node-id's of (pointers into) the virtual document that is being navigated:

- d *(down)*: $p' := d(p)$ assigns to p' the *first child* of p; if p is a leaf then $d(p) = \bot$ (null).
- r *(right)*: $p' := r(p)$ assigns to p' the *right sibling* of p; if there is no right sibling $r(p) = \bot$.
- f *(fetch)*: $l := f(p)$ assigns to l the *label* of p.

This minimal set of navigation commands is sufficient to completely explore arbitrary virtual documents. Additional commands can be provided in the style of [19]. E.g., we may include in $\mathbf{NC}$ a command for selecting certain siblings:

- *select* (σ_θ): $p' := \sigma_\theta(p)$ assigns to p' the first sibling to the right whose label satisfies θ (else $\bot$).

Definition 1 (Navigations) Let p_0 be the root for some document $t \in \mathbf{T}$. A *navigation* into t is a sequence $c =$

$$p'_0 := c_1(p_0), \ p'_1 := c_2(p_1), \ \ldots, \ p'_{n-1} := c_n(p_{n-1})$$

where each $c_i \in \mathbf{NC}$ and each p_i is a p'_j with $j < i$.

The *result* (or *explored part*) $c(t)$ of applying the navigation c to a tree t is the unique subtree comprising only those node-ids and labels of t which have been accessed through c. Depending on the context, $c(t)$ may also denote the final point reached in the sequence, i.e., p'_{n-1}. For notational convenience, we sometimes omit the pointer argument and simply write $c = c_1, \ldots, c_n$.   □

---

[3] $\mathbf{D}$ includes all "string data" like element names and character content.

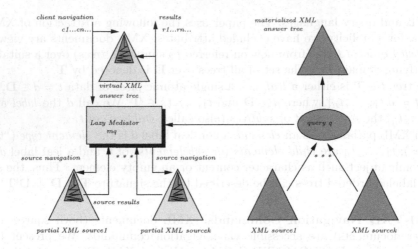

Fig. 2. Navigational interface of a lazy mediator

3   Query Evaluation Using Lazy Mediators

A *lazy mediator* m_q for a query or view definition[4] q operates as follows: The client browses into the virtual view exported by m_q by successively issuing DOM-VXD navigations on the view document exported by the mediator. For each command c_i that the mediator receives (Fig. 2), a minimal source navigation is sent to each source. Note that navigations sent to the sources depend on the client navigation, the view definition, and the state of the lazy mediator. The results of the source navigations are then used by the mediator to generate the result for the client and to update the mediator's state.

Query processing in the MIX mediator system involves the following steps:

Preprocessing: At compile-time, a XMAS mediator view v is first translated into an equivalent algebra expression E_v that constitutes the *initial plan*. The interaction of the client with the mediator may start by issuing a query q on v. In this case the preprocessing phase will compose the query and the view and generate the initial plan for $q' := q \circ v$.

Query Rewriting: Next, during the *rewriting phase*, the initial plan is rewritten into a plan $E'_{q'}$ which is optimized with respect to navigational complexity. Due to space limitations we do not present rewriting rules.

Query Evaluation: At run-time, client navigations into the virtual view, i.e., into the result of q' are translated into source navigations. This is accomplished by implementing each algebra operator op as a *lazy mediator* m_{op} that transforms incoming navigations (from the client or the operator above) into navigations that are directed to the operators below or the wrappers.

---

[4] We often use the terms *query* and *view definition* interchangeably.

```
CONSTRUCT <answer>                      % Construct the root element containing ...
            <med_home> $H               % ... med_home elements followed by
                       $S {$S}          % ... school elements (one for each $S)
            </med_home> {$H}            % (one med_home element for each $H)
          </answer> {}                  % create one answer element (= for each {})
WHERE homesSrc homes.home $H AND $H zip._ $V1 % get home elements $H and their zip code $V1
AND   schoolsSrc schools.school $S AND $S zip._ $V2 % ... similarly for schools
AND   $V1 = $V2                         % ... join on the zip code
```

Fig. 3. A XMAS query q

By translating each m_{q_i} into a plan E_{q_i}, which itself is a tree consisting of "little" lazy mediators (one for each algebra operation), we obtain a smoothly integrated, uniform evaluation scheme. Furthermore, these plans may be optimized wrt. required navigations by means of rewriting optimizers.

Example 1 (Homes and Schools) Fig. 3 shows a simple XMAS query which involves two sources, homeSrc and schoolsSrc, and retrieves all homes having a school within the same zip code region. For each such home the query creates a med_home element that contains the home followed by all schools with the same zip code. The body (WHERE clause) includes generalized path expressions, as in Lorel [1] and generalized OQL expressions [3]. Bindings to the variables are generated as the path expressions are matched against the document. In our example $H binds to home trees, reachable by following the path homes.home from the root of homesSrc; $S binds to school trees. The result of evaluating the body is a list of variable bindings.[5]

The head (CONSTRUCT clause) of the query describes how the answer document is constructed based on the variable bindings from the body. E.g., the clause <med_home> ... </med_home> {$H} dictates that for each binding h of $H exactly one med_home tree is created. For each such h, med_home contains h, followed by the list of all bindings s of $S such that (h, s) is contained in a binding of the body. For a more detailed exposition of XMAS see [16].   □

The XMAS Algebra. Each XMAS query has an equivalent XMAS algebra expression. The algebra operators input lists of variable bindings and produce new lists of bindings in the output. We represent lists of bindings as trees[6] to facilitate the description of operators as lazy mediators. For example, the list of variable bindings $[(\$X/x_1, \$Y/y_1), (\$X/x_2, \$Y/y_2)]$ is represented as the following tree

$$\text{bs[b[} X[x_1], Y[y_1] \text{], b[} X[x_2], Y[y_2] \text{]] .}$$

---

[5] XMAS also supports tree patterns in the style of XML-QL, e.g., <homes> $H: <home> <zip>$V1</zip> </home> </homes> IN homesSrc is the equivalent of the first line in the WHERE clause in Fig. 3.

[6] Variable bindings can refer to the same elements of the input, hence are implemented as *labeled ordered graphs*. This preserves node-ids which are needed for grouping, elimination of duplicates and order preservation.

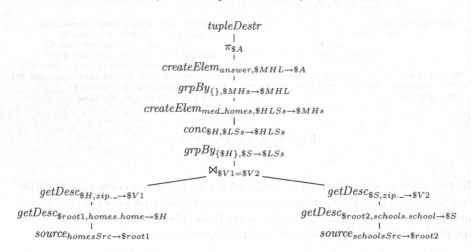

Fig. 4. Plan (algebra expression) E_q

Here, the bs[...] element holds a list of variable bindings b[...].

By b_i we denote the i-th element of bs; the notation $b_i + X[v]$ adds the binding (X/v) to b_i. $b_i.X$ denotes the value of X for b_i.

Algebra Operators. The XMAS algebra includes a set of operators conventional in database systems (σ, π, semi-/outer-/antisemi-join, $\times$, etc.) that operate on lists of bindings bs. Additionally, it contains operators that extend the nested relational algebras' nest/unnest operators with generalized path expressions and XML specific features such as access and creation of attribute/value pairs. The complete XMAS algebra is presented in [16]. Due to space limitations we only present operators that participate in the running example.

The semantics of algebra operators is given as a mapping from one or more input trees to the output tree. Let b_{in} and b_{out} denote variable bindings from the input and the output of the operators, respectively. The notation $op_{x_1,...,x_n \to y}$ indicates that op creates new bindings for y, given the bindings for $x_1, ..., x_n$.

- $getDesc_{e,re \to ch}$ extracts descendants of the parent element $b_{in}.e$ which are reachable by a path ending at the extracted node, such that this path matches the regular expression re. We consider the usual operators ".", "|", "*", etc. for path expressions; "_" matches any label (Fig. 4): For each input binding b_{in} and retrieved descendant d, $getDesc$ creates an output binding $b_{in} + ch[d]$. E.g., $getDesc_{H,zip._\to V1}$ evaluated on the list of bindings:

$$\text{bs[b[} H[\ home[addr[La\ Jolla],\ zip[91220]]]]$$
$$\text{b[} H[\ home[addr[El\ Cajon],\ zip[91223]]]] \text{]}$$

produces the list of bindings:

$$\text{bs[b[} H[\ home[addr[La\ Jolla],\ zip[91220]]],\ V1[91220]]$$
$$\text{b[} H[\ home[addr[El\ Cajon],\ zip[91223]]],\ V1[91223]] \text{]}$$

– $grpBy_{\{v_1,...,v_k\},v\rightarrow l}$ groups the bindings $b_{in}.v$ by the bindings of $b_{in}.v_1, \ldots,$ $b_{in}.v_k$ ($v_1,\ldots,v_k$ are the *group-by variables*). For each group of bindings in the input that agree on their group-by variables, one output binding $b[\ v_1[b_{in}.v_1],\ \ldots,\ v_k[b_{in}.v_k], l[\text{list}[coll]]]$ is created, where *coll* is the list of all values belonging to this group and list is a special label for denoting lists. For example, $grpBy_{\{\$H\},\$S\rightarrow\$LSs}$ applied to the input

bs[b[$H[\ home[addr[La\ Jolla],\ zip[91220]]],\ S[\ school[dir[Smith],\ zip[91220]]]]$
 b[$H[\ home[addr[La\ Jolla],\ zip[91220]]],\ S[\ school[dir[Bar],\ zip[91220]]]]$
 b[$H[\ home[addr[El\ Cajon],\ zip[91223]]],\ S[\ school[dir[Hart],\ zip[91223]]]]$]

will yield the output

bs[b[$H[\ home[addr[La\ Jolla],\ldots],LSs[\ list[school[dir[Smith],\ldots], school[\ldots]]]]$
 b[$H[\ home[addr[El\ Cajon],\ \ldots],\ LSs[\ list[school[dir[Hart],\ldots]]]]$]

– $conc_{x,y\rightarrow z}$ concatenates subtrees or lists of subtrees of $b_{in}.x$ and $b_{in}.y$, depending on their types. For each input tuple b_{in}, *conc* produces $b_{in}+z[conc]$, where *conc* is:
  • $\text{list}[x_1,\ldots,x_n,y_1,\ldots,y_n]$ if $b_{in}.x=\text{list}[x_1\ldots x_n]$ and $b_{in}.y=\text{list}[y_1\ldots y_n]$.
  • $\text{list}[x_1,\ldots,x_n,v_y]$ if $b_{in}.x=\text{list}[x_1\ldots x_n]$ and $b_{in}.y=v_y$.
  • $\text{list}[x,y_1,\ldots,y_n]$ if $b_{in}.x=v_x$ and $b_{in}.y=\text{list}[y_1\ldots y_n]$.
  • $\text{list}[v_x,v_y]$ if $b_{in}.x=v_x$ and $b_{in}.y=v_y$.

– $createElem_{label,ch\rightarrow e}$ creates a new element for each input binding. Here *label* is a constant or variable and specifies the name of the new element. Its subtrees are the subtrees of $b_{in}.ch$. Thus, for each input binding b_{in}, *createElem* outputs a binding $b_{in}+e[l[c_1,\ldots c_n]]$, where l is the value of $b_{in}.label$ and $c_1,\ldots,c_n$ are the subtrees of $b_{in}.ch$. E.g., $createElem_{med\_homes,\$HLSs\rightarrow\$MHs}$ where $\$HLSs$ results from $conc_{\$H,\$LSs\rightarrow\$HLSs}$ applied to the $\$H$ and $\$LSs$ in the output of the above $grpBy_{\{\$H\},\$S\rightarrow\$LSs}$ yields:

bs[b[$H[\ \ldots\ ],\ LSs[\ \ldots\ ],MHs[\ med\_home[\ school[dir[Smith],\ldots], school[\ldots]]]]$
 b[$H[\ \ldots\ ],\ LSs[\ \ldots\ ],MHs[\ med\_home[\ school[dir[Hart],\ldots]]]]$]

– *tupleDestr* returns the element e from the singleton list bs[b[$v[e]$]]
– $source_{url\rightarrow v}$ creates the singleton binding list bs[b[$v[e]$]] for the root element e at *url*.

Example 2 (XMAS→Algebra) Fig. 4 shows the algebraic plan for Fig. 3. □

Implementation of Operators as Lazy Mediators. XMAS algebra operators are implemented as lazy mediators. Each operator accepts navigation commands (sent from the "client operator" above) into its output tree and in response to each command c it (i) generates the required navigation sequence into its input tree(s), i.e., it sends navigation commands to the sources/operators below, and (ii) combines the results to produce the result of c. This computation model reminds of pipelined execution in relational databases. However there is

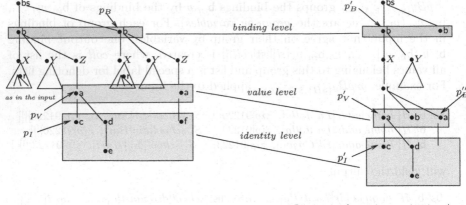

Fig. 5. Example navigations for $getDesc_{\$X,r.a\rightarrow\$Z}$

a new challenge: An incoming navigation command $c(p)$ may involve any previously encountered pointer p. Responding to $c(p)$ requires knowledge of the
input associations $a(p)$ of p. These associations encode sufficient information for
continuing the navigation, either down or right, from p.

Example 3 Consider the operator $getDesc_{X,r.a\rightarrow Z}$ that operates on the input
of Fig. 5. Given a node-id p_V at the *value level* of the output, the association
$a(p_V)$ contains the token v (to indicate that p_V is at the value level) and the
corresponding node-id p'_V in the input. A $d(p_V)$ will result in a $d(p'_V)$ sent below.
A $r(p_V)$ will result in a $\bot$. Similarly, given a node-id p_I at the *identity level* of
the output, the association $a(p_I)$ contains the token id and the corresponding
node p'_I. A $d(p_I)$ results in a $d(p'_I)$ and a $r(p_I)$ results in a $r(p'_I)$.

Finally note that a pointer p_B at the *binding level* requires two associated
pointers p'_B and p''_B, as shown in the Fig. 5. A command $r(p_B)$ will result in a
series of commands

$$p''_B := r(p''_B);\ l := f(p''_B)$$

until l becomes "a" or p''_B becomes $\bot$. In the second case the operator will proceed
from p'_B to the next input binding b and will try to find the next a node in the
x attribute of b.   □

The difficulty is that the operator has to know $a(p)$ for each p that may appear in
a navigation command and has to retrieve them efficiently. Maintaining association tables for each operator is wasteful because too many pointers will typically
have been issued and the mediator cannot eliminate entries of the table without
the cooperation of the client. Thus, the mediator does not store node-ids and

associations. Instead node-ids directly encode the association information $a(p)$ similar to *Skolem-ids* and *closures* in logical and functional languages, respectively. In Example 3, the node-id p_V is $\langle v; p_V' \rangle$, the node-id p_B is $\langle b; p_B', p_B'' \rangle$.

Note that the mediator is not completely stateless; some operators perform much more efficiently by caching parts of their input. For example,

- when the *getDesc* operator has a recursive regular path expression as a parameter, it stores part of the visited input. In particular, it keeps the input nodes that may have descendants which satisfy the path condition,
- the nested-loops join operator stores the parts of the inner argument of the loop. In particular, it stores the "binding" nodes along with the attributes that participate in the join condition.[7]

4   Managing Sources with Different Granularities

The lazy evaluation scheme described in the previous section is driven by the client's navigations into the virtual answer view. Thus, it can avoid unnecessary computations and source accesses. So far, we have assumed "ideal" sources that can be efficiently accessed with the fine grained navigation commands of DOM-VXD, and thus return their results node-at-a-time to the mediator. However, when confronting the real world, this fine granularity is often prohibitively expensive for navigating on the sources:

First, if wrapper/mediator communication is over a network then each navigation command results in a packets being sent over the wire. Similarly high expenses are incurred even if the wrapper and the mediator communicate via interprocess sockets. Second, if the mediator and wrapper components reside in the same address space and the mediator simply calls the wrapper, the runtime overhead may not be high, but the wrapper development cost still is, since the wrapper has to bridge the gap between the fine granularity of the navigation commands and the usually much coarser granularity at which real sources operate. Below we show how to solve this problem using a special buffer component that lets the wrapper *control the granularity* at which it exports data.

Example 4 (Relational Wrapper) Consider a relational wrapper that has translated a XMAS query into an SQL query. The resulting view on the source has the following format:

$$\mathsf{view}[\ \mathsf{tuple}[\mathsf{att}_1[v_{1,1}], \ldots, \mathsf{att}_k[v_{1,k}]], \ \cdots , \mathsf{tuple}[\mathsf{att}_1[v_{n,1}], \ldots, \mathsf{att}_k[v_{n,k}]]\ ]$$

i.e., a list of answer tuples with relational attributes att_j. Let the wrapper receive a r ($=right$) command while pointing to some tuple element of the source view. This will be translated into a request to advance the relational cursor and fetch the complete next tuple (since the tuple is the quantum of navigation in relational databases). Subsequent navigations into the attribute level att_j can then be

---

[7] We assume a low join selectivity and we do not store the attributes that are needed in the result, assuming that they will be needed relatively infrequently.

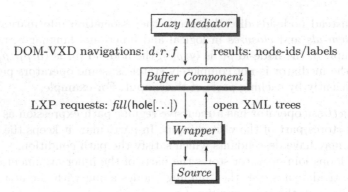

DOM-VXD navigations: d, r, f

results: node-ids/labels

LXP requests: $fill(\mathsf{hole}[\ldots])$

open XML trees

Fig. 6. Refined VXD architecture

answered directly by the wrapper without accessing the database. Thus, the wrapper acts as a *buffer* which mediates between the node-at-a-time navigation granularity of DOM-VXD and the tuple-at-a-time granularity of the source. □

The previous example illustrates that typical sources may require some form of buffering mechanism. This can also decrease communication overhead significantly by employing bulk transfers. E.g., a relational source may return chunks of 100 tuples at a time. Similarly, a wrapper for Web (HTML) sources may ship data at a page-at-a-time granularity (for small pages), or start streaming of huge documents by sending complete elements if their size does not exceed a certain limit (say 50K). Clearly, additional performance gains can be expected from such an architecture. In the following, we discuss how such extensions can be incorporated into the VXD framework.

Refined VXD Architecture: Buffers and XML Fragments. As motivated above, source results usually have to be buffered in order to reconcile the different access granularities of mediators and sources and to improve performance. One way to accomplish this without changing the architecture is by incorporating into *each* wrapper some ad-hoc buffering mechanism. While this has the advantage that the buffer implementation can be tailored to the specific source, it also leads to "fat" wrappers with increased development cost. Moreover, similar buffer functionality has to be reinvented for each wrapper in the system.

Therefore, instead of having each wrapper handle its own buffering needs, we introduce a more modular architecture with a separate generic buffer component that conceptually lies between the mediator and the wrapper (Fig. 6). The original mediator remains unchanged and interacts with the buffer using DOM-VXD commands. If the buffer cannot satisfy a request by the mediator, it issues a request to retrieve the corresponding node from the wrapper. The crux of the buffer component is that it stores *open (XML) trees* which correspond to a *partial* (i.e., incomplete) version of the XML view exported by the wrapper. The trees are open in the sense that they contain "holes" for unexplored parts of

the source view. When the mediator sends a navigation command to the buffer
component, the latter checks whether the corresponding node is available from
the buffer and if so immediately returns the result to the mediator. However,
if the incoming navigation "hits a hole" in the tree, then the buffer sends a *fill*
request to the wrapper. At this point, the granularity issue is resolved since the
wrapper answers the fill request by sending not only the single requested node
but possibly the whole XML tree rooted at the node or at least larger parts of
it, with further holes in place of the missing pieces.

Definition 2 (Holes, Open Trees) An element of the form $t = \text{hole}[id]$ is
called a *hole*; its single child id is the unique *identifier* for that hole. No assumption is made about the structure of id. We assume that $\text{hole} \in \mathbf{D}$ is a reserved
name. A tree $t \in \mathbf{T}$ containing holes is called *open* (or *partial*), otherwise *closed*
(or *complete*). Instead of $\text{hole}[id]$ we may simply write $*_{id}$.   □

Holes represent *zero or more unexplored sibling elements* of a tree:

Definition 3 (Represented Sublist) Given a tree $t = r[e_1, \ldots, e_n]$, we can
replace any subsequence $s_{i,k} = [e_{i+1}, \ldots, e_{i+k}]$ $(k \geq 0)$ in t by a hole $*_{i,k}$. In the
resulting open tree t', the hole $*_{i,k}$ is said to *represent the sublist* $s_{i,k}$ of t.   □

Example 5 (Holes) Consider the complete tree $t = r[a, b, c]$. Possible open
trees t' for t are, e.g., $r[*_1]$, $r[a, *_2]$, and $r[*_3, b, c, *_4]$. The holes represent the
following unexplored parts: $*_1 = [a, b, c]$, $*_2 = [b, c]$, $*_3 = [a]$, $*_4 = []$. Syntactically, one can substitute a hole by the list of children which it represents (assuming
that brackets around inner lists are dropped).   □

Since holes represent zero or more elements, the length of an open list is generally
different from the length of the complete list which it represents.

The Lean XML Fragment Protocol (LXP). LXP is very simple and comprises only two commands *get_root* and *fill*: To initialize LXP, the client (=buffer
component) sends the URI for the root of the virtual document, thereby requesting a handle for it:[8]

$$get\_root(\,URI\,) \longrightarrow \text{hole}[id]$$

This establishes the connection between the buffer (client) and the wrapper
(server). The wrapper answers the request by generating an identifier for the root
element. This id and all id's generated as responses to subsequent *fill* requests
are maintained by the wrapper. The main command of LXP is

$$fill(\text{hole}[id]) \longrightarrow [\mathbf{T}^*]\,.$$

---

[8] In general, sources do not export a single fixed XML view but, depending on the
sources capabilities, can accept different XML queries. In this case, the source generates a URI to identify the query result. We assume this step has been done before
starting the LXP.

When the wrapper receives such a *fill* request, it has to (partially) explore the part of the source tree, which is represented by the hole. Different versions of the LXP protocol can be obtained by constraining the way how the wrapper has to reply to the fill request. A possible policy would be to require that the wrapper returns list of the form $[e_1, \ldots, e_n, *_k]$, i.e., on the given level, children have to be explored left-to-right with at most one hole at the end of the list. On the other hand, LXP can be much more liberal, thereby providing interesting alternatives for query evaluation and propagation of results:

Example 6 (Liberal LXP) Let u be the URI of the complete tree $t=a[b[d,e],c]$. A possible trace is:

$$
\begin{array}{lll}
get\_root(u) = *_0 & \% \text{ get a handle for the root} \\
\quad fill(*_0) = [a[*_1]] & \% \text{ return a hole for } a\text{'s children} \\
\quad fill(*_1) = [b[*_2], *_3] & \% \text{ nothing to the left of } b; \text{ possibly more to the right} \\
\quad fill(*_3) = [c] & \% \text{ nothing left/right/below of } c \\
\quad fill(*_2) = [*_4, d[*_5], *_6] & \% \text{ there's one } d \text{ and maybe more around} \\
\quad fill(*_4) = [] & \% \text{ dead end} \\
\quad fill(*_5) = [] & \% \text{ also nothing here} \\
\quad fill(*_6) = [e] & \% \text{ another leaf}
\end{array}
$$

$\square$

The use of such a liberal protocol has several benefits, most notably, that results can be returned early to the mediator without having to wait before the complete source has been explored (this assumes that the DOM-VXD navigation commands are extended such that they can access nodes not only from left to right). When implemented as an asynchronous protocol, the wrapper can prefetch data from the source and fill in previously left open holes at the buffer.

Generic Buffer Algorithms. An advantage of the refined VXD architecture is that a single generic buffer component can be used for different wrappers. The buffer component has to answer incoming navigation commands and, if necessary, issue corresponding LXP requests against the wrapper. Fig. 7 depicts the algorithm which handles the down command $d(p)$ for returning a pointer to the first child of p.[9] Note that both the function $d(p)$ and the auxiliary function *chase_first(p)* are recursive. This is because they have to work correctly for the most liberal LXP protocol, in which the wrapper can return holes at arbitrary positions. To ensure correctness and termination of LXP, we only require that (i) the sequence of refinements of the open tree which the buffer maintains can be extended to the complete source tree using fill requests, and that (ii) "progress is made", i.e., a non-empty result list cannot only consist of holes, and there can be no two adjacent holes.

---

[9] The algorithm for $f(p)$ (fetch) is trivial and $r(p)$ is very similar to $d(p)$: replace $d(p)/r(p)$, $first\_child/right\_neighbor$, $children/right\_siblings$.

```
function d(p) {
    if not has_children(p) return ⊥      % can't go down: done!
    else
        p' := first_child(p);
        if not is_hole(p') return p'        % regular child: done!
        else                                % p' is a hole
            p'' := chase_first(p);          % chase first child
            if p'' ≠ ⊥ return p''           % found one: done!
            else            % remove the empty hole & redo without it:
                children(p) := children(p) \ {p'};
                return d(p);
}
```

```
function chase_first(p) {
    [x_1; ...; x_n] := fill(p);
    update_buffer_with([x_1; ...; x_n]);
    if n = 0
        return ⊥;
    else if not is_hole(x_1)
        return pointer_to(x_1);
    else
        return chase_first(x_1);
}
```

Fig. 7. Main buffer algorithm

Wrappers in the Refined VXD Architecture. In Example 4 we discussed a relational wrapper which communicates directly with the mediator, i.e., without an intermediate buffer component. The development cost of such a wrapper is quite high if one wants to avoid severe performance penalties due to the mismatching DOM vs. relational granularities. In contrast, the use of a buffer component provides the same performance benefits while also simplifying wrapper development significantly. The following example sketches the relational wrapper which has been developed for the MIXm system.

Relational LXP Wrapper. In order to be able to answer subsequent fill requests, the wrapper has to keep track of the hole id's it has generated. For example, the wrapper could just assign consecutive numbers and store a lookup table which maps the hole id's to positions in the source. Whenever feasible, it is usually better to encode all necessary information into the hole id and thus relieve the wrapper from maintaining the lookup table. For example, the MIXm relational wrapper uses hole identifiers of the form[10]

$$\text{hole}[db\_name.table.row\_number] \ .$$

When the wrapper receives a *get_root(URI)* command, it connects with the database specified in the URI and returns a handle to the root of the database, i.e., hole[*db_name*]. When receiving a *fill*(hole[*id*]) command, the wrapper can initiate the necessary updates to the relational cursor, based on the form of the *id*. In particular, the following structures are returned:

- at the *database level*, the wrapper returns the relational schema, i.e., the names of the database tables:[11]

$$fill(\text{hole}[db\_name]) \longrightarrow db\_name[\ table_1[\text{hole}[db\_name.table_1]], \ \dots \ ,$$
$$table_k[\text{hole}[db\_name.table_k]] \ ]$$

---

[10] It is transparent to the buffer component whether the hole identifier is sent as a nested XML element db_name[table[...]] or as a '.'-delimited character string.

[11] In the real system also column names/types and constraints are returned. We omit these details here.

– at the *table level*, the wrapper returns the first n tuples *completely* (n is a parameter) and leaves a hole for the remaining tuples (provided the are at least n rows in the table):

$$fill(\mathsf{hole}[db\_name.table_i]) \longrightarrow table_i[\ row_1[a_{1,1}[v_{1,1}],\ldots,a_{1,m}[v_{1,m}]],\ \ldots\ ,$$
$$row_n[a_{n,1}[v_{n,1}],\ldots,a_{n,m}[v_{n,m}]],$$
$$\mathsf{hole}[db\_name.table_i.(n+1)]\ ]$$

– at the *row level*, the wrapper returns the next n tuples (if available):

$$fill(\mathsf{hole}[db\_name.table_i.j]) \longrightarrow db\_name.table_i.j[\ row_{j+0}[\ldots],\ \ldots\ ,$$
$$row_{j+(n-1)}[\ldots],$$
$$\mathsf{hole}[db\_name.table_i.(j+n)]\ ]$$

Observe how the relational *wrapper controls the granularity* at which it returns results to the buffer. In the presented case, n tuples are returned at a time. In particular, the wrapper does not have to deal with navigations at the *attribute level* since it returns complete tuples without any holes in them.

Implementation Status. A Java implementation of the MIX mediator is available from [14] along with an interface that allows the user to interactively issue Java calls that correspond to the navigation commands. The mediator is complemented by a thin *client library* [16] that sits between the mediator and the client and allows transparent access to the virtual document through (a subset of) DOM. For other components and applications of the MIX system see [13].

References

1. S. Abiteboul, D. Quass, J. McHugh, J. Widom, and J. L. Wiener. The Lorel Query Language for Semistructured Data. *Intl. Journal on Digital Libraries*, 1(1):68–88, 1997.
2. P. Buneman, R. E. Frankel, and N. Rishiyur. An Implementation Technique for Database Query Languages. *ACM TODS*, 7(2):164–186, June 1982.
3. V. Christophides, S. Cluet, and G. Moerkotte. Evaluating Queries with Generalized Path Expressions. In *ACM SIGMOD*, pp. 413–422, 1996.
4. S. Cluet, C. Delobel, J. Simeon, and K. Smaga. Your Mediators Need Data Conversion! In *ACM SIGMOD*, pp. 177–188, 1998.
5. W. F. Cody, et.al. Querying Multimedia Data from Multiple Repositories by Content: the Garlic Project. In *VLDB*, pp. 17–35, 1995.
6. Document Object Model (DOM) Level 1 Specification. www.w3.org/TR/REC-DOM-Level-1/, 1998.
7. FLORID Homepage. www.informatik.uni-freiburg.de/~dbis/florid/.
8. H. Garcia-Molina, J. D. Ullman, and J. Widom. *Database System Implementation*. Prentice Hall, 1999.
9. T. Grust and M. H. Scholl. How to Comprehend Queries Functionally. *Journal of Intelligent Information Systems*, 12(2/3):191–218, Mar. 1999.
10. HERMES Homepage. www.cs.umd.edu/projects/hermes/.
11. B. Ludäscher, Y. Papakonstantinou, and P. Velikhov. A Framework for Navigation-Driven Lazy Mediators. In *ACM Workshop on the Web and Databases*, Philadelphia, 1999. www.acm.org/sigmod/dblp/db/conf/webdb/webdb1999.html

12. B. Mitschang, H. Pirahesh, P. Pistor, B. G. Lindsay, and N. Südkamp. SQL/XNF—Processing Composite Objects as Abstractions over Relational Data. In *ICDE*, pp. 272–282, Vienna, Austria, 1993.
13. MIX   (Mediation   of   Information   using   XML)   Homepage. www.npaci.edu/DICE/MIX/ and www.db.ucsd.edu/Projects/MIX/, 1999.
14. MIX*m* (MIX Mediator System). www.db.ucsd.edu/Projects/MIX/MIXm, 1999.
15. Y. Papakonstantinou, S. Abiteboul, and H. Garcia-Molina. Object Fusion in Mediator Systems. In *VLDB*, pp. 413–424, 1996.
16. P. Velikhov, B. Ludäscher, and Y. Papakonstantinou. Navigation-Driven Query Evaluation in the MIX Mediator System. Technical report, UCSD, 1999. www.db.ucsd.edu/publications/mixm.ps.gz.
17. XML-QL: A Query Language for XML. www.w3.org/TR/NOTE-xml-ql, 1998.
18. Extensible Markup Language (XML) 1.0. www.w3.org/TR/REC-xml, 1998.
19. XML Pointer Language (XPointer). www.w3.org/TR/WD-xptr.

Performance

Aggregate Aware Caching
for Multi-dimensional Queries

Prasad M. Deshpande* and Jeffrey F. Naughton

University of Wisconsin, Madison, WI 53706
{pmd, naughton}@cs.wisc.edu

Abstract. To date, work on caching for OLAP workloads has focussed on using cached results from a previous query as the answer to another query. This strategy is effective when the query stream exhibits a high degree of locality. It unfortunately misses the dramatic performance improvements obtainable when the answer to a query, while not immediately available in the cache, can be computed from data in the cache. In this paper, we consider the common subcase of answering queries by aggregating data in the cache. In order to use aggregation in the cache, one must solve two subproblems: (1) determining when it is possible to answer a query by aggregating data in the cache, and (2) determining the fastest path for this aggregation, since there can be many. We present two strategies – a naive one and a *Virtual Count* based strategy. The virtual count based method finds if a query is computable from the cache almost instantaneously, with a small overhead of maintaining the summary state of the cache. The algorithm also maintains cost-based information that can be used to figure out the best possible option for computing a query result from the cache. Experiments with our implementation show that aggregation in the cache leads to substantial performance improvement. The virtual count based methods further improve the performance compared to the naive approaches, in terms of cache lookup and aggregation times.

1 Introduction

On-Line Analytical Processing (OLAP) systems provide tools for analysis of multi-dimensional data. Most of the queries are complex, requiring the aggregation of large amounts of data. However, decision support applications need to be interactive and demand fast response times. Different techniques to speed up a query have been studied and implemented, both in research and industrial systems. These include precomputation of aggregates in the database, having specialized index structures, and caching in the middle tier.

While a great deal of work has been published on these issues, to our knowledge the published literature has not addressed the important issue of building an "active cache", one that can not only speed queries that "match" data in the cache, but can also answer queries that require aggregation of data in the cache. We show that a cache with such an ability is much more effective than a cache without such a capability. Intuitively, this is straightforward: aggregating cache-resident data is much faster than issuing a SQL query to a remote data source. However, in practice making this work is non-trivial.

---

* Work done while at NCR Corp.

C. Zaniolo et al. (Eds.): EDBT 2000, LNCS 1777, pp. 167–182, 2000.
© Springer-Verlag Berlin Heidelberg 2000

The first issue to be dealt with is that in such an active cache the lookup process is considerably more complex than it is in an ordinary cache, because it is not sufficient to see if the query result is in the cache. One must determine if the data in the cache is a sufficient basis from which to compute the answer to the query. This problem is especially difficult with fine granularity caching schemes such as chunk-based caching [DRSN98], query caching [SDJL96], and semantic caching [DFJST]. Obviously, this lookup must be fast — it is infeasible to spend a substantial amount of time deciding if a query can be computed from the cache, because it is possible that the lookup cost itself could exceed the time required to bypass the cache and execute the query at the remote backend database.

The second issue to be dealt with is that in such an active cache, there can be multiple ways in which to perform the aggregation required to answer the query. This situation arises due to the hierarchical nature of OLAP multidimensional data models — in general there are multiple aggregation paths for any query. The multiple aggregation paths complicate the cache lookup problem even further, since now not only is it necessary to determine if a query is computable from the cache, one must also find the best way of doing this computation.

In this paper, we propose solutions to both the cache lookup problem and the optimal aggregation path problem. Our implementation shows that with a small space overhead, we can perform much better than naive approaches. Overall, an active cache substantially outperforms a conventional cache (which does not use aggregation) for the representative OLAP workloads we studied.

Related Work In the field of caching for OLAP applications, [SSV] presents replacement and admission schemes specific to warehousing. The problem of answering queries with aggregation using views has been studied extensively in [SDJL96]. Semantic query caching for client-server systems has been studied in [DFJST]. [SLCJ98] presents a method for dynamically assembling views based on granular view elements which form the building blocks. Another kind of caching is chunk-based caching which is a semantic caching method optimized for the OLAP domain. Our previous paper [DRSN98] describes chunk based caching in detail. The different methods of implementing aggregations compared in this paper are based on a chunk caching scheme. A recent work on semantic caching is based on caching Multidimensional Range Fragments (MRFs), which correspond to semantic regions having a specific shape [KR99].

Paper Organization The remainder of the paper is organized as follows: Section 2 gives a brief description of the chunk based scheme; Section 3 presents an exhaustive search method for implementing aggregations; and Section 4 describes the virtual count based strategy. These methods are extended to incorporate costs in Section 5. Section 6 discusses replacement policies and Section 7 describes our experiments and results. The conclusions are presented in Section 8. Some details have been skipped in this paper due to space limitations. More details are available in [D99].

2   Chunk Based Caching

Chunk-based caching was proposed in [DRSN98]. In this section, we review chunk-based caching in order to make this paper self-contained. Chunk based caching takes advantage of the multi-dimensional nature of OLAP data. The dimensions form a multi-dimensional space and data values are points in that space. The distinct values for each dimension are divided into ranges, thus dividing the multi-dimensional space into chunks. Figure 1 shows a multidimensional space formed by two dimensions *Product* and *Time* and the chunks at levels (*Product, Time*) and (*Time*). The caching scheme uses chunks as a unit of caching. This works well since chunks capture the notion of semantic regions. Note that there can be chunks at any level of aggregation.

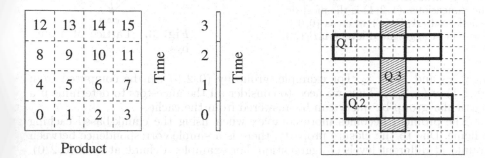

Fig. 1. Chunks at different levels.   **Fig. 2.** Reusing cached chunks.

In the chunk-based caching scheme, query results to be stored in the cache are broken up into chunks and the chunks are cached. When a new query is issued, the query is analyzed to determine what chunks are needed to answer it. The cache is probed to find these chunks. Depending on what chunks are present in the cache, the list of chunks is partitioned into two. One part is answered from the cache. The other part consists of the missing chunks which have to be computed from the backend. To compute the missing chunks, a single SQL statement is issued to the backend translating the missing chunk numbers into the selection predicate of the SQL query.

Example 1. Figure 2 shows three queries Q1, Q2 and Q3 which are issued in that order. Q3 can use some of the cached chunks it has in common with Q1 and Q2. Only the missing chunks (marked by the shaded area) have to be computed from the backend.

An important property we use later is the closure property of chunks described in [DRSN98]. This means that there is a simple correspondence between chunks at different levels of aggregation. A set of chunks at a detailed level can be aggregated to get a chunk at higher level of aggregation. For example, Figure 1 shows that chunk 0 of (*Time*) can be computed from chunks (0, 1, 2, 3) of (*Product, Time*).

3   Aggregations in the Cache

We now consider the problem of aggregation in more detail. In a multi-dimensional schema, there are many possible levels of aggregation, each of which corresponds to a different group-by operation. These group-bys can be arranged in the form of a lattice using the "can be computed by" relationship. This kind of structure has been extensively used in previous work [AAD+96][HRU96][SDN98].

For any group-by there are many group-bys from which it can be computed. In general, a group-by (x_1, y_1, z_1) can be computed from (x_2, y_2, z_2) if $x_1 \leq x_2$,

Example 2. Consider a schema with three dimensions A, B and C. Dimension B has a two level hierarchy defined on it, whereas A and C have a single level hierarchy. Figure 3 shows the lattice formed by these dimensions. (x, y, z) denotes the level on each of the dimensions. $(1, 2, 1)$ is the most detailed level $(A_1 B_2 C_1)$ whereas $(0, 0, 0)$ is the most aggregated level $(A_0 B_0 C_0)$.

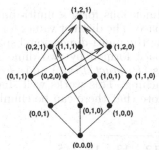

Fig. 3. Lattice of group-bys.

$y_1 \leq y_2$ and $z_1 \leq z_2$. For example, group-by $(0, 2, 0)$ can be computed from $(0, 2, 1)$ or $(1, 2, 0)$. Thus we need to consider all the ancestors to determine if a particular group-by query can be answered from the cache.

The problem becomes more complex when using the chunk-based caching scheme. Due to the closure property, there is a simple correspondence between chunks at different levels of aggregation. For example, a chunk at level $(0, 2, 0)$, say chunk 0, will map to a set of chunks at level $(1, 2, 0)$, say chunks 0 and 1. To compute chunk 0 of $(0, 2, 0)$ from $(1, 2, 0)$, we need both chunks 0 and 1 of $(1, 2, 0)$. It may happen that only chunk 0 of $(1, 2, 0)$ is present in the cache whereas chunk 1 is computable from other chunks. This implies that chunk 0 of $(0, 2, 0)$ is still computable from the cache. Thus to determine if a chunk of a particular group-by is computable from the cache, it is necessary to explore all paths in the lattice from that group-by to the base group-by. Figure 3 shows the different paths possible for computation of a chunk of $(0, 2, 0)$. Let us first examine a naive method of finding if a chunk is computable from the cache.

3.1   Exhaustive Search Method

The Exhaustive Search Method (ESM) is a naive implementation of finding if a chunk is computable from the cache. If a chunk is missing from the cache, it searches along all paths to the base group-by, to check if it can be computed from the cache. The algorithm is listed below:

Algorithm : ESM(Level, ChunkNumber)
Inputs: Level – Indicates the group-by level
              ChunkNumber – Identifies chunk that needs to be computed
```
if (CacheLookup(Level, ChunkNumber)) // Lookup in the cache
    return true;
For each Parent Group-by in the lattice
    ParentLevel = level of the Parent Group-by
    ParentChunkNumbersList = GetParentChunkNumbers(ChunkNumber, Level,
    ParentLevel)
    success = true;
    For each chunk number CNum in ParentChunkNumbersList
        if (!ESM(ParentLevel, CNum))
            success = false
            break
    if (success)
        return true
return false
```

In the above algorithm, *GetParentChunkNumbers()* is a function which maps a chunk at one level to a set of chunks at a more detailed level. This algorithm searches different paths and quits as soon as it finds a successful path.

Lemma 1. *Consider a schema having n dimensions, with hierarchies of size h_i on dimension i. Let $(l_1, l_2, \ldots l_n)$ denote the level of a group-by. Note that $(0, 0, \ldots 0)$ is the most aggregated level and $(h_1, h_2, \ldots h_n)$ is the base level. The number of paths in the lattice for a group-by at level $(l_1, l_2, \ldots l_n)$ to the base level is given by:*

$$\frac{(\Sigma_{i=1}^{n}(h_i - l_i))!}{\Pi_{i=1}^{n}(h_i - l_i)!}$$

Proof. The proof follows from a simple combinatorial argument. We will skip it due to space constraints.

The actual number of recursive calls to ESM is much higher than this because a single aggregate chunk maps to multiple chunks at a detailed level (through the *MapChunkNumbers()* function) and ESM has to be called on each of those chunks, i.e. there is a fanout along each step of the path.

Lemma 1 suggests that the complexity of determining if a chunk can be computed from the cache depends on the level of aggregation of the chunk. For highly aggregated chunks, the number of paths searched is higher since there are many ways to compute them. For example, for the most aggregated level $(0, 0, \ldots 0)$, it is $(h_1 + h_2 \ldots + h_n)!/(h_1! * h_2! * \ldots h_n!)$. Note that this is the worst case complexity. The algorithm will complete as soon as it finds one way to compute the chunk. The average complexity depends on the actual contents of the cache.

4   Virtual Count Based Method

There is a lot of room for improvement in the naive ESM method. Our strategy, the *Virtual Count* based method (VCM) is motivated by two observations:

1. As ESM searches along different paths, a lot of vertices are visited multiple times due to the lattice structure.
2. A lot of the work can be reused by maintaining some summary of the state of the cache in terms of some meta-information about each chunk.

Example 3. Consider a small subsection of a lattice as shown in Figure 4. Suppose ESM is searching for chunk 0 at level $(0, 0)$. Two of the paths from $(0, 0)$ intersect at $(1, 1)$. As ESM searches these two paths, it will search for each of chunks 0, 1, 2 and 3 at level $(1, 1)$ two times – once for each path. It does not reuse the work done previously.

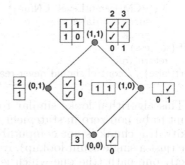

Fig. 4. Virtual counts.

In accordance with these observations, VCM maintains a count for each chunk at each group-by level. A chunk may be either directly present in the cache or may be computable through some path. Each path has to pass through some parent of that node in the lattice. Thus, the virtual count for a chunk is defined as:

Definition 1. Virtual Count: *The virtual count for a chunk indicates the number of parents of that node through which there is a successful computation path. The count is incremented by one if the chunk is directly present in the cache.*

The following property follows from the above definition:

Property 1. The virtual count of a chunk is non-zero if and only if it is computable from the cache.

Example 4. Figure 4 shows a very simple lattice with two dimensions having hierarchy size of 1 each. Level $(1,1)$ has 4 chunks, levels $(1,0)$ and $(0,1)$ have 2 chunks each and level $(0,0)$ has only 1 chunk. The figure shows the chunks that are present in the cache and the counts maintained by the VCM. Chunk 0 at level $(1,1)$ has count 1 since it is present in the cache and that is the only way to compute it. Chunk 1 at level $(1,1)$ is not computable, nor is it present in the cache, thus giving a count of 0. Chunk 0 at level $(1,0)$ has a count of 1 even though it is not present in the cache. This is because there is a successful computation path through 1 of its parents, i.e. level $(1,1)$. Chunk 0 at level (0,0) is present in the cache. Also, there are successful computation paths through two of its parents. Thus the count for chunk 0 at level (0,0) is 3.

Algorithm : VCM(Level, ChunkNumber)
Inputs: Level – Indicates the group-by level
           ChunkNumber – Identifies chunk that needs to be computed

```
if (Count(Level, ChunkNumber) == 0) // Count is the array of counts
    return false;                          ...                          (I)
if (CacheLookup(Level, ChunkNumber))
    return true;
For each Parent Group-by in the lattice
    ParentLevel = level of the Parent Group-by
    ParentChunkNumbersList = GetParentChunkNumbers(ChunkNumber, Level,
    ParentLevel)
    success = true;
    For each chunk number CNum in ParentChunkNumbersList
        if (!VCM(ParentLevel, CNum))
            success = false;
            break
    if (success)
        return true
assert(false) // control should never reach here
```

This algorithm looks similar to ESM in structure. However, the check for Count to be non-zero in statement (I) acts as a short circuit to reduce the complexity. If a chunk is not computable from the cache, VCM returns in constant time (just a single count lookup). If a chunk is indeed computable, VCM explores exactly one path (the one which is successful). Unsuccessful paths are rejected immediately without exploring completely. Compare this with the factorial number of paths for ESM.

4.1   Maintaining the Counts

Maintenance of the virtual counts makes lookups instantaneous. However, it adds an overhead when chunks are inserted or deleted from the cache since counts have to be updated at that time. The update algorithm while adding a chunk is listed below:

Algorithm : VCM_InsertUpdateCount(Level, ChunkNumber)
Inputs: Level − Indicates the group-by level
            ChunkNumber − Identifies chunk whose count needs to be incremented
Count(Level, ChunkNumber) = Count(Level, ChunkNumber) + 1
if (Count(Level, ChunkNumber) > 1) // Chunk was previously computable
    return
For each Child Group-by in the lattice
    ChildLevel = level of the Child Group-by
    ChildChunkNumber = GetChildChunkNumber(ChunkNumber, Level, ChildLevel)
    ChunkNumbersList = GetParentChunkNumbers(ChildChunkNumber, ChildLevel, Level)
    flag = true;
    For each chunk number CNum in ChunkNumbersList
        if (Count(Level, CNum) == 0)
            flag = false
            break
    if (flag)
        VCM_InsertUpdateCount(ChildLevel, ChildChunkNumber)

We will not go into formal proof of the correctness of the above update algorithm in maintaining virtual counts. However, we do comment on its complexity.

Lemma 2. *Suppose we are inserting a new chunk in the cache at level $(l_1, l_2, \ldots l_n)$. The number of counts updated is bounded by $n * \Pi_{i=1}^{n}(l_i + 1)$.*

Proof. The proof can be found in [D99].

The trick of the VCM algorithm is to maintain just sufficient information to determine if a chunk is computable, keeping the update cost minimal at the same time. The exact complexity of a single insert depends on the cache contents. The amortized complexity over all the inserts is much lower than this worst case complexity. This is because, the updates are propagated only when a chunk becomes newly computable. A chunk can become newly computable only once. It could be more if there are deletes also since a chunk can keep switching between computable and non-computable state. However we don't expect this to happen very often for each chunk. Typically a chunk insert will cause update to propagate to only one level. This is similar to B-Tree splits, where most page splits do not propagate more than one level. The counts also have to be updated when a chunk is thrown out of the cache. The algorithm for that is similar to the *VCM_InsertUpdateCount()* method both in implementation and complexity, so we will omit the details in this paper.

It can be shown from Lemma 1 and 2 that the worst case complexity of the ESM find is much higher compared to the update complexity of the VCM update. Again, due to space constraints we will skip the proof.

5   Cost Based Strategies

The ESM and the VCM algorithms find just one path for the computation of a chunk. Assuming a linear cost of aggregation, the cost of computing a chunk is proportional to the number of tuples aggregated. This assumption has been used previously, for solving the precomputation problem [HRU96][SDN98]. There may be multiple successful paths through which a chunk could be computed. Each path will have different cost of computation depending on what chunks are being aggregated along that path. Both ESM and VCM can be extended to find the least cost path.

Example 5. Consider the simple lattice shown in Figure 5. There are two paths for computation of chunk 0 at level $(0,0)$. One way is to aggregate chunk 1 at level $(1,0)$ and chunks 0 and 2 at level $(1,1)$. Another way is to aggregate chunks 0 and 1 at level $(0,1)$. The costs for these two options are different since the number of tuples being aggregated is different. In general, it is better to compute from a more immediate ancestor in the lattice, since group-by sizes keep reducing as we move down the lattice.

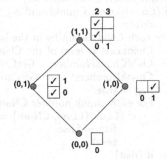

Fig. 5. Different costs of computation.

5.1   Cost Based ESM

The Cost based ESM (ESMC), instead of quitting after finding the first path, continues to search for more paths which might be of lesser cost. A listing of the ESMC algorithm is available in [D99]. The worst case complexity of ESMC is same as ESM. However, its average case complexity is much higher since it always explores all paths to find the minimum cost path. Whether this extra time is worth it depends on the time saved in aggregation. We present some experimental results which examine this in Section 7.

5.2   Cost Based VCM

The cost based VCM (VCMC) finds the best path for computing a chunk by maintaining cost information in addition to the count information. For each computable chunk, it stores the cost of the least cost path to compute it (`Cost` array) and the parent through which the least cost path passes (`BestParent` array). The find complexity is still constant time, which makes this method very attractive. The algorithm is similar to the VCM method and is listed in [D99]. The update algorithm is also similar to the one used by VCM. The only difference is that in VCMC an update is propagated in two cases – when a chunk becomes newly computable and when the least cost of computing a chunk changes. The worst case complexity of update remains the same, but the average complexity is slightly higher since an update is now propagated even when the least cost of a chunk changes.

Another advantage to maintaining the costs for the VCMC method is that it can return the least cost of computing a chunk instantaneously (without actually doing the aggregation). This is very useful for a cost-based optimizer, which can then decide whether to aggregate in the cache or go to the backend database.

6   Replacement Policies

The possibility of aggregating the cache contents to answer queries leads to interesting options for effectively using the cache space. In [DRSN98], we showed that a benefit based replacement policy works very well for chunks. In a simple cache, highly aggregated chunks have a greater benefit, since they are expensive to compute and thus are given a higher weight while caching. For aggregate aware caching schemes, it is much more difficult to associate a benefit with a chunk. There are two reasons:

1. Other than being used to answer queries at the same level, a chunk can potentially be used to answer queries at a more aggregated level.
2. Whether a chunk can be used to answer a query at a more aggregated level depends on the presence of other chunks in the cache. This is because an aggregated chunk maps to a set of chunks at a more detailed level and all those chunks need to be present in order to compute the aggregated chunk. This also means that the benefit of a chunk is not constant but keeps changing as the cache contents change.

A detailed discussion of these issues can be found in [D99]. We will just summarize them here.

Example 6. In Figure 6(a), chunk 0 at level (1,1) has a lower benefit than chunk 0 at level (1,1) in Figure 6(b). The presence of chunk 1 at level (1,1) in Figure 6(b) leads to a higher benefit to both chunks 0 and 1, since they can now be used to compute chunk 0 at level (0,1).

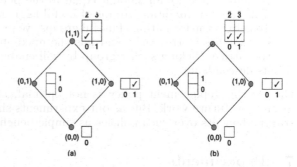

(a)   (b)

Fig. 6. Benefits.

6.1   Computing Benefits

The benefit of a newly computed chunk depends on how it has been computed.

1. *Cache computed chunk* – this is computed by aggregating other cached chunks. Its benefit is equal to the cost of this aggregation
2. *Backend chunk* – this is computed at the backend. Its benefit should also incorporate the cost of connecting to the backend, issuing a query and fetching results

Chunks which get computed at the backend should get a higher priority while caching than those which can be computed from other chunks already in the cache, since typically the overhead of fetching results from the backend is very high.

6.2   Forming Groups of Chunks

The optimal replacement policy should also try to form groups of useful chunks, since having a complete group leads to higher benefit for all chunks in the group as seen in Example 6. This is very difficult since it amounts to predicting what chunks are going to be inserted in the future. One way to solve this problem is to pre-compute entire group-bys and cache them. Since all the chunks in the group-by get cached, they can be used to compute any chunk at a higher aggregated level. In other words, pre-computing a group-by leads to the formation of useful group of chunks.

6.3   Two Level Policy

We propose the following policy in accordance with our observations:

- *Backend chunks* have higher priority and can replace *cache computed chunks*, but not the other way around. Replacement within each group is according to the normal benefit policy (i.e. highly aggregated chunks have higher benefit – same as that used in [DRSN98]).
- Whenever a group of chunks is used to compute another chunk, the clock value (we approximate LRU with CLOCK) of all the chunks in the group is incremented by an amount equal to the benefit of the aggregated chunk. This tries to maintain groups of useful aggregatable chunks in the cache.
- To help in the formation of useful groups, we pre-load the cache with a group-by that fits in the cache and has the maximum number of descendents in the lattice. Picking such a group-by will enable answering queries on any of its descendents.

Clearly this replacement policy is not optimal, and improving on it is fertile ground for future work. But as our experiments show, this policy provides substantial benefits over such policies as simple benefit based LRU.

7   Experiments

In this section, we describe the experiments used to evaluate the performance of the different schemes. We have a three tier system. The client issues queries to the middle tier which does caching of results. Both the client and the middle tier were running on a dual processor Pentium 133 MHz machine with 128 MB of main memory running SunOS 5.5.1. The backend database used was a commercial database system, running on a separate machine (a Sun UltraSparc 200 MHz with 256 MB of main memory running SunOS 5.5.1). A buffer pool size of 30 MB was used at the backend. The chunked file organization was achieved by building a clustered index on the chunk number for the fact file. The query execution times reported are the execution times at the middle tier.

All experiments were run on the APB-1 Schema [APB]. APB-1 is an analytical processing benchmark developed by the OLAP Council. APB has five

dimensions with hierarchies – *Product, Customer, Time, Channel* and *Scenario.*
Also, there is a measure *UnitSales* associated with the dimensions *Product, Customer, Time* and *Channel.* This mapping is stored in a fact table *HistSale.*

All queries are on the fact table *HistSale*, and ask for sum of *UnitSales* at different levels of aggregation. The number of nodes in the APB lattice is $(6 + 1) * (2 + 1) * (3 + 1) * (1 + 1) * (1 + 1) = 336$, since the hierarchy sizes are 6, 2, 3, 1 and 1 respectively. The data was generated using the APB data generator [APB], with the following parameters: number of channels = 10 and data density = 0.7. The table HistSale had about a million tuples, each of 20 bytes giving a base table size of about 22MB. The estimated size of the full cube for this schema is 902 MB. We experimented with cache sizes of 10 MB to 25 MB which is quite small compared to the size of the full cube.   We performed two kinds of experiments.   For one set (unit experiments) we used a very precise set of input queries, which were designed to bring out the best case, worst case and the average behavior. For the other set, we generated an artificial query stream. We describe the experiments in brief here. More details can be found in [D99].

7.1   Unit Experiments

The details of the first two experiments can be found in [D99]. We just summarize the results here.

Benefit of Aggregation This experiment demonstrates the benefit of implementing aggregations in the cache. We found that, on the average, aggregating in cache is about 8 times faster than computing at the backend. Note that this factor is highly dependent on the network, the backend database being used and the presence of indices and pre-computed aggregates.

Aggregation Cost Optimization This experiment measures how aggregation costs can vary along different paths in order to determine if cost based optimization is important. The difference between the fastest path and the slowest path is more for highly aggregated group-bys and lower for detailed group-bys. Experiments show that the average factor over all the group-bys was about 10.

Lookup Times In this experiment we measured the lookup times for all four algorithms ESM, ESMC, VCM and VCMC. We measured the lookup time for one chunk at each level of aggregation. The lookup time depends on the level of aggregation as well as on the cache contents. Table 1 lists the minimum, maximum and the average lookup times over all the group-bys for two cases: one where the experiment was run with an empty cache and the other where the cache was warmed up with all the base table chunks.

In both cases, the cache lookup times for VCM and VCMC are negligible. These methods explore a maximum of one path. The times for the ESM and ESMC are more interesting. When the cache is empty, none of the paths will be successful. However, both these methods have to explore all the paths.   For detailed level group-bys the lookup time is low since very few paths of computations exist. For aggregated group-bys the time is much higher due to explosion in the number of paths. This variation is one of the drawbacks of the exhaustive methods since query response time will no longer be consistent. VCM and VCMC do not have these problems.

When all the base table chunks are in the cache, lookup times for ESM becomes negligible, since the very first path it explores becomes successful (base table makes all paths successful). For ESMC, the lookup time is unreasonable when all the base level chunks are cached, since ESMC has to explore all the paths, to find the best cost path. The cost of each path itself becomes much higher, since each chunk on each path is computable and the ESMC is called recursively on it. We have ignored this fanout factor (one chunk at a particular level maps to a set of chunks at a more detail level) in estimating the complexity of the lookup. Even a savings in aggregation costs cannot justify such high lookup times. So we do not consider the ESMC method in any further experiments.

	Cache Empty			Cache Preloaded		
	Min	Max	Average	Min	Max	Average
ESM	0	106826	1896.1	0	44	4.54
ESMC	0	134490	2390	0	19826592	272598
VCM	0	0	0	0	62	6.32
VCMC	0	0	0	0	149	13.15

Table 1. Lookup times (ms).

Update Times The VCM and VCMC method incur an update cost while inserting and deleting chunks, since they have to maintain count and cost information. ESM and ESMC do not have any update cost. Lemma 2 suggests that update complexity is higher for more detail level chunks. To look at the worst case behavior we loaded all chunks of the base table – level (6,2,3,1,0) followed by all chunks at level (6,2,3,0,0). The update times vary while inserting different chunks, since how far an update propagates depends on what has been inserted in the cache previously. For example, while inserting the last chunk at level (6,2,3,1,0), update propagates all the way, since a lot of aggregate chunks become computable because of it. Table 2 shows the maximum, minimum and the average update time for the VCM and VCMC method. Even the maximum update time is quite feasible and on an average the cost is negligible. We can observe an interesting difference between VCM and VCMC. When inserting chunks at level (6,2,3,0,0), the update times for VCM are 0. All the chunks are already computable due to previous loading of level (6,3,3,1,0), so the updates do not propagate at all. However, for VCMC, insertion of chunks of (6,2,3,0,0) changes the cost of computation for all its descendents in the lattice. The cost information needs to be changed and the update costs reflects this.

	Loading (6,2,3,1,0)			Loading (6,2,3,0,0)		
	Min	Max	Average	Min	Max	Average
VCM	0	19	1.797	0	0	0
VCMC	1	36	5.427	0	15	10.09

Table 2. Update times (ms).

ESM	0
ESMC	0
VCM	32256*1 = 32 KB
VCMC	32256*6 = 194 KB

Table 3. Maximum Space Overhead.

Space Overhead The improved performance of VC based methods comes at the expense of additional memory required for the Count, Cost and BestParent arrays. The number of array entries is equal to total number of chunks at all possible levels. This might seem large, but it is feasible since the number of chunks is much smaller than the actual number of tuples. For example, in the schema used for our experiments, the base table had one million tuples of 20 bytes each. The total number of chunks over all the levels is 32256. Also, sparse array representation can be used to reduce storage for the arrays. Table 3 shows the maximum space overhead for the different methods assuming 4 bytes to store the cost and 1 byte each for the count and bestparent. Even for VCMC, the maximum overhead is quite small (about 0.97%) compared to the base table size. We can expect space overhead to scale linearly with the database size, since the number of chunks typically increases linearly assuming the average chunk size is maintained.

7.2   Query Stream Experiments

For these experiments, we generated a stream of queries using different parameters. These were similar to the ones used in [DRSN98]. For each experiment the cache was pre-loaded with a group-by as our "two-level policy". Performance is measured as an average over 100 queries. The cache sizes used ranged from 10 MB to 25 MB.

Generating a Query Stream The query stream is a mix of four kinds of queries – **Random, Drill down, Roll Up** and **Proximity** which try to model an OLAP workload. Roll-up, drill-down and proximity queries give rise to some locality in the query stream. While traditional caching can exploit proximity locality, we need active caches with aggregation to improve performance of roll-up queries. The query stream we used had a mix of 30% each of drill-down, roll-up and proximity queries. The rest of them (10%) were random queries.

Replacement Policies This experiment was designed to compare the "two level policy" described in Section 6 with the plain benefit based policy.   Figure 7 plots the percentage of queries which are complete hits in the cache for different cache sizes. By "complete hits" we mean queries which are completely answered from the cache, either directly or by aggregating other chunks. The average query execution times are plotted in Figure 8. As the cache size increases, the percentage of complete hits increases. There are two reasons: the cache can be pre-loaded with a larger group-by (so more queries can be answered by aggregating) and just more chunks are cached leading to better hit ratio in general. The results show that the "two level policy" performs better. The main reason for this is that it has a better complete hit ratio. For example, consider the case when the cache is large enough (25 MB) to hold the entire base table. The "two level policy" caches the the entire base table, leading to 100% complete hit ratio. The ratio is lower for the other case (since it throws away useful base chunks in favor of computed chunks), causing it to go to the backend for some queries.

Comparison of Different Schemes In this experiment, we compared the different approaches to caching: no aggregation, ESM and VCM based methods. Experiments in Section 7.1 showed that the lookup times for ESMC are unreasonable. Also, the lookup and update costs of VCMC are comparable to that of VCM. So we consider only ESM and VCMC. The case with no aggregations in the cache is considered to demonstrate the benefit of having an active cache. Fig 9 shows the average execution times for running the query stream described earlier. The "two level policy" was used for replacement for the ESM and VCMC methods. However, for the no aggregation case, the simple benefit based policy was used since detail chunks don't have any higher benefit in the absence of aggregation. Both ESM and VCMC outperform the no aggregation case by a huge margin. This is expected, since, without aggregation, the number of cache

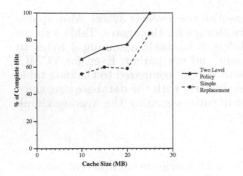

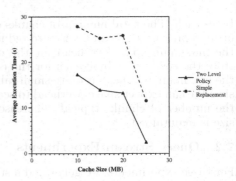

Fig. 7. Complete hit ratios.

Fig. 8. Average execution times.

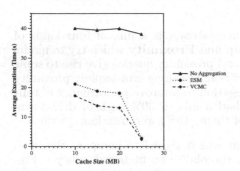

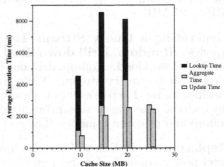

Fig. 9. Comparison of ESM and VCMC with No aggregation

Fig. 10. Time breakup. Left side bars represent ESM and right side represent VCMC.

misses are large. In fact only 31 out of the 100 queries are complete hits in the cache. For ESM and VCMC, the number of complete hits are much more.

VCMC outperforms ESM, with the difference being more for lower cache sizes. It might seem that the difference is not large. However, this is because of the fact that we are plotting the average execution times over all the queries. The queries which have to go the backend take disproportionately larger time and that affects the average. The difference between VCMC and ESM is more pronounced for queries which are complete hits. When the query stream has lot of locality we can expect to get many complete hits. So speeding up complete hit queries is critical for increased system throughput. Table 4 shows the percentage of queries that are complete hits and the speedup factor for these queries.

To further analyze the speedup, Figure 10 shows the average execution times for queries that hit completely in the cache. We split the total cost for each query into three parts: cache lookup time, aggregation time and update time (to

Cache Size (MB)	10	15	20	25
% of Complete Hits	66	74	77	100
Speedup factor (VCMC over ESM)	5.8	4.11	3.17	1.11

Table 4. Speedup of VCMC over ESM.

add the newly computed chunks). The bars on the left are for the ESM method and those on the right are for VCMC method. Even though it seems that the execution times are increasing for larger caches, note that the times cannot be compared across different cache sizes. This is because the set of queries which are complete hits is different for different cache sizes. At lower cache sizes, the speedup is more. This is because for smaller caches, the cache cannot hold a lot of chunks. So ESM has to spend a lot of time in finding a successful path of computation. This is reflected in very high lookup times. Also, there is a difference in the aggregation costs for ESM and VCMC, since VCMC considers costs to find the best path of computation. As the cache size is increased, the lookup time for ESM reduces, since there are more successful paths. In fact, for a cache size of 25 MB, the entire base table fits in memory and the first path it searches is a successful path. So the find time becomes negligible. The performance difference is now only due to the difference in the aggregation cost. We can also observe that the update times for VCMC method are very small. The update times, for a cache size of 25 MB, are slightly higher since it holds all the base level chunks. Whenever a new aggregated chunk is added or removed, it changes the costs of computation for its descendent chunks and these costs have to be updated. The find times for VCMC are negligible.

8   Conclusions

Providing a cache with the "active" capability of computing aggregates from cached data allows the cache to satisfy queries that would otherwise result in cache misses. Results from our implementation show that this can yield a substantial performance improvement over traditional caching strategies. The "two-level" policy works better than the simple benefit policy since it maintains useful groups of chunks and reduces accesses to backend. VCMC always performs better than ESM. When the cache size is small compared to the base (or "active" data size), the win of VCMC over ESM is more pronounced. A large part of this gain is due to savings in the find time and a smaller one due to aggregation time. When the cache is big enough to hold all base data and some more aggregated chunks, the gain in the find time is lost (since the first path chosen by ESM is successful). The improvement is now only due to the aggregation cost. So, in this case, we have a choice of using either ESM or VCMC depending on the locality in the query stream and the implementation effort one is willing to put in.

The area of active caching opens up a lot of opportunities for future work. One direction for such work would be to investigate the efficacy of such active caching approaches in workloads more general than those typically encountered in OLAP applications. There are also many interesting open issues for active caching for multidimensional workloads. One of the most interesting issues is that of cache replacement policies, since the problem is very complex for "active" caches.

References

AAD+96. S. Agarwal, R. Agrawal, P.M. Deshpande, A. Gupta, J.F. Naughton, R. Ramakrishnan, S. Sarawagi. On the Computation of Multidimensional Aggregates, *Proc. of the 22nd Int. VLDB Conf.*, 506–521, 1996.

APB. The Analytical Processing Benchmark available at *http://www.olapcouncil.org/* research/bmarkly.htm

DFJST. S. Dar, M. J. Franklin, B. T. Jonsson, D. Srivastava, M. Tan. Semantic Data Caching and Replacement, *Proc. of the 22nd Int. VLDB Conf.*, 1996.

DRSN98. P. M. Deshpande, K. Ramasamy, A. Shukla, J. F. Naughton. Caching Multidimensional Queries Using Chunks, *Proc of ACM SIGMOD* , 259–270, 1998.

D99. P. M. Deshpande. Efficient Database Support for OLAP Queries, *Doctoral Dissertation, University of Wisconsin, Madison.*, 1999.

HRU96. V. Harinarayanan, A. Rajaraman, J.D. Ullman. Implementing Data Cubes Efficiently, *Proc. of ACM SIGMOD* , 205–227, 1996.

KR99. Y. Kotidis, N. Roussopoulos. DynaMat: A Dynamic View Management System for Data Warehouses *Proc. of ACM SIGMOD* , 371–382, 1999.

RK96. R. Kimball. *The Data Warehouse Toolkit*, John Wiley & Sons, 1996.

RSC98. K. A. Ross, D. Srivastava, D. Chatziantoniou. Complex Aggregation at Multiple Granularities, *Int. Conf. on Extending Database Technology*, 263-277, 1998.

SDJL96. D. Srivastava, S. Dar, H. V. Jagadish and A. Y. Levy. Answering Queries with Aggregation Using Views, *Proc. of the 22nd Int. VLDB Conf.*, 1996.

SDN98. A. Shukla, P.M. Deshpande, J.F. Naughton. Materialized View Selection for Multidimensional Datasets, *Proc. of the 24th Int. VLDB Conf.*, 488–499, 1998.

SLCJ98. J. R. Smith, C. Li, V. Castelli, A. Jhingran. Dynamic Assembly of Views in Data Cubes, *Proc. of the 17th Sym. on PODS*, 274–283, 1998.

SSV. P. Scheuermann, J. Shim and R. Vingralek. WATCHMAN : A Data Warehouse Intelligent Cache Manager, *Proc. of the 22nd Int. VLDB Conf.*, 1996.

SS94. S. Sarawagi and M. Stonebraker. Efficient Organization of Large Multidimensional Arrays, *Proc. of the 11th Int. Conf. on Data Engg.*, 1994.

Performance and Availability Assessment for the Configuration of Distributed Workflow Management Systems*

Michael Gillmann[1], Jeanine Weissenfels[1], Gerhard Weikum[1], Achim Kraiss[2]

[1]University of the Saarland, Germany
{gillmann,weissenfels,weikum}@cs.uni-sb.de
http://www-dbs.cs.uni-sb.de/

[2]Dresdner Bank AG, Germany
achim.kraiss@dresdner-bank.com
http://www.dresdner-bank.com/

Abstract. Workflow management systems (WFMSs) that are geared for the orchestration of enterprise-wide or even "virtual-enterprise"-style business processes across multiple organizations are complex distributed systems. They consist of multiple workflow engines, application servers, and ORB-style communication servers. Thus, deriving a suitable configuration of an entire distributed WFMS for a given application workload is a difficult task.

This paper presents a mathematically based method for configuring a distributed WFMS such that the application's demands regarding performance and availability can be met while aiming to minimize the total system costs. The major degree of freedom that the configuration method considers is the replication of the underlying software components, workflow engines and application servers of different types as well as the communication server, on multiple computers for load partitioning and enhanced availability. The mathematical core of the method consists of Markov-chain models, derived from the application's workflow specifications, that allow assessing the overall system's performance, availability, and also its performability in the degraded mode when some server replicas are offline, for given degrees of replication. By iterating over the space of feasible system configurations and assessing the quality of candidate configurations, the developed method determines a configuration with near-minimum costs.

1 Introduction

1.1 Problem Statement

The main goal of workflow management systems (WFMSs) is to support the efficient, largely automated execution of business processes. Large enterprises demand the reliable execution of a wide variety of workflow types. For some of these workflow types, the availability of the components of the underlying, often distributed WFMS is crucial; for other workflow types, high throughput and short response times are mandatory. However, finding a configuration of the WFMS (e.g., with replicated

* This work was performed within the research project "Architecture, Configuration, and Administration of Large Workflow Management Systems" funded by the German Science Foundation (DFG).

C. Zaniolo et al. (Eds.): EDBT 2000, LNCS 1777, pp. 183-201, 2000.
© Springer-Verlag Berlin Heidelberg 2000

components) that meets all requirements is a difficult problem. Moreover, it may be necessary to adapt the configuration over time due to changes of the workflow load, e.g., upon adding new workflow types. Therefore, it is not sufficient to find an appropriate initial configuration; it should rather be possible to reconfigure the WFMS dynamically. The first step towards a (dynamic) configuration tool is the analysis of the WFMS to predict the performance and the availability that would be achievable under a new configuration.

The goal of our research is to build a configuration tool based on a system model that is able to predict the best configuration for a given workflow load. The configuration tool should optimize the ratio between performance and cost, or availability and cost, or even the combination of both, the so-called "performability".

1.2   Contribution

In this paper, we consider distributed WFMSs that consist of components like workflow engines, application servers, and communication servers such as ORBs. The WFMS can be configured such that each of these components may be replicated on different computers for availability and/or load partitioning. We present an analytic approach that considers both the performance and the availability of the entire WFMS in its assessment of a given configuration. The approach is based on stochastic methods [19, 20], specifically continuous-time Markov chains (CTMC), and shows the suitability of these models for a new application field. The developed analytic model allows us to rank the performance and availability of different configurations that use replicated components. Moreover, we can predict the performance degradation caused by transient failures and repair or downtime periods of servers (e.g., for upgrading software etc.). These considerations lead to the notion of "performability" [19], a combination of performance and availability metrics. From the analytic model we can also derive the necessary number of WFMS component replications to meet specified goals for performance and availability. So a crucial part of a configuration tool for distributed WFMS becomes analytically tractable, and no longer depends on expensive trial-and-error practice or the subjective intuition of the system administration staff.

1.3   Related Work

Although the literature includes much work on scalable WFMS architectures [1, 4, 5, 6, 12, 15], there are only few research projects that have looked into the quantitative assessment of WFMS configurations with regard to performance and availability. The work reported in [2, 3] presents several types of distributed WFMS architectures and discusses the influence of different load distribution methods on the network and workflow-server load, mostly using simulations. [18] presents heuristics for the allocation of workflow-type and workflow-instance data onto servers. Mechanisms for enhanced WFMS availability by replicating state data on a standby backup server have been studied in [9, 14]. None of this prior work has addressed the issue of how to configure a WFMS for given performance and availability goals.

The use of CTMC models in the context of workflow management has been pursued by [13]. This work uses the steady-state analysis of such models to analyze the efficiency of different outsourcing strategies in a virtual-enterprise setting. Our approach is more far-reaching in that we use methods for the transient analysis of

Markov chains to estimate the dynamic behavior of workflow instances and the resulting performance. In addition, we address also the availability and performability dimensions, which are beyond the scope of [13].

1.4   Outline

The rest of the paper is organized as follows. In Section 2, we introduce our model of a distributed WFMS. In Section 3, we describe how we can stochastically model the dynamic behavior of a workflow instance; we use a simplified e-commerce application as an illustrating example. In Sections 4 and 5, we develop the performance model and the availability model, respectively. In Section 6, we combine both models into the performability model that allows us to predict the influence of transient failures and downtime periods on the overall performance. Section 7 discusses how the presented models are integrated into the core of an automated configuration tool.

2   Architectural Model

In this section, we introduce an architectural model for distributed WFMSs. We basically follow the framework of [23]. Although the model is simple, it is powerful enough to capture the architecture models of most WFMS products and research prototypes in a reasonable way. Based on this model, we will introduce the central notions of the *system configuration* and the *system state* of a distributed WFMS.

A *workflow (instance)* is a set of *activities* that are spawned according to the control-flow specification of a given *workflow type*. An activity can either directly invoke an application, which is typical of automated activities, or it can first require the assignment to an appropriate human actor or organizational unit according to a specified worklist management policy.

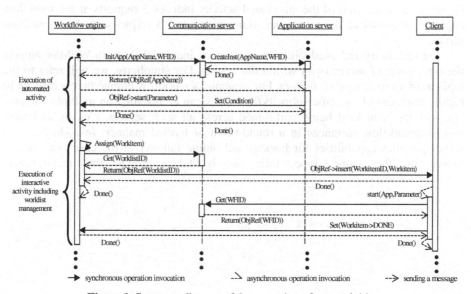

Figure 1: Sequence diagram of the execution of two activities

A distributed WFMS executes workflow instances in a decentralized manner: each workflow instance is partitioned into several *subworkflows* which may run on different *workflow engines*, for example, with one workflow engine per subworkflow type according to the organizational structure of the involved enterprises. Invoked applications of specific types run on dedicated *application servers*, for example, under the control of a Web application server and often with a database system as a backend. Finally, the communication within the underlying, often widely distributed and heterogeneous system environment is assumed to be handled by a special kind of *communication server*, for example, an object request broker (ORB) or a similar piece of middleware. These three types of WFMS components – workflow engines, application servers, and communication servers – will henceforth be viewed as abstract servers of specific types within our architectural model. For simplicity, we assume that each such server resides on a dedicated computer, and that all involved computers are connected by an intranet or the Internet. The situation where multiple servers run on the same computer can be addressed within our model, too, but would entail some technical extensions.

The interaction of the various components on behalf of a workflow instance is illustrated in the UML-style sequence diagram of Figure 1. Note that each activity involves exactly one workflow engine of a specific type, one application server of a given type, and the communication server. Each activity incurs a certain, activity-specific processing load on these servers. The first part of Figure 1 shows the sequence of the requests for the asynchronous execution of an automated activity. The second part of Figure 1 shows the sequence of the requests for an interactive activity. As that activity is executed on a client machine, the application server is not involved. The specific details of how many requests are sent at which timepoints between the various servers is not relevant, however, as far as the performance assessment and configuration planning is concerned. Rather we consider only the total load induced by an activity instance on each of the involved server types. So, in our example of Figure 1, the execution of the automated activity induces 3 requests at the workflow engine, 2 requests at the communication server, and 3 requests at the application server.

For scalability and availability reasons, many industrial-strength WFMSs support *the replication of server types* within the system. For simplicity, we will refer to the replicas of a server type as *servers*. For example, a workflow engine that is capable to handle instances of specific subworkflow types can be installed on multiple computers, with the total load being partitioned across all such servers, e.g., by assigning them subworkflow instances in a round-robin or hashed manner. In addition, each server provides capabilities for backup and online failover in the case that another server of the same type fails or is taken down for maintenance.

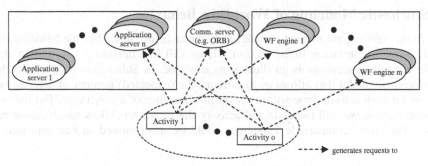

Figure 2: Architectural model of a distributed WFMS

In that case, the total load would be distributed across one less server, leading to (temporarily) degraded performance.

Figure 2 illustrates the presented architectural model: the WFMS consists of one type of communication server, m different types of workflow engines, and n different types of application server. The arcs denote service requests of workflow activities to the several server types. For example, the execution of an activity of type 1 requires work on the communication server, a workflow engine of type 1 and an application server of type n.

Each server of type x is assumed to have a failure rate λ_x and a repair rate μ_x. These rates correspond to the reciprocals of the mean time to failure and the mean time to repair, respectively. Here the notion of a failure includes downtimes for maintenance, and the repair time is the duration of a restart (including all necessary recovery steps) after a real failure or downtime in general.

Note that our architectural model could be easily extended to include more server types, for example, to incorporate directory services or worklist management facilities as separate servers if this were desired. The three server types made explicit in our model appear to be the most relevant ones for performance and availability assessment. Also note that we do not include clients as explicit components in the model, for the simple reason that client machines are usually not performance-critical. Rather the shared, and heavily utilized resources of servers usually form the bottlenecks in multi-user applications. Finally, we disregard all effects of human user behavior, e.g., their speed of reaction, intellectual decision making etc., for the assessment of workflow turnaround times, as these aspects are beyond the control of the computer system configuration.

We are now ready to define the central notion of the *system configuration* of a distributed WFMS. With k different server types, the system configuration of the WFMS is the vector of replication degrees $(Y_1,...,Y_k)$ for each server type; so Y_x is the number of servers of server type x that we have configured the system with. Because of server failures and repairs, the number of available servers of a given type varies over time. For a given point of time, we call the vector $(X_1,...,X_k)$ (with $X_x \leq Y_x$ for all $1 \leq x \leq k$) of the numbers of currently available servers of each server type the current *system state* of the WFMS.

3 Stochastic Modeling of Workflow Behavior

In this section, we present a model that stochastically describes the behavior of a single workflow instance. In Subsection 3.1, we will first introduce a simplified electronic-commerce scenario as an illustrating example. In Subsection 3.2, we develop the stochastic model that allows us to estimate the (expected) number of activity executions for each activity type within a workflow instance of a given type. For the sake of concreteness, we will use state and activity charts as a workflow specification language, but other, comparable languages could be incorporated in our approach as well.

3.1 Example Scenario

As an example of a workflow type, we present a simplified e-commerce scenario. To underline the completeness of our approach, we include the full spectrum of control flow structures, i.e., branching splits, parallelism, joins, and loops. The workflow is similar to the TPC-C benchmark for transaction systems [21], with the key difference that we combine multiple transaction types into a workflow and further enhance the functionality (see [7] for a full description of this workflow).

The workflow specification is given in the form of a state chart [10, 11]. This specification formalism has been adopted for the behavioral dimension of the UML industry standard [22], and it has been used for our own prototype system Mentor-lite [16, 24]. State charts specify the control flow between activities. A state chart is essentially a finite state machine with a distinguished initial state and transitions driven by event-condition-action rules (ECA rules). Throughout this paper, we assume that each workflow state chart has a single final state (i.e., one without outgoing edges). (If there were multiple final states, they could be easily connected to an additional termination state.) A transition from state s_i to state s_j, annotated with an ECA rule of the form $E[C]/A$, fires if event E occurs and condition C holds. The effect is that state s_i is left, state s_j is entered, and action A is executed. Conditions and actions are expressed in terms of variables that are relevant for the control and data flow among activities. In addition, an action A can explicitly start an activity, expressed by $st!(activity)$, and can generate an event E or modify a condition variable C (e.g., $fs!(C)$ sets the condition C to false). Each of the three components of an $E[C]/A$ triple may be empty.

Important additional features of state charts are nested states and orthogonal components. Nesting of states means that a state can itself contains an entire state chart. The semantics is that upon entering the higher-level state, the initial state of the embedded lower-level state chart is automatically entered, and upon leaving the higher-level state all embedded lower-level state charts are left. The capability for nesting states is especially useful for the refinement of specifications during the design process and for incorporating subworkflows. Orthogonal components denote the parallel execution of two state charts that are embedded in the same higher-level state (where the entire state chart can be viewed as a single top-level state). Both components enter their initial states simultaneously, and the transitions in the two components proceed in parallel, subject to the preconditions for a transition to fire.

Figure 3 shows the top-level state chart for our example workflow. Each state corresponds to an activity or one (or multiple, parallel) subworkflow(s), except for

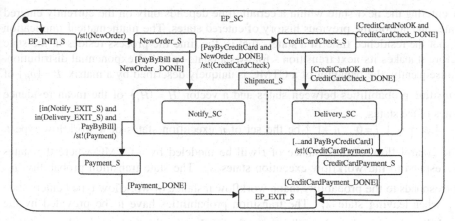

Figure 3: State chart of the electronic purchase (EP) workflow example

initial and final states. We assume that for every activity *act* the condition *act*_DONE is set to true when *act* is finished. So, we are able to synchronize the control flow so that a state of the state chart is left when the corresponding activity terminates. For parallel subworkflows, the final states of the corresponding orthogonal components serve to synchronize the termination (i.e., join in the control flow).

The workflow behaves as follows. Initially, the *NewOrder* activity is started. After the termination of *NewOrder*, the control flow is split. If the customer wants to pay by credit card, the condition *PayByCreditCard* is set and the *CreditCardCheck* activity checks the validity of the credit card. If there are any problems with the credit card, the workflow is terminated. Otherwise the shipment, represented by the nested top-level state *Shipment_S*, is initiated spawning two orthogonal/parallel subworkflows, specified in the state charts *Notify_SC* and *Delivery_SC* , respectively. After the termination of both subworkflows, the control flow is synchronized, and split again depending on the mode of payment. The workflow terminates in the finishing state *EP_EXIT_S*.

3.2   Stochastic Modeling

For predicting the expected load induced by the execution of a workflow instance, we have to be able to predict the control flow behavior of workflow instances. As workflows include conditional branches and loops, the best we can do here is to describe the execution   stochastically. Our goal thus is to estimate the number of activity invocations per workflow instance, for each activity type; from this estimate we can then derive the load induced by a workflow instance on the various server types. In the following, we will concentrate on workflows without nesting, and will come back to the general case later in Section 4 when we show how to incorporate subworkflows in the overall model.

A suitable stochastic model for describing the control flow within a simple workflow instance without nested subworkflows is the model of continuous-time, first-order Markov chains (CTMC) [19, 20]. A CTMC is a process that proceeds through a set of states in certain time periods. Its basic property is that the probability of entering the next state within a certain time depends only on the currently entered state, and not on the previous history of entered states. The mathematical implication is that the residence time in a state - that is, the time the process resides in the state before it makes its next transition - follows a (state-specific) exponential distribution. Consequently, the behavior of a CTMC is uniquely described by a matrix $P = (p_{ij})$ of transition probabilities between states and a vector $H = (H_i)$ of the mean residence times of the states.

Let $\{ s_i \mid i = 0 .. n-1 \}$ be the set of n execution states of a workflow type t. The control flow of an instance of t will be modeled by a CTMC where the states correspond to the workflow execution states s_i. The state transition probability p_{ij} corresponds to the probability that a workflow instance of workflow type t enters state s_j when leaving state s_i. The transition probabilities have to be provided by the workflow designer based on the semantics of the conditions between the workflow activities and the anticipated frequencies of business cases. If the entire workflow application is already operational and our goal is to reconfigure the WFMS (or investigate if a reconfiguration is worthwhile), then the transition probabilities can be derived from audit trails of previous workflow executions. The mean residence time H_i of a state i corresponds to the mean time that instances of workflow type t stay in the execution state s_i, i.e., the turnaround time of the corresponding activity (or the mean runtime of the corresponding nested subworkflow), and needs to be estimated or observed analogously. In accordance with the workflow specification, we assume that the CTMC has a single initial state s_0. In the initial state-probability vector of the CTMC, the probability is set to 1 for the initial state s_0 and to 0 for all other states. Moreover, we add a transition from the final execution state into an artificial absorbing state s_A. The transition probability of this transition is set to 1, and the residence time of the absorbing state is set to infinity.

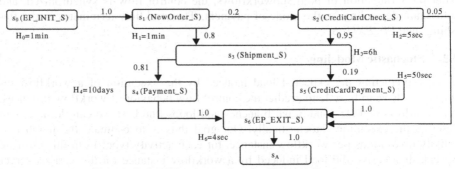

Figure 4: CTMC representing the EP workflow type

For workflow types with subworkflows, the subworkflows are represented by single states within the CTMC of the parent workflow. In the case of parallelism, the corresponding state represents all parallel subworkflows together. For the mean residence time of that state, we will use the maximum of the mean turnaround times of the parallel subworkflows.

Figure 4 gives an example for the CTMC representing the e-commerce workflow type of Figure 3. Besides the absorbing state s_A, the CTMC consists of seven further states, each representing the seven states of the workflow's top-level state chart. The values for the transition probabilities and the mean residence times are fictitious for mere illustration. With this CTMC model, we are now able to predict the expected number of invocations for each activity type, namely, the number of visits to the corresponding CTMC state before eventually reaching the absorbing state, using standard analysis techniques for Markov chains. We will provide more details in the following section, where we will also show how to derive the expected total load of a workflow instance.

4 Performance Model

In this section, we discuss the server-performance model. We proceed in four stages:

1. We analyze the *mean turnaround time* R_t of a workflow of a given type t, based on the analysis of state visit frequencies and the state residence times of the CTMC model. This analysis makes use of standard techniques for the transient behavior of Markov chains. (Note that the Markov chains in our approach are non-ergodic; so stationary state probabilities do not exist, and a steady-state analysis is not feasible.)

2. We determine *load* induced on each server type by a workflow instance of type t. We will model this load as the *expected number of service requests* to a server type. Technically, this is the most difficult step, and we will use a Markov reward model for this derivation.

3. We then aggregate, for each server type, the load over all workflow instances of all types (using the relative fractions of the various workflow types as implicit weights). The *total load* per server of a given server type is then obtained by dividing the overall load by the number of such servers (i.e., the server-type-specific degree of replication) in the configuration. In this stage we also derive the *maximum sustainable throughput* in terms of workflow instances per time unit.

4. Finally we derive, from the turnaround times of workflows and the total load per server, the *mean waiting times* of service requests caused by queueing at a heavily loaded server. This is a direct measure for the system's responsiveness as perceived by human users in interactions for the activities within a workflow. Overly high waiting times are an indication of a poorly configured system, and we can then identify the server type(s) that forms the bottleneck.

4.1 Workflow Turnaround Time

We derive the mean turnaround time of a workflow instance of type t by the transient analysis of the corresponding CTMC [20]. The mean turnaround time, R_t, is the mean time that the CTMC needs to enter the absorbing state for the first (and only) time, the so-called *first-passage time* of the absorbing state s_A.

The first-passage time of a CTMC state is generally computed by solving a set of linear equations [20] as follows. Assume that for all states s_i of the CTMC the probability that the first epoch at which the CTMC makes a transition into the absorption state s_A starting in state s_i is finite, is equal to one (which is the case for the specific CTMC models in our context of workflow management). Then, the mean first-passage time m_{iA} until the first transition of the CTMC into s_A starting in state s_i can be computed from the system of linear equations

$$-v_i m_{iA} + \sum_{j \neq A, \, j \neq i} q_{ij} m_{jA} = -1 \qquad , \quad i \neq A$$

where $v_i = 1/H_i$ is the rate of leaving state s_i, and $q_{ij} = v_i p_{ij}$ is the transition rate from state s_i to state s_j [20]. This linear equation system can be easily solved using standard methods such as the Gauss-Seidel algorithm.

4.2   Load (Service Requests) per Workflow Instance

The execution of a workflow instance spawns a set of activities, which in turn generate *service requests* to different server types. For example, the invocation of an activity incurs a certain initialization and termination load, and a processing load is induced during the entire activity, on involved workflow engine and application server type, and also on the communication server type. Let the matrix $L^t = \left(L_{xa}{}^t \right)$ denote the number of service requests generated on server type x by executing a single instance of the activity type a within an instance of workflow type t.

Consider the *EP* workflow type of our running e-commerce example. The corresponding CTMC has eight states in total, but the absorbing state s_A does not invoke an activity and thus does not incur any load. With three server types, the state-specific load vectors have three components each, and the entire load matrix L^{EP} is a 3×7 matrix.

In practice, the entries of the load matrix have to be determined by collecting appropriate runtime statistics.

4.2.1   Computing the Load of a Top-Level Workflow Instance Without Sub-workflows

To calculate the load that one workflow instance of a given type generates on the various server types, we use methods for the transient analysis of CTMC models. We will first disregard the possible existence of subworkflows, and will later augment our method to incorporate subworkflows.

The first, preparatory step is to eliminate the potential difficulty that the state residence times are non-uniform; there are standard techniques for transforming the CTMC into a uniform CTMC where the mean residence time is identical for all states and whose stochastic behavior is equivalent to that of the original model [20]. This is more of a technicality and serves to simplify the formulas. The actual analysis is based on a Markov reward model (MRM) which can be interpreted as follows: each time a state is entered and we spend some time there, we obtain a reward, and we are interested in the totally accumulated reward until we enter the absorbing state. This metric is known as the expected reward earned until absorption [20]. Here the reward that we obtain in each state is the number of service requests that are generated upon each visit of a state. (The term "reward" is somewhat misleading in our problem context, but it is the standard term for such models.) The expected number of service requests that an instance of the workflow type t generates on server type x can be computed by the formula

$$r_{x,t} = L_{x0}^t + \frac{1}{\nu^t}\left(\sum_{a \neq A} \sum_{z=0}^{\infty} \overline{p}_{0a}^t(z) \sum_{b \neq A, b \neq a} q_{ab}^t L_{xb}^t \right),$$

where $\nu^t = \max_{a \neq A}\left\{ \nu_a^t = 1/H_a^t \right\}$ is the maximum of the departure rates of the CTMC states with H_a^t denoting the state residence time of state s_a, $q_{ab}^t = \nu_a^t p_{ab}^t$ is the transition rate from state s_a to state s_b, and $\overline{p}_{0a}^t(z)$ is the taboo probability that the process will be in state s_a after z steps without having visited the absorbing state s_A starting in the initial state s_0. The taboo probabilities can be recursively computed from the Chapman-Kolmogorov equations

$$\overline{p}_{ab}^t(z) = \sum_{c \neq A} \overline{p}_{cb}^t \overline{p}_{ac}^t(z-1), \qquad a,b \neq A$$

starting with $\overline{p}_{00}^t(0) = 1$, and $\overline{p}_{0a}^t(0) = 0$ for $a \neq 0$, and with

$$\overline{p}_{ab}^t = \begin{cases} \dfrac{\nu_a^t}{\nu^t} p_{ab}^t, & b \neq a, \ a \neq A \\[2mm] 1 - \dfrac{\nu_a^t}{\nu^t}, & b = a, \ a \neq A \end{cases}$$

denoting the one-step transition probabilities of the CTMC after uniformization [20].

For an efficient approximation of $r_{x,t}$, the summation over the number of steps, z, has to be terminated when z exceeds a predefined upper bound z_{max}. The value of z_{max} is set to the number of state transitions that will not be exceeded by the workflow within its expected runtime with very high probability, say 99 percent. This value of z_{max} can be easily determined during the analysis of the CTMC.

4.2.2   Incorporation of Subworkflows

Once we add subworkflows, the expected turnaround time and the expected number of service requests generated by an instance of a workflow type t can be calculated in a hierarchical manner. For a CTMC state that represents a subworkflow or a set of parallel subworkflows, H_s^t corresponds to the mean turnaround time and the entries L_{xs}^t of the load matrix L^t correspond to the expected number of service requests for the entire set of nested subworkflows. Thus, the mean residence time H_s^t is approximately the maximum of the mean turnaround times of the parallel subworkflows $H_s^t = \max_{b \in S}\{R_b\}$, and the number of service requests L_{xs}^t for server type x equals the sum of the expected number of service requests generated by the parallel subworkflows $L_{xs}^t = \sum_{b \in S} r_{x,b}$.

Note that the maximum of the mean turnaround times of the parallel subworkflows is actually a lower bound of the mean residence time of the corresponding higher-level state. So the approximation is conservative with regard to the induced load per time unit.

4.3   Total Server Load and Maximum Sustainable Throughput

We associate with each workflow type t an arrival rate ξ_t which denotes the mean number of user-initiated workflows (of the given type) per time unit; the actual arrival process would typically be described as a Poisson process for systems with a relatively large number of independent clients (e.g., within an insurance company). By Little's law, the mean number of concurrently executing instances N^t_{active} of workflow type t is given by the product of the arrival rate ξ_t of new instances and the mean turnaround time R_t of a single instance of workflow type t: $N^t_{active} = \xi_t R_t$. The server-type-specific request arrival rate $l_{x,t}$ of a single instance of workflow type t is given by dividing the expected number of service requests to server type x, $r_{x,t}$, by the mean runtime R_t of an instance of t. Then the server-type-specific total load, i.e., its request arrival rate over all concurrently active instances of workflow type t is the product of $l_{x,t}$ with the mean number, N^t_{active}, of active workflow instances.

Finally, the request arrival rate l_x to server type x over all workflow types is obtained by

$$l_x = \sum_t N^t_{active} \frac{r_{x,t}}{R_t} = \sum_t \xi_t r_{x,t} \,.$$

With Y_x servers of server type x and uniform load distribution across these replicas, the total load per server (of type x) is $\tilde{l}_x = l_x / Y_x$. Note that this is actually the service request arrival rate. If we assume that each request keeps the server busy for a service time of length b_x on average, then the server's actual throughput is the maximum value $\hat{l}_x \le \tilde{l}_x$ such that $\hat{l}_x b_x \le 1$; for arrival rates such that $\tilde{l}_x b_x > 1$ the server could not sustain the load. So the maximum sustainable throughput (in terms of processed workflow instances per time unit) is given by the minimum of the $\hat{l}_x$ values over all server types x (i.e., the server type that saturates first).

4.4   Waiting Time of Service Requests

For analyzing the mean waiting time of service requests, we model each server type x as a set of Y_x M/G/1 queueing systems where Y_x is the number of server replicas of the server type. So we assume that service requests are, on average, uniformly distributed across all servers of the same type. This can be achieved by assigning work to servers in a round-robin or random (typically hashing-based) manner. In practice these assignments would typically be performed when a workflow instance starts, so that all subworkflows, activities, or invoked applications of the same type within that workflow instance are assigned to the same server instance for locality. While this realistic load partitioning policy may create temporary load bursts, the long-term (steady-state) load would be spread uniformly.

Each server is modeled only very coarsely by considering only its mean service time per service request and the second moment of this metric. Both of these server-type-specific values can be easily estimated by collecting and evaluating online statistics. We do not model the details of a server's hardware configuration such as CPU speed, memory size, or number of disks. Rather we assume that each server is a well-configured building block, and that we scale up the system by adding such building blocks. In particular, the CPU and disk I/O power of a server are assumed to be in balance, so that neither of these resources becomes a bottleneck while the other is way underutilized. Commercially available commodity servers for information systems in general are configured this way, and workflow management would fall into this category. Nevertheless, even if it turns out that one resource type always tends to be the bottleneck, our coarse-grained model is applicable under the assumption that the abstract notion of service time refers to the bottleneck resource within a server.

Let l_x be the arrival rate of service requests at server type x as derived in the previous subsection, b_x the mean service time of service requests at server type x, and $b_x^{(2)}$ the second moment of the service time distribution of service requests at server type x. The mean arrival rate of service requests at a single server of server type x is given by $\tilde{l}_x = l_x / Y_x$ where Y_x is the number of servers of server type x. Then the mean waiting time w_x of service requests at an individual M/G/1 server of type x is given by the standard formula [17]:

$$w_x = \frac{\tilde{l}_x b_x^{(2)}}{2(1 - \rho_x)}$$

where $\rho_x = \tilde{l}_x b_x$ is the utilization of the server. This mean waiting time is our main indicator of the responsiveness of the WFMS whenever user interactions take place.

The generalized case for configurations where multiple server types, say x and z, are assigned to the same computer is handled as follows: the server-type-specific arrival rates $\tilde{l}_x$ and $\tilde{l}_z$ are summed up, the server types' common service time distribution is computed, and these aggregate measures are fed into the M/G/1 model to derive the mean waiting time common to all server types on the same computer.

Note that our approach is so far limited to a homogenous setting where all underlying computers have the same performance capacity, but could be extended to the heterogeneous case by adjusting the service times on a per computer basis.

5 Availability Model

In this section we present the availability model for a distributed WFMS according to our architectural model of Section 2. We analyze the influence of transient component failures on the availability of the entire system.

5.1   CTMC for System States

Following the standard approach, our availability model is again based on continuous-time Markov chains (CTMC). The steady-state analysis of the CTMC delivers information about the probability of the current system state of the WFMS. Each state of the CTMC represents a possible system state of the WFMS. So a state of the

CTMC is a k-tuple with k being the number of different server types within the WFMS, and each entry of the tuple represents the number X_x of *currently available* servers of server type x at a given point of time. For example, the system state *(2,1,1)* means that the WFMS consists of three different server types and there are *2* servers of type *1*, *1* server of type *2*, and *1* server of type *3* currently running while the others have failed and are being restarted or have been taken down for maintenance. When a server of type x fails, the CTMC performs a transition to the system state with the corresponding value for server type x decreased by one. For example, the system state $(X_1,...,X_x,...,X_k)$ is left when a server of type x fails, and the system state $(X_1,...,(X_x-1),...,X_k)$ is entered. Analogously, when a server of type x completes its restart, the CTMC performs a transition into the state where the value for server type x is increased by one. The failure rates λ_x and the repair rates μ_x of the server types are the corresponding transition rates of the CTMC. This basic model implicitly assumes that the time spent in a state is exponentially distributed, but note that non-exponential failure or repair rates (e.g., anticipated periodic downtimes for software maintenance) can be accommodated as well, by refining the corresponding state into a (reasonably small) set of exponential states [20]. This kind of expansion can be done automatically once the distributions of the non-exponential states are specified.

With such a CTMC at hand, which can be shown to be ergodic, we are able to compute the steady-state probability for each state of the CTMC. Then the probability for the entire system being unavailable is simply the sum of the state probabilities over all those states where at least one server type is completely unavailable (i.e., has a zero entry in the X vector). We next present the details of the steady-state analysis of the CTMC in the following subsection.

5.2   Steady-State Analysis of the Availability-Model CTMC

Let k be the number of different server types, $Y = (Y_1,...,Y_k)$ the WFMS configuration, and let $X = \left\{ (X_1,...,X_k) \mid 0 \leq X_x \leq Y_x , 1 \leq x \leq k \right\}$ be the finite set of the system states of the WFMS.

We encode X into a set $\tilde{X}$ of integer values that denote the states of the CTMC of the previous subsection as follows:

$$(X_1, \text{K}, X_k) \text{ a } \sum_{j=1}^{k} X_j \prod_{l=1}^{j-1}(Y_l+1).$$

For example, for a CTMC with three server types, two servers each we encode the states (0,0,0), (1,0,0), (2,0,0), (0,1,0) etc. as integers 0, 1, 2, 3, and so on.

To derive the steady-state probabilities of the CTMC, we have to solve a system of linear equations

$$\pi Q = 0$$
$$\sum_i \pi_i = 1$$

where π_i denotes the steady-state probability of state $i \in \tilde{X}$, π is the vector (π_i), and Q is the infinitesimal generator matrix of the CTMC [19]. The generator matrix $Q = (q_{ij})$ with $i, j \in \tilde{X}$ is obtained by setting q_{ij} to the transition rate from the state $(X_1,...,X_k)$ corresponding to $i \in \tilde{X}$ into the state $(X_1',...,X_k')$ corresponding to $j \in \tilde{X}$.

The diagonal elements of Q are set to $q_{ii} = -\sum_{j \neq i} q_{ij}$. Note that $-q_{ii}$ is the rate at which

the system departs from state $i \in \tilde{X}$ [19]. The resulting linear equation system can again be solved easily by using standard methods such as the Gauss-Seidel algorithm.

As an illustrating example consider a scenario with three server types. Let server type *1* be the communication server, server type *2* be one type of workflow engine, and server type *3* be one type of application server. The failure rates are assumed as follows (where failures would typically be software-induced "Heisenbugs" [8] or

downtimes for maintenance): one failure per month (so $\lambda_1 = (43200 \text{ min})^{-1}$) for a

communication server, one failure per week (so $\lambda_2 = (10080 \text{ min})^{-1}$) for a workflow

engine, and one failure per day (so $\lambda_3 = (1440 \text{ min})^{-1}$) for an application server.

We further assume that the mean time to repair of a failed server is 10 minutes regardless of the server type, so the repair rates are $\mu_1 = \mu_2 = \mu_3 = (10 \text{ min})^{-1}$. Note

that these absolute figures are arbitrary, but the ranking of server types with respect to failure rates may reflect the maturity of the underlying software technologies. The entire WFMS is available when at least one server of each server type is running, and the WFMS is down when all server replications of at least one server type are down.

The CTMC analysis computes an expected downtime of 71 hours per year if there is only one server of each server type, i.e., no server is replicated. By 3-way replication of each server type, the system downtime can be brought down to 10 seconds per year. However, replicating the most unreliable server type, i.e., the application server type in our example, three times and having two replicas of each of the other two server types is already sufficient to bound the unavailability by less then a minute.

6 Performability Model

With the performance model alone we are able to predict the performance of the WFMS for a single, given system state. So changes of the system state over time caused by failures and repairs are not captured. In this section, we present a performability model that allows us to predict the performance of the WFMS with the effects of temporarily non-available servers (i.e., the resulting performance degradation) taken into account.

Our performability model is a hierarchical model constituted by a Markov reward model (MRM) for the availability CTMC of Section 5, where the state-specific rewards are derived from the performance model of Section 4. The probability of being in a specific system state of the WFMS is inferred from the availability model. As the reward for a given state of the availability CTMC, we use the mean waiting time of service requests of the WFMS in that system state. So we need to evaluate the performance model for each considered system state, rather than only for the overall configuration which now is merely the "upper bound" for the system states of interest. Then the steady-state analysis of the MRM [19] yields the expected value for the waiting time of service requests for a given WFMS configuration with temporary performance degradation induced by failures.

Let Y be a given system configuration and π_i be the steady-state probability for the system state $i \in \tilde{X}$ as calculated in Section 5. Let $w^i = \left(w_x^i\right)$ be the vector of the expected waiting times of service requests of all server types x for a given system state $i \in \tilde{X}$ as calculated in Section 4. Then the performability vector of the expected values of the waiting times of service requests $W^Y = \left(W_x^Y\right)$ for server types x under configuration Y and with failures taken into account, is obtained by conditioning the system-state-specific waiting time vectors w^i with the system state probabilities π_i , thus yielding $W^Y = \sum_{i \in \tilde{X}} w^i \pi_i$

The value of W^Y derived this way is the ultimate metric for assessing the performance of a WFMS, including the temporary degradation caused by failures and downtimes of server replicas. The system's responsiveness is acceptable if no entry of the waiting-time vector W^Y is above a critical tolerance threshold.

7 Configuration Tool

In this section, we sketch a configuration tool that we are currently developing based on the presented analytic models. We also discuss the integration of the tool into a given workflow environment.

7.1   Functionality and Architecture of the Configuration Tool

The configuration tool consists of four components: the *mapping* of workflow specifications onto the tool's internal models, the *calibration* of the internal models by means of statistics from monitoring the system, the *evaluation* of the models for given input parameters, and the computation of *recommendations* to system administrators and architects, with regard to specified performability goals.

For the mapping the tool interacts with a workflow repository where the specifications of the various workflow types are stored. In addition, statistics from online monitoring may be used as a second source (e.g., to estimate transition probabilities etc.). The configuration tool translates the workflow specifications into the corresponding CTMC models. For the evaluation of the models, additional parameters may have to be calibrated; for example, the first two moments of the server-type-specific service times have to be fed into the models. This calibration is again based on appropriate online monitoring. So both the mapping and calibration components require online statistics about the running system. Consequently, when the tool is to be used for configuring a completely new workflow environment, many parameters have to be intellectually estimated by a human expert. Later, after the system has been operational for a while, these parameters can be automatically adjusted, and the tool can then make appropriate recommendations for reconfiguring the system.

The evaluation of the tool's internal CTMC models is driven by specified performability goals. System administrators or architects can specify goals of the following two kinds: 1) a tolerance threshold for the mean waiting time of service requests that would still be acceptable to the end-users, and 2) a tolerance threshold for the unavailability of the entire WFMS, or in other words, a minimum availability level.

The first goal requires evaluating the performability model, whereas the second one merely needs the availability model. The tool can invoke these evaluations either for a given system configuration (or even a given system state if failures are not a major concern), or it can search for the minimum-cost configuration that satisfies both goals, which will be discussed in more detail in the next subsection. The cost of a configuration is assumed to be proportional to the total number of servers that constitute the entire WFMS, but this could be further refined with respect to different server types. Also, both kinds of goals can be refined into workflow-type-specific goals, by requiring, for example, different maximum waiting times or availability levels for specific server types.

The tool uses the results of the model evaluations to generate recommendations to the system administrators or architects. Such recommendations may be asked for regarding specific aspects only (e.g., focusing on performance and disregarding availability), and they can take into account specific constraints such as limiting or fixing the degree of replication of particular server types (e.g., for cost reasons).

So, to summarize, the functionality of the configuration tool comprises an entire spectrum ranging from the mere analysis and assessment of an operational system all the way to providing assistance in designing a reasonable initial system configuration, and, as the ultimate step, automatically recommending a reconfiguration of a running WFMS.

7.2   Greedy Heuristics Towards a Minimum-Cost Configuration

The most far-reaching use of the configuration tool is to ask it for the minimum-cost configuration that meets specified performability and availability goals. Computing this configuration requires searching the space of possible configurations, and evaluating the tool's internal models for each candidate configuration. While this may eventually entail full-fledged algorithms for mathematical optimization such as branch-and-bound or simulated annealing, our first version of the tool uses a simple greedy heuristics.

The greedy algorithm iterates over candidate configurations by increasing the number of replicas of the most critical server type until both the performability and the availability goals are satisfied. Since either of the two criteria may be the critical one and because an additional server replica improves both metrics at the same time, the two criteria are considered in an interleaved manner. Thus, each iteration of the loop over candidate configurations evaluates the performability and the availability, but adds servers to two different server types only after re-evaluating whether the goals are still not met. This way the algorithm avoids "oversizing" the system configuration.

8   Conclusion

In this paper, we have developed models to derive quantitative information about the performance, availability, and performability of configurations for a distributed WFMS. These models form the core towards an assessment and configuration tool. As an initial step towards evaluating the viability of our approach, we have defined a WFMS benchmark [7], and we are conducting measurements of various products and prototypes, including our own prototype coined Mentor-lite, under different configurations. These measurements are a first touchstone for the accuracy of our models. In addition, we have started implementing the configuration tool sketched in Section 7. This tool will be largely independent of a specific WFMS, using product-specific stubs for the tool's monitoring, calibration, and recommendation components. We expect to have the tool ready for demonstration by the middle of this year.

References

[1] G. Alonso, D. Agrawal, A. El Abbadi, C. Mohan, Functionality and Limitations of Current Workflow Management Systems, IEEE Expert Vol.12 No. 5, 1997

[2] T. Bauer, P. Dadam, A Distributed Execution Environment for Large-Scale Workflow Management Systems with Subnets and Server Migration, IFCIS Conf. on Cooperative Information Systems (CoopIS), Charleston, South Carolina, 1997

[3] T Bauer, P. Dadam, Distribution Models for Workflow Management Systems - Classification and Simulation (in German), Technical Report, University of Ulm, Germany, 1999

[4] A. Cichocki, A. Helal, M Rusinkiewicz, D. Woelk, Workflow and Process Automation, Kluwer Academic Publishers, 1998

[5] A. Dogac, L. Kalinichenko, M. Tamer Ozsu, A. Sheth (Eds.), Workflow Management Systems and Interoperability, NATO Advanced Study Institute, Springer-Verlag, 1998

[6] D. Georgakopoulos, M. Hornick, A. Sheth, An Overview of Workflow Management: From Process Modeling to Workflow Automation Infrastructure, Distributed and Parallel Databases Vol. 3 No. 2, 1995

[7] M. Gillmann, P. Muth, G. Weikum, J. Weissenfels, Benchmarking of Workflow Management Systems (in German), German Conf. on Database Systems in Office, Engineering, and Scientific Applications, Freiburg, Germany, 1999

[8] J. Gray, A. Reuter, Transaction Processing – Concepts and Techniques, Morgan Kaufmann, 1993

[9] C. Hagen, G. Alonso, Backup and Process Migration Mechanisms in Process Support Systems, Technical Report, Swiss Federal Institute of Technology (ETH), Zurich, Switzerland, 1998

[10] D. Harel, State Charts: A Visual Formalism for Complex Systems, Science of Computer Programming Vol. 8, 1987

[11] D. Harel, E. Gery, Executable Object Modeling with Statecharts, IEEE Computer Vol.30 No.7, 1997

[12] S. Jablonski, C. Bussler, Workflow Management, Modeling Concepts, Architecture, and Implementation, International Thomson Computer Press, 1996

[13] J. Klingemann, J. Waesch, K. Aberer, Deriving Service Models in Cross-Organizational Workflows, Int'l Workshop on Reasearch Issues in Data Engineering (RIDE), Sydney, Australia, 1999

[14] M. Kamath, G. Alonso, R. Günthör, C. Mohan, Providing High Availability in Very Large Workflow Management Systems, Int'l Conf. on Extending Database Technology (EDBT), Avignon, France, 1996

[15] C. Mohan, Workflow Management in the Internet Age, Tutorial, http://www-rodin.inria.fr/~mohan

[16] P. Muth, D. Wodtke, J. Weissenfels, G. Weikum, A. Kotz Dittrich, Enterprise-wide Workflow Management based on State and Activity Charts, in [5]

[17] R. Nelson, Probability, Stochastic Processes, and Queueing Theory, Springer-Verlag, 1995

[18] H. Schuster, J. Neeb, R. Schamburger, A Configuration Management Approach for Large Workflow Management Systems, Int'l Joint Conf. on Work Activities Coordination and Collaboration (WACC), San Francisco, California, 1999

[19] R. A. Sahner, K. S. Trivedi, A. Puliafito, Performance and Reliability Analysis of Computer Systems, Kluwer Academic Publishers, 1996

[20] H.C. Tijms, Stochastic Models, John Wiley and Sons, 1994

[21] Transaction Processing Performance Council, http://www.tpc.org/

[22] Unified Modeling Language (UML) Version 1.1, http://www.rational.com/uml/

[23] Workflow Management Coalition, http://www.wfmc.org/

[24] D. Wodtke, G. Weikum, A Formal Foundation For Distributed Workflow Execution Based on State Charts, Int'l Conf. on Database Theory (ICDT), Delphi, Greece, 1997

Evolution and Revolutions
in LDAP Directory Caches

Olga Kapitskaia[1], Raymond T. Ng[2], and Divesh Srivastava[3]

[1] Pôle Universitaire Léonard de Vinci, 92916 Paris, France
[2] University of British Columbia, Vancouver, BC V6T 1Z4, Canada
[3] AT&T Labs–Research, Florham Park, NJ 07932, USA
Olga.Kapitskaia@devinci.fr, rng@cs.ubc.ca, divesh@research.att.com

Abstract LDAP directories have recently proliferated with the growth of the Internet, and are being used in a wide variety of network-based applications. In this paper, we propose the use of generalized queries, referred to as *query templates*, obtained by generalizing individual user queries, as the semantic basis for low overhead, high benefit LDAP directory caches for handling declarative queries. We present efficient incremental algorithms that, given a sequence of user queries, maintain a set of potentially beneficial candidate query templates, and select a subset of these candidates for admission into the directory cache. A novel feature of our algorithms is their ability to deal with overlapping query templates. Finally, we demonstrate the advantages of template caches over query caches, with an experimental study based on real data and a prototype implementation of the LDAP directory cache.

1 Introduction

LDAP (Lightweight Directory Access Protocol) network directories have recently proliferated with the growth of the Internet, and a large number of directory server implementations are now available (see [8] for a survey). They are being used in a wide variety of network-based applications to store not only address books and contact information for people, but also personal profiles, network resource information, and policies. These systems provide a means for managing heterogeneity, while allowing for conceptual unity and autonomy across multiple directory servers, in a way far superior to what conventional relational or object-oriented databases can offer. To achieve fast performance and high availability in such systems, it is desirable to cache information close to the (client) applications that access the (server) directory (see, e.g., [6]). Recent studies (see, e.g., [14,11,4,5]) show that the use of semantic information in the client cache is advantageous to efficiently handle declarative queries. However, when individual user queries select just one or a few directory entries each, as is the case in many real LDAP applications that we have studied, these benefits come at a very high cost. The storage overhead of maintaining the meta-data that semantically describe the directory entries in the client cache becomes comparable to the size of the cached data, and the computational overhead of searching the meta-data to

C. Zaniolo et al. (Eds.): EDBT 2000, LNCS 1777, pp. 202–216, 2000.
© Springer-Verlag Berlin Heidelberg 2000

determine if a user query can be answered from the cache becomes prohibitive. Our paper describes a novel solution to this problem.

We propose the use of generalized queries, referred to as *query templates*, obtained by generalizing individual user queries, as the semantic basis for low overhead, high benefit LDAP directory caches for handling declarative queries.

For example, instead of keeping queries (tel=360-8777), (tel=360-8776), (tel=360-8786) and (tel=360-8785) to describe the contents of the cache, our approach could compute the query template (tel=360-87*), and maintain all entries that match this template in the client cache. In such a cache, the size of the semantic description is significantly reduced compared to query caching. Such an LDAP directory cache would then not only be able to efficiently answer a (previously posed) user query such as (tel=360-8777), but also a new query such as (tel=360-8751) that matches the query template.

In order to cache such query templates, our technique creates generalizations of different subsets of user queries. For example, given the above user queries, the query template (tel=360-877*) that generalizes the first two queries and the query template (tel=360-878*) that generalizes the next two queries would also be created as candidates. With each such candidate, we associate a cost and a benefit. Caching of high benefit, low cost candidate templates then results in substantially better cache utilization compared to conventional query caching.

In this paper, we consider the problem of dynamically maintaining a directory cache, given a sequence of user queries. We make the following contributions:

- We introduce the notion of an *LDAP query template*, which is an LDAP query that generalizes a set of user LDAP queries. We then describe the architecture of a *semantic LDAP directory cache*, which contains a set of directory entries, along with a semantic description of the cached data based on LDAP query templates (Section 2).
- We present incremental algorithms that create LDAP query templates by generalizing LDAP queries, and compute benefits and costs of these templates. To make effective use of the limited cache space, our algorithms account for the *overlap* between query templates (Section 3).
- We propose efficient algorithms that, given a sequence of user queries, maintain a set of potentially beneficial candidate query templates, and select a subset of these candidates for admission into the cache. Cache admission of query templates is done in a *revolutionary* fashion. Revolutions are typically followed by stable periods, where cache admission and replacement are done incrementally in an *evolutionary* fashion. New revolutions are initiated when the estimated benefit of the cached data drops substantially (Section 4).
- We validate the utility of our ideas with an experimental study, based on real data and a prototype implementation of the semantic LDAP directory cache. We show that template caching leads to considerably higher hit rates than query caching, while keeping the client-side computational overheads comparable to query caching (Section 5).

1.1 Related Work

The various approaches for utilizing semantic information about the data hidden in queries in the caching client can be broadly categorized into three groups: (a) view caching architectures, such as ADMS± [14] and Predicate Caching [11], that "hide" the overlap of query results; (b) "chunking" architectures, where the database is partitioned into groups of tuples, which are clustered together [5]; and (c) semantic caching architectures, where the cached data is dynamically divided into similar chunks, based on the actual queries that bring in the data [4]. All these approaches store data brought in by queries, using information from the queries to manage the cache, and avoid replicating data at the client. However, none of them use query generalizations as a basis for caching. Our caching architecture decouples the semantic cache description from the cached directory data, and is closer in spirit to the first group of architectures.

Prefetching data into memory to decrease expected response time of anticipated requests has been studied previously in the context of page server architectures (see, e.g., [1]). Prefetching methods use models of differing complexity, from associative memories [13] to probabilistic Markov-chain models [3,12]. To the best of our knowledge, ours is the first work to consider *generalizations* of user queries as the basis for prefetching data into and managing the contents of the client cache.

Cluet et al. [2] formally consider the problem of reusing cached LDAP directory entries for answering declarative LDAP queries, and present complexity results for conjunctive LDAP queries and query templates. They also design a sound and complete algorithm for determining whether a conjunctive LDAP query is cache-answerable using positive query templates. However, they do not consider the issues of query template creation, maintenance of their benefits, or cache admission and replacement algorithms, which are the focus of this paper.

2 LDAP Cache Architecture

In this section, we focus on the architecture of an LDAP directory cache. The novelty of our work is the decision to cache *LDAP query templates*, i.e., generalizations of user LDAP queries. We first define the notion of a query template and then describe the various components of the cache manager. Readers interested in the LDAP directory model are referred to [2].

2.1 LDAP Query Templates

In this paper, as in [2], we consider a query q to have two components: (a) a filter f_q that is a boolean combination of atomic filters on the schema attributes, and (b) attributes A_q that are in the projection list. A query is *conjunctive* when f_q is a conjunction (&) of atomic and negative atomic filters. Conjunctive queries are commonly used by LDAP directory-enabled applications. For this reason, in the rest of the paper, we focus attention on conjunctive queries.

LDAP applications often ask queries that instantiate one of a set of pre-defined "signatures". For example, a real-life LDAP messaging application deployed at AT&T Labs asks queries whose filters instantiate patterns such as (tel=$T), (mail=$M) and (& (objectClass=lip) (uniqueId=$U)), where $T is a telephone number, $M is an email address, and $U is a unique identifier of the messaging application subscribers.

Intuitively, LDAP templates can be thought of as LDAP queries (possibly with wildcard values) whose answers suffice to answer each of a set of user queries. Thus, both the queries with filters (tel=360-8*) and (tel=360-87*) are templates for the queries with filters (tel=360-8786), (tel=360-8776) and (tel=360-8750). Similarly, the query with filter (objectClass=lip) is a template for (&(objectClass=lip)(sn=kapitskaia)) and (&(objectClass=lip) (tel=360-8776)). This intuition is formalized below.

Definition 1 [Query Template] Consider an LDAP schema S, and a set of conjunctive LDAP queries $Q = \{q_1, \ldots, q_n\}$. A *query template* generalizing the set Q, denoted by t_Q, is an LDAP query, s.t. (a) for all directory instances I of schema S, $q_i(I) \subseteq t_Q(I), 1 \leq i \leq n$; and (b) t_Q is conjunctive. ∎

2.2   LDAP Cache Model

Our *semantic LDAP directory cache* contains a set of directory entries, along with a semantic description of the cached data.

The data stored in the cache is a subset of the data available at the directory server. We made the design decision to store each cached directory entry only once. We avoid the replication of entries by *merging* (i.e., taking the union of the (attribute, value) pairs of) the response entries with the same distinguished name that are brought in the cache as the results of different queries.

The semantic description consists of (a) the schema of the directory server, necessary for determining if an LDAP query can be answered from the cache [2]; and (b) a set of *actual query templates* (*AT*) describing the cached data. The presence of a query template t in AT indicates that every directory entry that is an answer to t is present in the cached directory entries. Further, each cached directory entry is guaranteed to be an answer to at least one of the actual query templates in AT.

Note that templates in the semantic description may *overlap*, i.e., a cached directory entry may be an answer to multiple query templates.

Cached Entries: Why Merging? When query caching systems associate query results with individual queries in the cache, it is possible that a directory entry that is an answer to multiple queries is stored multiple times in the cache. Our approach of avoiding the storage of redundant data in the cache, by merging the results of different queries, leads to a higher effective utilization of the cache. In addition, the merging of entries allows us to answer user LDAP queries by simply selecting data from the client cache, instead of performing expensive "joins" at the client cache. Since commercially available LDAP query processors efficiently answer selection-based queries, this decision allowed us to use a commercial LDAP directory server (Netscape Directory Server 3.1) in our prototype implementation.

Semantic Descriptions: What Kinds of Templates? The cached directory entries are semantically described by a set of LDAP query templates. We made the design decision to allow the templates to *overlap* with each other. Using semantically overlapping meta-data to describe the contents of a cache differs from the approach of Dar et al. [4], who maintain disjoint semantic regions. Our decision was motivated by the following considerations: computing disjoint LDAP query templates would introduce negation in the templates, considerably increasing (a) the complexity of *cache answerability*, i.e., determining whether an LDAP query can be answered from the cache (see [2] for details), and (b) the number of such disjoint templates, and hence the storage overhead of the meta-data. Further, we require that each (conjunctive) query template must be positive and projection-free. The rationale behind this decision is the work of Cluet et al. [2], who identified that the complexity of cache answerability is high when (a) the query templates contain negation, or (b) the query templates project attributes. When query templates are positive, conjunctive and projection-free, they showed that the cost of cache answerability is manageable in practice.

3   Creation and Maintenance of Query Templates

In this section, we present algorithms for computing query templates and their costs, and maintaining their benefits.

3.1   Creating Candidate Templates: Generalizing LDAP Queries

In this section, we describe an algorithm, `CompPairTemplates` (not shown), that efficiently computes a useful query template that generalizes a pair of LDAP queries. The algorithm uses a combination of:

- Explicitly specified generalization hierarchies on attribute domains, e.g., prefix matching on telephone numbers and suffix matching on e-mail addresses, to compute generalizations of atomic filters. For example, the atomic filters (`mail=olga@research.att.com`) and (`mail=divesh@research.att.com`) would generalize to the filter (`mail=*@research.att.com`).
- The natural hierarchy on conjunctive filters, based on the subset relationship between sets of conjuncts. For example, filters (`&(objectClass=lip)` `(mail=rng@research.att.com)`) and (`&(mail=olga@research.att.com)` `(gender=f)`) would generalize to the filter (`mail=*@research.att.com`).

Given a set of user LDAP queries, many possible query templates (each generalizing a different subset of the user queries) can be created. Keeping all possible templates can result in an inefficient use of the limited amount of cache space. Hence, only a fixed number, say n, of query templates, referred to as *candidate templates* (*CT*), are kept as candidates to be admitted into the cache in the future. The number n of templates to be kept can be determined adaptively.

3.2   Cost and Benefit of a Template

Each (candidate and actual) query template t is annotated with three statistical components: (i) $s(t)$: size of the result of t, (ii) $c(t)$: cost of execution of t, and (iii) $b(t)$: benefit of caching t.

The size $s(t)$ can be efficiently estimated, without evaluating t at the directory server, based solely on the statistics maintained about the directory entries at the client. In particular, pruned suffix trees [9,10] are very useful when estimating the sizes of string wildcard queries that constitute query templates.

The cost $c(t)$ is a measure of the total evaluation cost of the query template at the directory server, and the communication cost of transmitting the query and the query answer over the network. This can be estimated at the client using knowledge of the network and directory server parameters.

One would ideally like to measure the benefit of a template t as the sum of the costs $c(q_i)$ of future user queries q_i that could be answered using the result of t. Since future reference patterns are not available in advance, the probability of a future reference can be approximated from a past reference pattern using the history of user queries. However, maintaining the entire history of user queries is infeasible. Hence, we estimate the benefit of a template t using the benefits of available candidate templates that instantiate t. For a template t that is not instantiated by any candidate templates, we estimate the benefit $b(t)$ by its cost $c(t)$. In the next section, we describe Algorithm `ChooseCandidates` that incrementally maintains the benefits of templates in the cache.

These three components constitute a "profit" metric that our replacement policies use to find the most profitable templates to cache. The profit $p(t)$ of a template t is computed as: $p(t) = \frac{b(t)-c(t)}{s(t)}$. The rationale for choosing this profit metric will be given in Section 4.

3.3   Maintaining Templates

When a new query is asked, two kinds of actions are performed in the client cache that could potentially affect the subsequent contents of the cache:

- The benefits of the actual and candidate query templates need to be updated to reflect their utility in being able to answer the user query.
- New candidate templates may need to be generated, and their benefits and costs estimated.

The first kind of action is common to all caching architectures, and involves updating the replacement values of pages, objects or semantic regions (benefits and costs of query templates in the context of LDAP directory caches).

The second kind of action is novel to our LDAP cache architecture, and arises because of the central role played by query templates in our architecture. Algorithm `ChooseCandidates`, given in Figure 1(a), deals with this issue. Algorithm `ChooseCandidates` uses the user query q and the current set of candidate query templates $CT = \{ct_1, \ldots, ct_n\}$, to compute pair-wise generalizations of q with each query template in CT.

```
ChooseCandidates(q, CT) {
    /* CT = {ct₁, ..., ctₙ} */
    NT = ∅
    for each ctᵢ in CT
        ntᵢ = CompPairTemplates(ctᵢ, q)
        if (ntᵢ = ctᵢ)
            /*q: specialization of ctᵢ*/
            b(ctᵢ) = b(ctᵢ) + c(q)
        else if (ntᵢ ∈ NT)
            /* ntᵢ: template exists */
            b(ntᵢ) = max(b(ntᵢ),
                         b(ctᵢ) + c(q))
        else if (s(ntᵢ) < S)
            b(ntᵢ) = b(ctᵢ) + c(q)
            add ntᵢ to NT
    age each untouched ctᵢ
    NT = NT ∪ CT
    if (q ∉ NT and s(q) < S)
        b(q) = c(q)
        NT = NT ∪ q
    CT = {template with highest
          benefit in NT}
    choose (n − 1) additional
    templates with largest
    values of profit p(t) in NT
    return CT
}
```

(a) ChooseCandidates

```
Revolution(AT, CT) {
    /* compute CT' ⊆ AT ∪ CT */
    /* for admission */
    sort the tᵢ's using
        p(tᵢ)= (b(tᵢ)−c(tᵢ))/s(tᵢ)
    CT' = ∅
    repeat
        add the highest ranked
        remaining tᵢ that can
        fit in the available
        cache space to CT'
        adjust free space to
        reflect s(tᵢ)
        adjust benefits, costs,
        sizes of unselected
        templates in CT ∪ AT
        resort
    until (no more templates
           can be added)
    CT'' = template t in CT ∪ AT
           with highest value of
           b(t) − c(t)
    if (b(CT'') ≥ b(CT'))
        return CT''
    else return CT'
}
```

(b) Revolution

Fig. 1. Algorithms ChooseCandidates and Revolution

When the generalization of template t with query q is t itself, the result of t can be used to answer query q; in this case, the benefit $b(t)$ is updated by the execution cost $c(q)$ of the query. Untouched query templates in CT are aged by a suitably chosen aging factor. From the resulting set of (up to) $2n + 1$ templates (including query q itself), all templates whose size exceeds the cache size are discarded. Then (a) the template with the largest benefit is chosen, and (b) $n − 1$ additional templates with the largest profit $p(t) = \frac{b(t)−c(t)}{s(t)}$ are chosen.

3.4 Dealing with Overlap

To efficiently manage the cache, we need to compute the benefit of a set of templates (e.g., actual templates, or the set of candidate templates that can be used to replace the actual templates). This is complicated by the presence of overlap. With overlap, the benefit of a set of query templates can no longer be accurately estimated as the sum of the benefits of the individual templates. In general, the benefit of a set of query templates will be smaller than the sum of the benefits of the individual templates, but no smaller than the largest benefit. For example, the benefit $b(\{t_a, t_b\})$ of two query templates t_a and t_b is computed as $b(t_a) + b(t_b) - b(\&(t_a t_b))$. Computing $b(\&(t_a t_b))$ requires access to the history of user queries, which is not available. The key idea then is to use the *small* set CT of candidate query templates and their benefits in the cache to estimate the benefit of the overlap $b(\&(t_a t_b))$. We compute a conservative estimate of this overlap as the maximum benefit of a query template that instantiates $(\&(t_a t_b))$. By iteratively applying the above formula to compute $b(\{t_a, t_b\})$, we can obtain the benefit of a set of templates $b(\{t_{i_1}, \dots, t_{i_j}\})$.

4   Cache Processes

The component architecture of our semantic LDAP directory cache contains two principal architectural modules: (a) the cache manager, and (b) the data and meta-data cache. The components of the data and meta-data cache were discussed in previous sections. In this section, we describe the functionalities of the various components of the cache manager and their interactions during the various processes that manage the cached data. The principal functionality of the cache manager is the admission of the data into the cache and the replacement of the data from the cache. These functionalities are performed by two processes, one *revolutionary* and the other *evolutionary*. We discuss these in detail below.

4.1   Revolutions

Suppose that a user query is not cache-answerable. If the result of this query, fetched from the directory server by the cache manager, does not fit in the cache, the cache manager needs to determine how, if at all, to change the contents of the cache. Standard caching architectures, when faced with this situation, react by identifying low benefit pages, objects or semantic regions in the cache that, when evicted, would free up enough space. Our cache processes, in contrast, react by identifying high benefit candidate templates whose results fit in the cache, and discarding low benefit actual query templates, in a *revolutionary* fashion.

   We now formalize the goal of revolutionary change. Let $AT = \{at_1, \dots, at_k\}$ be the actual query templates corresponding to the cached directory entries, $CT = \{ct_1, \dots, ct_n\}$ be the candidate query templates, and S be the size of the cache. Among all subsets of the union of the actual and candidate templates $AT \cup CT$, choose a set CT' (for admission to the cache) such that *the residual benefit $b(CT') - c(CT')$ is maximized* subject to the constraint that $s(CT') \leq S$.

   To take advantage of the presence of the data in the cache when deciding on the new cache contents, we need to take the overlap between the candidate templates and the actual templates into account and modify the execution costs $c(t_i)$ of the templates in $AT \cup CT$ by replacing $c(t_i)$ by $c(\&t_i(!at_1)\dots(!at_k))$. A consequence of this modification is that each template in AT has its cost as 0.

Even in the absence of overlapping templates, this problem is equivalent to the KNAPSACK problem, which is NP-complete [7]. For the KNAPSACK problem, a standard greedy heuristic that delivers a competitive solution is based on selecting elements in decreasing order of b/s. This is the main reason why the profit metric used by our algorithms is computed as $\frac{b(t_i)-c(t_i)}{s(t_i)}$. The additional $c(t_i)$ component is based on the observations that: (a) the benefit of a candidate template needs to be offset by its execution cost, and (b) a candidate template may be selected to be an actual template even when there is no overlap between the candidate template and the currently cached data. Taking overlap into account, our greedy heuristic is presented in Algorithm Revolution in Figure 1(b).

4.2   Evolution

When revolutions are initiated on each user query, the overhead of maintaining the cache can become prohibitive. To reduce the cost of cache management, we combine our revolutionary approach with an *evolutionary* approach that modifies cache contents incrementally.

We now formalize the goal of evolutionary change for the LDAP cache architecture. Let $AT = \{at_1, \ldots, at_k\}$ be the set of actual query templates corresponding to the cached directory entries, and S be the size of the cache. Let q be the user query that is not cache-answerable, and suppose that the cache does not have enough available space, i.e., $s(AT \cup \{q\}) > S$.

The goal of evolutionary change can now be stated as follows. Among all subsets of AT, choose a set AT' to be evicted from the cache, such that: *the benefit $b(AT')$ is minimized* subject to the constraints that: (a) the total benefit $b(AT')$ of the evicted query templates should be lower than the benefit $b(q)$ of the newly inserted query, and (b) the result, $AT \setminus AT' \cup \{q\}$, after eviction of AT' and insertion of q should still fit in the cache.

Obtaining an exact solution for this optimization problem is computationally hard. Algorithm Evolution (not shown) provides a greedy, computationally efficient approximation to this problem, based on selecting elements in increasing order of the profit metric $p(t)$. Since the results of the selected templates are already in the cache, the $c(t)$ component of $p(t)$ can be set to 0.

4.3   A Hybrid Top Level Algorithm

Provided that the actual query templates have a "high enough" benefit, evolutionary changes to the cache are quite useful: the total estimated benefit of the cache is increased without incurring a significant computational overhead. However, when the actual query templates do not have a high enough benefit, it is more beneficial to change the contents of the cache in a revolutionary way. The candidate query templates that were generated, and whose benefits maintained, during evolutionary periods in the history of the cache, provide the source for an effective revolution. Such a revolution would hopefully be followed by a long period of stable cache contents, or evolutionary changes in the cache.

Our cache manager uses a hybrid algorithm that employs both revolutionary and evolutionary changes. An important question is when do revolutions get initiated. Intuitively, revolutions should be initiated when the benefit of the actual query templates becomes "too small". Instead of picking a constant threshold, we use an *adaptive* threshold, as follows. When Algorithm `ChooseCandidates` maintains the candidate templates, a subset of the candidate templates is chosen to constitute the *hypothetical* cache: (a) the size of the hypothetical cache is the same as that of the actual cache; and (b) the query templates HT that constitute the semantic description of the hypothetical cache are a subset of the candidate templates, selected *without* considering overlap (to enable efficient maintenance of HT). No data is fetched. A revolution is initiated when the benefit of the actual query templates falls below the estimated benefit of the hypothetical templates: $b(AT) < K * b(HT)$, for some normalization constant K. The value of K is dependent on the query workload and the degree of overlap between computed templates. In the experimental section, we provide an empirically determined value for this parameter for our data sets and workloads.

5   Experiments

5.1   Experimental Setup

We implemented a prototype of the LDAP directory cache that incorporates the algorithms presented in this paper. The prototype is written in C++ and uses Netscape's LDAP Directory Server 3.1 to manage the client cache. The client cache was run on a SPARC 20 running SunOS 5.7. We used Netscape's LDAP Directory Server 3.1 as our back-end directory server, on a lightly loaded Sun Ultra-1 (a faster machine than SPARC 20) running SunOS 5.5.1.

An important design goal of our prototype implementation is the use of a commercial LDAP directory server to store and access cached directory entries, which allows a simple mechanism for admitting entries into and replacing entries from the cache. Thus the entries are added to the cache using the API of the directory server that stores the cached entries. The merging of entries is performed automatically by the LDAP server. Our prototype also makes sure to (a) delete only non-overlapping entries from the cache and (b) use remainder queries to request entries from the server, for non cache-answerable user queries.

The reported results were obtained using synthetic workloads querying a real AT&T employee data set (approximatively 100000 entries). Following the methodology used in most caching experiments, we consider "hot-cold" workloads, with small hot regions that are hit by a significant fraction of the queries, and large cold regions that are hit much less often. As is common with many current LDAP applications, each query matched a single directory entry. We used an exact match query on the telephone number, e.g., (`tel=973-360-8776`), for this purpose. We used two workloads in our experiments, described below.

Uniform Hot-Cold: In the *uniform* hot-cold workload, we identified a portion of the directory data described by the query template (`tel=732-420-3*`), containing 217 directory entries, as the hot region, and the remaining data as the cold region. Queries were generated randomly, with $P\%$ of the queries uniformly distributed within the hot region, and $(100 - P)\%$ of the queries uniformly distributed within the cold region, for P values such as 70 and 90.

Hierarchical Hot-Cold: In the *hierarchical* hot-cold workload, we identified the directory data described by the template (tel=732-420*), containing 1796 directory entries, as the hot region, and the remaining data as the cold region. Furthermore, within the hot region, we identified the entries described by (tel=732-420-3*), as the "super-hot" region. Queries were generated as in the uniform hot-cold workload, with the following difference. Of the queries hitting the hot region, 90% were uniformly distributed within the super-hot region, while the others were uniformly distributed in the remaining part of the hot region.

5.2   Stability of the Benefit Computation

Recall that Algorithm ChooseCandidates maintains benefits of candidate templates. A natural question is whether this scheme is *stable*. Figure 2(a) shows how the benefit of a hot region changes, in response to the queries in a hot-cold workload. We consider two uniform (stable) workloads, one whose hot region has a hit rate of 90%, the other 50%. As can be seen, the benefit of the hot region is quite stable. We also consider a "moving" workload, where the first 5000 queries follow a uniform hot-cold workload with a 70% hit rate to the hot region, and the remaining 5000 queries follow a uniform hot-cold workload with a 30% hit rate to the hot region. As can be seen, the benefit of each half is stable, and the hot region's benefit rapidly adapts to the transition.

Figure 2(b) checks whether the profit metric behaves in the desired way. We consider the ratio of the profit of a sub-region of the hot region to that of the hot region as a whole. The lower curve shows that, when the "heat" of a hot region is uniformly distributed among its sub-regions, this ratio decreases, as the hit rate of the hot region increases. This is because, as an individual query hits the hot region, only one of the sub-regions has its benefit increased, while the others are aged. However, the benefit of the region, as a whole, also increases. The same reason also explains why the lower curve is always below 1. The upper curve in Figure 2(b) shows that, when the heat of a hot region is concentrated in a particular "super-hot" sub-region, the ratio of the super-hot sub-region's profit to that of the hot region *shows the opposite trend.*

These two curves collectively say the following: given a hot region where the heat is uniformly distributed among its sub-regions, our cache admission algorithms prefer selecting the entire hot region than each individual sub-region. On the other hand, if the heat of a hot region is concentrated in a sub-region, then our algorithms prefer selecting the "super-hot" sub-region.

5.3   Query Caching versus Template Caching

We now look at how template caching compares with query caching. For reasons of space, we show only the results for the uniform hot-cold workload of 1000

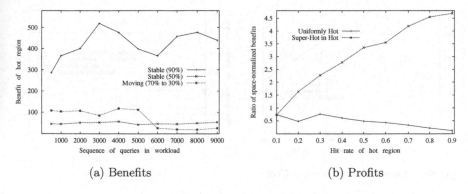

(a) Benefits   (b) Profits

Fig. 2. Benefit Maintenance for Query Templates

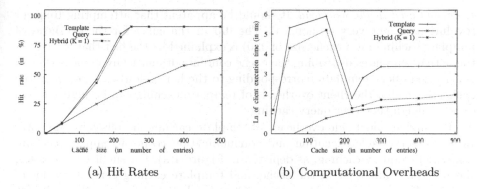

(a) Hit Rates   (b) Computational Overheads

Fig. 3. Query Caching versus Template Caching (Hit Rate and Client Costs)

queries. Figure 3(a) compares template caching with query caching on their hit rates. The *hit rate*, for a given cache size and query workload, measures the ratio of the cost of the queries that can be answered from the LDAP directory cache to the cost of all queries in the workload.

Notice that, as the cache size increases, the hit rates of both query caching and template caching increase. The hit rate of template caching peaks a little over 90% (which is roughly the number of queries hitting the hot region in the workload), at a cache size of 220 (which is roughly the size of the hot region in the workload). At the same cache size of 220, query caching, in contrast, has a hit rate only around 38%. In general, the hit rate of query caching remains much lower than that of template caching. This is due to the space overhead of query caching, when each query matches one (or a few) directory entries.

The advantage of template caching comes at a higher computational cost at the client, as depicted in Figure 3(b). This (considerable) client-side overhead is a consequence of attempting to perform revolutionary changes *each time a query*

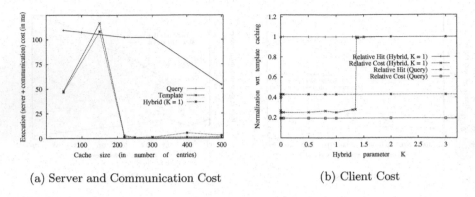

(a) Server and Communication Cost   (b) Client Cost

Fig. 4. Server- and Client-Side Costs of Caching

is encountered in the workload. It should be apparent that attempting frequent revolutions is not very economical. The dip in the curve for the overhead of template caching (at a cache size of 220) is explained by the fact that the size of the actual templates describing the cache contents dramatically reduces when a generalized query template (corresponding to the hot region) can now fit in the cache. Typically, the client overheads of template caching can be higher by an order of magnitude over query caching.

The higher client-side overheads of template caching are offset by the lower values of server-side execution and communication costs of template caching compared to query caching, as depicted in Figure 4(a). For smaller cache sizes, the hot spot cannot fit in the cache, and template caching generates a lot of server traffic, similar to query caching. Once the hot spot fits into the cache (at a cache size of 220), most queries can be answered from the cache, dramatically reducing the total server execution and communication costs.

Recall that, in Section 4.3, we suggested a hybrid approach that performs revolutions *only* when the total benefit of the cache contents becomes "low", i.e., $b(AT) < K * b(HT)$. The graphs in Figures 3 and 4(a) show how the hybrid approach compares with template and query caching when K is set to 1. As can be seen, the hybrid approach gives a hit rate almost as good as template caching. Also, its server-side execution and communication costs are very close to that of template caching. Yet, its client-side computational overhead is only a fraction of that of template caching.

5.4   Managing the Client-Side Computational Overhead

The client-side computational overhead of template caching is dominated by two components: (i) the cost of performing revolutions, and (ii) the cost of computing generalized templates. Both these costs can be tuned by adjusting the frequencies with which these tasks are performed.

Frequency of Revolutions: The frequency of performing revolutions is influenced by the value of the parameter K. Figure 4(b) shows how the choice of parameter K affects the hit rate and the overhead of the hybrid approach, for a cache size of 250 entries. Each point in the curves is normalized by the corresponding value obtained for template caching. Not shown on the graph is the case when K is very close to 0 (smaller than 10^{-15} in our experiments). Then, the hybrid approach behaves like query caching, resulting in low hit rate and low overhead. The interval of K between 10^{-15} and 1.37 is the most interesting, with the hit rate of hybrid caching as high as the hit rate of template caching, but with a significantly smaller cost. With $K > 1.37$ hybrid caching behaves like template caching. Thus, any value of K in the "interesting" interval is suitable, enabling easy tuning of the cache manager. Our results suggest that even performing revolutions infrequently still significantly enhances the overall effectiveness of the cache. Determining the range of optimal frequencies for performing revolutions is an interesting direction of future work.

Frequency of Generalizations: Due to the lack of space, we do not show the curves corresponding to our experiment on tuning the frequency of generalizations. Our results suggest that, in the case of a stable workload pattern, performing generalizations infrequently does not significantly affect the relative hit rate (no more than 5% in our experiments). Yet, the computational overhead drops significantly. However, when the pattern of user queries changes over time, generalizations have to be performed frequently for revolutions to be useful. When generalizations are performed often (up to once every 25 queries), the behavior of the cache manager is similar to that in the case of a stable workload. When generalizations are performed less often, we observed that the relative costs increased again, without any improvement in the relative hit rate. The reason is that, although (expensive) revolutions are being performed, beneficial generalized templates are created and admitted into the cache too late to have any utility. Determining the optimal frequency of performing generalizations is a topic of future work.

6   Conclusion

We explored the utility of LDAP query templates as the semantic basis for low overhead, high benefit LDAP directory caches. We demonstrated that the key ideas for effective caching are: (a) performing generalizations of LDAP queries; and (b) admitting such generalizations into the cache when their estimated benefits are sufficiently high. Our experiments illustrate that this revolutionary approach can lead to considerably higher hit rates, and lower server-side execution and communication costs, than conventional query caching, because of the admission of generalized query templates into the cache. The client-side computational overhead of revolutionary caching can be reduced in two ways. First, we can reduce the frequency with which revolutions are performed. Second, we can control the frequency with which query generalizations are computed. Each of these two schemes substantially reduces the computational overhead, with only a minimal drop in the hit rate. In combination, these two schemes make query template caching that much more effective.

Acknowledgements

We would like to thank Flip Korn and Misha Rabinovich for their comments on an earlier version of the paper.

References

1. P. Cao, E. W. Felten, A. R. Karlin, and K. Li. A study of integrated prefetching and caching strategies. In *Proceedings of ACM SIGMETRICS Conference*, pages 188–197, 1995.
2. S. Cluet, O. Kapitskaia, and D. Srivastava. Using LDAP directory caches. In *Proceedings of the ACM Symposium on Principles of Database Systems*, Philadelphia, PA, June 1999.
3. K. M. Curevitz, P. Krishnan, and J. S. Vitter. Practical prefetching via data compression. In *Proceedings of the ACM SIGMOD Conference on Management of Data*, pages 257–266, 1993.
4. S. Dar, M. J. Franklin, B. T. Jonsson, D. Srivastava, and M. Tan. Semantic data caching and replacement. In *Proceedings of the International Conference on Very Large Databases*, pages 330–341, Bombay, India, 1996.
5. P. M. Deshpande, K. Ramaswamy, A. Shukla, and J. F. Naughton. Caching multi-dimensional queries using chunks. In *Proceedings of the ACM SIGMOD Conference on Management of Data*, Seattle, WA, 1998.
6. M. J. Franklin. *Client data caching: A foundation for high performance object database systems*. Kluwer Academic Publishers, 1996.
7. M. R. Garey and D. S. Johnson. *Computers and Intractability: A Guide to the Theory of NP-Completeness*. W. H. Freeman and Company, 1979.
8. Innosoft. Innosoft's LDAP world implementation survey. Available from http://www.critical-angle.com/dir/lisurvey.html.
9. H. V. Jagadish, O. Kapitskaia, R. T. Ng and D. Srivastava. Multi-dimensional substring selectivity estimation. In *Proceedings of the International Conference on Very Large Databases*, 1999
10. H. V. Jagadish, R. T. Ng, and D. Srivastava. Substring selectivity estimation. In *Proceedings of the ACM Symposium on Principles of Database Systems*, Philadelphia, PA, June 1999.
11. A. M. Keller and J. Basu. A predicate-based caching scheme for client-server database architectures. *The VLDB Journal*, 5(1):35–47, 1996.
12. A. Kraiss and G. Weikum. Integrated document caching and prefetching in storage hierarchies based on markov-chain predictions. *The VLDB Journal*, 1998.
13. M. Palmer and S. Zdonik. FIDO: A cache that learns to fetch. In *Proceedings of the International Conference on Very Large Databases*, pages 255–264, 1991.
14. N. Roussopoulos, C. M. Chen, S. Kelley, A. Delis, and Y. Papakonstantinou. The ADMS project: Views "R" Us. *IEEE Data Engineering Bulletin*, June 1995.
15. P. Scheuermann, J. Shim, and R. Vingralek. WATCHMAN: A data warehouse intelligent cache manager. In *Proceedings of the International Conference on Very Large Databases*, 1996.

Industrial & Applications Track: Performance

Order Based Analysis Functions in NCR Teradata Parallel RDBMS

Ambuj Shatdal

NCR Corporation
5752 Tokay Blvd Ste 400, Madison, WI 53705, USA
ambuj.shatdal@ncr.com

Abstract. The decision-support (OLAP) applications commonly use order-based analysis functions like Rank, Cumulative Total, Moving Average. In past, the applications were forced to compute these important analysis functions outside the database. This resulted in loss of performance and inconvenience. In the NCR Teradata RDBMS V2R3.0.0, we have taken the lead by providing these functions as part of the extended SQL. In this paper we describe the feature and the algorithms. The feature allows computations on very large data sets and makes it significantly faster than what was previously possible.

1 Introduction

Order-based analysis functions like Rank, Cumulative Total, Moving Average are commonly used in the data-warehousing and decision-support (OLAP) applications. Since standard SQL and most relational databases do not have support for such functions, the applications are forced to compute these functions outside the database on a middle-tier server or a client machine. This results in performance loss because:

1. The computation is done on a relatively low-power client or middle-tier machine.
2. The extraction and reload of data is usually quite slow.
3. Further analysis of the results requires either reloading the data back in the database (over the network) or doing all the work on the client machine.
4. The function has to be computed independent of the rest of the query computation, which implies that the entire query can not be optimized as a whole.

Furthermore, in order to compute such functions one has to either write a client application from scratch, or use a middle-tier query tool that does the computation and express the query against it. Given a large data-warehouse, this may imply that there are several versions of these functions trying to do similar computation in a low-powered and inconvenient manner. Putting all the functionality in the central data-warehouse improves both performance and productivity.

These reasons motivated us to design and implement such functions in NCR Teradata RDBMS. In release V2R3.0.0, we have taken the lead by providing these functions as part of the extended SQL. The new feature allows significantly faster computation of such functions than what was possible and it also allows computation of such functions on very large data-sets not possible on a smaller client or middle-

C. Zaniolo et al. (Eds.): EDBT 2000, LNCS 1777, pp. 219–223, 2000.

tier machine. Considerable interest has been generated in our customers and partners for the new feature that goes to indicate that we made the right decision.

The analysis functions we implemented operate on ordered, and possibly grouped, relation. The uni-processor algorithm for computing such functions is simply:
1. Sort the records on the composite <grouping expression, order specification list>
2. Scan the records computing the function values

The natural parallel extensions of the above algorithm for a shared-nothing architecture result in following approaches, neither of which is satisfactory.
1. Sort the records globally (DeWitt et al [2]). Scan the records serially starting from the "smallest" processing unit successively to "next larger" processing units. This serialized scan will easily become a bottleneck in a large system.
2. Sort the records locally on each of the processing units. The function computation can be done while merging the locally sorted records to make a globally sorted result. Again, this approach has a serial bottleneck at the merge.

Hence we were challenged to design a shared-nothing algorithm that would overcome the above problems and be able to scale to hundreds of processing units. The algorithm overcomes the above serial bottlenecks using following techniques.
1. Intelligent use of the repartitioning step to successfully parallelize the scan.
2. By making the algorithm adaptive to the data it sees at runtime.

The only related works discussing integration of these functions in RDBMSs we are aware of are the RISQL functions [6] and the paper of Ramakrishnan et al [5] that describes the naïve algorithm and an alternative syntax. There are also proposals submitted to ANSI to make similar functionality part of the SQL standard [1]. We believe that ours is the first truly scalable and usable commercial implementation of this functionality that has been available since beginning of 1999.

2   Analysis Functions in NCR Teradata V2R3.0.0

An analysis function takes one or more arguments and an order-specification. For example, Moving Average takes an expression, a moving window size and an order-specification: MAVG(<expression>, <window size>, <order-specification-list>).

The order-specification-list is identical to an ORDER BY <order-specification-list>. We also introduced the new QUALIFY clause to be able to filter records based on function computation which allows the user to ask queries like "give me top 10 records". The functions can also be used in views, derived tables and insert-selects allowing for very complex requests. For details see Teradata SQL Reference [3].

There are two types of analysis functions: global functions, like Rank, whose value depends on all previous records and moving functions, e.g. Moving Sum, whose value depends on only previous N records. The following query provides an example:
SELECT StrName, SaleAmt, SaleDate, MAvg(SaleAmt, 7,SaleDate), Rank(SaleAmt)
FROM Sales, Stores
WHERE Sales.StoreId = Store.StoreId
GROUP BY StrName
QUALIFY Rank(SaleAmt) <= 5;

StrName	SaleAmt	SaleDate	MAvg(SaleAmt,7,SaleDate)	Rank(SaleAmt)
Green Bay	46121.00	98/07/24	37736.71	1
Green Bay	46120.00	98/07/31	37736.86	2
Green Bay	46119.00	98/07/17	37736.14	3
Green Bay	46119.00	98/07/10	37732.00	3
Green Bay	46113.00	98/07/03	34704.86	5
Los Angeles	103826.00	98/07/01	66923.14	1
Los Angeles	103822.00	98/07/22	75453.00	2
Los Angeles	103822.00	98/07/15	75449.57	2
Los Angeles	103821.00	98/07/08	75453.71	4
Los Angeles	103818.00	98/07/29	75452.71	5

Fig. 1. Partial output (of two stores only) for the query.

In the above query, the functions Rank and Moving Average are computed on the result of the join between the tables. The input is partitioned by StrName, i.e. the Rank and MAvg are computed within each Store. Then we apply the QUALIFY clause condition and return only those records that have Rank <= 5. Fig. 1 shows sample output of the query. Notice that only top 5 records are returned for each store, but the moving average has been computed over entire data.

The feature implementation has both parser and runtime components. In the parsing and optimization phase all the requested functions are groups into functions that can be evaluated simultaneously. Except for Rank, if order specification of one function is a left subset of another function, then both can be evaluated together.

In order to compute the functions, every set of records (determined by the grouping values, if any) has to be sorted. There are two alternatives.

1. Redistribute the data on <grouping expressions, order specification> using range partitioning and then locally sort the data resulting in a globally sorted result.
2. Redistribute the data on <grouping expressions> using hash partitioning and locally sort the partitioned data on <grouping expression, order specification>.

Hash partitioning alternative can achieve good performance only if the number of groups is significantly larger than number of processing units. Also, if the number of records is very small, the sampling and post-processing overhead involved in the range partitioning, described later, may make hash partitioning the better alternative.

It is hard to estimate number of groups except that when the processing is being done on a base table. In absence of certainty of using hash partitioning, we always choose range partitioning. This works well for two reasons.

1. Our runtime algorithm allows switching to hash partitioning if appropriate conditions are detected at runtime.
2. Using hash partitioning when unsuitable can result in significant performance loss.

The following describes the parallel runtime algorithm for evaluating all functions sharing a compatible order specification.

1. Prepare for sort, possibly requiring redistribution and on-the-fly aggregation.
2. Sort the records on <grouping expressions, order specification>.
3. Post-process, in parallel, after sort to enable parallel scan and evaluation of results.
4. Scan the records on all processing units in parallel computing the results.

For range partitioning the overhead for achieving successful parallelization in step 4 is limited to the on-the-fly-aggregation in 1st step and the 3rd step. The former requires only a little CPU and the later requires a few messages, a little CPU and possibly a little I/O (in case of moving functions).

In first step, if range partitioning is being done, then it samples the records and sends it to a designated processing unit. The designated processing unit analyzes the samples and either determines that hash partitioning is better or computes the partitioning table required for range partitioning.

If hash partitioning is chosen, either by optimizer or by the sample analysis, then the records are partitioned by hashing on the grouping expression. Furthermore, no partitioning is required for subsequent order specifications.

For range partitioning, computing aggregates on-the-fly for the first and last group is done after the records are received at a processing unit and before they are written.

Step 3 is needed only when we are doing range partitioning to enable parallel scan in the last step. It collects all the data to correctly initialize the scan. For example, the global functions (e.g. Rank) need to compute the aggregate value (in this case Count) for data on previous processing units. This is achieved by collecting the needed aggregate values from the on-the-fly aggregate data for the last groups accumulated during the 1st step. In order to compute the Moving functions in parallel, we replicate the minimum number of records necessary on to the previous processing unit.

The final step is straight forward as the previous computations have enabled the processing on all units to proceed independently and in parallel. For range partitioning case, the initialization of the scan uses the values obtained in step 3.

We briefly report the performance of the two approaches by computing two functions with different order specifications and returning the records that meet a qualification criterion. The applications are written using the Teradata DBS Preprocessor2 library in C [4]. The Teradata DBMS was running on a 2 node NCR Worldmark 4700 system (8 Pentium Pro CPU's). To minimize the network delays, we decided to put the client application on one of nodes.

In the traditional application, the SQL returns data ordered correctly using the ORDER BY for one function and then the first function is computed. The application then resorts the data using quicksort, computes the second function and restricts the records asking the equivalent of:

SELECT o_orderstatus, o_orderpriority, o_totalprice, o_orderdate,
            CSUM(1, o_totalprice), CSUM(o_totalprice, o_orderdate)
FROM ORDER /* TPCD ORDER Table [7] */
GROUP BY o_orderstatus, o_orderpriority
QUALIFY CSUM(1, o_totalprice) <= 10;
When using the new feature, we simply ask the above query in the application.

Table 1. Comparison of the traditional application vs. application using the new feature

Application	Number of Rows						
	5K	20K	80K	300K	1M	5M	30M
Traditional	0.92	2.52	10.24	71.03			
New Feature	1.28	1.65	3.82	11.98	42.26	249.82	2020.78

Table 1 shows the comparison of the two approaches for various data set sizes. We notice that the two-tier approach is faster at the smallest data set size (this is because an in-memory quicksort of a small data set might be faster than doing the same in the DBMS), but becomes worse for larger data set sizes. For 1 million records or more, the client runs out of memory and is unable to compute the functions.

3   Conclusions

We have shown that providing the order-based analysis functions in the DBMS is distinctly superior to previous alternative. To recap the main reasons:
1. Computation in the DBMS is significantly faster for all but smallest data sets.
2. We are able to analyze much larger data sets.
3. We are able to write complex analysis queries easily in "native" mode using SQL without having to write yet-another application or use a query tool.

In not too far a future all relational database vendors would need to provide similar functionality and the ANSI proposals [1] are a direction in that step. Hence there is a need to explore the domain of the alternative algorithms. Even though our algorithm gives us the best possible performance for our architecture, there exist alternative algorithms (a couple of them were pointed out earlier) which may be better suited to different architectures. A systematic study comparing algorithms for order-based function computation for different parallel architectures would be useful.

Optimizations of queries containing order-based functions, especially in a parallel environment, is another interesting and useful research area. We have touched upon the basics of optimizing the queries containing these functions. There are also feasible alternative plans that are candidate for optimizations, e.g.:
1. Computing functions with different order-specifications on the original data and then merge the results using a "join."
2. Using slower merge-join and getting the data in a sorted order for faster function computation, instead of, say a hash-join which would later require a sort.

Though we believe we have made a pioneering start by implementing the order-based analysis functions using a novel algorithm in a truly scalable parallel database system, there is scope for a lot of innovations and research in order to optimize the performance of these valuable functions.

The implementation of the new feature would not have been possible without the efforts of my NCR colleagues Ken McLean, Jan Nash, Marianne Ruegsegger, Steve Sheldon, Diana Thomas and the support of my supervisor Bill Putnam.

References

1. F. Zemke, et al. Proposal for OLAP functions. ANSI NCITS H2-99-155. April, 1999.
2. D. DeWitt, et al. Parallel External Sorting using Probabilistic Splitting. In Proc. of the PDIS Conference, Miami Beach, FL, December, 1991.
3. NCR Corporation. Teradata RDBMS For Unix SQL Reference, Volume 3, SQL Data Manipulation Language, Version 2 Release 3.0.0, Dec. 1998.
4. NCR Corporation. Teradata Application Programming with Embedded SQL for C, Cobol and PL/1, August 1997.
5. R. Ramakrishnan, et al. SRQL: Sorted Relational Query Language. In Proc. of SSDBM '1998, Capri, Italy, July 1998.
6. Red Brick Systems. Decision-Makers, Business Data, and RISQL. White Paper, Sep. 1995.
7. TPP Council. TPC benchmark D (decision support). Standard Specification 1.0. May 1995.

Performance of DB2 Enterprise-Extended Edition on NT with Virtual Interface Architecture

Sivakumar Harinath[1], Robert L. Grossman[1], K. Bernhard Schiefer[2], Xun Xue[2], and Sadique Syed[2]

[1] Laboratory of Advanced Computing, University of Illinois at Chicago, Chicago, IL 60607, USA
{sharin1, grossman }@uic.edu

[2] Database Technology, IBM Toronto Laboratory, 1150 Eglinton Avenue EastNorth York, Ontario M3C 1H7
{schiefer, xun, sadique} @ca.ibm.com

Abstract. DB2 Universal Database Enterprise-Extended Edition (DB2 UDB EEE) is a parallel relational database management system using a shared-nothing architecture. DB2 UDB EEE uses multiple nodes connected by an inter-connect and partitions data across these nodes. The communication protocol used between nodes of DB2 UDB EEE has historically been Transmission Control Protocol (TCP) / Internet Protocol (IP) but has now been extended to include the Virtual Interface (VI) Architecture. This paper discusses a new protocol termed Virtual Interface Protocol (VIP), built on top of the primitives provided by the VI Architecture. DB2 UDB EEE with VIP on a fast interconnect has shown significant improvement in reducing the elapsed time of queries when compared with TCP/IP over fast ethernet. This paper discusses the implementation and performance results on a Transaction Processing Council's Decision (TPC-D) support database.

1 Introduction

In contrast to traditional database queries, business intelligence queries are broadly concerned with extracting information from databases to facilitate decision making. These types of queries can be both compute and data intensive. Clusters of workstations are emerging as a powerful platform for performing these types of queries [3].

An important factor limiting the effectiveness of clusters has been the high latency of protocols such as TCP/IP which are commonly used to interconnect the workstations in a cluster. The Virtual Interface (VI) Architecture developed by a consortium led by Compaq, Intel, and Microsoft [2] is a specification for connecting workstations and peripherals, which reduces latency. The key idea is to move data directly from an application to the network interface controller (NIC) of the network interface hardware without going through the operating system [1].

C. Zaniolo et al. (Eds.): EDBT 2000, LNCS 1777, pp. 224-228, 2000.
© Springer-Verlag Berlin Heidelberg 2000

Clusters of workstations provide a natural shared-nothing architecture. With this type of architecture many operations can be performed in speeding up the overall computation. What is relevant here is that different workstations do not share a common memory but rather explicitly move data between the different memories. DB2 UDB EEE is based on this shared-nothing architecture [4, 5]. DB2 UDB EEE on Windows NT historically used TCP/IP for communication between the nodes. This paper discusses on improved performance of DB2 UDB EEE by utilizing the VI Architecture.

This paper is organized as follows. Section 2 describes the partitioning strategy used by DB2 UDB EEE. Section 3 describes the VI Architecture and how we integrated the VI Architecture for DB2 UDB EEE. Section 4 describes the experimental studies on the eight node and sixteen node clusters.

2 DB2 Universal Database

DB2 UDB EEE [4, 5, 6] is designed to support the very large databases that Business Intelligence applications often require. DB2 UDB EEE incorporates a highly scalable shared-nothing software architecture, which allows it to exploit symmetric multiprocessor (SMP) systems, clusters of SMP systems, MPP systems. This architecture enables DB2 UDB EEE to support very large databases by dividing the database into partitions, which can be stored and managed on separate nodes of a shared-nothing hardware platform. By searching these database partitions in parallel, elapsed times for queries can be dramatically reduced.

Nodes communicate over a interconnect and operate in parallel. The individual nodes can be either uniprocessor systems or SMP systems. In either case, each system node will have its own memory and access its own disks, but will share a scalable interconnect that always ensures point to point connectivity across the system.

3 Virtual Interface (VI) Architecture

The Virtual Interface (VI) Architecture [2], proposed by Compaq Computer Corporation, Intel Corporation and Microsoft Corporation, is a specification that defines industry-standard architecture for distributed messaging within a System Area Network (SAN). It is aimed at achieving low latency and high bandwidth communication between subsystems, with minimal Central Processing Unit (CPU) usage. The VI Architecture achieves this by providing direct access to the network interface hardware with appropriate hardware protection checks, there by avoiding the system-processing overhead inherent in traditional network architectures.

With the introduction of the VI Architecture DB2 UDB EEE on NT can communicate in a distributed messaging environment using low-latency, high speed SANs. The new interconnect fabrics that support the VI architecture are able to provide high bandwidth for transferring many messages, low latency for fast point-to-point delivery, and fault tolerance for ensuring messages reach their destination. The next section discusses few highlights of the experiments conducted. The full results, analysis, and detailed information on the implementation of DB2 UDB EEE on NT with VI Architecture as well as can be found in [7].

4 Implementation and Performance Results

Experiments were conducted on two cluster configurations – eight nodes and sixteen node DB2 UDB EEE clusters. A 100 Gigabyte/17 query TPC-D [8] database was used in our experiments. Each node of the eight node cluster was a four way with 200 MHz Pentium Pro ® processors, 2 GB of main memory, and 1 Megabyte (MB) of L2 cache. Each node of the sixteen node cluster was a four way with 400 MHz Pentium ® II Xeon™ processors, 1 GB of main memory, and 512 Kilobytes of L2 cache. Every node in both clusters contained a GigaNet's GNX 1000 card and Intel ® 100Mb/s Ethernet Cards. Each cluster was connected by two interconnects -- Giganet's GNX 5000 switch and also by Intel ® Express 10/100 Stackable Hub.

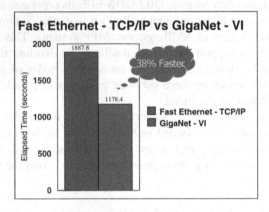

Fig 1. Elapsed time of TPC-D queries for sixteen node cluster

Figure 1 and Table 1 illustrate the performance of the VIP implementation in total elapsed time of all queries with experiments run on both the 8 and 16 node clusters. VIP performed better than TCP/IP on a per cluster basis and experienced better scalability characteristics over TCP/IP when the number of nodes increases.

The eight-node cluster was also used to simulate a test similar to the throughput test of the TPC-D benchmark [8]. One of the communication intensive queries (Query 17) was run as two streams, four streams and eight streams, simulating multiple users accessing the database. Fig. 2 shows the average query elapsed times of multi-stream invocations of this query. It was noticed that the VI implementation performed better as compared to TCP/IP. It was observed that VIP performs better when there is more data transfer between nodes, due either to communication intensive queries or high user loads.

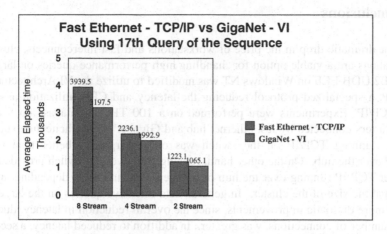

Fig 2. Elapsed time of multi-stream invocation of a communication intensive query

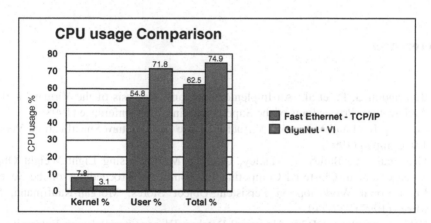

Fig 4. CPU activity during VIP and TCP/IP

Table 1. Elapsed time comparisons for 8 and 16 nodes

Interconnect/Nodes	Elapsed time for Eight Nodes	Elapsed time for Sixteen Nodes	Gain from node increase (%)
Fast Ethernet	3179.1	1887.8	40.6
VIA	2906.8	1178.4	59.5
Gain from VIA (%)	8.6	37.5	

Figure 3 presents the CPU activity during the time period this query was run. This clearly shows that the kernel CPU activity while using VIP is lower than in TCP/IP. These extra CPU cycles are utilized by the DB2 UDB EEE applications and there by results in faster completion of the queries.

5 Conclusions

With the dramatic drop in the price of workstations and fast interconnects, clusters of workstations are a viable option for handling high performance queries on large data sets. DB2 UDB EEE on Windows NT was modified to utilize the VI Architecture with the VIP, a specialized protocol reducing the latency and CPU utilization associated with TCP/IP. Experiments were performed on a 100 TPC-D database on 8 and 16 node clusters connected by fast ethernet hub and Giganet's VI Arhcitecture supported switch. Running TCP/IP on the switch was only marginally better than running TCP/IP over the hub. On the other hand, running VIP over the switch provided speed ups over TCP/IP running over the hub of between 10% and 89%, depending upon the query and the size of the cluster. In general, data intensive queries on the larger cluster had more dramatic improvements, since the overall reduction in latency, due to the larger number of connections, was greater. In addition to reduced latency, a secondary benefit was the reduced CPU utilization of VIP compared to TCP/IP allowed the queries to complete faster since more of the CPU was available for the query.

References

1. Buonandonna, P., et al.: An Implementation and Analysis of the Virtual Interface Architecture. Proceedings of the Supercomputing `98 Conference (1998)
2. Compaq, Intel and Microsoft: Virtual Interface Architecture Specification, Version 1.0. Compaq (1997)
3. Grossman, R., Bailey S., Hanley, D.: Data Mining Using Light Weight Object Management in Clustered Computing Environments. Proceedings of the Seventh International Workshop on Persistent Object Stores, Morgan-Kauffmann, San Mateo (1997) 237-249
4. IBM Corporation: DB2® Universal Database™ goes parallel with Enterprise and Enterprise-Extended Edition. IBM Corporation (1998)
5. IBM Corporation: IBM DB2® Universal Database™ on Windows NT Clusters. IBM Corporation (1998)
6. IBM Corporation: IBM DB2® Universal Database™ Administrator Guide, Version 5.2. IBM Corporation (1998)
7. H. Sivakumar H., et al: Improving the performance of DB2 UDB EEE with the Virtual Interface Protocol. LAC Tech Report 99-23TR, Laboratory for Advanced Computing, University of Illinois at Chicago (1999).
8. Transaction Processing Performance Council: TPC-D Benchmark Specification Version. (1998)

A Database Perspective on Building Large Applications
- Experience Report -

Joachim Thomas, Prithwish Kangsabanik
UBS AG Hochstr. 16, 4002 Basel, Switzerland
{<firstname>.<lastname>}@ubs.com

Abstract. Processing of large applications is inherently associated with database technology, since large applications usually require to process huge amounts of data. The banking sector was among the first commercial settings where large applications and database technology played an important role. This paper summarizes our experiences acquired through conducting a number of application projects at UBS AG. From this perspective, it points out chances and risks with modern software technology for building large database applications.

1 Introduction

Large applications are often tightly related to database technology, since they usually require to process huge amounts of data. The banking sector was one of the first commercial environments where large applications and database technology played an important role. Development started in the mid-60s with host-based applications that were being accessed exclusively via I/O terminals [1]. This was the beginning of an evolutionary process whose current state is characterized by n-tier architectures [22] with object-oriented processing facilities being more or less prevalent across the different layers [16, 17]. From its beginning, this evolution was torn between technical progress and the inherited "legacy". This dichotomy still prevails today.

Based on our practical experiences acquired through developing large applications as well as by consulting application developers, this paper points out chances and risks with commercially available software technology intended for building large applications that rely on database support to meet their information needs. Despite the empirical nature of our observations, we believe them to apply to many application scenarios, not only those to be found in banking environments.

Sect. 2 motivates a number of facts and impediments that must be dealt with when building large database applications today. In Sect. 3 we will discuss these problems referring to a sample application scenario taken from a project at UBS AG. Based on these experiences, Sect. 4 addresses key factors that determine the future setting for application development. Finally, Sect. 5 will summarize the central ideas of this paper.

2 Historic Evolvement

Large-scale application processing started with the advent of mainframe technology in the mid-60s [1]. Applications at this time were host-based; clients were I/O terminals (or terminals, for short). The connections between clients and hosts could be designed in a uniform and very simple ("slim") fashion. Application processing (including data management and access) was performed at a single site, just like development, maintenance, and evolution of applications. Over time, this clean and simple scenario became increasingly decentralized and complex. This development was motivated by new application requirements, by technological progress (different platforms with new functionalities/services), as well as organizational changes (acquisitions/mergers of companies and their generally diverse infrastructures for information processing).

This decentralization process resulted in n-tier architectures embodying basically three levels of processing (clients, middleware, backend). All tasks associated with (large)

C. Zaniolo et al. (Eds.): EDBT 2000, LNCS 1777, pp. 229-233, 2000.

applications - development, maintenance, evolution, processing - were spread across those layers. The following table summarizes some standards and technologies that represent the current state of the art at these levels.

Layer	Standards/Technologies	References
Client	OOA, OOD, Java	[6, 13, 20, 7, 25]
Middleware	Appl.servers, Distributed OO, JDBC, Mapping tools	[3, 5, 16, 17, 18, 19, 25]
Backend	Extended/Object-relational	[2, 11, 12, 15, 14, 21]

At first sight, these standards and products seem to be quite attractive for application development. However, we must keep in mind that legacy software in virtually all shapes and sizes is still commonplace and must be taken into account when building new systems. Moreover, the concepts shown above and their respective incarnations (i.e., software products) often do not match at one level of detail or another (cf., Sect. 3).

3   Problems in Current Application Development

Modern applications often adhere to n-tier architectures [22]. The technologies available in those tiers provide different semantic concepts with varying levels of abstraction. They either permit (or even require) to follow programming paradigms that do not necessarily match those to be found on neighbouring level(s). Fig. 1 illustrates this phenomenon referring to an OO application built on top of a relational DBMS and non-OO middleware. Discrepancies can be observed vertically (along the path from clients to backend) as well as horizontally, at each tier, among different applications.

The client level is dominated by OO concepts (classes, objects, attributes, etc.). Opposed to this, at the level of middleware, quite basic notions as, e.g., data items or messages prevail. If OO middleware [17] had been employed for the application, similar concepts as at the client could be encountered at the current level. In our example, the backend is constituted of a relational DBMS featuring classical relational notions as well as, e.g., user-defined functions (UDFs) or stored procedures [12].

(Business) Object Model

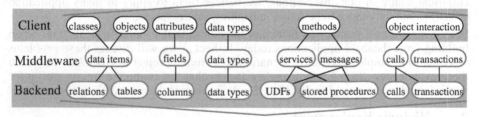

E/R Model

Fig. 1. Semantic discrepancies at clients, middleware, and backend

Certain notions appear on several levels (e.g., data types or transactions), however do not refer to identical concepts. Other concepts are named differently at various levels, however relate to similar semantic notions. For example, attributes at the client translate into fields at the middleware and columns at the backend. Finally, there are notions at a given level that may be associated with several concepts at the levels below. For example, a client method might be implemented as a middleware service or message which, in turn, might be mapped to UDFs or stored procedures at the backend DBMS.

Moreover, functionalities of different tiers are often insufficiently synchronized. As an example, consider a mapping tool that provides a cache for temporarily storing and manipulating objects that are derived from relational data. To synchronize cache and database processing, a proper integration of the activities at both sites is indispensable [4, 26]. However, we do not know of any mapping software offering this feature.

There is often no way to circumvent these facts in an elegant fashion. In such cases, the only workarounds are possible that are dictated by the particularities or shortcomings of software products or their underlying standards. Thus, choosing "the right" technologies for a given project is not an easy task, even more so, because it often requires to anticipate trends and evolutions of software products and standards. Other important factors are the existing system environment as well as new requirements posed by applications or application developers. Subsequently, we will outline these driving forces.

4   Choosing the Right Technologies

According to our experiences, there are three important factors to consider when selecting standards and products for conceptualizing and implementing large applications: *application requirements*, *current technologies*, and *heritage*. The term *heritage* relates to existing software infrastructure which may be *legacy* [10] or it may be *tradition*, i.e., although no more up-to-date, it can still compete with modern equivalents; consequently there is no desire to replace it. For example, a TP monitor might be considered as *tradition*; although acquired long ago, its functionality is still competitive and highly useful. However, pre-relational DBMS are *legacy*.

In the subsequent sections we will discuss important aspects of two of the above decision factors - *legacy* and *current technologies*. (We restrict our considerations to *legacy*, since, opposed to *tradition*, it might severely impede application development).

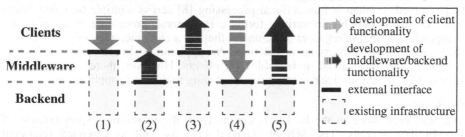

Fig. 2. New Applications and Legacy - common scenarios

4.1   Legacy

A quite appropriate and comprehensive definition of the term *legacy* can be found in the *Free On-Line Dictionary of Computing* [10]:

> *A computer system or application program which continues to be used because of the prohibitive cost of replacing or redesigning it and despite its poor competitiveness and compatibility with modern equivalents. The implication is that the system is large, monolithic and difficult to modify.*

Although there are technologies that promise to abstract from legacy (in particular CORBA, EJB), legacy semantics can only be masked to a limited extent. Therefore, migration paths must be determined case by case. Fig. 2 shows the scenarios when building database applications on top of legacy. The different cases are as follows:

(1)Client application built on top of existing middleware interfaces: This is a common and, depending on the middleware (e.g., CORBA services), a desirable scenario.

(2)Client application constructed on top of new middleware interfaces: This case is also common, for example, when a new application needs access to a mainframe DBMS via middleware interfaces that are tailored to the application's requirements.

(3) Terminal application built on top of middleware interfaces: This case is not very common, since "pure" terminal applications do not need middleware infrastructure.

(4) Client application implemented on top of backend interfaces: This case is also not very common. Instead, to access the backend DBMS, client applications usually rely on middleware interfaces for accessing database contents (cf., case (1)).

(5) Terminal application established on backend interfaces: This case is still common (e.g., automatic teller machines) and probably will prevail for non-graphical, mainly character-oriented applications.

4.2   Current Technologies

In the following, we concentrate on middleware and backend as mentioned in Sect. 2.

Middleware

The CORBA architecture provides facilities for developing middleware object services, running over heterogeneous hardware platforms. The recent EJB specification [24] permits to develop middleware services without concern for distribution, concurrency, or persistence. Recently, there are attempts to link both specifications [9].

Java middleware can connect to DBMSs via a common JDBC interface. However, in case of OO middleware accessing a non-OO (e.g., relational) DBMS, there is an impedance mismatch of data models. Mapping tools offer a solution to this problem by enabling application developers to map their business objects to relational tables.

From a DBMS perspective, there are several problems that are related to the coherency and optimization of processing between middleware and backend. One not yet satisfactorily solved problem is transactional processing [8] across multiple tiers that might store DB data, possibly in various formats. In general, processing at a tier is not independent of that of adjacent ones, unless there is a clear hierarchy of service interfaces that isolates processing in the tiers. An application should respect this strict service hierarchy to avoid undesirable side effects. However, there is currently no standard for such a service hierarchy for developing middleware applications.

Backend

Database processing at the backend benefits from the increasing expressiveness of DBMS data models. The SQL99 standard [12] as well as extended relational technology [2, 11, 21] have widened the scope of DBMS processing. Database systems can be used as simple data providers, featuring *universal access* to applications that perform complex processing logic. At the other end of the spectrum, a DBMS may offer full-fledged services to applications, thus acting as a *universal server*. In between both extremes, DBMS functionality may be used to only reduce structural discrepancies, or it may serve to narrow the gap between the semantics of the DBMS data model and the data models of the layers above. While this harmonization can be easily achieved for applications that are built *from scratch* (by supporting the client data model also at the levels of middleware and backend, e.g., "Java-relational DBMS" [23]), this problem remains to be solved for projects that are founded *on top* of existing infrastructure.

5   Summary

Large applications evolved from mainframe-based terminal solutions to n-tier architectures. Nowadays many approaches and technologies are available that support various aspects of application development and operation. Nevertheless, choosing the right technologies for projects remains a delicate task. There are three influence factors that must be considered in a comprehensive fashion - heritage, application requirements, and current technologies. We discussed two of these criteria and their manifestations from a database perspective, based on our experiences with application projects.

Despite many efforts to improve virtually all aspects of application development, a much better integration of these approaches is needed, not only at the level of implementation but also conceptually. We underlined this observation referring to our experiences from a number of large, up-to-date database application projects.

Acknowledgments

We thank Prof. T. Härder for his valuable comments and suggestions to this paper.

References

1. Amdahl, G.M., Blaauw, G.A., Brooks, F.P.: Architecture of IBM System/360, IBM Journal of Research and Development, Vol. 8, No. 2, April 1964, 87-101.
2. Carey, M., Chamberlin, D., Doole, D., Mattos, N., Narayanan, S., Rielau, S., Vance, B. O-O, what have they done to DB2?, Technical report, IBM Almaden Research Center, 1998.
3. Cobb, E.: Issues when making object middleware scalable, MiddlewareSpectra, May 1998
4. Deßloch, S., Leick, F.J., Mattos, N., Thomas, J.: The KRISYS Project - A Summary of What We have Learned so far, in: Stucky, W., Oberweis, A. (eds.): Datenbanksysteme in Büro, Technik und Wissenschaft, Springer (Informatik Aktuell), 1993, 124-143.
5. Edwards, J.: Let's Get Serious about Distributed Objects', Distributed Computing, 1998.
6. Gamma, E., Helm, R., Johnson, R., Vlissides, J.: Design Patterns: Elements of Reusable Object-Oriented Software, Addison Wesley, Reading, MA, 1995.
7. Gosling, J., McGilton, H.: The Java Language Environment: A White Paper, Sun Microsystems, Mountain View, CA, 1995.
8. Gray, J., Reuter, A.: Transaction Processing: Concepts and Techniques, Morgan Kaufmann, 1993.
9. Harkey, D., Burgett, K., Stone, T.: From e-Technology to e-Commerce - CORBA and EJB - How Their Specifications Relate, http://www.software.ibm.com/ad/cb/harkey-nov98.html
10. Howe, D.: Free On-Line Dictionary Of Computing, http://www.instantweb.com/~foldoc/contents.html.
11. Informix DataBlade Products, http://www.informix.com, 1997.
12. ISO Final Draft International Standard (FDIS) Database Language SQL -- Part 2. Foundation (SQL/Foundation), February 1999.
13. Jacobson, I., Christerson, M., Jonsson, P., Oevergaard, G.: Object-Oriented Software Engineering: A Use-Case-Driven Approach, Addison Wesley, MA, 1992.
14. Keller, W.: Object/Relational Access Layers - A Roadmap, Missing Links and More Patterns, EuroPLOP 1998.
15. McClure, S.: Object Database vs. Object-Relational Database", IDC Bulletin #14821E, August 1997.
16. Orfali, R., Harkey, D., Edwards J.: The Essential Client/Server Survival Guide, John Wiley, New York, 1996.
17. Orfali, R., Harkey, D., Edwards J.: The Essential Distributed Objects Survival Guide, John Wiley, New York, 1996.
18. Orfali, R., Harkey, D., Edwards J.: Instant Corba', John Wiley, New York, 1997.
19. OMG: The Common Object Request Broker: Architecture and Specification, Revision 2.0, Object Management Group, formal document 97-02-25, http://www.omg.org, July 1995, updated July 1996.
20. Rumburgh, J., Blaha, M., Premerlani, W., Eddy, F., Lorensen, W.: Object-Oriented Modeling and Design, Prentice Hall, Englewood Cliffs, NJ, 1991.
21. Stonebraker, M., Brown, P.: Object-Relational DBMSs: Tracking the Next Great Wave. Morgan Kaufmann Publishers, Inc., 1999.
22. Steiert, H.: Towards a component-based n-Tier C/S-architecture, Proc. of the third international workshop on Software architecture, 1998, 137 - 140.
23. JDBC 2.0 API, Sun Microsystems, 1998.
24. Enterprise Java Beans Specification 1.1, Public Draft 3, Sun Microsystems, 1999.
25. Szyperski, C.: Component Software, Addison Wesley Longman, Ltd., 1997
26. Thomas, J.: An Approach to Query Processing in Advanced Database Systems, DISDBIS16, infix-Verlag, 1996.

Data Warehousing

The Dynamic Data Cube

Steven Geffner, Divakant Agrawal, and Amr El Abbadi

Department of Computer Science
University of California
Santa Barbara, CA 93106
{sgeffner,agrawal,amr}@cs.ucsb.edu

Abstract. Range sum queries on data cubes are a powerful tool for analysis. A range sum query applies an aggregation operation (e.g., SUM, AVERAGE) over all selected cells in a data cube, where the selection is specified by providing ranges of values for numeric dimensions. We present the Dynamic Data Cube, a new approach to range sum queries which provides efficient performance for both queries and updates, which handles clustered and sparse data gracefully, and which allows for the dynamic expansion of the data cube in any direction.

1   Introduction

The data cube [1] is designed to provide aggregate information that can be used to analyze the contents of databases and data warehouses. A data cube is constructed from a subset of attributes in the database. Certain attributes are chosen to be *measure attributes*, i.e., the attributes whose values are of interest, while other attributes are selected as *dimensions* or *functional attributes*. The measure attributes are aggregated according to the dimensions. Range sum queries are useful analysis tools when applied to data cubes; a range sum query applies an aggregate operation (e.g., SUM, AVERAGE) to the measure attribute within the range of the query. Since the introduction of the data cube, there has been considerable research in the database community regarding the computation of data cubes [2], for choosing subsets of the data cube to precompute [3,4], for constructing estimates of the size of multidimensional aggregates [5] and for indexing precomputed summaries [6,7].

Ho, Agrawal, Megiddo and Srikant [8] have presented an elegant algorithm for computing range sum queries in constant time that we call the *prefix sum* approach. The approach is hampered by its update cost, which in the worst case requires recalculating all the entries in an array of the same size as the entire data cube. In a recent paper [9], we have presented an algorithm for computing range sum queries in data cubes that we call the *relative prefix sum* approach. The relative prefix sum method achieves a reduction in update complexity while maintaining constant time queries; nevertheless, it still incurs substantial update costs in the worst case.

Update complexity is often considered to be unimportant in current-day data analysis applications. These applications are oriented towards batch updates, and for a wide variety of yesterday's business applications that is considered sufficient.

C. Zaniolo et al. (Eds.): EDBT 2000, LNCS 1777, pp. 237-253, 2000.
© Springer-Verlag Berlin Heidelberg 2000

Batching updates, however, masks fundamental performance problems in updating data cubes. The prefix sum method is a good example of present-day cutting-edge data cube technology. During updates, it requires updating an array whose size is equal to the size of the entire data cube. It is easy to see that this model is not workable for many emerging applications, even under batch update conditions. Table 1 compares update costs for various methods of computing range sum queries in data cubes when the number of dimensions is 8. In the table, n is the size of each dimension, while d is the number of dimensions; thus, the size of the complete data cube is n^d. Even in the relatively smaller data cubes, the performance costs are striking. When $n=10^2$, the size of each dimension is only 100 elements; yet, with d=8, the full data cube is 10^{16} cells. To handle a single update at this data cube size, the prefix sum method requires on the order of 10^{10} times more instructions than the Dynamic Data Cube. On a hypothetical 500MIPS processor, excluding I/O and other costs and ignoring constants in the formulas, the prefix sum method may require more than 6 months of processing to update a single cell in the data cube; in such a case, even batch updating is not practical. The Dynamic Data Cube can update that same cell in under 0.008 seconds. Figure 1 presents the update functions in graphical form for a range of data cube sizes.

Table 1. Update cost functions by method. Values rounded to the nearest power of 10.

N	Update Cost Functions by Method, d=8			
	Full Data Cube $=n^d$	PS $=n^d$	RPS $=n^{d/2}$	DDC $=(\log_2 n)^d$
10	10^8	10^8	10^4	10^4
10^2	10^{16}	10^{16}	10^8	10^6
10^3	10^{24}	10^{24}	10^{12}	10^7
10^4	10^{32}	10^{32}	10^{16}	10^9

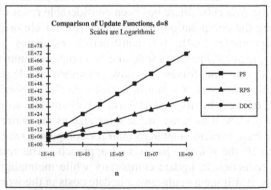

Fig. 1. Update functions. Scales are logarithmic.

In addition, for many application domains data is sparse or clustered. Examples include most geographically based information, such as geographically oriented business data (e.g., sales by region) and scientific measurements (e.g., carbon monoxide levels at various points on the Earth's surface). Still other applications require that data be allowed to grow dynamically in any direction, rather than in a single direction as with append-only databases. Currently popular techniques do not handle these cases well. For these and other potential application domains, we desire a method that achieves sublinear performance for both queries and updates. The method should permit the data cube to grow dynamically in any direction to suit the underlying data and should handle sparse or clustered data efficiently.

Contribution. We present the Dynamic Data Cube, a method that provides sublinear performance for both range sum queries and updates on the data cube. The method supports dynamic growth of the data cube in any direction; it gracefully manages clustered data and data cubes that contain large regions of empty space. Space requirements of the method may be constrained to within ε of the size of the data cube.

Paper Organization. The remainder of the paper is organized as follows. In Section 2, we present the model of the range sum problem and discuss several previous approaches. In Section 3, we introduce the *Basic Dynamic Data Cube* as a foundation for later sections. We present basic query and update methods. We conclude that the basic method still has considerable update complexity as the dimensionality of the data cube increases. In Section 4, we present the *Dynamic Data Cube*, which achieves sublinear complexity for both queries and updates. Section 5 addresses dynamic growth of the data cube. Section 6 concludes the paper.

2   Problem Statement and Previous Approaches

Assume the data cube has one measure attribute and d feature attributes (dimensions). Let D={1,2,...,d} denote the set of dimensions. Each dimension has size n_i that represents the number of distinct values in the dimension. Without loss of generality, assume each dimension has the same size; this allows us to present many of the formulae more concisely. Thus, let the size of each dimension be n, i.e. $n=n_1=n_2=...=n_d$. Initially we assume this size is known a priori; in Section 5 we will expand our analysis to dynamic environments. We can represent the d-dimensional data cube by a d-dimensional array A of size $n_1 \times n_2 \times ... \times n_d$, where $n_i \geq 2$, $i \in D$. In Figure 2, d=2. Each array element is called a *cell*; the total size of array A is n^d cells. The array has starting index 0 in each dimension. Each cell in array A contains the aggregate value of the measure attribute corresponding to a given point in the d-dimensional space formed by the dimensions. For notational convenience, in the two-dimensional examples we will refer to cells in array A as A[i,j], where i is the vertical coordinate and j is the horizontal coordinate. As Ho et. al. point out, the techniques presented here can also be applied to obtain COUNT, AVERAGE, ROLLING SUM, ROLLING AVERAGE, and any binary operator + for which there exists an inverse binary operator - such that a + b - b = a.

Array A

Index	0	1	2	3	4	5	6	7
0	3	5	1	2	2	4	6	3
1	7	3	2	6	8	7	1	2
2	2	4	2	3	3	3	4	5
3	3	2	1	5	3	5	2	8
4	4	2	1	3	3	4	7	1
5	2	3	3	6	1	8	5	2
6	4	5	2	7	1	9	3	3
7	2	4	2	2	3	1	9	1

Fig. 2. The data cube represented as an array A.

We observe the following characteristics of array A. Array A can be used by itself to solve range sum queries; we will refer to this as the *naive* method. Arbitrary range queries on array A can cost $O(n^d)$: a range query over the range of the entire array will require summing every cell in the array. Updates to array A take $O(1)$: given any new value for a cell, an update can be achieved simply by changing the cell's value in the array.

The *prefix sum* approach [8] achieves $O(1)$ complexity for queries and $O(n^d)$ complexity for updates. The prefix sum approach pre-computes many prefix sums of the data cube, which can then be used to answer ad hoc queries at run-time. Figure 3 shows the array P employed by the prefix sum approach. Each cell P[i,j] in array P stores the sum of all cells that precede it in array A, i.e., SUM(A[0,0]:A[i,j]). Using the prefix sum method, arbitrary range sum queries can be evaluated by adding and subtracting a constant number of cells in array P. In recent work, we presented the *relative prefix sum* approach [9]. The relative prefix sum approach achieves $O(1)$ complexity for queries and $O(n^{d/2})$ for updates.

Array P

Index	0	1	2	3	4	5	6	7
0	3	8	9	11	13	17	23	26
1	10	18	21	29	39	50	57	62
2	12	24	29	40	53	67	78	88
3	15	29	35	51	67	86	99	117
4	19	35	42	61	80	103	123	142
5	21	40	50	75	95	126	151	172
6	25	49	61	93	114	154	182	206
7	27	55	69	103	127	168	205	230

Fig. 3. Array P used in the prefix sum method.

Both the prefix sum approach and the relative prefix sum approach make use of a property of range sums in data cubes that is a consequence of the inverse property of addition. Figure 4 presents the essential idea: the sum corresponding to a range query's region can be determined by adding and subtracting the sums of various other regions, until we have isolated the region of interest. This technique requires a constant number of region sums that is related to the number of dimensions. We note that all such regions begin at cell A[0,0] and extend to some other cell in A. In the prefix sum method, the array P stores these region sums directly, and uses them to answer arbitrary queries as illustrated in Figure 4. In the relative prefix sum method, these sums are stored indirectly in a manner which improves update complexity.

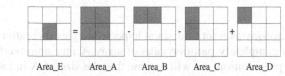

Fig. 4. An illustration of the two dimensional case:
SUM(Area_E)=SUM(Area_A)-SUM(Area_B)-SUM(Area_C)+ SUM(Area_D).

Array P

Index	0	1	2	3	4	5	6	7
0	3	8	9	11	13	17	23	26
1	10	18*	21	29	39	50	57	62
2	12	24	29	40	53	67	78	88
3	15	29	35	51	67	86	99	117
4	19	35	42	61	80	103	123	142
5	21	40	50	75	95	126	151	172
6	25	49	61	93	114	154	182	206
7	27	55	69	103	127	168	205	230

Fig. 5. Array P update example

While these methods each provide constant time queries, in the worst case they incur update costs proportional to the entire data space. This update cost results from the very dependencies in the data that allow these methods to work. As noted, the values of cells in array P are cumulative, in that they contain the sums of all cells in array A that precede them. Figure 5 shows the array P as the cell A[1,1] is about to be updated. The value of cell A[1,1] is a component of every P cell in the shaded region; thus, updating A[1,1] requires updating every P cell in the shaded region. In the worst case, when cell A[0,0] is updated, this cascading update property will require that every cell in the data cube be updated, or $O(n^d)$. The relative prefix sum method constrains cascading updates somewhat, but is still subject to this effect.

3   The Basic Dynamic Data Cube

In this section, we describe the Basic Dynamic Data Cube as a foundation for later sections. The method utilizes a tree structure which recursively partitions array A into *overlay boxes*. Each overlay box will contain information regarding relative sums of regions of A. By descending the tree and adding these sums, we will efficiently construct sums of regions that begin at A[0,0] and end at any arbitrary cell in A. To calculate complete region sums from the tree, we also make use of the inverse property of addition as illustrated in Figure 4. We will first describe overlays and then describe their use in constructing the Basic Dynamic Data Cube. As motivation to Section 4, we will analyze the performance of the basic tree and show that its update complexity is still problematic.

3.1   Overlays

We define an *overlay* as a set of disjoint hyperrectangles (hereafter called "boxes") of equal size that completely partition cells of array A into non-overlapping regions. For simplicity in presentation, we will assume that the size of A in each dimension is 2^i for some integer i. We denote the length of the overlay box in each dimension as k. We say that an overlay box is *anchored at* $(a_1, a_2, ..., a_d)$ if the box corresponds to the region of array A where the first cell (lowest cell index in each dimension) is $(a_1, a_2, ..., a_d)$; we denote this overlay box as $B[a_1, a_2, ..., a_d]$. The first overlay box is anchored at $(0, 0, ..., 0)$. An overlay box $B[a_1, a_2, ..., a_d]$ is said to *cover* a cell $(x_1, x_2, ..., x_d)$ in array A if the cell falls within the boundaries of the overlay box, i.e., if $\forall i((a_i \leq x_i) \text{ AND } (a_i+k > x_i))$.

Index	0	1	2	3	4	5	6	7
0				Y_1				Y_1
1				Y_2				Y_2
2				Y_3				Y_3
3	X_1	X_2	X_3	S	X_1	X_2	X_3	S
4				Y_1				Y_1
5				Y_2				Y_2
6				Y_3				Y_3
7	X_1	X_2	X_3	S	X_1	X_2	X_3	S

Fig. 6. Partitioning array A into overlay boxes.

Figure 6 shows array A partitioned into overlay boxes. Each dimension is subdivided in half; in this two-dimensional example, there are four resulting boxes. In the figure, k=4; i.e., each box in the figure is of size 4×4. The boxes are anchored at cells (0,0), (0,4), (4,0), and (4,4). Each overlay box corresponds to an area of array A of size k^d cells; thus, in this example each overlay box covers $4^2 = 16$ cells of array A. Each overlay box stores certain values. S is the subtotal cell, while X_1, X_2, X_3 are row sum cells in the first dimension and Y_1, Y_2, Y_3 are row sum cells in the second dimension. Each box stores exactly $(k^d - (k-1)^d)$ values; the other cells covered by the overlay box are not needed in the overlay, and would not be stored. Values stored in an overlay box provide sums of regions within the overlay box. Row sum values provide the cumulative sums of rows, in each dimension, of cells covered by the overlay box. Figure 7 demonstrates the calculation of row sum values; the row sum values shown in the figure are equal to the sum of the associated shaded cells in array A. Row sum value Y_1 is the sum of all cells within the overlay box in the row containing cell Y_1. Row sum value Y_2 is the sum of all cells within the overlay box in the row containing cell Y_2, plus Y_1. Row sum value X_1 is the sum of all cells within the overlay box in the column containing cell X_1. Row sum value X_2 is the sum of all cells within the overlay box in the column containing X_2, plus X_1. Note that row sum values are cumulative; i.e., X_2 includes the value of X_1, and X_n includes the values of $X_1..X_{n-1}$. Formally, given an overlay box anchored at $A[i_1, i_2, ..., i_d]$, the row sum value contained in cell $[i_1, i_2, ..., j, ..., i_d]$ is equal to $SUM(A[i_1, i_2, ..., i_d]:A[i_1, i_2, ..., j, ..., i_d])$. The subtotal value S is the sum of all cells in A covered by the overlay box. Formally, an overlay box anchored at $A[i_1, i_2, ..., i_d]$ has a subtotal value that is equal to $SUM(A[i_1, i_2, ..., i_d]:A[i_1+k-1, i_2+k-1, ..., i_d+k-1])$.

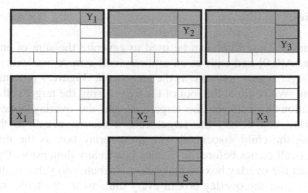

Fig. 7. Calculation of row sum values.

Index	0	1	2	3	4	5	6	7
0				11				15
1				29				33
2				40				48
3	15	29	35	51	16	35	48	66
4				10				15
5				24				31
6				42				47
7	12	26	34	52	8	30	54	61

Fig. 8. Array A partitioned into overlay boxes.

Figure 8 shows array A partitioned into overlay boxes of size 4×4. The subtotal in cell [3,3] is equal to the sum of all cells from A covered by the first overlay box, i.e. SUM(A[0,0] .. A[3,3]) = 51. The row sum in overlay cell [0,3] = A[0,0] + A[0,1] + A[0,2] + A[0,3] = 3+5+1+2 = 11. The row sum in overlay cell [1,3] = A[0,0] + A[0,1] + A[0,2] + A[0,3] + A[1,0] + A[1,1] + A[1,2] + A[1,3] = 3+5+1+2+7+3+2+6 = 29. Similarly, the row sum in overlay cell [3,0] = A[0,0] + A[1,0] + A[2,0] + A[3,0] = 3+7+2+3 = 15.

3.2   Constructing the Basic Dynamic Data Cube

We now describe the construction of the Basic Dynamic Data Cube, which organizes overlay boxes into a tree to recursively partition array A. The root node of the tree encompasses the complete range of array A. The root node forms children by dividing its range in each dimension in half. It stores a separate overlay box for each child. Each of its children are in turn subdivided into children, for which overlay boxes are stored; this recursive partitioning continues until the leaf level. Thus, each level of the tree has its own value for the overlay box size k; k is (n/2) at the root of the tree, and is successively divided in half for each subsequent tree level. We define the leaf level as the level wherein k=1. When k=1, each overlay box contains a single cell; since a single-cell overlay box contains only the subtotal cell, the leaf level contains the values stored in the original array A.

3.2.1   Queries.

The Basic Dynamic Data Cube can be used to generate the sum of any region of A which begins at A[0,0] and ends at an arbitrary cell c in A; we will refer to such a region as the *target region*, and to c as the *target cell*. Figure 9 presents a range sum query algorithm. We begin at the root of the tree. Using the target cell, the algorithm checks the relationship between the target cell and the overlay boxes in the node. When an overlay box covers the target cell, a recursive call to the function is performed using the child associated with the overlay box as the node parameter. When the target cell comes before the overlay box in any dimension, the target region does not intersect the overlay box and the box contributes no value to the sum. When the target cell is after the overlay box in every dimension, the target region includes the entire overlay box, and the box contributes its subtotal cell to the sum. Otherwise, the target region intersects the overlay box, and the box contributes a row sum value to the sum. Exactly one child will be descended at each level of the tree. This property follows from the construction of overlays. Overlay boxes completely partition array A into disjoint regions. Therefore, the target cell must fall within only one overlay box at a given level of the tree. Given a node and its overlay boxes, the target cell will fall within one box, and outside the others. Consider the boxes that do not enclose the target cell. Overlay boxes store the cumulative sums of rows in the region covered by the overlay box. Therefore, the contribution of these regions can be determined directly from the overlay box values; no descent is necessary. When the target cell falls within an overlay box, we must descend to the child associated with that overlay box. Therefore, exactly one child will be descended in the tree at any given node, and queries are of complexity O(log n).

```
/* Function CalculateRegionSum */
int CalculateRegionSum (DDCTreeNode h, Cell cell) {
    int sum=0;    /* running total of sum contributed by this
                    node and its subtrees */
    int i;        /* index variable */
    //naive code -- production code would only check
    //overlay boxes that intersect the target region
    for (i=0; i<NUM_OVERLAY_BOXES_PER_NODE; i++) {
        if (CellWithinBox(h.box[i], cell) {
            if (h is a leaf) sum+=h.box[i].subtotal;
            else if cell is coincident with a row sum cell
or
                the subtotal cell in h, sum+=that cell;
            else sum+=CalculateRegionSum(h.child[i], cell);
        } else {
            if (CellBeforeBox(h.box[i], cell)) sum+=0;
            else if (CellCompletelyAfterBox(h.box[i]))
                sum+=box.subtotal;
            else
                sum+=appropriate row sum value from this
overlay box;
        }
    }
    return sum;
}
```

Fig. 9. Query algorithm, Basic Dynamic Data Cube.

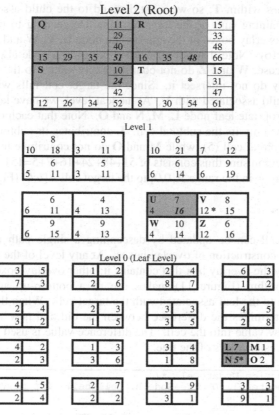

Fig. 10. Query example.

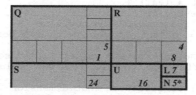

Fig. 10a. Individual components of the range sum.

An example of the query process is presented in Figure 10. We will calculate the region sum of the region that begins at A[0,0] and ends at cell * in the figure. For illustrative purposes only, we have labeled the overlay boxes for the four children of the root **Q**, **R**, **S** and **T**. Each of these overlay boxes contributes at most one value to the sum of the target region. Overlay box **Q** contributes its subtotal (51), since the target region includes all of the area covered by **Q**. **R** contributes its row sum value (48), which represents the sum of all the rows in **R** that are contained in the target region. Likewise, **S** contributes its row sum value (24). By summing these three values, the sum of all cells of A within the shaded region of the root node is obtained.

The target cell lies within **T**, so we must descend to the child associated with **T** to calculate the remaining sum of the target region. Descending to tree level one, we have labeled the overlay boxes of the appropriate node **U**, **V**, **W** and **Z**. **U** contributes its subtotal cell (16). Note that not all overlay boxes in a node always contribute to the sum; in this case, **W** and **Z** do not contribute any values to the sum of the target region, since they do not intersect it. Since the target cell falls within **V**, we must descend to the child associated with **V**. At the leaf level, we have labeled the overlay boxes of the appropriate leaf node **L**, **M**, **N** and **O**. Note that each overlay box at the leaf level contains only its the subtotal cell. **L** contributes its subtotal cell (7), and **N** contributes its subtotal cell (5), while **M** and **O** do not contribute to the target region sum. The total region sum thus consists of 51+48+24+16+7+5=151, which is the sum of all cells in array A in the range A[0,0] to the target cell A[6,6] (Figure 10a).

3.2.2   Updates.

The value of a cell can be updated by descending a single path in the tree. This follows from the construction of overlay boxes. At any level of the tree, an update to a cell affects only the overlay box that contains it; other overlay boxes are unaffected. The update algorithm (Figure 11) makes use of a bottom-up approach. It first traverses the tree to the leaf associated with the target cell. When the leaf is reached, the algorithm determines the difference between the old and new values of the cell, and stores the new value into the cell. The difference value is used to update overlay box values in ancestor nodes of the tree.

```
/* Function UpdateCell */
int UpdateCell(DDCTreeNode h, Cell cell, int newValue) {
    int oldValue;
    int difference;
    int i;
    i = the index of the overlay box in h that covers
cell;
    if (h is not a leaf) {
        difference=UpdateCell(h.child[i], cell, newValue);
        /*  difference=oldValue-newValue  */
        offset[] = offset of cell within h.box[i] in each
dimension;
        for each set of row sum values { /* d sets */
            add difference to all row sum values of index
greater than
            or equal to offset in that dimension
        }
        return difference;
    } else { /* h is a leaf */
        oldValue=h.box[i].subtotal;
        h.box[i].subtotal=newValue;
        return (oldValue-newValue); /* return difference */
    }
}
```

Fig. 11. Update algorithm, Basic Dynamic Data Cube.

Only one overlay box is updated at each tree level; therefore, the cost of updating the Basic Dynamic Data Cube is O(log n) plus the cost of updating the values in these overlay boxes. However, updates to overlay boxes can be expensive. As noted earlier, each overlay box contains $(k^d - (k-1)^d)$ values; however, for the two dimensional case we can observe from the figures that the number of row sum values, not including the subtotal cell, is equal to d(k-1). Thus, at the root level of the tree, each overlay box must store 2(n/2 -1) row sum cells, or O(n) cells. Row sum values are cumulative sums of rows. In the worst case, updating a single cell covered by an overlay box may require that every row sum value in the overlay box be updated; thus, updating the overlay row sum values becomes the dominant update cost. The worst-case update cost of the Basic Dynamic Data Cube becomes O(n) in the two-dimensional case. In the next section, we present a modification to the basic tree that improves update performance; the resulting structure has balanced, sublinear complexity for both queries and updates.

4   Improving Updates

It is clear that storing overlay values directly in arrays results in costly update characteristics. As noted, the high update complexity of the overlay boxes is a consequence of dependencies between successive row sum values. Recall from Figure 7 that row sum values are cumulative sums of rows of cells covered by an overlay box. The value in row sum cell X_1 is a component of the value of cells $X_2..X_k$; therefore, when the value in cell X_1 changes, the values in cells $X_2..X_k$ are affected. Thus, an update to a single cell may cause a cascading update throughout the array. The series of dependencies between row sum values is at the heart of this update problem, and leads to the cascading updates that we have described. If we could reduce the dependencies between row sums, the update cost for the tree as a whole can be significantly improved. The dependencies cannot be completely removed; the essence of the approach depends upon the existence of these dependencies, as illustrated in Figure 4. Instead, we propose a method of storing row sum values that ameliorates the series of dependencies between row sum values and as a consequence attains efficient, balanced update and query characteristics for the tree as a whole. Our method takes a recursive approach, the recursion being with respect to the number of dimensions in the data cube. We first present an efficient means of handling the two-dimensional base case, and then present the method by which higher dimensional data cubes can be recursively reduced to two dimensions.

4.1   The Two-Dimensional Case: The B^c Tree

We will analyze the two dimensional data cube as a special case of the d-dimensional data cube. We begin by examining the row sum values in the two dimensional data cube. An overlay for a two-dimensional data cube has two sets of row sum values, each of which is one-dimensional (Figure 6). Our goal is to reduce the cascading update that occurs when an individual row sum is updated. To this end, rather than store row sum values directly in an array, we will store them separately in an extension to the b-tree we call the *Cumulative B Tree* (B^c tree). There will be a separate B^c tree for each set of row sum values. The B^c tree is similar to a standard b-tree, with a few alterations. As in a standard b-tree, each node has a fixed maximum number of children (the *fanout*). Each node stores keys associated with the children, and data is stored in the leaves of the tree.

Figure 12 shows a B^c tree for one set of row sum values in an overlay box. The B^c tree modifies the standard b-tree in two ways. The first modification is with regard to keys. Each leaf of the B^c tree corresponds to one row sum cell. For the purposes of insertion and lookup, the key for each leaf is not equal to the data value in the cell, but rather is equal to the index of the cell in the one-dimensional array of row sum values. Thus, the leaves of the B^c tree are in the same order as the row sum cells in the overlay box. Recall that row sum values are cumulative sums of rows; in the B^c tree, we store the sum of each individual row separately, and generate cumulative row sums as needed. The first leaf in the figure corresponds to the first row sum cell. Its key is thus 1, and it stores the value 14, which is the sum of the cells in the first row of the overlay box. The second leaf corresponds to the second row sum cell; its key is thus 2, and its value is (23-14=9), which is the sum of the cells in the second row of the overlay box. B^c trees also augment the standard b-tree by storing additional values in interior nodes. Along with the traditional pointer to each child, interior nodes of the B^c tree maintain subtree sums (STS). For each node entry, the STS stores the sum of the subtree found by following the left branch associated with the entry. The fanout of the tree in the figure is three, so there are at most two STS values in each node; however, for fanout f there are (f-1) STSs. In this example, the root stores an STS of 33, which represents the sum of the leaf values in the left subtree below the root (14+9+10). The interior node with key 3 has an STS of 9, which represents the sum of the leaf values in its left subtree (9).

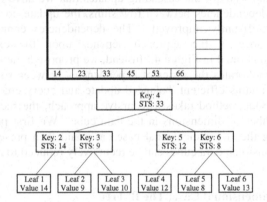

Fig. 12. One set of row sum values stored in a B^c tree.

A row sum value is obtained from the B^c tree in O(log k) steps, where k is the number of row sum values in the overlay box. To calculate the row sum value for a given cell, traverse the tree using the cell's index as the key. Before descending to a node's child, the algorithm sums each preceding STS in the node. The following example makes use of the B^c tree shown in Figure 12. Suppose we wish to find the value of row sum cell 5 in the overlay box. We start at the root, using 5 as the key. 5 is in the right subtree of the root. The STS of 33 precedes it, so we add 33 to our total and descend to the right child of the root. 5 is in the middle subtree of this node. The node has two STSs (12 and 8). The STS 12 precedes the subtree we will descend, so we add it to our total. The STS 8 is after the subtree we will descend, so we ignore it. We descend to the leaf, which contains the value 8, and add it to our total, yielding 33+12+8=53. We are storing the sums of individual rows in the leaves of the tree, and thus the value we have calculated is the row sum value that is required for the overlay box. Assuming the tree fanout is f, a constant value, the worst-case query time of the B^c tree requires ($f*log_f$ k), or O(log k).

We next describe the algorithm for updating row sum values in a B^c tree. The update complexity is O(log k). In Figure 12, suppose an update to the data cube causes the row sum cell 3 to change from 10 to 15. We will update the B^c tree, and hence the row sum value, to reflect this change using a bottom-up method. We begin by traversing down the tree to the leaf, where we note that the difference between the old and new values is +5. We update the value of cell 3 with the new value (15). As we return up the tree, we will update one STS value per visited node with the difference, when appropriate. In this case, we first ascend to the node with key 3 in tree level 1. We do not update the STS value of this node because the changed cell did not fall in its left subtree. We next ascend to the root. As the changed cell falls within the left subtree of the root, we update the STS value in the root with the difference, yielding (33+5=38). At most one STS value will be modified per visited node during the update process, since we only update the STS value corresponding to the subtree that contains the changed cell. Using the B^c tree to store overlay box values in the two-dimensional case thus provides both query and update complexity of O(log k).

4.2   Storing Overlay Box Values Recursively

The B^c tree breaks the barrier to efficient updates of row sum values in one dimension. We now consider the general case, where the dimensionality of the data cube is greater than two. We have already noted that a two-dimensional overlay box has two groups of row sum values, each of which is one-dimensional. In general, an overlay box of d dimensions has d groups of row sum values, and each group is (d-1) dimensional (Figure 13). The row sum values of a three-dimensional overlay consist of three planes, each of dimensionality two. We observe the fact that each group of row sum values has the same internal structure as array P. Recall that array P stores cumulative sums of cells in array A (Figure 3); row sum values store cumulative sums of rows within the overlay box. This concordance suggests that the two-dimensional row sum value planes be stored as two-dimensional data cubes using the techniques already described. Thus, the overlay box values of a d-dimensional data cube can be stored as (d-1)-dimensional data cubes using Dynamic Data Cubes, recursively; when d=2, we use the B^c tree to store the row sum values. Algorithms for query and update are as before, except that overlay box values are not accessed directly from arrays; rather, they are obtained from secondary trees.

4.3   Performance of the Dynamic Data Cube

The complete Dynamic Data Cube, including subtrees, has query complexity of $O(\log^d n)$ and update complexity of $O(\log^d n)$. Due to space limitations, the proof is available elsewhere; see our technical report at [10]. The technical report also describes an optimization that permits construction of Dynamic Data Cubes whose storage requirements are within ε of the storage required by the original array A.

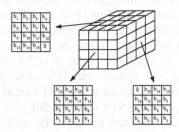

Fig. 13. Values stored in a three-dimensional overlay box (view is from lower rear).

5   Dynamic Growth of the Data Cube

The prefix sum and relative prefix sum methods do not address the growth of the data cube; instead, they assume that the size of each dimension is known a priori. For many potential applications, however, it is more convenient to grow the size of the data cube dynamically to suit the data. Furthermore, data may grow along any dimension in any direction relative to existing data in the cube. In other applications, data is sparse or clustered. Neither the prefix sum method nor the relative prefix sum method gracefully handles these situations. There are several difficulties. Neither approach makes any provision for empty or non-existent regions of cells within the data cube. Figure 14 shows an example of a cell, denoted *, being added to an existing data cube. Since empty regions are not allowed with these methods, the creation of cell * forces the further creation of all cells in the shaded region. This results in the first difficulty for these methods: since they must store all cells in the range of each dimension, a significant amount of storage space may be wasted for regions that are unpopulated. A more serious difficulty directly follows. For correctness of later queries, these methods would require that the values of cells in the shaded region be computed and stored when cell * is added. Furthermore, in a dynamic environment new cells may be added in any direction relative to existing cells. When the new cell precedes cells in the existing data cube, as in Figure 15, large regions of the cube may need to be updated.

Index	0	1	2	3	4	5	6	7	8	9	10
0	3	8	9	11	13	17	23	26			
1	10	18	21	29	39	50	57	62			
2	12	24	29	40	53	67	78	88			
3	15	29	35	51	67	86	99	117			
4	19	35	42	61	80	103	123	142			
5	21	40	50	75	95	126	151	172			
6	25	49	61	93	114	154	182	206			
7	27	55	69	103	127	168	205	230			
8											
9											*

Fig. 14. Creation of a new cell after existing cells.

			3	8	9	11	13	17	23	26
			10	18	21	29	39	50	57	62
*			12	24	29	40	53	67	78	88
			15	29	35	51	67	86	99	117
			19	35	42	61	80	103	123	142
			21	40	50	75	95	126	151	172
			25	49	61	93	114	154	182	206
			27	55	69	103	127	168	205	230

Fig. 15. Creation of a new cell before existing cells.

The Dynamic Data Cube is well suited to dynamic growth of the data cube due to the properties of the overlay box. Each overlay box covers some region in array A; when all the cells in that region of A are equal to zero, the overlay box values will also be equal to zero. We therefore need not store overlay boxes or subtrees associated with regions that are completely empty, since all row sums from such regions are zero. Accordingly, we can build the data cube incrementally over time using a Dynamic Data Cube. We begin with one node, the root, of size 2^d cells. Suppose information is to be added that falls in a cell that is outside the boundaries of the root; we call this *adding a new cell* (Figure 16a). When a new cell is added, we create a new root above the current root, thereby creating a new tree level. The new root has a size that is twice the size of the previous root in each dimension. The old root is placed as a child of the new root, and overlay box information is generated for it (Figure 16b). Data cube growth can occur in any direction. The parent grows the data space towards the new cell. Thus, the placement of the previous root in its new parent depends on the location of the new cell; to avoid certain forms of pathological growth, a round-robin approach may be used when resolving ambiguity. We do not allocate storage for the new sibling nodes of the previous root, however, since overlay boxes for these empty regions will have row sums that evaluate to zero. In the figures, the shaded areas represent regions for which no storage is allocated.

We continue to create new roots in this manner, doubling the size in each dimension for each successive root, until a root is created that encompasses the new cell. At this point, we traverse down the tree to the new cell, creating child nodes and associated overlay boxes as we descend (Figure 16c). Recall that only one overlay box at each tree level is affected by an update; therefore, we will create only one child node and overlay box per tree level during this process. No overlay box or subtree is instantiated for regions that are entirely empty. Should we encounter a non-existent overlay box during a query, we may conclude that its row sum values are all zero.

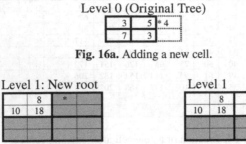

Level 0 (Original Tree)

Fig. 16a. Adding a new cell.

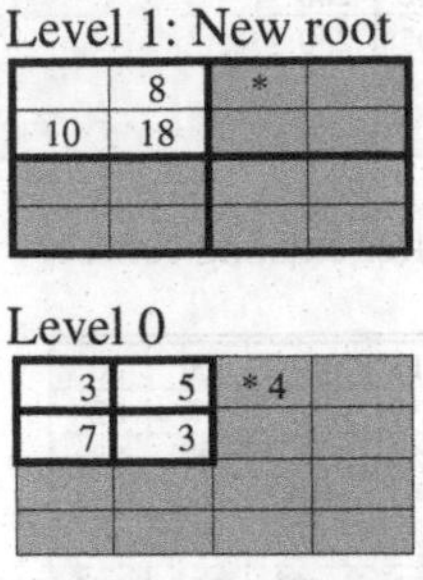

Level 1: New root

Level 1

Level 0

Level 0

Fig. 16b. New root created. 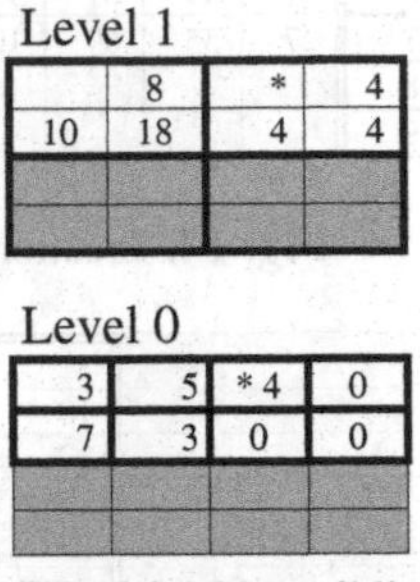   Fig. 16c. New sibling.

The B^c tree also supports incremental construction. Being derived from the standard b-tree, it gracefully handles growth of its data. As with the Dynamic Data Cube, we need not create all nodes in the B^c tree at instantiation. Even when a query seeks a cell that has not yet been inserted in the B^c tree, the B^c tree will still return the correct row sum value associated with that cell.

The properties of the Dynamic Data Cube are suited to clustered data and data that contain large, unpopulated regions. Where data does not exist, overlay boxes will not be instantiated; thus, the Dynamic Data Cube avoids the storage of empty regions. Since overlay boxes are self-contained, there is no cascading update problem associated with adding a new cell. The Dynamic Data Cube allows graceful growth of the data cube in any direction, making it suitable for applications that involve change or growth.

6   Conclusion

We present the Dynamic Data Cube, a method for handling range sum queries in data cubes that achieves sublinear performance complexity of $O(\log^d n)$ for both queries and updates. We discuss the properties of the Dynamic Data Cube that enable it to grow the data cube dynamically in any direction on any dimension, and its ability to handle sparse and clustered data gracefully. Space requirements of the DDC may be constrained to within ε of the size of the data cube. Table 2 presents the performance complexities of various methods of computing range sum queries.

The emphasis of this work is to reduce the prohibitive update cost in data cubes for applications that require a balance between updates and queries. In future work, we plan to explore modifying our approach to allow users to tune the method based on the relative importance of updates and queries.

Table 2. Performance complexities of various methods.

Method	Performance for input size N (N=n^d)	
	Query	Update
Naive approach	$O(n^d)$	$O(1)$
Prefix Sum [8]	$O(1)$	$O(n^d)$
Relative Prefix Sum [9]	$O(1)$	$O(n^{d/2})$
Dynamic Data Cube	$O(\log^d n)$	$O(\log^d n)$

References

[1]   J. Gray, A. Bosworth, A. Layman, H. Pirahesh. Data Cube: A relational aggregation operator generalizing group-by, cross-tabs and sub-totals. In *Proc. of the 12th Int'l Conference on Data Engineering*, pages 152-159, 1996.

[2]   S. Agarwal, R. Agrawal, P. M. Deshpande, A. Gupta, J. F. Naughton, R. Ramakrishnan, S. Sarawagi. On the computation of multidimensional aggregates. In *Proc. of the 22nd Int'l Conference on Very Large Databases*, pages 506-521, Mumbai (Bombay), India, September 1996.

[3]   V. Harinarayan, A. Rajaraman, J. D. Ullman. Implementing data cubes efficiently. In *Proc. of the ACM SIGMOD Conference on the Management of Data*, June 1996.

[4]   H. Gupta, V. Harinarayan, A. Rajaraman, J. Ullman. Index selection for OLAP. In *Proc. of the 13th Int'l Conference on Data Engineering*, Birmingham, U. K. April 1997.

[5]   A. Shukla, P. M. Deshpande, J. F. Naughton, K. Ramasamy. Storage estimation for multidimensional aggregates in the presence of hierarchies. In *Proc. of the 22nd Int'l Conference on Very Large Databases*, pages 522-531, Mumbai (Bombay), India, September 1996.

[6]   B. Salzberg, A. Reuter. Indexing for aggregation, 1996. Working Paper.

[7]   T. Johnson, D. Shasha. Hierarchically split cube forests for decision support: description and tuned design, 1996. Working Paper.

[8]   C. Ho, R. Agrawal, N. Megiddo, R. Srikant. Range Queries in OLAP Data Cubes. In *Proc. of the ACM SIGMOD Conference on the Management of Data*, pages 73-88, 1997.

[9]   S. Geffner, D. Agrawal, A. El Abbadi, T. Smith. Relative Prefix Sums: An Efficient Approach for Querying Dynamic OLAP Data Cubes. In *Proc. of the 15th International Conference on Data Engineering*, Sydney, Australia, March 1999.

[10]   S. Geffner, D. Agrawal, A. El Abbadi. Performance Characteristics of the Dynamic Data Cube. University of California, Santa Barbara, Computer Science Technical Report TRCS99-38, available at http://www.cs.ucsb.edu.

This research is partially supported by NSF under grant numbers IRI94-11330 and IIS98-17432.

OLAP Query Routing and Physical Design in a Database Cluster

Uwe Röhm, Klemens Böhm, and Hans-Jörg Schek

Database Research Group, Institute of Information Systems
ETH Zentrum, 8092 Zurich, Switzerland
{roehm|boehm|schek}@inf.ethz.ch

Abstract This article quantifies the benefit from simple data organization schemes and elementary query routing techniques for the PowerDB engine, a system that coordinates a cluster of databases. We report on evaluations for a specific scenario: the workload contains OLAP queries, OLTP queries, and simple updates, borrowed from the TPC-R benchmark. We investigate affinity of OLAP queries and different routing strategies for such queries. We then compare two simple data placement schemes, namely full replication and a hybrid one combining partial replication with partitioning. We run different experiments with queries only, with updates only, and with queries concurrently to simple updates. It turns out that hybrid is superior to full replication, even without updates. Our overall conclusion is that coordinator-based routing has good scaleup properties for scenarios with complex analysis queries.

1 Introduction

Practically any organization has accumulated large amounts of data. Increasingly, such data is becoming subject to complex analysis queries, also referred to as decision support queries or On-Line Analytical Processing queries (OLAP queries). Despite their complexity, users want those queries to be evaluated fast. Typically, materialized views and data warehousing technology are in use to meet this requirement. However, users more and more expect those queries to be evaluated on up-to-date data. View materializations help if updates and their propagation to materialized views do not delay the evaluation of queries. The main objective of our work within the PowerDB project at ETH Zurich is to reduce the slowdown of queries caused by updates. I.e., our vision of a 'next-generation OLAP platform' is that of a system allowing for efficient evaluation of short queries, updates, and complex analysis queries, without being in the way of each other.

The PowerDB architecture is a cluster of databases, i.e., a set of so-called *components* that run a DBMS, together with a coordinator. The approach pursued within the project is to build a simple yet clever coordinator: it can route queries to the least loaded component in case of replication, it can decompose and route complex queries in parallel to several components in case of partitioning and/or replication, and it can route updates to replica in parallel.

C. Zaniolo et al. (Eds.): EDBT 2000, LNCS 1777, pp. 254–268, 2000.

This current article investigates the capacities of routing in OLAP scenarios. We consider queries and simple concurrent updates that the component databases handle correctly without a global scheduler. We investigate admission control and routing techniques for complex analysis queries for different data placement schemes and under different update rates. We consider the case that there are streams of OLAP queries, OLTP queries, and simple updates, and we are interested in response times as well as throughput. Our objective is to assess simple techniques in quantitative terms, in order to have results that are sufficiently general.

In more detail, we proceed as follows: the first elementary but important question is under which circumstances queries should be evaluated concurrently, and when they better run after each other. Literature has coined the term *affinity* for two queries whose concurrent evaluation is better [17]. In the context of OLAP queries, it turns out that the number of cases where affinity occurs is limited. Furthermore, we have observed a phenomenon which we refer to as *obstruction*, i.e., two queries running concurrently execute much slower as if they run one after the other. In the body of the article, we say in which cases obstruction occurs.

Our next step is to evaluate simple data placement schemes and routing techniques for complex analysis queries. The alternative placement schemes considered are the following ones: the first one is full replication. The simplest routing technique is that the coordinator sends queries to the components one-at-a-time in a round-robin fashion. The second alternative called *hybrid* is a combination of replication and partitioning, i.e., we partition the biggest relation and replicate the other ones. Queries from the input stream that refer to the partitioned relation are evaluated one after the other. The rationale behind the second alternative is that most databases contain one relation that is significantly larger than the other ones. With hybrid, we expect a high degree of intra-query parallelism. The first alternative in turn leads to inter-query parallelism. The central question now is under which circumstances the speedup from intra-query parallelism is higher than the throughput improvement from inter-query parallelism. Our first result on affinity has told us that throughput increases linearly with full replication in a readonly environment (as the relative overhead is negligible), and our experiments confirm this. However, it turns out that hybrid is significantly better, e.g., with six nodes its throughput is a factor of 3 higher.

Finally, while complex analysis queries have been the motivation for this study, the more general scenario is that the transaction mix contains updates as well. As mentioned before, this current work considers a special case with regard to updates, namely transactions that contain one single update action. This restricted case gives us an idea regarding the influence of updates on query performance; at the same time, it is the most general case without explicitly taking global correctness into account. Our expectation is that hybrid is also better with updates, and our experiments confirm this. This is because the big relation also tends to be the one that is updated most frequently. The slowdown of the queries due to the kind of updates considered here is relatively moderate in both cases. For example, the throughput of hybrid decreases by 3% with six nodes and ten updates per second.

While related work has investigated affinity [17], much of this work has not taken OLAP queries into account. Furthermore, much empirical work on physical design has focused on partitioning without replication [6,8], and we have not found any conclusive answers to the important questions addressed above. To investigate these questions, we are building a full system, the PowerDB engine. For our evaluation, we have used data and queries from the TPC-R benchmark [16], which targets at platforms for OLAP.

This current work concentrates on query admission and routing issues and leaves aside scheduling. Arbitrary complex transactions with the need for a global scheduler are subject to future work. However, our own previous work has shown that scheduling at the coordinator level with parallelization yields good scalability [4,7,14]. — Furthermore, it should be clear that this article does not address query processing; instead, we rely on the query processing capabilities of off-the-shelf database technology.

The remainder of this article has the following structure: Section 2 gives an overview of our PowerDB architecture. In Section 3.1, we describe our physical design alternatives in more detail, followed by the corresponding query evaluation and routing strategies in Section 3.2. Section 4 contains our affinity study and the results of our performance evaluation of the two alternatives, full replication and hybrid design.

2   PowerDB System Architecture

2.1   Overview

The parallel architecture investigated in this current work is subject of a larger project of the Database Research Group at ETH Zurich called PowerDB. In short, PowerDB is a "database of databases". It uses relational databases for storage management. Figure 1 serves as an illustration. There is a distinguished node, the *coordinator*, and a number of other nodes, the *components*. Clients only interact with the coordinator. From the client point of view, there is one database schema. The coordinator passes updates and queries to the components

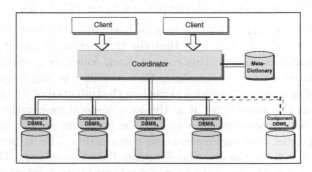

Fig. 1. System Architecture of PowerDB.

and collects the results. In more detail, the coordinator parallelizes, schedules and routes the queries, depending on the actual physical design. In case of updates, the coordinator is responsible for consistency of the data. A scheduler (cf. Figure 2) decides in which order to execute the queries. If several nodes can evaluate a query, a router chooses the target node. The coordinator has query-processing capabilities and is capable of evaluating several queries in parallel.

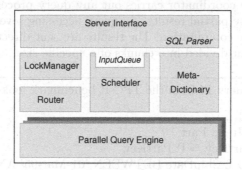

Fig. 2. Internal Structure of PowerDB.

Summing up, the coordinator is a database management system on top of database systems in that it consists of a SQL frontend, a metadictionary, a scheduler, a lock manager, a router and an execution engine (cf. Figure 2). We use the terms 'coordinator' and 'PowerDB engine' interchangeably. The hardware platform is a cluster of PCs; each PC runs an off-the-shelf relational DBMS. For the evaluation, the PowerDB cluster consists of up-to 6 Pentium-II computers (266 MHz), each equipped with 128 MBytes RAM and two 4 GBytes harddisks. We have used Oracle 8.0.4 as component DBMS on all PCs. A 100 MBit Ethernet LAN connects the nodes. The coordinator runs on a separate PC.

2.2   PowerDB Routing

This subsection describes the routing module and its interaction with other modules at the coordinator level in more detail. Clients communicate with PowerDB through a message-based interface. More precisely, clients issue SQL92-compliant statements. After parsing and validating an SQL statement, the SQL frontend generates a simple execution plan (see Example 1). The objective is to delegate the evaluation of the statement as much as possible to the component DBMSs. The execution plans do not specify the components that evaluate the plan. This is feasible since we will consider only simple placement alternatives that do not distinguish between components. So far, no further query optimization takes place. The SQL frontend then inserts the action into the scheduling queue.

To facilitate that the coordinator can accept new client requests while processing other ones, the PowerDB coordinator is multithreaded. The input queue is processed periodically, or as soon as it has a certain length. The scheduler determines a set of candidate components that can execute the current action from a correctness point of view. The router then selects the actual components from among the candidates. In the context of this current evaluation, we consider only simple query transactions consisting of a single SQL SELECT-statement and simple updates. Consequently, the scheduler does not impose any restrictions.

The execution engine is capable of executing multiple actions concurrently at different components. The main query execution strategy is query shipping: the component DBMSs are responsible for evaluating an SQL statement locally. The query engine at the coordinator carries out any query processing functionality necessary to combine partial results of a query accessing several nodes, e.g., set unions, or aggregate computation. The results are sent directly to the callback interface of the client divided into chunks of a specific size.

Example 1: Query 14 from the TPC-R benchmark looks as follows:

SELECT   SUM(...)
FROM   LineItem, Part
WHERE   L_PartKey = P_PartKey
          AND L_ShipDate BETWEEN '01-Mar-95' AND '01-Apr-95'

Plan A is the execution plan for full replication. ω is the wrap-operator known from middleware infrastructures for data integration [13]. The target node which shall execute the subtree with root ω_{node_x} is left unspecified. Now consider a data placement alternative that partitions relation LineItem over all components, and the components hold full replica of the other relations. With this design, the generated plan depends on the number of nodes. For instance, Plan B is for two nodes. It specifies that different nodes must execute the subqueries, and that the PowerDB query engine has to combine the partial results. Both with Plan A and Plan B, the router will fill in the placeholders for the target nodes.

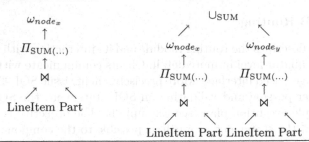

---

3   Physical Design and Routing of Complex Analysis Queries in a Database Cluster

3.1   Physical Design

Primitives for Physical Design. A fundamental problem in this context is the physical organization of data that yields good performance both with regard to queries and updates. The two primitives for physical design of individual relations that are specific to distribution are partitioning and replication [11]. *Partitioning*, i.e., data from a relation goes to different nodes, typically results in intra-query parallelism. *Replication* in turn leads to inter-query parallelism, as different nodes can evaluate queries in parallel. With replication, query-processing functionality at the coordinator is not necessary. But partitioning in general requires such functionality, at least if data is not shipped from one component to another.

Basic Alternatives Considered in this Study. In the following, we describe the basic alternatives for physical design that we consider in this context. Recall that we want to quantify the benefit from simple, elementary techniques for complex analysis queries. While literature has proposed other schemes for physical organization of databases as a whole, e.g., collocated joins [1] or multi-attribute declustering [5], we see such techniques as refinements of the basic alternatives described in the following.

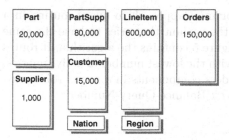

Full Replication. Our first basic alternative is full replication, i.e., each component contains a copy of each node. The coordinator does not process queries submitted by clients in any way; it routes the query to a component of its choice, and the component returns the result to the client. In Section 3.2, we discuss the different routing techniques considered.

Fig. 3. TPC-R with Full Replication.

Updates are processed in an eager, "update everywhere" fashion — Figure 3 serves as an illustration. The boxes correspond to the relations from the TPC-R database, the numbers are the numbers of tuples in the relation, and the different shades tell us which components hold a copy of the relation.

Hybrid Design. The second alternative, subsequently called *hybrid design*, is as follows: it partitions the biggest relation over all n nodes, and each node holds a copy of all the other relations (cf. Figure 4). With regard to query evaluation, there is a distinction between queries that refer to the partitioned relation and those that do not. In the first case, all components

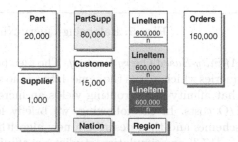

Fig. 4. TPC-R with Hybrid Design.

process the original query, and the coordinator computes the overall result. If the query does not contain aggregation, the overall result is simply the disjoint union of the intermediate results; computing the overall result in the other case is not difficult as well. If the query does not refer to the partitioned relation, their evaluation is as with full replication.

The rationale behind the second alternative is twofold: first, related work on physical organization of individual relations shows that partitioning is of advantage as long as partitions do not become too small [8]. In other words, we should partition the largest relation to obtain the optimal speedup. The other motivation is the heuristic that big relations are subject to frequent updates. With hybrid, each update of the big relation goes to only one component, as opposed to n components in the case of full replication.

3.2 Query Routing

The previous section has described the alternatives of physical design used in this study. Both approaches replicate at least some relations over all nodes. Hence, there are several components in the general case that can evaluate a query. To cope with this situation, different query routing algorithms are available [2,17,12,3]. In the following, we describe the routing schemes used in this study.

Balancing-Query-Number Routing. A common approach to query routing in a database cluster is round robin. We use the variant that tries to have the same number of active queries at each node. Figure 5 contains the algorithm. It routes a newly arrived query to the component with the lowest number of active queries. By using a stable sort algorithm it considers components in a round-robin way. [2] calls this routing strategy *BalanceQNr* ('Balance-Query-Number').

```
function BalanceQNr_Routing ( NodeList nodes, Action new_query ) : Node
begin
    // sort nodes by ascending load; if two nodes have the same number of queries,
    // the stable sort algorithm keeps them in the given order
    stable_sort( nodes, NumberOfQueriesComparison );
    return nodes[0]; // choose node with least load
end
```

Fig. 5. Balancing-Query-Number Routing Algorithm.

Affinity-Based Query Routing. The idea behind affinity-based routing is to assign queries which access the same data to the same component [17,3]. The rationale is that affinity-based routing yields an increased buffer-hit ratio and thus reduces I/O costs. In the following, we briefly look at existing affinity-based routing schemes and then describe a new algorithm targeted at our specific scenario.

[17,3] are simulation studies on affinity-based routing for OLTP scenarios. To decide if there is affinity between two queries, they only consider the data accessed by the queries, but not the nature of the access, i.e., 'scan' vs. 'random access'. But this differentiation is important. For example, consider two queries which do an aggregation over a relation. As they access exactly the same data, a simple affinity-based routing algorithm would assign them to the same node. However, assume that evaluation of the queries is scan-based. In order to avoid

flushing the database buffer, current database systems do not use the normal database buffer for pages read during a scan [10]. The effect is that two queries with scan-based evaluation do not benefit from each other. Even worse, scanning the same disk may lead to obstruction[1].

```
function AffinityBased_Routing ( NodeList nodes, Action newquery ) : Node
begin
  stable_sort( nodes, NumberOfQueriesComparison );
  foreach node in nodes do
    boolean affinity := true;
    foreach activequery in node.activeQueries do
      affinity := affinity and (AffinityMatrix[newquery][activequery]>0);
    od
    if ( affinity = true ) then
        return node;
  od
  return NULL;
end
```

Fig. 6. Affinity-Based Routing Algorithm.

Consequently, the nature of the data access matters. Our improved affinity-based routing strategy reflects this. Figure 6 contains it in pseudo-code. The core of the algorithm is the *affinity matrix*, which states how much the concurrent execution of two queries is faster than their sequential evaluation. The values incorporate both data affinity and nature of access. The algorithm routes a newly arrived query to a component whose active queries have affinity with the new one. We will present the matrix in Subsection 4.1.

"Short Queries ASAP". Our affinity investigations will motivate another routing algorithm called *Short-Queries-As-Soon-As-Possible*, which we will describe at the end of Subsection 4.1.

4   Performance Evaluation

In this section, we present the results of an extensive evaluation of our data placement and routing alternatives with the TPC-R benchmark and the PowerDB system. Subsection 4.1 contains our findings regarding affinity. Subsection 4.2 compares different query routing algorithms. It shows that affinity-based routing improves throughput only marginally, and that sequential evaluation of complex queries is superior. Therefore, Subsection 4.3 compares the two physical design alternatives using sequential routing only. Subsection 4.3 investigates the performance impact of simple updates.

---

[1] With the TPC-R benchmark, queries Q_1 and Q_6 both scan the central fact table (LineItem) in order to compute certain aggregates. The concurrent execution of both queries at the same node is 25% slower than the sequential execution.

Experimental Setup. The TPC Benchmark R [16] is the successor of the TPC-D benchmark. It consists of 22 OLAP queries and two data modification streams, called "refresh functions". Given a scaling factor sf, the first one (RF1) inserts $sf * 1500$ new orders and corresponding lineitems into the database, while the second refresh function (RF2) deletes them. We have used the query stream corresponding to the query sequence O(00) of the specification. Each component has the complete data set of the TPC-R benchmark with scaling factor 0.1. The data and the indexes sum up to a database size of about 300 MBytes for each component. With the hybrid approach, the LineItem relation has been partitioned over the components according to the L_OrderKey attribute.

4.1 Affinity

This subsection presents and explains the so-called *affinity matrix* of the TPC-R benchmark used in the affinity-based routing algorithm as described in Figure 6. In a nutshell, each cell of the affinity matrix contains the affinity value of a pair of queries. To come up with the affinity matrix, we have looked at the characteristics of the queries, i.e., size of relations, selectivity of predicates, execution plan, obtained from the query optimizer. We have evaluated query pairs for which we

Query	Q_1	Q_2	Q_3	Q_4	Q_5	Q_6	Q_7	Q_8	Q_9	Q_{10}	Q_{11}
Runtime	53s	11s	190s	123s	327s	181s	345s	57s	211s	127s	31s

Query	Q_{12}	Q_{13}	Q_{14}	Q_{15}	Q_{16}	Q_{17}	Q_{18}	Q_{19}	Q_{20}	Q_{21}	Q_{22}
Runtime	235s	25s	43s	77s	16s	14s	106s	20s	64s	79s	13s

Table 1. Runtimes of single TPC-R Queries.

have expected a relatively high degree of affinity. We have run such queries both sequentially and concurrently. In more detail, the affinity matrix gives us the effect of concurrent query evaluation on mean response time (MRT):

$$affinity(Q_x, Q_y) = 100 - \frac{MRT(Q_x\|Q_y) * 100}{MRT(Q_x; Q_y)}$$

The affinity value represents the improvement (in percent) of mean response time by concurrent execution of two queries. The faster the concurrent execution is compared to the sequential one, the higher is the affinity value. In the formula, $MRT(Q_x\|Q_y)$ denotes the mean response time of Q_x and Q_y executed concurrently, and $MRT(Q_x; Q_y)$ stands for the mean response time of Q_x and Q_y where Q_y is executed after Q_x. I.e.,

$$MRT(Q_x; Q_y) = \frac{ExecutionTime(Q_x) + ResponseTime(Q_y, [Q_x])}{2}$$

$ResponseTime(Q_y, [Q_x])$ is the response time of Q_y whose execution starts after evaluation of Q_x. In other words,

$$ResponseTime(Q_y, [Q_x])) = ExecutionTime(Q_x) + ExecutionTime(Q_y)$$

Table 2 is the affinity matrix for the TPC-R queries we have measured (cells of unmeasured pairs are left blank). To compensate runtime fluctuations, we only consider affinity values higher of at least 2%, otherwise, there is a '-'. As can been seen, the matrix is only sparsely populated, i.e., affinity rarely occurs.

	Q_1	Q_2	Q_3	Q_4	Q_5	Q_6	Q_7	Q_8	Q_9	Q_{10}	Q_{11}	Q_{12}	Q_{13}	Q_{14}	Q_{15}	Q_{16}	Q_{17}	Q_{18}	Q_{19}	Q_{20}	Q_{21}	Q_{22}	
Q_1	-	10%					-													-			Q_1
Q_2																							Q_2
Q_3	-	32%	15%	6%	-	4%		-		-			3%	-		-	-		-	-	-		Q_3
Q_4	3%	2%	35%	15%	26%	-	10%	10%		23%	-			3%	4%		-			-	-		Q_4
Q_5	-		-	29%	-	-		-	9%			-				-	21%				-		Q_5
Q_6	-		-	7%	32%	-		-	-		26%				-				-				Q_6
Q_7		-	-		-	31%		-	-			-		-			-			-			Q_7
Q_8		6%	15%	25%	30%											6%		-					Q_8
Q_9		-	-	-	-	-	10%		-					-					-			-	Q_9
Q_{10}		8%	8%	32%	10%	19%	-	-	-			19%	-			-			-	-		-	Q_{10}
Q_{11}																							Q_{11}
Q_{12}		-	-	6%	18%	-		-	-			33%				2%	-			-			Q_{12}
Q_{13}		31%	37%	36%			-			2%				8%									Q_{13}
Q_{14}					-										8%								Q_{14}
Q_{15}					2%										-								Q_{15}
Q_{16}							4%			6%						7%			-		33%		Q_{16}
Q_{17}	5%	47%	47%	48%		48%	4%			2%			5%						9%		44%		Q_{17}
Q_{18}	-		-	-		-		-	-				-			-	-			-	-	-	Q_{18}
Q_{19}		44%	42%	46%		46%	4%					-				12%							Q_{19}
Q_{20}	-	23%	20%	32%	24%	36%	-					2%	4%			8%	6%	17%	3%	2%	3%		Q_{20}
Q_{21}	-		-	5%	13%	-				-			-				-			-	-	8%	Q_{21}
Q_{22}		42%	44%	45%			-	4%				2%											Q_{22}
	Q_1	Q_2	Q_3	Q_4	Q_5	Q_6	Q_7	Q_8	Q_9	Q_{10}	Q_{11}	Q_{12}	Q_{13}	Q_{14}	Q_{15}	Q_{16}	Q_{17}	Q_{18}	Q_{19}	Q_{20}	Q_{21}	Q_{22}	

Table 2. Affinity Matrix of TPC-R Queries.

The affinity matrix is not symmetric. To explain this, we have a closer look at a relatively high value in the matrix. For instance, it is of advantage to assign Q_{17} to a component that currently evaluates Q_3, but the opposite is not. There is a large runtime difference between these queries, i.e., Q_3 with 160 seconds versus Q_{17} with 4 seconds (cf. Table 1). In other words, the improvement is not the consequence of query evaluations favoring each other, but of a reduced waiting period. Hence, mean response time does not adequately reflect affinity if there is such a large runtime difference. As the effect described above is typical, we conclude that exploiting affinity systematically should not bring any significant improvement. Subsequent experiments with affinity-based routing policies will validate this claim.

"Short Queries ASAP." TPC-R consists of a mix of queries some of which are complex analysis queries, some of which are short queries. As a consequence of our evaluation on affinity, we suggest the so-called "Short-Queries-As-Soon-As-Possible" routing policy (ShortQueriesASAP) given in Figure 7. In order

---

if (*query in the head of the input queue is a long query*)
   evaluate query on a component that currently does not evaluate any query
else if (*query in the head of the input queue is a short query*)
   evaluate query on a component that either is not evaluating any query,
   or that is currently evaluating a long query, but no other short query

---

Fig. 7. Short-Queries-ASAP Routing Policy.

to minimize the waiting period of short queries, the *ShortQueriesASAP* policy allows them to be executed concurrently with one other query. Only long queries have to wait in the input queue until a free node is available. Note that this is indeed a routing algorithm. It does not schedule the queries, i.e., sort the input queue.

4.2 Routing Algorithms

To evaluate our alternative routing algorithms, we have executed a stream of TPC-R queries on the database cluster with full replication. The query stream corresponds to the query sequence O(00) of the TPC-R specification. The three routing strategies are *Balance-the-Number-Of-Queries*, *Short-Queries-ASAP* and *Affinity-Based-Routing*. With regard to Balance-the-Number-of-Queries, we have measured the following variants: one without a maximum load per node, subsequently referred to as *BalanceQNr*, and one with at most one query per node, referred to as *Sequential*.

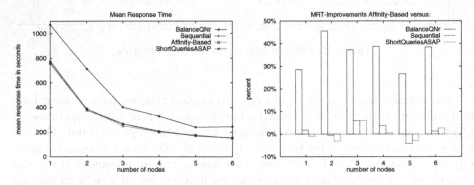

Fig. 8. Comparison of Routing Strategies with Full Replication.

As shown in Figure 8, sequential evaluation is among the best strategies. As expected, affinity-based routing improves the mean response time only slightly, e.g., for three components by 6% compared to sequential routing. The simple routing policy Short-Queries-ASAP introduced in the previous Subsection performs quite reasonable, but there is no general performance gain versus sequential or affinity-based. As the values for Sequential, Short-Queries-ASAP and Affinity-Based routing are always very close, the right diagram in Figure 8 "zooms in" and displays the relative difference between the alternatives. Figure 8 also tells us that the concurrent execution of multiple queries at one node (BalanceQNr) is clearly suboptimal. The mean response time of BalancingQNR-routing is 30% to 40% slower than sequential or affinity-based routing.

4.3 Physical Database Design Alternatives

After investigating the different routing algorithms, we now compare the two design alternatives full replication and hybrid design. We first study query performance in isolation, we then investigate the effect of concurrent updates on query streams. From now on, the routing strategy is always the sequential one.

Query Performance   For this experiment, we have issued the set of the 22 TPC-R queries as one batch to the coordinator, and have measured the runtime of each query separately. Figure 9 shows the mean response time and throughput of the TPC-R queries with the two design alternatives for different numbers of components.

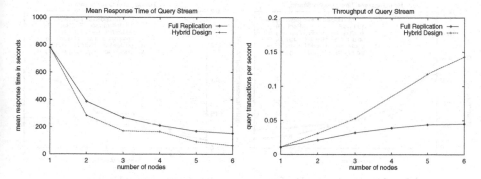

Fig. 9. Querying Performances of Physical Database Design Alternatives.

The hybrid design improves throughput significantly: With a system size of six nodes, the throughput is three times better compared to full replication. The reason is that due to the partitioning of the LineItem relation 17 of the 22 TPC-R queries gained intra-query parallelism.

The throughput improvement of the PowerDB cluster with full replication is linear with the number of nodes (see Figure 9) as one might have expected. E.g., with six components the mean response time of the TPC-R is approximately a sixth of the response time with one node. The same is true for the throughput, which is about five times higher. However, the performance improvement with hybrid is better, and the reason is as follows: the LineItem relation is partitioned into smaller fragments. This allows the component to use more efficient execution plans. We have verified this for some queries. Oracle has taken the reduced size of the LineItem partitions into account; the smaller partitions allow for in-memory sorting. Hence, the system has generated execution plans with merge joins whenever possible. The reduced cost of the join and the better caching behaviour of smaller partitions together with increased intra- and inter-query parallelism yield a throughput improvement of 12 with six components.

Query Performance with Concurrent Updates   Finally, we study the effect of concurrent updates on query performance. In this experiment, we have measured the throughput of the 22 TPC-R queries with different rates of concurrent updates. We have configured the coordinator to run up to one query and update concurrently at each component. Since we do not consider concurrency control issues, we have not used the TPC-R refresh functions for this experiment. Instead, we have used a stream of single-update transactions on LineItem. With full replication, such updates affect all components, while queries run on a single component. With hybrid, the situation is the reverse. Due to the single-action transactions, no conflict check is necessary. The results presented here are valuable to assess the performance with both designs under concurrent updates. To allow for easier comparison, we have included the runtimes of the pure query streams from Section 4.3 (no concurrent updates) in Figure 10 (cf. Line A).

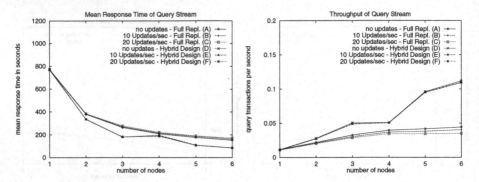

Fig. 10. Querying Performances with Concurrent Updates.

With both design alternatives, query performance decreases by about 10% with a concurrent stream of 10 updates per second. Increasing the update rate to 20 updates per second did not yield a much bigger deterioration. The slowest mean response time was about 20% slower than without updates. The overall results are the same as the ones for the scenario without updates. With a system size of six nodes, the throughput with the hybrid design is about three times higher, compared to full replication. Furthermore, the hybrid design proved more robust with regard to concurrent updates: the slowdown of the query stream is much less than with full replication. For example, with six nodes and 20 updates per second, the query performance of hybrid design (F) is 98% of the performance without updates (D), while it is at 79% with full replication (C).

5   Related Work

The bottomline of this section is that, even though admission control and routing are well-known concepts that have been investigated some time ago, previous research has not addressed these issues for OLAP queries.

Transaction Routing. In literature, the term 'transaction routing' normally means 'query routing': only with queries there typically is a choice of sites where to execute the transaction. — Carey et al. [2] address the problem of routing queries in a distributed (shared-nothing) database system with full replication. Based on the classification of queries into either CPU-bound or I/O-bound, they propose two algorithms: *BNQRD* ("Balance the Number of Queries by Resource

Demands") routes queries to the site with the smallest number of queries of the same class, while *LERT* ("Least Estimated Response Time") uses estimates of the I/O and CPU demand to route a query such that the estimated response time is minimized. The improvement of both algorithms is in the 10% − 20% range. [15] refines this approach by classifying queries not only into CPU- or I/O bound, but also into a finite set of types based on their resource demands, i.e., CPU, memory, and I/O considered separately for each disk. However, such classifications do not help in scenarios where all queries are I/O bound, e.g., queries that carry out scans over relations.

[17] presents an *affinity-based* approach to transaction routing. Incoming transactions are classified into affinity groups based on their pattern of page references. With this routing scheme, there is a component assigned to each affinity group, and each transaction goes to the component of its group. The classification is static, and does not consider changes of workload patterns. Several works extended this approach, e.g., [3] additionally introduced average response time goals for each class. However, all the classifications do not take the kind of access into account, but only the data referenced. Thus, if two queries scan the same large table, obstruction occurs. Finally, for a general classification framework of different routing strategies see [12].

Admission Control. Other related work has investigated admission/load control for a single database system. [9] presents a conflict-driven approach for automatic load control. Its algorithm prevents data-contention trashing by monitoring a performance metric, the so-called *conflict rate*, and by reacting to critical system states by postponing the execution of newly arriving transactions or aborting transactions currently running.

6   Conclusions

This work has shown that simple techniques for physical design and for routing in a database cluster architecture lead to significant performance improvements. Our scenario included OLAP queries, OLTP queries, and updates taken from the TPC-R benchmark. It has produced results that confirm our work on PowerDB, but that are also interesting in themselves: we have found out that affinity of queries is not larger than in scenarios others have considered earlier, i.e., OLTP queries only. On the other hand, we have observed that complex analysis queries may obstruct each other. This means that the system should not try to evaluate queries concurrently. Regarding a parallel architecture, we have evaluated two basic alternatives for data organization, full replication and hybrid, together with different routing schemes. It turns out that hybrid is superior to full replication in all the scenarios considered, and its speedup is more than linear. However, we should point out that the size of the biggest relation in the database limits the speedup obtained with hybrid. For a very large number of components, a combination of our elementary alternatives is probably appropriate. Finally, updates consisting of only one update per transaction lead to a very moderate slowdown of the query stream, e.g., 2% in one particular setting. This leads us to the overall conclusion that coordinator-based routing has good scaleup properties for scenarios with complex analysis queries. For the evaluation, we have used the PowerDB prototype, an implementation of a 'database of databases' based on off-the-shelf hardware and software components. In the future, we will investigate the effects of combining scheduling with routing. This includes full transaction support as well as reordering of the input queue.

References

1. C.K. Baru, et al. Dbs2 parallel edition. *IBM Systems Journal*, 34(2), 1995.
2. Michael J. Carey, Miron Livny, and Hongjun Lu. Dynamic task allocation in a distributed database system. In *Proceedings of the 5th IEEE Int. Conf. on Distributed Computing Systems (ICDCS), Denver, Colorado*, May 1985.
3. D. Ferguson, et al. Satisfying response time goals in transaction processing systems. In *Proceedings of the 2nd Int. Conf. on Parallel and Distributed Information Systems, San Diego*, 1993.
4. T. Grabs, K. Böhm, and H.-J. Schek. A document engine on a db cluster. *High Performance Transaction Systems Workshop (HPTS)*, Sept. 1999.
5. S. Ghandeharizadeh, D.J. DeWitt, and W. Qureshi. A performance analysis of alternative multi-attribute declustering strategies. In *Proceedings of the 1992 ACM SIGMOD Conference, San Diego, California*, pages 29–38, 1992.
6. H.V. Jagadish, L.V. Lakshmanan, and D. Srivastava. Snakes and sandwiches: Optimal clustering strategies or a warehouse. In *Proceedings of the 1999 ACM SIGMOD Conference, Philadelphia*, pages 37–48, June 1999.
7. H. Kaufmann and H.-J. Schek. Extending tp-monitors for intra-transaction parallelism. In *Proceedings of PDIS'96, Miami*, December 1996.
8. M. Mehta and D.J. DeWitt. Data placement in shared-nothing parallel database systems. *VLDB Journal*, 6(1):53–721, 1997.
9. Axel Moenkeberg and Gerhard Weikum. Conflict-driven load control for the avoidance of data-contention trashing. In *Proceedings of the 7th IEEE Int. Conf. on Data Engineering (ICDE), Kobe, Japan*, pages 632–639, 1991.
10. Oracle Corporation. *Oracle8 Server Concepts, Release 8.0, Chapter 5*, 1997.
11. M. T. Özsu and P. Valduriez. *Principles of Distributed Database Systems*, chapter 7–9. Prentice Hall, 1991.
12. Erhard Rahm. A framework for workload allocation in distributed transaction processing systems. *Systems Software Journal*, 18:171–190, 1992.
13. U. Röhm and K. Böhm. Working together in harmony — an implementation of the corba object query service and its evaluation. In *Proc. of the 15th IEEE Int. Conf. on Data Engineering, Sydney, Australia*, March 1999.
14. M. Rys, M. C. Norrie, and H.-J. Schek. Intra-transaction parallelism in the mapping of an object model to a relational multi-processor system. In *Proc. of the 22nd Int. Conf. on Very Large Databases, Mumbai, India*, 1996.
15. A. Thomasian. A performance study of dynamic load balancing in distributed systems. In *Proceedings of the 7th IEEE Int. Conf. on Distributed Computing Systems (ICDCS), Berlin, Germany*, 1987.
16. Transaction Processing Performance Council. Tpc-r benchmark specification rev. 1.0.1. Technical report, July 1999.
17. P. S. Yu, et al. Analysis of affinity based routing in multi-system data sharing. *Performance Evaluation*, 7:87–109, 1987.

Materialized View Selection
for Multi-cube Data Models

Amit Shukla, Prasad M. Deshpande, and Jeffrey F. Naughton

{amit,pmd,naughton}@cs.wisc.edu
University of Wisconsin - Madison, Madison WI 53706, USA

Abstract. OLAP applications use precomputation of aggregate data to improve query response time. While this problem has been well-studied in the recent database literature, to our knowledge all previous work has focussed on the special case in which all aggregates are computed from a single cube (in a star schema, this corresponds to there being a single fact table). This is unfortunate, because many real world applications require aggregates over multiple fact tables. In this paper, we attempt to fill this lack of discussion about the issues arising in multi-cube data models by analyzing these issues. Then we examine performance issues by studying the precomputation problem for multi-cube systems. We show that this problem is significantly more complex than the single cube precomputation problem, and that algorithms and cost models developed for single cube precomputation must be extended to deal well with the multi-cube case. Our results from a prototype implementation show that for multi-cube workloads substantial performance improvements can be realized by using the multi-cube algorithms.

1 Introduction

Online Analytical Processing (OLAP) systems use the *multidimensional model*, which expands the row and column approach of the relational model into multiple categories of data called dimensions. Dimensions such as time, product, line item, and geography categorize and summarize facts, like unit sales. We refer to this summarization as *aggregation*. Array arithmetic can be used to efficiently access cells and slices of the data. This results in support for complex analytical queries and applications. Other functionality supported by OLAP servers include functions that analyze, forecast, model, and answer "what if" questions about the data. They also have built-in functions for mathematical, financial, statistical, and time-series manipulation.

OLAP systems require fast interactive multidimensional data analysis of aggregates. To fulfill this requirement, database systems frequently statically precompute aggregate views on some subset of dimensions and their corresponding hierarchies. Virtually all OLAP products resort to some degree of precomputation of these aggregates. In order to understand the issues involved in precomputation, let us first look at how multidimensional data providers structure their data model. The most common approach used by OLAP products is called the *multi-cube* structure [8]. In this approach, the application designer segments the database into a set of multidimensional structures each of which is composed of a subset of the overall number of dimensions in the database. Products such as Oracle Express, Microstrategy DSS Suite, Informix Metacube and Microsoft OLAP services

C. Zaniolo et al. (Eds.): EDBT 2000, LNCS 1777, pp. 269–284, 2000.
© Springer-Verlag Berlin Heidelberg 2000

all use the multi-cube approach. Unfortunately, to date, the research community has virtually ignored the precomputation problem over multi-cubes, concentrating instead on the simpler single–cube model. To our knowledge, this is the first paper to address the precomputation problem in the context of multi-cube domains. Thus, queries which access multiple cubes are not taken into account when making a decision of what group bys to precompute.

The goal of this paper is twofold. First, to understand the ramifications of having a multi-cube data model, and second to understand the precomputation problem when there are queries which access multiple cubes. We examine existing techniques, and propose new techniques which can be utilized to solve this problem. We show that the multi-cube aggregate selection problem is significantly more complex than the single cube computation problem, and that algorithms and cost models developed for single cube precomputation must be extended to deal well with the multi-cube case. Our results show that for multi-cube workloads substantial performance improvements can be realized by using multi-cube algorithms instead of previously proposed single cube algorithms.

1.1 An Example Schema

In this paper, for clarity of exposition we will assume a Relational approach to OLAP. This means that each "cube" of a multi-cube model corresponds to a fact table. However, the material presented in this paper is not restricted to the relation model.

Consider a schema which consists of three dimensions, CustID, ProdID, and TimeID. They identify a customer, a product, and the time (in months). The schema has three fact tables. The first is Sales, a row of which captures the dollar sales and unit sales of a particular product by a certain store in some month. The second fact table is ProdCost, and it captures the cost of products on a month by month basis. The third table captures the shipping cost of products to various customers, and is called ShipCost.

Sales(ProdID, CustID, TimeID, Sales, UnitsSold)
ProdCost(ProdID, TimeID, PCost)
ShipCost(CustID, TimeID, SCost)

A user can specify "derived" or computed metrics, which are formed as a combination of other metrics. If the component metrics belong to different fact tables, then a join is required to generate the derived metric. For example, a "derived metric" called *Profit* = (Sales - UnitsSold * (PCost + SCost)), which is obtained from the natural join of the ProdCost and Sales tables along the ProdID, TimeID dimensions. Any queries which involve the Profit metric will require a join to be performed, unless the join is precomputed. For example, the following query requires a join:

SELECT Sales.CustID, SUM(Sales - UnitsSold * (PCost + SCost))
FROM ProdCost, ShipCost, Sales
WHERE ProdCost.ProdID = Sales.ProdID AND ProdCost.TimeID = Sales.TimeID
AND ShipCost.CustID = Sales.CustID AND ProdCost.TimeID = Sales.TimeID
GROUP BY Sales.CustID

1.2 Related Work

To find a set of aggregates to materialize, [7] proposes a greedy algorithm that attempts to maximize the benefit per unit space. They prove that if the largest aggregate view occupies a fraction f of the space available for precomputation, then the aggregates picked by the greedy algorithm have a benefit at least $(0.63-f)$ times the benefit of the optimal set of views for the same amount of space. The greedy algorithm restricts itself to a single cube data model.

Other related work includes [10] where the authors explore efficient algorithms for aggregate selection for single cube schemas. In [5], the authors consider the selection of views and indexes together. [6] presents a theoretical framework for the view-selection problem, and proposes a general algorithm and several heuristics. [13] surveys techniques proposed for determining what aggregates should be precomputed. When lattices are so large that even scanning them once is expensive, a different approach to precomputation is needed. [2] examine lattices with 10^{13} aggregate views. For such lattices, they provide heuristics to determine what views should be precomputed based a set of views the user supplies. All these papers ([13,5,6,2]) examine the aggregate selection problem in the context of a single cube. Finally, Shukla discusses aggregate selection algorithms in detail in [11].

1.3 Paper Organization

In section 2 we describe the lattice framework and cost model for the aggregate selection problem. We also describe an existing aggregate selection algorithm. Section 3 discusses the issues that arise when joining multiple cubes and precomputing their joins. Section 4 presents greedy algorithms for aggregate selection for multi-cube schemas. We carry out an experimental evaluation of the different precomputation algorithms in Section 5, and present insights into the problem of aggregate selection. Section 6 presents our conclusions.

2   Previous Work on Precomputation

In this section we first discuss the lattice framework for multidimensional datasets. This framework was first proposed by Harinarayan et al. [7]. Next we present the cost model for single cube schemas proposed by [7], and used in subsequent research [13,5,2,10]. In order to handle multi-cube schemas, we extend the single cube cost model to account for join costs required to compute derived metrics. Shukla et al. [10] had proposed an average query cost metric which makes visualization of the "goodness" of the aggregate set selected for precomputation easier. We repeat a description of average query cost in Section 2.4.

2.1 Lattice Framework for Multidimensional Datasets

Queries on multidimensional datasets can be modeled by the data cube operator. For distributive function such as sum, min, max, etc., some group bys can be computed from the precomputed result of another group by. In the example Sales table of Section 1.1, the aggregate on (ProdID, CustID) can be used to answer a query on (ProdID). This relation between aggregate views can be used to place them within a lattice framework as proposed in [7]. Aggregates are vertices of an n-dimensional cube. The following properties define a hypercube lattice $\mathcal{L}$ of aggregates.

(a) There exists a partial order $\preceq$ between aggregate views in the lattice. For aggregate views u and v, $v \preceq u$ if and only if v can be answered using the results of u by itself.

(b) There is a base view in the lattice, upon which every view is dependent. The base view is the database.

(c) There is a completely aggregated view "ALL", which can be computed from any other view in the lattice.

The aggregate selection problem is equivalent to selecting vertices from the underlying hypercube lattice. For example, the lattice $\mathcal{L}$ in Figure 1 represents the cube of the schema described in Section 1.1. The three dimensions ProdID, CustID, TimeID are represented by P, C, T respectively, and an aggregate view is labeled using the names of the attributes it is aggregated on. For example, view PC is aggregated on attributes ProdID and CustID. In Figure 1, if an edge connects two views, then the *higher* view can be used to precompute the other view. For example, there is an edge between PC and P. This means that PC can be used to compute P. If there is no precomputation, a query on P (ProdID) has to be answered using the base data, PCT (Sales table). When there are multiple cubes, we have a collection of lattices from which aggregates have to be picked for precomputation.

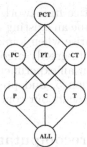

Fig. 1. The hypercube lattice corresponding to the example in Section 1.1.

2.2   The Cost Model

We use the cost model proposed by [7], in which the cost of answering a query (time of execution) is assumed to be equal to the number of tuples in the aggregate used to answer the query. An experimental validation of this cost model is provided in [7], where the authors used experiments on TPC-D Benchmark data. They found that there is an almost linear relationship between size and running time of a query. In summary, we assume that the cost of answering a query q is equal to the number of tuples read to return the answer.

2.3   The Benefit Metric

Informally, the *benefit of an aggregate view v* is computed by adding up the savings in query cost for each view w (including v), over answering it from the base view. If a set $\mathcal{S}$ of aggregate views is chosen for materialization, the benefit of $\mathcal{S}$ is the sum of the benefits of all views in $\mathcal{S}$. This is similar to the metric used by [7].

We now formally define the benefit of an aggregate view. If $\mathcal{S}$ is a set of aggregates that have already been selected for precomputation, the *benefit* of a view v is concerned with how materializing v improves the cost of computing other views, including itself. Let $\mathcal{C}(v)$ be the cost of computing another view from v. Looking back to our cost model, $\mathcal{C}(v)$ is the number of tuples in v. The benefit of v with respect to the $\mathcal{S}$, $\mathcal{B}(v, \mathcal{S})$, is defined below.

1. For each aggregate view $u \preceq v$, $\mathcal{B}_u$ is defined as:
   1.1 Let w be the least cost view in $\mathcal{S}$ such that $u \preceq w$
   1.2 If $\mathcal{C}(v) < \mathcal{C}(w)$, then $\mathcal{B}_u = \mathcal{C}(w) - \mathcal{C}(v)$, else $\mathcal{B}_u = 0$
2. $\mathcal{B}(v, \mathcal{S}) = \sum_{u \preceq v} \mathcal{B}_u$

In short, for each view u that is a descendant of v, we check to see if computing u from v is cheaper than computing u from any other view in the set $\mathcal{S}$. If this is the case, then precomputing v benefits u. Since all aggregates can be computed from the (unaggregated) base data, in step 1.1 we can always find a least cost aggregate view w (the base data in the worst case).

Definition 1. *The benefit per unit space of a view v is defined as:*

$$\mathcal{B}_s(v, \mathcal{S}) = \frac{\mathcal{B}(v, \mathcal{S})}{|v|}, \text{ where } |v| \text{ is the size of } v$$

2.4 Average Query Cost

Next, consider a set of lattices $\mathcal{L}$ with n views, $v_1, \ldots, v_n$. There are n different *templates* for queries, one for each view: $\mathcal{Q}_1, \mathcal{Q}_2, \ldots, \mathcal{Q}_n$. Let there be a set $\mathcal{S}$ of aggregate views precomputed, so that a query of view v_i can be most cheaply answered from a view u_i, $u_i \in \mathcal{S}$. Let queries on $\mathcal{S}$ occur with probabilities $p_1, p_2, \ldots, p_n$, then the *average query cost* is defined as:

$$\frac{1}{n} \cdot \sum_{i=1}^{n} p_i \mathcal{C}(u_i), \tag{1}$$

where $\mathcal{C}(u_i)$ is the cost of answering a query $\mathcal{Q}_i$ on a view v_i. In [10], we show that maximizing the benefit of a set $\mathcal{S}$ of aggregate views is the same as minimizing their average query cost.

2.5 Aggregate Selection

PickAggregates is a greedy algorithm proposed by Ullman etal. [7] to select aggregates for precomputation based on the above benefit model. The inputs to PickAggregates are: space – the amount of space available for precomputation, and $\mathcal{A}$, a set initially containing all aggregates in the lattice, except the base table. The output is $\mathcal{S}$, the set of aggregates to be precomputed. The algorithm is as follows:

Algorithm PickAggregates
WHILE (space > 0) **DO**
    w = aggregate having the maximum benefit per unit space in $\mathcal{A}$
    IF (space $- |w| > 0$) **THEN**
        space = space $- |w|$
        $\mathcal{S} = \mathcal{S} \cup w$
        $\mathcal{A} = \mathcal{A} - w$
    ELSE
        space = 0
    Update the benefit of affected nodes in the lattice
$\mathcal{S}$ is the set of aggregates picked by BPUS

The notion of benefit used by the above algorithm was described in Section 2.3. PickAggregates attempts to maximize the benefit of the set of aggregates picked. The authors prove that if the largest aggregate view occupies a fraction f of the space available for precomputation, then the aggregates picked by BPUS have a benefit at least $(0.63 - f)$ times the benefit of the optimal set of views for the same amount of space.

3   Issues in Multi-cube Models

In order to discuss precomputation for multi-cube data models, it is necessary to define the semantics of queries over multi-cube models. For concreteness, in this section we discuss the issues that arise in queries over multi-cube models, and state the conventions we will follow when dealing with queries over multi-cubes. We start by looking at the semantics of multidimensional queries.

3.1   Multidimensional Query Semantics

The multidimensional model expands the row and column approach of the relational model into multiple categories of data called dimensions. Dimensions such as time, product, line item, and geography categorize and summarize facts, like unit sales. Users can ask analytical queries using a multidimensional query tool. A multidimensional query consists of the dimensions of interest (such as time, product), the fact to be summarized (like unit sales), and conditions (such as time equals january 1999). If the query accesses multiple cubes, then the data model implicitly specifies the procedure to join the two cubes. Therefore, in this paper we adopt standard multidimensional semantics [12], which state that one should join on all the dimensions common to the cubes being joined.

Definition 2. *The columns used to join two fact tables are called their "join dimensions". The join dimensions between two tables include all their common dimensions.*

For example, from the schema of section 1.1, the join dimensions between Sales and ProdCost are ProdID, TimeID. Based on this definition of join dimensions, we can define our notation for uniquely identifying a group by.

Definition 3. *Let D_i represent a dimension, F_j represent a distributive aggregation function such as sum, min, max, and M_k represent a metric. Then the results of the query*get $D_1, \ldots, D_n, F_1(M_1), \ldots, F_r(M_r)$, *can be represented compactly as* $(D_1, \ldots, D_n)_{F_1(M_1), \ldots, F_r(M_r)}$

For example using this definition, the query: get ProdID, CustID, SUM(Sales) will be represented by $(ProdID, CustID)_{SUM(Sales)}$. In order to simplify the notation, we assume that if the aggregation function is not specified, then it is SUM. Therefore, the above query can be rewritten as $(ProdID, CustID)_{Sales}$. A corollary of this assumption by multidimensional query tools is that multidimensional queries are restricted to a subset of SQL in that one cannot express different ways of joining two fact tables - one always has to join on all the common dimensions.

3.2   Precomputed Joins

Let us look at the benefits of precomputing aggregates that result from joining multiple cubes. Our goal is to investigate the approach of computing the join of all the cubes. Precomputing the join of all the cubes creates a single large table that is in effect the "universal relation" [14], of which the multiple fact tables are projections. We scrutinize this approach to understand if it will enable us to apply single-table aggregate selection algorithms immediately. We show that this approach is fraught with hazards.

Consider the tables from the schema of Section 1.1. At a first glance, it seems as if we can extend the idea of precomputation of aggregates formed from a single fact table to precomputing aggregates formed from joins between fact tables. If we perform an *equi-join* between the two tables ShipCost and Sales,

SELECT Sales.CustID, Sales.ProdID, Sales.TimeID, SUM (Sales), SUM (SCost)
FROM Sales, ShipCost
WHERE Sales.CustID = ShipCost.CustID
AND Sales.TimeID = ShipCost.TimeID
GROUP BY Sales.CustID, Sales.ProdID, Sales.TimeID

to obtain a new table T_e with the schema T_e(CustID, ProdID, TimeID, S_Sales, S_SCost). This new table T_e can be precomputed and materialized in the database. However, T_e can be used only by queries which require a join of Sales and ShipCost. That is, T_e cannot be used to answer queries which access only one of the joined tables. This leads us to examine whether we can use full outer joins between tables to solve this problem.

When we perform the natural join between two tables ShipCost and Sales, only tuples from ShipCost that have matching tuples in Sales – and vice versa – appear in the result. Hence, tuples without a "related tuple" are eliminated from the result. *Outer joins* [3] were proposed to be used when one wants to retain all tuples from both tables being joined. In our example, an outer join between ShipCost and Sales would include tuples from both tables that join with each other as well as tuples that belong to only ShipCost, and only Sales, whether or not they have matching tuples in the other relation. Now, suppose that we perform a full outer join between the ShipCost and Sales tables.

SELECT Sales.CustID, Sales.ProdID, Sales.TimeID, SUM (Sales), SUM (SCost)
FROM Sales, ShipCost
WHERE Sales.ProdID(+) = ShipCost.ProdID(+)
AND Sales.TimeID(+) = ShipCost.TimeID(+)
GROUP BY Sales.CustID, Sales.ProdID, Sales.TimeID

In the above SQL, the (+) notation is used to denote an outer join. The outer join results in a new table T_o with the schema T_o(CustID, ProdID, TimeID, S_Sales, S_SCost). The queries (TimeID)$_{SCost}$ and (TimeID)$_{Sales}$ can be answered using the following SQL statements:

SELECT TimeID, SUM (SCost)
FROM T_o
WHERE SCost is NOT NULL
GROUP BY TimeID

SELECT TimeID, SUM (Sales)
FROM T_o
WHERE Sales is NOT NULL
GROUP BY TimeID

On the other hand, to answer a query on (CustID, TimeID)$_{Sales}$ requires the SQL.

SELECT CustID, TimeID, SUM (Sales)
FROM T_o
WHERE Sales is NOT NULL
AND SCost is NOT NULL
GROUP BY CustID, TimeID

For one derived metric, there are three possible aggregates which can be queried. Let us look at what happens when we join in a third table, ProdCost to T_o using an outer join. The aggregates which can be queried are: $(TimeID)_{Sales}$, $(TimeID)_{Sales,SCost}$, $(TimeID)_{PCost}$, $(TimeID)_{SCost,PCost}$, $(TimeID)_{SCost,Sales}$, and $(TimeID)_{PCost,Sales}$, $(TimeID)_{SCost,PCost,Sales}$. If we try to precompute aggregates from T_o, it is not clear which aggregate should be precomputed. The table used by $(TimeID)_{Sales}$ cannot be used to answer $(TimeID)_{Sales,SCost}$. Hence both aggregates have to considered separately by an aggregate selection algorithm for precomputation. This negates the advantage of having a single lattice. Besides, this goes against the data model design, which splits this one table into multiple tables for reasons of efficient storage, and to avoid the various anomalies associated with denormalized schemas. Clearly, it makes sense to precompute the natural join and compute the derived metric. In the above example, we would precompute $T_{\bowtie}$ = T_e(CustID, ProdID, TimeID, Profit), where Profit = (Sales - UnitsSold*(SCost - PCost)). This avoids the repetition of SCost for each ProdID, and repeating the PCost for each CustID.

From this discussion it is clear that the single universal relation like table approach is fraught with difficulty. This single table must be materialized from a full multi-way outer join. It is likely to be very large, and to contain a lot of redundant information. Finally, mapping multidimensional queries to this single table is likely to be inefficient because each aggregate requires a *slightly* different NULL value filtering, and the NULL filtering itself must be performed. Accordingly, we look for alternative approaches to speeding up OLAP queries using precomputation in section 4.

3.3   Multi-cube Join Quirks

Let us look at the various issues that arise when multiple-cubes are joined, and their join is precomputed. The basis of star schema data modelling is that the dimensions determine the measures and there are no other dependencies. That is, the metrics in a table are functionally dependent on the dimensions. If the base data consists of *aggregate views* of some base schema, then we cannot synthesize a lost dimension using joins. Let us assume that the following functional dependencies exist: $CPT \rightarrow Sales$; $PT \rightarrow PCost$, where C, P, and T stand for CustID, ProdID, and TimeID respectively. But if the tables in the database are actually:

    SalesNoTime(ProdID, CustID, Sales, UnitsSold)
    ProdCost(ProdID, TimeID, PCost)

Then, one cannot join the two tables to get $(TimeID)_{Sales}$. We call such an aggregate a *"phantom"* table since it can be obtained from the original data, but not from the derived view.

Another interesting quirk arises when performing a join between two tables; one cannot aggregate out a join column before performing the join. This leads to a lossy join in the sense that we lose the ability to distinguish which tuple should be in the result. For example, in the following schema,

    Sales(ProdID, CustID, TimeID, Sales, UnitsSold)
    CustCost(ProdID, CustID, TimeID, Cost)

with the functional dependencies $CPT \rightarrow Sales$, $PTC \rightarrow Cost$, if the join columns are ProdID (P), CustID (C), and TimeID (T), then we cannot join the aggregate $(CustID, ProdID)_{Sales}$ with $(ProdID, CustID, TimeID)_{Cost}$ to compute the result of a query. This importance of the need for this discussion will become clearer when we consider join benefits of aggregate nodes in a lattice.

3.4   The Subset Assumption

Now we discuss the subset assumption, and show how query semantics can be ambiguous without it. Consider a query which joins the ProdCost and ShipCost tables from the schema described in Section 1.1. The functional dependencies are: $PT \rightarrow PCost$, $CT \rightarrow SCost$. Neither of these two fact tables is contained in the other. This leads to interesting queries such as $(Customer)_{PCost}$ which are ambiguous since they can be obtained using either of the following two SQL statements.

```
SELECT ShipCost.Customer,  SUM (PCost)
FROM ShipCost, ProdCost
WHERE ShipCost.Time = ProdCost.Time
GROUP BY ShipCost.Customer
```

```
SELECT ShipCost.Customer, T1.Sum_PCost
FROM ShipCost, (SELECT SUM(PCost) AS Sum_PCost  FROM ProdCost) T1
```

The first SQL query joins the two tables on their join dimensions, which leads to an answer which may not have any meaning. The second SQL query computes the total product cost and repeats it for each customer. This might be more accurate in capturing what the user wants since the product cost is not dependent on the Customer attribute. We define "dimensional containment", which makes it easier to define what joins will result in meaningful results.

Definition 4. *When the dimensions of one fact table T_1 are a subset of the dimensions of another fact table T_2, then T_2 is said to dimensionally contain T_1.*

Since query semantics are ambiguous without it, we assume that when two or more tables are joined, one of the tables dimensionally contains the others. For example, from Section 1.1, the Sales table dimensionally contains both ShipCost and ProdCost. Tables dimensionally contained by the Sales table can be joined through it to answer queries. For example, a query such as $(CustID)_{PCost}$ can be unambiguously answered using the following SQL:

```
SELECT Sales.CustID,  SUM (ProdCost.PCost)
FROM Sales, ProdCost
WHERE Sales.Product = ProdCost.Product
AND Sales.Time = ProdCost.Time
GROUP BY Sales.CustID
```

Next we examine the precomputation problem for multi-cube systems. We start with a framework for multidimensional datasets.

4   New Aggregate Selection Techniques for Multi-cubes

In this section we first extend the cost model to account for the benefits of aggregates arising from the existence of multiple cubes. Then, we propose aggregate selection algorithms based on the new benefit model.

4.1   Benefits across Multiple Cubes

Let us look at the lattices $\mathcal{L}_1$, $\mathcal{L}_2$ for two cubes with schemas $T_1(A,B,M_1)$ and $T_2(A,B,C,M_2)$, where A, B, C are the dimensions, and M_1, M_2 are the measures. To obtain an aggregate containing a derived metric composed of metrics from both cubes, we have to join the two tables. In the multi-cube scenario, each precomputed aggregate can potentially have a join benefit in addition to the simple benefit

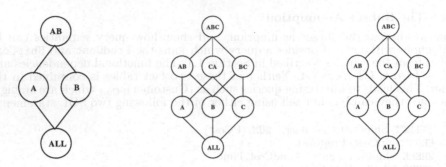

Fig. 2. Lattice $\mathcal{L}_1$ **Fig. 3.** Lattice $\mathcal{L}_2$ **Fig. 4.** Lattice $\mathcal{L}_{\bowtie}$

described in section 2.3. The benefit of the aggregate $\mathcal{L}_2$(A,B) is larger because any aggregate which required the join of $\mathcal{L}_1$(A,B) with $\mathcal{L}_2$(A,B,C) can now be obtained by joining $\mathcal{L}_1$(A,B) with $\mathcal{L}_2$(A,B). Thus, the precomputation of $\mathcal{L}_2$(A,B) has a benefit to its children in $\mathcal{L}_2$, and a benefit to the aggregates having derived metrics which result from a join. Let us quantify this join benefit.

We assume that joins are performed using a hash join based algorithm. So, if nodes $\mathcal{L}_1$(A,B) and $\mathcal{L}_2$(A,B) are joined to answer the query, then we assume that each node is scanned and partitioned on the join dimensions, and written to disk. Then these partition are read in to perform the join. Therefore, counting only I/O costs (as we have been doing so far), the join cost is approximately equal to $2(|\mathcal{L}_1(A,B)| + |\mathcal{L}_2(A,B)|)$. The derived metric results in a virtual lattice $\mathcal{L}_{\bowtie}$ (see Figures 2, 3, and 4). The aggregate $\mathcal{L}_2$(A,B) benefits $\mathcal{L}_{\bowtie}$(A,B) and all its descendants. The cost savings from precomputing $\mathcal{L}_2$(A,B) (ie, the benefit of $\mathcal{L}_2$(A,B)) are computed as follows: $2(|\mathcal{L}_1(A,B)| + |\mathcal{L}_2(A,B,C)|) - 2(|\mathcal{L}_1(A,B)| + |\mathcal{L}_2(A,B)|)$ which is equal to $2(|\mathcal{L}_2(A,B,C)| - |\mathcal{L}_2(A,B)|)$. The benefit per unit space of $\mathcal{L}_2$(A,B) increases by

$$\mathcal{J}_s(\mathcal{L}_2(A,B),\mathcal{S}) = \frac{2(|\mathcal{L}_2(A,B,C)| - |\mathcal{L}_2(A,B)|)}{|\mathcal{L}_2(A,B)|} * (\# \text{ benefited nodes in other lat.})$$

where $\mathcal{J}_s$ denotes the join benefit of $\mathcal{L}_2(A,B)$, and $\mathcal{S}$ is the set of aggregates already selected for precomputation. In addition, the number of nodes in $\mathcal{L}_1$ benefited by the precomputation of $\mathcal{L}_2(A,B)$ is 4 (namely, $\mathcal{L}_1(A,B)$, $\mathcal{L}_1(A)$, $\mathcal{L}_1(B)$, and $\mathcal{L}_1(ALL)$. From the discussion in section 3.3 about multi-cube join semantics, one should note however that the number of benefitted join nodes can be zero. For example, neither $\mathcal{L}_1(A)$ nor $\mathcal{L}_2(A)$ have any join benefit since joining either node with a node in the other lattice does not lead to a semantically valid answer. Thus we can define the total benefit of $\mathcal{L}_2(A,B)$ as: $\mathcal{B}_s(\mathcal{L}_2(A,B),\mathcal{S}) + \mathcal{J}_s(\mathcal{L}_2(A,B),\mathcal{S})$ We define the *principal* lattice as the lattice that dimensionally dominates all the other tables in the join. For example, $\mathcal{L}_2$ is the principal lattice for the derived metric obtained by joining $\mathcal{L}_2(A,B,C)$ with $\mathcal{L}_1(A,B)$ (see Figure 3). Aggregates from lattice $\mathcal{L}_1$ cannot be used in a join to obtain any nodes in $\mathcal{L}_{\bowtie}$ as it violates the rule that one cannot aggregate out a join column before performing the join (see section 3.3). Thus, only aggregates from the principal lattice can be used, and the dimensions of the least aggregated node of the principal node must contain the join dimensions. For example, the least aggregated node of $\mathcal{L}_2$ than can be used is (A,B).

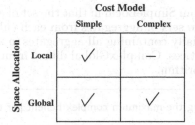

Fig. 5. The different multi-cube algorithm strategies

4.2   Aggregate Selection for Multi-cubes

Now we present three algorithms that pick aggregates for schemas having multi-cube data models. There are two different parameters that we vary to obtain different algorithms for aggregate selection. The first is the space allocation strategy, which can be either *local* or *global*. Local space allocation means that the available space for precomputation is divided up among the cubes, and aggregate selection algorithms are then run on each cube. Global space allocation means that space is not divided among the cubes, and aggregate selection algorithms pick the best aggregates from all cubes simultaneously. The second parameter is the cost model. The cost model can be *simple* (as described in section 2.3, which doesn't consider derived metrics and virtual cubes, or *complex* (as described in section 4.1, which accounts for the benefit arising from the joins required by derived metrics. The complex cost model was described in Section 4.1. The algorithms which result from varying these two parameters can be classified using the grid in Figure 5.

We will refer to the four algorithms by combining the type of cost model followed by the space allocation strategy. For example, *ComplexGlobal* refers to the algorithm which uses the complex cost model and a global space allocation strategy. The algorithm which results from using the complex cost model and a local space allocation strategy doesn't make sense since the cost model captures benefits across cubes, but the space allocation is local to each cube. Therefore, we don't discuss the *ComplexLocal* algorithm. We will study the SimpleLocal, SimpleGlobal, and ComplexGlobal algorithms. The experimental studies will compare the Simple and Complex cost models to quantify the improvement in query response time obtained by using the complex cost model.

The algorithm SimpleLocal works by dividing the space among the cubes, and then executing the algorithm PickAggregates on each cube. The inputs to PickAggregates are: space – the amount of space available for precomputation, and $\mathcal{A}$, a set initially containing all aggregates in the lattice, except the base table. The output is $\mathcal{S}$, the set of aggregates to be precomputed. The algorithm is as follows:

Algorithm PickAggregates
WHILE (space > 0) **DO**
      w = aggregate having the maximum simple benefit per unit space in $\mathcal{A}$
      IF (space − $|w|$ > 0) **THEN**
            space = space − $|w|$
            $\mathcal{S} = \mathcal{S} \cup w$
            $\mathcal{A} = \mathcal{A} - w$
      ELSE
            space = 0
      Update the benefit of affected nodes in the lattice
$\mathcal{S}$ is the set of aggregates picked by BPUS

SimpleGlobal differs from SimpleLocal in that the set of aggregates it has to choose from is the union of the sets of aggregates from each cube. Therefore, for Simple-Global, $\mathcal{A}$, is a set initially containing all aggregates in all the lattices, except the base tables of those lattices. ComplexGlobal differs from SimpleGlobal only in the second step of the algorithm.

---

w = aggregate having the maximum complex benefit per unit space in $\mathcal{A}$

The series of steps required to update the benefits of the aggregates in the lattices for ComplexGlobal is interesting. Thus a brief description is presented next.

Algorithm UpdateBenefits

   IF the aggregate is picked from a virtual lattice
         Update aggregates in the virtual lattice
         A node in the Principal lattice has a reduced benefit
   ELSE
         Update aggregates in the lattice
         Update the cheapest parent for any affected Virtual lattices
             also update the benefit of the previous cheapest parent.

Let us examine these steps in a little more detail. At each step the greedy algorithm picks the aggregate with the highest benefit. If the aggregate v with the maximum benefit is from a virtual lattice, then we have to first update all descendants of v to see if they can now be computed less expensively using v. The benefit of all the ancestors of v also has to be reduced since they no longer benefit the computation of v or any of its descendants which were updated. Now the benefits of the nodes which benefited v in the principal lattice have to be reduced because they no longer benefit v or its descendants.

On the other hand, if the aggregate u is picked from a non-virtual cube, then its descendants have to be updated since it might be cheaper to compute them using u. Ancestors of u also have to be updated to reduce their benefit (if any) to u. If u belongs to the cube $\mathcal{P}$, then aggregates in a virtual cube $\mathcal{V}$, for which $\mathcal{P}$ is the *principal* lattice, also have to be updated. Any aggregates v in $\mathcal{V}$ for which it is now cheaper to use u should be updated to reflect this information. In addition, the benefit of the previous aggregate used to compute v should be reduced if it is cheaper to compute v using u.

We can show that the greedy algorithm never performs too badly. In fact, if f is the ratio of the size of the largest aggregate to the amount of space available for precomputation, it can be shown that the benefit of the greedy algorithm is at least $(0.63 - f)$ of the benefit of the optimal algorithm. (0.63 arises from $(e-1)/e$, where e is the base of the natural logarithm). The proof is very similar to that presented for the greedy algorithm in [7], so we do not present it here. The algorithm *PBS* proposed in [10] can be used for lattices which are SR-hypercube (see [10]). In addition, the lattice must not be the principal lattice for some derived metric.

5   Experimental Evaluation

In this section we quantify the improvement in average query cost (average query response time) that can be achieved by the use of the complex cost model. We

Fact Table	Size (Tuples)	Component Dimensions	Metrics
Budget	250,000	Prod, Cust, Scenario, Time	UnitSales, DollarSales
Inv	50,000	Prod, Cust, Channel, Time	Inventory
ProdCost	221,000	Prod, Scenario, Time	ProductCost
Sales	146,000	Prod, Cust, Channel, Scenario, Time	UnitSales, DollarSales
ShipCost	64,000	Cust, Scenario, Time	ShippingCost

Table 1. The APB-1 benchmark schema

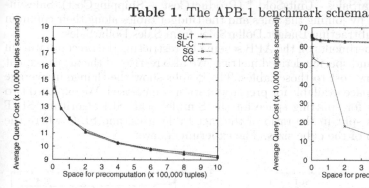
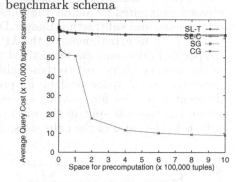

Fig. 6. The average query cost as space is varied for experiment 1 (2 tables, no derived metrics).

Fig. 7. The average query cost as space is varied for experiment 2 (3 tables, 1 derived metric).

used the schema for the APB-1 benchmark [1]. APB-1 is the industry standard benchmark defined by the OLAP council [1], which has most of the major OLAP vendors as members. The APB-1 benchmark database consists of five dimensions, Product, Customer, Channel, Scenario, and Time. The Product, Customer, and Time dimensions have 6, 2, and 3 level hierarchies defined on them respectively, while the channel and scenario dimensions don't have any hierarchies (only 1 level). The dimensions and their levels followed by the number of distinct values in parenthesis are described next. The Product dimension has 6 levels: Code (9000), Class (900), Group (100), Family (20), Line (7), and Division (2). The Customer dimension has 2 levels: Store (900) and Region (100). The Channel and Scenario dimensions have 1 level each (no hierarchy), and 10, 3 distinct values respectively. The Time dimension has three levels, Month (24), Quarter (8), and Year (2). There are five fact tables, Budget, Inv, ProdCost, Sales, and ShipCost. The Budget table contains the budgeted (scenario = 'Budget') UnitSales, and DollarSales of a product to a customer in a given month. The inventory is stored in the Inv table by product, customer, sales channel, and time. The ProdCost table stores product costs by product, scenario, and time, while ShipCost stores the shipping cost by customer, scenario and time. Lastly, the Sales table contains the actual sales of a product to a customer using some channel in some month. The five fact tables, their dimensions, and their sizes (in tuples) are shown in Table 1. We used the analytical formulas presented in [9] to estimate the size of aggregates formed by the cube operator. For example, consider a relation R having attributes A, B, C and D. Suppose we want to estimate the size of the group by on attributes A and B. If the number of distinct values of A is n_A and that of B is n_B, then the number of elements in $A \times B$ is $n_e = n_A n_B$. Let $|\mathcal{D}|$ be the number of tuples in the fact table. Using these values and an assumption that tuples are uniformly distributed, the number of elements in the group by on A and B is: $n_e - n_e(1 - 1/n_e)^{|\mathcal{D}|}$. This is similar to what is done in relational group by size estimation. All the experiments vary the amount of space used for precomputation, and plot the average query cost as a function of the amount of space.

The two derived metrics are *Profit*, and *Sales increase*. Profit is computed by joining the Sales, ProdCost and ShipCost tables along their common dimensions, with Profit = DollarSales - UnitsSold * (ProductCost + ShippingCost). Sales increase is computed by joining the Sales and the Budget tables along their common dimensions, and subtracting Budget.DollarSales from Sales.DollarSales.

We ran four experiments on the APB schema by restricting the precomputation to specific tables, and specific derived metrics. We also restricted the measurement of the average query cost to those tables. The graphs show the change in average query cost as the space available for precomputation is increased. We explored two different strategies for splitting space for the SimpleLocal (SL) algorithm, SL-T where the space is split in the ratio of the fact table sizes, and SL-C where the split is in the ratio of the cube sizes. The experiments are:

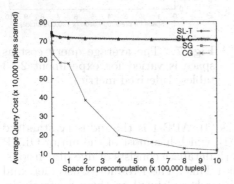

Fig. 8. The average query cost as space is varied for experiment 3 (4 tables, 2 derived metrics).

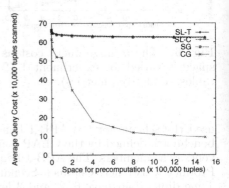

Fig. 9. The average query cost as space is varied for experiment 4 (5 tables, 2 derived metrics).

- Expt 1: The schema contains the Sales, Budget tables, and no derived metrics. This experiment studies the effect of multiple fact table without any derived metrics. Since there are no derived metrics, SimpleGlobal and ComplexGlobal pick the same set of aggregates. The graph is shown in Figure 6.
- Expt 2: The schema contains the Sales, ShipCost, ProdCost tables, and one derived metric (Profit). In this experiment we study the effect of a derived metrics formed from three fact tables. The graph is shown in Figure 7.
- Expt 3: The schemas consists of the Sales, ShipCost, ProdCost, Budget tables, and two derived metrics (Profit and Sales increase). In this experiment we study the effect of having two derived metrics. The graph is shown in Figure 8.
- Expt 4: This schema consists of the entire APB-1 database, and contains all five fact tables, and two derived metrics (Profit and Sales increase). The graph is shown in Figure 9.

In plotting these graphs we have assumed that queries uniformly access all aggregates in all lattices. The graphs show that as the space is increased, the average query cost reduces rather rapidly at first, and then the rate of decrease of average query cost reduces significantly. We can see that ComplexGlobal outperforms any of the other algorithms because it precomputes nodes in the lattice resulting from the virtual fact table having the derived metrics. For example, let us look at Figure 7. The sudden reduction in average query cost when the space changes from 100,000 to 200,000 tuples occurs because a detailed level aggregate of the virtual lattice now fits and is picked for precomputation. This results in a large decrease in the average query cost since queries on a large number of aggregates in the virtual lattice can now be computed using the detailed level aggregate instead of performing a join. The reduction in the average query cost is not as dramatic in Figures 8 and 9 because there are two virtual lattices, and there are actually two drops in the average query cost corresponding to the picking of detailed level aggregates from the two virtual lattices. As we can see from Figure 9, the average query cost of the set of aggregates picked using the simple cost model can be four times the average query cost of the set of aggregates picked using ComplexGlobal.

6   Conclusions

Precomputing aggregates on some subsets of dimensions and their corresponding hierarchies can substantially reduce the response time of a query. While this problem has been well-studied in the recent database literature, to our knowledge we are the first to study aggregate selection for multi-cube data models which compute aggregates over multiple cubes. In this paper, we analyzed the multi-cube precomputation problem in detail. We showed that this problem is significantly more complex than the single cube precomputation problem, and that algorithms and cost models developed for single cube precomputation must be extended to deal well with the multi-cube case. We proposed three different algorithms, SimpleLocal, SimpleGlobal, and ComplexGlobal which pick aggregates for precomputation from multi-cube schemas. Our results from a prototype implementation show that for multi-cube workloads substantial performance improvements can be realized by using multi-cube algorithms instead of the previously proposed single cube algorithms. In particular, the complex cost model considers join costs, leading to a much better set of aggregates picked for aggregation.

To conclude, we discuss which algorithm is appropriate for a given schema. The algorithm of choice will depend on the existence of derived metrics which require fact table joins to be performed. In the absense of derived metrics, the complex cost model reduces to the simple cost model. Further, if the lattice is a SR-hypercube lattice [10], the algorithm PBS proposed by [10] can be used. For non-SR-hypercube lattices, either SimpleLocal or SimpleGlobal can be used. If the schema contains derived metrics, ComplexGlobal should be used.

References

1. APB-1 Benchmark, Release II, November 1998. Available from http://www.olapcouncil.org/research/bmarkly.htm.
2. E. Baralis, S. Paraboschi, E. Teniente. Materialized View Selection in a Multidimensional Database, *Proc. of the 23rd Int. VLDB Conf.*, 1997.
3. R. Elmasri, S. Navathe, *Fundamentals of Database Systems*, The Benjamin/Cummings Publishing Company, Inc., 1989.

4. J. Gray, A. Bosworth, A. Layman, H. Pirahesh. Data Cube: A Relational Aggregation Operator Generalizing Group-By, Cross-Tab, and Sub-Totals, *Proc. of the 12th Int. Conf. on Data Engg.*, pp 152-159, 1996.
5. H. Gupta, V. Harinarayan, A. Rajaraman, J.D. Ullman. Index Selection for OLAP. *Proc. of the 13th ICDE*, 208–219, 1997.
6. H. Gupta. Selection of Views to Materialize in a Data Warehouse. *Proc. of the Sixth ICDT*, 98–112, 1997.
7. V. Harinarayan, A. Rajaraman, J.D. Ullman. Implementing Data Cubes Efficiently, *Proc. ACM SIGMOD Int. Conf. on Man. of Data*, 205–227, 1996.
8. Nigel Pendse and Richard Creeth, The Olap Report. Information available from http://www.olapreport.com/.
9. A. Shukla, P.M. Deshpande, J.F. Naughton, K. Ramasamy, Storage Estimation for Multidimensional Aggregates in the Presence of Hierarchies, *Proc. of the 22nd Int. VLDB Conf.*, 522–531, 1996.
10. A. Shukla, P.M. Deshpande, J.F. Naughton, Materialized View Selection for Multidimensional Datasets, *Proc. of the 24th Int. VLDB Conf.*, 1998.
11. A. Shukla, Materialized View Selection for Multidimensional Datasets, *Ph.D. Dissertation, University of Wisconsin - Madison*, 1999.
12. Erik Thomsen, *Olap Solutions : Building Multidimensional Information Systems*, John Wiley & Sons, 1997.
13. J.D. Ullman, Efficient Implementation of Data Cubes Via Materialized Views A survey of the field for the 1996 KDD conference.
14. J.D. Ullman, Principles of Database and Knowledge–base Systems, Volume II, Computer Science Press, 1988.

Semistructured Data

On Bounding-Schemas for LDAP Directories

Sihem Amer-Yahia[1], H. V. Jagadish[2], Laks V. S. Lakshmanan[3], and Divesh Srivastava[1]

[1] AT&T Labs–Research, Florham Park, NJ 07932, USA
[2] University of Michigan, Ann Arbor, MI 48109, USA
[3] Concordia University, Montreal, QC H3G 1M8, Canada and IIT–Bombay, India
{sihem,divesh}@research.att.com, jag@eecs.umich.edu, laks@cs.concordia.ca

Abstract As our world gets more networked, ever increasing amounts of information are being stored in LDAP directories. While LDAP directories have considerable flexibility in the modeling and retrieval of information for network applications, the notion of schema they provide for enabling consistent and coherent representation of directory information is rather weak. In this paper, we propose an expressive notion of *bounding-schemas* for LDAP directories, and illustrate their practical utility. Bounding-schemas are based on lower bound and upper bound specifications for the content and structure of an LDAP directory. Given a bounding-schema specification, we present algorithms to efficiently determine: (i) if an LDAP directory is legal w.r.t. the bounding-schema, and (ii) if directory insertions and deletions preserve legality. Finally, we show that the notion of bounding-schemas has wider applicability, beyond the specific context of LDAP directories.

1 Introduction

X.500 style directories have proliferated with the growth of the Internet, and are being used to keep track of a wide variety of information such as corporate white pages about people and organizations, network resources and policies [1], and operating system resources. The dominant protocol for accessing such information is the lightweight directory access protocol (LDAP), and such directories have come to be known as LDAP directories. In a nutshell, an LDAP directory consists of nodes (referred to as directory entries) organized in a forest, with each directory entry containing a set of (attribute, value) pairs for some entity, and the hierarchy (forest) of entries typically reflecting real-world organizational and functional classifications. LDAP directory applications then retrieve entries that match (a boolean combination of) conditions on individual attributes, the retrieval typically scoped to some subtree of the hierarchy.

In most directory applications, entities of the same type may be quite heterogeneous. For example, person john may have no e-mail address (or may have deliberately suppressed it) and no cell phone number, person jack may have a single e-mail address and several cell numbers, while person mary may have multiple e-mail addresses and cell numbers. In such situations, relational databases

C. Zaniolo et al. (Eds.): EDBT 2000, LNCS 1777, pp. 287–301, 2000.
© Springer-Verlag Berlin Heidelberg 2000

have used null values, with limited success, in an attempt to capture the heterogeneity. A possible solution might be to treat e-mail address as a set-valued attribute; however, this suffers from the disadvantage of introducing an additional level of indirection for accessing an e-mail address, and it is also very inefficient in representation if only a small fraction of persons have multiple e-mail addresses. Defining sub-types of `person` based on the existence of certain attributes, while sometimes useful, can cause the number of sub-types to become combinatorial in the number of attributes. Given the pervasive heterogeneity of entities represented in the directory, traditional class definitions and traditional class inheritance are both inappropriate as directory schema elements.

LDAP directories facilitate the modeling of heterogeneous real-world entities using two complementary approaches. First, an attribute associated with an *object class* (a term used in the LDAP literature for a weak notion of class) may be denoted to be an *allowed* attribute, permitting each entity that belongs to that object class to specify zero or more distinct values for this attribute. Thus, e.g., `cellularPhone` can be specified to be an allowed attribute of object class `person`. Second, an object class can be denoted as *auxiliary*, permitting an entity to belong to zero or more auxiliary object classes, and to specify (possibly multiple) values for the attributes of the auxiliary object classes. This is in contrast to requiring, as is traditionally the case in object-oriented databases, that an entity belong to a single, most-specific class in a class hierarchy. Thus, e.g., an object class `online`, with allowed attribute `mail`, can be denoted as auxiliary, and both a `person` entity and an `organization` entity can additionally belong to object class `online`.

LDAP schemas, while very flexible, are too weak for their intended usage of enabling information to be represented in the directory in a consistent fashion. One cannot restrict inappropriate combinations of object classes. For example, one cannot *prohibit* a `person` from also belonging to the auxiliary object class `packetRouter`. Similarly, even though entities are structured in a forest, usually with some principles in mind, there is no way to specify the principles that have been followed. For example, we might want to require that each `organization` have a `person` as a descendant, and prohibit any `person` from having an `organization` as a child. There is no mechanism for stating and enforcing such schema specifications in the LDAP model. The purpose of this paper is to address such limitations, thereby ensuring that applications have a coherent view of the directory data. We make the following contributions:

– We propose a rich and useful notion of schema called *bounding-schemas*, that restricts legal directory instances, without sacrificing the flexibility offered by the LDAP model (Section 2). The key idea is to specify lower bounds and upper bounds on both (i) Content Schema: what attributes and object classes to expect for any entity type, and (ii) Structure Schema: what hierarchical relationships to expect between entity types represented in the directory.
– We present algorithms to efficiently determine: (i) if an LDAP directory is *legal*, i.e., it satisfies the bounding-schema (Section 3), and (ii) if directory updates preserve legality (Section 4).

– We demonstrate that the notion of bounding-schemas has wider applicability, beyond the specific context of LDAP directories, to semi-structured data models (Section 5).

For brevity, we focus on the core ideas in this paper, and refer the reader to the online technical report [4] for additional details, and for a treatment of the issue of checking consistency of bounding schemas.

1.1 Motivating Example

We now describe a simple corporate white pages directory to motivate the need for bounding-schemas in LDAP directories. More sophisticated directories, such as those for directory-enabled network (DEN) applications, also exhibit similar needs for bounding-schemas.

An organization like AT&T employs a diverse collection of persons, such as researchers, developers, managers, secretaries, consultants, summer students, short term visitors, etc. These persons work in a wide variety of organizational units, across the organization. A corporate white pages directory needs to represent information both about the individual persons and the organizational units, in order to support a variety of queries. LDAP directories are very well suited for white pages directories, and are used extensively for this purpose.

As an example, a corporate white pages LDAP directory could consist of an entry for each employee, and one for each organization unit. Information about an entity is represented as a set of (attribute, value) pairs in the directory entry corresponding to the entity. For instance, the entry corresponding to person laks may contain, among other (attribute, value) pairs, two values for the attribute mail. The values of the special attribute objectClass denote the various types associated with the entity. The hierarchical organization of the directory entries in the corporate white pages reflects a natural organizational hierarchy. Employees directly belonging to an organization unit are created as children entries of the entry corresponding to the organizational unit. Thus, persons sihem and laks might directly belong to the databases organizational unit, and indirectly belong to the attLabs organizational unit, which may be an ancestor of databases in the directory.

Schema specifications are important to ensure coherency of data, and to reflect the principles used in structuring the data in the directory. One useful "content schema" specification for ensuring a certain basic level of consistency among the various employees is to *require* that each person entry in the directory specify values for the attributes name and uid. Again, while person entries can additionally belong to facultyMember, it is natural to *forbid* an orgUnit from also belonging to facultyMember. Similarly, "structure schema" specifications would *require* that each orgUnit have at least one person as a descendant, and *forbid* person entries from having children entries.

This combination of lower bound (required) and upper bound (complement of forbidden) schema specifications gives rise to the notion of bounding-schemas for directories. Bounding-schemas ensure coherency of data, while permitting considerable heterogeneity in the directory instance.

2   Bounding-Schemas

The directory data model centers around the notions of attributes and object classes. We assume infinite sets $\mathcal{A}, \mathcal{C}$ of attributes and object classes, as well as a set $\mathcal{T}$ of types. Each type $t \in \mathcal{T}$ has an associated domain, denoted $dom(t)$. We use $dom(\mathcal{T})$ to abbreviate $\bigcup_{t \in \mathcal{T}} dom(t)$. Without loss of generality, we assume that the attribute `objectClass` is in $\mathcal{A}$.

Directory Instance: Just as the relational model uses relations as a single uniform data structure, the directory model uses a *forest* as a single data structure. We call nodes of this forest *directory entries*. Each entry may "hold" information in the form of a set of (attribute, value) pairs. Informally, an entry may be regarded as an entity and an object class as an entity type. These intuitions are formalized below. We assume an infinite set $\mathcal{R}$ of objects called directory entries.

Definition 1 [Directory Instance]   A *directory instance* $\mathcal{D} = (R, class, val, N)$ is such that:

1. $R \subset \mathcal{R}$ is a finite set of directory entries.
2. the function $class : R \rightarrow 2^{\mathcal{C}}$ associates with each directory entry a finite, non-empty set of object classes from $\mathcal{C}$, to which the entry belongs.
3. $val : R \rightarrow 2^{\mathcal{A} \times dom(\mathcal{T})}$ is a function that associates with each directory entry r a finite set of (attribute, value) pairs such that: (a) each attribute value of r is of the right type, and (b) the object classes that r belongs to must be the values of r's `objectClass` attribute.
4. $N \subset R \times R$ is a binary relation, such that the graph (R, N) is a forest.[1]   ∎

Directory Schema: A directory schema consists of two components, reflecting the nature of directory instances. The first component is a *content schema*, which says what attributes and object classes to expect for entity types represented in the directory, and is itself subdivided into two parts: an *attribute schema* and a *class schema*. The second component is a *structure schema*, which says what hierarchical relationships to expect between entity types represented in the directory. These components are formally presented below.

Definition 2 [Attribute Schema]   An *attribute schema* $\mathbf{A} = (C, A, \alpha_r, \alpha_a)$ consists of: (1) a finite set of object classes $C \subset \mathcal{C}$, (2) a finite set of attributes $A \subset \mathcal{A}$, (3) a function $\alpha_r : C \rightarrow 2^A$ that specifies the *required* attributes for each object class, and (4) a function $\alpha_a : C \rightarrow 2^A$ that specifies the *allowed* attributes for each object class. We require that $\alpha_r(c) \subseteq \alpha_a(c), \forall c \in C$.   ∎

Attribute schemas are part of the standard LDAP schema specification. The intuition is that a directory entry that belongs to a given object class must have

---

[1] In an LDAP directory, each entry is associated with a "distinguished name", and the set of distinguished names induces the forest structure. For the purpose of this paper, this abstraction of the forest is adequate.

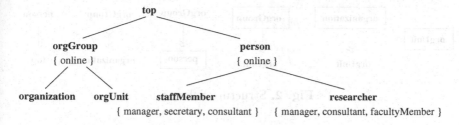

Fig. 1. Class Schema

one or more values for each of the required attributes of the class, and may have zero or more values for the additional allowed attributes of the class.

Since a directory entry can belong to multiple object classes, the attribute schema is not sufficient by itself to identify which attributes cannot occur in an entry, or which attributes cannot co-occur. The class schema, described next, will help us resolve this issue. LDAP directories distinguish between *core* object classes[2] and *auxiliary* object classes. Notationally, we assume that the classes C are partitioned into infinite sets C_c of core classes and C_x of auxiliary classes.

Definition 3 [Class Schema]   A *class schema* $\mathbf{H} = (C, E, \text{Aux})$ consists of:

- A finite set of core object classes $C_c = C \cap C_c$, which includes top.
- A binary relation $E \subset C_c \times C_c$, such that the graph (C_c, E) is a tree with top as its root. Informally, the tree (C_c, E) represents a single inheritance hierarchy of core classes. Each entry must belong to some core object class. If an entry e belongs to core object class c_i, and c_j is the parent of c_i, then e is required to belong to c_j as well. We denote this by $c_i - \boxed{c_j}$. Also, for core object classes c_i and c_j, when neither of c_i and c_j is a superclass of the other, an entry e cannot belong to both c_i and c_j. We denote this by $c_i \nrightarrow c_j$.
- A set of auxiliary classes $C_x = C \cap C_x$.
- A function Aux : $C_c \rightarrow 2^{C_x}$ that associates a set of auxiliary classes with each core class. Informally, an entry that belongs to a core class c may also belong to classes in Aux(c). ∎

Figure 1 depicts a possible class schema for the white pages directory application. The core object classes form a single inheritance hierarchy, e.g., we can see that organization $-\boxed{\text{orgGroup}}$ and organization $\nrightarrow$ person hold. The auxiliary object classes associated with each core object class are indicated in parentheses. Thus, according to this class schema, if an entry laks belongs to core class researcher, it must also belong to core classes person and top, and may additionally belong to auxiliary classes facultyMember and online.

We have focused on the different components of a directory's content schema so far. We present the structure schema next.

---

[2] Core object classes are referred to as "structural" object classes in the LDAPv3 proposed standard [15,14]. We use the term "core" class to avoid confusion with the structure schema of a directory.

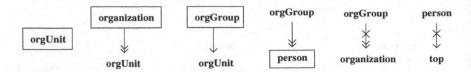

Fig. 2. Structure Schema

Definition 4 [Structure Schema] A *structure schema* is a triple $\mathbf{S} = (C_r, E_r, E_f)$ of *required object classes* C_r, *required structural relationships* E_r, and *forbidden structural relationships* E_f, defined as follows:

- $C_r \subseteq C_c$ is a subset of core object classes. We use the notation $\boxed{c}$ to denote that $c \in C_r$. Informally, $\boxed{c}$ says that there must be at least one directory entry one of whose core object classes is c.
- $E_r \subseteq C_c \times \{ch, de, pa, an\} \times C_c$ is a relation. We use the notations $c_i \longrightarrow \boxed{c_j}$, $c_i \longrightarrow\!\!\!\rightarrow \boxed{c_j}$, $\boxed{c_j} \longrightarrow c_i$, and $\boxed{c_j} \longrightarrow\!\!\!\rightarrow c_i$ to denote triples of the form (c_i, ch, c_j), (c_i, de, c_j), (c_i, pa, c_j) and (c_i, an, c_j), respectively, in E_r.
  Informally, $c_i \longrightarrow \boxed{c_j}$ says each entry that belongs to object class c_i must have at least one entry that belongs to object class c_j as its child. Other patterns have an analogous meaning.
- $E_f \subseteq C_c \times \{ch, de\} \times C_c$ is a relation. We use the notation $c_i \not\rightarrow\!\!\!\rightarrow c_j, c_i \not\rightarrow\!\!\!\rightarrow c_j$ to denote triples of the form $(c_i, ch, c_j), (c_i, de, c_j)$ in E_f.
  Informally, $c_i \not\rightarrow\!\!\!\rightarrow c_j$ says for no pair of entries, say e_i and e_j, that belong to object classes c_i and c_j respectively, can e_j be a child of e_i. $c_i \not\rightarrow\!\!\!\rightarrow c_j$ has a similar meaning. ∎

For the white pages directory, the structure schema is depicted in Figure 2. For example, the required structural relationship orgGroup $\longrightarrow\!\!\!\rightarrow$ $\boxed{\text{person}}$ intuitively says that every organizational group must (directly or indirectly) employ a person. Such a person could additionally belong to either of the object classes researcher or staffMember; the structure schema does not mandate either. Similarly, the forbidden structural relationship person $\not\rightarrow\!\!\!\rightarrow$ top says that a person cannot have any child in a legal directory instance.

Definition 5 [Directory Schema] A *directory schema* $\mathcal{S} = (\mathbf{A}, \mathbf{H}, \mathbf{S})$ consists of an attribute schema $\mathbf{A}$, a class schema $\mathbf{H}$, and a structure schema $\mathbf{S}$. ∎

Taken together, the three components of a directory schema can be regarded as specifying a *lower bound* (i.e., what must be present in a directory instance) and an *upper bound* (i.e., what is allowed, or equivalently, what is forbidden). Thus, the directory schema is indeed a *bounding-schema*.

Informally, a directory instance is *legal* w.r.t. a given schema provided it lies within the "bounds" imposed by the different components of the schema. We have presented the intuition above, and suppress formal details because of space limitations; these are available in the technical report [4].

3 Testing Legality of Directory Instances

The principal reason for specifying a directory schema is to ensure consistent and coherent representation of information in the directory. This is guaranteed by testing legality of instances.

3.1 Content Schema

Testing that a directory instance is legal with respect to the content schema, i.e., the attribute and class schemas, can be performed on each directory entry independently. Essentially, the test involves verifying that each directory entry contains the *required* object class co-occurrences and attributes, and only contains the *allowed* object class co-occurrences and attributes.

Testing that an entry e satisfies the class schema can be performed in a straightforward manner in time $O(|class(e)| + \max_{c \in C_c}(|\text{AUX}(c)|) * depth(\mathbf{H}))$, where $|class(e)|$ is the number of object classes that entry e belongs to, $depth(\mathbf{H})$ is the depth of the core class hierarchy, and $\max_{c \in C_c}(|\text{AUX}(c)|)$ denotes the maximum number of auxiliary classes associated with any core class in the schema.

Testing that an entry e satisfies the attribute schema can be performed in a straightforward manner in time $O(|val(e)| + \sum_{c \in class(e)}(|\alpha_a(c)|))$, where $|val(e)|$ is the number of (attribute, value) pairs of e, and $|\alpha_a(c)|$ denotes the number of allowed attributes associated with object class c.

3.2 Structure Schema

Testing that a directory instance is legal with respect to the structure schema, in particular the required and forbidden structural relationships, involves checking a set of binary relationships between directory entries. A straightforward approach would compare every pair of (parent, child) entries and every pair of (ancestor, descendant) entries, against the structure schema. This approach has the following drawbacks:

- It takes time $O((|E_r|+|E_f|)*|\mathcal{D}|^2)$, where E_r is the set of required structural relationships, and E_f is the set of forbidden structural relationships. This is quadratic in the size of the directory instance $\mathcal{D}$.
- An important problem concerning legality is efficiently testing its preservation under directory updates. The above approach offers little insight into this problem.

We now present an elegant and efficient technique for testing legality against the structure schema. First, we focus only on the required and forbidden structural relationships, E_r and E_f, of $\mathbf{S}$. The key idea behind our technique for testing legality of a directory instance $\mathcal{D}$ against (E_r, E_f) is to translate each relationship in E_r and each relationship in E_f into a hierarchical selection query in the directory query language introduced in [10]. We then show that $\mathcal{D}$ is legal w.r.t. (E_r, E_f) if and only if *each of the hierarchical selection queries thus*

Schema Element	Hierarchical Selection Query
$c_i \longrightarrow \boxed{c_j}$	$(-$ $($objectClass$=c_i)$ $(c$ $($objectClass$=c_i)$ $($objectClass$=c_j)))$
$\boxed{c_j} \longrightarrow c_i$	$(-$ $($objectClass$=c_i)$ $(p$ $($objectClass$=c_i)$ $($objectClass$=c_j)))$
$c_i \longrightarrow\!\!\!\!\rightarrow \boxed{c_j}$	$(-$ $($objectClass$=c_i)$ $(d$ $($objectClass$=c_i)$ $($objectClass$=c_j)))$
$\boxed{c_j} \longrightarrow\!\!\!\!\rightarrow c_i$	$(-$ $($objectClass$=c_i)$ $(a$ $($objectClass$=c_i)$ $($objectClass$=c_j)))$
$c_i \not\!\!\rightarrow c_j$	$(c$ $($objectClass$=c_i)$ $($objectClass$=c_j))$
$c_i \not\!\!\rightarrow\!\!\!\!\rightarrow c_j$	$(d$ $($objectClass$=c_i)$ $($objectClass$=c_j))$
$\boxed{c}$	$($objectClass$=c)$

Fig. 3. Translating Structure Schema to Hierarchical Selection Queries

obtained (and hence their disjunction) is empty. It was established in [10] that every hierarchical selection query Q can be evaluated very efficiently, with an I/O complexity of $O(|Q| * |\mathcal{D}|)$, where $|Q|$ is the size of the query Q, when the directory entries are sorted. This forms the basis for an efficient test for legality w.r.t. (E_r, E_f).

Consider the required structural relationship orgGroup $\longrightarrow\!\!\!\!\rightarrow \boxed{\text{person}}$ from our white pages directory. Recall that $c_i \longrightarrow\!\!\!\!\rightarrow \boxed{c_j}$ says each entry that belongs to object class c_i must have at least one descendant entry that belongs to object class c_j. The hierarchical selection query $(d$ (objectClass=orgGroup) (objectClass=person)) retrieves each directory entry that belongs to object class orgGroup provided that it has at least one descendant entry that belongs to object class person. The following hierarchical selection query retrieves the remaining directory entries that belong to object class orgGroup:

Q_1: $(-$ (objectClass=orgGroup)
          $(d$ (objectClass=orgGroup)(objectClass=person)))

Observe that a directory instance $\mathcal{D}$ is legal w.r.t. the required structural relationship orgGroup $\longrightarrow\!\!\!\!\rightarrow \boxed{\text{person}}$ if and only if the query Q_1 evaluated against $\mathcal{D}$ is empty. The other required structural relationships in E_r can be translated to hierarchical selection queries [10] in an analogous manner.

Consider now a forbidden structural relationship of the form person $\not\!\!\rightarrow\!\!\!\!\rightarrow$ top from our white pages directory. Recall that $c_i \not\!\!\rightarrow\!\!\!\!\rightarrow c_j$ says for no pair of entries, say e_i and e_j, that belong to object classes c_i and c_j respectively, can e_j be a descendant of e_i. Thus, the query

Q_2: $(c$ (objectClass=person) (objectClass=top))

evaluated against $\mathcal{D}$ is empty if and only if $\mathcal{D}$ is legal w.r.t. person $\not\!\!\rightarrow\!\!\!\!\rightarrow$ top. The other forbidden structural relationship in E_f can be translated to a hierarchical selection query analogously. The complete set of translations from relationships in E_r and E_f to hierarchical selection queries is provided in Figure 3.

Finally, we focus on the required object classes C_r of **S**. Recall that $\boxed{c}$ says that there must be at least one directory entry one of whose object classes is c.

As an example, a requirement such as $\boxed{\text{orgUnit}}$, from our white pages directory, is satisfied by $\mathcal{D}$ iff the query:

Q_3: (objectClass=orgUnit)

evaluated against $\mathcal{D}$ is non-empty. So, $\mathcal{D}$ is legal w.r.t. C_r if and only if each of the selection queries thus obtained (and hence their conjunction) is *non-empty*.

To summarize, efficient legality testing of $\mathcal{D}$ against the structure schema **S** is based on reductions to the directory queries of [10], which are known to be efficiently evaluable.

Theorem 1. (Legality Testing) *Consider a directory instance $\mathcal{D}$ and a directory schema $\mathcal{S} = (\mathbf{A}, \mathbf{H}, \mathbf{S})$. Testing if $\mathcal{D}$ is legal w.r.t. $\mathcal{S}$ can be performed in time* $O(|\mathcal{D}| * (\max_{e \in \mathcal{D}}(|class(e)|) + \max_{c \in C_c}(|\text{AUX}(c)|) * depth(\mathbf{H}) + \max_{e \in \mathcal{D}}(|val(e)|)$ $+ \max_{e \in \mathcal{D}}(\sum_{c \in class(e)}(|\alpha_a(c)|)) + |\mathbf{S}|)).$ ∎

4   Testing Legality Against Updates

In this section, we describe how to efficiently check whether updates to the directory instance preserve legality.

4.1   Granularity of Updates for Testing Legality

The entries in an LDAP directory instance are organized in a forest. LDAP directories require that newly created entries must either be roots in the forest, or must be children of existing directory entries. Similarly, LDAP directories allow only leaf entries to be deleted from the forest; a directory entry that has descendants cannot be deleted, unless all its descendants are first deleted.

We consider "update transactions", consisting of a *sequence* of distinct directory entry insertions and deletions. Our goal is to incrementally determine whether such an update transaction would preserve legality. A key question before we can proceed with checking preservation of legality under updates is: what is a meaningful granularity of updates for testing legality?

Testing legality at the granularity of a single directory entry insertion or deletion is not a robust choice, under the notion of a directory schema. The problem is that violation of legality caused by one update operation may be reversed by another update operation in the same transaction, which is awkward. Consider for example, a directory instance that is updated by adding a new orgUnit entry as a child of another orgUnit entry, and by adding a few person entries as children of the newly created orgUnit, such that the updated directory instance is legal. However, if one were to test for legality immediately after the new orgUnit entry had been added, the required structural relationship orgGroup $\longrightarrow\!\!\!\!\!\rightarrow$ $\boxed{\text{person}}$ would be violated, because none of its person child entries has been added yet.

While one could use the entire sequence of directory entry insertions and deletions as the granularity for testing preservation of legality, such an approach is neither modular, nor does it allow an elegant characterization of cases where incremental legality checking is possible. For the purpose of our analysis, we propose abstracting a directory update transaction as inserting a set of subtrees into, and deleting a set of subtrees from, the forest, where no two subtree roots form an (ancestor, descendant) pair. This abstraction has a very desirable modularity property as shown by the following result.

Theorem 2. *Let S be a directory schema, and $\mathcal{D}$ a legal instance of S. Consider an update transaction $\mathcal{U}$ that is a sequence of distinct directory entry insertions into and deletions from $\mathcal{D}$. Let $\mathcal{D}'$ denote the directory instance obtained by applying $\mathcal{U}$ to $\mathcal{D}$. Let $\Delta\mathcal{D}_1, \ldots, \Delta\mathcal{D}_n$ denote the subtrees inserted into $\mathcal{D}$ as a result of $\mathcal{U}$, and $\Delta\mathcal{D}_{n+1}, \ldots, \Delta\mathcal{D}_m$ denote the subtrees deleted from $\mathcal{D}$ as a result of $\mathcal{U}$. Let $\mathcal{D}_i, 1 \leq i \leq m$ denote the instance obtained by updating $\mathcal{D}_{i-1}$ by (adding or deleting, as appropriate) $\Delta\mathcal{D}_i$, where $\mathcal{D} = \mathcal{D}_0$ and $\mathcal{D}' = \mathcal{D}_m$.*

Then $\mathcal{D}'$ is legal w.r.t. S iff each of $\mathcal{D}_i, 1 \leq i \leq m$, is legal w.r.t. S. ∎

Intuitively, the above result says that independent of the actual sequence of directory entry insertions and deletions in the update transaction, we can check for legality by first inserting subtrees corresponding to inserted directory entries (checking legality after each subtree insertion), and then deleting subtrees corresponding to deleted directory entries (checking legality after each subtree deletion). This abstraction helps us characterize cases where incremental legality checking is possible. Hence, we restrict our attention to directory updates that consist of the insertion or deletion of a *single* subtree. We denote the updated directory instance by $\mathcal{D} + \Delta\mathcal{D}$ for insertions, by $\mathcal{D} - \Delta\mathcal{D}$ for deletions, and by $\mathcal{D} \pm \Delta\mathcal{D}$ when the nature of the update is unimportant.

4.2 Incremental Testing of Legality

Consider a schema $S = (\mathbf{A}, \mathbf{H}, \mathbf{S})$, and an instance $\mathcal{D}$ that is legal w.r.t. S.

Testing whether the update $\Delta\mathcal{D}$ preserves legality, i.e., $\mathcal{D} \pm \Delta\mathcal{D}$ is legal, with respect to the content schema $(\mathbf{A}, \mathbf{H})$ can always be performed efficiently. Insertion of a subtree $\Delta\mathcal{D}$ preserves legality w.r.t. $(\mathbf{A}, \mathbf{H})$ iff $\Delta\mathcal{D}$, viewed as a directory instance, is legal w.r.t. $(\mathbf{A}, \mathbf{H})$. Deletion of $\Delta\mathcal{D}$ cannot violate legality w.r.t. $(\mathbf{A}, \mathbf{H})$. These are consequences of the fact that legality w.r.t. the content schema can be tested by independently checking each entry in the instance.

Incrementally testing whether an update $\Delta\mathcal{D}$ preserves legality with respect to the structure schema $\mathbf{S} = (C_r, E_r, E_f)$ is more complex. Legality of $\mathcal{D} \pm \Delta\mathcal{D}$ cannot, in general, be tested by simply examining $\Delta\mathcal{D}$ itself. Consider for example, a legal directory instance that is updated by adding a new orgUnit entry as a child of a person entry, and adding a few person entries as children of the newly created orgUnit. The updated directory instance $\mathcal{D} + \Delta\mathcal{D}$ is clearly not legal, since it violates both $\boxed{\text{orgGroup}} \longrightarrow \text{orgUnit}$ and person $\not\to$ top. However, neither of these violations can be detected by solely examining $\Delta\mathcal{D}$. In general, we may need to examine $\mathcal{D} + \Delta\mathcal{D}$ (for insertions), $\mathcal{D} - \Delta\mathcal{D}$ (for deletions), $\Delta\mathcal{D}$, or even nothing, depending on the specific structural relationship.

Suppose we want to incrementally test whether the insertion $\Delta\mathcal{D}$ preserves legality w.r.t. the relationship orgGroup $\longrightarrow\!\!\!\rightarrow$ [person]. We can make effective use of the hierarchical selection query corresponding to the structural relationship, for this purpose. For the above structural relationship, the corresponding hierarchical selection query is given by Q_1 (from Section 3.2), reproduced below:

Q_1: $(-$ (objectClass=orgGroup)
           $(d$ (objectClass=orgGroup)(objectClass=person)$)$$)$

The result of Q_1 should be empty for the relationship orgGroup $\longrightarrow\!\!\!\rightarrow$ [person] to be satisfied. Denote by $Q[\mathcal{D}]$ the result of applying query Q on a directory instance $\mathcal{D}$. Suppose $Q_1[\mathcal{D}] = \emptyset$. Then, we can show that $Q_1[\mathcal{D} + \Delta\mathcal{D}] = \emptyset$ if and only if $Q_1[\Delta\mathcal{D}] = \emptyset$. The rationale is that adding $\Delta\mathcal{D}$ to $\mathcal{D}$ cannot make any entries of $\mathcal{D}$ violate the relationship. Thus, the only way $\mathcal{D} + \Delta\mathcal{D}$ could violate the required structural relationship is if $\Delta\mathcal{D}$ violated it.

As another example, consider the relationships [orgGroup] $\longrightarrow$ orgUnit and person $\rightarrow\!\!\!\times\!\!\!\rightarrow$ top. Consider deleting a subtree. We can show that, in these cases, no check needs to be performed after the deletion; in other words, as long as the original instance satisfies these relationships, no deletion can violate them. Deletion could, however, violate the relationship orgGroup $\longrightarrow\!\!\!\rightarrow$ [person]; in this case, we may have to check for the satisfaction of the relationship in the entire updated instance, $\mathcal{D} - \Delta\mathcal{D}$.

We now formalize these intuitions. Consider a (required or forbidden) structural relationship κ, and let Q_κ be the hierarchical selection query such that an instance $\mathcal{D}$ is legal w.r.t. κ if and only if $Q_\kappa[\mathcal{D}] = \emptyset$. We would like to efficiently determine whether or not $Q_\kappa[\mathcal{D} \pm \Delta\mathcal{D}] = \emptyset$, taking advantage of the knowledge that $Q_\kappa[\mathcal{D}] = \emptyset$. The key idea is to identify a query expression $\delta Q_\kappa(\Delta\mathcal{D}, \mathcal{D} \pm \Delta\mathcal{D})$ that is syntactically identical to Q_κ, except that each sub-expression of δQ_κ may be evaluated on any one of $\emptyset$, $\Delta\mathcal{D}$, and $\mathcal{D} + \Delta\mathcal{D}$ (in the case of insertion) or $\mathcal{D} - \Delta\mathcal{D}$ (in the case of deletion).

Definition 6 [Incremental Testing of Legality]   Let κ, Q_κ and δQ_κ be defined as above. Then, we define the following:

- κ is *incrementally testable against insertion* if at least one sub-expression of δQ_κ is evaluated on $\emptyset$ or on $\Delta\mathcal{D}$. We call δQ_κ the Δ^+-*query* for κ.
- κ is *incrementally testable against deletion* if at least one sub-expression of δQ_κ is evaluated on $\emptyset$ or on $\Delta\mathcal{D}$. We call δQ_κ the Δ^--*query* for κ. ∎

Figure 4 lists the various required and forbidden structural relationships in (E_r, E_f), indicates whether or not they are incrementally testable against insertion or deletion, and gives the corresponding δQ_κ query expressions. (For brevity, we have used the attribute oc instead of objectClass.) The following result establishes its correctness.

Theorem 3. (Incremental Testing of Legality) *A structural relationship is incrementally testable for legality against insertion or deletion iff it is so indicated in Figure 4.* ∎

κ	Y/N	δQ_κ for Insertions
$c_i \longrightarrow \boxed{c_j}$	yes	$(-\ (\text{oc}=c_i)\,[\Delta\mathcal{D}]\ (c\ (\text{oc}=c_i)\,[\Delta\mathcal{D}]\ (\text{oc}=c_j)\,[\Delta\mathcal{D}]))$
$\boxed{c_j} \longrightarrow c_i$	yes	$(-\ (\text{oc}=c_i)\,[\Delta\mathcal{D}]\ (p\ (\text{oc}=c_i)\,[\Delta\mathcal{D}]\ (\text{oc}=c_j)\,[\mathcal{D}+\Delta\mathcal{D}]))$
$c_i \longrightarrow\!\!\!\rightarrow \boxed{c_j}$	yes	$(-\ (\text{oc}=c_i)\,[\Delta\mathcal{D}]\ (d\ (\text{oc}=c_i)\,[\Delta\mathcal{D}]\ (\text{oc}=c_j)\,[\Delta\mathcal{D}]))$
$\boxed{c_j} \longrightarrow\!\!\!\rightarrow c_i$	yes	$(-\ (\text{oc}=c_i)\,[\Delta\mathcal{D}]\ (a\ (\text{oc}=c_i)\,[\Delta\mathcal{D}]\ (\text{oc}=c_j)\,[\mathcal{D}+\Delta\mathcal{D}]))$
$c_i \rightarrow\!\!\!\times\!\!\!\rightarrow c_j$	yes	$(c\ (\text{oc}=c_i)\,[\mathcal{D}+\Delta\mathcal{D}]\ (\text{oc}=c_j)\,[\Delta\mathcal{D}])$
$c_i \rightarrow\!\!\!\times\!\!\!\rightarrow\!\!\!\rightarrow c_j$	yes	$(d\ (\text{oc}=c_i)\,[\mathcal{D}+\Delta\mathcal{D}]\ (\text{oc}=c_j)\,[\Delta\mathcal{D}])$
		δQ_κ for Deletions
$c_i \longrightarrow \boxed{c_j}$	no	$(-\ (\text{oc}=c_i)\ (c\ (\text{oc}=c_i)\ (\text{oc}=c_j)))\,[\mathcal{D}-\Delta\mathcal{D}]$
$\boxed{c_j} \longrightarrow c_i$	yes	$(-\ (\text{oc}=c_i)\,[\emptyset]\ (p\ (\text{oc}=c_i)\,[\emptyset]\ (\text{oc}=c_j)\,[\emptyset]))$
$c_i \longrightarrow\!\!\!\rightarrow \boxed{c_j}$	no	$(-\ (\text{oc}=c_i)\ (d\ (\text{oc}=c_i)\ (\text{oc}=c_j)))\,[\mathcal{D}-\Delta\mathcal{D}]$
$\boxed{c_j} \longrightarrow\!\!\!\rightarrow c_i$	yes	$(-\ (\text{oc}=c_i)\,[\emptyset]\ (a\ (\text{oc}=c_i)\,[\emptyset]\ (\text{oc}=c_j)\,[\emptyset]))$
$c_i \rightarrow\!\!\!\times\!\!\!\rightarrow c_j$	yes	$(c\ (\text{oc}=c_i)\,[\emptyset]\ (\text{oc}=c_j)\,[\emptyset])$
$c_i \rightarrow\!\!\!\times\!\!\!\rightarrow\!\!\!\rightarrow c_j$	yes	$(d\ (\text{oc}=c_i)\,[\emptyset]\ (\text{oc}=c_j)\,[\emptyset])$

Fig. 4. δQ_κ Query Expressions for Insertions and Deletions

In an analogous fashion, we can show that the required object classes C_r in the structure schema **S** are incrementally testable for insertion. If we had the ability to associate each $\boxed{c_i}$ with the number of entries that belong to c_i, then C_r would also be incrementally testable for deletion. We skip the details.

5 Discussion

5.1 Possible Embellishments

There are many conceivable, and potentially useful, schema elements that are not part of the bounding-schema proposal. Here, we rationalize our design decisions.

Multiple Inheritance: Since attribute names are drawn from a single universal namespace, and since there are no methods associated with objects in the directory model, multiple inheritance is not difficult to implement. However, using multiple inheritance to achieve the objective of allowing entries to belong to multiple object classes will lead to a combinatorial explosion in the number of object classes in the schema. By contrast, auxiliary object classes offer an elegant and flexible means to achieve the same objective while avoiding such an explosion.

Structural Relationships on Attributes: The co-occurrence and structural relationships that we have considered in the paper have all been with respect to object classes that must or must not occur. In addition, one could consider having requirements on attributes that must or must not occur in an entry based upon other attributes in the same entry, or in structurally related entries. Similarly, we could have requirements on object classes that must or must not occur at an entry based on attributes that occur in structurally related entries.

Most of these relationships can be captured in a two-step manner through co-occurrence and structural relationships on object classes followed by the attribute schema specification on object classes. Such a two-step formulation is actually preferable (and arguably more natural) in terms of encapsulation and modularity at the object class level. As such, even though we believe that the work presented in this paper could be extended to deal with co-occurrence and structural relationships on attributes, we have chosen not to do so.

Numeric Restrictions: By default, each entry in an LDAP directory can have multiple values for each attribute. Often, it is useful to specify that particular attributes may have only a single value. For example, we may require that a **person** entry have at most a single value for the **socialSecurityNumber** attribute. For this purpose, LDAP provides a schema specification wherein particular attributes can be declared to be "single-valued". Such a specification is clearly orthogonal to the requirements captured by our bounding-schema, and can easily be incorporated in our framework.

Keys: Keys are a critical part of the schema for a relational database. In other data models, including object-oriented and semi-structured models, the role of keys is sometimes just as important, but often less emphasized. For LDAP directories, the distinguished name of an entry serves as a key, uniquely identifying an entry at any point in time. Other notions of keys can easily be incorporated in our framework as values of attributes. However, given the relatively loose notion of an object class, any notion of a key in an LDAP directory must be unique across all entries in the directory instance, not just within a single object class. Specification of keys is again orthogonal to our definition of a bounding-schema.

Complex Integrity Constraints: In the case of a relational database, there is a well-understood notion of a schema, distinct from integrity constraints. The former includes specification of each table name, the column names and types for each column, identification of keys, and of (at least certain basic kinds of) functional dependencies. Everything else is considered an integrity constraint. In the case of an LDAP directory, clearly, object classes, attributes, and types belong in a schema. What attributes and object classes must co-occur and cannot co-occur are also legitimate parts of the schema. Finally, there is the issue of structural relationships. Clearly, some basic specifications on what types of nodes can appear below what other types of nodes are critical schema components. These we have included in our schema specification language. On the other hand, there is no end to the complexity of assertions that could be made about structural relationships. By design, we have chosen to draw the line at a fundamental set of structure schema specifications, and relegate more complex assertions to the status of integrity constraints.

5.2 Related Work

Schema plays a central role in the design and administration of databases. In fact, the presence of a schema is a central property that distinguishes an organized database from an arbitrary collection of data. A crucial difference between bounding-schemas and schema specification in traditional (relational and object-oriented) databases is that schemas for traditional databases are *rigid*, i.e., they allow very little flexibility in what constitutes a legal instance. As a consequence, even simple changes typically require a heavy-weight schema evolution process. In contrast, many kinds of schema evolution, such as adding a new allowed attribute to an object class, or adding a new auxiliary object class to the auxiliary object classes associated with a core object class is extremely lightweight in LDAP, involving *no* modifications to existing directory entries.

More recently, the notion of semi-structured databases has been proposed, which permit more flexible schemas than traditional databases [2,5]. The dominant notion here is one of (discovered) descriptive, rather than prescriptive, schema. Several alternatives have been proposed to specify the schema, and then to compare a schema with a database instance. Schema could be specified as a graph with simulation used for comparison [6], specified as a graph with a finite automaton used for comparison [9], or specified as a monadic Datalog program with program evaluation used for comparison [12]. The need for approximate schema has also been observed in [12], leading to explicit descriptions of lower and upper bound schemas (see [13] for more details).

In the directory context, while flexibility remains a central objective, schema is meant to be prescriptive, as opposed to the semi-structured world discussed above. There is considerable activity surrounding the enhancement of the current LDAPv2 standard [16], with at least some of these enhancements relating to richer schema specification. There are a variety of embellishments incorporated in different proposals, including [15,14]. These include: the notion of a single inheritance hierarchy of core object classes, the notion of auxiliary object classes, and the notion of an extensible object that allows all possible attributes.

5.3   A Wider Applicability of Bounding-Schemas

Path constraints have been proposed for semi-structured databases based on labeled paths where the path length is fixed [7], and based on regular expressions that constrain the destination of the path [3]. These path constraints do not suffice for expressing relationships of the form $c_i \longrightarrow \boxed{c_j}$ and $c_i \rightarrowtail c_j$, where the path length between c_i and c_j can be arbitrary.

Such required and forbidden structural relationships may be very useful in semi-structured databases. For example, one might want to specify that each person node *must* have a (descendant) name node, without having to fix the length of the path between these nodes. As another example, while one might want to allow a country node to have child corporation nodes (national corporations could be modeled thus), a corporation node to have child country nodes (international corporations could be modeled thus), and a corporation node to have child corporation nodes (conglomerates could be modeled thus), but one might want to *forbid* a country node to be a descendant of another country node. Thus, in principle, our notions can be used to usefully enhance the notion of schema for semi-structured databases.

Acknowledgements

The research of H. V. Jagadish was supported in part by NSF grant IIS-9986030. The research of Laks V. S. Lakshmanan was supported in part by grants from NSERC and NCE/IRIS/NSERC.

References

1. Directory enabled networks ad hoc working group. http://www.murchiso.com/den/.
2. S. Abiteboul. Querying semi-structured data. In *Proceedings of the International Conference on Database Theory*, pages 1–18, 1997.
3. S. Abiteboul and V. Vianu. Regular path queries with constraints. In *Proceedings of the ACM Symposium on Principles of Database Systems*, pages 122–133, 1997.
4. S. Amer-Yahia, H. V. Jagadish, L. V. S. Lakshmanan, and D. Srivastava. On bounding-schemas for LDAP directories. Tech. Report, Concordia University, Montreal, November 1999. http://www.cs.concordia.ca/~faculty/laks/edbt00Sub.ps.gz.
5. P. Buneman. Semistructured data. In *Proceedings of the ACM Symposium on Principles of Database Systems*, pages 117–121, 1997.
6. P. Buneman, S. Davidson, M. Fernandez, and D. Suciu. Adding structure to unstructured data. In *Proceedings of the International Conference on Database Theory*, pages 336–350, Delphi, Greece, 1997.
7. P. Buneman, W. Fan, and S. Weinstein. Path constraints in semistructured and structured databases. In *Proceedings of the ACM Symposium on Principles of Database Systems*, pages 129–138, 1998.
8. R. Elmasri and S. B. Navathe. *Fundamentals of Database Systems*. Benjamin/Cummings Publishers, second edition, 1994.
9. R. Goldman and J. Widom. DataGuides: Enabling query formulation and optimization in semistructured databases. In *Proceedings of the International Conference on Very Large Databases*, 1997.
10. H. V. Jagadish, L. V. S. Lakshmanan, T. Milo, D. Srivastava, and D. Vista. Querying network directories. In *Proceedings of the ACM SIGMOD Conference on Management of Data*, Philadelphia, PA, June 1999.
11. A. Kemper and G. Moerkotte. *Object-oriented database management applications in engineering and computer science*. Prentice Hall, 1994.
12. S. Nestorov, S. Abiteboul, and R. Motwani. Extracting schema from semistructured data. In *Proceedings of the ACM SIGMOD Conference on Management of Data*, pages 295–306, 1998.
13. D. Suciu. Managing web data. SIGMOD'99 tutorial., 1999.
14. M. Wahl, A. Coulbeck, T. Howes, and S. Kille. Lightweight directory access protocol (v3): Attribute syntax definitions. Request for Comments 2252. Available from ftp://ds.internic.net/rfc/rfc2252.txt, Dec. 1997.
15. M. Wahl, T. Howes, and S. Kille. Lightweight directory access protocol (v3). Request for Comments 2251. Available from ftp://ds.internic.net/rfc/rfc2251.txt, Dec. 1997.
16. W. Yeong, T. Howes, and S. Kille. Lightweight directory access protocol. Request for Comments 1777. Available from ftp://ds.internic.net/rfc/rfc1777.txt, Mar. 1995.

Approximate Graph Schema Extraction
for Semi-structured Data

Qiu Yue Wang, Jeffrey Xu Yu, and Kam-Fai Wong

Department of Systems Engineering and Engineering Management,
The Chinese University of Hong Kong, Hong Kong, China
{qywang,yu,kfwong}@se.cuhk.edu.hk

Abstract Semi-structured data are typically represented in the form of
labeled directed graphs. They are self-describing and schemaless. The
lack of a schema renders query processing over semi-structured data expensive. To overcome this predicament, some researchers proposed to
use the structure of the data for schema representation. Such schemas
are commonly referred to as graph schemas. Nevertheless, since semistructured data are irregular and frequently subjected to modifications,
it is costly to construct an accurate graph schema and worse still, it is difficult to maintain it thereafter. Furthermore, an accurate graph schema
is generally very large, hence impractical. In this paper, an approximation approach is proposed for graph schema extraction. Approximation
is achieved by summarizing the semi-structured data graph using an incremental clustering method. The preliminary experimental results have
shown that approximate graph schemas were more compact than the
conventional accurate graph schemas and promising in query evaluation
that involved regular path expressions.

1 Introduction

Semi-structured data arise in many applications, such as scientific databases,
world-wide-web, and data integration from various data sources [1,4]. They differ
from structured data in traditional databases in that the data are not confined
by a rigid schema which is defined in advance, and often exhibit irregularities.
Furthermore, these data evolve rapidly under the WWW environments.

Typical models proposed for managing such data are labeled directed graphs
[20,2,3], which are schemaless and self-describing, e.g. Fig. 1 shows a sample
Object Exchange Model (OEM)[20] data graph. To cope with the irregularities of semi-structured data, regular path expressions are widely used in query
languages for semi-structured systems [2,3,15,13]. However, the lack of schema
poses great difficulties in query optimization. For example, to process a query
embedded with regular path expressions, query evaluation inevitably involves an
exhaustive search over the complete data graph.

Based on automata equivalence, DataGuide is proposed [10]. It is a concise
and accurate graph schema for the data graph in terms of label paths. Its accuracy lies in that the schema and the data have the same sets of label paths, and

C. Zaniolo et al. (Eds.): EDBT 2000, LNCS 1777, pp. 302–316, 2000.
© Springer-Verlag Berlin Heidelberg 2000

its conciseness lies in that every label path in the schema is unique. However for large cyclic graphs, constructing a DataGuide may require exponential time and result in a DataGuide which is much larger than the original data graph. In general, it is expensive to construct and maintain an accurate graph schema for a data graph when the data are irregular and evolve rapidly. Furthermore, an accurate schema may be too large and hence impractical for query optimization. In [11], several heuristic-based strategies are proposed to build approximate DataGuides by merging "similar" portions of the DataGuide during construction. However these strategies are situation specific. [17] and [18] aim to type objects in the data set approximately by combining objects with similar type definitions, instead of constructing an approximate structural summary for the data graph. Their approximation methods are sensitive to the predetermined external parameters (such as the threshold θ, the number of clusters K, etc.); and it is hard to decide the optimal values for different data graphs in advance.

In this paper, we propose to construct an approximate graph schema by clustering objects with similar incoming and outgoing edge patterns using an incremental conceptual clustering method [8]. Our approach has the following unique features. No predetermined parameters are required to approximate the schema. It is cheap to construct and maintain the resultant schema and it is small in size. Moreover, we propose a query evaluation strategy for processing regular path expression queries with assistance of the schema.

The rest of the paper is organized as follows. The background knowledge is outlined in Sect. 2. Section 3 introduces the accurate graph schema, namely DataGuide. In Sect. 4, the algorithm to extract the approximate graph schema is given. Section 5 describes the query evaluation strategies and Sect. 6 presents the preliminary experimental results. Finally, Section 7 concludes the paper.

2   Preliminaries

2.1   OEM

In this study, we deal with semi-structured database based on the Object Exchange Model (OEM). It adapts easily to other graph-structured data models.

An OEM database is a labeled directed graph, $G = (V, E)$ where V is a set of vertices and $E \subseteq V \times V$. A sample OEM database is shown in Fig. 1. Each vertex in the graph represents an object which has a unique object identifier (oid) and a value. A value may be atomic or complex. Atomic objects do not have any outgoing edges. Complex objects have outgoing edges pointing to its subobjects. An OEM database might have multiple entry points from which data will be accessed. Each entry point has a unique name. Without loss of generality, we assume that an OEM database has a single entry point denoted as *root*. A label path of an OEM object o is a sequence of one or more dot-separated labels, $l_1.l_2 \cdots l_n$, such that a path of n edges $(e_1 \cdots e_n)$ from o can be traversed where edge e_i has label l_i. An OEM database is self-describing, i.e. all the schematic information is embedded in the labels. It can cope with data irregularities and

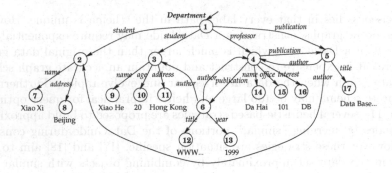

Fig. 1. An OEM data graph

incompleteness. For example, in Fig. 1, both objects 2 and 3 are *student* objects; but object 2 has no *age* while object 3 has one. For another example, *publication* objects 5 and 6 are at different levels.

2.2   Regular Path Expressions

Due to the irregularities of semi-structured data or partial knowledge about the data, users need to use regular path expressions for querying [2,3,15,13]. In [13], wild cards are used to denote arbitrary sequence of links. In [2,3,15], regular expression symbols are used to express the set of paths that may be of arbitrary length. In this paper, a regular path expression is defined as follows.

$$P ::= l \parallel \epsilon \parallel P.P \parallel P|P \parallel P* \parallel (P)$$

where l denotes a string value for edge labels and ϵ is for an empty string. Concatenation, union and closure are denoted as ., | and * respectively. In addition, a special symbol "_" is used to match any edge labels. We abbreviate "_*" with "#". A query with a regular path expression "*select P*" is to retrieve all the objects reachable from the *root* in the graph via a label path satisfying the regular path expression P. For example, the query "*select #.publication.title*" is to find all the objects reachable via any label path ended with "publication.title". In Fig. 1, the result of this query is {12, 17}. It is important to know that without any structural information, evaluation of the query would result in searching the entire data graph. Conversely, with the assistance of a schema, the query can be efficiently processed by accessing only the appropriate subgraph.

2.3   Graph Schema

For semi-structured data, the notion of a graph schema is formally introduced and studied in [5]. By definition, a graph database G_d conforms to a graph schema G_s if there is a simulation from G_d to G_s, informally that is, whenever there is an edge in G_d, there is a corresponding edge with the same label in G_s.

Such a schema is known as an upper-bound schema since the set of label paths in G_s is a superset of the label paths in G_d. A graph database G_d may conform to multiple graph schemas. For example, Fig. 2 shows four graph schemas for the data graph of Fig. 2(a): namely, the data graph itself, minimal graph schema with a single vertex, a graph schema resulted from clustering similar outgoing and incoming edge patterns and a graph schema with the same path set as the database. In Fig. 2(c) and (d), each vertex in the graph schema is denoted by its *extent*.[1] Notice that different schemas have different expressiveness for the data.

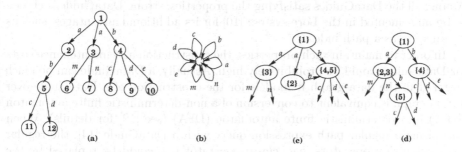

Fig. 2. A Data Graph and its Graph Schemas. (a) a data graph; (b) a minimal schema; (c) an approximate schema; and (d) a strong DataGuide.

Graph schemas can be useful to optimize regular path expression queries [7,14]. In general, evaluating a regular path expression query, Q, with assistance of schema information, G_s, is done in two steps.

- **Step-1**: the query Q is rewritten with the schema G_s into a query Q^s.
- **Step-2**: the query Q^s is evaluated against the underlying database, G_d.

The total cost of query evaluation consists of two parts: $cost(Q, G_s)$ for the first step, and $cost(Q^s, G_d)$ for the second step. It is beneficial to adopt G_s for pruning Q only when $cost(Q, G_s) + cost(Q^s, G_d) < cost(Q, G_d)$.[2] Given Q and G_d, $cost(Q, G_s)$ is proportional to the size of G_s, and $cost(Q^s, G_d)$ is related to the accuracy or expressiveness of G_s. Consider the example database shown in Fig. 2(a). If a schema G_s is minimal in size (i.e. Fig. 2(b)), query optimization with G_s would be cost ineffective for $cost(Q^s, G_d) = cost(Q, G_d)$ since G_s has no effect on pruning the query in the first step. On the other hand, if G_s is the database itself, which contains all information about the database, it would not be cost-effective either since $cost(Q, G_s) \approx cost(Q, G_d)$. Therefore, in practice, the guiding principle in extracting schema from a database is to balance between the size and accuracy of the resultant schema.

---

[1] The extent of a vertex in G_s is the set of vertices in G_d that simulate to it.
[2] $cost(Q, G_d)$, the cost of naive query evaluation, i.e. without optimization.

3   An Accurate Graph Schema

DataGuide proposed in [10] is a concise and accurate graph schema for the underlying data graph in terms of label paths. It means that compared with the original data graph there is no missing, duplicate, or false path in the DataGuide. In other words, it requires that each label path in the data graph appears exactly once in the schema and each label path in the schema must exist in the data graph. Such properties enable checking whether a given label path of length n exists in the data graph by traversing at most n objects in the DataGuide. Among all the DataGuides satisfying the properties, strong DataGuide is chosen to be implemented in the Lore system [10] for its additional advantages, such as it can serve as a path index.

In order to maintain such properties, the construction and maintenance costs for DataGuides could be prohibitively high. Actually, a DataGuide can be much larger than the data graph it models for the construction of a DataGuide over a data graph is equivalent to conversion of a non-deterministic finite automaton (NFA) to a deterministic finite automaton (DFA) (see [19] for details). When optimizing a regular path expression query with a DataGuide [14], the regular path expression operators, e.g. *closure* operator ($*$), could be replaced by the actual set of possible matching paths. However, the path expansion would be costly if the DataGuide was sizeable. When the size of DataGuide is close to or even larger than that of the original data graph, it will be undesirable to prune the query with the DataGuide.

Based on the above observations, we propose to extract an approximate graph schema from the data. Such a graph schema is small in size and cheap to construct and maintain. We further investigate its effectiveness in optimizing regular path expression queries experimentally.

4   Approximate Graph Schema

In the following, we outline the construction of an approximate schema using the incremental conceptual clustering algorithm in COBWEB [8]. Under our approach, the approximate graph schema of a rooted OEM data graph, G_d, is a rooted graph $G_s^c = (V_c, E_c)$ where V_c is a set of vertices and $E_c \subseteq V_c \times V_c$. The root of G_s^c is denoted as $root_c$. Each vertex in G_s^c is an extracted concept and is associated with a set of objects (oids) in G_d that belong to the concept. Each edge is labeled with a string which represents the relationship between the two corresponding concepts. Let v_i be a vertex in G_d which has at least one outgoing edge,[3] and $\overline{v}_i$ be a vertex in G_s^c. We use $A(v_i)$ and $R(v_i)$ to denote the sets of labels associated with the outgoing edges and incoming edges of a vertex v_i, respectively. For a vertex $\overline{v}_i$ in G_s^c, $R(\overline{v}_i) = \bigcup_{v_i \in \overline{v}_i} R(v_i)$, and $A(\overline{v}_i) = \bigcup_{v_i \in \overline{v}_i} A(v_i)$, since $\overline{v}_i$ in G_s^c represents a set of vertices in G_d.

---

[3] Only complex objects in the OEM data graph are considered in the clustering algorithm. All the atomic objects are clustered into a virtual concept in the schema.

On one hand, a guiding principle in the clustering is to predict $R(\overline{v}_i)$ and $A(\overline{v}_i)$ as accurately as possible. For each label l in $R(\overline{v}_i) \cup A(\overline{v}_i)$, the predictability is reflected by the conditional probability $P(l|\overline{v}_i)$. The higher is the probability, the more probable that an object v_i included in $\overline{v}_i$ has an edge labeled l. Another principle, minimizing the size of the G_s^c is to minimize the number of appearances of each label l. This is equivalent to maximizing the predictiveness of l, which is reflected by the conditional probability $P(\overline{v}_i|l)$. The higher is the predictiveness, the more probable that an object, v_i having an edge labeled with l, is in $\overline{v}_i$. The tradeoff between predictability and predictiveness for a label l associated with an edge of $\overline{v}_i$ and the expected tradeoff for all the labels of $\overline{v}_i$ are defined as $T(l, \overline{v}_i)$ and $E(\overline{v}_i)$ respectively as follows.

$$T(l, \overline{v}_i) = P(l|\overline{v}_i) \cdot P(\overline{v}_i|l)$$

$$E(\overline{v}_i) = \frac{1}{|R(\overline{v}_i) \cup A(\overline{v}_i)|} \sum_{l \in R(\overline{v}_i) \cup A(\overline{v}_i)} T(l, \overline{v}_i)$$

where $|X|$ is the cardinality of the set X. The utility function, U, for clustering is defined on the overall partition quality as follows.

$$U = \frac{1}{K} \sum_{i=1}^{K} E(\overline{v}_i)$$

where K is the number of clusters in the partition.

Each object in G_d is clustered into a vertex in G_s^c one at a time. The edges between the vertices in G_s^c are built accordingly while the data graph G_d is traversed and each object in G_d is assigned to a vertex in G_s^c. At the beginning, there is only one vertex, $root_c$, in G_s^c to which we simply assign the *root* object of G_d. Thereafter, for each time we visit a vertex v_j from v_i (which is assigned to $\overline{v}_i$) along the edge labeled with l, we will perform the following steps. If v_j has not been assigned to any vertex in G_s^c, it will be assigned to a vertex $\overline{v}_j$ which results in the highest utility. $\overline{v}_j$ can be either an existing vertex in G_s^c or a newly created one. [4] An edge labeled with l from $\overline{v}_i$ to $\overline{v}_j$ will be added to G_s^c.[5] The algorithm is outlined below using a depth-first traversal strategy.

procedure traverse($v_i, \overline{v}_i$)
begin
    foreach $< v_i, v_j >$ with a label l in G_d
        if v_j has not been assigned to $\overline{v}_j$ in G_s^c **then**
            let $\overline{v}_j$ be a vertex in G_s^c which will result in a max utility value;
            assign v_j to $\overline{v}_j$;
            traverse($v_j, \overline{v}_j$);
        endif
        add $< \overline{v}_i, \overline{v}_j >$ with a label l into G_s^c;
    endfor
end

---

[4] In this way, the number of vertices in G_s^c is formed automatically.
[5] Multiple edges with the same label are ignored.

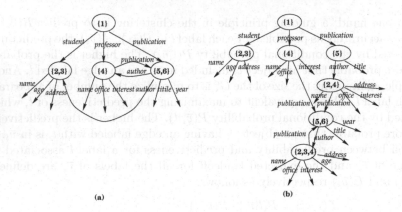

(a)   (b)

Fig. 3. (a) The approximate schema G_s^c; and (b) the strong DataGuide of Fig. 1.

Unlike a strong DataGuide which is constructed by merging paths that reach the same source target set,[6] the construction of G_s^c is based on clustering the objects with similar incoming and outgoing edge sets. There may be duplicate or false paths in G_s^c. For example, Fig. 3 shows the approximate schema, G_s^c, and the strong DataGuide for the data graph in Fig. 1. As we can see, in G_s^c, the label path *publication.year* is false and *publication.author* is duplicated, and there is no duplicate or false path in the DataGuide. However the DataGuide is much larger, even larger than the data graph.

5 Query Evaluation

A regular path expression query can be represented as an operator tree. Each leaf node in the tree is a *scan* operator; and each non-leaf node is a regular expression operator: *concatenation* (.), *union* (|) or *closure* (∗). For example, Q_1 is a regular path expression query on the data graph in Fig. 2(a). The operator tree for Q_1 is shown in Fig. 4(a). The string value in each *scan* node is the label to be matched.

Q_1: select #.e

5.1 Naive Query Evaluation

A depth-first traversal algorithm like that in [2] is used to evaluate a regular path expression query on a graph. Each node on the operator tree is implemented as an iterator[12]. It is invoked with an input value (oid) and returns one output value (oid) at a time on request by its parent. With an input oid, a *scan* node

---

[6] A source target set is a set of objects reachable by traversing the label path in the source data graph.

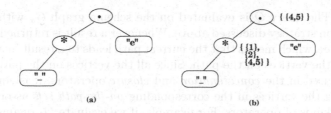

Fig. 4. The operator tree and restricted operator tree for Q_1

scans the set of outgoing edges of the object and retrieves all oids of its subobjects following the specified label. A *concatenation* node concatenates its left and right children by passing the output values of the left child to the right child. Like a relational nested-loop join, for each oid returned by the left child—referred to as *via_oid*, it invokes the right child with the *via_oid* and retrieves all the return values from the right child. A *union* node retrieves the union set of results from the children. The unary operator *closure* node has only one child. With the input oid o_i, it retrieves all the oids reachable from o_i by concatenating any number of the child. The concatenations are realized in a depth-first traversal manner with a stack, in which all the *via_oids* of the concatenations from the input object to the return object are stored.

5.2   Query Evaluation with Schema

The general way of evaluating a regular path expression query with schema information consists of two steps: rewriting the query with the schema and then evaluating the rewritten query over the database. Various techniques have been proposed for rewriting a query [7,14]. In [7], a query is represented as an automaton. The rewritten query is the cross-product of the query automaton and the graph schema. Thus the closure state is expanded into a subgraph of the schema contributing to the results. [14] evaluates the query on the schema, and replaces the closure operator ($*$) with the union ($|$) of all possible paths in the schema that would lead to the results. Although the two methods are based on different representations of the query, i.e. automata or regular expressions, they are similar in nature. For example, if we represent queries with regular path expressions, the rewritten query of Q_1 with the schema shown in Fig. 2(c) is the same for both techniques:

Q_1^s: select $(a.b|b).e$

However, if the schema is sizeable and there are exponential number of paths in the matching subgraph, the rewritten query could become very large and impractical. To overcome this predicament, we propose to restrict the query with the set of vertices in the schema that are on the paths leading to the results—i.e. *on-the-path set*. Based on this, the query evaluation algorithm is as follows:

- **Step-1** The query Q is evaluated on the schema graph G_s with the naive evaluation strategy discussed above. Whenever a result is returned by the operator tree, which means that the current path leads to a result, mark the tree with all the vertices on the path. Since all the vertices on the path, *via_oids*, are captured in the *concatenation* and *closure* operators, it is equivalent to recording the vertices in the corresponding *on-the-path sets* associated with the two kinds of operators. For example, if we evaluate Q_1 against G_s^c (Fig. 2(c)), the restricted query tree of Q_1 is shown in Fig. 4(b). Recall that each vertex in the schema represents a set of objects in the underlying database, which is referred to as its extent. We define the extent of the *on-the-path set* as the union of the extents of all the vertices in the *on-the-path set*.
- **Step-2** With the assistance of the *on-the-path set*, we can use the naive evaluation strategy to evaluate Q against the underlying database G_d with minor modifications, i.e. all the vertices traversed are ensured to be in the extent of the *on-the-path set*. For example, only the vertices in the set of $\{1,2,4,5\}$ are traversed when the restricted query Q_1 (see Fig. 4(b)) is evaluated over the database shown in Fig. 2(a).

Since we use the set of vertices instead of the set of paths to restrict the query, G_s^c is sometimes more effective than DataGuide in query optimization. For example, when the G_s^c shown in Fig. 2(c) is used to optimize the query Q_1, the query is restricted to the subgraph $\{\{1\},\{2\},\{4,5\} \}$ in G_s^c, i.e. the subgraph $\{1,2,4,5\}$ in G_d; on the other hand, when the DataGuide shown in Fig. 2(d) is used to optimize Q_1, the query is restricted to the subgraph $\{1,4\}$ in G_d. In this case, DataGuide is more accurate than G_s^c. Conversely, for the query *"select a.#.m"*, G_s^c is more accurate because it restricts the query to the subgraph $\{1,3\}$ while DataGuide the subgraph $\{1,2,3\}$. Here we can see that DataGuide and G_s^c have different accuracy with respect to the query.

6   Performance Study

The graph schema extracted by our algorithm, G_s^c, is approximate in terms of label paths. This means it may contain duplicate and false paths. We conducted some experiments to evaluate its effectiveness in query optimization of regular path expressions. The results were compared with that of the DataGuide, which is an accurate graph schema. First, we compared the size of the approximate graph schema with the size of the accurate graph schema over various data graphs. Second, we investigated the effectiveness of the schemas by comparing the query costs for evaluating a regular path expression query between the naive strategy, and those with G_s^c optimization and with DataGuide optimization. Since the algorithm is incremental, it is sensitive to the initial order of the input objects. As such breadth-first and depth-first traversal orders may result in different G_s^c. Thus, we have also evaluated and compared both orders, breadth-first G_s^c (denoted as $b\_G_s^c$) and depth-first G_s^c (denoted as $d\_G_s^c$).

The experiments were based on the synthetic data generated using two methods.

- The first set of synthetic data were generated from some input graph schema specifications. Using input graph schemas to generate synthetic data, the feasibility of the algorithm for extraction of embedded schema from the data graph could be assessed by comparing the resultant G_s^c with the input graph schema; and also meaningful queries over the data graph could be designed.
- To further investigate the performance of G_s^c and DataGuide over a wider range of graph-structured data, we used the method proposed in [10] to generate numerous data graphs. But we could not figure out meaningful queries for such graph in advance. Thus, we chose a label path randomly in the generated data graph to form a regular path expression query for query evaluation.

The size of a graph were measured by the number of complex objects ($CObjs$) and the number of edges ($Links$) in the graph. A query evaluation system was implemented using the strategies described in Sect. 5. The query cost was simply measured by the number of objects scanned since we assumed no clustering in the graph database and every object scanned would incur a random page access.

6.1   Synthetic Data with Input Graph Schemas

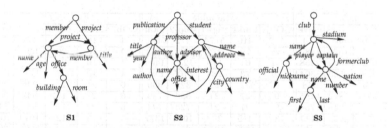

Fig. 5. The Input Graph Schemas for Synthetic Data

Some of the input graph schemas used to generate the data are shown in Fig. 5. The following parameters were associated with each vertex and edge of the input graph schema:

- the maximum number of objects in the vertex;
- the probability that the objects in the vertex having a specific outgoing edge— *probability of the edge*;
- the maximum number of a specific outgoing edge for an object in the vertex— *fan-out of the edge*;

Initially, the system generated the maximum number of objects for each vertex in the input graph schema. For each outgoing edge of the vertex, a subset of the objects was chosen randomly according to the *probability of the edge*, e.g. if the probability was equal to 0.5, then only half of the objects in the vertex had that edge. The number of that edge for an object was bounded by the *fan-out of the edge*. According to the input graph schema, the edge randomly pointed to an object in the referred vertex. The output data graph was the one traversed from the *root* object. Thus all the objects in the data graph were ensured reachable from the *root*.

It is impossible to explore all possible graph schemas and queries. It is also rather difficult to define the types of them formally. In our experiments, we used the three input graph schemas shown in Fig. 5 to generate the synthetic data and applied the following test queries to them.

$Q1$: select #.member.#.office
$Q2$: select #.author.address
$Q3$: select club.#.player.name

Schema $S1$ was a cyclic graph schema with only one cycle between two vertices at the same level. Schema $S2$ was a simple acyclic graph schema with a small number of distinct label paths. Schema $S3$ was a cyclic graph schema with cycles between two vertices at different levels.

Table 1. Sizes and Query Costs

	DB			DataGuide					$b\_G_s^c/d\_G_s^c$				
No	CObjs	Links	naive	CObjs	Links	step-1	step-2	total	CObjs	Links	step-1	step-2	total
1a	236	668	914	152	410	5174	472	5646	4	10	26	472	498
1b	487	1520	1880	30	79	272	999	1271	4	10	26	999	1025
1c	612	1840	2358	24	61	176	1233	1409	4	10	26	1237	1263
1d	828	2580	3304	29	73	284	1705	1989	4	10	26	1713	1739
2a	374	1274	948	9	27	21	329	350	6	21	17	246	263
2b	541	1882	1485	9	27	21	688	709	6	21	17	543	560
2c	668	2216	1754	9	27	21	723	744	6	21	17	595	612
3a	779	2973	2117	139	419	303	1074	1377	5	13	12	1074	1086
3b	508	1905	1319	583	1788	1279	653	1932	5	13	12	653	665
3c	967	3578	2551	1799	5416	3888	1257	5145	5	13	12	1257	1269

The results for the sizes of the approximate and accurate graph schemas and query costs are shown in Table 1.[7] By varying the parameters on the vertices and edges of the input graph schema, different DBs (databases) could be generated from the same schema, where $DB1x$, $2x$, $3x$ are from $S1$, $S2$ and $S3$ respectively. We could see that the size of G_s^c was close to the input graph schema; in particular, G_s^cs for $DB1x$ and $3x$ were the same as the schemas $S1$ and $S3$, respectively, and G_s^cs for $DB2x$ were one vertex more than $S2$. However, the size of the DataGuide could be much larger, e.g. $DB3b$, $3c$, due to data irregularity. The total cost for evaluating the query with the schemas is the sum of the costs for two steps. The approximate graph schema was promising for query optimization. The small size of G_s^c resulted in much less cost in the first step than the cost using the DataGuide. While for most test cases the costs in the second step

---

[7] Since $b\_G_s^c$ and $d\_G_s^c$ were identical for all test cases, we placed them in one column.

Table 2. Parameters for Generating the DB Graphs

DB	Height	Lab/lev	Fanout	Full	Obj/lev	BackFreq	BackLev	Random Path
1	5	2	10	N	200	-	-	b.d.f.h.k
2	5	4	10	N	200	-	-	b.f.l.p.s
3	5	4	20	N	200	-	-	d.g.j.n.t
4	5	2	10	N	200	10	0	b.d.f.h.k
5	5	4	10	N	200	10	0	b.f.l.n.u
6	5	4	20	N	200	10	0	d.i.j.n
7	5	2	10	N	200	10	2	b.d.f.h.k
8	5	4	10	N	200	10	2	b.f.l.n.u
9	5	4	20	N	200	10	2	d.g.j.n.t
10	8	2	10	N	200	-	-	b.d.g.i.j.m.n.q
11	8	2	10	N	200	10	0	b.d.g.h.j.m
12	8	2	10	N	200	10	2	b.d.g.h.j.m

for G_s^c were almost the same as that for DataGuide, in other cases the costs in the second step for G_s^c were less ($Q2$ on $DB2a, 2b, 2c$) or more ($Q1$ on $DB1c, 1d$) than that for DataGuide. The reason was that they had different accuracy for the data graph as discussed in Sect. 5. For example, for $Q2$ on $DB2x$, there were two kinds of authors with different attributes, i.e. one was professors and the other students. However, only students had the attribute "address". G_s^c restricted the search space to the set of students only but the DataGuide restricted to the set of professors and students.

6.2   Synthetic Data for General Graphs

To further study the performance, we adopted the method given in [10] to generate more general data graphs. The set of parameters for graph generation were briefly described below (for details see [10]):

- *Height:* maximum level number. Level n includes all objects whose shortest path from the *root* is of length n.
- *Lab/lev:* the number of unique labels on outgoing edges for each level. The sets of labels for different levels are disjoint.
- *Fan-out:* maximum number of outgoing edges from any complex object.
- *Full:* a boolean value to indicate whether the number of outgoing edges for each object is equal to *Fan-out* (Y) or can be less (N).
- *Obj/lev:* an integer value. The maximum number of objects for a level is equal to this value multiplied by the level number.
- *BackFreq:* the portion of outgoing edges that are redirected to objects in previous levels.
- *BackLev:* the number that the redirected level is above the current level, e.g. 0 means the same level as the current level.

Table 3. The Sizes

	DB		DataGuide		$b\_G_s^c$		$d\_G_s^c$	
No	CObjs	Links	CObjs	Links	CObjs	Links	CObjs	Links
1	638	3441	31	62	6	19	6	19
2	638	3441	172	624	11	63	8	47
3	1039	10820	224	880	9	55	6	32
4	630	3404	75	160	8	39	11	60
5	630	3404	221	808	17	131	21	168
6	1014	10572	1563	6737	15	333	20	431
7	629	3397	428	934	6	26	8	35
8	629	3397	362	1287	9	72	17	136
9	1039	10820	-	-	7	65	7	66
10	3902	21482	252	503	9	31	9	31
11	3894	21445	2269	5512	13	95	17	140
12	3895	21448	187951	525262	13	87	17	143

Table 2 shows the parameters that we used to generate various data graphs. The "Random Path" column shows a random label path from the *root* in each generated data graph. Based on that, a regular path expression query was formed and evaluated over the data graph.

Table 4. The Query Costs

DB		DataGuide			$b\_G_s^c$			$d\_G_s^c$			Query
No	naive	step-1	step-2	total	step-1	step-2	total	step-1	step-2	total	
1	1464	72	243	315	18	215	233	18	215	233	#.f.h.k
2	1754	450	435	885	56	443	499	38	443	481	#.f.#.s
3	2712	493	1139	1632	24	1110	1134	16	1110	1126	#.n.t
4	1448	160	243	403	23	216	239	40	214	254	#.f.h.k
5	1323	460	110	570	48	110	158	62	111	173	#.l.n.u
6	2082	3152	201	3353	40	109	149	53	100	153	#.j.u
7	1446	1002	842	1844	18	814	832	23	814	837	#.f.h.k
8	1321	776	408	1184	25	690	715	58	690	748	#.l.n.u
9	2722	-	-	-	19	1897	1916	19	1897	1916	#.n.t
10	13516	642	4508	5150	44	4465	4509	44	4465	4509	#.i.j.#.q
11	7851	4544	118	4662	30	109	139	41	109	150	#.g.h
12	7853	-	-	-	30	3847	3877	45	4580	4625	#.g.h

The sizes of the schemas and the query cost results were tabulated in Table 3 and Table 4, respectively. While the size of the DataGuide varied greatly with some changes on the parameters, e.g. increasing the *lab/lev* (from $DB1$ to $DB2$), or increasing the *height* from ($DB1$ to $DB10$), the size of the approximate graph schema only changed slightly. Also back links could cause a dramatic increase in the size of the DataGuide, e.g. DB10, 11, and 12, and some even failed in constructing a DataGuide, e.g. DB9. But back links had minor effects on the size of approximate graph schemas. On the other hand, for random queries, the experiment results showed that the expressiveness of the approximate graph schema was satisfactory in restricting the search space of the regular path expression queries.

7 Conclusion

Semi-structured data are represented as labeled directed graphs and queried with regular path expressions. The accurate graph schema, DataGuide, which does not contain missing, duplicate or false paths in the schema, is not effective for optimization of a wide range of regular path expression queries due to the fact that its size can be much larger than the original data graph. In this paper, we proposed an approximate graph schema based on an incremental clustering method which clusters vertices with similar incoming and outgoing edge patterns. Our experimental studies showed that for different data graphs the sizes of approximate graph schemas were smaller than that of accurate graph schemas. Also, for regular path expression queries, query optimization with the approximate graph schema outperformed the accurate graph schema. In the near future, we plan to

- explore various approximate graph schemas [19] and conduct an extensive performance study in order to evaluate their effectiveness.
- investigate different query evaluation strategies using the schema [6,16,9].

Acknowledgments. This project is partially supported by the National Science Foundation, China (NSFC) under the contract no. 69633020 and by the Chinese University of Hong Kong, under the Strategic Grant programme (project no.: 44M5007).

References

1. S. Abiteboul. Querying semi-structured data. In *Proceedings of the International Conference On Database Theory*, 1997.
2. S. Abiteboul, D. Quass, J. McHugh, J. Widom, and J. Wiener. The lorel query language for semi-structured data. *International Journal on Digital Libraries*, 1(1):68–88, 1997.
3. P. Bueman, S. Davidson, G. Hillebrand, and D. Suciu. A query language and optimization techniques for unstructured data. In *Proceedings of ACM SIGMOD International Conference on Management of Data*, 1996.
4. P. Buneman. Semistructured data. In *Proceedings of PODS*, 1997.
5. P. Buneman, S. Davidson, M. Fernandez, and D. Suciu. Adding structure to unstructured data. In *Proceedings of International Conference on Database Theory*, 1997.

6. V. Christophides, S. Cluet, and G. Moerkotte. Evaluating queries with generalized path expressions. In *Proceedings of ACM SIGMOD International Conference on Management of Data*, 1996.
7. M. Fernandez and D. Suciu. Optimizing regular path expressions using graph schemas. In *Proceedings of International Conference on Data Engineering*, 1998.
8. D. Fisher. Knowledge acquisition via incremental conceptual clustering. In J. Shavlik and T. Dietterich, editors, *Readings in Machine Learning*. Morgan Kaufmann Publishers, 1990.
9. G. Gardarin, J. Gruser, and Z. Tang. Cost-based selection of path expression processing algorithms in object-oriented databases. In *Proceedings of the 22nd International Conference on Very Large Data Bases*, 1996.
10. R. Goldman and J. Widom. Dataguides: Enabling query formulation and optimization in semistructured databases. In *Proceedings of the 23rd International Conference on Very Large Data Bases*, 1997.
11. R. Goldman and J. Widom. Approximate dataguides. Technical report, Stanford University, 1998.
12. G. Graefe. Query evaluation techniques for large databases. *ACM Computing Surveys*, 25(2):73–170, 1993.
13. D. Konopnicki and O. Shmueli. W3qs:a query system for the world wide web. In *Proceedings of the International Conference on Very Large Data Bases*, 1995.
14. J. McHugh and J. Widom. Compile-time path expansion in lore. Technical report, Stanford University, 1998.
15. A. Mendelzon, G. Mihaila, and T. Milo. Querying the world wide web. In *Proceedings of the Fourth Conference on Parallel and Distributed Information Systems*, 1996.
16. A. Mendelzon and P. Wood. Finding regular simple paths in graph databases. *SIAM Journal of Computing*, 24(6):1235–1258, 1995.
17. S. Nestorov, S. Abiteboul, and R. Motwani. Inferring structure in semistructured data. In *Proceedings of the Workshop on Management of Semistructured Data*, 1997.
18. S. Nestorov, S. Abiteboul, and R. Motwani. Extracting schema from semistructured data. In *Proceedings of ACM SIGMOD International Conference on Management of Data*, 1998.
19. S. Nestorov, J. Ullman, J. Wiener, and S. Chawathe. Representative objects: Concise representations of semistructured, hierarchical data. In *Proceedings of International Conference on Data Engineering*, 1997.
20. Y. Papakonstantinou, H. Garcia-Molina, and J. Widom. Object exchange across heterogeneous information sources. In *Proceedings of International Conference on Data Engineering*, 1995.

A Data Model for Semistructured Data with Partial and Inconsistent Information

Mengchi Liu[1] and Tok Wang Ling[2]

[1] Department of Computer Science, University of Regina
Regina, Saskatchewan, Canada S4S 0A2
mliu@cs.uregina.ca
[2] School of Computing, National University of Singapore
Lower Kent Ridge Road, Singapore 119260
lingtw@comp.nus.edu.sg

Abstract With the recent popularity of the World Wide Web, an enormous amount of heterogeneous information is now available online. As a result, information about real world objects may spread over different data sources and may be partial and inconsistent. How to manipulate such semistructured data is thus a challenge. Previous work on semistructured data mainly focuses on developing query languages and systems to retrieve semistructured data. Relatively less attention has been paid to the manipulation of such data. In order to manipulate such semistructured data, we need a data model that is more expressive than the existing graph-based and tree-based ones to account for the existence of partial and inconsistent information from different data sources. In this paper, we propose such a data model for semistructured data that allows partial and inconsistent information and discuss how to manipulate such semistructured data.

1 Introduction

With the recent popularity of the World Wide Web, an enormous amount of heterogeneous information is now available online. As a result, information about real world objects may spread over different data sources. Such information may be partial (incomplete) and inconsistent in the data that come from various sources. The need to manipulate such kind of semistructured data has become more and more important. Previous work on semistructured data mainly focuses on developing query languages and systems to retrieve semistructured data, such as W3QS [12], WebSQL [26], WebLog [19], UnQL [9], Lorel [2]. WebOQL [4], and Florid [15]. For surveys, see [1,14]. How to manipulate semistructured data coming from various sources has also received some attention [3,6,11,10,21,28]. Earlier proposals are based on simple graph-based data models such as OEM [29] or tree-based data models such as the one in [8], which fail to account for the existence of partial and inconsistent information. For example, most academic people should have a Bibtex database to keep references. While two or more persons work together on a paper, an immediate problem is how to merge multiple Bibtex databases. Although all Bibtex databases have similar structures,

C. Zaniolo et al. (Eds.): EDBT 2000, LNCS 1777, pp. 317–331, 2000.
© Springer-Verlag Berlin Heidelberg 2000

the values in these databases may be partial or inconsistent. The typical case is the *authors* of a paper. Someone likes to list all authors in full names, but others may just indicate the first one or two authors. Even for one author, the order of first name (or initial) and last name may be different. Furthermore, partial data for the same record may be missing or inconsistent. Therefore, how to obtain information as complete as possible from these sources, i.e., their union, how to get the common information from different data sources, i.e., their intersection, or how to find the information that is in the first data source but not in the second one, i.e., their difference, are interesting questions. In other words, we need a set of operations to manipulate such semistructured data.

In the past decade, the similar problem, that is, manipulating data with partial and/or incomplete information, has been investigated in depth in the context of relational, complex object and multiple databases [5,7,13,16,17,18,22,23,27,30]. Specific operations such as union, intersection [5] and join [7] are introduced to manipulate such data. However, these works focus on typed data and support only homogeneous sets and tuples. Thus, it is difficult to directly apply them on semistructured data, where although the data may have some structure, the structure is not as rigid, regular, or complete as that required by traditional database systems [1].

In this paper, we propose a novel semistructured data model to reflect the existence of partial and inconsistent information. We also study how to manipulate such semistructured data with a set of operations. In particular, we focus on three operations, *union*, *intersection* and *difference*, and discuss their semantic properties.

The rest of the paper is organized as follows. Section 2 defines our semistructured data model. Section 3 discusses how to manipulate semistructured data and the semantic properties. Section 4 summarizes and points out further research issues.

2   Semistructured Data Models

In this section, we introduce our data model to represent semistructured data. The data model consists of *semistructured data* which are built from *objects*. We assume the existence of a set $\mathcal{M}$ of markers, a set $\mathcal{A}$ of attribute labels, and a set $\mathcal{U}$ of constants such that $\mathcal{M}$ and $\mathcal{A} \cup \mathcal{U}$ are disjoint.

Definition 1. The notion of *objects* is defined as follows:

(1) Constants in $\mathcal{U}$ are objects called *atomic* objects.
(2) Markers in $\mathcal{M}$ are objects called *marker* objects.
(3) There is a special object $\perp$.
(4) If $O_1, ..., O_n, (n > 1)$ are distinct objects, then $O_1|...|O_n$ is an object called *or-value*.
(5) If $O_1, ..., O_n, (n \geq 0)$ are distinct objects, then $\langle O_1, ..., O_n \rangle$ is an object called *partial set*.

(6) If $O_1, ..., O_n, (n \geq 0)$ are distinct objects, then $\{O_1, ..., O_n\}$ is an object called *complete set*.

(7) If $O_1, ..., O_n, (n \geq 0)$ are objects and $A_1, ..., A_n$ are distinct attribute labels, then $O \equiv [A_1 \Rightarrow O_1, ..., A_n \Rightarrow O_n]$ is an object called *tuple*. We denote O_i by $O.A_i$. We also assume that $O.A = \perp$ for an attribute A not in $\{A_1, ..., A_n\}$.

We use $\perp$ for null/unknown object. For example, in a tuple representing a person, if the age of the person is unknown, then we use $[..., age \Rightarrow \perp, ...]$.

As we are dealing with the manipulations of semistructured data from different sources, it is possible that we have conflicting information. In this case, we use an *or-value* to record the conflicting result. For example, the or-value $21|22$ in the tuple $[..., age \Rightarrow 21|22, ...]$ implies the age is 21 or 22 as there is a conflict right now and it is not clear that any one of these two values is correct. It is up to the user to solve the conflicts.

The *markers* are used to identify/refer to an object uniquely. They are similar to *object identifier* in OEM (Object Exchange Model) [2], but different in nature. An *object identifier* is attached to each object, even to each constant in OEM. In contrast, *markers* in our data model can be used to identify complex objects. For example, in a Bibtex database, markers correspond to the keys [20]; in a Web page, markers correspond to URLs. See Examples 1 and 2.

Besides null/unknown and inconsistent values, it is quite common that partial rather than complete information is provided for a set. For example, in a Bibtex file, someone may only give partial authorship such as *"Bob and others"* to indicate *"Bob, et al."* are the authors. In this case, the set that contains *"Bob"* is partial and should be represented with $\langle "Bob" \rangle$ to indicate that the set only provides partial authorship. In particular, the empty partial set $\langle \rangle$ indicates that it is a set but we do not know what is in it. It contains more information than $\perp$. On the other hand, if we know the complete authorship such as *"Bob and Tom"*, then the set that contains *"Bob"* and *"Tom"* is complete and should be represented in our data model as $\{"Bob", "Tom"\}$. The empty set $\{\}$ indicates there is nothing in it, which is quite different from $\langle \rangle$. The notions of partial and complete set were first introduced in ROL [24] and later extended in Relationlog [25]. They are used to represent the open and closed world assumption on sets in a database.

We now define the notion of semistructured data as follows.

Definition 2. Let $m_1, ..., m_n \in \mathcal{M}$ be markers with $n > 0$, $m \equiv m_1|...|m_n$, and O an object. Then $m : O$ is a *semistructured data*. When $n = 1$ and O does not contain or-values or marked objects, it is called *real*. Otherwise, it is called *virtual*.

Real semistructured data are the ones that can exist in the real world while virtual ones are those generated with our operations, union, intersection, and difference as defined in Section 3. Just like in the object-oriented paradigm, objects with similar properties are grouped into a class.

For example, a Bibtex file can be viewed as a set of real semistructured data while a Web page can be viewed as a single real semistructured data.

Example 1. Consider the following bib file with two cross-reference entries:

```
@InBook{Bob,
   author  = "Bob and others",
   title   = "Oracle",
   crossref = DB}

@Book{DB,
   booktitle = "Database",
   editor    = "John",
   year      = 1999}
```

They can be represented as two semistructured data as follows:

Bob: [*type* ⇒ *"InBook"*, *author* ⇒ ⟨*"Bob"*⟩, *title* ⇒ *"Oracle"*, *crossref* ⇒ *DB*]
DB: [*type* ⇒ *"Book"*, *booktitle* ⇒ *"Database"*, *editor* ⇒ *"John"*, *year* ⇒ 1999]

where *Bob* and *DB* are markers, and ⟨*"Bob"*⟩ is a partial set which indicates *"Bob"* is one of the authors.

Example 2. Consider the following simplified Web page:

```
<html>
<head><title>CSDept</title></head>
<body>
<h2>People</h2>
<ul>
<li><a href="faculty.html">      Faculty </a>
<li><a href="staff.html">        Staff  </a>
<li><a href="students.html">     Students</a>
</ul>
<h2><a href="programs.html"> Programs<a></h2>
<h2><a href="research.html"> Research<a></h2>
</body>
</html>
```

Suppose *www.cs.uregina.ca* is the URL of this web page. Then it can be represented as a semistructured data in our data model as follows:

www.cs.uregina.ca : [
    Title ⇒ *CSDept*,
    People ⇒ {[*Faculty* ⇒ *faculty.html*],
              [*Staff* ⇒ *staff.html*],
              [*Students* ⇒ *students.html*]},
    Programs ⇒ *programs.html*,
    Research ⇒ *research.html*
    ]

where *www.cs.uregina.ca, faculty.html, staff.html, students.html, programs.html, research.html* are markers, and the rest are attribute labels.

Note that our semistructured data model can capture more information than the existing semistructured data models such as OEM [2] and labeled tree model [9] since null/unknown, *or-value*, *partial* and *complete* set objects are supported.

3 Manipulation of Semistructured Data

In this section, we discuss how to manipulate semistructured data. Consider the following semistructured data that represent two Bibtex items from two different bib files:

$B80 : [type \Rightarrow "Article", title \Rightarrow "Oracle", author \Rightarrow "Bob", year \Rightarrow 1980]$
$B82 : [type \Rightarrow "Article", title \Rightarrow "Oracle", year \Rightarrow 1980, journal \Rightarrow "IS"]$

The first tuple has a null value for the attribute *journal* whereas the second has a null value for the attribute *author*. They have different markers. Let us assume that articles can be identified by their type and title. Then the two semistructured data can be combined, that is, their union, based on the *type* and *title* attributes to obtain more information shown as follows:

$B80|B82 : [type \Rightarrow "Article", title \Rightarrow "Oracle", author \Rightarrow "Bob",$
$year \Rightarrow 1980, journal \Rightarrow "IS"]$

where $B80|B82$ means that the two Bibtex terms from two different bib files have different markers that refer to the same article.

Similarly, the information common in them, that is, their intersection based on the *type* and *title* attributes, is as follows:

$\perp : [type \Rightarrow "Article", title \Rightarrow "Oracle", year \Rightarrow 1980]$

where $\perp$ as a marker indicates that the two Bibtex terms have different markers that refer to the same article but we do not care what they are in terms of their common information.

Finally, the information in the first semistructured data but in not the second except the type and title, that is, the difference between the first and second based on the *type* and *title* attributes, is as follows:

$B80 : [type \Rightarrow "Article", title \Rightarrow "Oracle", author \Rightarrow "Bob"]$

In order to formalize these operations on semistructured data, we first introduce the following notions.

Definition 3. An object O_1 is *less informative* than an object O_2, denoted by $O_1 \unlhd O_2$, if and only if one of the following holds:

(1) $O_1 = O_2$
(2) $O_1 = \perp$
(3) $O_1 \equiv O_1'|...|O_m'$ and $O_2 \equiv O_1'|...|O_n'$ with $1 \leq m < n$

(4) O_1 is a partial set and O_2 is a partial or complete set, and for each $O \in O_1 - O_2$, there exists $O' \in O_2 - O_1$ such that $O \trianglelefteq O'$

(5) O_1 and O_2 are both tuples such that for each attribute A in O_1, $O_1.A \trianglelefteq O_2.A$

The less informative relationship is used to express the fact that one object is part of another object. It is used to determine when two objects can be manipulated and to show the properties of the operations. The special treatment of sets in (4) of Definition 3 guarantees that the less informative relationship is a partial order as in [25].

The following are several examples:

$$a \trianglelefteq a \qquad \{a\} \trianglelefteq \{a\} \qquad [A \Rightarrow a] \trianglelefteq [A \Rightarrow a] \qquad \text{by}(1)$$
$$\bot \trianglelefteq a \qquad \bot \trianglelefteq \{a\} \qquad \bot \trianglelefteq [A \Rightarrow a] \qquad \text{by}(2)$$
$$a_1 \trianglelefteq a_1|a_2 \qquad a_1|a_2 \trianglelefteq a_1|a_2|a_3 \qquad a_1|a_2|a_3 \trianglelefteq a_1|a_2|a_3 \qquad \text{by (3) or (1)}$$
$$\langle a_1 \rangle \trianglelefteq \langle a_1, a_2 \rangle \qquad \langle a_1 \rangle \trianglelefteq \{a_1, a_2\} \qquad \{a_1, a_2\} \trianglelefteq \{a_1, a_2\} \qquad \text{by (4) or (1)}$$
$$[A \Rightarrow a] \trianglelefteq [A \Rightarrow a, B \Rightarrow b] \qquad [A \Rightarrow \langle a_1 \rangle] \trianglelefteq [A \Rightarrow \langle a_1, a_2 \rangle, B \Rightarrow b] \qquad \text{by (5)}$$

Definition 4. A semistructured data $m_1 : O_1$ is *less informative* than a semistructured data $m_2 : O_2$, denoted by $m_1 : O_1 \trianglelefteq m_2 : O_2$, if and only if $m_1 \trianglelefteq m_2$ and $O_1 \trianglelefteq O_2$.

We extend the notion to sets of semistructured data as follows.

Definition 5. Let S_1 and S_2 be sets of semistructured data. Then S_1 is *less informative* than S_2, denoted by $S_1 \trianglelefteq S_2$ if and only if for each $D_1 \in S_1 - S_2$ there exists a $D_2 \in S_2 - S_1$ such that $D_1 \trianglelefteq D_2$.

It turns out that the less informative relationship has the following property.

Proposition 1. The less informative relationship is a partial order.

Definition 6. Let O_1 and O_2 be two objects and $K = \{A_1, ..., A_m\}$ a set of attributes. Then O_1 and O_2 are *compatible* with respect to K if and only if one of the following holds:

(1) both are constants and are equal
(2) both are markers and are equal
(3) both are or-values that do not contain $\bot$ and are equal set-wise.
(4) both are complete sets and are equal
(5) both are tuples and are equal or $O_1.A_i$ and $O_2.A_i$ are compatible with respect to K for $1 \leq i \leq m$

In other words, two objects are compatible with respect to K if they are other than $\bot$ and are equal, or they have compatible K value when they are tuples.

In our data model, the set K of attributes in the above definition is similar to the notion of the key in the relational data model, but can be non-atomic. It is used to identify objects. If two different objects are compatible, then we treat them as the different aspects of the same object so that we can manipulate them using operations to be introduced shortly.

The following pairs of objects are compatible with respect to $K = \{A, B\}$:

a	and	a	by (1)
m	and	m	by (2)
$a|b$	and	$b|a$	by (3)
$\{a_1, a_2\}$	and	$\{a_1, a_2\}$	by (4)
$[A \Rightarrow a_1, B \Rightarrow \{b_1, b_2\}, C \Rightarrow c_1]$	and	$[A \Rightarrow a_1, B \Rightarrow \{b_1, b_2\}, C \Rightarrow c_2]$	by (5)

The following pairs of objects are not compatible with respect to $K = \{A, B\}$:

$\perp$	and	$\perp$
a	and	$\perp$
a_1	and	a_2
$a_1|a_2$	and	$a_1|a_2|a_3$
$\langle a_1 \rangle$	and	$\langle a_1, a_2 \rangle$
$\langle a_1 \rangle$	and	$\{a_1, a_2\}$
$\langle a_1 \rangle$	and	$\{a_2, a_3\}$
$[A \Rightarrow a_1, B \Rightarrow \perp, C \Rightarrow \{c_1\}]$	and	$[A \Rightarrow a_1, B \Rightarrow \perp, C \Rightarrow \{c_1\}]$
$[A \Rightarrow \perp, B \Rightarrow b_1, C \Rightarrow \{c_1\}]$	and	$[A \Rightarrow \perp, B \Rightarrow b_2, C \Rightarrow \{c_1\}]$

Two $\perp$ are not compatible because two different occurrences may not denote the same real-world entity; a and $\perp$ are not compatible because $\perp$ may not mean a; $a_1|a_2$ and $a_1|a_2|a_3$ are not compatible because $a_1|a_2$ means the value is either a_1 or a_2 while $a_1|a_2|a_3$ means the value is either a_1, a_2 or a_3; $\langle a_1 \rangle$ and $\langle a_1, a_2 \rangle$ are not compatible because our knowledge about the two partial sets is different: $\langle a_1 \rangle$ means the set contains a_1 while $\langle a_1, a_2 \rangle$ means the set contains a_1 and a_2.

As shown in the above examples, two identical objects may not be compatible if they involve $\perp$.

Definition 7. Let $S_1 \equiv m_1 : O_1$ and $S_2 \equiv m_2 : O_2$ be two semistructured data and $K = \{A_1, ..., A_k\}$, $k \geq 1$. Then S_1 and S_2 are *compatible* with respect to K if and only if O_1 and O_2 are compatible with respect to K.

Consider the two semistructured data again:

$B80 : [type \Rightarrow "Article", title \Rightarrow "Oracle", author \Rightarrow "Bob", year \Rightarrow 1980]$
$B82 : [type \Rightarrow "Article", title \Rightarrow "Oracle", year \Rightarrow 1980, journal \Rightarrow "IS"]$

They are compatible with respect to $K = \{type, title\}$, but not compatible with respect to $K' = \{type, title, author\}$ or $K'' = \{type, title, author, year\}$.

The main goal of this paper is to define how to manipulate semistructured data when given a set of attributes. Now we introduce the *union* operation which is used to get more information from two objects representing the same real-world entity. It is similar to the union operation in [5], the join operation in [7], and the grouping operation in [25], but it handles partial and inconsistent information.

Definition 8. Let $K = \{A_1, ..., A_m\}$ be a set of attributes, and O_1 and O_2 two objects. Then their *union* based on K, denoted by $O_1 \cup_K O_2$, is defined as follows:

(1) $O_1 \cup_K O_1 = O_1$, $O_1 \cup_K \perp = O_1$

(2) If O_1 and O_2 are distinct partial sets, then

$O_1 \cup_K O_2 = \langle O \mid O \in O_1,\ \nexists O' \in O_2,\ O$ and O' are compatible wrt K, or
$O \in O_2,\ \nexists O' \in O_1,\ O$ and O' are compatible wrt K, or
$\exists O' \in O_1, \exists O'' \in O_2,\ O'$ and O'' are compatible wrt K,
$O = O' \cup_K O'' \rangle$

(3) If O_1 is a partial set and O_2 is a complete set such that $O_1 \trianglelefteq O_2$, then
$O_1 \cup_K O_2 = O_2$

(4) If O_1 and O_2 are distinct tuples that are compatible with respect to $A_1, ..., A_m$ and $A_1, ..., A_n$ are all attributes in them, then
$O_1 \cup_K O_2 = [A_1 \Rightarrow O_1.A_1 \cup_K O_2.A_1, ..., A_n \Rightarrow O_1.A_n \cup_K O_2.A_n]$

(5) In all other cases, $O_1 \cup_K O_2 = O_1 | O_2$

Example 3. The following are several examples where $K = \{A, B\}$:

$a \cup_K a = a$	by (1)
$\{a\} \cup_K \{a\} = \{a\}$	by (1)
$[C \Rightarrow c] \cup_K [C \Rightarrow c] = [C \Rightarrow c]$	by (1)
$a \cup_K \perp = a$	by (1)
$\langle a \rangle \cup_K \langle b \rangle = \langle a, b \rangle$	by (2)
$\langle a_1, a_2 \rangle \cup_K \{a_1, a_2, a_3\} = \{a_1, a_2, a_3\}$	by (3)
$[A \Rightarrow a_1, B \Rightarrow b_1, C \Rightarrow \langle c_1 \rangle] \cup_K [A \Rightarrow a_1, B \Rightarrow b_1, C \Rightarrow \{c_1, c_2\}]$	
$= [A \Rightarrow a_1, B \Rightarrow b_1, C \Rightarrow \{c_1, c_2\}]$	by (4)
$a_1 \cup_K a_2 = a_1 | a_2$	by (5)
$a_1 \cup_K \{a_1\} = a_1 | \{a_1\}$	by (5)
$a_1 \cup_K [A \Rightarrow a_1] = a_1 \mid [A \Rightarrow a_1]$	by (5)
$a_1 \cup_K a_2 | a_3 = a_1 | a_2 | a_3$	by (5)
$\{a_1, a_2\} \cup_K \{a_1, a_2, a_3\} = \{a_1, a_2\} | \{a_1, a_2, a_3\}$	by (5)

Note that the union of two partial sets is still a partial set as we still do not know if the result is complete. The union of two distinct complete sets however generates an or-value as shown in the last case above. Assuming that these two sets represent authors of the same paper, then their union indicates there is a conflict in them. Using the union of the traditional set theory cannot detect such a conflict.

To find common information in objects that represent the same real-world entity, we need to use the *intersection* operation which is defined as follows.

Definition 9. Let $K = \{A_1, ..., A_m\}$ be a set of attributes, and O_1 and O_2 two objects. Then their *intersection* based on K, denoted by $O_1 \cap_K O_2$, is defined as follows:

(1) $O_1 \cap_K O_1 = O_1$

(2) If O_1 and O_2 are distinct or-values such that $O'_1, ..., O'_n$ are common in them with $n \geq 1$, then $O_1 \cap_K O_2 = O'_1 | ... | O'_n$

(3) If O_1 and O_2 are distinct partial sets or one of them is complete, then
$$O_1 \cap_K O_2 = \langle O \mid \exists O' \in O_1, \exists O'' \in O_2, \ O' \text{ and } O'' \text{ are compatible wrt } K,$$
$$O = O' \cap_K O'' \rangle$$

(4) If O_1 and O_2 are distinct complete sets, then
$$O_1 \cap_K O_2 = \{O \mid \exists O' \in O_1, \exists O'' \in O_2, \ O' \text{ and } O'' \text{ are compatible wrt } K,$$
$$O = O' \cap_K O'' \}$$

(5) If O_1 and O_2 are distinct tuples that are compatible with respect to K and $A_1, ..., A_n$ are all attributes in them, then
$$O_1 \cap_K O_2 = [A_1 \Rightarrow O_1.A_1 \cap_K O_2.A_1, ..., A_n \Rightarrow O_1.A_n \cap_K O_2.A_n]$$

(6) In all other cases, $O_1 \cap_K O_2 = \perp$

Note that the intersection of two partial sets or a partial set and a complete set is a partial set as we are not sure if the result is complete. However, the intersection of complete sets is a complete set as we know exactly what are the common elements in two complete sets.

Example 4. The following are several examples where $K = \{A, B\}$:

$a \cap_K a = a$	by (1)
$\{a\} \cap_K \{a\} = \{a\}$	by (1)
$[C \Rightarrow c] \cap_K [C \Rightarrow c] = [C \Rightarrow c]$	by (1)
$a_1 \cap_K a_1 | a_2 = a_1$	by (2)
$\langle a_1, a_2 \rangle \cap_K \langle a_1, a_2, a_3 \rangle = \langle a_1, a_2 \rangle$	by (3)
$\langle a_1, a_2 \rangle \cap_K \{a_1, a_2, a_3\} = \langle a_1, a_2 \rangle$	by (3)
$\langle a_1, a_2 \rangle \cap_K \{a_3\} = \langle \rangle$	by (3)
$\{a_1, a_2\} \cap_K \{a_1, a_2, a_3\} = \{a_1, a_2\}$	by (4)
$\{a_1, a_2\} \cap_K \{a_3\} = \{\}$	by (4)
$[A \Rightarrow a_1, B \Rightarrow b_1, C \Rightarrow \langle c_1 \rangle] \cap_K [A \Rightarrow a_1, B \Rightarrow b_1, C \Rightarrow \{c_1, c_2\}]$	
$= [A \Rightarrow a_1, B \Rightarrow b_1, C \Rightarrow \langle c_1 \rangle]$	by (5)
$a_1 \cap_K \perp = \perp$	by (6)
$a_1 \cap_K a_2 = \perp$	by (6)
$a_1 \cap_K [A \Rightarrow a_1] = \perp$	by (6)
$[A \Rightarrow a_1, B \Rightarrow b_1, C \Rightarrow c_1] \cap_K [A \Rightarrow a_2, B \Rightarrow b_2, C \Rightarrow c_2] = \perp$	by (6)

Proposition 2. The union and intersection operations are commutative.

To obtain information in the first object but not in the second, we can use the *difference* operation defined as follows.

Definition 10. Let $K = \{A_1, ..., A_m\}$ be a set of attributes, and O_1 and O_2 two objects. Then their *difference* based on K, denoted by $O_1 -_K O_2$, is defined as follows:

(1) If O_1 is an object other than a partial or complete set, then $O_1 -_K O_1 = \bot$

(2) If O_1 and O_2 are distinct or-values such that $O'_1, ..., O'_n$ are all objects in O_1 but not in O_2 with $n \geq 1$, then $O_1 -_K O_2 = O'_1|...|O'_n$

(3) If O_1 is a partial set and O_2 is a partial or complete set, then
$$O_1 -_K O_2 = \langle O \mid O \in O_1, \not\exists O' \in O_2, \ O \text{ and } O' \text{ are compatible wrt } K, \text{ or}$$
$$\exists O' \in O_1, \exists O'' \in O_2, \ O' \text{ and } O'' \text{ are compatible wrt } K,$$
$$O{=}O' -_K O''\rangle$$

(4) If O_1 is a complete set and O_2 is a partial or complete set, then
$$O_1 -_K O_2 = \{O \mid O \in O_1, \not\exists O' \in O_2, \ O \text{ and } O' \text{ are compatible wrt } K, \text{ or}$$
$$\exists O' \in O_1, \exists O'' \in O_2, \ O' \text{ and } O'' \text{ are compatible wrt } K,$$
$$O{=}O' -_K O''\}$$

(5) If O_1 and O_2 are distinct tuples that are compatible with respect to K and $B_1, ..., B_n$ all attributes in O_1 other than $A_1, ..., A_m$, then
$$O_1 -_K O_2 = [A_1 \Rightarrow O_1.A_1, ..., A_m \Rightarrow O_1.A_m,$$
$$B_1 \Rightarrow O_1.B_1 -_K O_2.B_1, ...B_n \Rightarrow O_1.B_n -_K O_2.B_n]$$

(6) In all other cases, $O_1 -_K O_2 = O_1$

Note that we keep the value of K in the result as it provides the identity for the result.

Example 5. The following are several examples where $K = \{A, B\}$:

$$a -_K a = \bot \hspace{8cm} \text{by (1)}$$
$$a -_K \bot = a \hspace{8cm} \text{by (6)}$$
$$a_1|a_2 -_K a_1 = a_2 \hspace{7cm} \text{by (2)}$$
$$\langle a_1, a_2\rangle -_K \langle a_2, a_3\rangle = \langle a_1\rangle \hspace{5.5cm} \text{by (3)}$$
$$\langle a_1, a_2\rangle -_K \{a_1, a_2\} = \langle\rangle \hspace{5.5cm} \text{by (3)}$$
$$\{a_1, a_2\} -_K \langle a_3\rangle = \{a_1, a_2\} \hspace{5cm} \text{by (4)}$$
$$\{a_1, a_2\} -_K \{a_1, a_2\} = \{\} \hspace{5.5cm} \text{by (4)}$$
$$[A \Rightarrow a_1, B \Rightarrow b_1, C \Rightarrow c_1|c_2, D \Rightarrow \{d_1, d_2\}] -_K [A \Rightarrow a_1, B \Rightarrow b_1, C \Rightarrow c_2]$$
$$= [A \Rightarrow a_1, B \Rightarrow b_1, C \Rightarrow c_1, D \Rightarrow \{d_1, d_2\}] \hspace{2.5cm} \text{by (5)}$$
$$[A \Rightarrow a_1, B \Rightarrow \langle b_1\rangle] -_K [A \Rightarrow a_2, B \Rightarrow \langle b_2\rangle, C \Rightarrow c_2]$$
$$= [A \Rightarrow a_1, B \Rightarrow \langle b_1\rangle] \hspace{6cm} \text{by (6)}$$

Definition 11. Let $K = \{A_1, ..., A_m\}$ be a set of attributes, $D_1 = m_1 : O_1$ and $D_2 = m_2 : O_2$ two semistructured data. Then their *union*, *intersection* and *difference* based on K, denoted by $D_1 \cup_K D_2$, $D_1 \cap_K D_2$, and $D_1 -_K D_2$, are defined as follows:

$$D_1 \cup_K D_2 = m_1 \cup_K m_2 : O_1 \cup_K O_2$$
$$D_1 \cap_K D_2 = m_1 \cap_K m_2 : O_1 \cap_K O_2$$
$$D_1 -_K D_2 = m_1 -_K m_2 : O_1 -_K O_2$$

Definition 12. Let $K = \{A_1, ..., A_m\}$ be a set of attributes, S_1 and S_2 two sets of semistructured data. Then their *union*, *intersection* and *difference* based on K, denoted by $S_1 \cup_K S_2$, $S_1 \cap_K S_2$, and $S_1 -_K S_2$ are defined as follows:

$S_1 \cup_K S_2 = \{D_1 \in S_1 \mid \not\exists D_2 \in S_2$ such that D_1 and D_2 are compatible wrt $K\}$
$\qquad \cup \{D_2 \in S_2 \mid \not\exists D_1 \in S_1$ such that D_1 and D_2 are compatible wrt $K\}$
$\qquad \cup \{D_1 \cap_K D_2 \mid D_1 \in S_1, D_2 \in S_2$ such that D_1 and D_2 are compatible wrt $K\}$

$S_1 \cap_K S_2 = \{D_1 \cap_K D_2 \mid D_1 \in S_1, D_2 \in S_2$ such that D_1 and D_2 are compatible wrt $K\}$

$S_1 -_K S_2 = \{D_1 \in S_1 \mid \not\exists D_2 \in S_2$ such that D_1 and D_2 are compatible wrt $K\}$
$\qquad \cup \{D_1 -_K D_2 \mid D_1 \in S_1, D_2 \in S_2$ such that D_1 and D_2 are compatible wrt $K\}$

Example 6. Consider the following two sets of semistructured data which are essentially two Bibtex files, one of which (S_1) contains pure journal papers and the other (S_2) contains both journal and conference papers.

$S_1 = \{B80: [type \Rightarrow "Article", title \Rightarrow "Oracle",\ auth \Rightarrow "Bob",\ year \Rightarrow 1980\quad],$
$\qquad S78: [type \Rightarrow "Article", title \Rightarrow "Ingres",\ auth \Rightarrow "Sam", jnl \Rightarrow "TODS"],$
$\qquad A78: [type \Rightarrow "Article", title \Rightarrow "Datalog", auth \Rightarrow "Ann", year \Rightarrow 1978\quad],$
$\qquad J88: [type \Rightarrow "Article", title \Rightarrow "DOOD",\ auth \Rightarrow "Joe",\ jnl \Rightarrow "JLP"\quad]\}$

$S_2 = \{B82: [type \Rightarrow "Article", title \Rightarrow "Oracle",\ auth \Rightarrow "Bob",\ year \Rightarrow 1980\quad],$
$\qquad A78: [type \Rightarrow "Article", title \Rightarrow "Datalog", auth \Rightarrow "Tom", year \Rightarrow 1978\quad],$
$\qquad P90: [type \Rightarrow "Article", title \Rightarrow "DOOD",\ auth \Rightarrow "Pam", jnl \Rightarrow "JLP"\quad],$
$\qquad S85: [type \Rightarrow "Article", title \Rightarrow "NF2",\quad auth \Rightarrow "Sam", year \Rightarrow 1985\quad],$
$\qquad T79: [type \Rightarrow "InProc", title \Rightarrow "RDB",\quad auth \Rightarrow "Tom", conf \Rightarrow "PODS"],$
$\qquad A75: [type \Rightarrow "InProc", title \Rightarrow "NF2",\quad auth \Rightarrow "Ann", year \Rightarrow 1975\quad],$
$\qquad S76: [type \Rightarrow "InProc", title \Rightarrow "Ingres",\ auth \Rightarrow "Sam", conf \Rightarrow "EDBT"]\}$

Let $K = \{type, title\}$. Then their union, intersection and difference based on K are as follows:

$S_1 \cup_K S_2$
$= \{S78: [type \Rightarrow "Article", title \Rightarrow "Ingres",\ auth \Rightarrow "Sam", jnl \Rightarrow "TODS"\quad]\}$
$\cup \{S85: [type \Rightarrow "Article", title \Rightarrow "NF2",\quad auth \Rightarrow "Sam", year \Rightarrow 1985\quad],$
$\qquad T79: [type \Rightarrow "InProc", title \Rightarrow "RDB",\quad auth \Rightarrow "Tom", conf \Rightarrow "PODS"],$
$\qquad A75: [type \Rightarrow "InProc", title \Rightarrow "NF2",\quad auth \Rightarrow "Ann", year \Rightarrow 1975\quad],$
$\qquad S76: [type \Rightarrow "InProc", title \Rightarrow "Ingres",\ auth \Rightarrow "Sam", conf \Rightarrow "EDBT"]\}$
$\cup \{B80: [type \Rightarrow "Article", title \Rightarrow "Oracle",\ auth \Rightarrow "Bob",\ year \Rightarrow 1980\quad] \cup_K$
$\qquad B82: [type \Rightarrow "Article", title \Rightarrow "Oracle",\ auth \Rightarrow "Bob",\ year \Rightarrow 1980\quad],$
$\qquad A78: [type \Rightarrow "Article", title \Rightarrow "Datalog", auth \Rightarrow "Ann", year \Rightarrow 1978\quad] \cup_K$
$\qquad A78: [type \Rightarrow "Article", title \Rightarrow "Datalog", auth \Rightarrow "Tom", year \Rightarrow 1978\quad],$
$\qquad J88: [type \Rightarrow "Article", title \Rightarrow "DOOD",\ auth \Rightarrow "Joe",\ jnl \Rightarrow "JLP"\quad] \cup_K$
$\qquad P90: [type \Rightarrow "Article", title \Rightarrow "DOOD",\ auth \Rightarrow "Pam", jnl \Rightarrow "JLP"\quad]\}$

$= \{S78 \qquad : [type \Rightarrow "Article", title \Rightarrow "Ingres",\ auth \Rightarrow "Sam", jnl \Rightarrow "TODS"\quad],$
$\quad S85 \qquad : [type \Rightarrow "Article", title \Rightarrow "NF2",\quad auth \Rightarrow "Sam", year \Rightarrow 1985\quad],$
$\quad T79 \qquad : [type \Rightarrow "InProc", title \Rightarrow "RDB",\quad auth \Rightarrow "Tom", conf \Rightarrow "PODS"],$
$\quad A75 \qquad : [type \Rightarrow "InProc", title \Rightarrow "NF2",\quad auth \Rightarrow "Ann", year \Rightarrow 1975\quad],$
$\quad S76 \qquad : [type \Rightarrow "InProc", title \Rightarrow "Ingres",\ auth \Rightarrow "Sam", conf \Rightarrow "EDBT"\quad],$
$\quad B80|B82: [type \Rightarrow "Article", title \Rightarrow "Oracle",\ auth \Rightarrow "Bob", year \Rightarrow 1980\quad],$
$\quad A78 \qquad : [type \Rightarrow "Article", title \Rightarrow "Datalog", auth" Ann"|"Tom", yr \Rightarrow 1978\quad],$
$\quad J88|P90: [type \Rightarrow "Article", title \Rightarrow "DOOD",\ auth \Rightarrow "Joe"|"Pam", jnl \Rightarrow JLP]\}$

$S_1 \cap_K S_2$

$= \{B80: [type \Rightarrow "Article", title \Rightarrow "Oracle", \ auth \Rightarrow "Bob", \ year \Rightarrow 1980 \ ] \ \cap_K$
    $\quad B82: [type \Rightarrow "Article", title \Rightarrow "Oracle", \ auth \Rightarrow "Bob", \ year \Rightarrow 1980 \ ],$
    $\quad A78: [type \Rightarrow "Article", title \Rightarrow "Datalog", auth \Rightarrow "Ann", year \Rightarrow 1978 \ ] \ \cap_K$
    $\quad A78: [type \Rightarrow "Article", title \Rightarrow "Datalog", auth \Rightarrow "Tom", year \Rightarrow 1978 \ ],$
    $\quad J88: [type \Rightarrow "Article", title \Rightarrow "DOOD", \ auth \Rightarrow "Joe", \ jnl \Rightarrow "JLP"] \ \cap_K$
    $\quad P90: [type \Rightarrow "Article", title \Rightarrow "DOOD", \ auth \Rightarrow "Pam", jnl \Rightarrow "JLP"]\}$
$= \{ \ \perp : [type \Rightarrow "Article", title \Rightarrow "Oracle", \ auth \Rightarrow "Bob", year \Rightarrow 1980],$
    $\quad A78: [type \Rightarrow "Article", title \Rightarrow "Datalog", year \Rightarrow 1978 \qquad\qquad],$
    $\quad \perp \ : [type \Rightarrow "Article", title \Rightarrow "DOOD", \ jnl \Rightarrow "JLP" \qquad\qquad]\}$

$S_1 -_K S_2$

$= \{S78: [type \Rightarrow "Article", title \Rightarrow "Ingres", \ auth \Rightarrow "Sam", jnl \Rightarrow "TODS"]\}$
$\cup \ \{ B80: [type \Rightarrow "Article", title \Rightarrow "Oracle", \ auth \Rightarrow "Bob", \ year \Rightarrow 1980 \quad] \ -_K$
    $\quad B82: [type \Rightarrow "Article", title \Rightarrow "Oracle", \ auth \Rightarrow "Bob", \ year \Rightarrow 1980 \quad],$
    $\quad A78: [type \Rightarrow "Article", title \Rightarrow "Datalog", auth \Rightarrow "Ann", year \Rightarrow 1978 \quad] \ -_K$
    $\quad A78: [type \Rightarrow "Article", title \Rightarrow "Datalog", auth \Rightarrow "Tom", year \Rightarrow 1978 \quad],$
    $\quad J88: [type \Rightarrow "Article", title \Rightarrow "DOOD", \ auth \Rightarrow "Joe", \ jnl \Rightarrow "JLP" \quad] \ -_K$
    $\quad P90: [type \Rightarrow "Article", title \Rightarrow "DOOD", \ auth \Rightarrow "Pam", jnl \Rightarrow "JLP" \quad]\}$
$= \{S78: [type \Rightarrow "Article", title \Rightarrow "Ingres", \ auth \Rightarrow "Sam", jnl \Rightarrow "TODS"],$
    $\quad B80: [type \Rightarrow "Article", title \Rightarrow "Oracle" \qquad\qquad\qquad\qquad\qquad],$
    $\quad \perp \ : [type \Rightarrow "Article", title \Rightarrow "Datalog", auth \Rightarrow "Ann" \qquad\qquad],$
    $\quad J88: [type \Rightarrow "Article", title \Rightarrow "DOOD", \ auth \Rightarrow "Joe" \qquad\qquad\qquad]\}$

Note that the two semistructured data with title *"Ingres"* (also *"NF2"*) are not compatible as one has type *"Article"* and the other has type *"InProc"*.

As the above example shows, the union operation combines sets of semistructured data and records inconsistency in the meantime, the intersection operation finds common information in sets of semistructured data and indicates inconsistency in the meantime, while the difference operation finds the information in the first set of semistructured data but in not the second set.

The user can then solve the inconsistency based on the results.

The *union, intersection,* and *difference* operations have the following properties.

Proposition 3. Let S_1 and S_2 be sets of semistructured data and K a nonempty set of attributes. Then

(1) $S_1 \ \trianglelefteq \ S_1 \cup_K S_2, \quad S_2 \ \trianglelefteq \ S_1 \cup_K S_2$
(2) $S_1 \cap_K S_2 \ \trianglelefteq \ S_1, \quad S_1 \cap_K S_2 \ \trianglelefteq \ S_2$
(3) $S_1 -_K S_2 \ \trianglelefteq \ S_1$
(4) $S_1 \ = \ (S_1 -_K S_2) \ \cup_K \ (S_1 \cap_K S_2)$

Proposition 4. Let S_1, S_2 be sets of semistructured data and K_1 and K_2 nonempty sets of attributes. Then $K_1 \subseteq K_2$ implies the following:

(1) $S_1 \cup_{K_2} S_2 \ \trianglelefteq \ S_1 \cup_{K_1} S_2$
(2) $S_1 \cap_{K_1} S_2 \ \trianglelefteq \ S_1 \cap_{K_2} S_2$
(3) $S_1 -_{K_1} S_2 \ \trianglelefteq \ S_1 -_{K_2} S_2$

For example, let $K_1 = \{type, title\}$ and $K_2 = \{type, title, author\}$. Then for the two sets of semistructured data in Example 6, $S_1 \cup_{K_2} S_2 \trianglelefteq S_1 \cup_{K_1} S_2$, $S_1 \cap_{K_1} S_2 \trianglelefteq S_1 \cap_{K_2} S_2$, and $S_1 -_{K_1} S_2 \trianglelefteq S_1 -_{K_2} S_2$.

4 Conclusion

The need for manipulating semistructured data naturally arises in real-world applications. In this paper, we present a novel approach for representing and manipulating semistructured data with partial and inconsistent information. Three powerful operations: *union, intersection,* and *difference,* are defined and their semantic properties are discussed in detail. This work provides a firm foundation in discussing the semantics of semistructured data in which heterogeneous data may come from various data sources with partial and inconsistent information.

Our work can be extended by adding other important operations to make it complete for query and manipulate semistructured data. Besides the operations in the nested relational and complex object data models, we need the *expand* operation that can be used to expand the markers to semistructured data for further manipulation. We also intend to investigate how to implement the semistructured data model and use it for various practical semistructured data applications. Finally, we would like to develop rule-based languages for such semistructured data model based on Complex Object Calculus [5], Datalog extensions such as Relationlog [25] and deductive object-oriented database languages such as ROL [24].

References

1. S. Abiteboul. Querying Semistructured Data. In *Proceedings of the International Conference on Data Base Theory,* pages 1–18. Springer-Verlag LNCS 1186, 1997.
2. S. Abiteboul, D. Quass, J. McHugh, J. Widom, and J. L. Wiener. The Lorel Query Language for Semistructured Data. *Intl. Journal of Digital Libraries,* 1(1):68–88, 1997.
3. J. L. Ambite, N. Ashish, G. Barish, G.A. Knoblock, S. Minton, P.J. Modi, I. Muslea, A. Philpot, and S. Tejada. ARIADNE: A system for constructing mediators for internet sources. In *Proceedings of the ACM SIGMOD International Conference on Management of Data,* 1998.
4. G. Arocena and A. Mendelzon. WebOQL: Restructuring Documents, Databases and Webs. In *Proceedings of the International Conference on Data Engineering,* pages 24–33. IEEE Computer Society, 1998.
5. F. Bancilhon and S. Khoshafian. A Calculus for Complex Objects. *J. Computer and System Sciences,* 38(2):326–340, 1989.
6. C. Beeri, G. Elber, T. Milo, Y. Sagiv, O. Shmueli, N. Tishby, Y. Kogan, D. Konopnicki, P. Mogilevski, and N. Slonim. Websuite – A tool suite for harnessing web data. In *Proceedings of the International Workshop on the Web and Databases,* 1998.
7. O. P. Buneman, S. B. Davidson, and A. Watters. A Semantics for Complex Objects and Approximate Answers. *J. Computer and System Sciences,* 43(1):170–218, 1991.

8. P. Buneman, S. Davidson, M. Fernandez, and D. Suciu. Adding Structure to Unstructured Data. In *Proceedings of the International Conference on Data Base Theory*, pages 336–350. Springer-Verlag LNCS 1186, 1997.
9. P. Buneman, S. Davidson, G. Hilebrand, and D. Suciu. A Query Language and Optimization Techniques for Unstructured Data. In *Proceedings of the ACM SIG-MOD International Conference on Management of Data*, pages 505–516, 1996.
10. S. S. Chawathe, H. Garcia-Molina, J. Hammer, K. Ireland, Y. Papakonstantinou, J. D. Ullman, and J. Widom. The TSIMMIS Project: Integration of Heterogeneous Information Sources. In *Proceedings of the 10th Meeting of the Information Processing Society of Japan*, pages 7–18, 1994.
11. W. W. Cohen. Integration of Heterogeneous Databases without Common Domains Using Queries Based on Textual Similarity. In *Proceedings of the ACM SIGMOD International Conference on Management of Data*, pages 201–212, 1998.
12. O. Shmueli D. Konopnicki. W3QS: A Query System for the World-Wide Web. In *Proceedings of the International Conference on Very Large Data Bases*, pages 54–65, Zurich,Switzerland, 1995. Morgan Kaufmann Publishers, Inc.
13. L.G. Demichiel. Resolving Database Incompatibility: An Approach to Performing Relational Operations over Mismatched Domains. *IEEE Transactions on Knowledge and Data Engineering*, 1(4):485–493, 1989.
14. D. Florescu, A. Levy, and A. Mendelzon. Database Techniques for the World-Wide Web: A Survey. *SIGMOD Record*, 26(3), 1997.
15. R. Himmeroder, G. Lausen, B. Ludascher, and C. Schlepphorst. On a declarative semantics for web queries. In *Proceedings of the International Conference on Deductive and Object-Oriented Databases*, pages 386–398, Switzerland, 1997. Springer-Verlag LNCS.
16. R. Hull and G. Zhou. A Framework for Supporting Data Integration Using the Materialized and Virtual Approaches. In *Proceedings of the ACM SIGMOD International Conference on Management of Data*, pages 481–492, 1996.
17. T. Imielinski and W. L. Jr. Incomplete Information in Relational Databases. *Journal of ACM*, 31(4):761–791, 1984.
18. W. L. Jr. On Databases with Incomplete Information. *Journal of ACM*, 28(1):41–70, 1981.
19. L. V. S. Lakshmanan, F. Sadri, and I. N. Subramanian. A Declarative Language for Querying and Restructuring the Web. In *Proceedings of the 6th International Workshop on Research Issues in Data Engineering*, 1996.
20. L. Lamport. *Latex User Guide and Reference Manual*. Addison Wesley, 2 edition, 1994.
21. A. Y. Levy, A. Rajaraman, and J. J. Ordille. Querying heterogeneous information sources using source descriptions. In *Proceedings of the International Conference on Very Large Data Bases*, pages 251–262. Morgan Kaufmann Publishers, Inc., 1996.
22. L. Libkin. A Relational Algebra for Complex Objects based on Partial Information. In *Proceedings of the Conference on Mathematical Foundations of Programming Semantics*, pages 26–41, Rostock, Germany, 1991. Springer-Verlag LNCS 495.
23. L. Libkin. Normalizing Incomplete Databases. In *Proceedings of the ACM Symposium on Principles of Database Systems*, pages 219–230, San Jose, California, 1995.
24. M. Liu. ROL: A Deductive Object Base Language. *Information Systems*, 21(5):431 – 457, 1996.
25. M. Liu. Relationlog: A Typed Extension to Datalog with Sets and Tuples. *Journal of Logic Programming*, 36(3):271–299, 1998.

26. A. Mendelzon, G. Mihaila, and T. Milo. Querying the World Wide Web. In *Proceedings of the First International Conference on Parellel and Distributed Information System*, pages 80–91, 1996.

27. A. Motro and I. Rakov. Estimating the Quality of Data in Relational Databases. In *Proceedings of the 1996 Conference on Information Quality*, pages 94–106, 1996.

28. K. Munakata. Integration of Semistructured Data Using Outer Joins. In *Proceedings of the Workshop on Management of Semistructured Data*, 1997.

29. Y. Papakonstantinou, H. Garcia-Molina, and J. Widom. Object Exchange across Heterogeneous Information. In *Proceedings of the International Conference on Data Engineering*, pages 251–260. IEEE Computer Society, 1995.

30. F. S. C. Tseng, A. L. P. Chen, and W. P. Yang. Answering Heterogeneous Databases Queries with Degrees of Uncertainty. *Distributed and Parallel Databases*, 1(3):281–302, 1993.

Data Mining

Mining Classification Rules from Datasets with Large Number of Many-Valued Attributes

Giovanni Giuffrida[1], Wesley W. Chu[1], and Dominique M. Hanssens[2]

[1] Dept. of Computer Science, Univ. of California, Los Angeles
`giovanni@cs.ucla.edu`, `wwc@cs.ucla.edu`
[2] Anderson Grad. School of Manag., Univ. of California, Los Angeles
`dominique.hanssens@anderson.ucla.edu`

Abstract Decision tree induction algorithms scale well to large datasets for their univariate and divide-and-conquer approach. However, they may fail in discovering effective knowledge when the input dataset consists of a large number of uncorrelated many-valued attributes. In this paper we present an algorithm, Noah, that tackles this problem by applying a multivariate search. Performing a multivariate search leads to a much larger consumption of computation time and memory, this may be prohibitive for large datasets. We remedy this problem by exploiting effective pruning strategies and efficient data structures. We applied our algorithm to a real marketing application of *cross-selling*. Experimental results revealed that the application database was too complex for C4.5 as it failed to discover any useful knowledge. The application database was also too large for various well known rule discovery algorithms which were not able to complete their task. The pruning techniques used in Noah are general in nature and can be used in other mining systems.

1 Introduction

Decision tree induction algorithms, such as C4.5 [15], are characterized by the following two properties:

(i) *Univariate splitting.* The partitioning criteria is based on a single variable at a time. Therefore, for n independent variables, n partitions are compared with each other. The variable that generates the partition with the best statistical significance is chosen as the next *test* [15].

(ii) *Divide–and–Conquer approach.* After a univariate split, each child node covers only a subset of the initial dataset. Thus, subsequent splits are based on the remaining portions of the training set.

Although these two properties are the backbone of the efficient implementation of decision tree induction algorithms, they limit their learning ability in certain situations. In this paper, we first discuss this shortcoming in more details. Then, we present a rule discovery algorithm, Noah, that performs a more exhaustive search than C4.5 because it uses a *multivariate* approach. We introduce effective pruning strategies to control the combinatorial explosion of the multivariate

C. Zaniolo et al. (Eds.): EDBT 2000, LNCS 1777, pp. 335–349, 2000.
© Springer-Verlag Berlin Heidelberg 2000

search. Then, we discuss the application of Noah to a real marketing cross-selling application. The application dataset was too large to be processed by CN2 [4], Ripper [5], CBA [11], and Apriori [1] and too complex for C4.5 to induce useful knowledge.

2   Preliminaries

The goal of a classifier is to *learn* a body of knowledge $\mathcal{M}$ from an input dataset I. The derived knowledge $\mathcal{M}$ can then be used to *predict* (i.e., classify) new tuples. Let us consider a set of n *independent* variables $X_1, \ldots, X_n$ such that each X_k takes on values from a domain D_{X_k}. In addition, we have another variable X_c, called the *class variable*, whose domain is $D_C = \{c_1, \ldots, c_m\}$, with m being the number of classes. The task of a classifier is:

(i) Given a training dataset I consisting of a set of *(n+1)-tuples*: $(t_1, \ldots, t_n, c)$, where $t_k \in D_{X_k}$ $(k = 1, \ldots, n)$ and $c \in D_C$;

(ii) Construct a mapping $\mathcal{M} : (D_{X_1}, \ldots, D_{X_n}) \to D_C$.

$\mathcal{M}$ can now be used to predict the class of new tuples. Thus, given a n-tuple $t' = (t'_1, t'_2, \ldots, t'_n)$, such that $t'_i \in D_{X_i}, i = 1, \ldots, n$, the predicted class c' will be: $c' = \mathcal{M}(t')$.

Let "$X = v$" be a *term* where X is an independent variable and v one of its values, $v \in D_X$. A term "$X = v$" *covers* a tuple t when the attribute X in t has value v.[1] Let a *pattern* be a *conjunction* of *terms*. A pattern ρ *covers* a tuple t when *all* the terms in ρ cover t. A rule r is a statement of the form: "if ρ then Φ" where ρ is a pattern and Φ is a class distribution. r covers a tuple t when ρ covers t. The *support* of r, $supp(r)$, is the number of tuples in I covered by ρ. Φ is the class distribution over the tuples covered by r. Φ is represented as a vector of m counters, i.e., one counter for each class, of the form: $[n_1, n_2, \ldots, n_m]$, where each n_i is the number of tuples in the training set that are (1) covered by r and (2) whose class attribute is c_i. Thus, $supp(r) = \sum_i n_i$. The *confidence* of a rule "if ρ then Φ" is a measure of *goodness* of the rule, it is function of Φ and is often based on the *entropy* concept [15]. (More details on the "confidence" in Noah are discussed later.)

3   Shortcomings of Tree Induction Algorithms

Let us now discuss the shortcomings of the univariate and divide-and-conquer approaches used in C4.5.

Shortcomings of the univariate splitting. Consider the database of Figure 1(a) where "PLAY?" is the class attribute. We can synthesize it as: *"We do not play tennis when it is hot and highly humid at the same time; we play in all other*

---

[1] We assume only discrete variables.

TEMP	HUMID.	PLAY?
hot	normal	yes
hot	medium	yes
hot	dry	yes
cool	high	yes
mild	high	yes
v_hot	high	yes
hot	high	no
hot	high	no
hot	high	no

(a) The training set

(b) The tree produced by C4.5

Fig. 1: The univariate approach of C4.5 fails to discover the evidence that (hot,high) leads to no

circumstances." We ran C4.5[2] over this dataset; it induced the *one-node* tree shown in Figure 1(b). Basically, C4.5 does not find any good predictive variable, among Temp and Humidity, to split the database upon. Therefore, it is unable to learn the strong rule: "if Temp=hot and Humid=high then No." Thus, C4.5 overlooks this piece of knowledge which is described by the *interaction* of the two independent variables. Consequently, the tree in Figure 1(b) misclassifies the tuple <hot,high> which should be classified as "No."

Shortcomings of the divide-and-conquer approach. Let us now consider the training set in Figure 2(a). By running C4.5 over it, we get the tree shown in Figure 2(b). This is a perfect tree because each leaf covers only tuples of the same class. However, C4.5 did not discover the rule r_1:"if Humid=high then No." This is because r_1 is *subsumed* by the more general rule r_2:"if Temp=hot then No" that was discovered by choosing Temp as the splitting variable at the first iteration. Consequently, when we classify the new tuple <cool,high>, C4.5 uses the rightmost leaf of the tree in Figure 2(b) and predicts "Yes." In the training set, however, there is much more evidence of "if Humid=high then No" than "if Temp=cool then Yes", therefore, it would make more sense to classify the input tuple as "No."

These two shortcomings penalize C4.5 when dealing with datasets that have a large number of uncorrelated many-valued variables[3] where each variable, when taken alone, has low predictive power. Under such circumstances the knowledge can be scattered among many rectangular portions of the input relation which are difficult to be learned by C4.5. As discussed in Section 5, C4.5 was not able to derive a meaningful tree from a database of a real-world application with a

---

[2] We used Release 8 of C4.5 available at www.cse.unsw.edu.au/~quinlan with all default settings.

[3] Intuitively, a "many-valued variable" is a variable that takes on values from a large domain.

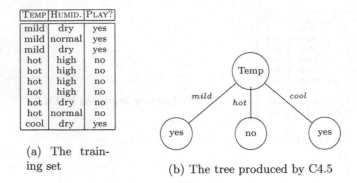

TEMP	HUMID.	PLAY?
mild	dry	yes
mild	normal	yes
mild	dry	yes
hot	high	no
hot	high	no
hot	high	no
hot	high	no
hot	dry	no
hot	normal	no
cool	dry	yes

(a) The train-
ing set

(b) The tree produced by C4.5

Fig. 2: The Divide-and-Conquer approach of C4.5 fails to discover subsumed patterns

large number of many-valued attributes. This motivated us to develop the Noah rule discovery algorithm that performs a more exhaustive search than C4.5.

By running Noah over the dataset of Figure 1(a) we get the rule: "if Temp=hot and Humid=high then No (conf=1, supp=3)." Noah uses this rule when asked to classify the new case <hot,high> and correctly outputs "No" as the predicted class. From the dataset of Figure 2(a), Noah discovers, among others, the rule: "if Humid=high then No." When asked to classify the new tuple <cool,high>, Noah uses this rule and properly classifies the new tuple as "No."

Performing a multivariate search leads to a much larger consumption of computation time and memory, this may be prohibitive for large datasets. We remedied to this problem by exploiting effective pruning strategies and efficient data structures.

4   The NOAH Algorithm

Noah is based on the well known level-wise approach used by many rule induction systems. This approach was first proposed by Agrawal *et al.* [1] in their *Apriori* algorithm for discovering association rules. In such an approach, rules are refined in a general-to-specific fashion. That is, rules are derived by progressively refining their pattern at each iteration. The main strength of this algorithm is its ability of pruning *infrequent* patterns in a hierarchical way (refer to [12] for a nice formalization of this problem).

The Noah algorithm is outlined in Figure 3. We first perform a reordering of the terms in the input relation (line 1 of the algorithm in Figure 3), which is described in detail in Section 4.1. The set R_k, containing all k-term rules, is initialized to $\emptyset$ at the beginning of each iteration (line 2). The set S_k (line 4) contains all possible k-patterns created from the current tuple t at the k-th iteration ($k = 1, 2, \dots$). In turn, for each pattern ρ of S_k the set T_k of all subpatterns of ρ with cardinality $k-1$ is computed. The **if** statement of line 6 tests

```
input    : Input Database I
output   : A Set of Rules R_final

1   TermReordering( I );
    R_final ← ∅;
    k ← 1;
    while k = 1 or R_{k-1} ≠ ∅ do
2       R_k ← ∅;
3       foreach tuple t ∈ I do
4           S_k ← {k-patterns from t};
            foreach pattern ρ ∈ S_k do
5               T_k ← {(k-1)-patterns from ρ};
6               if (T_k ⊆ R_{k-1}) or (k = 1) then
7                   if there is not a rule with pattern ρ in R_k then
8                       R_k ← R_k ∪ { "if ρ then [0,0,...,0]" };
                    end
9                   increment t.class of the rule whose pattern is ρ;
                end
            end
        end
10      R_k ← R_k/{ρ ∈ R_k | supp(ρ) < minSupp};
        S ← {ρ ∈ R_k | conf(ρ) ≥ minConf};
11      R_k ← R_k/S;
12      R_final ← R_final ∪ S;
13      Prune R_k by Confidence Upper Bound (see Section 4.2);
14      Prune R_k by Term Dependency (see Section 4.3);
        increment k;
    end
```

Fig. 3: The Noah algorithm

the existence of all such sub-patterns: If all elements of T_k exist in R_{k-1} (line 6) and a rule with pattern ρ does not already exist in R_k (line 7), then a new rule with pattern ρ is created and inserted into R_k (line 8). The class distribution of the rule with pattern ρ is then updated (line 9).

Once all tuples in the input set I have been visited, a set of k-term rules is contained in R_k. We then prune meaningless rules in R_k as follows: For each rule in R_k we first perform the minimum support pruning (line 10) as in *Apriori*. Then, as proposed by [2], we remove from R_k all rules having confidence greater than the $minConf$ threshold (line 11) and store them in R_{final} (line 12). Notice that Noah uses a different strategy from other induction systems, such as CN2 and Ripper, that always look for the most overall confident rules. In Noah, the user sets a lower bound for the rule confidence ($minConf$). Every rule whose confidence is greater than $minConf$ is considered satisfactory. While this strategy may penalize the overall accuracy of the system, it provides early stop of rule growing and thus reduces the computation complexity and improves the scalability. Furthermore, this allows the implementation of the pruning-ahead "confidence upper bound" strategy (discussed in Section 4.2). Similarly to the minimum support concept, the rationale to setup $minConf$ is application-dependent. Then, two other pruning techniques are invoked (lines 13 and 14). They are based on the "confidence upper bound" and "term dependency concepts, their details are discussed in Section 4.2 and 4.3, respectively.

After the pruning process, Noah starts a new iteration. This process continues as long as R_k contains rules to be refined. Since we never partition the input dataset in Noah, all rules are always induced from the entire training set. This alleviates the *small disjunct problem* [9,7].

4.1   Terms Reordering

To optimize rule lookup, all terms from the training set are ordered according to their support. Thus, a new version of the input dataset is created where each term is replaced by a numerical id that corresponds to the sorted order. Such a *tokenized* representation enables Noah to implement a *bit index* structure to fast test existence of *conjunctions* of terms (line 6 of the algorithm in Fig. 3).

4.2   Pruning Rules by "Confidence Upper Bound"

Recall that in Noah the user specifies a minimum value for the rule confidence (*minConf*). Once the confidence of a rule is larger than *minConf* the rule will not be further refined. This property allows us to prune rules ahead by estimating, after each iteration, whether or not a certain rule will ever satisfy the minimum confidence constraint.

In Noah, the rule confidence $\mathcal{C}(P)$ is computed as:

$$\mathcal{C}(P) = 1 - \frac{-\sum_i^k p_i \ln(p_i)}{\ln(k)} \qquad (1)$$

where P is the class probability distribution $(p_1, p_2, \dots, p_k)$ and k is the number of classes. The numerator in (1) is the entropy of the class probability distribution. The $\ln(k)$ in the denominator is used to normalize the entropy so that its value falls in the range 0 to 1. For a given rule, the larger the value of $\mathcal{C}$ the more *confident* we are about that rule.

In the following we will restrict our study to the two-class case (i.e., $k = 2$). We first need to prove the following proposition.

PROPOSITION 1 The confidence $\mathcal{C}$ of a given rule is monotonically increasing w.r.t. the absolute difference between p_1 and p_2 (where p_1 and p_2 are the probability of the first and second class, respectively).

Proof. We proceed by rewriting (1) in terms of $\Delta = |p_1 - p_2|$. Let us first consider the case $p_1 \geq p_2$. We have:

(i) $p_1 + p_2 = 1$, for the axiom of probabilities.
(ii) $\Delta = p_1 - p_2$.

After some manipulations of these two equations, we have $p_1 = \frac{1+\Delta}{2}$ and $p_2 = \frac{1-\Delta}{2}$. By substituting p_1 and p_2 into (1) we rewrite $\mathcal{C}$ as function of Δ. For the two class case, we have:

$$\hat{\mathcal{C}}(\Delta) = 1 - \frac{-\frac{1+\Delta}{2}\ln(\frac{1+\Delta}{2}) - \frac{1-\Delta}{2}\ln(\frac{1-\Delta}{2})}{\ln(2)} \qquad (2)$$

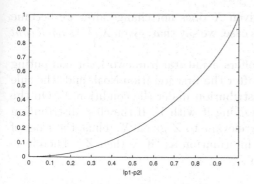

1. Given a rule r, being c_1 and c_2 the population of the first and second class of r, respectively;
2. Let $d = c_1 + c_2 - minSupp$;
3. Let $c_{small} = min(c_1, c_2)$;
4. Let $c_{large} = max(c_1, c_2)$;
5. Let $c_{small} = c_{small} - d$;
6. if $c_{small} < 0$ then $c_{small} = 0$;
7. Let $tot = c_{small} + c_{large}$;
8. Let $p_1 = c_{small}/tot$;
9. Let $p_2 = c_{large}/tot$;
10. if $\mathcal{C}([p_1, p_2]) < minConf$, then drop the rule r;

Fig. 4: Rule Confidence is a monotonically increasing function of $|p_1 - p_2|$

Fig. 5: The CUB pruning algorithm

The sign of the first derivative of (2) is always positive in the interval $(0, 1)$, therefore $\hat{\mathcal{C}}$ is monotonically increasing. The plot in Fig. 4 shows the monotonicity of $\hat{\mathcal{C}}$ w.r.t. $p_1 - p_2$. In the same manner, we can prove the monotonicity of $\hat{\mathcal{C}}$ for the case of $p_1 < p_2$. □

In our pruning strategy we combine the results of this proposition with the well known property that rule support does not increase after each rule specialization. For example, say that $minSupp = 100$ and $minConf = 0.75$. Let us assume that after some iterations Noah found the rule r "if ... then $[c_1 = 30, c_2 = 80]$." The confidence $\mathcal{C}$ of r is 0.59 and its support is 110. Thus, r covers only 10 tuples more than the specified $minSupp$ threshold. From Proposition 1 we know that the larger the difference between the two class probabilities, the higher is the rule confidence $\mathcal{C}$. Therefore, in the most optimistic case, r is specialized in such a way that 10 tuples with class attribute c_1 are not covered anymore. This maximizes the difference between the two class probabilities and, consequently, the confidence of r. Thus, we get the distribution $[c_1 = 20, c_2 = 80]$. The confidence based on this distribution is 0.72. We refer to such confidence value as the *Confidence Upper Bound* (CUB) of r. Now, since CUB is smaller then $minConf$, we drop r at this point as none of its possible specializations will have confidence larger than $minConf$ and support larger than $minSupp$ at the same time.

The algorithm of this pruning strategy for a two-class case is shown in Fig. 5. An important aspect of this pruning technique is that it does not introduce any loss of information, i.e., it pruned ahead rules which will be anyhow pruned later.

4.3   Pruning Rules by Term Dependency

This pruning strategy is based on the concept of *informational relevance* discussed by Pearl [14] and, in part, proposed by Bayardo [2] for *Apriori*. Recall that a proposition Z is said to be *conditionally independent* of Y given X if:

$$P(Z \mid X) = P(Z \mid X, Y) \tag{3}$$

The *conditional probability* of Z given X does not change after we become aware of the new proposition Y. In this case, we say that: given X, Y *is irrelevant* to Z.

The level-wise approach of Noah offers a natural framework for computing the probabilities of (3). Suppose that after the first iteration Noah finds the rule "if X then Z" where Z is the class distribution under the condition X. On the second iteration, Noah refines X by *and*-ing it with Y. If the class distribution of this new rule is still Z, then Y is irrelevant to Z given X. Thus, the rule "if X and Y then Z" provides the same information as "if X then Z." Therefore, Noah drops the rule "if X and Y then Z."

EXAMPLE 1 Consider a medical database containing the variables Sex and Pregnant. Consider the rule: "if Pregnant=Yes then Z." Refining the pattern of this rule to include the term "Sex=Female" is a waste of time since someone who is pregnant is always a female. Thus, "Sex=Female" is irrelevant for "Z", once we know the fact that "Pregnant=Yes."   □

Notice that "Pregnant=No" does not give us information on the sex of the individual, i.e., both men and women can be non-pregnant. Thus, there is no *functional dependency* between the two variables. In fact, the dependency applies only for certain configuration of these variables. Therefore, the case discussed in the previous example will not be captured by the well known notion of functional dependency—which has been extensively studied in databases.

Noah uses such dependencies among certain configurations of the input variables to cut the search space. We do not need to compare the entire distribution before and after a refinement, in fact, we only need to measure variations of the rule support for the given refinement. Noah relaxes (3) with an *almost equal* concept by means of the user-defined *minDepRatio* parameter. For example, say $minDepRatio = 0.9$ and consider a pattern ρ and a term y. If

$$\frac{supp(\rho \cup \{y\})}{supp(\rho)} > minDepRatio \qquad (4)$$

then Noah discards the rule "if ρ and y then $\ldots$". In other words, if at least 90% of the tuples covered by ρ are also covered by $\rho \cup \{y\}$, then y is considered "irrelevant given ρ."

Once an irrelevance between a pattern ρ and a term y has been discovered, we also check whether ρ and y are *equivalent* as follows. If:

$$\frac{supp(\rho \cup \{y\})}{supp(y)} > minDepRatio \qquad (5)$$

then also ρ is irrelevant given y. Thus ρ and y are equivalent. In other words, ρ is a necessary and sufficient condition for y. By summarizing, given a pattern ρ and a term y:

 − if (4) holds and (5) does not hold, then y is irrelevant given ρ;
 − if both (4) and (5) hold, then y is equivalent to ρ;

Table 1. Number of rules pruned by min-supp (ms) and term dependency (ti) per iteration on datasets from UCI repository ($minSupp = 1\%$, $minDepRatio = 90\%$)

Iter.N.	Vote		Heart		Ann		Hypo		Soybean		Adult		House		Tae		Process		Insurance	
↓	ms	td	ms	td	ms	td	ms	td	ms	td	ms	td	ms	td	ms	td	ms	td	ms	td
#1	0	0	134	0	932	0	772	0	2	0	22018	0	2408	0	0	0	110	0	0	0
#2	98	32	1374	147	9214	2509	8200	3800	478	2607	3845	433	117	381	0	67	432	2065	0	2062
#3	694	304	314	430	18	1	130	123	2766	1699	465	52	1	20	0	13	369	338	0	2201
#4	512	388	66	139			3	2	2161	3052	31	1					100	318	0	148
#5	446	461	3	17					541	1778	7	0					10	59	0	4
#6	116	154	0	2					65	299									0	1
#7	17	9							0	13										
Tot.→	1883	1348	1891	735	10164	2510	9105	3925	6013	9448	26366	486	2526	401	0	80	1021	2780	0	4416

In case y is equivalent to ρ Noah discards all rules discovered so far that contain y in their antecedent. This is because for each such a rule there will be another rule containing ρ, in place of y, that provides the same information.

Experimental results based on large application datasets showed that such pruning is very effective. This is because often databases need to be *de-normalized* prior to be processed by rule induction algorithms and such de-normalization creates many *dependences* among the terms in the databases.

We also tested this pruning strategy for ten datasets from the UCI repository using a minimum support of 1% and a dependency ratio of 90%. The number of rules pruned for each dataset by both the minimum support and the term-dependency pruning are summarized in Table 1. For each dataset (columns "Vote," "Heart," "Ann," etc. in Table 1) we report the number of rules pruned, at each iteration, by minimum support (columns "ms") and by term dependency (columns "td"). The number of rules pruned by the minimum support are reported just for comparison. For instance, for the "Vote" dataset, on the third iteration (row "#3"), 694 rules are pruned by the minimum support versus 304 rules pruned by term dependency. The last row shows the total number of rules pruned by each method.

Conversely to the "Confidence Upper Bound" earlier discussed, the term dependency pruning produces some loss of information. In fact, we drop a rule when its specialized version yields to a class distribution which is "close enough" to the more general version of the rule. The $minDepRatio$ is set by the user according to the current application. This pruning can be easily *switched off* by setting $minDepRatio$ to 1.

5   Application of Data Mining for Cross-Selling

In this section, we discuss the use of Noah for a marketing *cross-selling* application. In a cross selling activity, a company tries to sell additional products or services to its current customers. A fundamental task for a successful cross-selling activity is the accurate identification of the best prospects for a given product. Since the company acts among current customers, it has already a considerable amount of individual level data that may support such a task.

The Database. The database provided to us has a total of 41, 400 records (number of customers) and 221 attributes. The total number of possible values of all the attributes combined together is 53, 137. Furthermore, a large amount of missing and/or noisy values are presented in the dataset. We split the dataset into a training set of 27, 703 tuples and a hold-out sample of 13, 697 tuples. Almost all of the attributes are discrete; some of them have a large domain (e.g., "zip" and "city").

5.1   Data Mining with Noah for the Cross-Selling Problem

The company we are studying offers a portfolio of five possible services to its customers. We classified each customer either as "Single" (if he/she purchased only one service) or "Multiple" (if he/she purchased more than one service). Our goal is the accurate prediction of the correct class—"Multiple" or "Single"— of each customer. From a managerial perspective, we need to pinpoint those customers who are more inclined to have multiple services as they constitute the target of the cross-selling. Differently from common prediction problems, not only do we need to predict the class for each customer, we also need to associate a confidence measure to each prediction. Such confidence measures allow us to rank prospects in a *gain chart* form (discussed below) in order to target them differently. For example, we may decide to call over the phone (an expensive marketing process) prospects classified as "Multiple" with high confidence as opposed to mail a standard flyer (a cheaper marketing process) to those predicted as "Multiple" with low confidence. This allows the company to properly allocate available resources to maximize its return from the marketing campaign.

To address this problem, we first ran Noah on the input training set. It found a total of 4, 135 rules—the training dataset was of 27, 703 tuples, we set $minSupp = 0.5\%$ and $minConf = 0.75$. We then *classified* each customer in the hold-out sample by using the discovered rules. Notice that rules discovered by Noah are not mutually exclusive, therefore, multiple rules can cover a specific tuple during classification. We select the rule with the highest confidence in this case. We then labelled each customer in the hold-out with the best class suggested by the rule and the confidence of the rule.

Out of the entire hold-out sample, rules discovered by Noah covered a total of 6, 224 customers (the rest are predicted by the most populated class, the *default* rule, computed over the original distribution). We arranged Noah predictions on a gain chart as follows: we created 10 (almost) equal-size clusters of hold-out customers (i.e., quantiles of about 10%). Each cluster contains customers whose prediction confidence falls within a specified range. In other words, we fixed the confidence range for each cluster in the gain chart to accommodate about 10% of the covered customers within that cluster. We then sorted those clusters according to the confidence range in a descending order. Then, for each cluster we computed the accuracy of our prediction for all customers belonging to that cluster. The resulting gain chart is shown in Table 2. For instance, for the cluster number 1, we set a confidence range of 0.850–1.000, the total number of customers whose associated prediction confidence falls in that range is

Table 2. The gain chart created using Noah

Cl. Rank	Conf. range	Cl. Size	Hits	Accuracy	%Pop	%Covered
1	0.850–1.000	646	581	89.94%	4.72%	10.38%
2	0.830–0.850	657	538	81.89%	4.80%	10.56%
3	0.818–0.830	679	572	84.24%	4.96%	10.91%
4	0.805–0.818	647	531	82.07%	4.72%	10.40%
5	0.795–0.805	642	509	79.28%	4.69%	10.31%
6	0.788–0.795	576	454	78.82%	4.21%	9.25%
7	0.777–0.788	601	460	76.54%	4.39%	9.66%
8	0.766–0.777	656	499	76.07%	4.79%	10.54%
9	0.758–0.766	592	431	72.80%	4.32%	9.51%
10	0.750–0.758	528	386	73.11%	3.85%	8.48%

646 (column "Cl. Size"), of which 581 (column "Hits") are correctly predicted. This means an accuracy of 89.94% (column "Accuracy"). The column "%Pop" contains the proportion of the number of customers in the cluster over the total size of the hold-out sample ($\frac{\text{Cl. Size}}{13697}$). Whereas "%Cover" is computed over the total number of covered customers ($\frac{\text{Cl. Size}}{6224}$). As expected, the accuracy of each cluster worsens as the confidence range goes down. Notice the anomaly of the 2nd cluster whose accuracy drops to 81.89%, which is worse than the 3rd and 4th cluster.

The overall results were deemed very satisfactory by marketing domain experts. As already mentioned, the actual utilization of such findings consists of a set of different marketing strategies that are applied to the different clusters depending on the cluster accuracy. Since we are working with current customers, each of them can be precisely pinpointed (i.e., his/her phone number, address, etc.).

5.2   Experimental Results Using Other Mining Algorithms

We performed our experiments on a Linux OS with a 266 MHz Pentiun PC with 128 Mbytes of physical memory and 128 Mbytes of virtual memory. Our experiments revealed that our application dataset is intractable for CN2[4], Ripper[5], Apriori[6], and CBA[7] as all of them failed in their execution for lack of memory.

On the other hand, C4.5 was able to complete its task but the discovered decision tree was very poor. We first tried C4.5 with the original dataset. C4.5 discovered a decision tree with 54, 575 nodes which, after pruning, was reduced to a single-node tree—that corresponds to always predict the most populated class. After *massaging* the input training set, e.g., removing some many-valued variables and/or converting others to different types, C4.5 was only able to produce the two-level tree shown in Figure 6. Basically, C4.5 identified only the variable "FirstService" which stores the first service (out of five available) each customer subscribed to. The classification accuracy results of applying C4.5 are shown in Table 3. For the training set, the error before pruning is 11.5%

---

[4] Downloaded from http://www.cs.utexas.edu/users/pclark/software.html.
[5] To be requested at http://www.research.att.com/~wcohen/ripperd.html
[6] Downloaded from http://fuzzy.cs.uni-magdeburg.de/~borgelt.
[7] Downloaded from http://www.comp.nus.edu.sg/~dm2.

Table 3. The results of applying C4.5 to the application dataset

Results from training set (27703 items)				Results from validation set (13697 items)			
Before Pruning		After Pruning		Before Pruning		After Pruning	
Tree Size	Error	Tree Size	Error	Tree Size	Error	Tree Size	Error
58144	3183 (11.5%)	6	8747 (31.6%)	58144	5444 (39.7%)	6	(4321) 31.5%

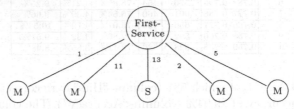

Fig. 6: The tree generated from C4.5 from the application database

over $58,144$ tree nodes; the error, after pruning, increased to 31.6% over only six nodes. This is a symptom of the complexity of the input dataset whose knowledge was initially captured by an over-fitted tree with a large number of poorly populated leaves. This tree was then pruned down to a much smaller tree with a much larger error. The over-fitting is also witnessed by the opposite behavior on the validation set: the unpruned tree produces a larger error than the pruned tree.

A gain chart (Table 4) can be drawn based on the output of C4.5. It can be obtained by attaching to each predicted class the accuracy of the corresponding leaf in the decision tree. Comparing Tables 2 and 4, we note that the output from Noah is superior in many aspects to the one from C4.5. For instance, with C4.5, we cannot partition customers in more than five clusters since that is the total number of leaf nodes in the generated tree. Furthermore, we cannot create the quantile representation of the gain chart, as we did with Noah. This reduces the flexibility for cross-selling planning. Accuracy is in general higher for Noah. Noah accuracy over the best $4,448$ customers[8] is 82.24% (this is obtained by averaging the accuracy of clusters 1 to 7). Whereas, the accuracy for the best $4,195$ customers in C4.5 (i.e., the ones belonging to cluster 1) is 76.4%.

Comparison over the entire hold-out sample. In Table 2 we only reported the customers who are covered by some *good* rule discovered by Noah (i.e., rules with confidence greater than the *minConf* threshold set to 0.75). They are a total of $6,224$ customers from the hold-out sample. The rest of them, i.e., $13697 - 6224 = 7473$, are predicted by low confidence rules and/or the *default* rule. In C4.5 there is no concept of default rules as all the cases are classified by some leaf. Therefore, for the sake of completeness, we now discuss the performance of C4.5 and Noah over the entire hold-out sample (i.e., $13,697$ records). Noah performs slightly better than C4.5 over the entire hold-out sample. In fact, C4.5 reports an error of $4,321$ cases (see Table 3) which yields an accuracy of $\frac{13697-4321}{13697} = 68.4\%$

---

[8] By "best customer" here we mean a customer whose class we can accurately predict.

Table 4. The gain chart created using C4.5

Cl. Rank	Leaf Conf.	Cl. Size	Hits	Accuracy	%Pop	%Covered
1	0.76	4195	3205	76.40%	30.63%	30.63%
2	0.74	1321	972	73.58%	9.64%	9.64%
3	0.67	3069	2055	66.96%	22.41%	22.41%
4	0.63	2656	1681	63.29%	19.39%	19.39%
5	0.61	2456	1463	59.57%	17.93%	17.93%

whereas Noah misclassifies a total of $4,040$ cases which yields an accuracy of $\frac{13697-4040}{13697} = 70.5\%$. It is important to note that the accuracy lower bound (or *baseline*) of the dataset is 63.9%, that is, if we always guess "Multiple" (i.e., the most populated class in the training set) we correctly predict 63.9% of the cases in the hold-out sample (any useful classifier has to beat this value). Thus, the percentage improvement over the baseline is $\frac{68.4-63.9}{63.9} = 7\%$ for C4.5 versus the $\frac{70.5-63.9}{63.9} = 10.3\%$ of Noah.

For this specific application, an important contribution of Noah is the possibility of creating the gain chart shown in Table 2 which properly supports the cross-selling activity. Basically, with Noah we are able to locate those portions of the dataset where an accurate prediction is possible, that is, where some robust knowledge can be elicited. This matches with the cross-selling problem where we do not need to target the entire population of customers. With Noah we are able to predict (clusters of) customers with accuracy up to almost 90% (see Table 2). C4.5 is far from that level and its outcome was considered of no interest by domain experts.

In terms of learning time, C4.5 performs much faster than Noah. C4.5 took about 8 minutes to complete its task[9] whereas Noah completed in about 4 hours. The main reasons are: Noah performs a multivariate search for rules, it never partitions the dataset and always keeps it as an external file.

6   Related Work

Both KDS [8,6] and CBA [11] are very closely related to our work as they mine classification rules in a *Apriori* [1] style. The focus of KDS is for the SQL implementation of the learning procedure. CBA provides a sophisticated classification procedure. An extensive comparison of accuracy performance with C4.5 on a set of UCI datasets is discussed in [11]. Both KDS and CBA do not treat the problem of mining datasets with large number of attributes. Basically, Noah is an extension of KDS to handle large number of many-valued attributes.

Bayardo *et al.* [3] discuss an extension of *Apriori*, called "Dense-Miner," to discover classification rules. They introduce the concept of "minimum improvement" that, basically, discards rules that provide only minor confidence improvement (or just deterioration) over a more general version of the rule. They also propose a pruning by "confidence upper bound," similar to the one we described. However, they use an "association form" for the classification rules:

---

[9] We used all standard parameters when running C4.5.

$\rho \Rightarrow y$, where ρ is a pattern and y is a class term. Their definition of rule confidence is $C = \frac{supp(\rho \cup \{y\})}{supp(\rho)}$ which is different from the one used in Noah, therefore the proposed solutions are different.

Our "term dependency" pruning resembles closely the "(near) equivalence" strategy proposed by Bayardo [2]. However, in Noah we extended it with the concept of "equivalence" between terms.

Lent *et al.* [10] also propose a classifier based on *Apriori*-like association rules. They propose an algorithm to cluster *similar* association rules into a more descriptive rule. They however limit their approach to only two terms in the rule antecedent.

SLIQ [13], SPRINT [16], and MIND [17] induce classification trees from databases residing on disk. They are based on the univariate and divide-and-conquer principles of C4.5 discussed earlier. Thus, they will exhibit similar drawbacks as of C4.5.

7   Conclusions

In this paper we presented an algorithm to mine classification rules from datasets with a large number of many-valued attributes. In such datasets knowledge may be scattered among many uncorrelated rectangular portions of the input dataset. The univariate and divide-and-conquer approach of C4.5 may fail in discovering knowledge under such circumstances. We presented an algorithm, Noah, that discovers classification rules by following a multivariate approach. The combinatorial explosion related to the multivariate search is controlled by optimized data structures and efficient pruning strategies. These strategies are quite general and may be exploited by other learning algorithms as well. We have successfully applied Noah to a real application of cross-selling marketing based on a dataset of $41,400$ records and 221 attributes. C4.5 failed in discovering useful knowledge from this dataset. Applying the same dataset on other rule discovery algorithms, such as CN2, Ripper, Apriori, and CBA, failed due to a lack of memory. Our future work agenda includes an improved classification procedure and the application of Noah to other large dataset domains. Noah does not require the dataset to reside in main memory during learning. This provides a basics for a tighter integration of Noah with DBMS which is currently under study.

References

1. R. Agrawal, H. Mannila, R. Srikant, H. Toivonen, and A.I. Verkamo. Fast discovery of association rules. In *Advances in Knowledge Discovery and Data Mining*. AAAI Press / The MIT Press, 1996.
2. R.J. Bayardo. Brute-force mining of high-confidence classification rules. In D. Heckerman, H. Mannila, D. Pregibon, and R. Uthurusamy, editors, *Proceedings of the Third International Conference on Knowledge Discovery and Data Mining (KDD-97)*. AAAI Press, 1997.

3. R.J. Bayardo, R. Agrawal, and D. Gunopulos. Constraint-based rule mining in large, dense databases. In *Proc. of the 15th Int'l Conf. on Data Engineering*, pages 188–197, 1999.
4. P. Clark and T. Niblett. The CN2 induction algorithm. *Machine Learning*, 3:261–283, 1989.
5. W.W. Cohen. Learning trees and rules with set-valued features. In *Proceedings of the Thirteenth National Conference on Artificial Intelligence AAAI-96*. AAAI press/ The MIT press, August 1996.
6. L. G. Cooper and G. Giuffrida. Turning datamining into a management science tool: New algorithms and empirical results. *Management Science*, 2000 (To appear).
7. P. Domingos. Linear-time rule induction. In E. Simoudis, J. W. Han, and U. Fayyad, editors, *Proceedings of the Second International Conference on Knowledge Discovery and Data Mining (KDD-96)*, page 96. AAAI Press, 1996.
8. G. Giuffrida, L. G. Cooper, and W. W. Chu. A scalable bottom-up data mining algorithm for relational databases. In *10th International Conference on Scientific and Statistical Database Management (SSDBM '98)*, Capri, Italy, July 1998. IEEE Publisher.
9. R.C. Holte, L.E. Acker, and B.W. Porter. Concept learning and the problem of small disjuncts. In *Proceedings of the Eleventh International Joint Conference on Artificial Intelligence*, Detroit, (MI), 1989. Morgan Kaufmann.
10. B. Lent, A. Swami, and J. Widom. Clustering association rules. In *Proceedings of the Thirteenth International Conference on Data Engineering (ICDE '97)*, Birmingham, UK, 1997.
11. B. Liu, W. Hsu, and Y. Ma. Integrating classification and association rule mining. In R. Agrawal, P. Storloz, and G. Piatetsky-Shapiro, editors, *Proceedings of the Fourth International Conference on Knowledge Discovery and Data Mining (KDD-98)*, page 80. AAAI Press, 1998.
12. H. Mannila and H. Toivonen. Levelwise search and borders of theories in knowledge discovery. *Data Mining and Knowledge Discovery*, 1, November 1997.
13. M. Mehta, R. Agrawal, and J. Rissanen. SLIQ: A fast scalable classifier for data mining. *Lecture Notes in Computer Science*, 1057, 1996.
14. Judea Pearl. *Probabilistic Reasoning in Intelligent Systems: Networks of Plausible Inference*. Morgan Kaufmann, San Mateo, California, 1988.
15. J. R. Quinlan. *C4.5 : Programs for Machine Learning*. Morgan Kaufmann, San Mateo, California, 1993.
16. J. C. Shafer, R. Agrawal, and M. Mehta. SPRINT: A scalable parallel classifier for data mining. In T. M. Vijayaraman, Alejandro P. Buchmann, C. Mohan, and Nandlal L. Sarda, editors, *VLDB 1996*, Mumbai (Bombay), India, September 1996. Morgan Kaufmann.
17. M. Wang, B. Iyer, and J. S. Vitter. Scalable mining for classification rules in relational databases. In *Proceedings of International Database Engineering and Application Symposium (IDEAS'98)*, Cardiff, Wales, U.K., July 1998.

Efficient Discovery of Functional Dependencies and Armstrong Relations

Stéphane Lopes, Jean-Marc Petit, and Lotfi Lakhal

Laboratoire LIMOS, Université Blaise Pascal - Clermont-Ferrand II
Campus Universitaire des Cézeaux
24 avenue des Landais
63177 Aubière cedex, France
{slopes,jmpetit,llakhal}@libd2.univ-bpclermont.fr

Abstract In this paper, we propose a new efficient algorithm called Dep-Miner for discovering minimal non-trivial functional dependencies from large databases. Based on theoretical foundations, our approach combines the discovery of functional dependencies along with the construction of *real-world Armstrong relations* (without additional execution time). These relations are small Armstrong relations taking their values in the initial relation. Discovering both minimal functional dependencies and real-world Armstrong relations facilitate the tasks of database administrators when maintaining and analyzing existing databases. We evaluate Dep-Miner performances by using a new benchmark database. Experimental results show both the efficiency of our approach compared to the best current algorithm (i.e. Tane), and the usefulness of real-world Armstrong relations.

1 Introduction and Motivation

Functional dependencies, introduced in [11], are by far the most common integrity constraints in the real world [26,21]. They are very important when designing or analyzing relational databases. Discovering functional dependencies hidden in a database has been addressed by various approaches, among which we quote [24,31,25,18].

Armstrong relations, introduced in [16], are closely related to functional dependencies: such relations exactly satisfy a set of functional dependencies. They can show both the existence and the nonexistence of functional dependencies for a given relation [15,24,25]. Algorithms for computing Armstrong relations from functional dependencies are given in [6,24,14,12]. In this paper, we introduce the concept of *real-world Armstrong relations*. Such relations are small Armstrong relations only populated with values actual from the initial relation.

Discovering both minimal functional dependencies and real-world Armstrong relations could greatly facilitate the tasks of database administrators (DBA) when maintaining existing databases and reorganizing their schemas. We call such a reorganization logical tuning: for instance, the DBA could assess relevance of discovered functional dependencies by using small relations sampling the initial

C. Zaniolo et al. (Eds.): EDBT 2000, LNCS 1777, pp. 350–364, 2000.
© Springer-Verlag Berlin Heidelberg 2000

relations, and once these dependencies are proved to be useful, he can perform relation normalization. The motivation behind normalization is to remove the problems that are caused by the update anomalies and redundancies [26,21].

For addressing the problem of discovering minimal non-trivial functional dependencies, a theoretical framework is proposed in [25,26]. The underlying approach is based on the concept of agree set [6]. This set groups all the attributes having the very same values for a given couple of tuples. From agree sets, maximal sets[1] are derived, and from maximal sets, all minimal non-trivial functional dependencies can be generated.

In this paper, we propose a new efficient algorithm called Dep-Miner for discovering agree sets, maximal sets, left-hand sides (LHS) of minimal non-trivial functional dependencies and real-world Armstrong relations. Our approach is defined under the assumption of limited main memory resources and its feasibility does not depend on the volume of handled data. Since database accesses are only performed during the computation of agree sets, Dep-Miner takes in input a small representation of a relation, called *stripped partition databases* derived from [13,32,18]. From them, new characterizations of agree sets are given. These characterizations show that stripped partition databases are information-aly equivalent to relations in our context and provide efficient algorithms for discovering agree sets from large relations. From agree sets, a characterization of maximal sets is introduced. Then, a levelwise algorithm[2] is proposed for computing the LHS of minimal non-trivial functional dependencies. It is based on the characterization of LHS as the set of minimal transversals of a simple hypergraph [25,26]. An existence condition for real-world Armstrong relation is given as well as the algorithm for generating such a relation.

Evaluations of Dep-Miner performances are achieved by using a new benchmark database. Experimental results show both the efficiency of the approach compared to the best current algorithm (i.e. Tane [18]), and the usefulness of real-world Armstrong relations. Indeed, we observed that these relations were small sizes and thus form a good sampling of the initial relation.

Paper organization. In section 2, some definitions and results in relational database theory are presented. Our approach is detailed in section 3 and two versions of the algorithm Dep-Miner are presented. In section 4, we explain how to achieve Armstrong relations with the algorithms Dep-Miner. Section 5 details experimental results and section 6 concludes the paper by giving further research work.

2 Basic Definitions

This section is devoted to setting the groundwork of our approach. It briefly resumes definitions and results from relational database theory, which are relevant in our context [26,3,21].

---

[1] Also called *intersection generators* in [6] or *meet-irreducible sets* in [17,14].
[2] This kind of algorithm has been extensively used in data mining [4,29,27].

Let R be a *relation schema*. If $X \subseteq R$ and t is a tuple, we denote by $t[X]$ the restriction of t to X.

A *functional dependency* over R is an expression $X \to A$ where $X \subseteq R$ and $A \in R$. The functional dependency $X \to A$ *holds* in a relation r (denoted by $r \models X \to A$) if and only if $\forall t_i, t_j \in r$, $t_i[X] = t_j[X] \Rightarrow t_i[A] = t_j[A]$. A functional dependency $X \to A$ is *minimal* if A is not functionally dependent on any proper subset of X. The functional dependency $X \to A$ is *trivial* if $A \in X$. We denote by $dep(r)$ the set of all functional dependencies that hold in r: $dep(r) = \{X \to A / X \cup A \subseteq R, r \models X \to A\}$. Let F and G be two sets of functional dependencies, F is a *cover* of G if $F \models G$ (this notation means that each dependency $f \in G$ holds in any relation satisfying all the dependencies in F) and $G \models F$.

For complementing previous definitions, agree sets, maximal sets and LHS sets are introduced.

Let t_i and t_j be tuples and X an attribute set. The tuples t_i and t_j *agree* on X if $t_i[X] = t_j[X]$. The *agree set* of t_i and t_j is defined as follows: $ag(t_i, t_j) = \{A \in R / t_i[A] = t_j[A]\}$. If r is a relation, $ag(r) = \{ag(t_i, t_j) / t_i, t_j \in r, t_i \neq t_j\}$.

A maximal set is an attribute set X which, for some attribute A, is the largest possible set not determining A. We denote by $max(dep(r), A)$ the set of maximal sets for A w.r.t. $dep(r)$:
$max(dep(r), A) = \{X \subseteq R / r \not\models X \to A \text{ and } \forall Y \subseteq R, X \subset Y, r \models Y \to A\}$; and
$MAX(dep(r)) = \bigcup_{A \in R} max(dep(r), A)$.

From maximal sets, functional dependencies can be inferred as follows [25]:

The set of LHS of functional dependencies w.r.t. $dep(r)$ and an attribute A is denoted by $lhs(dep(r), A)$: $lhs(dep(r), A) = \{X \subseteq R / r \models X \to A \text{ and } \forall X' \subset X, r \not\models X' \to A\}$. The set $\{X \to A / X \in lhs(dep(r), A), A \in R\}$ is a cover of $dep(r)$.

For finding LHS of functional dependencies from maximal sets, the notion of hypergraph is to be introduced. A collection $\mathcal{H}$ of subsets of R is a *simple hypergraph* if $\forall X \in \mathcal{H}, X \neq \emptyset$ and $(X, Y \in \mathcal{H}$ and $X \subseteq Y \Rightarrow X = Y)$ [8]. Elements of $\mathcal{H}$ are called the *edges* of the hypergraph and elements of R are the *vertices* of the hypergraph. The collection $cmax(dep(r), A)$ of complements of maximal sets $max(dep(r), A)$ is a simple hypergraph. A *transversal* T of $\mathcal{H}$ is a subset of R intersecting all the edges of $\mathcal{H}$, i.e. $T \cap E \neq \emptyset, \forall E \in \mathcal{H}$. A *minimal transversal* of $\mathcal{H}$ is a transversal T such that it does not exist a transversal T', $T' \subset T$. The collection of minimal transversals of $\mathcal{H}$ is denoted by $\mathrm{Tr}(\mathcal{H})$. Minimal transversals of simple hypergraph are related to LHS of functional dependencies: $\mathrm{Tr}(cmax(dep(r), A)) = lhs(dep(r), A)$.

3   Dep-Miner Algorithm

Our approach is depicted in figure 1: from the initial relation, a stripped partition database is extracted; using such partitions, agree sets are computed; and thus, maximal sets are generated. On the one hand, they are used to build Armstrong relations. On the other hand, deriving their complements is straightforward and

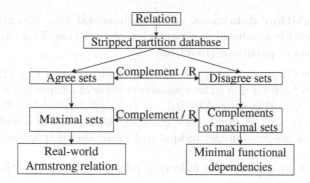

Fig. 1. General framework

then LHS of functional dependencies are computed. Let us notice that approaches presented in [24,19,25,26] fit in this general framework without necessarily covering all the presented steps. Moreover, they operate by loading the dealt data in main memory without a special emphasis on the computation of agree sets. Algorithm 1 (see below) presents the different steps of Dep-Miner.

Algorithm 1. Dep-Miner: Discovering minimal functional dependencies and real-world Armstrong relations

Input: a relation r

Output: minimal functional dependencies and real-world Armstrong relation for r

  1: AGREE_SET: computes agree sets from r
  2: CMAX_SET: derives complements of maximal sets from agree sets
  3: LEFT_HAND_SIDE: computes LHS of functional dependencies from complements of maximal sets
  4: FD_OUTPUT: outputs functional dependencies
  5: ARMSTRONG_RELATION: builds real-world Armstrong relation from maximal sets and R

3.1   Finding Agree Sets

A naive algorithm for computing agree sets in a relation r works as follows: for each couple of tuples (t_i, t_j) in r, compute $ag(t_i, t_j)$ as defined in the previous section. If p is the number of tuples in the relation and n is the number of attributes, the time complexity of this algorithm is in $O(np^2)$. When p is large, the algorithm becomes impractical due to the number of couples (plus the overhead due to the cost of $ag(t_i, t_j)$).

We propose a new approach to compute agree sets which aims to decrease the number of candidate couples. For meeting such needs, we reduce the initial relation using the concept of *stripped partition database* and new characterizations of agree sets are proposed in order to minimize the number of couples. Furthermore, an interesting aspect would be to avoid the cost of $ag(t_i, t_j)$.

From stripped partition databases, two algorithms are proposed: the former implements the new approach to compute agree sets; the latter provides an optimization of the previous algorithm which is more efficient when handling large relations.

Stripped partition databases. The fundamental idea underlying our approach is to provide a reduced representation of a relation. This can be achieved using the notion of partitions [13,32,18].

Partitions. Two tuples t_i and t_j are *equivalent* with respect to a given attribute set X if $t_i[A] = t_j[A] \forall A \in X$. The *equivalence class* of a tuple $t_i \in r$ with respect to a given set $X \subseteq R$ is defined by $[t_i]_X = \{t_j \in r / t_i[A] = t_j[A], \forall A \in X\}$. The set $\pi_X = \{[t]_X / t \in r\}$ of equivalence classes is a *partition* of r under X. In the sequel, we use a positive integer unique to t as an identifier for each tuple t.

Example 1. Let us consider the following relation representing the assignment of employees to departments.

Tuple No.	empnum	depnum	year	depname	mgr
1	1	1	85	Biochemistry	5
2	1	5	94	Admission	12
3	2	2	92	Computer Sce	2
4	3	2	98	Computer Sce	2
5	4	3	98	Geophysics	2
6	5	1	75	Biochemistry	5
7	6	5	88	Admission	12

For briefness, attributes empnum, depnum, year, depname, mgr are renamed A, B, C, D, E respectively. The partition associated to attribute A is: $\pi_A = \{\{1,2\}, \{3\}, \{4\}, \{5\}, \{6\}, \{7\}\}$.

Stripped partitions. Such partitions group equivalence classes having a size greater than one. In fact, when an equivalence class encompasses a single element, the associated tuple does not share the values of the considered attribute set with any other tuple in the relation. The stripped partition for an attribute set X is defined by: $\widehat{\pi_X} = \{c \in \pi_X / |c| > 1\}$

Example 2. The stripped partition for attribute A is achieved by removing equivalence classes of size one: $\widehat{\pi_A} = \{\{1,2\}\}$.

Stripped partition databases. The new representation of a relation is called a stripped partition database. It encompasses stripped partitions for each attribute. Let r be a relation over R. A *stripped partition database* $\widehat{r}$ of r is defined as follows: $\widehat{r} = \bigcup_{A \in R} \widehat{\pi_A}$.

Computing stripped partition database from a relation is straightforward (it would correspond to the pre-processing phase in a data mining context).

Characterizing agree sets. We firstly need to define the set MC of maximal equivalence classes induced by a stripped partition database.

Maximal equivalence classes. Let $\widehat{r}$ be a stripped partition database. The set MC of maximal equivalence classes of $\widehat{r}$ is defined as follows:
$MC = Max_\subseteq \{c \in \widehat{\pi} / \widehat{\pi} \in \widehat{r}\}$.

Example 3. Continuing our example, the set of maximal equivalence classes is the following:
$MC = \{\{1, 2\}, \{1, 6\}, \{2, 7\}, \{3, 4, 5\}\}$.

For building agree sets, we only consider couples of tuples belonging to a common equivalence class of MC (because tuples in two different equivalence classes disagree for each attribute of R). This results from the lemma 1 which proves the correctness of algorithm 2 presented below.

Lemma 1. *[22] Let r be a relation. $ag(r) = \bigcup_{c \in MC} ag(c)$.*

The first algorithm. The first proposed algorithm (see below algorithm 2) results from the lemma 1. It operates as follows: The first step (line 1) computes the maximal equivalence classes from a stripped partition database. Then, for each maximal equivalence class, all possible couples of tuples are generated (lines 4 to 7). Corresponding agree sets are then computed (lines 8 to 12): an attribute is added to the agree set of two tuples if these tuples are in a common equivalence class in the stripped partition for this attribute. Finally, the set of agree sets is updated (lines 13 to 24).

Algorithm 2. AGREE_SET: Computes agree sets from stripped partition databases

Input: the stripped partition database $\hat{r}$ of a relation r
Output: the agree sets of r: $ag(r)$
 1: $MC := Max_{\subseteq}\{c \in \widehat{\pi_A}/\widehat{\pi_A} \in \hat{r}\}$
 2: $ag(r) := \emptyset$
 3: $couples := \emptyset$
 4: **for all** maximal equivalence classes $c \in MC$ **do**
 5:      **for all** couple $(t, t') \in c$ **do**
 6:          $couples := couples \cup (t, t')$
 7:          $ag(t, t') := \emptyset$
 8: **for all** $\widehat{\pi_A} \in \hat{r}$ **do**
 9:      **for all** equivalence class $c \in \widehat{\pi_A}$ **do**
10:          **for all** $(t, t') \in couples$ **do**
11:              **if** $t \in c$ and $t' \in c$ **then**
12:                  $ag(t, t') := ag(t, t') \cup A$
13: **for all** couple $(t, t') \in couples$ **do**
14:      $ag(r) := ag(r) \cup ag(t, t')$

Example 4. From the set MC, the generated couples are:
$\{(1, 2), (1, 6), (2, 7), (3, 4), (3, 5), (4, 5)\}$.
This algorithm discovers the following agree sets: $ag(r) = \{\emptyset, A, BDE, CE, E\}$.

Compared with the naive algorithm, the number of couples is reduced and the cost of $ag(t, t')$ is avoided. However, the proposed algorithm requires storing all couples that can generate agree sets. Since the number of these couples can be very great, we cannot assume that they always fit into main memory. The solution used to avoid this problem is computing agree sets as soon as a fixed number of couples was generated. More precisely, when a threshold (associated to the number of tuples) is reached, corresponding agree sets are computed from the current set of couples. This set is then deleted and the process continues by examining the remaining couples.

However, the computation can be time consuming and the algorithm becomes less efficient when the number of couples is great, i.e. when equivalence classes are large or when they are numerous. We propose therefore another characterization of agree sets which originates to a new algorithm more efficient in such a case.

Another characterization of agree sets. The fundamental idea under this new characterization of agree sets is to preserve, for each tuple, the identifiers of equivalence classes in which the considered tuple appears. Then, computing the agree set of two tuples can be merely performed by achieving the intersection of their identifier set, and getting the associated attributes.

Let us assume that $\widehat{\pi_A} = \{\widehat{\pi_{A,0}}, \ldots, \widehat{\pi_{A,k}}\}$. We denote by $ec(t)$ the set of identifiers of equivalence classes in which the tuple t appears: $ec(t) = \{(A, i)/A \in R \text{ and } t \in \widehat{\pi_{A,i}}\}$

Example 5. In our example, for attribute E, $\widehat{\pi_E} = \{\widehat{\pi_{E,0}}, \widehat{\pi_{E,1}}, \widehat{\pi_{E,2}}\}$, where $\widehat{\pi_{E,0}} = \{1, 6\}, \widehat{\pi_{E,1}} = \{2, 7\}, \widehat{\pi_{E,2}} = \{3, 4, 5\}$
For the second tuple, the indentifier set is $ec(2) = \{(A, 0), (B, 1), (D, 1), (E, 1)\}$

We can now give a characterization of agree sets.

Lemma 2. *[22] Let t_i and t_j be two tuples. $ag(t_i, t_j) = \{A \in R/\exists k \text{ s.t. } (A, k) \in ec(t_i) \cap ec(t_j)\}$.*

Example 6. Let us consider $ec(1) = \{(A, 0), (B, 0), (D, 0), (E, 0)\}$ and $ec(2) = \{(A, 0), (B, 1), (D, 1), (E, 1)\}$. Since $ec(1) \cap ec(2) = \{(A, 0)\}$, $ag(1, 2) = A$.

The second algorithm. From lemma 2, we propose a second algorithm for exhibiting agree sets (see below algorithm 3). The first step (lines 2 to 5) states the relationship between tuples and equivalence classes: for each tuple in the stripped partition database, the equivalence classes in which the considered tuple appears are preserved (line 5). In the second step (lines 6 to 9), agree sets are computed: for each couple in maximal equivalence classes, the agree set of the couple is computed from the relationships previously stated (line 9).

3.2   Finding Maximal Sets

For exhibiting maximal sets from agree sets, we introduce a new characterization[3] of the set of maximal sets for the attribute A: $max(dep(r), A)$.

---

[3] In [25], a similar result is used for yielding complements of maximal sets from complements of agree sets (disagree sets). However, it is not explicitly stated contrarily to Lemma 3.

Algorithm 3. AGREE_SET 2: Computes agree sets from stripped partition databases
Input: the stripped partition database $\hat{r}$ of a relation r
Output: the agree sets of r: $ag(r)$
1: $ag(r) := \emptyset$
2: **for all** $\hat{\pi}_A \in \hat{r}$ **do**
3:     **for all** equivalence class $\hat{\pi}_{A,i} \in \hat{\pi}_A$ **do**
4:         **for all** tuple $t \in \hat{\pi}_{A,i}$ **do**
5:             $ec(t) := ec(t) \cup (A, i)$
6: $MC := Max_{\subseteq}\{c \in \hat{\pi}_A/\hat{\pi}_A \in \hat{r}\}$
7: **for all** maximal equivalence classes $c \in MC$ **do**
8:     **for all** couple $(t, t') \in c$ **do**
9:         $ag(r) := ag(r) \cup \{A \in R/\exists j \text{ s.t. } (A, j) \in ec(t) \cap ec(t')\}$

Lemma 3. *[22]* $max(dep(r), A) = Max_{\subseteq}\{X \in ag(r)/A \notin X, X \neq \emptyset\}$.

As mentioned in section 2, we need to compute complement of maximal sets for achieving LHS of minimal functional dependencies. Algorithm 4 yields complements of maximal sets from agree sets. Its correctness results from lemma 3.

Firstly, we compute maximal sets for each attribute in R (lines 1 to 2): for an attribute A in R, agree sets which do not contain A and which are maximal with respect to inclusion are added to the set of maximal sets (line 2). Finding the complement of maximal sets (lines 3 to 6) is straightforward.

Algorithm 4. CMAX_SET: Computes complement of maximal sets
Input: the agree sets over r: $ag(r)$
Output: complements of maximal sets: $CMAX(dep(r))$
1: **for all** attributes $A \in R$ **do**
2:     $max(dep(r), A) := Max_{\subseteq}\{X \in ag(r)/A \notin X\}$
3: **for all** attributes $A \in R$ **do**
4:     $cmax(dep(r), A) := \emptyset$
5:     **for all** $X \in max(dep(r), A)$ **do**
6:         $cmax(dep(r), A) := cmax(dep(r), A) \cup (R \setminus X)$

Example 7. When applied to our example, the previous algorithm yields the following results for attribute A:
$max(dep(r), A) = \{BDE, CE\}$ and $cmax(dep(r), A) = \{AC, ABD\}$.

3.3   Finding Left-Hand Sides of Functional Dependencies

Minimal transversals of the simple hypergraph $cmax(dep(r), A)$ provide LHS of minimal functional dependencies (see section 2). We propose a new levelwise algorithm (see algorithm 5) for computing minimal transversals of a simple hypergraph.

The set L_i of candidate sets of size i is initialized with attributes appearing in $cmax(dep(r), A)$. The collection of minimal transversals is computed (from lines 4 to 8): for each set l in L_i, we test if l is a transversal (line 5). In this case, l is saved (line 5) in LHS_i of LHS of minimal functional dependencies of size i and removed (line 6) from L_i (all supersets of l are non minimal transversals). Next level is generated (line 7) by adapting the *Apriori-gen* function [4].

Algorithm 5. LEFT_HAND_SIDE: Computes LHS of minimal functional dependencies

Input: complements of maximal sets: $CMAX(dep(r))$
Output: the LHS of minimal functional dependencies: $lhs(dep(r))$
1: **for all** attributes $A \in R$ **do**
2:     $i := 1$
3:     $L_i := \{B/B \in X, X \in cmax(dep(r), A)\}$
4:     **while** $L_i \neq \emptyset$ **do**
5:         $LHS_i[A] := \{l \in L_i/l \cap X \neq \emptyset, \forall X \in cmax(dep(r), A)\}$
6:         $L_i := L_i \setminus LHS_i[A]$
7:         $L_{i+1} := \{l'/|l'| = i+1 \text{ and } \forall l \subset l'/|l| = i, l \in L_i\}$
8:         $i := i + 1$
9:     $lhs(dep(r), A) := \bigcup_i LHS_i[A]$

Example 8. We obtain the following sets:
$lhs(dep(r), A) = \{A, BC, CD\}$, $lhs(dep(r), B) = \{AC, AE, B, D\}$,
$lhs(dep(r), C) = \{AB, AD, AE, C\}$, $lhs(dep(r), D) = \{AC, AE, B, D\}$,
$lhs(dep(r), E) = \{B, C, D, E\}$.

These set leads to the following minimal funtional dependencies:

$r \models BC \rightarrow A$	$r \models AB \rightarrow C$	$r \models B \rightarrow D$
$r \models CD \rightarrow A$	$r \models AD \rightarrow C$	$r \models B \rightarrow E$
$r \models AC \rightarrow B$	$r \models AE \rightarrow C$	$r \models C \rightarrow E$
$r \models AE \rightarrow B$	$r \models AC \rightarrow D$	$r \models D \rightarrow E$
$r \models D \rightarrow B$	$r \models AE \rightarrow D$	

4   Generating Real-World Armstrong Relations

Exhibiting functional dependencies could yield a huge amount of results and taking advantages of them is far from trivial. Generally, all the functional dependences cannot be taken into account to normalize the relational schema. In fact, only some inferred functional dependencies are relevant when modifying the database structure [26]. Two reasons justify that:

1. Some functional dependencies could accidentally hold in a relation extension which represents the state of the data at a given time. There is no guarantee for the validity of these dependencies in another relation extension.
2. Functional dependencies can express two things [7,28]: either an association of attributes which represents relevant information which is interesting to preserve, or just an integrity constraint between the data.

For making decision of discarding a functional dependency or not, possible alternatives are:

1. requesting the DBA to make such a decision;
2. using clues given by a workload of SQL statement for example by studying duplicate attribute sequences [23];
3. providing some help to the DBA for example with a sample of the initial relation.

The next step of our approach fits in the latter trend.

Let us notice that a rather similar issue is also addressed by recent data mining approaches because discovered knowledge could be so voluminous that it could not be directly used [20,5,30]. Nevertheless, we do not provide a comparison between these approaches and ours because proposed solutions widely differ.

An algorithm to construct an Armstrong relation from maximal sets is proposed in [6,24]. Let us assume that $C = \{X_0, \ldots, X_n\}$ where $X_0 = R$ and $X_i \in MAX(dep(r))$. Each $X_i \in C$ is associated with the tuple t_i defined as follows:

$$t_i[A] = \begin{cases} 0 & \text{if } A \in X_i, \\ i & \text{if } A \notin X_i. \end{cases} \tag{1}$$

The relation $r = \{t_0, \ldots, t_n\}$ is an Armstrong relation of size $|MAX(dep(r))|+1$.

Under similar assumptions, real-world Arsmtrong relations are built up from an initial relation. We firstly present what we mean by real-world Armstrong relation:

Informally, a real-world Armstrong relation is an Armstrong relation satisfying the three following properties:

1. it is an equivalent representation of the initial relation as regards functional dependencies;
2. its values are taken among those of the initial relation;
3. its size is often smaller of several orders of magnitude than the size of the initial relation.

Definition 1. *Let r be a relation over R. A real-world Armstrong relation $\bar{r}$ over R is defined as follows:*

1. *$\bar{r}$ is an Armstrong relation satisfying $dep(r)$;*
2. *$|\bar{r}| = |MAX(dep(r))| + 1$;*
3. *$\forall A \in R, \forall t_i \in \bar{r}, t_i[A] \in \pi_A(r)$ where $\pi_A(r)$ is the projection of r on A.*

The existence of a real-world Armstrong relation depends on the number of distinct values for each attribute in the relation r: That leads to the following result.

Proposition 1. *[22] Let r be a relation over R. A real-world Armstrong relation $\bar{r}$ over R exists if and only if $\forall A \in R, |\pi_A(r)| \geq |\{X \in MAX(dep(r))/A \notin X\}| + 1$.*

This condition means that, in the initial relation, each attribute must necessarily have enough different values in order to construct real-world Armstrong relations. Under this condition, we can build them as follows:

Suppose $C = \{X_0, \ldots, X_n\}$ where $X_0 = R$ and $X_i \in MAX(dep(r))$. For each $X_i \in C$, associate the tuple t_i such that: $\forall A \in R, \pi_A(r) = \{v_{A0}, \ldots, v_{Ak}\}$

$$t_i[A] = \begin{cases} v_{A0} & \text{if } A \in X_i, \\ v_{Ai} & \text{if } A \notin X_i. \end{cases} \tag{2}$$

Example 9. From our example, the following Armstrong relation and real-world Armstrong relation can be generated from $MAX(dep(r)) \cup R$

empnum	depnum	year	depname	mgr	empnum	depnum	year	depname	mgr
0	0	0	0	0	1	1	85	Biochemistry	5
0	1	1	1	1	1	5	94	Admission	12
2	0	2	0	0	3	1	92	Biochemistry	5
3	3	0	3	0	4	2	85	Geophysics	5

Let us underline that real-world Armstrong relation is more informative than the other one. As shown in the next section, their sizes can be significantly smaller than the size of the initial relation.

5   Performances

To test the performances of our algorithms, we performed several experiments on an Intel Pentium II with a CPU clock rate of 350 Mhz, 256 MB of main memory and running Windows NT 4. We implemented the algorithms using the C++ language and STL (Standard Template Library). Attribute sets are implemented as bit vectors to provide set operations in constant time. The DBMS accesses are done by ODBC to remain independent of the DBMS. We used two DBMSs during the tests: Oracle and MS Access.

Firstly, we give an overview of the Tane algorithm against which we compare the performances of Dep-Miner. Then, we present the new benchmark database used for the tests and show the obtained results.

5.1   The Tane Algorithm

Several algorithms for discovering functional dependencies have been presented [24,31,25]. However, the Tane algorithm [18] is the best current algorithm for the discovery of minimal non-trivial functional dependencies. Moreover, Tane can also provide approximate functional dependencies. It partitions the set of tuples of a relation according to their attribute values. Thus it preserves the information about which tuples agree on a set of attributes. To check if a functional dependency holds, it verifies whether the tuples agree on the right-hand side whenever they agree on the left-hand side. The approach is based on a levelwise algorithm [27]. Functional dependencies are searched starting with dependencies having small left-hand side (i.e. from dependencies that are not likely satisfied). It prunes the search space as soon as possible.

For the tests, due to the limitation of the downloadable version of Tane (available at [2]) to relations with less than 32 attributes and the fact that Tane is implemented in C under Linux, we have implemented our version of Tane in order to compare it with Dep-Miner.

5.2   The Benchmark Database

We generated synthetic data sets (i.e. relations) in order to control various parameters during the tests. By this way, the pros and cons for the two algorithms can be studied in more depth.

We firstly create a table with $|R|$ attributes in the database and then insert $|r|$ tuples. Each inserted value depends on the parameter c which is the rate of identical values. It controls the number of identical values in a column of the table. For example, if c has a value of 50% for an attribute and the number of tuples is 1000, this means that each value for this attribute is chosen between 500 possible values.

5.3   Experiments with Synthetic Data

In this section, we present experimental results obtained with generated data. Tests were made on various relations classified in three groups: data sets without constraints, data sets with parameter c set to 30% and data sets with parameter c fixed to 50%. Due to the lack of space, only the second dataset will be presented here (see figure 2). The full set of tests (result tables and figures) can be found in [22].

The number of attributes varies from 10 to 60 and the number of tuples from 10,000 to 100,000. The execution times (in seconds) are shown in figure 2,

In these tests, we compare two versions of Dep-Miner to Tane. The former (called Dep-Miner) implements algorithm 2 for computing agree sets. The latter (called Dep-Miner 2) implements algorithm 3 to perform the very same task.

For discovering functional dependencies, Dep-Miner is faster than Tane in all cases. The difference grows along with the number of attributes. Dep-Miner 2 is more efficient than Tane when the number of attributes or the number of tuples are large.

For Armstrong relations, we observe that their size is small compared with the size of the original relations. Most of the times, the number of tuples in generated real-world Armstrong relations varies from $1/100$ to $1/10,000$ compared with the number of tuples of the original relations.

6   Conclusion

In this paper, we propose a new approach intended for a twofold objective: discovering minimal non-trivial functional dependencies holding in a given relation;

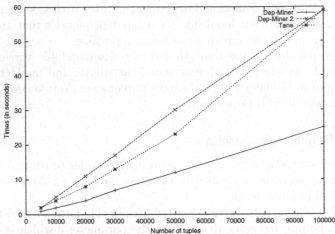

Fig. 2. Execution times (in seconds) for correlated data (30%)

achieving a real-world Armstrong relation, which can be seen as a loss-less sample of the initial relation.

The approach fits in a theoretical framework proposed in [24,25,26] for addressing the very same issue. Nevertheless, it differs from related work because we put the emphasis on the efficiency of the discovery of functional dependencies and real-world Armstrong relations. In this context, new solutions are proposed by using techniques originated by data mining. Each step of the approach is provided with formal foundations ensuring the correctness of the underlying algorithms.

The main benefit of our twofold discovery approach is that the DBA is provided with two different representations. On one hand functional dependencies could be used for normalizing existing relation schemas. On the other hand, real-world Armstrong relations are particularly useful for better understanding relation schemas, and aiding to select only relevant functional dependencies among the whole (and possibly voluminous) set of extracted dependencies.

Perspectives for Database Administration. Reducing database administration functions is recognized as being a new challenge in database community. In this context, the aim of the so-called "plug and play databases" is facilating the database administrator tasks and dealing with information discovery [9]. For example, in the context of the *AutoAdmin* project [1], physical database design is investigated for tuning index definitions in order to improve performances of the system [10].

In a similar way, existing logical database constraints should be fully understood. Providing the DBA with such a knowledge is particularly critical not only for improving application performances but also for guaranteeing data consistency. We believe that promising applications of the presented work fit in such a research direction.

Acknowledgments. We thank Rosine Cicchetti for her help during the writing of this paper.

References

1. Autoadmin Project, Microsoft research, database group,
   http://www.research.microsoft.com/db.
2. WWW page http://www.cs.helsinki.fi/research/fdk/datamining/tane.
3. Serge Abiteboul, Richard Hull, and Victor Vianu. *Foundations of Databases*. Addison Wesley, 1995.
4. Rakesh Agrawal and Ramakrishnan Srikant. Fast algorithms for mining association rules in large databases. In *Proceedings of the Twentieth International Conference on Very Large Databases, Santiago de Chile, Chile*, pages 487–499, 1994.
5. Roberto Bayardo and Rakesh Agrawal. Mining the most interesting rules. In *Proceedings of the Fifth International Conference on Knowledge Discovery & Data Mining, San Diego, CA, USA*, 1999.
6. Catriel Beeri, Martin Dowd, Ronald Fagin, and Richard Statman. On the structure of Armstrong relations for functional dependencies. *Journal of the ACM*, 31(1):30–46, 1984.
7. Catriel Beeri and Michael Kifer. An integrated approach to logical design of relational database schemes. *ACM Transaction on Database Systems*, 11(2):134–158, 1986.
8. Claude Berge. *Graphs and Hypergraphs*. North-Holland Mathematical Library 6. American Elsevie 1976, 2d rev. ed. edition, 1976.
9. Philip A. Bernstein, Michael L. Brodie, Stefano Ceri, David J. DeWitt, Michael J. Franklin, Hector Garcia-Molina, Jim Gray, Gerald Held, Joseph M. Hellerstein, H. V. Jagadish, Michael Lesk, David Maier, Jeffrey F. Naughton, Hamid Pirahesh, Michael Stonebraker, and Jeffrey D. Ullman. The Asilomar report on database research. *SIGMOD Record*, 27(4):74–80, 1998.
10. Surajit Chaudhuri and Vivek R. Narasayya. Autoadmin 'what-if' index analysis utility. In *Proceedings of the ACM SIGMOD International Conference on Management of Data, Seattle, Washington, USA*, pages 367–378, 1998.
11. E. F. Codd. Further normalization of the data base relational model. Technical Report 909, IBM Research, 1971.
12. Ethan Collopy and Mark Levene. Evolving example relations to satisfy functional dependencies. In *Proceedings of the International Workshop on Issues and Applications of Database Technology*, pages 440–447, 1998.
13. Stavros S. Cosmadakis, Paris C. Kanellakis, and Nicolas Spyratos. Partition semantics for relations. *Journal of Computer and System Sciences*, 33(2):203–233, 1986.
14. János Demetrovics, Leonid Libkin, and Ilya B. Muchnik. Functional dependencies in relational databases: A lattice point of view. *Discrete Applied Mathematics*, 40:155–185, 1992.
15. Ronald Fagin. Armstrong databases. Technical Report 5, IBM Research Laboratory, 1982.
16. Ronald Fagin. Horn clauses and database dependencies. *Journal of the ACM*, 29(4):952–985, 1982.
17. Georg Gottlob and Leonid Libkin. Investigations on Armstrong relations, dependency inference, and excluded functional dependencies. *Acta Cybernetica*, 9(4):385–402, 1990.

364   Stéphane Lopes, Jean-Marc Petit, and Lotfi Lakhal

18. Ykä Huhtala, Juha Kärkkäinen, Pasi Porkka, and Hannu Toivonen. Efficient discovery of functional and approximate dependencies using partitions. In *Proceedings of the Fourteenth IEEE International Conference on Data Engineering*, pages 392–401, 1998.
19. Martti Kantola, Heikki Mannila, Kari-Jouko Räihä, and Harri Siirtola. Discovering functional and inclusion dependencies in relational databases. *International Journal of Intelligent Systems*, 7:591–607, 1992.
20. Mika Klemettinen, Heikki Mannila, Pirjo Ronkainen, Hannu Toivonen, and A. Inkeri Verkamo. Finding interesting rules from large sets of discovered association rules. In *Proceedings of the Third International Conference on Information and Knowledge Management, Gaithersburg, Maryland*, pages 401–407, 1994.
21. Mark Levene and Georges Loizou. *A Guided Tour of Relational Databases and Beyond*. Springer-verlag London Limited, 1999.
22. Stéphane Lopes, Jean-Marc Petit, and Lotfi Lakhal.   Efficient discovery of functional dependencies and armstrong relations (complete version) http://libd2.univ-bpclermont.fr/publications.   Technical report, LIMOS, 1999.
23. Stéphane Lopes, Jean-Marc Petit, and Farouk Toumani. Discovery of "interesting" data dependencies from a workload of SQL statements (poster). In Jan M. Zytkow and Jan Rauch, editors, *Proceedings of the Principles of Data Mining and Knowledge Discovery, Prague, Czech Republic*, volume 1704, pages 430–435, 1999.
24. Heikki Mannila and Kari-Jouko Räihä. Design by example: An application of Armstrong relations. *Journal of Computer and System Sciences*, 33(2):126–141, 1986.
25. Heikki Mannila and Kari-Jouko Räihä. Algorithms for inferring functional dependencies from relations. *Data and Knowledge Engineering*, 12(1):83–99, 1994.
26. Heikki Mannila and Kari-Jouko Räihä. *The Design of Relational Databases*. Addison Wesley, 1994.
27. Heikki Mannila and Hannu Toivonen. Levelwise search and borders of theories in knowledge discovery. *Data Mining and Knowledge Discovery*, 1(3):241–258, 1997.
28. V.M. Markowitz and J.A. Makowsky. Identifying extended entity-relationship object structures in relational schemas. *IEEE Transactions on Software Engineering*, 16(8):777–790, 1990.
29. Nicolas Pasquier, Yves Bastide, Rafik Taouil, and Lotfi Lakhal. Discovering frequent closed itemsets for association rules. In *Proceedings of the Seventh International Conference on Database Theory, Jerusalem, Israël*, pages 398–416, 1999.
30. Nicolas Pasquier, Yves Bastide, Rafik Taouil, and Lotfi Lakhal. Mining bases for association rules using galois closed sets (poster). In *Proceedings of the Sixteenth IEEE International Conference on Data Engineering, February 29 - March 3, San Diego, CA, USA*. IEEE Computer Society, 2000.
31. Iztok Savnik and Peter A. Flach. Bottom-up induction of functional dependencies from relations. In *Proceedings of the AAAI-93Workshop on Knowledge Discovery in Databases*, pages 174–185, 1993.
32. Nicolas Spyratos. The partition model: A deductive database model. *ACM Transaction on Database Systems*, 12(1):1–37, 1987.

Athena: Mining-Based Interactive Management of Text Databases

Rakesh Agrawal, Roberto Bayardo, and Ramakrishnan Srikant

IBM Almaden Research Center
San Jose, CA, U.S.A.
ragrawal@acm.org, bayardo@alum.mit.edu, srikant@us.ibm.com

Abstract We describe Athena: a system for creating, exploiting, and maintaining a hierarchy of textual documents through interactive mining-based operations. Requirements of any such system include speed and minimal end-user effort. Athena satisfies these requirements through linear-time classification and clustering engines which are applied interactively to speed the development of accurate models.

Naive Bayes classifiers are recognized to be among the best for classifying text. We show that our specialization of the Naive Bayes classifier is considerably more accurate (7 to 29% absolute increase in accuracy) than a standard implementation. Our enhancements include using Lidstone's law of succession instead of Laplace's law, under-weighting long documents, and over-weighting author and subject.

We also present a new interactive clustering algorithm, C-Evolve, for topic discovery. C-Evolve first finds highly accurate cluster digests (partial clusters), gets user feedback to merge and correct these digests, and then uses the classification algorithm to complete the partitioning of the data. By allowing this interactivity in the clustering process, C-Evolve achieves considerably higher clustering accuracy (10 to 20% absolute increase in our experiments) than the popular K-Means and agglomerative clustering methods.

1 Introduction

People and organizations are amassing more and more data in the form of unstructured or semi-structured textual documents, due mostly to the flourishing of e-mail and world-wide web usage. Systems that manage text databases typically provide support for keyword queries and manual arrangement of documents into a hierarchical ("folder") structure. Benefits of a folder hierarchy include the ability to quickly locate a document without having to remember the exact keywords contained in that document, and the ability to easily browse a set of related documents. Unfortunately, the task of maintaining coherent folders is time consuming, and often unused or under-used as a result. For example, many if not most e-mail users simply allow their messages to accumulate in the inbox where these messages remain until they are deleted. As a result, the benefits of a well-maintained folder hierarchy are never realized. Outside the e-mail context,

C. Zaniolo et al. (Eds.): EDBT 2000, LNCS 1777, pp. 365–379, 2000.
© Springer-Verlag Berlin Heidelberg 2000

web search engines such as Yahoo! [27] and several e-commerce sites with large product catalogs provide and maintain hierarchical categorizations to enhance the usability of search results and to facilitate browsing.

In this paper, we present a system henceforth referred to as Athena[1] that simplifies the process of hierarchical document organization through text mining algorithms. Athena is currently implemented on top of Lotus Notes [14] to support the management of e-mail and discussion databases, though the concepts apply equally well to other document repositories including collections of web pages or text files. Important functionality of Athena includes:

- *Topic Discovery*: Decompose an unorganized collection of documents into groups so that each group consists of documents on the same topic.
- *Hierarchy Reorganization*: Reorganize a hierarchical collection of documents into another hierarchy.
- *Hierarchy Population and Inbox Browsing*: Use the information contained in the current populated hierarchy to organize documents in Inbox by topic and/or automatically route new documents. Documents that fit in multiple categories can optionally be routed to (or displayed under) several categories.
- *Hierarchy Maintenance*: Identify misfiled documents in a node of the hierarchy and detect concept drift within a node.

A more detailed description of the Athena functionality is given in [1].

Classification and clustering are the two basic building blocks used for implementing the above functionality. These technologies have been studied extensively in the areas of statistics, data-mining, information retrieval, and machine learning. However, standard techniques performed poorly for our application. For example, Naive Bayes classifiers [6] are recognized to be among the best for classifying text. We found that by specializing Naive Bayes for our application, we could reduce the number of errors by 30 to 60% (with 7 to 29% absolute increase in accuracy) when compared to a standard implementation. Our enhancements include using Lidstone's law of succession instead of Laplace's law, under-weighting long documents, and weighting author and subject.

Clustering algorithms applied in this domain must be fast to avoid taxing the patience of the user. We present a new linear-time interactive clustering algorithm, C-Evolve, for topic discovery. C-Evolve first finds highly accurate cluster digests (partial clusters), gets user feedback to merge/correct these digests, and then uses the classification algorithm to complete the partitioning of the data. By allowing interactivity in the clustering process, C-Evolve is considerably more accurate (10 to 20% absolute increase in accuracy in our experiments) than K-Means [21] as well as agglomerative clustering methods [21].

Paper Layout In the rest of this section, we discuss related work on systems for routing or clustering email or text documents. (We discuss related work in

---

[1] Automated Text HiErarchy maNAgement

clustering or classification algorithms in Sections 3 and 4.) We describe the technical details of the classification component in Section 2, along with experimental results justifying our design decisions. Section 3 goes into the technical details of the clustering component, and also provides an empirical evaluation of its efficacy. Section 4 concludes with a summary and directions for future work.

Related Work There have been at least three previous proposals on the development of classification models for the purpose of routing e-mail, either in general [4] [25] or for the special case of junk-mail [23]. Other systems provide agents that assist e-mail users by predicting an action the user is likely to take [15] [19]. None of these proposals address the task of textual database organization outside of routing incoming documents.

Other related work includes the Scatter/Gather system [5], which uses on-line clustering to assist the user in browsing large collections of documents. While Scatter/Gather does not directly address the problem of creating and maintaining a lasting document organization, many of the requirements of our systems are similar, such as the need for fast, on-line algorithms capable of extracting useful information from text, and the need to involve the user in the process of applying these algorithms. We make a more detailed comparison of our system to Scatter/Gather in a later section. SONIA [24] uses agglomerative text clustering to organize the results of queries to networked information sources, and Naive Bayes classification to organize new documents within an existing categorization scheme.

2   Classification Component

Athena's classification component is used for hierarchy reorganization, document routing, and identification of misfiled documents. We decided to base our classifier on the Naive-Bayes model [6] for the following reasons:

- Naive-Bayes classifiers are very competitive with other techniques for text classification [3] [12] [11] [20] [16].[2]
- They stabilize quickly [8], which supports automated hierarchy reorganization with a limited number of examples.
- They are fast. They can be constructed quickly with a single pass over the documents, making them suitable for on-line model creation; they also quickly classify incoming documents [3].
- They are simple to update in the presence of document additions or deletions, making them easy to maintain.

---

[2] We also experimented with using the SPRINT decision-tree classifier [26], but found it had low accuracy in this domain due to the small number of examples per class and the large feature space.

The basic Naive-Bayes classifier estimates the posterior probability of class C_i given a document d via Bayes' rule:

$$\Pr(C_i|d) = \frac{\Pr(d|C_i) \times \Pr(C_i)}{\Pr(d)}$$

We ignore $\Pr(d)$ since it is the same for all classes. $\Pr(C_i)$ is estimated by:

$$\Pr(C_i) = \frac{\text{Number of documents in class } C_i}{\text{Total number of documents in the dataset}}$$

To estimate $\Pr(d|C_i)$, we "naively" assume that all the words in the document occur independently to get

$$\Pr(d|C_i) = \prod_{w \in d} \Pr(w|C_i)$$

Let $n(C_i, w)$ be the number of occurrences of word w in class C_i (counting multiple occurrences), and $n(C_i) = \sum_w n(C_i, w)$ the total number of words in class C_i. Then the maximum likelihood estimate for $\Pr(w|C_i)$ is simply $n(C_i, w)/n(C_i)$. However, using this estimate would give a probability of zero for any word that does not occur in the class, and thus result in $\Pr(d|C_i)$ being zero for any document d that contained a word not present in class C_i. The standard approach to address this problem (e.g. [3] [18] [10]) is to smooth the maximum likelihood estimate with Laplace's law of succession [6] to get

$$\Pr(w|C_i) = \frac{n(C_i, w) + 1}{n(C_i) + |V|} \tag{1}$$

where $|V|$ is the size of the vocabulary (i.e., the number of distinct words in the dataset). The above formula is the result of assuming that all possible words are *a priori* equally likely (see [22] for details).

Following [16], we use the multinomial form of the Naive Bayes classifier where each document is treated as a bag of words rather than a set of words to yield better accuracy.

2.1   Enhancing the Naive-Bayes Classifier

We first specialized the standard Naive-Bayes classifier by applying techniques such as under-weighting long documents and over-weighting author and subject [2]. To over-weight subject (author) by w times, we treated the subject (author) as if each of the words in the subject (author) had occurred w times rather than just once. To prevent long documents from dominating the folder profile, we under-weighted documents with more then l words (for some threshold l) by treating each word as if it had occured only $l/n(d)$ times, where $n(d)$ is the number of words in the document. The weights and thresholds were determined by using a part of the training set as a validation set. These enhancements cumulatively yielded upto 3% accuracy improvements in our experiments.

	Small Class	Large Class
Vocabulary	10,000	10,000
Number of Words	1000	100,000
Number of occurrences of word w	10	1000
$\Pr(w|c)$ w/o correction	1%	1%
$\Pr(w|c)$ with correction	0.1%	0.91%

Fig. 1. Skew due to Laplace Correction

In search for ideas for larger improvements in accuracy, we examined the words that had the maximum impact on the classification of a document. These words can be found by looking at the ratio of $\Pr(w|c)/\Pr(w|c')$, where c is the class Athena chose and c' the class for which $\Pr(w|c')$ is highest. Investigation of some misclassified documents revealed that the probability estimate of some words was being highly skewed by the Laplace correction. Figure 1 explains this skew with an example. Word w has a maximum likelihood estimate of 1% in both classes. However, after applying the Laplace correction, it is considered 9 times more likely to appear in the large class as in the small class. Hence we suspected that the Laplace correction was creating a strong bias towards larger classes.

Lidstone's law of succession We then replaced Laplace's law of succession with Lidstone's law of succession. For positive λ, we estimate $\Pr(w|C_i)$ to be

$$\Pr(w|C_i) = \frac{n(C_i, w) + \lambda}{n(C_i) + \lambda|V|} \tag{2}$$

This class of probability estimates is due to the actuaries G.F. Hardy [7] and G.J. Lidstone [13] at the turn of the century. The above estimate is a linear interpolation of the maximum likelihood estimate $n(C_i, w)/n(C_i)$ and the uniform prior $1/|V|$. This can be seen by rewriting (2) with the substitution $\mu = n(C_i)/(n(C_i) + \lambda|V|)$:

$$\Pr(w|C_i) = \mu \frac{n(C_i, w)}{n(C_i)} + (1 - \mu)\frac{1}{|V|}$$

Note that if $\lambda = 1$, the Lidstone correction is identical to the Laplace correction. In their attempt to improve the accuracy of Naive Bayes, Kohavi et al [9] also experimented with Lidstone correction using the datasets available in the UCI repository.None of these datasets consists of textual data. They found that using $\lambda = 1/\text{total records}$, they could slightly reduce the average absolute error (by 1%, from 19.59% to 18.58%) compared to Laplace correction.

Empirical Evaluation We ran experiments on the datasets shown in Table 1. A, B, C and D refer to four email datasets, while Reuters is the single-category

Dataset	#Folders	#Docs	#Docs/Folder Avg ± Std. Dev.	#Words/Folder Avg ± Std. Dev.	Vocabulary
A	53	768	14 ± 25	4K ± 4K	15K
B	38	1,039	25 ± 34	10K ± 17K	23K
C	204	2,995	15 ± 23	5K ± 9K	39K
D	15	964	64 ± 47	18K ± 13K	15K
Reuters	82	11,367	138 ± 517	15K ± 36K	24K

Table 1. Dataset Characteristics

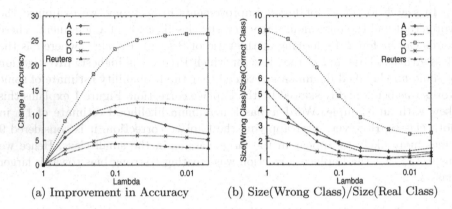

(a) Improvement in Accuracy   (b) Size(Wrong Class)/Size(Real Class)

Fig. 2. Lidstone Correction

version of Distribution 1.0 of Reuters-21578[3]. Notice that three of the four email datasets have a very large number of classes, ranging from 38 to 204, and very few examples per class, ranging from 25 to just 14 documents. All our accuracy numbers were computed using 10-fold cross-validation.

Figure 2(a) shows the change in accuracy as we vary λ in the Lidstone correction, relative to the accuracy for the Laplace correction ($\lambda = 1$). The accuracy improved by 4% to 26%, with the largest gains on those datasets where the accuracy numbers were low. The number of errors was reduced by between 25% and 60% on these datasets (details given later in Table 2). The optimal value of λ varied between 0.2 and 0.01, depending on the dataset.

Recall our hypothesis that the reason for the improvement in accuracy due to decreasing λ is the bias towards large classes produced by the Laplace correction. To verify this hypothesis, we need to measure the size bias of the classifier. For any misclassified documents d, let C_m be the misclassified class and C_r the right class. We use the geometric mean of $n(C_m)/n(C_r)$ over all misclassified documents as a measure of the size bias of the classifier. Figure 2(b) shows that the size bias decreases dramatically with decreasing λ, confirming our hypothesis. At $\lambda = 1$, the misclassified class is between 2 and 9 times larger than the right class. At the optimal λ values for the datasets, the ratio is between 1 and 2.5.

---

[3] Available from http://www.research.att.com/ lewis

Dataset	Number of Classes	Standard	Lidstone	Final	Reduction in Errors	Top 3 classes
A	53	60.5 ± 5.7	71.5 ± 6.3	72.4 ± 5.4	30%	84.4 ± 5.5
B	38	66.2 ± 5.4	84.8 ± 1.7	86.9 ± 2.4	61%	95.1 ± 2.0
C	204	47.0 ± 3.0	74.4 ± 1.9	76.1 ± 2.3	55%	88.1 ± 2.7
D	15	81.6 ± 4.2	88.6 ± 3.2	88.9 ± 1.8	40%	98.1 ± 1.6
Reuters	82	79.9 ± 1.3	84.8 ± 1.0	85.2 ± 1.2	26%	94.8 ± 0.7

Table 2. Accuracy $\pm$ Standard Deviation

Note that dataset C, for which decreasing λ gave the most dramatic gains, also has the largest change in the size bias, decreasing from 9 to 2.5.

Given the sensitivity of accuracy to the value of λ, Athena uses an automatic procedure to select the optimal value of λ on a per-dataset basis. We use a portion of the training set as a validation set, and compute the accuracy of the classifier over this validation set for various values of λ to obtain the optimal value.

Recent work by McCallum et al. [17] uses both the uniform prior and a global prior (the frequency distribution over the entire dataset) to smooth the maximum likelihood estimate. Their algorithm uses expectation maximization to assign weights to each of these distributions on a per-class basis. This procedure typically requires a dozen or so iterations over the data, which can be expensive.

Summary of Results Table 2 shows the accuracy of the classifier for several versions:

- *Standard:* Standard Naive Bayes classifier with Laplace correction
- *Lidstone:* Classifier using Lidstone correction instead of Laplace correction, with the optimal value of λ determined automatically using part of the training set as a validation set.
- *Final:* Classifier using Lidstone correction that additionally over-weights author and subject, and under-weights long documents.
- *Reduction in Errors* between the Standard version and the Final version.
- *Top 3 classes:* Accuracy of the classifier when the classifier is judged correct if any of the top 3 choices were correct.

We observe large gains in accuracy due to Lidstone's correction, and small (but useful) gains in accuracy due to over-weighting author and subject, and under-weighting long documents. The increase in absolute accuracy ranged from 7 to 29% for the email datasets, with a 30 to 61% reduction in the number of errors. We also note that the classifier accuracy is significantly higher when considering the top three classes. These accuracies can be achieved by applications which make multiple recommendations for document routing (e.g. [25]), allowing the user to make the final selection. Additionally, in this application domain, many documents naturally belong to multiple classes. Multiple classifications of a document can be useful for informing the user of this possibility.

3   Clustering Component

The clustering component is responsible for topic discovery within an unorganized collection of documents. We have developed an interactive approach to clustering which involves iteratively presenting the user with a perusable number of related documents that suggest how a specified folder might be decomposed. We call such a set of documents a cluster digest. This term is borrowed from the Scatter/Gather system [5], which uses on-line text clustering to assist the user in browsing a document collection. In Scatter/Gather, cluster digests are presented to the user to determine which documents in the collection are worth browsing. Unlike Scatter/Gather, Athena does not produce a complete clustering before forming the cluster digests. Instead, it applies a novel algorithm that produces the digests directly. This results in response times suitable for on-line application, with equivalent or better results. The algorithm can also produce these digests incrementally, allowing the incorporation of feedback from the user into the clustering model before producing additional results, and avoiding any need for the user to specify a desired number of clusters apriori.

There are multiple proposals for text clustering, with many of the most popular and effective belonging to the agglomerative class [21]. A drawback of this class of algorithms is they are at best of quadratic runtime complexity, limiting their usefulness in on-line applications such as ours. To overcome this limitation, Scatter/Gather uses a complex intermixing of iterative partitional clustering algorithms (e.g. K-Means) and an agglomerative scheme. The basic idea is to apply the inferior but fast partitional clustering algorithm until the document set has been decomposed to a point where agglomerative clustering can be used efficiently. Because we found that a complete clustering typically contains too many errors to be useful for reorganizing a document collection, we instead opted to develop a new algorithm that very quickly produces only the cluster digests for topic discovery, and leaves further document partitioning to the classifier. Our experiments reveal that this approach is considerably more accurate.

Our algorithm can be thought of as "evolving" one cluster digest at a time. After evolving a new digest, it is presented to the user who can discard irrelevant documents, move documents between the digests, and even discard a digest entirely. After these modifications are made, additional digests can be mined from the remaining documents at the user's request. In implementing clustering in this manner, the user need not specify up-front an exact number of clusters to discover.

3.1   Algorithm Details

The pseudo-code for the digest evolution routine appears in Figure 4. We call the algorithm C-Evolve(n), where the variable n specifies the number of cluster digests to evolve simultaneously. (Only the best of this set is returned.) This algorithm is called once for each cluster desired by the user.

Input variables:
   A set D of input documents.
   A set P of previously-discovered cluster digests (possibly empty).
   An integer n specifying the number of clusters to evolve simultaneously.
   An integer DIGEST_SIZE bounding the number of documents in a cluster.
Return value:
   A cluster digest consisting of at most DIGEST_SIZE documents from D.
Score Function: See algorithm description.
Algorithm:
   1. Remove documents within the digests of P from D.
   2. Initialize a cluster C_1 with a random document from D.
   3. For $i = 2 \ldots n$
      Initialize a cluster C_i with the document d in D that minimizes the following:
      $\max(\forall_{j=1 \ldots i-1} \text{ sim}(d, C_j))$
   4. For $i = 1 \ldots n$
      Let cluster C_i' contain the top $\min(|C_i| + 1, \text{DIGEST\_SIZE})$ scoring
      documents d according to score(d, C_i, P)
   5. If there exists some $i = 1 \ldots n$ such that $C_i \neq C_i'$,
      (a) $C_i := C_i'$ for all $i = 1 \ldots n$
      (b) goto step 4.
   6. Return the cluster C_i out of $C_1 \ldots C_n$ that maximizes the following:
      $\min(\forall_{d \in C_i} \text{ score}(d, C_i, P))$

Fig. 3. The C-Evolve(n) algorithm for evolving a cluster digest.

The pseudo-code makes use of a similarity function, $sim()$, that returns a
floating point value between 0 and 1 (with 1 indicating maximum similarity).
This function must accept either a single document or a set of documents for each
of its two arguments. In our experiments, we use the Scatter/Gather approach for
computing similarities: Similarity of a document pair is given by cosine distance
between vectors of term frequencies, with term frequencies damped by the square
root function. Similarity of two clusters is then given by the average pair-wise
similarity between their documents.

Another function used by the pseudo-code, $score()$, accepts a document, a
cluster digest C, and a set of cluster digests P. The return value of this function
is maximized when the document is highly similar to cluster C, and highly dissimilar to those clusters within P. We use the method below for computing such
a value, though C-Evolve can use other scoring functions with these properties.

$$\text{score}(d, C, P) = \begin{cases} \min(\forall_{C_p \in P} [\text{sim}(d, C) - \text{sim}(d, C_p)]) & \text{if } P \text{ non-empty,} \\ \text{sim}(d, C) & \text{otherwise} \end{cases}$$

The first three steps of the algorithm perform initialization, which involves
removing documents from the input set that already belong to previously-discovered cluster digests, and seeding the n clusters with documents that are dissimilar to each other. This seeding policy spreads the search for a good cluster
digest across the document space.

Step 4 grows the clusters one document at a time until the maximum size is reached and clusters stop changing. By virtue of the scoring function, this step not only attempts to maximize similarity between documents within a given cluster, but also dissimilarity between the evolving cluster and previously discovered clusters. This ensures that, even though the algorithm is not performing a complete partitioning of the input documents, the evolving digests are likely to discover a topic that is not already represented by the existing ones. Note that this scheme is not entirely greedy – that is, a document added to the cluster may disappear from it in a later iteration. Even though a document may score highly during an early iteration, as the cluster evolves it may no longer score so highly. This feature ensures such documents are removed to improve the final result.

Athena employs C-Evolve with the parameter n set to 6. This setting was chosen because it yielded good results, and it is small enough to guarantee response times of a few seconds given a document collection of a thousand documents, a cluster digest size of 10-20, and a Java based implementation.

There is no simple way to obtain a tight bound on the iterations performed by C-Evolve(n) since the clusters can continue to evolve after reaching the desired size. In practice, however, the number of iterations performed after the cluster digest has reached the desired size is typically small, usually well under 5. This amounts to a linear average-case complexity assuming the cluster digest size and the value of n are bounded by constants. If desired, the number of iterations can be hard-bounded by a small constant to guarantee linear complexity in the worst-case. If the user desires a larger cluster digest, e.g. one that is proportional to the collection size instead of bounded by a constant, the procedure can be modified to grow the cluster more than a single document at a time. We have found that slow cluster growth is most helpful during the early iterations of the procedure, so growth can be accelerated during later iterations in order to guarantee linear complexity without significantly compromising the results.

3.2   Evaluation

In this section, we compare C-Evolve with more traditional clustering methods including K-Means and Hierarchical Agglomerative Clustering [21]. Our first suite of experiments evaluates how well C-Evolve performs when finding cluster digests compared to these other (appropriately modified) techniques. Because agglomerative and K-Means clustering fully partition the input documents, in order to produce cluster digests, we modified them to return the most central documents of each cluster. The second suite of experiments evaluates how well C-Evolve, when applied interactively with the classifier from the previous section, compares to these other clustering methods when fully partitioning the input documents.

Agglomerative clustering algorithms work by placing each document in its own cluster, and then iteratively merging the pair of most similar clusters until the desired number of clusters remain. In our implementation, cluster similarity is given by average pair-wise similarity between the documents from each cluster. We use the same document similarity function (cosine distance) and document representation (term frequencies damped by the square-root function) for all clustering algorithms to ensure a fair comparison. This algorithm is exactly the "reference" clustering algorithm used in Scatter/Gather [5].

K-Means clustering seeds each initial cluster (the number of which equals the number of desired clusters) with a single randomly chosen document. A pass is made over the input documents and each document is placed moved into the cluster that is most similar to it. This process repeats until the clusters stop changing, at which point they are returned.

We used e-mail collections to evaluate these algorithms, obtained from co-workers who diligently file their e-mail, along with the standard Reuters-21578 benchmark data[4] in order to show the results apply more generally. (Table 1 shows some of the characteristics of these datasets.) For each data-set, we selected at most 100 documents from each folder/category to prevent folders with many documents (e.g. those compiled from an active mailing list) from excessively slowing the agglomerative algorithms[5] and overly skewing the input distribution. For the Reuters data, each document was placed into a "folder" corresponding to the first topic to which it is assigned.

Evaluating Topic Discovery We assume that the organization provided by the folder hierarchy from each data-set is the "true" clustering of the data. For each data-set, fifty trials were performed, where for each trial, six folders were selected at random from a given data-set and the documents intermixed. Each clustering algorithm was then run on the resulting document collection and made to identify three cluster digests containing 11 documents each.

We chose to identify a smaller number of cluster digests than the number of true clusters in order to determine the sensitivity of agglomerative and K-Means clustering to the number of clusters identified – in real world applications, the true number of clusters is unknown, so the number of clusters the user chooses to identify is unlikely to be the same as the true number of clusters. To demonstrate that knowledge of the true number of clusters does not necessarily improve the results, we also have agglomerative and K-Means clustering identify six cluster digests and return the best three of the result. (The best cluster digests are those which maximize average pair-wise similarity).

For each set of cluster digests provided by an algorithm for a given run, we compute two "goodness" metrics. The first is digest purity: we want each digest to contain only documents from a single one of the true clusters. Purity of a digest is therefore defined as the maximum number of documents within

---

[4] Available at http://www.research.att.com/ lewis/reuters21578.html

[5] Experiments were run by e-mail database owners on their personal machines in order to maintain their privacy. This required our experiments to complete over a single evening so that their machines were free for regular work during the day.

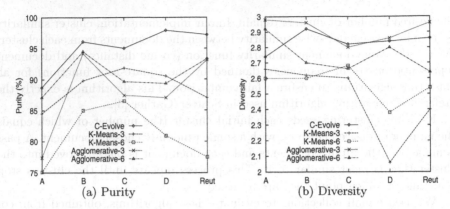

Fig. 4. Purity and Diversity Results for the Cluster Digests

the digest that belong to the same true cluster, divided by the total number of documents within the digest. Another metric is digest diversity: we want each digest to present a topic that is distinct from the others. Cluster diversity is therefore the number of true clusters covered by the dominant class from each cluster digest. This implies the maximum diversity score is 3 since we apply the algorithms to find only 3 digests in this experiment.

The results of the experiment appear in Figure 4. As can be seen, C-Evolve is superior to all other schemes with respect to the purity metric. With respect to diversity, it is superior to all but the agglomerative algorithm which identifies three clusters before returning the digests of each. Surprisingly, the algorithms which attempt to identify the true number of clusters do not fare any better than their counterparts which identify only three clusters.

Evaluating Interactive Clustering After a set of topics is discovered, Athena allows the user to populate these topics with additional documents by applying the classifier from the previous section. We evaluate how well this technique works when attempting to fully recover the true clustering by completely partitioning the input documents. For these experiments, we select 5 folders at random from each data-set and intermix the documents to form the algorithm input. Once again, fifty trials are performed on each data-set and the results averaged.

For this experiment, we have the K-Means and Agglomerative clustering algorithms attempt to identify the true number of clusters (5 in this case). For each cluster identified, each document is considered an "error" if its class does not match the dominant class of the cluster. Following [24], we compute the accuracy of a given clustering as one minus the error rate.

We apply C-Evolve repeatedly until each folder is discovered (a folder is said to be discovered by a digest if the dominant class of the digest matches that of the folder). Typically, the number of digests identified in order to discover all folders exceeds the true number of clusters by only one or two. We compute errors

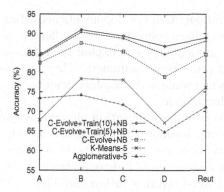

Fig. 5. Accuracy Results

for this approach by first summing up the total number of documents in each digest that do not belong to the dominant class of the digest. This error value is then added to the number of errors produced by the classifier in populating the clusters with the remaining documents. To simulate user-corrections, before applying the classifier, we remove any errors from the cluster digests and merge cluster digests that discover the same folder. We also evaluate the effect of having the system present the user with a small number of randomly-selected examples for manual correction of Athena's classification before the classifier is applied in order to broaden the training set. We tried both 5 documents per folder and 10 documents per folder. Each document presented to the user by Athena is counted as an error if the suggested class is not the folder to which the document actually belongs.

As can be seen in Figure 5, our interactive approach to clustering leads to substantial improvements in accuracy over standard clustering techniques. Manual correction of Athena's classification of a small number of randomly-selected examples before applying the classifier leads to further improvement. Note that we obtain these results even though we provide the traditional clustering techniques with knowledge of the true number of clusters. The fact that such improvements are possible suggests that a "true" clustering as envisioned by an end-user who organizes documents rarely matches the true clustering as defined by any statistical technique. By allowing interactivity in the clustering process, our approach allows the user to guide the algorithm towards a more desirable partitioning of the input documents.

4   Conclusions and Future Work

We addressed the problem of simplifying the process of hierarchical document organization and management through text mining algorithms. Using classification and clustering as the basic building blocks, our Athena system provides rich functionality for automatic creation and maintenance of hierarchical text databases. Using Athena, users can discover topics in their unorganized collection of documents and partition the documents according to these topics. They can reorganize a hierarchical collection into a different hierarchy by giving only few documents as examples. They can exploit the information contained in their current hierarchy to route new documents. They can also find misfiled documents and identify when some node in a hierarchy may need reorganization due to concept drift within a node.

The implementation of this application placed new requirements on the classification and clustering technology, making the use of standard solutions inadequate. For classification, we enhanced the basic Naive-Bayes algorithm with several features including the use of Lidstone's law of succession, under-weighting long documents, and over-weighting author and subject. These enhancements led to 7 to 29% absolute increase in accuracy on our real-life test data sets.

We also developed a new interactive clustering algorithm. This algorithm first finds highly accurate cluster digests (partial clusters), obtains user feedback to merge/correct these digests, and then uses the classification algorithm to complete the partitioning of the data. In our experiments, this new algorithm resulted in 10-20% increase in absolute accuracy over k-means and agglomerative clustering. While strict classification and clustering algorithms have been well-studied in previous work, this interactivity dimension has received comparably little attention. We feel further research directed towards cooperation between on-line data-mining algorithms and the end-user will prove fruitful.

Acknowledgements We would like to thank Andreas Arning, Ashok Chandra, Dimitris Gunopulos, Howard Ho, Sunita Sarawagi, John Shafer and Magnus Stensmo for their contributions to the design of Athena.

References

1. R. Agrawal, R. Bayardo, and R. Srikant.   Athena: Mining-based interactive management of text databases.   Research Report RJ 10153, IBM Almaden Research Center, San Jose, CA 95120, July 1999.   Available from http://www.almaden.ibm.com/cs/quest.
2. C. Apte, F. Damerau, and S.M. Weiss. Automated Learning of Decision Rules for Text Categorization. *ACM Transactions on Information Systems*, 1994.
3. S. Chakrabarti, B. Dom, R. Agrawal, and P. Raghavan. Using Taxonomy, Discriminants, and Signatures for Navigating in Text Databases. In *Proc. of the 23rd Int'l Conf. on Very Large Databases*, pages 446–455, 1997.
4. W.W. Cohen. Learning Rules that Classify E-Mail. In *Proc. of the 1996 AAAI Spring Symposium on Machine Learning in Information Access*, 1996.
5. D.R. Cutting, K.R. David, J.O. Pedersen, and J.W. Tukey. Scatter/Gather: A Cluster-based Approach to Browsing Large Document Collections. In *Proc. of the 15th Intl ACM SIGIR Conf. on Research and Development in Information Retrieval*, 1992.
6. I.J. Good. *The Estimation of Probabilities: An Essay on Modern Bayesian Methods.* M.I.T. Press, 1965.
7. G. Hardy. Correspondence. *Insurance Record*, 1889.

8. R. Kohavi. Scaling Up the Accuracy of Naive-Bayes Classifiers: a Decision-Tree Hybrid. In *Proc. of the Second Int'l Conf. on Knowledge Discovery and Data Mining*, 1996.

9. R. Kohavi, B. Becker, and D. Sommerfield. Improving simple bayes. In *The 9th European Conference on Machine Learning, Poster Papers*, 1997.

10. P. Kontkanen, P. Myllymaki, T. Silander, and H. Tirri. BAYDA: Software for Bayesian Classification and Feature Selection. In *Proc. of the Fourth Int'l Conf. on Knowledge Discovery and Data Mining*, 1998.

11. K. Lang. News Weeder: Learning to Filter Net-News. In *Proc. of the 12th Int'l Conf. on Machine Learning*, pages 331–339, 1995.

12. D.D. Lewis and M. Ringuette. A comparison of two learning algorithms for text categorization. In *In Third Annual Symposium on Document Analysis and Information Retrieval*, pages 81–92, 1994.

13. G. Lidstone. Note on the general case of the Bayes-Laplace formula for inductive or a posteriori probabilities. *Trans. Fac. Actuaries*, 8:182–192, 1920.

14. Lotus Notes. http://www.notes.net.

15. P. Maes. Agents that Reduce Work and Information Overload. *Communications of the ACM*, 37(7):31–40, 1994.

16. Andrew McCallum and Kamal Nigam. A Comparison of Event Models for Naive Bayes Text Classification. In *AAAI-98 Workshop on "Learning for Text Categorization"*, 1998.

17. Andrew McCallum, Ronald Rosenfeld, Tom Mitchell, and Andrew Ng. Improving Text Classification by Shrinkage in a Hierarchy of Classes. In *Intl. Conf. on Machine Learning*, 1998.

18. Tom M. Mitchell. *Machine Learning*, chapter 6. McGraw-Hill, 1997.

19. T.R. Payne and P. Edwards. Interface Agents that Learn: An Investigation of Learning Issues in a Mail Agent Interface. *Applied Artificial Intelligence*, 11:1–32, 1997.

20. M. Pazzani and D. Billsus. Learning and Revising User Profiles: The identification of interesting web sites. *Machine Learning*, 27:313–331, 1997.

21. E. Rasmussen. *Information Retrieval: Data Structures and Algorithms*, chapter Clustering algorithms, pages 419–442. Prentice Hall, Englewood Cliffs, NJ, 1991.

22. E.S. Ristad. A Natural Law of Succession. Technical report, Princeton University, 1995. Research Report CS-TR-495-95.

23. M. Sahami, S. Dumais, D. Heckerman, and E. Horvitz. A Bayesian Approach to Filtering Junk E-mail. In *Proc. of the AAAI'98 Workshop on Learning for Text Categorization*, Madison, Wisconsin, 1998.

24. M. Sahami, S. Yusufali, and M.Q.W. Baldonado. Sonia: A service for organizing networked information autonomously. In *Proc. of the Third ACM Conference on Digital Libraries*, pages 200–209, 1998.

25. R. Segal and J. Kephart. MailCat: An Intelligent Assistant for Organizing E-Mail. In *Proc. of the Third Int'l Conf. on Autonomous Agents*, 1999.

26. John Shafer, Rakesh Agrawal, and Manish Mehta. SPRINT: A Scalable Parallel Classifier for Data Mining. In *Proc. of the 22nd Int'l Conference on Very Large Databases*, Bombay, India, September 1996.

27. Yahoo! http://www.yahoo.com.

Industrial & Applications Track: XML

Tamino – An Internet Database System

Harald Schöning[1] and Jürgen Wäsch[2]

[1] Software AG, Uhlandstraße 12, D-64297 Darmstadt, Germany
Harald.Schoening@softwareag.com
[2] GMD – Integrated Publication and Information Systems Institute (IPSI),
Dolivostraße 15, D-64293 Darmstadt, Germany
waesch@darmstadt.gmd.de

Abstract. Software AG's Tamino is a novel database server designed to fit the needs of electronic business and worldwide information exchange via the Internet. It is not just an on-top solution based on a database system originally designed for use in other application areas. Rather, it is entirely designed for the specific scenario of HTTP-based access to data represented in XML. These data can stem from various sources, and can be combined on the fly when a corresponding request is encountered. This paper sketches the architecture and the functional features of Tamino, and justifies its various design decisions.

1 Introduction and Requirements

Currently, one of the emerging application areas of information technology is electronic commerce, in particular business-to-business commerce. Data such as orders and invoices, but also product descriptions and statistical data are exchanged between companies worldwide. The traditional EDI is not capable of mastering the necessary openness and flexibility which allows a company to spontaneously establish data exchange with an arbitrary other company.

One pre-requisite for the new forms of e-business is that data are accessible via the Web. Software AG's Tamino is an advanced database system which stores data "next to the Web" and makes them accessible via HTTP and the eXtensible Markup Language (XML) [1]. In this paper, we discuss the requirements for XML-based information management and present the overall architecture of Tamino.

Native Management of XML Data. As more and more information is represented and exchanged using XML, the need to store and transactionally manage such information in a database system is obvious. Unfortunately, existing database concepts fail to cope with the flexibility and extensibility of XML.

(Object-)relational database systems cannot map the nested, potentially recursive structure of XML documents adequately, especially in cases where no schema is known. Hence, they can store complex XML documents only as large text fields, but SQL does not provide adequate operators to query the structural aspects of them. The same holds for the text extensions integrated into some object-relational systems. Object-oriented database systems have more powerful means to store XML documents in a manner that reflects their structure. However, the query languages offered (e.g., OQL) are typically not suited for retrieval in recursive structures. A

C. Zaniolo et al. (Eds.): EDBT 2000, LNCS 1777, pp. 383-387, 2000.

database server tailored to XML-based e-business has to *natively* support the special characteristics of XML data, i.e., XML syntax, semantics and schemas.

The Need for a New Query Language. XML defines a logical data model of its own, using ordered labeled trees as main data structure. This new data model results in a need for a new query language which is tailored to the specific needs of XML.

There have been several proposals for such a query language [2]. One of these, XQL [3], is widely accepted and has been implemented in several systems, e.g., ODI's eXcelon [4], GMD's XQL/PDOM Engine [5], and Tamino. XQL is strongly related to the pattern language XPath [6] and supports the notions of hierarchy, sequence, and position. Elements and attributes can be searched, based on their context and content. In contrast to XPath, XQL also provides means to compose and combine XML documents on the fly. XQL is closed, i.e., it delivers XML as result of all queries. Standardisation of an XML query language is currently under way within W3C's XML query language working group [7].

Internet and Intranet as Integral Parts of the Database System. Most Web and e-business applications operate on top of the HTTP protocol, the basic building block of Intranets and the Internet. For database systems operating in these environments it is mandatory to be accessible via HTTP. This does not only imply some means to pass queries and data from the database system to the web server and vice versa. Far more, integration into the philosophy of HTTP-based communication is required. This comprises query facilities through URLs (not just an interpreter running on the Web server's site which translates URL syntax to SQL), update by means of HTTP requests and very efficient information passing between Web servers and the database system (without intermediate transformation).

Integration of Multiple Data Sources via XML. XML-centric access to a single database's data is very useful for Web and e-business applications, provided that all the relevant data really are present in this single database. This, however, is not the case in most typical scenarios. Often, it is not feasible to maintain consistent copies of the operational data just for Web access. Hence, the database access via HTTP must include gateway functionality (1) to combine data from multiple sources on the fly when required by a user request and (2) to forward data modifications to external data sources. The user or the calling application should not notice the distribution of data, but just see a uniform XML document without recognizing the sources of data.

2   Tamino Overview

Software AG's Tamino differs from many other system by the fact that it can store XML documents "natively" (without transforming them into another format), but still is a scalable full-fledged database system. In this section, the most relevant XML-centric features of Tamino and its architecture are presented.

Inserting and Retrieving XML Documents. All requests to Tamino can be shipped via HTTP. A URL specifies the database to be used and the location of a document inside the database. Several keywords have been defined to specify the kind of re-quest (e.g., insertion, deletion, update, query). A XML document can be stored without defining a schema, i.e., it is sufficient if it is well-formed. In addition, even non-XML documents (e.g., images, DTDs, etc.) can be stored via HTTP. Tamino uses Web server extensions with very fast communication channels to the database.

Tamino's query language is based on XQL A dedicated query language for XML (as opposed to enhanced SQL) is essential in order to cope with the characteristics of XML. Tamino adds text retrieval capabilities and multi-document queries to XQL.

Tamino's Data Map. For many application areas, a set of DTDs has been defined and all incoming documents validate against one of these DTDs. In this case, Tamino can be used to decompose documents at storage time and compose them at query time as an alternative to native storage. On an element or attribute basis, one can define how the element or attribute shall be stored, or how it is to be retrieved. There are several options:

- The element or attribute can be stored in Tamino itself (the most common case). In this case, no conversion into another data model will be performed. As shown in [8], storing XML in relational systems can lead to unacceptable performance.
- The element or attribute can be mapped to an SQL database. In this case, the designer will specify how to map the element to a table, row, and column. The SQL database can be an external database, which is accessible via Tamino's *X-Node*, or it can be Tamino's built-in SQL database. Thus, Tamino can access existing data sources to integrate company data into new XML-based applications.
- The element or attribute can be mapped to a user-defined function, i.e., the function is called with the data as input (when inserting an element) or as output (on retrieval). The function can be used to access other data sources (e.g., ERP systems), to send mail, etc. The administrator can define how these relate together, i.e., whether data stored are the same as those delivered. While this is an unusual feature in the context of databases, it is quite useful to access volatile information sources (e.g., stock rates or date and time).

The chosen mapping is stored in a repository called *Data Map*. Note that a single document can be mapped to multiple data sources (including Tamino itself). Thus, Tamino does not act as a pure XML wrapper, but as integrator of distributed data. To optimize this, Tamino supports the storage of documents with suppressed markup. If this option is chosen, the markup will be recomputed on retrieval.

Indexing in Tamino. The Data Map also contains the indexing information. For each type of documents, i.e., those with the same DTD, a dedicated indexing strategy can be applied. Full text indexing can be specified on element level. Such an index covers the element and all its descendants. As a consequence, indexing the root element with a full text index results in the document being full-text indexed.

Tamino can also have indexes that are tailored to the data type which matches best the element's or attribute's content. A "number" attribute, for example, would match the Integer data type. Note that XML itself has no data types for element contents. Types for an element or attribute must manually be defined in the Data Map. Data-type aware indexes are a prerequisite for efficiently answering queries such as "List the books that cost below $20".

Overall Architecture. Tamino comprises a database engine called *X-Machine* dedicated to the handling and storage of XML data. This is a full-fledged database system including query optimization, transactions, concurrency control, etc. A high-speed channel between one or multiple web servers and Tamino serves as the primary interface to the Intranet and Internet. In addition, XML data can be accessed from Tamino applications directly without employing a web server.

A component called *X-Node* is responsible for pushing incoming data to external systems (via standard interfaces such as ODBC and OLE-DB) or extracting the data from these systems as defined in the Data Map. X-Node also acts as a transaction manager for the external systems, thus, guaranteeing data consistency. All data available in a company can be combined into the uniform XML view. As a special case, data cannot only be forwarded to external data sources, but also to relational tables stored in Tamino itself. This facilitates efficient handling of a set of data via both the XML interface and the SQL interface. Hence, these data stored in Tamino can directly be accessed by standard SQL tools, but can also be used by the X-machine without involving the overhead of crossing system boundaries.

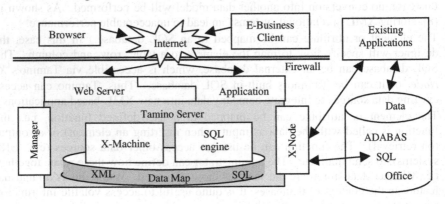

Fig. 1. Architecture of Tamino.

The X-Machine. The *X-Machine* comprises an XQL parser, which analyses and optimizes the XQL queries. Some parts of an XQL query can be evaluated on schema level (e.g., the possible existence of a certain element type in a document). These are evaluated first to reduce the scope of the query. Then, using the Data Map, usable indexes are discovered, and the most promising indexes are selected and used to find an initial set of documents. These are then checked against the remaining filters (the XQL term for selection predicates) and resolved against the external data sources. The latter task is done by the *Object Composer*. Note that some resolution against external data sources might have to be done before all filters can be applied, because the filters reference the external data. The Object Composer has to take care of access paths (indexes) defined on the external databases in this case. All other external data access is postponed until the qualifying documents have been identified. For incoming documents, the processing is similar. These documents are parsed and then, using the data map, distributed to the affected data sources by the *Object Processor*.

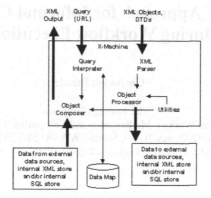

Fig. 2. Architecture of the X-Machine.

3   Conclusions

Software AG is positioning Tamino as an XML-centric information server for electronic business, accessible via HTTP. Although it provides integration with other data sources, Tamino's key differentiator is native storage and retrieval of well-formed or valid XML documents, along with the integrated management of Internet objects and SQL data, transaction support, high performance, and high scalability.

Many IT companies, in particular database vendors, are carrying out XML projects. Vendors of object-oriented database systems have introduced XML interfaces. Most relational database vendors (e.g., Oracle, IBM, and Informix) are working on extensions to handle XML data, too, but their XML support is limited at the moment and it remains to be seen if performance for queries and updates will be acceptable, especially when reasonably complex XML documents are processed [8].

Software AG's Tamino, however, follows a different approach. Tamino does not provide just a converter for XML or a XML mapping to an existing product. Instead, it natively speaks XML. Comparisons with a well-known commercial relational system offering XML-related tools has proven Tamino's superior performance.

References

1. T. Bray et al: Extensible Markup Language (XML) 1.0. W3C Recommendation, February 10, 1998, http://www.w3.org/TR/1998/REC-xml-19980210.html.
2. W3C Query Languages Workshop. Boston, 1998, http://www.w3.org/TandS/QL/QL98/.
3. Jonathan Robie: XQL FAQ, 1999, http://metalab.unc.edu/xql/.
4. Object Design: eXcelon, http://www.odi.com/excelon/.
5. Gerald Huck et al: Lightweight Persistency Support for the Document Object Model. OOPSLA Workshop "Java and Databases: Persistence Options", Denver, CO, Nov 1999.
6. James Clark et al: XML Path Language (XPath) Version 1.0. W3C Proposed Recommendation, October 8, 1999, http://www.w3.org/TR/xpath.
7. W3C XML Query Language Working Group, http://www.w3.org/XML/Group/Query
8. D. Florescu et al: A Performance Evaluation of Alternative Mapping Schemes for Storing XML Data in a Relational Database. Rapport de Recherche No. 3680 INRIA, August 1999.

A Systematic Approach for Informal Communication During Workflow Execution

Christoph Bussler

The Boeing Company
Phantom Works – Mathematics and Computing Technology
P. O. Box 3707, m/s 7L-70, Seattle, WA 98124-2207, U. S. A.
christoph.bussler@pss.boeing.com

Abstract. Informal communication is often necessary during workflow execution despite all attempts to define workflow types completely. Traditionally, workflow participants use an e-mail system to communicate informally during (formal) workflow execution. However, the use of two independent software systems causes a set of significant problems due to the systems' autonomy: a disjoint data set makes common management and history analysis impossible. This paper analyzes the problems and suggests a systematic approach for informal communication. An extended workflow architecture is reported on that implements informal coordination with a WFMS's workflow concepts.

1 Uncoordinated Informal Communication

In the ideal world pre-defined workflow tasks as part of a pre-defined complex workflow type are self-sufficient. All for the execution of workflow tasks required data is defined within the workflow type and provided to the workflow participant during workflow execution. In addition, workflow participants possess the necessary knowledge and experience to perform assigned workflow tasks completely. Many workflow management systems (WFMSs) can support the ideal world (see [6] for a list).

Unfortunately, WFMS deployment shows that it is in general neither possible to provide complete information to a workflow participant nor to have completely knowledgeable workflow participants. If a workflow participant is missing information or knowledge then he uses other available technology to acquire what he misses or he simply walks over to one of his colleagues' office. It turns out that the main medium of choice by workflow participants for informal communication in the distributed organization is the corporate e-mail system.

Section 2 describes some of the problems related to e-mail-based informal communication in context of workflow management. Section 3 presents the concepts of coordinated informal communication based on the idea that a workflow management system is used as the communication tool. Section 4 describes the implementation of the enhanced workflow architecture based on a commercially available WFMS.

C. Zaniolo et al. (Eds.): EDBT 2000, LNCS 1777, pp. 388–392, 2000.
© Springer-Verlag Berlin Heidelberg 2000

2   Problems of E-Mail-Based Informal Communication

Using e-mail for informal communication has the following two major problems. First, the workflow participant has to keep track of the informal communication by himself. In practical terms, when a workflow participant sends an e-mail, receives an answer, replies to it, etc. a thread of e-mails develops which is related to a workflow task. This relationship is neither maintained by the e-mail system nor by the WFMS. It has to be maintained manually by the workflow participant since the two systems are completely autonomous with respect to each other.

Second, the workflow history cannot show who participated in the informal communication because it took place in an e-mail system. Since the content of the communication is not accessible either from a workflow analysis tool it cannot be analyzed to see if more information needs to be supplied to the workflow task in the future. Of course, for analysis purpose the workflow participant can be asked to provide the e-mail thread, but he might have deleted it already.

Even though informal communication can be achieved by using an e-mail system, many problems are caused by this approach. These problems disappear if informal communication is part of workflow execution instead.

3   WFMS-Coordinated Informal Communication

3.1   Informal Communication Concepts

An informal communication is related to one workflow task. Each workflow task can have none or one informal communication. An informal communication is a set of conversations. Each conversation is a sequence of messages and responses and is taking place between a workflow participant and a conversation partner. This allows that a workflow participant and a conversation partner exchange several messages back and forth until the topic of the conversation is discussed sufficiently.

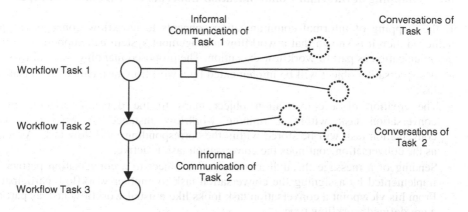

Fig. 1. Relationship between workflow task, informal communication and conversations

Since there can be several conversations going on as part of the informal communication of a workflow task, a workflow participant can discuss with several conversation partners simultaneously. Figure 1 depicts the situation in an example with three workflow tasks. Workflow task 1 has three conversations, workflow task 2 has two conversations and workflow task 3 does not have any informal communication attached to it.

The lifecycle of a conversation is very basic. In total, a conversation can be in one of several states as depicted in Figure 2.

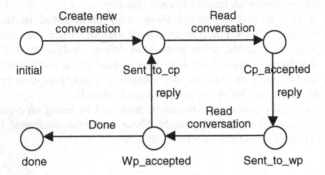

Fig. 2. States of a conversation task

Initially a conversation is in state "initial". As soon as a workflow participant creates a conversation it is in state "sent_to_cp" (for "sent to conversation partner"). As soon as the conversation partner accepted the conversation, it is in state "cp_accepted" (for "conversation partner accepted"). If he replies, the conversation is in state "sent_to_wp" (for "sent to workflow participant"). He either declares the conversation finished (in state "done") or replies causing the continuation of the life-cycle.

3.2   Mapping of Informal Communication Concepts to Workflow Concepts

If the mapping of informal communication concepts to workflow concepts can be achieved then it is shown that a workflow management system can support informal communication as part of workflow execution. The proposed mapping is as follows:

- A conversation object will be implemented by a workflow task called conversation task.
- The creation of a conversation object maps to the dynamic creation of a conversation task within a running workflow instance. A pointer to the conversation task will be stored within the corresponding workflow task. As long as the conversation continues the conversation task is active.
- Sending of a message through a conversation object to a conversation partner is implemented by assigning the conversation task to another workflow participant. From his viewpoint a conversation task looks like a usual workflow task as part of a pre-defined workflow type.
- Opening and typing in the reply to a message maps to accepting a workflow task and typing in the reply. Pressing the reply button will dynamically re-assign the

same conversation task back to the workflow participant without finishing the conversation task. This allows that a workflow participant and a conversation partner can exchange several messages and replies based on the same conversation task within the workflow instance. An ongoing conversation is therefore the continued re-assignment of the same conversation task to one of the conversation partners.

Informal communication is available by default and does not require any modeling activity by a workflow modeler.

4   Informal Communication Enhanced Workflow Architecture

The above outlined architecture is implemented with the workflow system InConcert [1], [5]. InConcert provides the possibility to add workflow tasks dynamically to running workflow instances. This supports the dynamic creation of conversation tasks. The identifier of a workflow task can be externalized so that it can be referenced. A subtype "conversation task" can be built from the natively available type "workflow task". Objects can be extended by attributes so that the conversation task type can be extended as required by e.g. a message.

InConcert cannot know about the meaning of "conversation tasks". Therefore the execution semantics has to be extended so that conversation tasks perform according to their definition. This additional execution semantics is code added to the workflow system and called appropriately by the user interface. The following gives an overview of the additional functionality.

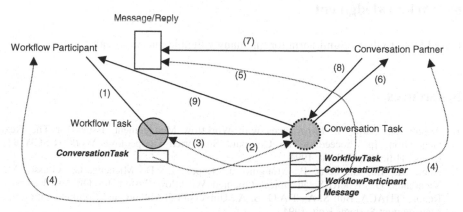

Fig. 3. Detailed object structure and object behavior of conversations and workflow tasks

If a workflow participant starts a new conversation in context of a workflow task, an instance of "conversation task" is created (1), see Figure 3. Its unique identifier is stored in one of the *ConversationTask* attributes of the workflow task (2). Its *WorkflowTask* attribute contains the unique identifier of the workflow task (3). The workflow participant's name as well as the conversation partner's name will be stored in *WorkflowParticipant* and *ConversationPartner*, respectively (4). As soon as the workflow participants indicates that he wants to send the message to the conversation partner, the message is stored in *Message* (5) and the conversation task is assigned to the conversation partner (6).

If a conversation partner replies to a message from a workflow participant, he modifies the message (7) and selects the reply button on the interface (8). This triggers an update of the *Message* attribute and a re-assignment of the conversation task to the workflow participant (stored in *WorkflowParticipant*) (9).

As long as a conversation task is assigned to one of the conversation participants (workflow participant or conversation partner) the other one does only have read access. This is required to ensure the consistency of the *Message* content.

5   Related Work

[3] describes the integration of two systems, WooRKS (a workflow management system) [2] and UTUCS (User to User Communication Support) [4]. While WooRKS is a workflow management system UTUCS is a system supporting conversations. According to [3] UTUCS is used to handle exceptional situations during workflow execution. In contrast, the approach presented in this paper supports conversations in any situation (exceptional as well as non-exceptional). Furthermore, conversations are completely implemented within a WFMS avoiding the integration problems of two independently built systems. Common management and history analysis is possible when following this approach.

6   Acknowledgment

I would like to thank Sunil Sarin for his many valuable questions and comments.

References

1. Abbott, K.; Sarin, S.: Experiences with Workflow Management: Issues for The Next Generation. In: Proceedings on Computer-Supported Cooperative Work (CSCW'94), Chapel Hill, NC, U. S. A., 1994
2. Ader, M.; Lu, G.; Pons, P.; Monguio, J.; Lopez, L.; De Michelis, G.; Grasso, M.; Vlondakis, G.: WooRKS, an Object Oriented Workflow System for Offices. Technical Report ITHACA, Bull S. A., T.A.O. S. A., Università di Milano, and Communication and Management Systems Unit, 1994
3. Agostini, A.; De Michelis, G.; Grasso, M.; Patriarca, S.: Reengineering a Business Process with an Innovative Workflow Management System: a Case Study. In: Collaborative Computing, Chapman & Hall, Vol. 1, No. 3, 1994
4. Agostini, A.; De Michelis, G.; Patriarca, S.; Tinini, R.: A Prototype of an Integrated Coordination Support System. In: Computer Supported Cooperative Work. An International Journal, Vol. 2, No. 4, 1994
5. InConcert Process Designer's Guide. Software Release 3.6. InConcert, Inc., 1997
6. Jablonski, S.; Bussler, C.: Workflow Manage-ment - Modeling Concepts, Architecture and Implementation. International Thomson Computer Press, September 1996

Spatial & Temporal Information

Temporal View Self-Maintenance*

Jun Yang and Jennifer Widom

Computer Science Department, Stanford University
{junyang,widom}@db.stanford.edu, http://www-db.stanford.edu/

Abstract View *self-maintenance* refers to maintaining materialized views without accessing base data. Self-maintenance is particularly useful in data warehousing settings, where base data comes from sources that may be inaccessible. Self-maintenance has been studied for nontemporal views, but is even more important when a warehouse stores temporal views over the history of source data, since the source history needed to perform view maintenance may no longer exist. This paper tackles the self-maintenance problem for temporal views. We show how to derive auxiliary data to be stored at the warehouse so that the warehouse views and auxiliary data can be maintained without accessing the sources.

The temporal view self-maintenance problem is considerably harder than the nontemporal case because a temporal view may need to be maintained not only when source data is modified but also as time advances, and these two dimensions of change interact in subtle ways. We also seek to minimize the amount of auxiliary data required, taking into account different source capabilities and update constraints that are common in temporal warehousing scenarios. While our framework and algorithms are presented using a true temporal data model, our results apply directly to the ad-hoc temporal support (i.e., timestamp attributes in the standard relational model) commonly found in data warehouses today.

1 Introduction

A *data warehouse* is a repository of data that has been extracted and integrated from multiple operational *data sources* for efficient querying and analysis. Many warehouse applications are *temporal* in nature, i.e., they are based not only on the up-to-date source information, but also on the history of the data at the sources. On the other hand, operational sources usually do not store their entire history. While some sources may store partial history, many *nontemporal* sources store only the current state of their data. For example, a company's sales department database might keep track of the current pending orders, and remove orders once they are filled. Nevertheless, the company analysts might want to pose queries over all orders that have ever been submitted.

Data warehouses typically materialize *views* to support the expected queries of warehouse users and applications. In [12] we presented a temporal data warehousing framework in which the warehouse materializes and incrementally main-

---

* This work was supported by DARPA and the Air Force Rome Laboratories under contracts F30602-95-C-0119 and F30602-96-1-0312.

C. Zaniolo et al. (Eds.): EDBT 2000, LNCS 1777, pp. 395–412, 2000.

tains temporal views over the history of source data. Since sources may be non-temporal, we cannot expect to be able to query them for the source data history that may be needed to maintain temporal warehouse views. The solution is to make the views *self-maintainable* by storing *auxiliary data* at the warehouse so that the warehouse data as a whole can be maintained without accessing any source data. The notion of materialized view self-maintenance was introduced for nontemporal views in [2,6,9]. In this paper, we tackle the self-maintenance problem for temporal views. Note that while self-maintenance for nontemporal views may largely be a matter of convenience or efficiency, for temporal views over nontemporal sources self-maintenance usually is required.

The temporal version of the view self-maintenance problem poses significant challenges not found in the nontemporal version. Temporal views may be affected not only by data updates, but also as time advances. For example, in the sales department database, an order that was placed yesterday may not be considered "old" now, but will turn old if it remains outstanding after 30 days. To make temporal views self-maintainable, we must consider both dimensions of change (data and time), and more importantly, their potential interactions. As we shall see, the auxiliary data required for handling both dimensions of change is not simply the union of the data required for handling the two dimensions independently.

Although our results on temporal view self-maintenance apply to temporal databases in general, we shall use temporal data warehousing as the motivation and setting for our work. An obvious brute-force solution to the self-maintenance problem is to store the entire history of all source data at the warehouse. Because history grows monotonically, this solution eventually fails when the warehouse runs out of storage space. Even if storage is not a concern, it is helpful to identify the historical data not required for view maintenance and move it off-line in order to speed up regular operations. In this paper, we seek to minimize the amount of auxiliary data needed for temporal view self-maintenance, taking into account different source capabilities and update constraints that are common in warehousing scenarios. We consider not only nontemporal sources, but also more powerful sources that represent time and allow retroactive updates, possibly within a fixed-length *update window*. For example, the payroll department of a company may maintain a database that records the days that each employee has worked. It may be possible to modify the time records within last seven days, but once records become more than a week old they are considered permanent. We shall address how the length of the update window affects the amount of auxiliary data needed for self-maintenance. Moreover, note that in this example each employee tuple (indicating time at work) may be "alive" for multiple disjoint time periods. In our earlier sales department example, each order tuple is "alive" for only one time period. Whether a source tuple can be "alive" for a set of periods versus a single period also has a dramatic impact on the amount of auxiliary data needed.

We base our work on a true temporal data model and a temporal query language equivalent to a subset of TSQL2 [3]. However, we must emphasize that our results are very applicable to existing warehouses and operational sources with ad-hoc temporal support. These systems typically store temporal information as normal attributes in the relational model, and query it using SQL. An ad-hoc temporal warehouse usually materializes the entire history of all source data, and leaves it to the administrator to control the purging of unneeded historical data [5]. By solving the self-maintenance problem, our work provides a way to automatically identify and remove warehouse data no longer needed for view maintenance.

Due to space limitations, this printed version presents only a subset of our framework, algorithms, and results from the full version of this paper [13]. The omitted material is outlined briefly in Section 7, but we refer the interested reader to [13] for details and full discussion.

2   Preliminaries

2.1   Data Model and View Definition Language

Our temporal data model is essentially the *Bitemporal Conceptual Data Model* [8] restricted to the valid-time dimension. The time domain $\mathbb{T}$ is a set of *time instants*, or *chronons*, isomorphic to the natural numbers. A temporal relation schema has the form $(A_1, A_2, ..., A_m, \mathbb{T})$, where the A_i's are *explicit attributes* and $\mathbb{T}$ is the implicit *time attribute*. Explicit attributes form a key. Values for explicit attributes come from regular value domains. The value for the time attribute is a nonempty set of time instants drawn from $\mathbb{T}$. The time attribute also can be viewed as a set of maximal, nonoverlapping time periods, each encoded by a pair of start and end time instants.

Intuitively, a temporal relation $R(A_1, A_2, ..., A_m, \mathbb{T})$ records the history of a nontemporal relation $R^{nt}(A_1, A_2, ..., A_m)$. A temporal tuple $r \in R$ is interpreted as follows: the nontemporal tuple $r^{nt} = \langle r.A_1, r.A_2, ..., r.A_m \rangle$ is present in the state of R^{nt} at time instant t iff $t \in r.\mathbb{T}$. In other words, the time attribute records the times during which the tuple is "alive". We require that $r.\mathbb{T}$ does not extend beyond t_{now}, the current time. However, the last time period of $r.\mathbb{T}$ may end with a special symbol NOW, meaning that r^{nt} is alive in the current snapshot of R^{nt}, and will continue to stay alive as time advances. A detailed discussion of our treatment of NOW can be found in [12].

We now define the five operators in our basic temporal relational algebra. In the following, R, R_i, S are temporal relations, r, r_i, s are tuples from the respective relations, and A_R, A_{R_i}, A_S denote the sets of explicit attributes in their schemas. Let $r.A$ denote the part of r containing values for the attributes in a set A. To facilitate definition, we define a helper function $h(R, r', A) \overset{\text{def}}{=} \bigcup_{(r \in R \;\wedge\; r.A = r'.A)} r.\mathbb{T}$, which returns the union of the time attributes of all tuples in R that agree with tuple r' on the attributes in A.

- Selection: $\sigma_p(R) \overset{\text{def}}{=} \{r \mid r \in R \ \wedge \ p(r)\}$
- Join: $\bowtie_p(R_1, ..., R_n) \overset{\text{def}}{=} \{\langle r_1.A_{R_1}, ..., r_n.A_{R_n}, c\rangle \mid r_1 \in R_1 \ \wedge ... \wedge \ r_n \in R_n$
$\wedge \ p(r_1, ..., r_n) \ \wedge \ c = r_1.\text{T} \cap ... \cap r_n.\text{T} \ \wedge \ c \neq \varnothing\}$
- Projection: $\pi_A(R) \overset{\text{def}}{=} \{\langle r.A, c\rangle \mid r \in R \ \wedge \ c = h(R, r, A)\}$
- Difference: $R - S \overset{\text{def}}{=} \{\langle r.A_R, c\rangle \mid r \in R \ \wedge \ c = r.\text{T} - h(S, r, A_R) \ \wedge \ c \neq \varnothing\}$
- Union: $R \cup S \overset{\text{def}}{=} \{\langle u, c\rangle \mid (\exists r \in R : u = r.A_R \ \wedge \ c = r.\text{T} \cup h(S, r, A_R))$
$\vee \ (\exists s \in S : u = s.A_R \ \wedge \ c = s.\text{T} \cup h(R, s, A_R))\}$

The predicate p used in the temporal selection and join operators may be a standard nontemporal predicate referencing explicit attributes, a temporal predicate referencing the time attribute T and/or the special symbol NOW, or a combination of both, connected via Boolean operators $\wedge$, $\vee$, and $\neg$. We briefly describe some of the temporal predicates we consider. TS represents the start time of the earliest period in T; TE represents the end time of the last period in T. TS and TE can be compared to any time instant $t \in \mathbb{T}$ using the operators $=$, $>$, $<$, etc. They also can be compared to a NOW-relative time such as NOW − 3 weeks. During query evaluation, temporal predicates are evaluated with the implicit binding NOW $= t_{now}$, where t_{now} is the current time. Predicate (T overlaps $[t_s, t_e]$) tests whether the time attribute overlaps the period $[t_s, t_e]$; predicate (T contains $[t_s, t_e]$) tests whether it contains $[t_s, t_e]$. Again, t_s and t_e may be NOW-relative. Finally, length(T) returns the sum of the lengths of the periods in T, which can be compared to any constant length (such as 1 year).

2.2   Temporal Data Warehouse

Each data source has a number of *source relations* monitored and exported by an *extractor* [11]. Conceptually, for each source relation, the temporal warehouse has a corresponding *temporal base relation* representing the source relation's history. In this paper, we assume that our temporal view is defined over the conceptual temporal base relations, and that we are provided with updates to these relations using, e.g., the techniques in [12]. We do not assume or require that the temporal base relations actually exist. The results in this paper show how to modify the temporal view definition and/or materialize additional views in order to make the temporal warehouse fully self-maintainable.

Maintenance of temporal views involves two procedures: *view refresh* and *change propagation* [12]. View refresh is the procedure for updating temporal views with respect to time advances. Since it is generally inefficient to update views at every clock tick, view refresh usually is triggered either implicitly by a request to access the view contents, or explicitly by a request from the warehouse administrator. Change propagation is the procedure for updating views with respect to data changes. Source updates are detected by the extractor and converted to updates on the corresponding temporal base relations, which then trigger change propagation at the warehouse. To make a temporal warehouse self-maintainable, we must ensure that the warehouse contains all data needed for both view refresh and change propagation.

	OrdID	T
r_1	1	$[09/01, 09/11]$
r_2	2	$[09/22, 09/27]$
r_3	3	$[09/23, 09/28]$
r_4	4	$[09/24, 09/29]$
r_5	5	$[09/25, \text{NOW}]$

Fig. 1. Contents of R on 10/01.

	Emp	Dept	T
s_1	A	marketing	$[09/14, 09/18] \cup [09/21, 09/25]$
s_2	A	sales	$[09/28, \text{NOW}]$
s_3	B	sales	$[09/23, 09/25] \cup [09/28, \text{NOW}]$
s_4	C	payroll	$[09/28, \text{NOW}]$
s_5	D	sales	$[09/14, 09/18] \cup [09/28, \text{NOW}]$

Fig. 2. Contents of S on 10/01.

Sources with temporal support often allow retroactive updates within some *update window*. Formally, an update window is a NOW-relative time period of the form $[\text{NOW} - l, \text{NOW}]$, where $l \geq 0$. An update μ on a tuple r with update window $[\text{NOW} - l, \text{NOW}]$ may modify the value of $r.\text{T}$ in any arbitrary way within $[\text{NOW} - l, \text{NOW}]$. However, the part of $\mu(r).\text{T}$ before $\text{NOW} - l$ must remain the same as the original $r.\text{T}$. As an important special case, a nontemporal source has an update window of $[\text{NOW}, \text{NOW}]$, i.e., only the current state of the data can be updated. An update of explicit attributes becomes two updates of time attributes, as will be seen in Example 4, so we need not consider updates of explicit attributes separately. In practice, updates to a relation R are processed in batches $\bigtriangledown R$ and $\triangle R$, which together describe the net effect of the updates as $R \leftarrow R - \bigtriangledown R \cup \triangle R$.

Besides the update-window constraint, we also consider the *single-period constraint* which is common in warehousing scenarios. This constraint requires the time attribute of a source history tuple to be a single time period rather than a set of time periods. For instance, the single-period constraint holds for the order history in the sales department example given earlier, but does not hold for the employee work history in the payroll department example.

2.3 Examples

In this section, we provide examples that yield insight into temporal view self-maintenance. Examples 1–3 illustrate how various constraints affect the amount of auxiliary data needed. Example 4 considers a temporal selection view with a composite predicate. We intentionally provide several examples that are simple and easy to follow, but the general case can be quite complicated and subtle, as we shall see in Example 5.

Example 1. (Update window $[\text{NOW}, \text{NOW}]$, single-period constraint) Consider a conceptual temporal base relation that records the order history for a sales department. A simplified version, $R(\text{OrdID}, \text{T})$, is shown in Fig. 1. The granularity of the time domain is one day, and the current time is 10/01. Each order tuple is "alive" when the order is pending. We assume that orders are pending for only one time period. For example, $r_1.\text{T} = [09/01, 09/11]$ means order 1 was submitted on 09/01 and filled on 09/12.

Suppose the customer service department has a policy of calling customers two days after their order has been filled to make sure they have received the shipment. For this purpose, we define a temporal warehouse view $V \stackrel{\text{def}}{=}$

$\sigma_{\text{TE=NOW-3 days}}(R)$. Currently on 10/01, only r_3 is in the view. However, data in addition to V itself may need to be stored at the warehouse if we want to correctly maintain V when time advances and/or R is updated, without relying on historical data retrieved from the source.

Consider time advances first. Say that NOW has changed from 10/01 to 10/02. As a result, r_4 will satisfy (TE = NOW − 3 days) and should be inserted into V. To be able to perform this insertion on 10/02, we must store r_4 in advance.

Now, let us also take source updates into account. Assume that the sales department database only allows updates at the current time, i.e., its update window is [NOW, NOW]. Suppose on 10/01, order 5 gets filled and is removed from the sales department database. This source deletion translates into an update on the temporal base relation R as $\triangledown R = \{\langle 5, [10/01, \text{NOW}]\rangle\}$, which changes r_5 to $r_5' = \langle 5, [09/25, 09/30]\rangle$. (See [12] for details on how this translation is performed.) Then, when time advances to 10/03, r_5' will be in V. In order to compute r_5', we need to store r_5 in advance, because r_5'.T cannot be derived from $\triangledown R$ alone.

To summarize, to make V self-maintainable, we must store not only r_3, which is currently in V, but also r_4 and r_5, which could potentially contribute to V after going through some sequence of time advances and/or data updates. On the other hand, we need not store r_1 or r_2. On 10/01, r_1.TE and r_2.TE are already less than NOW − 3 days. Since NOW always grows bigger as time advances, (TE = NOW − 3 days) will never become true unless T is updated. Both r_1.T and r_2.T have terminated far before the start of the update window, and new time instants cannot be added to r_1.T or r_2.T because that would create disjoint time periods, violating the single-period constraint.

In this example, the fact that we need to save r_4 and r_5 but not r_1 or r_2 is intuitively quite obvious. However, the reasoning involved is illustrative of the techniques underlying our results, which apply to much more complex views. □

Example 2. (Update window [NOW−7 days,NOW], single-period constraint) The setup is identical to Example 1, except now we assume that the source has an update window of [NOW − 7 days, NOW], which therefore includes r_2.TE. Thus, in addition to storing r_3, r_4, and r_5, we must store r_2, because it is possible for a source update on 10/01 to retroactively change r_2.T to [09/22, 09/28], which satisfies (TE = NOW − 3 days). We need not store r_1 since r_1.TE lies well before the update window and the single-period constraint still holds.   □

Example 3. (Update window [NOW − 7 days, NOW], no single-period constraint) Continuing with Example 2, suppose that we also drop the single-period constraint. Now, r_1 must be stored as well: we could update the value of r_1.T inside the current update window to [09/27, 09/28], resulting in r_1.T = [09/01, 09/11] ∪ [09/27, 09/28] which satisfies (TE = NOW − 3 days).   □

Example 4. (Composite selection predicate) Consider a conceptual temporal base relation $S(\text{Emp}, \text{Dept}, \text{T})$, which records the set of days worked by a given employee in a given department. The corresponding source relation is stored in the payroll department database, with an update window of $[\texttt{NOW} - 7\,\texttt{days}, \texttt{NOW}]$. Fig. 2 shows the current contents of S on 10/01. Suppose the manager of the sales department wants to keep an eye on the inexperienced employees, i.e., those who have worked in the department for fewer than five days altogether. Accordingly, we define a temporal warehouse view $U \overset{\text{def}}{=} \sigma_{\texttt{Dept}=\texttt{sales}} \wedge \texttt{length(T)} < 5\,\texttt{days}(S)$.

First, note that in order to maintain U, we need not store any S tuples that do not already satisfy $(\texttt{Dept} = \texttt{sales})$. The truth value of this predicate is not affected by time advances or updates of T. As for updates of explicit attributes, they are naturally modeled as pairs of updates of T. For example, if employee A moves from the sales department back to the marketing department on 10/01, this update of Dept will translate into $\triangledown R = \{\langle \texttt{A}, \texttt{sales}, [10/01, \texttt{NOW}]\rangle\}$ and $\triangle R = \{\langle \texttt{A}, \texttt{marketing}, [10/01, \texttt{NOW}]\rangle\}$. (Again, see [12] for details.) $\triangledown R$ will update s_2.T to $[09/28, 09/30]$, while $\triangle R$ will update s_1.T to $[09/14, 09/18] \cup [09/21, 09/25] \cup [10/01, \texttt{NOW}]$. Neither $\triangledown R$ nor $\triangle R$ will change the truth value of $(\texttt{Dept} = \texttt{sales})$ for any tuple. Therefore, we need not store s_1 or s_4 because these tuples can never satisfy $(\texttt{Dept} = \texttt{sales})$ in the future.

Among the remaining tuples, s_2 is already in U. To make U self-maintainable, we must also store s_3, but not s_5. The reason is as follows. Although the current value of s_3.T indicates that employee B already has worked in the sales department for seven days, it is possible that on 10/01 the payroll department realizes that there is a mistake in the records: employee B has in fact been on leave since 09/28. Thus, a correction is made, and s_3.T is updated to $[09/23, 09/25]$, which now satisfies $(\texttt{length(T)} < 5\,\texttt{days})$. On the other hand, for employee D, the part of s_5.T outside the update window is already five days long. No matter how we modify the value of s_5.T within the update window, the length of s_5.T will still be at least five days. Moreover, the length of a time attribute will never decrease as time advances. Therefore, we need not store s_5. $\qquad\square$

Example 5. (Seemingly simple selection) Consider a view $W \overset{\text{def}}{=} \sigma_{\texttt{TE}=t}(R)$, where R is the same as in Example 2, and t is some fixed time instant, say, 12/25. It turns out that in order to make W self-maintainable, we need to store $\sigma_q(R)$, where q is:

$$(\texttt{TE} = t) \vee \big((\texttt{NOW} - 8\,\texttt{days} = t) \wedge (\texttt{TE} \geq t) \wedge (\texttt{TS} \leq t)\big)$$
$$\vee \big((\texttt{NOW} - 7\,\texttt{days} \leq t) \wedge (\texttt{TE} \geq \texttt{NOW} - 8\,\texttt{days})\big)$$

Given the above definition of q, it is not terribly difficult to verify that $\sigma_q(R)$ indeed makes W self-maintainable. However, a number of subtleties exist, and it should be evident to the reader that coming up with a proper q is not a trivial process. How do we find q automatically for arbitrary selection predicates? How do we guarantee that $\sigma_q(R)$ is self-maintainable? How do we know whether $\sigma_q(R)$ contains the minimum amount of information required? The rest of this paper provides a systematic approach to answering these questions. $\qquad\square$

3   General Approach

Because of space limitations, we only consider temporal selection views in this version of the paper. Results for temporal join, aggregation, and *snapshot-reducible* [10] views (including projection, difference, and union) are presented in the full version of this paper [13].

As we have seen in the examples, even selection views may not be self-maintainable without storing auxiliary information. To make a temporal selection view $\sigma_p(R)$ self-maintainable, we derive a "superview" $\sigma_{\alpha(p)}(R)$ by relaxing the selection predicate from p to $\alpha(p)$. Instead of the original view, we materialize and maintain the superview. The superview must contain not only the current contents of the original view, but also all tuples with the potential of contributing to the original view after going through a sequence of time advances and/or data updates. Furthermore, the superview must itself be self-maintainable. In the remainder of this paper, we study how to find the smallest superview that meets these requirements.

As mentioned in Section 2.2, contents of a temporal view are affected by two types of changes: time advances and data updates. Since these two types of changes can interact in rather intricate ways, we first consider them separately. We show how to derive $\alpha^t(p)$ such that $\sigma_{\alpha^t(p)}(R)$ is self-maintainable with respect to time advances, and $\alpha^\mu(p)$ such that $\sigma_{\alpha^\mu(p)}(R)$ is self-maintainable with respect to data updates. Then, we show how to combine $\alpha^t(p)$ and $\alpha^\mu(p)$ together to derive $\alpha(p)$ such that $\sigma_{\alpha(p)}(R)$ is self-maintainable with respect to both time advances and data updates. As we will see, simply taking the disjunction of $\alpha^t(p)$ and $\alpha^\mu(p)$ is not sufficient.

Before delving into the details we must introduce some additional notation. Recall that temporal predicates are always evaluated with a binding for NOW. We use $[p]_t(r)$ to denote that predicate p is evaluated on tuple r with the binding NOW $= t$. If the $[\cdot]_t$ notation is omitted, p is evaluated with the default binding NOW $= t_{now}$, where t_{now} is the current time. Similarly, $[\mu]_t(r)$ denotes that update μ is applied to r at time t.

4   Handling Time Advances: α^t

In this section we ignore data updates and concentrate on the problem of making a temporal selection view self-maintainable with respect to time advances alone. At the very least, the superview must contain enough information to maintain the original view as time advances. Therefore, we must relax the selection predicate to select also the tuples that could satisfy the original predicate at a future time, leading to the following definition of $\bar{\alpha}^t$ as our first guess for α^t.

Definition 1. *($\bar{\alpha}^t$) Let t_{now} be the current time and p a selection predicate. Define $\bar{\alpha}^t(p)$ as a selection predicate over a temporal tuple r:* $(\bar{\alpha}^t(p))(r) \stackrel{def}{=} \exists t \geq t_{now} : [p]_t(r)$.

Intuitively, $\bar{\alpha}^t(p)$ selects all and only those tuples that either satisfy p now or could satisfy p in the future if there are no data updates. Any correct superview of $\sigma_p(R)$ must necessarily contain all these tuples because they are either in $\sigma_p(R)$ already or might be added to $\sigma_p(R)$ as time advances. In effect, $\bar{\alpha}^t$ provides a lower bound for α^t, but we still need to ensure the self-maintainability of the superview. With $\bar{\alpha}^t$ defined, we can now be more precise about what constitutes a "correct" definition of α^t.

Definition 2. *(Correct α^t) Let p be a selection predicate. A definition of α^t is correct if the following properties hold: (i) $p \rightarrow \alpha^t(p)$; (ii) $\bar{\alpha}^t(p) \rightarrow \alpha^t(p)$; (iii) $\bar{\alpha}^t(\alpha^t(p)) \rightarrow \alpha^t(p)$.*

The arrow notation denotes logical implication. Property (i) ensures that the superview contains the original view. Property (ii) ensures that the superview contains enough information to maintain the original view with respect to time advances. Property (iii) ensures that the superview also contains enough information to maintain itself with respect to time advances, i.e., the superview is self-maintainable with respect to time advances. Strictly speaking, either (i) or (ii) is redundant: (i) follows from (ii), and (ii) follows from (i) and (iii). Nevertheless, it is instructive to list all three properties because each one translates into a different intuitive requirement.

A trivially correct definition of α^t simply sets $\alpha^t(p)$ to **true** for any p, which corresponds to the simple solution of always materializing complete temporal base relations. Fortunately, we can do better. By Def. 1, $\bar{\alpha}^t$ already satisfies Properties (i) and (ii) of Def. 2. We still need to verify that Property (iii) holds; that is, $\bar{\alpha}^t(p)$ should select not only all tuples with the potential of satisfying p, but also those with the potential of satisfying $\bar{\alpha}^t(p)$ itself in the future. It turns out that $\bar{\alpha}^t$ is idempotent, i.e., $\bar{\alpha}^t(p) \leftrightarrow \bar{\alpha}^t(\bar{\alpha}^t(p))$. Therefore, $\bar{\alpha}^t$ is a correct definition of α^t; in fact, it is the best α^t that we can hope for, as shown by the following theorem. (All proofs are omitted due to space constraints.)

Theorem 1. *(Correctness & minimality of $\bar{\alpha}^t$) $\bar{\alpha}^t$ is a correct definition of α^t. Furthermore, it is minimal: given any correct definition of α^t, $\bar{\alpha}^t(p) \rightarrow \alpha^t(p)$ for any selection predicate p.*

Theoretically, then, $\bar{\alpha}^t$ is an ideal definition of α^t. Computationally, however, it is problematic. Def. 1 cannot be evaluated by typical query engines because it contains an existentially quantified variable t over an infinite domain $\mathbb{T}$. Therefore, we will devise $\hat{\alpha}^t$ as a computationally feasible alternative to $\bar{\alpha}^t$. To compute $\hat{\alpha}^t(p)$ for a composite predicate p, we first apply DeMorgan's Laws to push all negations in p down to the level of atomic predicates. Then, for each atomic or negated atomic predicate q in p, we replace q with a quantifier-free predicate logically equivalent to $\bar{\alpha}^t(q)$ that can be evaluated by typical query engines. In the full version of this paper [13], we provide tables that specify $\hat{\alpha}^t$ for all atomic and negated atomic predicates in our temporal predicate language. We separately handle the general case where T may be a set of time periods and the special case where the single-period constraint holds. Computing $\hat{\alpha}^t$ thus involves nothing more than pushing all negations down and looking up the appropriate $\hat{\alpha}^t$ specifications. The formal definition of $\hat{\alpha}^t$ is given below, followed by a theorem stating its correctness and an example showing its computation.

Definition 3. *($\hat{\alpha}^t$) Let p be a selection predicate with negations pushed down to the level of atomic predicates. We define $\hat{\alpha}^t(p)$ inductively on the structure of p. If p is an atomic or negated atomic predicate, $\hat{\alpha}^t(p)$ is defined as a quantifier-free predicate logically equivalent to $\bar{\alpha}^t(p)$ (specified in [13]). $\hat{\alpha}^t(p_1 \vee p_2)$ is defined as $\hat{\alpha}^t(p_1) \vee \hat{\alpha}^t(p_2)$. $\hat{\alpha}^t(p_1 \wedge p_2)$ is defined as $\hat{\alpha}^t(p_1) \wedge \hat{\alpha}^t(p_2)$.*

Theorem 2. (Correctness of $\hat{\alpha}^t$) *$\hat{\alpha}^t$ is a correct definition of α^t according to Def. 2.*

Example 6. Recall Example 4. We demonstrate how to compute $\hat{\alpha}^t(p_1 \wedge p_2)$, where p_1 is (Dept = sales) and p_2 is (length(T) < 5 days). Here T may be a set of time periods. According to the specifications in [13], $\hat{\alpha}^t(p_1)$ is (Dept = sales), while $\hat{\alpha}^t(p_2)$ is (length(T) < 5 days). Therefore, $\hat{\alpha}^t(p_1 \wedge p_2)$ is (Dept = sales) $\wedge$ (length(T) < 5 days), which happens to be $p_1 \wedge p_2$.

Intuitively, if a tuple does not satisfy $p_1 \wedge p_2$ now, it cannot possibly satisfy $p_1 \wedge p_2$ in the future without data updates. For (Dept = sales), time advances have no effect on the truth value of a nontemporal predicate; for (length(T) < 5 days), length(T) never decreases as time advances.   □

Minimality of $\hat{\alpha}^t$. By Def. 3, $\hat{\alpha}^t$ is equivalent to $\bar{\alpha}^t$ for all atomic predicates. Therefore, according to Thm. 1, $\hat{\alpha}^t$ is also the minimal definition of α^t for atomic predicates. For composite predicates, Def. 3 preserves the minimality of $\hat{\alpha}^t$ over disjunction. Intuitively, $p_1 \vee p_2$ will be true in the future iff either p_1 or p_2 will be true in the future. On the other hand, Def. 3 does not always preserve minimality over conjunction. Intuitively, if $p_1 \wedge p_2$ will be true in the future, then both p_1 and p_2 will be true in the future. However, the converse does not hold because p_1 and p_2 may not become true at the same time. Formally, $\bar{\alpha}^t(p_1 \wedge p_2) \rightarrow \bar{\alpha}^t(p_1) \wedge \bar{\alpha}^t(p_2)$, but the converse may or may not be true. Example 6 happened to be one where minimality is preserved over conjunction. The following example illustrates the loss of minimality over conjunction.

Example 7. Consider a predicate $p_1 \wedge p_2$, where p_1 is (NOW > 10/02) and p_2 is (TE = NOW − 3 days). According to the specifications in [13], $\hat{\alpha}^t(p_1)$ is true, since NOW will eventually move past 10/02 as time advances. Also, $\hat{\alpha}^t(p_2)$ is (TE ≥ NOW − 3 days) $\wedge$ (TE is not NOW). Intuitively, if TE is some fixed time instant on or after the current value of NOW − 3 days, p_2 will eventually become true when NOW − 3 days catches up with TE in time. On the contrary, if TE is before NOW − 3 days, p_2 will never become true since NOW − 3 days only grows bigger as time advances. Furthermore, a tuple whose TE is NOW can never satisfy p_2 because NOW always comes after NOW − 3 days. Hence, both $\hat{\alpha}^t(p_1)$ and $\hat{\alpha}^t(p_2)$ are minimal, as expected.

By Def. 3, $\hat{\alpha}^t(p_1 \wedge p_2)$ is $\hat{\alpha}^t(p_1) \wedge \hat{\alpha}^t(p_2)$, which reduces to (TE ≥ NOW − 3 days) $\wedge$ (TE is not NOW). Unfortunately, we have relaxed the original predicate too much. To see why, suppose that the current time is 10/01, and there is a tuple whose TE = 09/29. This tuple currently satisfies $\hat{\alpha}^t(p_1 \wedge p_2)$, but it will never satisfy $p_1 \wedge p_2$. The reason is that p_1 will be true only after 10/02, while p_2 will be true only on 10/02. □

To alleviate the loss of minimality, it is possible to refine $\hat{\alpha}^t$ by first augmenting the conjunction with additional predicates that logically follow from the conjunction, and then applying $\hat{\alpha}^t$ to the augmented conjunction. For instance, we can augment $p_1 \wedge p_2$ in Example 7 with (TE > 09/29), which follows from $p_1 \wedge p_2$. Applying $\hat{\alpha}^t$ to the augmented conjunction $p_1 \wedge p_2 \wedge$ (TE > 09/29) and simplifying the result, we get (TE ≥ NOW − 3 days) ∧ (TE is not NOW) ∧ (TE > 09/29). This predicate is indeed a minimal α^t for $p_1 \wedge p_2$ and will correctly rule out the tuple whose TE = 09/29.

To automatically infer predicates that follow from a given conjunction a temporal theorem prover would be needed. However, without such a theorem prover our framework is still correct: although $\hat{\alpha}^t$ may not be minimal for certain conjunctive predicates, $\hat{\alpha}^t$ is still a correct definition of α^t. The practical implication of a nonminimal $\hat{\alpha}^t$ is that some tuples may be saved unnecessarily. However, such cases are relatively unusual.

5   Handling Data Updates: α^μ

We now turn to the problem of making a temporal selection view self-maintainable with respect to data updates alone. Similar to handling time advances, for a view $\sigma_p(R)$ our approach is to relax the selection predicate to $\alpha^\mu(p)$ such that $\sigma_{\alpha^\mu(p)}(R)$ is self-maintainable with respect to data updates. As a first step, we define $\bar{\alpha}^\mu(p)$ to select all tuples that either satisfy p now or may satisfy p after an update. Recall that we need only consider updates to time attributes (Section 2.2).

Definition 4. *($\bar{\alpha}^\mu$) Let t_{now} be the current time and p a selection predicate. Suppose that the update window is* [NOW − l, NOW]. *Define $\bar{\alpha}^\mu(p)$ as a selection predicate over a temporal tuple r: $(\bar{\alpha}^\mu(p))(r) \stackrel{def}{=} \exists \mu$ in $[t_{now} - l, t_{now}] : p(\mu(r))$. Here, μ is an update of* T *that may possibly leave* T *unchanged but may not change* T *to ∅.*

Intuitively, $\sigma_{\bar{\alpha}^\mu(p)}(R)$ contains the contents of $\sigma_p(R)$ plus enough auxiliary information to maintain $\sigma_p(R)$ with respect to data updates, and nothing more. When an update arrives, we check whether it is for a tuple stored in $\sigma_{\bar{\alpha}^\mu(p)}(R)$. If so, we have enough information to apply the update and maintain the view. If not, we know that this update cannot cause any tuple to satisfy p, because all tuples with the potential of satisfying p after an update are stored in $\sigma_{\bar{\alpha}^\mu(p)}(R)$.

A nice duality exists between α^μ for data updates and α^t for time advances. The following definitions and theorems are identical in form to those in Section 4. We first formalize the notion of a correct α^μ using $\bar{\alpha}^\mu$, and show that $\bar{\alpha}^\mu$ is a correct definition of α^μ and also the minimal one. We then define $\hat{\alpha}^\mu$ as a computable alternative to $\bar{\alpha}^\mu$, in the same manner as we have defined $\hat{\alpha}^t$.

Definition 5. *(Correct α^μ) Let p be a selection predicate. A definition of α^μ is correct if the following properties hold: (i) $p \to \alpha^\mu(p)$; (ii) $\bar{\alpha}^\mu(p) \to \alpha^\mu(p)$; (iii) $\bar{\alpha}^\mu(\alpha^\mu(p)) \to \alpha^\mu(p)$.*

Theorem 3. *(Correctness & minimality of $\bar{\alpha}^\mu$) $\bar{\alpha}^\mu$ is a correct definition of α^μ. Furthermore, it is minimal: given any correct definition of α^μ, $\bar{\alpha}^\mu(p) \to \alpha^\mu(p)$ for any selection predicate p.*

Definition 6. *($\hat{\alpha}^\mu$) Let p be a selection predicate with negations pushed down to the level of atomic predicates. We define $\hat{\alpha}^\mu(p)$ inductively on the structure of p. If p is an atomic or negated atomic predicate, $\hat{\alpha}^\mu(p)$ is defined as a quantifier-free predicate logically equivalent to $\bar{\alpha}^\mu(p)$ (specified in [13]). $\hat{\alpha}^\mu(p_1 \vee p_2)$ is defined as $\hat{\alpha}^\mu(p_1) \vee \hat{\alpha}^\mu(p_2)$. $\hat{\alpha}^\mu(p_1 \wedge p_2)$ is defined as $\hat{\alpha}^\mu(p_1) \wedge \hat{\alpha}^\mu(p_2)$.*

Theorem 4. *(Correctness of $\hat{\alpha}^\mu$) $\hat{\alpha}^\mu$ is a correct definition of α^μ according to Def. 5.*

For atomic predicates and their negations, $\hat{\alpha}^\mu$ is minimal. For composite predicates, minimality is preserved over disjunction, but not over conjunction. The reasoning is analogous to the reasoning for $\hat{\alpha}^t$. A complete set of tables of $\hat{\alpha}^\mu$ specifications can be found in [13]. Besides the single-period constraint, update window [NOW $- l$, NOW] also plays an important role in $\hat{\alpha}^\mu$ specifications. Most $\hat{\alpha}^\mu$ specifications contain references to l; a smaller l makes them more selective, particularly when $l = 0$.

Example 8. To illustrate the importance of constraints, we explain $\hat{\alpha}^\mu$(TE $=$ NOW $- 3$ days) under different constraints. Note how $\hat{\alpha}^\mu$ becomes more and more selective as we add the single-period constraint and decrease the length of the update window.

Update window [NOW $- 7$ days, NOW], *no single-period constraint.* Note that NOW $- 3$ days is inside the update window. Thus, for any tuple r, we can always update the part of r.T within the current update window to end at $t_{now} - 3$ days. Therefore, $\hat{\alpha}^\mu$(TE $=$ NOW $- 3$ days) is true, as specified in [13].

Update window [NOW $- 7$ days, NOW], *single-period constraint.* NOW $- 3$ days is still inside the update window, but we can no longer apply an arbitrary update since we need to make sure that T remains a single period afterwards. Specifically, if r.TE $<$ NOW $- 8$ days, we cannot modify r.T because any update within [NOW $- 7$ days, NOW] would create another disjoint period in r.T. On the other hand, as long as r.TE $\geq$ NOW $- 8$ days, we can make (TE $=$ NOW $- 3$ days) true by updating the part of r.T within the update window to be $[t_{now} - 7$ days, $t_{now} - 3$ days]. This update will not create more periods in r.T, because $[t_{now} - 7$ days, $t_{now} - 3$ days] is connected to the part of r.T before the update window, if any. Therefore, $\hat{\alpha}^\mu$(TE $=$ NOW $- 3$ days) is (TE $\geq$ NOW $- 8$ days).

Update window [NOW, NOW], *single-period constraint.* Again, because of the single-period constraint, we can update a tuple r only if r.TE lies within or next to the update window. Thus, all we can do is terminate r.T right before the current update window, i.e., on $t_{now} - 1$ day, which is still not enough to satisfy (TE $=$ NOW $- 3$ days). Therefore, $\hat{\alpha}^\mu$(TE $=$ NOW $- 3$ days) remains (TE $=$ NOW $- 3$ days). □

6   Combining Time Advances and Data Updates: α

Finally, we tackle the problem of making a temporal selection view self-maintainable with respect to both time advances and data updates. For a view $\sigma_p(R)$, our goal is to derive $\alpha(p)$ by relaxing the original selection predicate p such that $\sigma_{\alpha(p)}(R)$ is a self-maintainable superview of $\sigma_p(R)$. Following the same path that we have taken when deriving α^t and α^μ, we first define $\bar{\alpha}$ as a lower bound for α.

Definition 7. *($\bar{\alpha}$) Let t_{now} be the current time and p a selection predicate. Suppose that the update window is $[\text{NOW} - l, \text{NOW}]$. Define $\bar{\alpha}(p)$ as a selection predicate over a temporal tuple r:*

$$(\bar{\alpha}(p))(r) \stackrel{def}{=} \exists t_1 \geq t_{now} : \exists \mu_1 \text{ in } [t_1 - l, t_1] :$$
$$\exists t_2 \geq t_1 : \exists \mu_2 \text{ in } [t_2 - l, t_2] : \dots$$
$$\exists t_n \geq t_{n-1} : \exists \mu_n \text{ in } [t_n - l, t_n] :$$
$$\exists t_{n+1} \geq t_n : [p]_{t_{n+1}}([\mu_n]_{t_n}(\dots([\mu_2]_{t_2}([\mu_1]_{t_1}(r)))\dots))$$

Here, $n \geq 0$, and each μ_i is an update of T that may possibly leave T unchanged but may not change T to $\varnothing$.

The sequence of t_i's and μ_i's in the definition is interpreted as follows. First, time advances from t_{now} to t_1, and an update μ_1 is applied to r at t_1. Then, time advances from t_1 to t_2, and μ_2 is applied at t_2, etc. Finally, after μ_n has been applied at t_n, time advances to t_{n+1} and p becomes true. Intuitively, a tuple r satisfies $\bar{\alpha}(p)$ iff r will satisfy p after going through a finite sequence of interleaving time advances and data updates. The sequence is effectively empty when $n = 0$ and $t_1 = t_{now}$. Therefore, $\sigma_{\bar{\alpha}(p)}(R)$ contains the current contents of $\sigma_p(R)$ plus enough auxiliary information to maintain $\sigma_p(R)$, and nothing more. Using $\bar{\alpha}$, we now formally define what constitutes a correct α, and show that $\bar{\alpha}$ is a correct α as well as the minimal one.

Definition 8. *(Correct α) Let p be a selection predicate. A definition of α is correct if the following properties hold: (i) $p \to \alpha(p)$; (ii) $\bar{\alpha}(p) \to \alpha(p)$; (iii) $\bar{\alpha}(\alpha(p)) \to \alpha(p)$.*

Theorem 5. *(Correctness & minimality of $\bar{\alpha}$) $\bar{\alpha}$ is a correct definition of α. Furthermore, it is minimal: given any correct definition of α, $\bar{\alpha}(p) \to \alpha(p)$ for any selection predicate p.*

Since Def. 7 uses an unbounded number of existential quantifiers, we need to find a computable alternative to $\bar{\alpha}$. We shall take the same approach as before, defining $\hat{\alpha}$ inductively starting from atomic predicates and their negations. However, even for a simple atomic or negated atomic predicate p, finding the quantifier-free predicate equivalent to $\bar{\alpha}(p)$ is a difficult and sometimes extremely tricky task. Fortunately, we can use the quantifier-free versions of $\bar{\alpha}^t$ and $\bar{\alpha}^\mu$ derived in the previous sections to compute the quantifier-free version of $\bar{\alpha}$, instead of deriving it directly from Def. 7. Now, the question becomes, how should we define $\bar{\alpha}$ in terms of $\bar{\alpha}^t$ and $\bar{\alpha}^\mu$?

A first simple guess is $\bar{\alpha}(p) \leftrightarrow \bar{\alpha}^t(p) \vee \bar{\alpha}^\mu(p)$. Recall that $\sigma_{\bar{\alpha}^t(p)}(R)$ contains enough information to maintain $\sigma_p(R)$ with respect to time advances, and $\sigma_{\bar{\alpha}^\mu(p)}(R)$ contains enough information to maintain $\sigma_p(R)$ with respect to data updates. Therefore, $\sigma_{\bar{\alpha}^t(p) \vee \bar{\alpha}^\mu(p)}(R)$ contains enough information to maintain $\sigma_p(R)$ with respect to either time advances or data updates. This definition may seem reasonable, but it turns out to be incorrect, as illustrated by the following example.

Example 9. Let p be the predicate (TE = NOW − 3 days). Suppose that the update window is [NOW, NOW] and T may contain only a single period. This scenario was considered first in Example 1. As we have seen in Examples 7 and 8, respectively, $\bar{\alpha}^t(p)$ is (TE ≥ NOW − 3 days) ∧ (TE is not NOW), and $\bar{\alpha}^\mu(p)$ is (TE = NOW − 3 days). Hence, $\bar{\alpha}^t(p) \vee \bar{\alpha}^\mu(p)$ is (TE ≥ NOW − 3 days) ∧ (TE is not NOW). However, $\bar{\alpha}^t(p) \vee \bar{\alpha}^\mu(p)$ may miss some tuples with the potential of satisfying p. Specifically, $r_5 = \langle 5, [09/25, \text{NOW}] \rangle$ from Fig. 1 does not satisfy $\bar{\alpha}^t(p) \vee \bar{\alpha}^\mu(p)$, but in Example 1 it was shown to be necessary for the maintenance of $\sigma_p(R)$.

The problem is that $\bar{\alpha}^t(p) \vee \bar{\alpha}^\mu(p)$ selects tuples that can satisfy p either through time advances or through data updates, but it fails to select tuples that can satisfy p through a sequence of interleaving time advances and data updates. For instance, as discussed in Example 1, r_5 satisfies p by going through a data update on 10/01 first, and then through an advance of time from 10/01 to 10/03. Thus, r_5 is missed by $\bar{\alpha}^t(p) \vee \bar{\alpha}^\mu(p)$. Another way to see the problem is by observing that $\sigma_{\bar{\alpha}^t(p) \vee \bar{\alpha}^\mu(p)}(R)$ is not self-maintainable. In particular, the update on 10/01 will change r_5 to $r'_5 = \langle 5, [09/25, 09/30] \rangle$, which satisfies $\bar{\alpha}^t(p) \vee \bar{\alpha}^\mu(p)$. Since $\sigma_{\bar{\alpha}^t(p) \vee \bar{\alpha}^\mu(p)}(R)$ does not contain r_5, it will be not be maintainable when this update occurs. □

The real source of the problem is that when we relax a selection predicate by $\bar{\alpha}^t$, we may introduce auxiliary data that is not maintainable with respect to data updates, and similarly, when we relax a selection predicate by $\bar{\alpha}^\mu$, we may introduce auxiliary data that is not maintainable with respect to time advances. This analysis suggests the following procedure for computing $\bar{\alpha}(p)$. Initially, we set the answer predicate p' to p. Of course, $\sigma_{p'}(R)$ may not be self-maintainable yet, so we relax p' using $\bar{\alpha}^t$ and $\bar{\alpha}^\mu$, i.e., we replace p' with $\bar{\alpha}^\mu(\bar{\alpha}^t(p'))$. By relaxing p', we may have introduced more auxiliary data into $\sigma_{p'}(R)$ which needs to be maintained. Therefore, we must replace p' with $\bar{\alpha}^\mu(\bar{\alpha}^t(p'))$ again. This process is repeated until p' no longer changes, and at this point $\sigma_{p'}(R)$ is self-maintainable. Thm. 6 below indicates that $\bar{\alpha}(p)$ is indeed logically equivalent to p' as computed by the above procedure.

Theorem 6. *(Fixed-point formulation of $\bar{\alpha}$) Let p be a selection predicate. $\bar{\alpha}(p) \leftrightarrow (\bar{\alpha}^\mu \circ \bar{\alpha}^t)^*(p)$, where $(\bar{\alpha}^\mu \circ \bar{\alpha}^t)^*(p)$ denotes the fixed point of applying $\bar{\alpha}^t$ and $\bar{\alpha}^\mu$ to p.*

Thm. 6 provides us a way to compute $\bar{\alpha}(p)$, although a number of practical issues still remain. To evaluate $(\bar{\alpha}^\mu \circ \bar{\alpha}^t)^*(p)$, we must use $\hat{\alpha}^t$ and $\hat{\alpha}^\mu$, the computable alternatives to $\bar{\alpha}^t$ and $\bar{\alpha}^\mu$ defined in Sections 4 and 5. As we have seen, $\hat{\alpha}^t$ and $\hat{\alpha}^\mu$ are not always equivalent to $\bar{\alpha}^t$ and $\bar{\alpha}^\mu$ for conjunctive predicates. The fixed-point iteration may introduce conjunctions into the relaxed predicate even if the original predicate is atomic. Thus, during the iteration, we may want to augment the relaxed predicate in order to improve the minimality of the result, using the technique introduced in Section 4. Moreover, testing the termination condition of the fixed-point iteration involves testing the logical equivalence of temporal predicates. Therefore, if we wish to automate the fixed-point computation, we will again need a theorem prover for our temporal language. Since we do not want to rely on the existence of such a theorem prover, we have computed $\bar{\alpha}$ manually for all atomic predicates and their negations, as specified in [13]. Care has been taken to ensure that all results are indeed minimal.

Example 10. As an example of the fixed-point computation, we show how to use $\hat{\alpha}^t$ and $\hat{\alpha}^\mu$ to derive $\bar{\alpha}(p)$, where p is (TE = NOW − 3 days). As in Example 9, we assume that the update window is [NOW, NOW] and the single-period constraint holds. First, we apply $\hat{\alpha}^t$ to p. According to the specifications in [13], $\hat{\alpha}^t(p)$ is:

$$(\text{TE} \geq \text{NOW} - 3 \text{ days}) \land (\text{TE is not NOW})$$

Next, we apply $\hat{\alpha}^\mu$ to $\hat{\alpha}^t(p)$. According to [13], $\hat{\alpha}^\mu(\text{TE} \geq \text{NOW} - 3 \text{ days})$ remains (TE ≥ NOW − 3 days), while $\hat{\alpha}^\mu(\text{TE is not NOW})$ becomes (TS < NOW). Thus, $\hat{\alpha}^\mu(\hat{\alpha}^t(p))$ is:

$$(\text{TE} \geq \text{NOW} - 3 \text{ days}) \land (\text{TS} < \text{NOW})$$

Since this predicate is different from p, we must continue the fixed-point iteration. According to [13], $\hat{\alpha}^t(\text{TE} \geq \text{NOW} - 3 \text{ days})$ remains (TE ≥ NOW − 3 days), while $\hat{\alpha}^\mu(\text{TS} < \text{NOW})$ becomes **true**. Thus, $\hat{\alpha}^t(\hat{\alpha}^\mu(\hat{\alpha}^t(p)))$ is:

$$(\text{TE} \geq \text{NOW} - 3 \text{ days})$$

Subsequent applications of $\hat{\alpha}^\mu$ and $\hat{\alpha}^t$ all yield the same predicate. Therefore, $(\hat{\alpha}^\mu \cap \hat{\alpha}^t)^*(p)$ is (TE ≥ NOW − 3 days).

Notice that the steps in the fixed-point computation correspond to the sequence of interleaving time advances and data updates that may cause a tuple to satisfy the original predicate. For instance, suppose that the current time is 10/01 and there is a tuple r with $r.\text{T} = [10/01, \text{NOW}]$. Currently, r satisfies $\hat{\alpha}^t(\hat{\alpha}^\mu(\hat{\alpha}^t(p)))$, but not $\hat{\alpha}^\mu(\hat{\alpha}^t(p))$. The difference between $\hat{\alpha}^t(\hat{\alpha}^\mu(\hat{\alpha}^t(p)))$ and $\hat{\alpha}^\mu(\hat{\alpha}^t(p))$ is an application of $\hat{\alpha}^t$, hinting that an advance of time will make r satisfy $\hat{\alpha}^\mu(\hat{\alpha}^t(p))$. Indeed, when time advances to 10/02, r satisfies $\hat{\alpha}^\mu(\hat{\alpha}^t(p))$. However, r still does not satisfy $\hat{\alpha}^t(p)$. This time, $\hat{\alpha}^\mu(\hat{\alpha}^t(p))$ and $\hat{\alpha}^t(p)$ differ by an application of $\hat{\alpha}^\mu$, hinting that a data update is required. Indeed, this update subtracts [10/02, NOW] from $r.\text{T}$, changing it to [10/01, 10/01]. Now, r satisfies $\hat{\alpha}^t(p)$. Finally, an advance of time from 10/02 to 10/04 causes r to satisfy p.

The above reasoning can be generalized to show that any tuple that currently satisfies (TE ≥ NOW − 3 days) will eventually satisfy (TE = NOW − 3 days) after going through the sequence of time advances and data updates corresponding to the steps in the fixed-point computation. We have in effect a proof of the minimality of (TE ≥ NOW − 3 days); that is, (TE ≥ NOW − 3 days) is a quantifier-free predicate equivalent to $\bar{\alpha}(\text{TE} = \text{NOW} - 3 \text{ days})$. ☐

From the specifications of $\hat{\alpha}$ for atomic predicates and their negations, we can proceed to define $\hat{\alpha}$ for composite predicates. Like $\hat{\alpha}^t$ and $\hat{\alpha}^\mu$, $\hat{\alpha}$ is minimal for predicates with no conjunctions, but it does not preserve minimality over conjunction. If needed, we can improve $\hat{\alpha}$ using the technique of augmenting predicates in Section 4.

Definition 9. ($\hat{\alpha}$) *Let p be a selection predicate with negations pushed down to the level of atomic predicates. We define $\hat{\alpha}(p)$ inductively on the structure of p. If p is an atomic or negated atomic predicate, $\hat{\alpha}(p)$ is defined as a quantifier-free predicate logically equivalent to $\bar{\alpha}^t(p)$ (specified in [13]). $\hat{\alpha}(p_1 \vee p_2)$ is defined as $\hat{\alpha}(p_1) \vee \hat{\alpha}(p_2)$. $\hat{\alpha}(p_1 \wedge p_2)$ is defined as $\hat{\alpha}(p_1) \wedge \hat{\alpha}(p_2)$.*

Theorem 7. *(Correctness of $\hat{\alpha}$) $\hat{\alpha}$ is a correct definition of α according to Def. 8.*

Example 11. To conclude this section, we derive superviews for all example views in Section 2.3. For Examples 1–4, we also verify that the superviews indeed contain all and only those tuples of Fig. 1 and 2 required for self-maintenance as identified by our analysis in Section 2.3.

   Example 1. With update window [NOW, NOW] and the single-period constraint, $\hat{\alpha}(\text{TE} = \text{NOW} - 3\text{ days})$ is $(\text{TE} \geq \text{NOW} - 3\text{ days})$, as specified in [13]. Hence, the superview of V is $\sigma_{\text{TE} \geq \text{NOW} - 3\text{days}}(R)$, which contains r_3, r_4, and r_5.

   Example 2. With update window [NOW $-$ 7 days, NOW] and the single-period constraint, $\hat{\alpha}(\text{TE} = \text{NOW} - 3\text{ days})$ is $(\text{TE} \geq \text{NOW} - 8\text{ days})$ according to [13]. Hence, the superview of V is $\sigma_{\text{TE} \geq \text{NOW} - 8\text{days}}(R)$, which contains r_2, r_3, r_4, and r_5.

   Example 3. With update window [NOW $-$ 7 days, NOW] and no single-period constraint, $\hat{\alpha}(\text{TE} = \text{NOW} - 3\text{ days})$ is true according to [13]. Hence the superview is R.

   Example 4. With update window [NOW$-$7 days, NOW] and no single-period constraint, $\hat{\alpha}(\text{Dept} = \text{sales})$ remains $(\text{Dept} = \text{sales})$ and $\hat{\alpha}(\text{length}(\text{T}) < 5\text{ days})$ is $(\text{length}(\text{T} - [\text{NOW} - 7\text{ days}, \text{NOW}]) < 5\text{ days})$ according to [13]. Therefore, $\hat{\alpha}(\text{Dept} = \text{sales} \wedge \text{length}(\text{T}) < 5\text{ days})$ is $(\text{Dept} = \text{sales}) \wedge (\text{length}(\text{T} - [\text{NOW} - 7\text{ days}, \text{NOW}]) < 5\text{ days})$. The superview of U is $\sigma_{\text{Dept}=\text{sales} \wedge \text{length}(\text{T}-[\text{NOW}-7\text{ days}, \text{NOW}]) < 5\text{ days}}(S)$, which contains s_2 and s_3.

   Example 5. With update window [NOW $-$ 7 days, NOW] and the single-period constraint, $\hat{\alpha}(\text{TE} = t)$ is q according to [13]. Hence, the superview of W is $\sigma_q(R)$. □

7 Additional Issues and Related Work

Omitted from this paper due to space constraints, the full version [13] also addresses the following issues:

- Self-maintenance of temporal join, aggregation, and *snapshot-reducible* [10] views
- Algorithms for incrementally maintaining temporal views and auxiliary data
- Exploiting the case where source updates result in "pure" deletions and insertions instead of timestamp modifications of existing tuples
- Handling infinitely wide source update windows

– Dealing with the *coalescing effect* [3] of temporal projection
– Extending our framework to handle views with bag semantics

A number of papers are related to temporal view self-maintenance to some degree. Reference [7] explored view maintenance in the *chronicle* model, which makes several assumptions that simplify self-maintenance. First, the model does not support NOW. Each tuple is timestamped with a single time instant rather than a set. Operators of the algebra are all snapshot-reducible. Finally, chronicles are append-only and no retroactive updates are allowed; using our terminology, the update window is [NOW, NOW]. It is possible to handle the chronicle model as a special case in our framework.

Reference [1] considered the maintenance of relational queries whose selection predicate may reference NOW. They also used the idea of superviews to make selection views self-maintainable. Under their data model, updates to the time attribute are modeled as pure deletions and insertions. Therefore, as we show in [13], it suffices to consider only the dimension of time advances. Moreover, they assumed that NOW could not be stored in data, and there were no update-window constraints. These assumptions further simplify the problem in their case.

The full version of this paper [13] contains a more comprehensive discussion of related work, including nontemporal view self-maintenance [2,6,9], warehouse data expiration [5], and temporal constraint checking [4].

References

1. L. Bækgaard and L. Mark. Incremental computation of time-varying query expressions. *IEEE Trans. on Knowledge and Data Engineering*, 7(4):583–590, 1995.
2. J. A. Blakeley, N. Coburn, and P.-Å. Larson. Updating derived relations: Detecting irrelevant and autonomously computable updates. *ACM Trans. on Database Sys.*, 14(3):369–400, 1989.
3. M. H. Böhlen, C. S. Jensen, and R. T. Snodgrass. Evaluating the completeness of TSQL2. In *Proc. of the 1995 Intl. Workshop on Temporal Databases*, pages 153–174, 1995.
4. J. Chomicki. Efficient checking of temporal integrity constraints using bounded history encoding. *ACM Trans. on Database Sys.*, 20(2):148–186, 1995.
5. H. Garcia-Molina, W. J. Labio, and J. Yang. Expiring data in a warehouse. In *Proc. of the 1998 Intl. Conf. on Very Large Data Bases*, pages 500–511, 1998.
6. A. Gupta, H. V. Jagadish, and I. S. Mumick. Data integration using self-maintainable views. In *Proc. of the 1996 Intl. Conf. on Extending Database Technology*, pages 140–144, 1996.
7. H. V. Jagadish, I. S. Mumick, and A. Silberschatz. View maintenance issues for the chronicle data model. In *Proc. of the 1995 ACM Symp. on Principles of Database Sys.*, pages 113–124, 1995.
8. C. S. Jensen, M. D. Soo, and R. T. Snodgrass. Unifying temporal models via a conceptual model. *Information Sys.*, 19(7):513–547, 1994.

9. D. Quass, A. Gupta, I. S. Mumick, and J. Widom. Making views self-maintainable for data warehousing. In *Proc. of the 1996 Intl. Conf. on Parallel and Distributed Information Sys.*, pages 158–169, 1996.

10. R. T. Snodgrass. The temporal query language TQuel. *ACM Trans. on Database Sys.*, 12(2):247–298, 1987.

11. J. Widom. Research problems in data warehousing. In *Proc. of the 1995 Intl. Conf. on Information and Knowledge Management*, pages 25–30, 1995.

12. J. Yang and J. Widom. Maintaining temporal views over non-temporal information sources for data warehousing. In *Proc. of the 1998 Intl. Conf. on Extending Database Technology*, pages 389–403, 1998.

13. J. Yang and J. Widom. Temporal view self-maintenance in a warehousing environment. Technical report, Computer Science Department, Stanford University, 1999.
http://www-db.stanford.edu/pub/papers/yw-tempsm.ps.

A Unified Approach for Indexed and Non-indexed Spatial Joins

Lars Arge[1*], Octavian Procopiuc[1**], Sridhar Ramaswamy[2], Torsten Suel[3], Jan Vahrenhold[4***], and Jeffrey Scott Vitter[1**]

[1] Center for Geometric Computing, Department of Computer Science, Duke University, Durham, NC 27708–0129. {large,tavi,jsv}@cs.duke.edu

[2] Epiphany, 2300 Geng Road, Palo Alto, CA. sridhar@epiphany.com

[3] Computer and Information Science, Polytechnic University, 6 MetroTech Center, Brooklyn, NY 11201. suel@photon.poly.edu

[4] Westfälische Wilhelms-Universität, Institut für Informatik, 48149 Münster, Germany. jan@math.uni-muenster.de

Abstract Most spatial join algorithms either assume the existence of a spatial index structure that is traversed during the join process, or solve the problem by sorting, partitioning, or on-the-fly index construction. In this paper, we develop a simple plane-sweeping algorithm that unifies the index-based and non-index based approaches. This algorithm processes indexed as well as non-indexed inputs, extends naturally to multi-way joins, and can be built easily from a few standard operations. We present the results of a comparative study of the new algorithm with several index-based and non-index based spatial join algorithms. We consider a number of factors, including the relative performance of CPU and disk, the quality of the spatial indexes, and the sizes of the input relations. An important conclusion from our work is that using an index-based approach whenever indexes are available does not always lead to the best execution time, and hence we propose the use of a simple cost model to decide when to follow an index-based approach.

1 Introduction

Geographic Information Systems (GIS) have generated considerable interest in the commercial and research database communities over the last decade. A GIS typically supports the management and manipulation of spatial data types such as points, lines, polylines, polygons, and surfaces. Since the amount of data that needs to be managed is often quite large, GISs are usually disk-based systems.

* Supported in part by National Science Foundation grants EIA–9870734 and EIA–9972879.

** Supported in part by the U.S. Army Research Office under grant DAAH04–96–1–0013 and by the National Science Foundation under grants CCR–9522047 and EIA–9870734.

*** This work was done while a Visiting Scholar at Duke University.

C. Zaniolo et al. (Eds.): EDBT 2000, LNCS 1777, pp. 413–429, 2000.

One of the fundamental operations on spatial data is the *spatial join*, which combines two relations based on some spatial criterium. The most common case is the *spatial overlay join* where the *intersect* predicate is used for joining the input relations. Spatial objects can be quite complex, and their accurate representation can require a large amount of memory. Since manipulating such large objects can be cumbersome and expensive, it is customary to *approximate* spatial objects and manipulate the approximations as much as possible. The most common technique is to bound each spatial object by the smallest axis-parallel rectangle that completely contains it, called the *minimal bounding rectangle* (MBR). Spatial overlay joins can then be performed in two steps [28]:

- **Filter Step:** The spatial operation is first performed on the MBR representation, i.e., the first step is to identify all intersecting pairs of MBRs.
- **Refinement Step:** The exact representations of the objects corresponding to each such pair of MBRs are used to validate the results.

In this paper, we focus on the filter step. (For the rest of the paper, we use the term "spatial join" to refer to the filter step of the spatial join, unless explicitly stated otherwise.) This step has been studied extensively by a number of researchers, and most existing work can be broadly categorized into two approaches. The first approach relies on the existence of a spatial index structure (e.g., an R-tree or R*-tree) that is traversed during the join process. The second approach does not use any existing index structures, but instead uses techniques such as partitioning, sorting, or on-the-fly construction of indexes.

The first contribution of this paper is a simple spatial join algorithm, called *Priority Queue-Driven Traversal* (or *PQ* for short), that combines the index-based and non-index based approaches. The algorithm can be built from a few standard operations, and can process indexed as well as non-indexed inputs. It can also easily be extended to handle certain multi-way joins.

Our second contribution is to show that using an index-based spatial join whenever indexes are available does not always yield the fastest execution time. This is mainly due to the difference between the performance of sequential and random I/O. We propose the use of a cost model that explicitly takes this difference into account when choosing which approach to use.

The third contribution is an extensive comparative study of several index-based and non-index based spatial joins. We present experiments on three different hardware platforms representing the typical range in CPU and disk performance of current workstations. Our experiments use real-world data sets scaling up to tens of millions of spatial objects. Most previous studies consider only input sizes in the tens or at most hundreds of thousands. We consider both the number of disk block accesses and the actual execution time, thus quantifying the effect of random versus sequential disk accesses, as well as the quality of the index structures, on the performance. In contrast, most previous work focuses on only one of the two measures.

The remainder of this paper is organized as follows. In Section 2, we provide a brief summary of related work on spatial joins. In Section 3, we describe the algorithms we considered for the comparative study. Section 4 describes our new algorithm PQ. Section 5 describes our experimental platform, and in Section 6 we present and discuss the experimental results. Finally, Section 7 offers some concluding remarks.

2   Previous Work

Early Work. Orenstein [29] uses a transformational approach based on space-filling curves, and then performs a sort-merge join along the curve to solve the join problem. In another transformational approach [6], the MBRs of two-dimensional spatial objects are transformed into points in four dimensions. These points are stored in a multi-attribute data structure such as the grid file [27], which is then used to perform the join. An efficient algorithm for the rectangle intersection problem based on plane-sweeping was proposed by Güting and Schilling [13], who observed that real data sets from VLSI applications tend to obey a so-called *square-root rule*, i.e., in a set of N rectangles there are only $O(\sqrt{N})$ rectangles that intersect a given vertical or horizontal line. Rotem [32] proposes a spatial join algorithm based on the join index of Valduriez [37] and a grid file.

Spatial Index-Based Approaches. Several join algorithms have been proposed that use spatial index structures such as the R-tree [14], R^+-tree [34], R^*-tree [7], or PMR quad-tree [33]. Brinkhoff, Kriegel, and Seeger [8] propose an algorithm based on R^*-trees that performs a carefully synchronized depth-first traversal of the two trees to be joined. An optimized version of this algorithm was described in [16]. Günther [12] studies the tradeoffs between using join indexes and spatial indexes for the spatial join. He concludes that a join index approach is better for low join selectivities, while for higher join selectivities, spatial indexes perform better. Hoel and Samet [15] propose to use PMR quad-trees for the spatial join and compare it against members of the R-tree family. Lo and Ravishankar [21] discuss the case where only one of the relations has an index. They construct an index for the other relation on the fly, by using the existing index as a starting point (or *seed*). Afterwards, the tree join algorithm of [8] is used to perform the actual join. Another algorithm for the case where only one relation has an index was recently proposed by Mamoulis and Papadias [24], who also discuss how to perform multiple joins occurring in more complex spatial queries.

Non Index-Based Approaches. Recently a lot of work has focused on the case where neither of the input relations has an index. Lo and Ravishankar [22] propose to first build indexes using spatial sampling techniques, and then use the tree join algorithm of [8] to compute the join. Another recent paper [20] proposes an algorithm based on a filter tree structure. Patel and DeWitt [30] and Lo and Ravishankar [23] both propose *hash*-based algorithms that use a spatial partitioning function to subdivide the input such that each partition fits in memory. Patel and DeWitt then use a standard plane-sweeping technique to perform the join for each partition, while Lo and Ravishankar use an indexed nested loop join. Arge et al. [4] propose an algorithm based on plane-sweeping and partitioning along a single axis that guarantees an asymptotically optimal number of disk accesses in the worst case. The algorithm is essentially an improved version of the algorithm of Güting and Schilling [13]. As shown in [4], for common data sets the partitioning steps are never executed, and the algorithm thus reduces to an initial sort followed by a plane sweep.

3   Description of the Algorithms

In this section, we describe the previously known algorithms that we compare in our study. We implemented two non-index based algorithms, the *Partition-based Spatial Merge Join* (*PBSM*) of Patel and DeWitt [30] and the *Scalable Sweeping-based Spatial Join* (*SSSJ*) of Arge et al. [4], as well as an index-based algorithm, the synchronized R-tree traversal (*ST*) of Brinkhoff et al. [8].

3.1   Scalable Sweeping-Based Spatial Join (SSSJ)

The Scalable Sweeping-based Spatial Join (*SSSJ*) algorithm [4] combines an optimized internal memory plane-sweep algorithm with a partitioning along a single dimension that makes the algorithm provably robust against worst-case data distributions.

Plane-Sweeping. We first briefly describe the internal memory plane-sweep algorithm, which is used as a component in all four algorithms that we implemented. A plane-sweep algorithm solves a two-dimensional geometric problem by moving a vertical or horizontal *sweep-line* across the data, processing each object as it is reached by the sweep-line (see, e.g., [31]). Clearly, for any pair of intersecting rectangles, there exists a horizontal line that passes through both rectangles, and thus only rectangles located on the same sweep-line (or rather, the intervals corresponding to their projections onto that line) need to be tested for intersection. This observation is used in plane-sweeping to reduce the join problem to a (dynamic) one-dimensional interval intersection problem. Arge et al. [4] experimentally compared four internal memory data structures for storing the intervals corresponding to rectangles cut by the same sweep-line, including two methods called Striped-Sweep and Forward-Sweep. Forward-Sweep has been used in several previous implementations of spatial join algorithms (see, e.g., [8,30]), while Striped-Sweep was shown in [4] to be by a factor of 2 to 5 faster than the other methods for most real-life data sets. We refer to [4] for a detailed discussion of these algorithms and their performance.

Structure of SSSJ. After initially sorting the two sets of input MBR's based on y-coordinates, a plane-sweep is performed by reading both sorted inputs sequentially while maintaining two internal memory interval data structures. This approach works efficiently as long as the data structures do not grow beyond the size of the available internal memory. It was observed by Arge et al. [4] that even for very large real-life data sets, the maximum size of the data structures will be relatively small. To handle cases where the structures do not fit in memory, *SSSJ* combines the plane-sweep approach with an I/O-optimal algorithm based on the distribution sweeping technique [5,11]. In all experiments performed for this study the data structures were always significantly smaller than the available internal memory, and thus *SSSJ* essentially consists of a sorting step followed by a single scan over the data.

Implementation. Our implementation of SSSJ is the same as that in [4], and is based on external memory multiway mergesort and the internal memory algorithm Striped-
Sweep. For data sets of the size we used, and excluding the output of the intersections, *SSSJ* performs two sequential read passes, one non-sequential read pass (while merging), and two sequential write passes over the data.

3.2   Partition-Based Spatial Merge Join (PBSM)

Partition-based Spatial Merge Join (*PBSM*) [30] is a hash-join algorithm that consists of a partitioning step followed by a plane-sweep step. In the partitioning step the objects from both input sets are distributed to a number of *partitions* such that each partition is likely to fit into internal memory. Then intersections within each partition are computed using the Forward-Sweep algorithm.

Since a copy of each input rectangle is assigned to each partition that it intersects, it can be difficult to compute a priori the number p of partitions that are needed. To avoid overfull partitions in the case of clustered data, a larger number $t \gg p$ of *tiles* is created to which the rectangles are distributed. The algorithm then assigns the t tiles to the p partitions by enumerating the tiles in row-major order and applying a hash function (e.g., round-robin); see [30] for details. Excluding the reporting of the intersections, *PBSM* usually performs two sequential read passes and one non-sequential write pass over the data.

Implementation. Our implementation of *PBSM* followed closely that of Patel and DeWitt [30]. Although we estimated the available internal memory very conservatively, we observed several partitions exceeding the internal memory size. Handling these partitions caused a fairly large number of page faults, which slowed down the internal memory part of the algorithm. We were able to alleviate this problem by increasing the number of tiles from 32×32 (as suggested by Patel and DeWitt) to 128×128, and this number of tiles was used throughout all experiments.

3.3   Synchronized R-tree Traversal (ST)

One of the most widely studied spatial join algorithms using R-trees was proposed by Brinkhoff et al. [8], and it has been used as a benchmark in several recent experimental studies [16,21,23,30]. The main idea is to perform a synchronized depth-first traversal of two trees storing the MBR's of the two data sets. For each pair of nodes in the tree whose bounding rectangles intersect, the algorithm computes all pairs of children whose bounding rectangles intersect, and then recurses. Finally, the intersections are reported once the search reaches the leaves.

If the MBR's in the two sets to be joined are distributed in approximately the same way, then all nodes from both trees are involved in the join operation. Assuming that each node occupies exactly one page, the total number of nodes in the R-trees is clearly a lower bound on the number of page requests for dense data sets. We refer to this number as the "optimal" number of page accesses. Recently, Huang, Jing, and Rundensteiner [16] proposed an algorithm based on breadth-first traversal that is reported to take approximately the same amount of CPU time as *ST*, while performing an almost optimal number of I/O operations (if a sufficiently large buffer pool is available).

Implementation. Since ST usually visits R-tree nodes more than once, it benefits from the use of a buffer pool storing previously touched nodes. In other spatial join experiments buffer pools occupying between 0.5 MB and 1 MB [8,16,24] or between 2 MB and 24 MB [30] have been used. Having 24 MB of internal memory available (see Section 5.1), we decided to give *ST* as much advantage as possible by using a buffer pool of size 22 MB (the remaining 2 MB were used for internal memory computations). Pages were replaced using the *least recently used* (LRU) policy. Following the recommendations of Brinkhoff et al. [8], we computed intersections between MBR's in two R-tree nodes using the Forward-Sweep algorithm, while considering only rectangles overlapping the intersection of the MBR's of the nodes under consideration.

For all R-tree experiments, we used packed R-trees that had been bulk-loaded using the Hilbert heuristic [17]. The maximum fanout was set to 400, corresponding to a page size of 8192 bytes (see Section 5.1). Following recommendations by DeWitt et al. [10], we were careful not to pack all nodes to 100% of capacity, since that might result in too much overlap between bounding rectangles on the same level, and thus decrease the quality of the index. Instead, we filled each node to 75% and included additional rectangles only if they did not increase the area already covered by the node by more than 20%. For our data sets, the resulting trees had an average packing ratio of around 90%.

4 Priority Queue-Driven R-tree Traversal (PQ)

In this section, we describe our new spatial join algorithm called *Priority Queue-Driven Traversal* (*PQ*). The main advantage of this algorithm is that it combines the index-based and non-index-based approaches in a way such that inputs in either representation can be processed using the same algorithm. The algorithm incorporates aspects of the plane-sweep approach of *SSSJ* as well as the tree traversal idea of *ST*.

Structure of PQ. A non-indexed input is processed by *PQ* in essentially the same way as in *SSSJ*; the MBR's are first sorted and then feed into a plane-sweep algorithm. If an input has a spatial index structure, such as an R-tree, the algorithm will exploit this structure and directly extract the data in sorted order according to the direction of the plane-sweep. The extracted data is directly fed into the plane-sweep algorithm. The other input to the sweep can be extracted in the same way from another index structure or read from a sorted non-indexed input.

PQ can be thought of as an extension of $SSSJ$ to the case of indexed inputs: it utilizes the same sorting and plane-sweep components as SSSJ, but adds an "index adapter" which extracts data from a spatial index structure in sorted order. In the following we describe how this extraction is performed by means of a tree traversal. A somewhat similar way of traversing the indexed data in sorted order was proposed by Kitsuregawa, Harada, and Takagi [19] in the context of joining two relations indexed by a k-d-tree. Here we present a conceptually simpler algorithm based on a priority queue.

The main idea in our traversal algorithm is to run a horizontal sweep-line through the nodes of the R-tree. To do so, we maintain a priority queue initially containing the bounding rectangle of the root of the tree. We advance the sweep-line by extracting the rectangle with minimum lower y-coordinate from the priority queue. If this rectangle is a bounding rectangle of an internal node of the R-tree, then we load all bounding rectangles of its children from disk and insert them in the priority queue. If the rectangle is a bounding rectangle stored within a leaf (i.e., the MBR of some spatial object), then we feed it into the plane-sweep algorithm, which performs the actual join. Figure 1 shows the basic structure of the algorithm for extracting elements in sorted order.

Algorithm *Extract_Next_Item:*
/* We have a priority queue P for bounding rectangles organized by their lower y-coordinate. Initially, P contains only the bounding rectangle of the root. */

    while P is not empty
        Extract the minimum element r from P
        if r is an internal node of the tree
            Read the children of r and insert them into P
        else
            Return(r)
    endwhile
    Return("End of input")

Fig. 1. Algorithm for extracting the next item from the index in sorted order.

We point out that while the version of PQ described here will always access all nodes of the index structure, the algorithm can be modified so that it only visits those parts that can result in intersections; the details of this (slightly more complicated) version are omitted from this paper. This modification is important for cases where one of the relations is very sparse or localized (see the discussion in Section 6.3), but has no influence on performance for any of the experiments in this paper.

The presentation of PQ given here assumes that the priority queue never grows larger than the amount of internal memory available. Note, however, that

PQ can be modified to handle overflow gracefully by using an external priority queue [2,9], and that it can also be combined with the partitioning step along one dimension that *SSSJ* performs in the case of an overflow of the interval data structure. We omit these details here since they are only needed for unusual worst-case input distributions.

One key feature of *PQ* is that it touches each node of the R-tree at most once. Thus, the algorithm achieves an "optimal" number of page accesses to the tree (provided that the size of the priority queue never grows beyond the available internal memory). Since *PQ* can process both indexed and non-indexed inputs, it can also easily be extended to multi-way intersection joins. For example, a 3-way intersection join can be performed by feeding the output of a two-way join directly into another join with a third (indexed or non-indexed) input.[1]

Implementation. *PQ* use the same internal memory components as *SSSJ* (see Section 3.1). For the priority queue, we chose the heap-based implementation provided by the *C++ Standard Template Library* (STL) [26]. To optimize the performance and reduce the space requirements of the priority queue, we actually maintained two priority queues: one for the bounding rectangles of the internal nodes and one for the data rectangles in the leaves. Since the only information needed for processing an internal node is its position on disk and the lower y-coordinate of its bounding box, we maintained the internal nodes by storing tuples of the form $(y, \text{page ID})$ in the first queue. For data MBR's however, we need to store four coordinates and an ID. During the algorithm, the next MBR to be processed can be found by comparing the first elements of the two queues.

As the priority queues grow larger, the individual access operations (*add* and *extract_min*) get noticeably slower, even though each operation on a heap storing N objects takes at most $O(\log N)$ comparisons. To increase the performance of the priority queue, we therefore used the following strategy: Whenever we loaded an R-tree leaf from disk, we sorted its rectangles by their lower y-coordinates and inserted only the first rectangle from this sorted sequence into the priority queue. Whenever we extracted a rectangle corresponding to a leaf from the queue, we added the next rectangle from that leaf (if any) to the queue. This technique does not significantly decrease the total space requirement, since all data rectangles of a given leaf have to be loaded into internal memory in order to perform the initial sort. However, by reducing the size of the priority queue, we save $O(\lg B)$ time per priority queue operation.

5   Experimental Platforms

In this section, we describe the experimental set-up for our studies, providing detailed information on the hardware, software, and data sets that were used.

---

[1] However, for more complicated multi-way joins which do not correspond to n-way intersections, it is not clear how to extend the algorithm in an elegant fashion; see [25] for a discussion of such cases.

5.1   Hardware Platforms

To cover a wide range of CPU speeds and disk transfer rates, we performed experiments on three different system configurations—refer to Table 1. The first system (also used in [4,16]) is a combination of a relatively slow processor and a fast disk. The second system has a fast processor (slightly faster than the one used in [24]) and a disk with high transfer rate but relatively slow average access time. The third is a state-of-the-art workstation, with both a fast processor and a fast disk. All machines were equipped with 64 MB of internal memory and the amount of free internal memory was at least 24 MB.

Table 1. Hardware configurations used in our experiments.

	Workstation (Model)	CPU (MHz)	Hard Disk (Model)	Size (GB)	Buffer (KB)	Read (ms)	Throughput (peak, MB/s)
1	SUN Sparc 20	50	ST-32550N (Barracuda)	2.1	512	8.0	10
2	SUN Ultra 10	300	ST-34342A (Medalist)	4.3	128	12.5	33.3
3	DEC Alpha 500	500	ST-34501W (Cheetah)	4.4	512	7.7	40

The page size on Machines 2 and 3 was 8 KB, while Machine 1 had a page size of 4 KB. In order to obtain comparable results, we used 8 KB per R-tree node in all experiments. Thus, on Machine 1 we always requested two blocks per I/O-operation.

5.2   Software Environment

We implemented the algorithms in C++ using the *Transparent Parallel I/O Programming Environment* (TPIE) [3], a templated library that supports high-level, yet efficient implementations of external memory algorithms.

In TPIE, the actual page transfers between disk and internal memory is performed by a so-called Block Transfer Engine (BTE). One implementation employs the `read` and `write` system calls, which improve the performance of purely stream-based algorithms like *PBSM* or *SSSJ*. Hence, we used this BTE in our experiments with these algorithms, and in order to take advantage of the sequential disk access pattern, we used a logical page size of 512 KB. For our R-tree implementation, however, we chose a BTE that performs memory-mapped I/O operations using `mmap` system calls, thus bypassing the operating system's buffer cache in a way similar to using a raw disk device (as done in many commercial database systems [36, p. 535]).

We compiled all programs using the `GNU C++` compiler (version 2.8), with -O2 level of optimization.

5.3   Data Sets

The TIGER/Line data set from the US Bureau of the Census [35] is one of the standard benchmarks for spatial databases. Its current distribution consists of

six CD-ROMs of data. We extracted the hydrographic and road features of the
entire United States and created six data sets of different sizes (see Table 2).
The two smallest sets consist of the state of New Jersey (NJ) and New York
(NY), respectively. These sets were also used in our previous experiments with
PBSM and *SSSJ* [4]. The data on the first disk (DISK1) covers 15 states from
the Eastern US. The data on disks 4-6 (DISK4-6) covers the Western half of the
US, while the data on disks 1-3 (DISK1-3) covers the Eastern half. Our largest
data set is obtained from all six disks (DISK1-6).

The sizes given in Table 2 refer to files containing the MBRs of each feature.
Each MBR occupies 20 bytes (16 bytes for the corner coordinates, 4 bytes for the
ID), and each output item is a pair of IDs corresponding to overlapping MBRs.

Table 2. Bounding rectangles of the TIGER/Line 97 data sets.

Category		NJ	NY	DISK1	DISK4-6	DISK1-3	DISK1-6
"Road"	Objects	414,442	870,412	6,030,844	11,888,474	17,199,848	29,088,173
	Data	7.9 MB	16.6 MB	115.0 MB	226.7 MB	328.0 MB	554.8 MB
	R-tree	8.3 MB	17.7 MB	122.8 MB	245.8 MB	352.5 MB	598.4 MB
"Hydro"	Objects	50,853	156,567	1,161,906	3,446,094	3,967,649	7,413,353
	Data	1.0 MB	3.0 MB	22.1 MB	65.7 MB	75.6 MB	141.4 MB
	R-tree	1.1 MB	3.3 MB	25.0 MB	74.6 MB	85.5 MB	160.2 MB
Output	Objects	130,756	421,110	3,197,520	8,554,133	9,378,642	17,938,533
	Data	1.0 MB	3.2 MB	24.4 MB	65.3 MB	71.6 MB	136.9 MB

In addition to the disk space required to hold the original data and the spatial
index, we need scratch space for temporary files created during the preprocessing.
Since bulk loading an R-tree requires a sorting step, we had to store both the
unsorted and the sorted stream of rectangles on the local disk. Together with the
spatial index, the overall space requirement was a little more than three times
the size of the original data set, and therefore we were unable to construct the
R-trees for the largest data sets on Machine 1.

6   Experimental Results

In this section, we present some of the results of an extensive experimental study
of the performance of the four algorithms described in the previous sections.
We measured I/O cost, internal computation time, and memory requirements.
We consider two different measures of the I/O cost: the total number of I/O
operations performed, and the actual time taken by the I/O operations. The first
set of experiments, discussed in the next section, considers the internal memory
requirements of the new *PQ* join algorithm and verifies that its data structures
indeed fit in internal memory. In Section 6.2 we compare the performance of the
two index-based algorithms (*PQ* and *ST*). Finally, in Section 6.3 we compare
the running times of all four algorithms.

6.1 Memory Requirements of PQ

The space requirements of PQ on the different data sets are shown in Table 3. The space requirement is measured as the size of the sweep-line data structures plus the size of the priority queues. The latter includes the actual STL priority queues as well as the buffers needed to hold the currently active sorted lists of MBR's as described in Section 4. We see that even though the priority queue is significantly larger than the sweep-line structure, it nevertheless easily fits in memory even on the largest data set. In particular, the size of the priority queue is always less than 1% of the total data set.

Table 3. Maximal memory usage (in MB) for the PQ Join algorithm

Data Structure	NJ	NY	Disk1	Disk4-6	Disk1-3	Disk1-6
Priority Queue	0.32	0.76	1.44	2.72	3.65	4.99
Sweep Structure	0.09	0.10	0.12	0.15	0.17	0.20
Total	0.41	0.86	1.56	2.87	3.82	5.19

6.2 Comparison of Indexed Joins

A common measure for the I/O efficiency of index-based algorithms is the number of pages requested by read or write operations. In this section, we consider the I/O efficiency of the index-based join algorithms ST and PQ under this measure and compare the results to the actual running times of the algorithms.

Page Accesses. In Table 4, we show the number of pages requested by ST and PQ. We give the total number of page requests as well as the average number of requests per R-tree node. These numbers are independent of the machine used, since internal memory and logical page sizes are identical for all machines. The "lower bound" refers to the number of pages occupied by the indexes.

Table 4. Number of pages requested during joining.

Method	Requests	NJ	NY	Disk1	Disk4-6	Disk1-3	Disk1-6
Lower Bound	Total	1,198	2,706	18,917	41,011	56,061	97,096
	Avg.	1.00	1.00	1.00	1.00	1.00	1.00
PQ Join	Total	1,198	2,706	18,917	41,011	56,061	97,096
	Avg.	1.00	1.00	1.00	1.00	1.00	1.00
ST Join	Total	1,196	2.704	27,001	66,937	63,823	112,323
	Avg.	1.00	1.00	1.43	1.63	1.14	1.16

As expected, the number of page requests for PQ is optimal. In fact, PQ is guaranteed to be optimal as long as its data structures fit into internal memory. The numbers for ST, on the other hand, vary quite widely. There are two factors that affect the number of page accesses of ST: the heuristic for restricting the search space and the depth first-search traversal mechanism. The first factor decreases the set of pages that need to be touched, while the second results in many pages being requested more than once. For the small data sets (NJ and NY), the entire indexes fit in the buffer pool, so no page needs to be requested more than once *from disk*. Furthermore, we can directly see the positive effect of restricting the search space since the number of pages requested by *ST* is actually slightly less than the "lower bound". As the trees become larger than the buffer pool, the number of page requests increases significantly, with each page being requested between 1.14 and 1.63 times on the average.

Estimated Running Times. The simple method of counting the number of disk accesses has been used in several papers on index-based spatial joins in order to compare the performance of spatial join algorithms; see, e.g., [8,16,24]. The estimate for the running time is commonly obtained by multiplying the number of page requests by the average disk block read access time, and then adding the measured internal computation time. In Figure 2(a)–(c) we show the resulting estimated running times for *ST* and *PQ* on all three machines. Here and in the following, we suppress the results for NJ for reasons of readability. The total CPU cost is the sum of the amounts of time spent in *user* and *system* mode as reported by the `getrusage` function call. This time was added to the I/O cost estimated as described above.

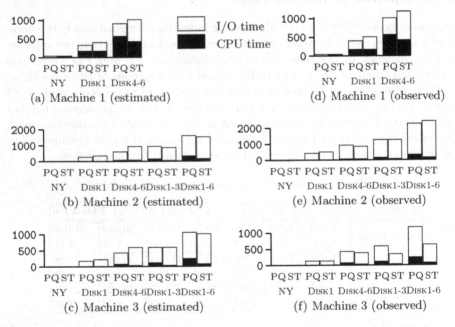

Fig. 2. Join costs (in seconds) for all machines: estimated (a)–(c) and observed (d)–(f).

Using the estimated running times, there is no clear winner between the two algorithms. On Machine 1, with the slowest processor and a relatively fast disk, *PQ* seems to have a slight advantage. On the two faster machines, however,

PQ does significantly more CPU work, while ST spends more time on I/O. The higher CPU cost of PQ is mainly due to the various internal memory data structures.

Actual Running Times. The above estimates are based on the assumption that page requests are random. While this may be true in some situations (e.g., index structures that are built in an ad-hoc fashion, or database servers that handle multiple interfering requests), it is not clear to what degree it applies to packed or bulk-loaded spatial index structures where neighbors in the index are often located closely together on the disk.

To investigate whether such issues significantly affect performance, we considered the actual running times of ST and PQ. We made sure that no other processes were running on the machines, and measured the overall running time using the `gettimeofday` function call. The CPU usage time was determined as before, but the I/O cost was now determined by calculating the difference between the overall running time and the CPU usage time. The measured running times of PQ and ST are shown in Figure 2(d)–(f). Note that they are significantly different from the estimated times in Figure 2(a)–(c). In particular, on Machine 3, which has both the fastest CPU and disk, ST is significantly faster than PQ on the larger data sets, while the estimated times are nearly equal.

To explain the above behavior, we note that most R-tree bulk-loading algorithms—including the one we used—construct an index structure in a sequential bottom-up fashion that causes all children of a node to be allocated sequentially. Thus, if there is only one process allocating pages, it is most likely that the children will be laid out sequentially on disk, and, in the best case, may even reside on the same track. ST traverses the trees in a depth first search manner, which means that all leaf nodes having the same parent are loaded consecutively. Since the leaves are by far the largest part of the tree, ST could perform significant amounts of sequential I/O on the bulk-loaded trees. PQ, on the other hand, basically performs random I/Os that do not depend on the way the tree is layed out on disk. As the sweep-line of PQ is advancing, nodes are read more or less randomly from the different parts of the tree that intersect with the sweep-line. This effect becomes more pronounced as the size of the tree increases. However, we expect that the performance of ST will degrade on systems running multiple processes with interfering requests, whereas the behavior of PQ should be roughly the same. An indication of such an effect can be found in the relative performance of ST on Machine 2. The on-disk buffer on this disk is significantly smaller than that of the other machines (128 KB vs. 512 KB), and on this machine we do not observe the same relative advantage of ST over PQ. Finally, note that the running times on Machine 1 are mainly determined by the internal computation times, since this machine has a fast disk and a fairly slow processor.

6.3 Running Times for All Algorithms

We now compare the measured running times of all four algorithms, the index-based ST and PQ algorithms and the non-index-based $PBSM$ and $SSSJ$ algorithms. Since $SSSJ$ and $PBSM$ access the data in a highly sequential fashion, we did not include them in the comparison between estimated and measured running times. The sequential access should give these algorithms an advantage relative to *PQ* and *ST*. On the other hand, *SSSJ* and *PBSM* access the data multiple times.

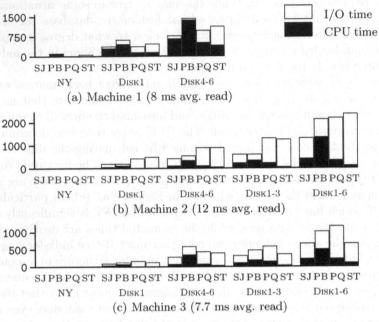

Fig. 3. Observed join costs (in seconds) for all machines.

The results are shown in Figure 3. With the exception of one experiment, *SSSJ* (SJ) always outperforms all other algorithms in terms of total running time even though it performs the largest number of I/Os. This difference in performance can be explained by taking the difference between random and sequential I/O into account. If, based on the disc specifications, we assume that a random read takes on average 10 times as much time as a sequential read and that a sequential write takes on average 1.5 times as much time as a sequential read, *SSSJ* performs the equivalent of $3n + (2n) * 1.5 = 6n$ sequential reads (*SSSJ* performs a total of 3 reads and 2 writes of the entire data), while *PQ* performs the equivalent of $10n$ sequential reads.

Note however, that in some cases index-based algorithms may not have to read the entire input data. This can happen when the join is performed between small localized portions of the input data sets, e.g., when joining hydrographic features from the state of Minnesota and road features of the entire United States. Here, *SSSJ* will still sort both data sets, though only a small clustered portion of the road relation needs to participate in the join. In such a case, index-based algorithms such as *ST* or *PQ*, which only traverse the relevant parts of an index, may be significantly more efficient.

In summary, *PQ* suffers in performance because it naively chooses to use an index whenever it one available. From the above arguments, we can see that, for the given disk configuration, it is advantageous to use the index only when the join involves less than 60% of the leaf nodes. An estimate of this number can be obtained using, e.g., the spatial histograms developed in [1]. Using such a cost-based approach to choose between the index-based and non-index based algorithms, PQ should have the best overall execution time in most cases.

We also comment on the relationship between our experiments and a similar set of experiments performed by Patel and DeWitt [30]. Their experiments, which compare $PBSM$ and ST, were conducted on a machine with a relative CPU/disk performance similar to our Machine 1. Our results match their observation that for such a configuration, the index-based ST is faster than the non-index based PBSM (see Figure 3(a)). (On the other hand, if the time spent on constructing the index is taken into consideration, the tree-based join ST is slower than $PBSM$.) Furthermore, our experiments extend their results in two ways. First, we demonstrate that the relative performance of spatial join algorithms depends heavily on the size of the data sets and the relative performance of the CPU and the I/O subsystems. Second, we show how index layout on disk can significantly influence the performance. The latter relates to whether one should take index loading time into consideration when comparing index-based spatial join algorithms. As we have seen, ST benefits from the layout produced by a good bulk-loading algorithm, and its performance may degrade if the R-tree is updated frequently after bulk loading.[2] Thus, it seems fair to take into account the costs for building or periodic rebuilding. On the other hand, since bulk loading essentially consists of (external) sorting of the data, there would have been no possibility of improving over the sorting based $SSSJ$, unless the cost of building or periodic rebuilding is amortized over several spatial join operations.

7   Conclusions and Open Problems

In this paper, we presented a simple algorithm that unifies the index based and non-index based spatial join approaches. Under reasonable assumptions about the input data, our algorithm is guaranteed to perform an optimal number of I/O operations. We also presented the results of an extensive set of experiments on real-life data that shows that it is important to take into account the difference between sequential and random I/O when designing spatial join algorithms for massive data sets.

The performance of the index-based algorithms depends heavily on the properties of the spatial index structure. Not surprisingly, tightly packed space-efficient index structures perform better than structures that achieve a lower space utilization or that do not map adjacent leaves of the tree to consecutive locations on disk. It remains an open problem to incorporate these properties of bulk-loaded index structures into testbeds and performance models for spatial join algorithms.

---

[2] Note, however, that Kim and Cha [18] have recently described how to locally reorganize the tree during updates to maintain a good layout of sibling nodes.

Acknowledgments

We thank Jignesh Patel for clarifications on implementation details of PBSM.

References

1. S. Acharya, V. Poosala, and S. Ramaswamy. Selectivity estimation in spatial databases. In *Proc. SIGMOD Intl. Conf. on Management of Data*, pages 13–24, 1999.

2. L. Arge. The buffer tree: A new technique for optimal I/O-algorithms. In *Proc. Workshop on Algorithms and Data Structures, LNCS 955*, pages 334–345, 1995. A complete version appears as BRICS technical report RS-96-28, University of Aarhus.

3. L. Arge, R. Barve, O. Procopiuc, L. Toma, D. E. Vengroff, and R. Wickeremesinghe. *TPIE User Manual and Reference (edition 0.9.01a)*. Duke University, 1999. The manual and software distribution are available on the web at http://www.cs.duke.edu/TPIE/.

4. L. Arge, O. Procopiuc, S. Ramaswamy, T. Suel, and J. S. Vitter. Scalable sweeping-based spatial join. In *Proc. Intl. Conf. on Very Large Databases*, pages 570–581, 1998.

5. L. Arge, O. Procopiuc, S. Ramaswamy, T. Suel, and J. S. Vitter. Theory and practice of I/O-efficient algorithms for multidimensional batched searching problems. In *ACM-SIAM Symp. on Discrete Algorithms*, pages 685–694, 1998.

6. L. Becker, K. Hinrichs, and U. Finke. A new algorithm for computing joins with grid files. In *Proc. IEEE Intl. Conf. on Data Engineering*, pages 190–197, 1993.

7. N. Beckmann, H.-P. Kriegel, R. Schneider, and B. Seeger. The R*-tree: An efficient and robust access method for points and rectangles. In *Proc. SIGMOD Intl. Conf. on Management of Data*, pages 322–331, 1990.

8. T. Brinkhoff, H.-P. Kriegel, and B. Seeger. Efficient processing of spatial joins using R-trees. In *Proc. SIGMOD Intl. Conf. on Management of Data*, pages 237–246, 1993.

9. G. S. Brodal and J. Katajainen. Worst-case efficient external-memory priority queues. In *Proc. Scandinavian Workshop on Algorithms Theory, LNCS 1432*, pages 107–118, 1998.

10. D. J. DeWitt, N. Kabra, J. M. Patel, and J.-B. Yu. Client-server Paradise. In *Proc. Intl. Conf. on Very Large Databases*, pages 558–569, 1994.

11. M. Goodrich, J.-J. Tsay, D. E. Vengroff, and J. S. Vitter. External-memory computational geometry. In *Proc. IEEE Symp. on Foundations of Computer Science*, pages 714–723, 1993.

12. O. Günther. Efficient computation of spatial joins. In *Proc. IEEE Intl. Conf. on Data Engineering*, pages 50–59, 1993.

13. R. H. Güting and W. Schilling. A practical divide-and conquer algorithm for the rectangle intersection problem. *Information Sciences*, 42:95–112, 1987.

14. A. Guttman. R-trees: A dynamic index structure for spatial searching. In *Proc. SIGMOD Intl. Conf. on Management of Data*, pages 47–57, 1984.

15. E. G. Hoel and H. Samet. A qualitative comparison study of data structures for large linear segment databases. In *Proc. SIGMOD Intl. Conf. on Management of Data*, pages 205–214, 1992.

16. Y.-W. Huang, N. Jing, and E. Rundensteiner. Spatial joins using R-trees: Breadth-first traversal with global optimizations. In *Proc. Intl. Conf. on Very Large Databases*, pages 396–405, 1997.
17. I. Kamel and C. Faloutsos. On packing R-trees. In *Proc. Intl. Conf. on Information and Knowledge Management*, pages 47–57, 1993.
18. K. Kim and S. K. Cha. Sibling clustering of tree-based spatial indexes for efficient spatial query processing. In *Proc. ACM Intl. Conf. Information and Knowledge Management*, pages 398–405, 1998.
19. M. Kitsuregawa, L. Harada, and M. Takagi. Join strategies on KD-tree indexed relations. In *Proc. IEEE Intl. Conf. on Data Engineering*, pages 85–93, 1989.
20. N. Koudas and K. C. Sevcik. Size separation spatial join. In *Proc. SIGMOD Intl. Conf. on Management of Data*, pages 324–335, 1996.
21. M.-L. Lo and C. V. Ravishankar. Spatial joins using seeded trees. In *Proc. SIGMOD Intl. Conf. on Management of Data*, pages 209–220, 1994.
22. M.-L. Lo and C. V. Ravishankar. Generating seeded trees from data sets. In *Proc. Intl. Symp. on Spatial Databases, LNCS 951*, pages 328–347, 1995.
23. M.-L. Lo and C. V. Ravishankar. Spatial hash-joins. In *Proc. SIGMOD Intl. Conf. on Management of Data*, pages 247–258, 1996.
24. N. Mamoulis and D. Papadias. Integration of spatial join algorithms for joining multiple inputs. In *Proc. SIGMOD Intl. Conf. on Management of Data*, pages 1–12, 1999.
25. N. Mamoulis, D. Papadias, and Y. Theodoridis. Processing and optimization of multiway spatial joins using R-trees. In *Proc. Symp. on Principles of Database Systems*, pages 44–55, 1999.
26. D. R. Musser and A. Saini. *STL Tutorial and Reference Guide: C++ Programming with the Standard Template Library*. Addison-Wesley, 1996.
27. J. Nievergelt, H. Hinterberger, and K. C. Sevcik. The grid file: An adaptable, symmetric multikey file structure. *ACM Trans. on Database Systems*, 9(1):38–71, March 1984.
28. J. A. Orenstein. A comparison of spatial query processing techniques for native and parameter spaces. In *Proc. SIGMOD Intl. Conf. on Management of Data*, pages 343–352, 1990.
29. J. A. Orenstein and F. A. Manola. PROBE spatial data modeling and query processing in an image database application. *IEEE Trans. on Software Engineering*, 14(5):611–629, May 1988.
30. J. M. Patel and D. J. DeWitt. Partition based spatial-merge join. In *Proc. SIGMOD Intl. Conf. on Management of Data*, pages 259–270, 1996.
31. F. P. Preparata and M. I. Shamos. *Computational Geometry: An Introduction*. Springer, Berlin, 2nd edition, 1988.
32. D. Rotem. Spatial join indices. In *Proc. IEEE Intl. Conf. on Data Engineering*, pages 500–509, 1991.
33. H. Samet. *The Design and Analysis of Spatial Data Structures*. Addison-Wesley, 1990.
34. T. Sellis, N. Roussopoulos, and C. Faloutsos. The R^+-tree: A dynamic index for multi-dimensional objects. In *Proc. Intl. Conf. on Very Large Databases*, pages 507–518, 1987.
35. *TIGER/Line*^{TM} *Files, 1997 Technical Documentation*. Washington, DC, September 1998. http://www.census.gov/geo/tiger/TIGER97D.pdf.
36. U. Vahalia. *UNIX Internals: The New Frontiers*. Prentice Hall, 1996.
37. P. Valduriez. Join indices. *ACM Trans. on Database Systems*, 12(2):218–246, June 1987.

Parametric Rectangles: A Model for Querying and Animation of Spatiotemporal Databases*

Mengchu Cai, Dinesh Keshwani, and Peter Z. Revesz

University of Nebraska-Lincoln, Lincoln, NE 68588, USA

Abstract We propose *parametric rectangles* — cross products of intervals whose end points are functions of time — as a new data model for representing, querying, and animating spatiotemporal objects with continuous and periodic change. We prove that the model is closed under relational algebra and new spatiotemporal operators and that relational algebra queries can be evaluated in PTIME in the size of any input quadratic non-periodic parametric rectangle database. Finally, we also describe the implementation in our PReSTO database system.

1 Introduction

Many spatiotemporal objects such as clouds, cars, deserts, lakes, planets, ships and tornados change position or shape continuously and also sometimes periodically. Although in the last decade substantial research was done independently in spatial [16,22] and temporal [18] data modeling, continuously changing objects require new data models that can capture the interdependency of the spatial and temporal extents of these objects.

We introduce a new approach to modeling spatiotemporal objects based on the use of n-dimensional parametric rectangles (or boxes), which are moving objects specified as the cross product of intervals that are parallel to the axes and whose endpoints are functions of time. In our model, each spatiotemporal object is represented by a finite set of parametric rectangles. We provide a PTIME evaluable query language by generalizing the relational algebra to our model. We also add to the query language some spatiotemporal operators like *block, collide, deflect, granulate, scale* and *shift* that facilitate novel applications.

An advantage of our model is the combination of efficient querying with efficient animation of objects. Most other spatiotemporal data models have difficulty combining effectively these two functions (see Section 7). We implemented a system –PReSTO (short for *Parametric Rectangle Spatio-Temporal Objects*)– that proves that the combination is effective in practice as well as theory.

The paper is structured as follows. Section 2 describes the parametric rectangle data model and illustrates how to represent spatiotemporal objects in this model. Section 3 defines the query language by generalizing relational algebra and proves that the evaluation of queries is in PTIME in the size of the database.

---

* The third author was supported by NSF grant IRI-9625055 and a Gallup Research Professorship. Contacts: revesz@cse.unl.edu and http://cse.unl.edu/~revesz

C. Zaniolo et al. (Eds.): EDBT 2000, LNCS 1777, pp. 430–444, 2000.

Section 3 also introduces some new operators for spatiotemporal queries. Section 4 describes the animation approach. Section 5 presents implementation results. Section 6 discusses the mapping from raster-based spatiotemporal objects to 2D parametric rectangles. Finally, Section 7 covers related work.

2 Parametric Rectangle Data Model

2.1 Parametric Rectangles

A n-dimensional rectangle is the cross product of n intervals, each in a different dimension. If the lower and upper bounds of the intervals are functions of time, then the rectangle is called a *parametric rectangle*. Formally, let $\mathbf{R}$ denote the set of real numbers, and $\mathbf{R}^+$ the set of non-negative real numbers.

Definition 1. A n-dimensional *parametric rectangle* r is a tuple:

$$\langle x_1^[, \ x_1^], \ldots, x_n^[, \ x_n^], \ from, \ to \rangle$$

where for each $i = 1, \ldots, n$, the lower and the upper bounds of an interval in the ith dimension, denoted $x_i^[$ and $x_i^]$, are functions $(\mathbf{R}^+ \to \mathbf{R})$ of time t applicable when $t \in [from, \ to]$, and $from$ and to are constants in $\mathbf{R}^+$.

The semantics of r, denoted by $sem(r)$, is a polyhedron in $n+1$ dimensional space defined as follows:

$$sem(r) = \{ \ (x_1, \ldots, x_n, t) \mid \forall_{1 \le i \le n} \ x_i \in [x_i^[(t), \ x_i^](t)], \ t \in [from, \ to] \}$$

We call m-degree those parametric rectangles in which the bounds are at most m-degree polynomial functions of time. We also call $m = 1$ and $m = 2$ degree parametric rectangles linear and quadratic, respectively.

Example 1. The semantics of the parametric rectangle $r = \langle 5 - t, 10 + t, 4 - t, 6 + t, 0, 3 \rangle$, is the polyhedron in x, y and t dimensions as shown in Figure 1.

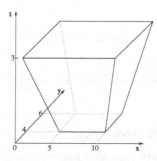

Fig. 1. Semantics of the Parametric Rectangle

Example 2. Suppose that a sail boat which at time $t = 0$ occupies the space $9 \le x \le 19$, $10 \le y \le 20$ first moves east with a speed of 5 ft/sec until $t = 10$. Then it goes northeast until $t = 20$, with a speed of 10 ft/sec in both the x and y axes. Finally, it goes north with a speed of 8 ft/sec until $t = 25$. We can represent the sail boat by 3 parametric rectangles, as shown in Table 1.

Table 1. Parametric rectangles for the sail boat

x^l	x^j	y^l	y^j	from	to
$9 + 5t$	$19 + 5t$	10	20	0	10
$59 + 10(t - 10)$	$69 + 10(t - 10)$	$10 + 10(t - 10)$	$20 + 10(t - 10)$	10	20
159	169	$110 + 8(t - 20)$	$120 + 8(t - 20)$	20	25

Example 3. Suppose that a plane drops a bomb at $t = 0$ to hit a target as shown in Figure 2. The bomb can be represented by a quadratic parametric rectangle as shown in Table 2.

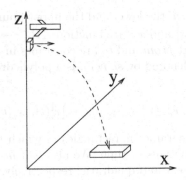

Fig. 2. The trajectory of the bomb

Table 2. Parametric rectangles for the bomb

x^l	x^j	y^l	y^j	z^l	z^j	from	to
t	$t + 1$	t	$t+1$	$100 - 9.8t^2$	$102 - 9.8t^2$	0	3.19

2.2 Periodic Parametric Rectangle

Some spatiotemporal objects can also move periodically, for example, shuttle buses and planets in the solar system. It is not possible to finitely represent these periodic objects by the parametric rectangles that we have discussed so far. Hence we extend the parametric rectangle concept to *periodic parametric rectangle* by adding a parameter as follows:

Definition 2. A *periodic parametric rectangle* r is a tuple of the form

$$\langle x_1^[, x_1^], \ldots, x_n^[, x_n^], from, to, period \rangle$$

where *period* is a non-negative integer constant such that $period = 0$ or $period \geq (to - from)$, and all the other parameters are as in Definition 1.

The semantics of r is the semantics of a set of parametric rectangles $r_0, r_1, \ldots$ such that $r_0 \equiv \langle x_1^[, x_1^], \ldots, x_n^[, x_n^], from, to \rangle$ and r_k exists between $from + k * period$ and $to + k * period$. Further, r_k at time t is identical to r_0 at time $t - k * period$. More precisely:

$$sem(r) \equiv sem(\bigcup_{k \geq 0} \{\langle\, x_1^[(t - k * period), x_1^] (t - k * period), \ldots, x_n^[(t - k * period),$$
$$x_n^] (t - k * period), from + k * period, to + k * period \,\rangle\})$$

In particular, when $period = 0$, then $sem(r) \equiv sem(\{r_0\})$.

We call *non-periodic* parametric rectangles those in which $period = 0$.

Example 4. Suppose there is a shuttle bus running every 30 minutes around a route as shown in Figure 3. We can represent it by 6 periodic parametric

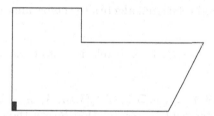

Fig. 3. Route of shuttle bus

rectangles, in a relation *shuttle*, as shown in Table 3.

Table 3. Periodic parametric rectangles for the *shuttle* relation

$x^[$	$x^]$	$y^[$	$y^]$	$from$	to	$period$
0	1	$6t$	$6t + 1$	0	5	30
$5(t - 5)$	$1 + 5(t - 5)$	30	31	5	9	30
20	21	$30 - 4(t - 9)$	$31 - 4(t - 9)$	9	11.5	30
$20 + 6(t - 11.5)$	$21 + 6(t - 11.5)$	20	21	11.5	19	30
$65 - 5(t - 19)$	$66 - 5(t - 19)$	$20 - 4(t - 21)$	$21 - 4(t - 21)$	19	24	30
$40 - 8(t - 24)$	$41 - 8(t - 24)$	0	1	24	29	30

2.3   Parametric Rectangle Database

Definition 3. Let $\mathcal{P}$ denote the set of all parametric rectangles, and $\mathcal{U}$ a finite set of attributes. Let $A_1, \ldots, A_k$ be elements of $\mathcal{U}$. For each A_i there is an attribute domain $Dom(A_i)$ associated with it. Let $\square$ be a special attribute such that $Dom(\square) = \mathcal{P}$ and $\square.x_i$ the interval for the ith dimension. A *parametric rectangle tuple* r on $\square, A_1, \ldots, A_k$ is a tuple in $Dom(\square) \times Dom(A_1) \times \ldots \times Dom(A_k)$.

The semantics of a parametric rectangle tuple $r = \langle r_1, a_1, \ldots, a_k \rangle$ is the cross product of the semantics of the parametric rectangle r_1 with the values $a_1, \ldots, a_k$.

A *parametric rectangle relation* is a finite set R of parametric rectangle tuples. The semantics of R is the union of the semantics of each tuple in R. An instantiation of R at time t_1, denoted by $R(t_1)$ is the union of instantiations of all tuples in R at time t_1. A *parametric rectangle database* is a finite set of parametric rectangle relations. In the following, by relations we mean parametric rectangle relations.

3   Querying Parametric Rectangle Databases

3.1   Relational Algebra for the Parametric Rectangle Model

In this section we extend relational algebra to the parametric rectangle database model.

Definition 4. Let R_1 and R_2 be two relations over the same set of attributes $\square, A_1, \ldots, A_k$.

- *projection* ($\hat{\pi}_Y$) Let $Y \subseteq \{\square, \square.x_1, \ldots, \square.x_n, A_1, \ldots, A_k\}$. The projection of R_1 on Y, denoted by $\hat{\pi}_Y(R_1)$, is a relation R over the attributes Y such that

$$R = \{r : \exists r_1 \in R_1, \forall A \in Y, \text{ the values of } A \text{ in } r \text{ and } r_1 \text{ are equal}\}$$

- *selection* ($\hat{\sigma}$) Let E be the conjunction of a set of comparison predicates in the form $A\,\theta\,c$ or $A\,\theta\,B$, where c is a constant, $A, B \in \{A_1, \ldots, A_k\}$, $\theta \in \{=, <, <=, >, >=\}$ and A,B are distinct. The selection $\hat{\sigma}_E(R_1)$ is a relation R containing the parametric rectangle tuples in R_1 whose attribute values satisfy E.
- *intersection* ($\hat{\cap}$) The intersection of R_1, R_2, denoted by $R_1 \hat{\cap} R_2$, is a relation R over attributes $A_1, \ldots, A_k$ such that

$$sem(R) = sem(R_1) \cap sem(R_2)$$

- *union* ($\hat{\cup}$) The union of R_1, R_2, denoted by $R_1 \hat{\cup} R_2$, is a relation R over attributes $A_1, \ldots, A_k$ that contains all tuples in R_1 and R_2.

$$sem(R) = sem(R_1) \cup sem(R_2)$$

- *difference* ($\hat{-}$) The difference of R_1, R_2, denoted by $R_1 \hat{-} R_2$, is a relation R over attributes $A_1, \ldots, A_k$ such that

$$sem(R) = sem(R_1) \setminus sem(R_2)$$

- *complement* ($\hat{\neg}$) Let R be a relation with only the $\square$ attribute. The complement of R, denoted by $\hat{\neg} R$ is also a parametric rectangle relation R' with the $\square$ attribute, such that

$$sem(R') = \{(x, y, t) : (x, y, t) \notin sem(R)\}$$

The unary operators have higher precedence than the binary operators. Intersection ($\hat{\cap}$) has higher precedence than union ($\hat{\cup}$) and difference ($\hat{-}$). A *relational algebra expression* over parametric rectangle databases is built up in the standard way, using the operators in Definition 4.

Theorem 1. *For any fixed n, any relational algebra expression can be evaluated in PTIME in the size of the input quadratic non-periodic parametric rectangle database, where each parametric rectangle is within the same n dimensions.* $\square$

Theorem 2. *Linear periodic parametric rectangle databases are closed under the relational algebra operators.* $\square$

Example 5. Suppose there is a ship represented by the relation *ship*, and a torpedo has just been fired towards the ship. The torpedo is represented by the relation *torpedo*. The relations are shown in Table 4.

Table 4. Parametric rectangles for the *ship* , *torpedo* and *hit* relations

ship

x^l	x^j	y^l	y^j	$from$	to	$period$
$20 + t$	$30 + t$	20	25	0	25	0

torpedo

x^l	x^j	y^l	y^j	$from$	to	$period$
45	48	$45 - t$	$51 - t$	0	25	0

hit

x^l	x^j	y^l	y^j	$from$	to	$period$
45	48	$45 - t$	25	20	25	0

Query: "Will the torpedo hit the ship?"
ship $\hat{\cap}$ *torpedo*
We can evaluate the intersection and represent it by a parametric rectangle relation *hit* as shown in Table 4.

Example 6. Suppose that the relation *clouds* has an attribute *humidity* which indicates the humidity of the cloud, and the clouds with humidity greater than 60 percent are called rain clouds.

Query: "Which of the clouds are rain clouds?"

$\hat{\sigma}_{humidity \geq 60}(clouds)$

Let *region* be a relation with an additional attribute *temperature*. Suppose that it rains when a rain cloud moves into a region where the temperature is between 0 and 20 degrees.

Query : "Which region is most likely to get rain?"

$\hat{\pi}_{\square}(\hat{\sigma}_{humidity \geq 60}(clouds)) \hat{\cap} \hat{\pi}_{\square}(\hat{\sigma}_{(temperature \geq 0 \wedge temperature \leq 20)}(region))$

Example 7. Consider the *shuttle* relation in Example 4. Let the relation *bus_stop* represent a bus-stop along the route of the shuttle bus. Suppose the relation *passenger* represents a man walking toward the bus-stop during some part of the day.

Query: "Will the passenger be able to catch the bus?"

$(shuttle \hat{\cap} bus\_stop) \hat{\cap} passenger$

Example 8. The nine planets of the solar system revolve around the sun in periodic orbits. They are represented by 3D periodic parametric rectangle relations *Mercury, Venus, ..., Pluto*. The motion of a comet is represented by the periodic relation *comet*.

Query: "Will the comet ever collide with any of the planets?"

$(Mercury \hat{\cup} Venus \hat{\cup} ... \hat{\cup} Pluto) \hat{\cap} comet)$

3.2   Block Operator

Some spatiotemporal applications need operators that are not provided in relational algebra. Let us consider the following example.

Example 9. There is a growing forest fire whose shape is approximated by the parametric rectangle tuple $\langle 4, 4, 20 + t, 20 + 0.5t, 0, 20, 0 \rangle$. A plane drops foam to extinguish the fire. Let us assume that the foam is represented by the tuple $\langle 20, 25, 20 - t, 25, 0, 20, 0 \rangle$. Let *fire* and *foam* be relations, containing the above tuples. Suppose that parts of the fire are extinguished when they meet the foam. Other parts continue to grow as before.

Query: "At time $t = 15$, what part of the forest is still on fire?"

Figure 4 (left) shows the instantiation of $fire - foam$ at time $t = 15$. The result does not correctly answer the query, because it fails to consider that some parts of the fire stop growing when they are extinguished.

To allow us to answer queries like the one above, we introduce a new operator called *block* that applies only to non-periodic 2D parametric rectangle relations. Note that the semantics of such relations allows us to view each non-periodic 2D parametric rectangle as a set of moving points (x, y) where x and y are linear functions of t.

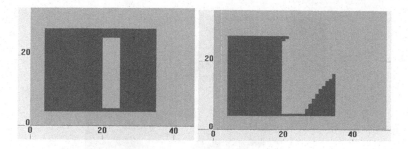

Fig. 4. The forest fire example with difference (left) and block (right)

Definition 5. Let R_1 and R_2 be two relations. R_1 *block* R_2 till some time t_k, denoted by $block(R_1, R_2, t_k)$, is the instantiation at t_k of the set of moving points in R_2 that did not intersect with R_1 any time before or at t_k. Formally,

$$block(R_1, R_2, t_k) = \{ ((x(t_k),\ y(t_k)) \mid \exists \ \langle x^[, x^], y^[, y^], from, to \rangle \in R_2,$$
$$0 \le \alpha \le 1,\ 0 \le \beta \le 1,$$
$$x = \alpha x^[+ (1 - \alpha)x^],\ \ y = \beta y^[+ (1 - \beta)y^],$$
$$\nexists t'\ from \le t' \le t_k \le to,\ (x(t'), y(t')) \in R_1(t') \}$$

Here is an efficient algorithm to approximate the result of *block* operation by recursion. In the algorithm we use a threshold *max_depth* to guarantee the termination of the recursion. Let R_1 and R_2 be the two input relations.

Procedure block(R_1, R_2, t_k)
    for each tuple $r_2 \in R_2$ **do**
        $R' = R' \cup blockrect(R_1, r_2, t_k, 0)$
    return R'

Procedure blockrect (R_1, r_2, t_k, d)
    if $\{r_2\} \cap R_1 = \emptyset$ **then return** $\{r_2\}$ at t_k
    else if at t_k $\{r_2\} \subseteq R_1$ **then return** $\emptyset$.
    else if $d < max\_depth$ **then** partition r_2 into quadrants r_{21}, r_{22}, r_{23}, r_{24}
        return $blockrect(R_1, r_{21}, t_k, d+1) \cup \ldots \cup blockrect(R_1, r_{24}, t_k, d+1)$

Now the forest fire query in Example 9 (see also Figure 4) can be written as:

$$block(foam, fire, 15)$$

Example 10. Suppose that *tornado* is a relation that represents the movement of a tornado in an area represented by the relation *region*.
Query: "What is the trajectory of the tornado at time t = 20?"
block(tornado, region, 20)
The result of the query, evaluated in the PReSTO system, is shown in Figure 5.

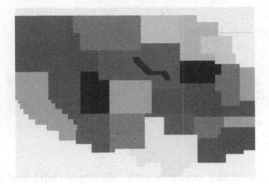

Fig. 5. Result of $block(tornado, region, 20)$ in the PReSTO system

3.3 Collide Operator

Another possible interaction between spatiotemporal objects is collision. Here we only consider the elastic collision between spatiotemporal objects which do not change their extent, that is, in them $x^\lceil$ and $x^\rfloor$ and also $y^\lceil$ and $y^\rfloor$ have the same coefficients of t. (An elastic collision is one in which both momentum and energy are conserved.) Suppose two objects are represented by the parametric rectangles r_1 and r_2 with an attribute *mass*. We define the collision of r_1 and r_2, denoted by $collide(r_1, r_2)$, as follows:

$$collide(r_1, r_2) = \begin{cases} \{r_1, \ r_2\} & \text{if } r_1 \cap r_2 = \emptyset \\ \{r_1', \ r_1'', \ r_2', \ r_2''\} & \text{otherwise} \end{cases}$$

where r_1' and r_2' represent r_1 and r_2 before collision and r_1'' and r_2'' represent them after the collision. It is easy to see that all parameters of r_1' and r_2', except to, are the same as those of r_1 and r_2 respectively. r_1'' and r_2'' are computed by the following algorithm. r_1 and r_2 can be viewed as spherical masses, with the x and y components of each one's velocity equal to its coefficients of t in $x^\lceil$ and $y^\lceil$ respectively.

1. Compute the time of the collision $t_c = \min_{r \in r_1 \cap r_2}(r.from)$, then $r_1''.from = r_2''.from = t_c$.
2. Let LC be the line joining the centers of the two objects at $t = t_c$. Decomposite the velocity of r_1 and r_2 along LC and the direction orthogonal to LC as shown in Figure 6.
3. Consider the collision as a "head-on" collision [5] between the objects along the LC. Compute the velocities of r_1 and r_2 along the LC after the collision by momentum and energy conservation equations. The velocities of r_1 and r_2 along the direction orthogonal to the LC do not change.
4. Let v_x and v_y denote the components of the velocity of r_1 after collision on the x and y axes, respectively.

$$r_1''.x^[= v_x(t - t_c) + r_1.x^[(t_c) \quad r_1''.x^] = v_x(t - t_c) + r_1.x^](t_c)$$
$$r_1''.y^[= v_y(t - t_c) + r_1.y^[(t_c) \quad r_1''.y^] = v_y(t - t_c) + r_1.y^](t_c)$$

The bound functions of r_2'' are computed similarly.

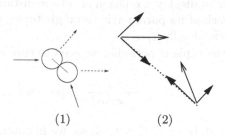

(1) (2)

Fig. 6. (1) Line joining centers (LC) at t_c (dotted) (2) Collision along LC

3.4   Deflect Operator

Given a linear 2D parametric rectangle r, the deflect operator, $deflect(r, \theta)$, changes the direction of r (that is, the direction of its center point) counter-clockwise by the angle θ. The resulting parametric rectangle r' is on the same interval $[from, to]$ as r and can be computed as follows. At $t = from$, r and r' are the same, and at $t > from$ they have the same width and height but different locations. Then find (v_x, v_y), the speed of the center of r along the x and y axes, and φ, the angle between the direction of r and the x-axis. The speed of the center of r' is $v_x' = \sqrt{v_x^2 + v_y^2} \cos(\varphi + \theta)$, $v_y' = \sqrt{v_x^2 + v_y^2} \sin(\varphi + \theta)$. From this we can specify the bounds of r'.

For example, if $r = \langle 4t - 10,\ 6t + 10, -t - 5,\ t + 5,\ 0,\ 10 \rangle$, then the operation $deflect(r, tan^{-1}(\frac{3}{4}))$ gives $r' = \langle 3t - 10,\ 5t + 10, 2t - 5,\ 4t + 5,\ 0,\ 10 \rangle$.

3.5   Scale Operator

For an n-dimensional parametric rectangle r, the scale operator, denoted by $scale(r, i, \alpha)$, will change $x_i^[$ into $x_i^[- \frac{\alpha}{2}(\Delta x_i)$ and $x_i^]$ into $x_i^] + \frac{\alpha}{2}(\Delta x_i)$ where $\Delta x_i = x_i^] - x_i^[$.

3.6   Temporal Operators

Given a parametric rectangle tuple $r = \langle x_1^[, x_1^], \ldots, x_n^[, x_n^], from, to \rangle$, the operator $shift(r, \beta)$ sets the time back β units. The result of this operator is the tuple: $\langle x_1^[(t+\beta), x_1^](t+\beta), \ldots, x_n^[(t+\beta), x_n^](t+\beta), from - \beta, to - \beta \rangle$. We also define the operator $granulate(r, \alpha)$ to change the time units to be $alpha$ times the current one. The result is: $\langle x_1^[(\frac{t}{\alpha}), x_1^](\frac{t}{\alpha}), \ldots, x_n^[(\frac{t}{\alpha}), x_n^](\frac{t}{\alpha}), \alpha from, \alpha to \rangle$.

4   Animation of Parametric Rectangle Databases

By animation, we mean a display of the instantiation of the relations in the database at successive time instants. Parametric rectangle databases can be easily animated. In order to display a relation at a time instant t_i, we need to first perform a check on each of its parametric rectangle tuples as follows:

If the tuple has $period = 0$, $t'_i = t_i$

Otherwise, since the tuple is periodic, we need to compute t'_i such that

$$t'_i = ti - \lfloor \frac{t_i - from}{period} \rfloor \cdot period$$

Now we can check if $from \leq t'_i \leq to$. If so, we instantiate the variable t by t'_i and obtain a rectangle defined by $\langle x^\lfloor(t'_i), x^\rfloor(t'_i), y^\lfloor(t'_i), y^\rfloor(t'_i) \rangle$.

Proceeding in this manner, we obtain a set of rectangles corresponding to the relation at time t_i. These can be displayed using standard graphics routines.

5   Implementation Results

We implemented the query language and animation algorithm in PReSTO (short for *Parametric Rectangle Spatio-Temporal Objects*) using Microsoft Visual C++.

Table 5 shows the execution times for the evaluation of three examples from Section 3. The torpedo-ship example was extended and the solar system example was projected into 2D. The results are shown in . The PReSTO system ran in Windows NT, on a 266 MHz Pentium II PC with 64 MB RAM.

Table 5. Query Evaluation Times

Example	Number of Tuples	Running Time (milliseconds)
torpedo-ship (Ex. 5 extended)	12	60
shuttle bus (Ex. 7)	35	200
solar system (Ex. 8 in 2D)	513	7500

We provided a graphical user interface through which the user can specify the following parameters: the name of the parametric rectangle relation, the initial time, the time period, the number of time-steps and the minimum delay time, which controls the speed of the animation. Each snapshot of the relation is displayed as soon as the animation algorithm returns the corner vertices of the rectangles to be displayed. The animation is extremely fast. Hence we did not include animation time as a part of the running time.

To demonstrate the animation capability of PReSTO, we have included two snapshots of a cloud moving over the United States, as shown in Figure 7.

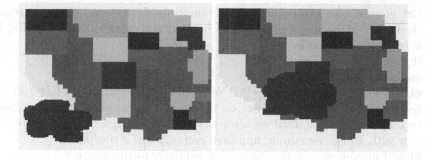

Fig. 7. Cloud at $t = 25$ (left) and $t = 182$ (right) in the PReSTO system

6 Mapping of Spatiotemporal Objects to Parametric Rectangles

Given the initial and final raster snapshots of a spatiotemporal object, we present an algorithm which runs in time linear in the size of the raster images, to approximate its motion by parametric rectangles.

For simplicity, let us assume that the given raster images are square, say $Init\_Pic[i, i]$, $Final\_Pic[f, f]$ where i, f are powers of 2. Also, we know the coordinates of the left lower corners of both images.

Without loss of generality, suppose $i \geq f$.

Procedure mapping
Input: $Init\_Pic[i, i]$, $Final\_Pic[f, f]$, t_{init}, t_{final}
Output: Parametric Rectangle Relation

1. We rectangulate the raster images as follows (See Figure 8):
   (a) Take the bigger image (here $Init\_Pic[i, i]$) and divide it into squares of size $r \times r$, where r equals $\frac{2i}{f}$. The number of such parametric rectangles will be $(\frac{i}{r})^2$. The number of rows of squares will be $\frac{i}{r}$.
   (b) For each of the squares, if the majority of the raster points of the square are within the object, mark the square as 'On'.
   (c) For each row of squares, combine adjacent squares that are marked 'On', to get one or more rectangles in each row.
   (d) Repeat Steps (a), (b) and (c) for the smaller image (here $Final\_Pic[f, f]$), using $r = 2$.

   Note: Step 1 will ensure that both $Init\_Pic$ and $Final\_Pic$ have the same number of rows of rectangles.
2. Next, we pair rectangles of the initial image with those of the final image. Assume that Step 1 results in the structures $Init[]$ and $Final[]$, where $Init[k]$ and $Final[k]$ refer to the kth row of rectangles in the initial and final images respectively. Repeat the following for each k:

Let m and n be the number of rectangles in $Init[k]$ and $Final[k]$ respectively. Let us assume $Init[k]$ has m horizontal rectangles, and $Final[k]$ has n horizontal rectangles

if $m = n$ then we simply pair the jth rectangle of $Init[k]$, with the jth rectangle of $Final[k]$ for $1 \leq j \leq m$.

else if $m < n$ then, let $d = \lfloor \frac{m}{n} \rfloor$. We pair the first rectangle of $Init[k]$ with the first d rectangles of $Final[k]$, the second rectangle with the second d rectangles and so on until we come to the mth rectangle of $Init[k]$, which we pair with all the remaining unpaired rectangles of $Final[k]$.

else if $m > n$, we can do the pairing similarly to the above.

3. Finally we compute the output relation, which consists of parametric rectangles corresponding to each pair of rectangles.
   (a) Suppose the rectangles in a pair are $[x_1, x_2] \times [y_1, y_2]$ and $[x_1', x_2'] \times [y_1', y_2']$, where the first one is from $Init[]$ and the second from $Final[]$.
   (b) Let the parametric rectangle corresponding to this pair be

$$\langle x^{[}, x^{]}, y^{[}, y^{]}, from, to \rangle$$

Clearly, $from = t_{init}$ and $to = t_{final}$. We know that $x^{[}$ is a linear function of t, say $at + b$. This implies that

$x^{[}(t_{init}) = a\, t_{init} + b$ and $x^{[}(t_{final}) = a\, t_{final} + b$

We also know that $x^{[}(t_{init}) = x_1$ and $f_l(t_{final}) = x_1'$. Since we know x_1, x_1', t_{init} and t_{final}, we can determine $x^{[}$. Similarly, we can determine $x^{]}, y^{[}$ and $y^{]}$.

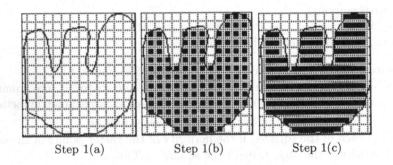

| Step 1(a) | Step 1(b) | Step 1(c) |

Fig. 8. Rectangulation of the image

Note: In the above algorithm, if the raster images dimensions are not powers of two, then we can use standard algorithms [10] to stretch or shrink a given image to a square image with dimension as the nearest power of 2. Our mapping provides a highly accurate approximation for a reasonable time interval. If the approximation is needed over larger intervals, it would be necessary to provide more snapshots during the interval, and call the algorithm for each sub-interval.

7   Related Work

Constraint databases with rational linear or real polynomial constraints can be used to represent spatiotemporal objects with continuous change [13,17]. They can be queried by relational algebra, which is quite powerful, although it cannot express some queries like parity and transitive closure [1].

The parametric 2-spaghetti data model [7] generalizes the 2-spaghetti data model [16] by allowing the corner vertices to be represented as linear functions of time. The parametric 2-spaghetti data model cannot represent polynomial (Example 3) and periodic (Example 4) parametric rectangles and cannot be queried by relational algebra, because it is not closed under intersection [7]. However, this model can represent linear constraint databases over two spatial and one temporal dimension [7] and can be used to animate such databases [6].

[8] represents spatiotemporal objects by a composition of a reference spatial extent at some reference time and various types of transformation functions. In this model, it is easy to obtain any snapshot of a spatiotemporal object, making animation straightforward. However, in some cases this model also may not be closed under intersection [8], and the query complexity may be high.

[9] defines continuously moving points and regions and an extended SQL query language on these objects. However, changing of object shape (shrinking and growing) and animation are not considered in this model.

[21] can only represent spatiotemporal objects with discrete change. This model can be queried by an extended relational algebra. [11] proposes another spatiotemporal data model based on constraints in which, like in [21], only discrete change can be modeled. An SQL based query language is also presented.

There are many data models to represent and query only temporal or only spatial data. For example, [2,12,19] can represent temporal objects with discrete change and periods. These models can be queried by either relational algebra or Datalog. Some other purely temporal or purely spatial data models are reviewed in [16,18,22]. We also did not deal with issues like visual query languages [3], indefinite information [15], query processing [4], nearest neighbor [14] and approximate queries [20]. We are currently investigating extensions in these directions.

References

1. M. Benedikt, G. Dong, L. Libkin, and L. Wong. Relational Expressive Power of Constraint Query Languages. *Journal of the ACM*, 45:1, pp. 1-34, 1998.
2. E. Bertino, C. Bettini, E. Ferrari, and P. Samarati. An Access Control Model Supporting Periodicity Constraints and Temporal Reasoning. *ACM Transactions on Database Systems*, 23:3, pp. 231-285, 1998.
3. C. Bonhomme, C. Trépied, M-A. Aufaure, R. Laurini. A Visual Language for Querying Spatio-Temporal Databases. *Proc. 7th ACM Symposium on Geographic Information Systems*, 34-39, Kansas City, MO, November 1999.
4. A. Brodsky, J. Jaffar, M. Maher. Towards Practical Query Evaluation for Constraint Databases. *Constraints*, 2:3-4, pp. 279-304, 1997.

5. M. Casco Associates. *Linear Momentum and Collisions: A Mechanics Course*, available at http://www.mcasco.com/p1lmc.html.

6. J. Chomicki, Y. Liu, and P.Z. Revesz. Animating Spatiotemporal Constraint Databases. In: *Proc. Workshop on Spatio-Temporal Database Management*, Springer-Verlag LNCS 1678, pp. 224-241, Edinburgh, Scotland, Sept. 1999.

7. J. Chomicki and P.Z. Revesz. Constraint-based Interoperability of Spatiotemporal Databases, *Geoinformatica*, 3:3, 1999. (Preliminary version In: *Proc. International Symposium on Large Spatial Databases*, Springer-Verlag LNCS 1262, pp. 142-161, Berlin, Germany, July 1997.)

8. J. Chomicki and P.Z. Revesz. A Geometric Framework for Specifying Spatiotemporal Objects. In: *Proc. International Workshop on Time Representation and Reasoning*, pp. 41-46, Orlando, Florida, May 1999.

9. M. Erwig, R.H. Güting, M.M. Schneider and M. Vazirgiannis. Spatio-Temporal Data Types: An Approach to Modeling and Querying Moving Objects in Databases. In: *Proc. ACM Symposium on Geographic Information Systems*, November 1998.

10. R. Gonzalez, R. Woods. *Digital Image Processing*, Addison-Wesley, 1998.

11. S. Grumbach, P. Rigaux, and L. Segoufin. Spatio-Temporal Data Handling with Constraints. In: *Proc. 6th ACM Symposium on Geographic Information Systems*, November 1998.

12. F. Kabanza, J-M. Stevenne, and P. Wolper. Handling Infinite Temporal Data. *Journal of Computer and System Sciences*, 51:1, pp. 1-25, 1995.

13. P. C. Kanellakis, G. M. Kuper, and P.Z. Revesz. Constraint Query Languages. *Journal of Computer and System Sciences*, 51:1, pp. 26-52, 1995.

14. G. Kollios, D. Gunopulos, and V.J. Tsotras. Nearest Neighbor Queries in a Mobile Environment. In: *Proc. Workshop on Spatio-Temporal Database Management*, Springer-Verlag LNCS 1678, pp. 119-134, Edinburgh, Scotland, September 1999.

15. M. Koubarakis and S. Skiadopoulos. Tractable Query Answering in Indefinite Constraint Databases: Basic Results and Applications to Querying Spatio-Temporal Information. In: *Proc. Workshop on Spatio-Temporal Database Management*, Springer-Verlag LNCS 1678, pp. 204-223, Edinburgh, Scotland, September 1999.

16. R. Laurini and D. Thompson. *Fundamentals of Spatial Information Systems*. Academic Press, 1992.

17. P.Z. Revesz. *Introduction to Constraint Databases*. Springer-Verlag, 1999.

18. A. Tansel, J. Clifford, S. Gadia, S. Jajodia, A. Segev, and R.T. Snodgrass. *Temporal Databases: Theory, Design, and Implementation*. Benjamin/Cummings Inc., Redwood City, California, 1993.

19. D. Toman, J. Chomicki, and D.S. Rogers. Datalog with Integer Periodicity Constraints. *Proc. International Symposium on Logic Programming*, pp. 189-203, Ithaca, New York, 1994.

20. D. Vasilis, M. Christos, and S. Spiros. A Provably Efficient Computational Model For Approximate Spatiotemporal Retrieval. In: *Proc. 7th ACM Symposium on Geographic Information Systems*, pp. 40-46, Kansas City, Missouri, November 1999.

21. M. F. Worboys. A Unified Model for Spatial and Temporal Information. *Computer Journal*, 37:1, pp. 25-34, 1994.

22. M. F. Worboys. *GIS: A Computing Perspective*, Taylor & Francis, 1995.

Systems & Applications

An Architecture for Archiving and Post-Processing Large, Distributed, Scientific Data Using SQL/MED and XML

Mark Papiani, Jasmin L. Wason, and Denis A. Nicole

Department of Electronics and Computer Science,
University of Southampton, Southampton, SO17 1BJ, UK.
{mp|jlw98r|dan}@ecs.soton.ac.uk

Abstract. We have developed a Web-based architecture and user interface for archiving and manipulating results of numerical simulations being generated by the UK Turbulence Consortium on the United Kingdom's new national scientific supercomputing resource. These simulations produce large datasets, requiring Web-based mechanisms for storage, searching and retrieval of simulation results in the hundreds of gigabytes range. We demonstrate that the new DATALINK type, defined in the draft SQL Management of External Data Standard, which facilitates database management of distributed external data, can help to overcome problems associated with limited bandwidth. We show that a database can meet the apparently divergent requirements of storing both the relatively small simulation result metadata, and the large result files, in a unified way, whilst maintaining database security, recovery and integrity. By managing data in this distributed way, the system allows post-processing of archived simulation results to be performed directly without the cost of having to rematerialise to files. This distribution also reduces access bottlenecks and processor loading. We also show that separating the user interface specification from the user interface processing can provide a number of advantages. We provide a tool to generate automatically a default user interface specification, in the form of an XML document, for a given database. The XML document can be customised to change the appearance of the interface. Our architecture can archive not only data in a distributed fashion, but also applications. These applications are loosely coupled to the datasets (in a many-to-many relationship) via XML defined interfaces. They provide reusable server-side post-processing operations such as data reduction and visualisation.

1   Introduction

We have been working with the UK Turbulence Consortium [1] to provide an architecture for archiving and manipulating the results of numerical simulations. One of the objectives of the consortium is to improve collaboration between groups working on turbulence by providing a mechanism for dissemination of data to members of the turbulence modelling community. The consortium is now running simulations on

C. Zaniolo et al. (Eds.): EDBT 2000, LNCS 1777, pp. 447-461, 2000.

larger grid sizes than has previously been possible, using the United Kingdom's new national scientific supercomputing resource.[1] One complete simulation, comprising perhaps one hundred timesteps, requires a total storage capacity of some hundreds of gigabytes. This necessitates new Web-based mechanisms for storage, searching and retrieval of multi-gigabyte datasets that are generated for each timestep in a simulation. In particular, an architecture is required that can minimise bandwidth usage whilst performing these tasks.

The Caltech Workshop on Interfaces to Scientific Data Archives [2] identified an urgent need for infrastructures that could manage and federate active libraries of scientific data. The workshop found that whilst databases were much more effective than flat files for storage and management purposes, trade-offs existed as the granularity of the data objects increased in size. If a database is being created to manage metadata describing scientific results, then ideally the database should also be used to store the actual scientific result data in a unified way. However for large output files it becomes costly and inefficient to store the data as binary large objects (BLOBS) within the database.

We describe a solution that uses an implementation of the new SQL:1999 (formerly known as SQL3, see for example [3]) DATALINK type, defined in *SQL Management of External Data (SQL/MED)* [4], to provide database management of scientific metadata and large, distributed result files simultaneously with integrity. We apply this technology to the Web, by providing a user-interface to securely manage large files in a distributed scientific archive, despite limited bandwidth.

A database table containing an attribute defined as a DATALINK type can store a URL that points to a file on a remote machine. Once a URL has been entered into the database, software running on the remote machine ensures that the file is treated as if it was actually stored in the database, in terms of security, integrity, recovery and transaction consistency. We use this mechanism to allow large result files to be distributed across the Web.

Our system generates a user interface, from a specification defined in Extensible Mark-up Language (XML) [5], to a database that supports DATALINKs. We have created an XML Document Type Definition (DTD) to define the structure of the XML file.

Our architecture provides the following features for scientific data archiving:

1. *The system can be accessed by users of the scientific archive, who may have little or no database or Web development expertise.* Users are presented with a dynamically generated HTML query form that provides a search interface akin to Query by Example (QBE) [6]. We generate this interface automatically from an XML user interface specification file (XUIS). The XUIS specifies the Web interface to a particular object-relational database (which may contain BLOBS and DATALINK types). This file is constructed automatically using metadata extracted from the da-

---

[1] A 576 processor Cray T3E-1200E situated at the University of Manchester, which forms part of the *Computer Services for Academic Research (CSAR)* service run on behalf of the UK Research Councils. http://www.csar.cfs.ac.uk/

tabase catalogue but can be customised to provide specialised features in the interface.

2. *The default interface specification adds a novel data browsing facility to maintain a Web-based feel.* Contrary to Manber's statement that finding ways to include browsing in even relational databases would be a great step [7], we show that one simple way to browse relational databases is to follow relationships between tables, implied by referential integrity constraints defined in the database catalogue. We use this principle to provide hypertext links in displayed results that access related information.

3. *Large result files can be archived at (or close to) the point where they are generated.* For the UK Turbulence Consortium, this means that files can be archived at the Manchester site on a local machine that is connected via a high-speed link to the supercomputer. By entering the URLs of these files into a DATALINK column of a remote database (via a Web-based interface to the remote database), database security and integrity features can then be applied to the files. An alternative to this, which achieves similar database security and integrity for result files, is to use a Web interface to upload a file across the Internet and then store it as a BLOB in a centralised archive at the new location. However, this alternative is not feasible for large files due to limited Internet bandwidth. Even if a file can be transferred to a centralised site, additional processing cost is incurred (which is not present with the DATALINK mechanism) when loading the file as a BLOB type into the database.

4. Because simulation results are stored in unmodified files, *existing post-processing applications, that use standard file I/O techniques, can be applied to the files without having to rewrite the applications.* An alternative would be to modify applications to first access result objects from a database but this would be very undesirable for many scientific users who often apply post-processing codes written in FORTRAN.

5. The Caltech workshop [2] recommended 'cheap supercomputers for archives'. The report suggests that research is necessary to establish whether high-performance computing resources, built from commodity components, are viable for data-intensive applications (as well as compute-intensive applications, as has been shown to be the case in for example, the Beowulf project [8]). *We are using our architecture to build a large scientific archive from commodity components, with many distributed machines acting as file servers for a single database.* Security, backup and integrity of the file servers can be managed using SQL/MED. This arrangement can provide high performance in the following areas:

   • Data can be distributed so that it is physically located closest to intensive usage.

   • Data distribution can reduce access bottlenecks at individual sites.

   • Each machine provides a distributed processing capability that allows multiple datasets to be post-processed simultaneously. Suitable user-directed post-processing, such as array slicing and visualisation, can significantly reduce the amount of data that needs to be shipped back to the user. Post-processing codes that have been archived by our system can be associated with remote data files using the XUIS. This allows dynamic server-side execution of the stored applications, with chosen datasets as input parameters.

The rest of this paper is structured as follows. Section 2 begins with a high level description of our architecture. We next describe how we use XML to specify customisable user interfaces with searching and browsing capabilities. We explain the functionality that SQL/MED brings to our architecture. Sections 3 describes some related work. Finally section 4 draws some conclusions from our work.

2   System Architecture and User Interface

This section starts with a high level view of our architecture. We then describe how XML is used to specify the functionality of the user interface. We show how our system supports two kinds of information retrieval, searching and browsing. We illustrate four different types of browsing links that our system can include automatically in Web pages displaying query results. 'DATALINK browsing' is particularly important in our architecture for managing large, distributed scientific data files. We therefore provide an overview of the DATALINK type defined in the draft SQL/MED standard. We also describe how the user interface can be customised through modifications to the XUIS, and how post-processing codes can extend the functionality of the interface by the inclusion of 'operations' in the XUIS.

2.1 System Architecture

The architecture of our system is shown in Fig 1. It consists of a database server host (located at Southampton University) and a number of file server hosts that may be located anywhere on the Internet. All of these hosts have an installed Web server to allow HTTP (or HTTPS – HTTP plus Secure Socket Layer) communications directly from a Web browser client.

A user of our system initially connects to the Web server on the database server host. The URL of our system invokes a Java Servlet [9] program. Separate threads within the Servlet process handle requests from multiple Web browser clients. Each user is first presented with a login screen. Once a user has been verified interaction with the database is possible via HTML pages that are dynamically generated by our Servlet code. These pages consist of HTML forms, Javascript and hypertext links.

The database server stores metadata describing the scientific information such as, simulation titles, descriptions and authors. This data is stored locally in the database and is accessed by our Servlet code using Java Database Connectivity (JDBC) [10]. The data is represented by tables with attributes defined as standard SQL-types, BLOB types, or CLOB (character large object) types. The latter types are used in our system to store *small* image/video files, executable code binaries or *small* ASCII files containing source code or descriptive material for the turbulence simulations.

For scientific data archiving, an essential feature of our interface is the novel use of remote file severs which store files referenced by attributes defined as DATALINK SQL-types. These file servers manage the *large* files associated with simulations, which have been archived where they were generated. When the result of a database access yields a DATALINK value, our interface presents this to the user as a hypertext link that can be used to download the referenced file. The URL contains an encrypted key that is prefixed to the required file name. This key is verified by DATALINK file manager code (running on the file server host) which intercepts attempts to access any files controlled by the remote database. Without this key, files cannot be accessed, either via the locally installed Web server or directly from the file system by a locally connected user. As well as allowing a user to simply download a dataset, our interface also allows user-selected post-processing codes to execute on the remote file server host to reduce the volume of data returned.

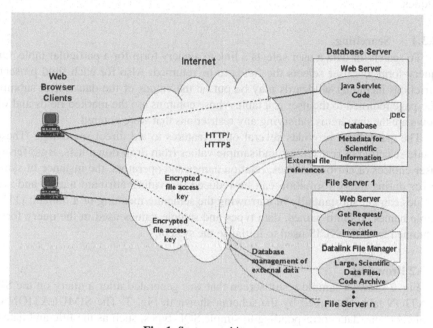

Fig. 1. System architecture

2.2 XML Specification of the User Interface

Our system is started by initialising the Java Servlet code with an XUIS. This initialisation can take several seconds but it is a one-off cost that is not repeated during subsequent requests from users. A default XUIS can be created prior to system initialisation using a tool that we provide. This tool, written in Java, uses JDBC to extract data and schema information from the database being used to archive simulation results. This default XUIS conforms to a DTD that we have created. The default XUIS can be customised prior to system initialisation. The XUIS contains table names, column names, column types, sample data values for each column, and details of primary keys and foreign keys that participate in referential integrity constraints. The XUIS also allows aliases to be defined for table and column names.

In the following sections we explain how this information is used to provide an interface with searching and browsing capabilities and how it facilitates customisation of the interface and dynamic execution of post-processing applications.

2.3   Searching and Browsing Data

After logging in users of our interface can begin to locate information in the scientific archive by searching or browsing data or by using a combination of both techniques.

2.3.1   Searching

To search for data a user selects a link to a query form for a particular table. On the query form, the user selects the fields to be returned. Also for each field present, restrictions including wildcards may be put on the values of the data. After submission the page returned to the user is a table whose columns are the marked fields and whose rows are the data items satisfying any restrictions that were entered.

The query form provides several other features to aid direct searching. These include selection of restrictions and sample values from drop-down lists. By offering the user choices of attribute names, relation names and operators, the instance of syntactic error during query formation can be reduced. Providing attribute names and sample values can aid substantially in narrowing the semantic meaning of a domain [11]. The table names, column names, data types and sample values used in the query form are obtained from the XUIS used to initialise the system.

2.3.2 Browsing

Fig. 2 shows a sample result screen that was generated after a query on the SIMULATION table described by the schema shown in Fig. 3. The SIMULATION result table contains data corresponding to simple SQL-types, such as the title and date for a simulation. It also contains a number of hypertext links. Our interface automatically inserts several different types of link that we describe below.

The SIMULATION result table (Fig. 2) displays a link on *each* AUTHOR_KEY attribute. This is because AUTHOR_KEY is a foreign key in the SIMULATION table that references the AUTHOR table (see Fig. 3). Selecting a link on an AUTHOR_KEY value will retrieve full details of the author by displaying the appropriate row from the AUTHOR table.

The inverse relationship provides a *primary key link* to a table in which the primary key value appears as a foreign key. Each individual SIMULATION_KEY value of Fig. 2 contains *a primary key link*. Because primary keys may appear in several tables as a foreign key, there may be a choice of tables to browse to. Selecting one of these values will return all the rows that the key appears in from one of the referenced tables. The particular table is indicated in the currently checked radio button in the column header.

The table of data returned by our software interface may be quite large. Cells associated with simple values, such as numbers or short character strings, display the actual values. As well as simple types, we also use BLOB and CLOB types, to store small files that can be uploaded over the Internet. Cells associated with these types display a *LOB link* to the object. Clicking on such a link causes the data associated with the cell to be rematerialised and returned to the client. The link displays the size of the object in bytes, which may help users decide whether they want to retrieve the object. For example, Fig. 3 indicates that the DESCRIPTION attribute in the SIMU-LATION table is a CLOB type. Selecting the hypertext links on the DESCRIPTION fields in Fig. 2 will retrieve the description and display it directly in the browser window since it contains character data. For BLOB data (e.g. a stored image or executable) selecting the link will allow the user to retrieve the data as a file.

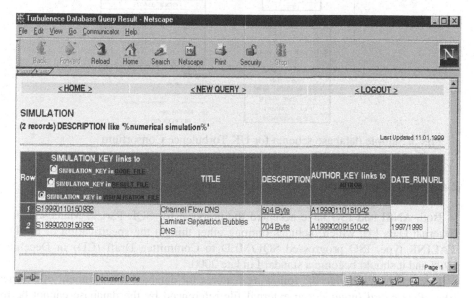

Fig. 2. Result table from querying SIMULATION table

The sample schema of Fig. 3 also contains three attributes of the DATALINK SQL-type. These DATALINK attributes serve the main purpose of our architecture – to archive large scientific data via the Web. The attributes in the Turbulence Consortium schema are used for storing result files, code files, and visualisation files. These values are displayed as a filename in a result table, with a hypertext link that contains an encrypted key, required to access the file from the remote file server (see section 2.4).

Hyperlinks on BLOB/CLOB and DATALINK types are included in the interface if the XUIS specifies a column as consisting of one of these types. Foreign key and primary key links are included in the XUIS by default if referential integrity constraints are available in the database metadata. If metadata describing referential integrity is not available, the XUIS can still be customised to include these hypertext links.

454   Mark Papiani, Jasmin L. Wason, and Denis A. Nicole

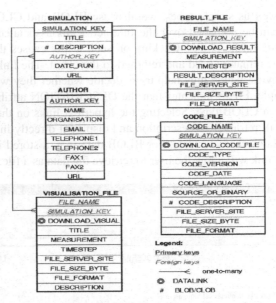

Fig. 3. Sample database schema for UK Turbulence Consortium

2.4   SQL Management of External Data: The New DATALINK Type

Both ANSI and ISO have accepted the proposal for SQL Part 9: Management of External Data [4], which includes (among other things) the specification of the DATALINK type. ISO progressed SQL/MED to Committee Draft (CD) in December 1998 and it should become a standard in late 2000.

DATALINKs provide the following features for database management of external files: *Referential Integrity* (an external file referenced by the database cannot be renamed or deleted), *Transaction Consistency* (changes affecting both the database and external files are executed within a transaction. This ensures consistency between a file and its metadata), *Security* (file access controls can be based on the database privileges) and *Coordinated Backup and Recovery* (the database management system can take responsibility for backup and recovery of external files in synchronisation with the internal data).

Our interface uses an implementation of the DATALINK type that is available with IBM's DB2 Database. This uses a DB2 database to store the data associated with standard types internally, plus DATALINK specific software running on the remote file servers to manage external data. This software processes SQL *INSERT, UPDATE* and *DELETE* statements that affect DATALINK columns, to link and unlink files for the database. It manages information about linked files, and previous versions of linked files for recovery purposes. It also intercepts file system commands to ensure that registered files are not renamed, deleted and optionally, check the user's access authority.

A DATALINK value can be entered via a standard SQL *INSERT* or *UPDATE* statement. If read permission is managed by the database, an SQL *SELECT* statement retrieves the value in the form:

`http://host/filesystem/directory/access_token;filename`

The file can then be accessed from the filesystem in the normal way using the name: *access_token;filename*, or, by using the full URL if the file is placed on a Web server (as in our system). The access tokens have a finite life determined by a database configuration parameter. This can be set to expire after an interval.

2.5 Interface Customisation Through XUIS Modification

The XUIS can be customised to provide aliases for table names and column names as well as user-defined sample values. It is also possible to prevent tables or columns being displayed in the query forms and results, by removing them from the XUIS. Hypertext links for navigation between tables can also be added or removed by modification of the XUIS. A fragment of the XML for the XUIS is shown below:

```
<table name="AUTHOR" primaryKey= "AUTHOR.AUTHOR_KEY">
  <tablealias>Author</tablealias>
  <column name="AUTHOR_KEY" colid="AUTHOR.AUTHOR_KEY">
    <type><VARCHAR/><size>30</size></type>
    <pk><refby tablecolumn="SIMULATION.AUTHOR_KEY"/></pk>
      <samples>
        <sample>A19990110151042</sample>
        <sample>A19990209151042</sample>
```

Initial feedback from users indicated that they would like to replace the keys displayed in the results with more meaningful data. The XUIS can be modified to specify a 'substitute column' to be displayed in the results in place of foreign keys. The substitute column is a user-specified column from the table that the foreign key references. For example, the AUTHOR_KEY attributes in the SIMULATION table of Fig. 2 can be replaced by, say, the NAME attribute from the referenced AUTHOR table. These values still provide a browsing link to the full author details. The XUIS can also be customised to replace primary keys with the names of linked tables.

2.6 Suitable Processing of Data Files Prior to Retrieval: 'Operations'

McGrath [12] asserts that users of scientific data servers usually only require a selected part of a dataset that is typically stored in a large complex file, and that it is critical therefore, to provide a means to identify data of interest, and to be able to retrieve the selected data in a useable format. Referring back to our system architecture of Fig.1 we see the Web servers on the remote file servers can process a standard HTTP 'Get request' to return a complete result file to the client (if the encrypted file access key is correct). This is the functionality that we have described so far. However, Fig. 1 also shows that a Java Servlet can be invoked on the file server to handle the incoming request.

Our architecture allows the XUIS to be modified to allow post-processing applications that have been archived using DATALINK values to be dynamically executed server-side to reduce the data volume returned to the user. These applications can consist of Java classes or any other executable format, suitable for the file server host on which the data resides, including C, FORTRAN and scripting languages. These applications do not have to be specially written for our architecture (in fact, *operations* stored *as* DATALINKs can be downloaded separately for standalone execution elsewhere) and they can be packaged in a number of different formats including various compressed archive formats (such as tar.Z, gz, zip, tar etc.). The only restriction is that the initial executable file accepts a filename as a command line parameter. This filename will correspond to the name of a dataset to be processed. Archived applications are associated with a number of archived datasets using a mark-up syntax that we have defined for 'operations' in the XUIS. If the application allows other user-specified parameters, the syntax for *operations* has been defined so that an HTML form will be created to request these parameters at invocation time. The XML syntax we have defined for *operation* parameters is similar to that used for HTML forms. Applications that correspond to *operations* do not have to be stored as DATALINKs. They can also be specified in the XUIS in the form of URLs that refer to CGI programs or Servlets that run on the file server host to provide a post-processing capability. A fragment of the XML for an *operation* is shown below:

```
<column name="DOWNLOAD_RESULT"
        colid ="RESULT_FILE.DOWNLOAD_RESULT">
    <type><DATALINK/></type>
    <operation name="GetImage" type="JAVA"
          filename="GetImage.class" format="jar"
          guest.access="true" column="false">
        <if>
            <condition colid="RESULT_FILE.SIMULATION_KEY">
                <eq>'S19990110150932'</eq></condition>
        </if>
        <location>
            <database.result
                colid="CODE_FILE.DOWNLOAD_CODE_FILE">
                <condition colid="CODE_FILE.CODE_NAME">
                    <eq>'GetImage.jar'</eq>
                </condition>
            </database.result>
        </location>
        <parameters>
            <param>
                <variable>
                    <description>DO you require FORTRAN
                        or JAVA Sample Code?</description>
                    <input type="radio"
                        name="output_format"
                        value="Fortran" >FORTRAN
                    </input>
                </param>
```

An example of the processing associated with an *operation* stored as a DATALINK follows. Fig. 4 shows the result of a query on the RESULT_FILE table from the schema of Fig. 3. The columns containing a cog icon in the column header present the user with operations to execute against the preceding DATALINK column containing dataset result files.

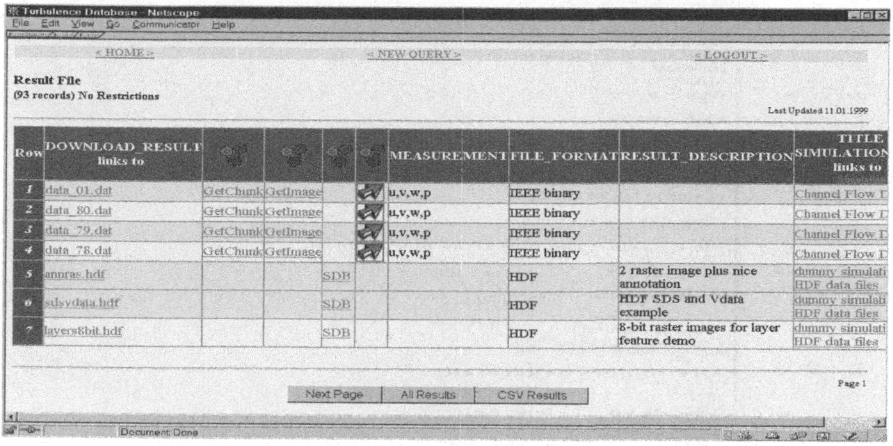

Fig. 4. Result table showing 'operations' available for post-processing datasets

Selecting the 'GetImage' hyperlink corresponding to the DATALINK value containing 'data_01.dat' produces a screen that describes what the operation does, and requests that the user specifies (via text boxes, radio buttons etc.) any input parameters that were defined for the operation in the XUIS. The information contained in this form was specified in the XUIS and the operation itself is stored as a DATALINK in the CODE_FILE table of the schema shown in Fig. 3. The example 'GetImage' operation extracts a user-specified slice from a dataset corresponding to a simulation of turbulence in a 3-D channel and returns a GIF image of a user-selected velocity component or pressure from the flow field. The result (applied to 'data_01.dat') is shown in Fig 5. When the user submits the request this initiates a sequence of processing. The location of the DATALINK file corresponding to the dataset to be processed and the location of the DATALINK file corresponding to the 'GetImage' *operation* along with the selected parameter values, are passed to a Servlet running on the file server host. This Servlet also receives other information (stored as hidden fields in the HTML form that was initially specified in the XUIS, such as the executable type for the operation (e.g. FORTRAN, C, Java) and whether the application is contained in an a compressed archive format.

The Servlet then makes external system calls to unpack the application in the temporary directory created for the user and to execute the application with the given dataset filename and other command line arguments. The Servlet redirects standard output and standard error from the executable to files in the temporary directory.

When the application ends any output is returned to the user as illustrated in Fig. 5. The user is also given the opportunity to download any files that are created by the application. Since the 'GetImage' *operation* produces GIF images, which the browser understands, these are also displayed on the Web page.

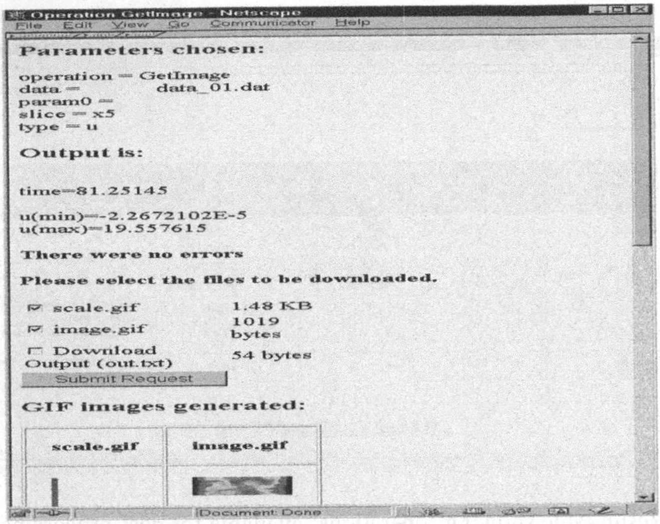

Fig. 5. Output from 'operation' execution

When the user hits 'submit request' in the results page of Fig. 5 a multipart HTTP response is used to return all the requested files to the user, and the temporary directory and all of its contents are deleted. If the user does not download the files in this way the temporary directories are removed periodically when they are no longer being used. This is monitored by keeping track of active Servlet sessions IDs.

As well as incorporating stored operations with XML defined interfaces, the system also allows authorised users to upload abirary Java programs for secure server-side execution, to post-process datasets stored on the file server hosts. (In Fig. 4 this facility is requested using the arrow icon.)

3   Related Work

There has been a substantial body of research in the area of graphical interfaces to databases. A comprehensive survey can be found in [13]. Most of the systems that incorporate data browsing are applied to database models that have *explicit* relationships between objects in the database. Such database models include entity-relationship (E-R) and object-oriented data models (see for example the PESTO interface described in [14]). Our data browsing technique does not rely on explicit relationships defined in the data model, but extracts implied relationships from the relational model to dynamically include hyperlinks in results. Our interface is automatically generated, requiring no HTML page maintenance. As such, we do not rely on our scientific user-base having Web and database development experience. Our interface also allows customisation through changes to XML mark-up. Furthermore our interface can manage distributed data through the DATALINK SQL-type and be extended by the inclusion of executable code described by XML mark-up.

NCSA's *Scientific Data Service* (SDS) [15] [12] provides a Web-based interface targeted at manipulating scientific datasets. It consists of a CGI program for browsing data in a number of scientific formats such as the Hierarchical Data Format (HDF) (http://hdf.ncsa.uiuc.edu). This CGI program is written in C and provides functionality such as visualisation and extraction of subsets of data specifically written for the supported scientific data formats. However SDB does not provide sophisticated storage and search capabilities for archiving and selecting the data files that it can process. It assumes that these files are simply placed in a directory structure belonging to the Web server. We were able, however, to incorporate SDB as an 'operation' in our interface by the inclusion of simple mark-up in the XUIS that specified SDB for post-processing result files in HDF format. This allows SDB to benefit from our secure data management architecture and search capabilities. The XML fragment to include the 'SDB' *operation* is shown below:

```
<operation name="SDB" type="" filename=""
           format="" guest.access="true" column="false">
  <if><condition colid="RESULT_FILE.FILE_FORMAT">
           <eq>'HDF'</eq>
      </condition></if>
  <location>
      <URL> http://dns.ecs.soton.ac.uk/cgi-bin/SDB</URL>
  </location>
  <description>NCSA Scientific Data Browser</description
</operation>
```

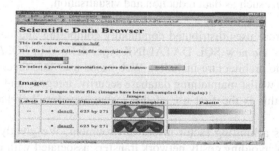

Fig. 6. NCSA'S SDB [15] has been specified as an 'operation' in the XUIS

4   Conclusions

We have constructed a prototype system to meet a requirement of the UK Turbulence Consortium to make available to authorised users, large result files from numerical simulations, with a total storage requirement in the hundreds of gigabyte range. We also archive applications that can be dynamically invoked to post-process data. A demonstration is available at http://www.hpcc.ecs.soton.ac.uk/~turbulence.

Our interface is specifically aimed at users with a scientific background who are not familiar with SQL. As such, we aim to help users locate scientific data files of interest, using an intuitive searching and browsing mechanism in keeping with a Web-based look and feel. One of the implications of this is that we automate the interface construction so that it requires little database or Web development experience to install and access. This is a generic, schema-driven system that can be used to manage many different types of large, distributed data archives. We achieve the automated construction by allowing the user interface specification to be defined in an XML file used to initialise the system and by providing a tool that can generate a default XML specification. Separating the user interface specification from the user interface processing can provide a number of further advantages:

- The user interface, although schema driven can be customised to use aliases for table and column names and to present different sample values. Tables and attributes can also be hidden from view.
- Hypertext links to related data can be specified in the XML even if there are no referential integrity constraints defined for the database.
- Different Users (or classes of user) can have different XML files thereby providing them with different user interfaces to the same data.
- For scientific data archiving a major benefit, facilitated by the XML user interface specification, is the capability to associate 'operations' with database columns, so that a user can extend the interface by including standard post-processing codes. These applications are loosely coupled to the datasets via XML defined interfaces. They provide reusable server-side post-processing operations such as data reduction and visualisation.

Our architecture uses distributed commodity computing and non-proprietary technologies such as the new SQL DATALINK type, defined in SQL/MED. We demonstrate a complete architecture including Web-based user interface for archiving large, distributed files whilst maintaining database security, integrity and recovery. As far as we are aware, this is the first use of this technology for Web-based scientific data archiving.

Bandwidth is a limiting factor in our environment. We greatly reduce bandwidth requirements by avoiding costly network transfers associated with uploading data files to a centralised site and by allowing data reduction through post-processing. Data distribution also reduces retrieval bottlenecks at individual sites.

5   Acknowledgements

The UK Turbulence Consortium (EPSRC Grant GR/M08424) provided data for this project. IBM's DB2 Scholars programme provided us with DB2 licenses. The DB2 Data Protection and Recovery Team at IBM were extremely helpful when responding to questions regarding DB2's DATALINK implementation.

References

1. Sandham, N.D. and Howard, R.J.A. Direct Simulation of Turbulence Using Massively Parallel Computers. *In:* A. Ecer *et al.*, *eds. Parallel Computational Fluid Dynamics '97*, Elsevier, 1997.
2. Williams, R., Bunn, J., Reagan, M., and Pool, C., T. *Workshop on Interfaces to Scientific Data Achives*, California, USA, 25-27 March, 1998, Technical Report CACR-160, CALTECH, 42pp.
3. Eisenberg, A. and Melton, J., SQL:1999, formerly known as SQL3. *SIGMOD Record*, 28(1), March, 1999.
4. Mattos, N., Melton, J. and Richey, J. Database Language SQL-Part 9:Management of External Data (SQL/MED), ISO/IEC Committee Draft, CD 9075-9, December, 1988. ftp://jerry.ece.umassd.edu/isowg3/dbl/YGJdocs/ygj023.pdf
6. Jim Bray, J., Paoli, J. and Sperberg-McQueen, C., M. *eds.* Extensible Markup Language (XML) 1.0, W3C Recommendation, 10 February, 1998. http://www.w3.org/TR/REC-xml
7. Zloof M.M. Query By Example. *American Federation of Information Processing (AFIPS) Conf. Proc.*, Vol. 44, National Computer Conference, 1975, 431-8.
8. Manber, U. Future Directions and Research Problems in the World Wide Web. *Proc ACM SIGMOD Conf.*, Montreal, Canada, June 3-5, 1996, 213-15.
9. Warren, M., S., *et al.* Avalon: An Alpha/Linux Cluster Achieves 10 Gflops for $150k. Gordon Bell Price/Performance Prize, Supercomputing 1998. http://cnls.lanl.gov/avalon/
10.Davidson, J., D., and Ahmed, S. Java Servlet API Specification, Version 2.1a, November, 1988. http://java.sun.com/products/Servlet/index.html
10. White, S., Hapner, M. JDBC 2.0 API, Sun Microsystems Inc., Version 1.0, May, 1998.
11. Haw D., Goble, C., A., and Rector, A., L. GUIDANCE: Making it easy for the user to be an expert. *Proc. 2nd Int. workshop on User Interfaces to Databases*, Ambleside, UK, 13-15th July, 1994, 19-44.
12. McGrath, R., E. *A Scientific Data Server: The Conceptual Design. White Paper*, NCSA, University of Illinois, Urbana-Champaign, January, 1997.
13. Catarci, T., Costabile, M., F., Levialdi, S., and Batini, C. Visual Query Systems for Databases: A Survey. *Journal of Visual Languages and Computing*, 8, 1997, 215-60.
14. Carey, M., J., Haas, L., M., Maganty, V., and Williams, J., H. PESTO: An Integrated Query/Browser for Object Databases. *Proc. VLDB Int. Conf.*, India, 3-6 September, 1996, 203-14.
15. Yaeger, N. *A Web Based Scientific Data Access Service: The Central Component of a Lightweight Data Archive*, National Center for Supercomputing Applications, University of Illinois, Urbana-Champaign. http://hopi.ncsa.uiuc.edu/sdb/sdb.html

Persistent Client-Server Database Sessions

Roger S. Barga, David B. Lomet, Thomas Baby, and Sanjay Agrawal

Microsoft Research, Microsoft Corporation
One Microsoft Way, Redmond, WA 98052
barga@microsoft.com

Abstract. Database systems support recovery, providing high database availability. However, database applications may lose work because of a server failure. In particular, if a database server crashes, volatile server state associated with a client application's session is lost and applications may require operator-assisted restart. This prevents masking server failures and degrades application availability. In this paper, we show how to provide persistent database sessions to client applications across server failures, without the application itself needing to take measures for its recoverability. This offers improved application availability and reduces the application programming task of coping with system errors. Our approach is based on (i) capturing client application's interactions with the database server and (ii) materializing database session state as persistent database tables that are logged on the database server. We exploit a virtual database session. Our procedures detect database server failure and re-map the virtual session to a new session into which we install the saved old session state once the server has recovered. This integrates database server recovery *and* transparent session recovery. The result is persistent client-server database sessions that survive a server crash without the client application being aware of the outage, except for possible timing considerations. We demonstrate the viability of this approach by describing the design and implementation of Phoenix/ODBC, a prototype system that provides persistent ODBC database sessions; and present early results from a performance evaluation on the costs to persist and recover ODBC database sessions.

1 Introduction

The Application Availability Problem Database systems support fault-tolerance and high availability by recovering quickly from system failures. However, recovery has been restricted to the database system and has ignored applications interacting with the database at the time of failure. Currently, those applications either fail, resulting in an application outage, or must cope with database failures for themselves, assuming they survive the database crash. The former compromises application availability and can increase operational complexity. The latter either severely restricts application flexibility or increases its complexity.

C. Zaniolo et al. (Eds.): EDBT 2000, LNCS 1777, pp. 462-477, 2000.

When an application fails because of a database system crash, organizations responsible for the application need to quickly bring the application back on line. In the enterprise-computing world, time is quite literally money and the high cost of downtime drives awareness. While database recovery ensures that the database state is consistent, an application retaining state across database transactions can have consistency requirements that are not captured at the database transaction boundary. Further, parts of the application state may be lost during a crash. Restoring and continuing application execution is all too frequently a very complex and time-consuming operational problem.

In some system configurations, an application can survive a database server crash. For example, when the application executes on a client machine while the database is on a separate server. This permits the application to include logic to deal with database crashes and hence avoid an application outage. However, handling errors is a very difficult part of getting applications right. Dealing with database failures at the application level is tedious and error-prone, even when the application stays alive.

Our Approach Coping with system failures to minimize application outages and to avoid application program complexity thus presents a very large problem for robust enterprise computing. Our goal is to simultaneously improve application availability and simplify application logic. We accomplish that by having the *system* take responsibility for application persistence across system failures. It is the *system* that acts to ensure that the application will be recoverable and be able to continue execution after a crash. The goal is to provide application persistence across system crashes without the application taking any measures to ensure its own survival. We call this *transparent* application recoverability.

The work we describe in this paper aims to provide application recovery at modest system implementation cost and at arm's-length from the database system and its recovery manager. This work focuses on providing transparent application recovery in a client/server context, but without introducing a substantial recovery manager or extensively modifying an existing database system's recovery manager. The advantage of this is that we can layer our middleware infrastructure on many SQL database systems, hence providing persistent applications for them all.

Phoenix/ODBC We have implemented the prototype system Phoenix/ODBC to explore the utility and practicality of persistent ODBC client-server database sessions. These sessions persist across database server failures. The application exploiting Phoenix/ODBC interacts with it as it would with a normal ODBC driver. And, except for issues of performance, which we discuss later, the application program does not detect a difference between Phoenix/ODBC and a database vendor supplied ODBC driver in the absence of a database system crash. Thus, Phoenix/ODBC is *transparent* during normal operation and in the absence of database system failures.

Should the database system server crash, i.e. the DBMS running on a separate server machine, the typical ODBC driver provides no graceful way for the application to cope with the server failure. Indeed, the SQL/CLI standard [ANSI SQL/CLI] provides no defined semantics as to what should happen to an application should a SQL database system crash. At best, the application is notified of the server failure and must "pull itself together" to deal with the server failure. At worst, the application hangs waiting for ODBC to respond to its last (and interrupted) request. However, with Phoenix/ODBC, a SQL database system crash and recovery merely results in a delayed response to an ODBC request. Once the database system recovers, the application's request returns normally, and the application can continue its execution. Thus Phoenix/ODBC is also *transparent* during database system crashes in that the application is not even aware of the crash, and need take no special measures to deal with it.

Phoenix/ODBC performs three main functions to provide persistent database sessions:

1. It ensures that volatile session state will persist across server failures. Phoenix/ODBC materializes volatile session state on the database server as database tables. Phoenix/ODBC persists result sets, messages, and database updates that effect volatile session state. Phoenix/ODBC intercepts application requests going to the server and identifies session state that must be stored on stable storage, and then creates permanent tables on the underlying database to record this state. If the database system crashes, then the session state contained in these tables will automatically be recovered. Some state information is also saved on the client, but need not be persistent there because we are not protecting against client failures. This state permits the synchronization of recovered server state with the client state.

2. It provides a virtual database session to isolate client applications from database server failures. Clients connect to the Phoenix/ODBC virtual session, and Phoenix/ODBC maps that session to an underlying ODBC database session. Should a failure occur, the underlying ODBC database session is lost. However, once the database server has recovered, Phoenix/ODBC re-maps the virtual session to a new post-crash ODBC session. It associates the saved session state of the pre-crash ODBC session with this new post-crash session.

3. Fast recovery after a failure is critical for high application availability as short outages may go unnoticed by the human user. Phoenix/ODBC detects potential database server failures and, in the event the database crashed, transparently reinstalls database session state from which normal processing can resume. It re-syncs the recovered session state with the state of the client application, presenting the illusion that no failure has occurred.

The result is persistent client-server database sessions that can survive a server crash without the client application being aware of the outage, except for possible timing considerations. Equally important, from an implementation perspective, Phoenix/ODBC requires no changes to the database, native ODBC drivers, or client application. Phoenix/ODBC continues the trend of expending system resources to conserve more expensive and error-prone human resources.

This paper makes three primary contributions: 1) It describes a generic method for persisting database sessions. 2) It demonstrates that persistent database sessions are practical, based on the design and implementation of Phoenix/ODBC. 3) Finally, it presents initial performance results from our prototype implementation that suggests the response time cost of using Phoenix/ODBC is usually modest.

2   ODBC Background

ODBC (Open Data Base Connectivity) is a standard application programming interface (API) by which a client application accesses the data in the database. ODBC enables any application to access any database that supports this standard via SQL by using a standard collection of call points.   Vendors support ODBC by providing a driver, a client stub, specifically designed for their particular database system.   The ODBC driver's application interface adheres to the ODBC standard. All ODBC drivers support the same call points, regardless of what database engine is on the back end.

The ODBC driver interaction with the database system is customized to the specific database engine. This interaction requires the use of proprietary communication protocols, SQL language message formats, and result set representations. Using ODBC, applications don't have to be customized to or even aware of the proprietary aspects of accessing the data they are using. The driver makes any necessary translations in sending SQL statements to the DBMS and presents the results back to the application in a standard way, including standard return codes.

ODBC Components   The ODBC infrastructure consists of two components that mediate between the client and database system storing the data, as follows:

- **Driver:**An ODBC driver is a dynamic link library that responds to calls an application makes to the ODBC API.   If SQL statements from the application contain ANSI or ODBC SQL syntax not supported by the database, the driver translates the statements into database-specific SQL syntax and then passes the statement to the server. When the database responds with a result set, the driver reformats it in the reverse direction into a standard ODBC result set.

- **Driver Manager**: The ODBC driver manager is a Microsoft provided layer that manages the communication between the application and the appropriate ODBC driver. The driver manager selects the driver for a particular database when the application first connects to the server, then passes all ODBC function calls coming from the application to this ODBC driver. The driver manager also handles some ODBC function calls directly, and detects and handles some errors.

An Illustrative ODBC Client-Server Session   To illustrate the use of ODBC interface and likely result were a database server failure to occur, we consider the following example, illustrated in Figure 1. Our database session is similar to those in the TPC-H benchmark, and involves three tables: a master customer table, a detail orders table, and a summary invoice table. The task is to extract the appropriate records for a customer with the last name "Smith," find that customer's current orders, and then aggregate the order totals into the invoice summary table. This client application might be coded as follows:

1. Create an ODBC database session by opening a connection to a named database server, follow the standard protocol to log on the server, then issue a series of ODBC function calls to set application specific attributes on the database connection.
2. Submit an ODBC function containing a SQL statement to create a result set from the customer table (**A**) consisting of records with a last name of 'Smith'.
3. Issue fetch commands to retrieve records from result set until appropriate customer is found.
4. Submit an ODBC function containing a SQL statement to open a cursor on the orders table (**B**) for orders matching this customer's ID.
5. Issue fetch commands to retrieve all matching order detail records for this customer ID.
6. Calculate the aggregate of those order detail records.
7. Submit an ODBC function containing a SQL statement to update the invoices table (**C**) with the aggregate.
8. Issue an ODBC function call to close the connection to the database, terminating the ODBC session.

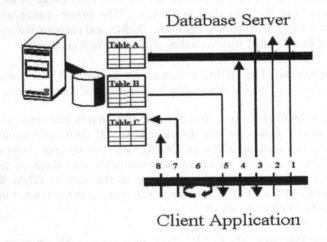

Fig.1. Client application using ODBC to access a customer order database.

Server Failure Behavior The ODBC standard leaves undefined what behavior the client application can expect should the database server to which it has a connection fail. Consider what the effects of a server failure might involve:

- **Detecting Server Failure:** ODBC functions may simply *"hang"* when the server fails. The user does not know whether the server is busy, the connection slow, or if a database failure has occurred. Once a database failure is verified the application must be terminated manually.

- **Application Availability**: Once a database server failure has been detected and the application terminated, the application must be restarted, a new ODBC session established, and new connections to the database opened. Partial execution can leave the application state confused, requiring long outages to reconstruct the application state. This too can require manual intervention.
- **Loss of Transient State.** If a failure occurs after the application has created volatile server state, for example result sets from SQL statements or temporary tables holding results or user input, this state is lost. Moreover, it may be impossible to reliably re-create this state because subsequent database updates have changed the subset of the data upon which the lost state depends.

Even should the client application be able to continue execution after a server failure, for an application to cope with the failure requires additional complex and subtle code to deal with these problems. This increases application complexity, delays application deployment, contributes to application bugs, and reduces overall application availability. This is where Phoenix/ODBC comes in.

3   Phoenix/ODBC

Overview Phoenix/ODBC provides persistent database sessions to client applications that interact with databases using ODBC. These sessions can survive a database server crash without the client application being aware of the outage, except for possible timing considerations. The design of Phoenix/ODBC is based on application message logging, in which all application requests going from the client to the database server are intercepted. Phoenix/ODBC records statements that alter session context, such as statement 1 in the example presented in the previous section. It rewrites selected SQL statements to create persistent database tables that capture the server's SQL session state, before passing the request on to the native ODBC driver (result sets of statements 2 and 4 will be made to persist). Phoenix/ODBC intercepts database server responses, variously caching, filtering, and reshaping result sets, and synchronizing with state materialized on the database server (partially delivered result sets in statements 3 and 5 are synchronized to provide seamless delivery). We exploit an ODBC virtual database session to isolate client applications from database server failures. When Phoenix/ODBC detects a database server failure it re-maps the virtual session to a newly created session into which, once the server has recovered, it installs the persistent state information of the pre-crash session. After the client application has successfully terminated, Phoenix/ODBC cleans up all persistent structures on the database server that were created to store database session state (statement 8), dropping all tables and stored procedures. Phoenix/ODBC integrates database server recovery *and* transparent session recovery. The result is persistent client-server ODBC database sessions that survive a server crash without the client application being aware of the outage, except for possible timing considerations.

Wrapping the ODBC API Phoenix/ODBC intercepts application requests and makes volatile session state persistent without requiring changes to the database system, native ODBC driver, or any special application programming. Wrapping the ODBC API is the key to this end.

Our goal for Phoenix/ODBC was to provide persistent database sessions to client applications executing on Microsoft's Windows/NT, without the application itself needing to take measures for its recoverability. While the implementation specifics may differ, we believe our approach is also applicable to ODBC clients executing in other environments. We also wanted to avoid requiring modifications to either the database system or native ODBC drivers. Hence, the code for Phoenix/ODBC is completely contained within an enhanced Microsoft ODBC driver manager. As described in Section 2, the driver manager manages communications between an application and the ODBC drivers it uses. All application requests are first sent to the driver manager which then routes the requests to the native ODBC driver. Despite the variety of commercial database servers and available ODBC drivers, they are all managed on Microsoft systems by a common driver manager.

The *Phoenix-enhanced* driver manager wraps the call points of database vendor provided ODBC drivers in the same way as the original driver manager. It creates a surrogate for each function in the ODBC API that intercepts the client application ODBC request on its way to the ODBC driver. Actions that Phoenix/ODBC must take to analyze the request and provide for the persistence of volatile session state are performed in the surrogate, prior to passing the application request on to the native driver. This approach to providing server database sessions that survive system crashes is completely transparent to other system components. It requires no changes to native ODBC drivers, client application programs, or SQL database systems.

Decomposing and Persisting Application ODBC State The first step towards providing ODBC persistent database sessions is to decompose session state into separate elements, each of which can be managed as a distinct data object. These elements of session state have different lifetimes and recovery requirements that we exploit. Session state includes:

- **Session Context:** One element of this is the set of client specifiable attributes of the ODBC session, including the connect request, user login information, and default database settings. Database server specific information is also included, e.g., user identification, current database, user temporary objects, such as temporary tables and stored procedures, and unacknowledged messages sent by the server to the client.
- **Results of SQL Statement Execution:** SQL statements return one of the following: i) a result set for a SELECT statement; ii) a global cursor which can be referenced outside the SQL statement; iii) return codes, which are always integer values; iv) return messages for SQL updates; v) output parameters, which can be either data or a cursor variable;
- **Database Procedures:** Procedures can be stored at the server, consisting of one or more SQL statements that have been precompiled.

- **SQL Command Batch:** This is a group of two or more SQL statements, or a single SQL statement that has the same effect as a group of two or more SQL statements.

While there are subtleties to each element of an applications ODBC state, handling SQL results is particularly challenging. We describe how they are treated next in some detail.

Result Sets A result set is made persistent by being stored as a persistent SQL table. Seamless delivery of results is ensured by re-accessing this table after a failure, then re-establishing the place where pre-crash delivery was interrupted. When Phoenix/ODBC intercepts an application request, it performs a one-pass parse to determine request type. If the application request is a SQL statement that generates a result set, Phoenix/ODBC takes the following steps to ensure this result will be recoverable in case of server failure.

Step 1: *Phoenix/OBDC determines the structure of the SQL statement result set, i.e. the names of attributes, their types, and the order in which they appear in each returned tuple.* Since Phoenix/ODBC need only know the result format in order to create a persistent table for it, Phoenix/ODBC only requires the result set *metadata*. The metadata describes the number of columns in the result, the types of those columns, their names, precision, nullability, and so on. Because it is essential to minimize expensive network traffic between the server and client, we want to acquire this metadata with a single round trip to the server with minimum data transfer and with minimum server impact. To do this, Phoenix/ODBC appends the clause "WHERE 0=1" to the original SQL statement. It sends this modified query to the server via the native ODBC driver. ODBC delivers the result set metadata as a prefix to the delivery of the result data. This Phoenix/ODBC "trick" guarantees that the query will not be executed and that no result data will actually be returned, minimizing both server load and message size. Only query compilation is performed on the server, and only the metadata is returned in the reply message.

Step 2: *A table is created at the server to hold the result generated by the SQL statement.* Once a response is returned from the server indicating the rewritten SQL statement has successfully executed, Phoenix/ODBC reads the metadata and reformats it into a CREATE TABLE statement. It then sends the CREATE statement to the database server to create an empty persistent table at the server to hold the result set. This table is part of a special Phoenix database, it is not a temporary table.

Step 3: *The result set is stored in the just created persistent table at the server.* What is materialized depends on both the SQL statement and on how the application requests the results set from the server. With ODBC, the "how" is determined by the statement options specified prior to executing a SELECT.

Default Result Set When the ODBC default values are used as the options, the database server sends the result set in the most efficient way possible. The server assumes that the application will fetch all the rows from the result set promptly. Therefore, the database server sends all rows from the result set and the client application must buffer any rows that are not used immediately but may be needed later. This is referred to as a default result set.

To materialize a default result set, Phoenix/ODBC sends the database server a request to execute the original SQL statement and stores its result in the persistent table created at Step 2 Phoenix/ODBC creates the following stored procedure to do this, using ANSI-standard SQL:

CREATE PROCEDURE P (@T string) AS
INSERT
    <original SQL statement>
INTO T

The advantage of using a stored procedure is that all data is moved locally at the server, not sent first to the client. It involves a single round-trip message from client to server; rather than having data moving across the network. The action is itself an atomic SQL statement, i.e. it executes in a separate transaction. Once the server has returned a response indicating the procedure was successfully executed, the result set is stable and will persist across server failures. Next, Phoenix/ODBC issues the SQL statement SELECT * FROM T to open the table and returns control to the application for normal processing.

Step 4: To ensure seamless delivery of the result set, Phoenix/ODBC keeps track of the current location in the now persistent result set. Should a failure occur, subsequent database recovery ensures the result set exists after the failure. Phoenix/ODBC resumes access to the result set at the remembered location of the last access before the database system failure.

Cursors The SQL language permits results to be returned in ways other than via default result sets. An application can control delivery of results at a finer granularity by exploiting *cursors*, two forms of which we discuss briefly: keyset cursors and dynamic cursors. An application's SQL query may return no rows, a few rows, or millions of rows. The user is unlikely to want to see millions of rows. Fetching and buffering millions of rows is usually a waste of time and resources. Server cursors, such as keyset and dynamic, allow an application to fetch results a block of rows at a time from an arbitrarily large result set. The application is permitted to "navigate" through the result set via a server cursor. A server cursor allows the application to fetch any other block of rows, including the next n rows, the previous n rows, or n rows starting at a certain row number. The server fills each block fetch request only as needed. Some server cursors also allow an application to update or delete fetched rows. If the row data changes between the time the SQL cursor definition statement is executed and the time the row is fetched by the application, the updated row data is returned. These features of server cursors present unique challenges for Phoenix/ODBC.

A *keyset cursor* captures the set of rows that satisfy a query at the time the cursor is opened and it permits those rows to be accessed and updated. If a keyset cursor is requested, Phoenix/ODBC materializes only the keys of the result set rows in the persistent database table. When the application requests a row from the result set, Phoenix/ODBC reads the key from the table and SELECTs the record from the database using this key. If the row data has been changed or the record itself deleted, the updated row data is returned. Phoenix/ODBC transparently supports keyset cursors, but now the cursors persist across failures.

A *dynamic cursor* specifies a logical predicate (the *WHERE* clause) that defines the rows of interest. The set of rows fetched changes dynamically as rows are inserted and deleted. If a *dynamic cursor* is requested, Phoenix/ODBC again materializes the keys of the result set rows in a persistent database table, exactly as it did for keyset cursors. Now, however, when the next row is fetched, it is not necessarily the row with the next key as an insertion may have occurred. Thus, a fetch causes Phoenix/ODBC to use the last record key seen by the application and the next record key from the table to *SELECT* a *range* of rows from the database server. If records have been inserted into this range, Phoenix/ODBC fetches them and presents the appropriate row to the application. Again, Phoenix/ODBC transparently supports dynamic cursors, but now the cursor persists across failures.

Data Modification Statements "Results" A server failure can also occur while the application is attempting to modify data in tables using a data manipulation statement (insert, update, and delete). While there is no result set, there is state associated with a data manipulation statement, namely the number of tuples affected by the modification. In addition, for purposes of recovery it is necessary to determine whether the statement successfully executed or not; that is, we require *testable state*. Our approach is to intercept the application request and *wrap* a transaction around the data modification statement. Within this transaction we add an insert statement after the data manipulation statement to record the outcome (number of tuples affected) in a Phoenix-managed table. In the event of a server crash, Phoenix/ODBC can probe this table to determine the status of the application request; if the request completed Phoenix/ODBC simply returns the outcome logged in this table to the application, else Phoenix/ODBC resubmits the original application request.

Message "Results" When the database server commits a transaction and then fails before it can send a response to the client, that message will be lost to the client. Phoenix/ODBC prevents lost messages by including the transaction reply buffers in its persistent session context. The database server writes both the commit record and reply buffer to a Phoenix database table before committing the transaction and replying to the client. On database recovery, Phoenix/ODBC will deliver the reply buffer to the client, thus avoiding the lost message.

Temporary Objects SQL applications often declare temporary database tables to serve as program work spaces, and temporary stored procedures to execute the same task (sequence of SQL statements) several times in a session. In the event of a database server failure temporary objects would be lost. Our approach for persisting temporary objects is to intercept application requests to create temporary tables or temporary stored procedures, then rewrite the request to create a persistent table or persistent stored procedure. Phoenix/ODBC records the name of all persistent tables and stored procedures created, and all subsequent references to the temporary object will be intercepted and redirected to the corresponding permanent object. Upon normal session termination, Phoenix/ODBC will explicitly remove these tables and stored procedures.

Virtual ODBC Sessions   There are two notions of session within the ODBC framework. A client application has an ODBC session with which it interacts. On behalf of the application, ODBC establishes database sessions, called connections with database systems accessed during the ODBC session. When a server crashes, the database session does not survive the crash. The server's failure can also corrupt and hence lead to the termination of the client application's ODBC session as well.

To provide persistent sessions, Phoenix/ODBC insulates the client application from these underlying sessions. Instead, the client connects to a Phoenix/ODBC session. This is possible because Phoenix/ODBC is an extension of the Driver Manager and "wraps" native ODBC drivers. The Phoenix virtual session is mapped to an ODBC session. The ODBC session establishes a database session via an ODBC connection. This connection is identified by a *connection handle*. Phoenix/ODBC maps this connection handle to a virtual connection handle before returning it to the application. Should a crash occur, Phoenix/ODBC establishes a new connection with the database server and remaps the virtual connection handle to the handle for the new connection.

A Phoenix/ODBC session interrupted by a server crash will hence have two connections to the database at the crashed server, the pre-crash session and the post-crash session. The pre-crash session information is normally volatile and hence is lost when the server crashes. Phoenix/ODBC takes steps to materialize this volatile state as persistent tables at the server. Thus, the application sees a database session that is virtual in that the volatile state is trivial and the substantive state is mapped to persistent tables. After a crash, Phoenix/ODBC creates the post-crash database session, again with a trivial volatile state, and reconnects this post-crash session to the persistent tables built during the pre-crash session.

To mask Phoenix/ODBC activity required to (i) establish persistent tables on the server, (ii) to ping for server recovery, and (iii) re-create session state, Phoenix/ODBC establishes a private database connection. When an application interrogates its virtual connection, it only sees the activity on the connection to which its virtual connection is mapped, not the activity on the private connection. The mapped connection activity mimics the application's use of a normal ODBC connection.

Server and Session Crash Recovery   Phoenix/ODBC detects server failures (i) by intercepting communications errors raised by the ODBC driver or (ii) by timing out application requests. Once a potential problem is detected, Phoenix/ODBC must re-contact the server. Phoenix/ODBC uses a private database connection to *'ping'* the server and periodically attempts to reconnect to the database. If after a period of time Phoenix/ODBC is unable to connect to the server, it assumes the database system crashed and passes the communication error on to the application.

If successful, Phoenix/ODBC must determine if the database system actually crashed or whether there is simply a communication failure or delay. We want to discover whether our database session, which will be erased in a crash, still exists. There is no explicit test for this. We test a proxy for this, i.e. we test whether a special temporary table created by Phoenix/ODBC for the session still exists. Temporary tables exist only within a session and are deleted when a session terminates for any reason.

Recovery of the ODBC virtual database session is separated into two phases. First, Phoenix/ODBC transparently reconnects the application to the database server and re-associates saved information with these new database connections. Phoenix/ODBC reinstalls each client connection to the database system using the original connection request and login information, then issues a series of calls to the database server in order to reinstall application specified ODBC connection options. Once complete, Phoenix/ODBC binds these new connections to the virtual database session. Second, Phoenix/ODBC reinstalls SQL state. Phoenix/ODBC first verifies that all application state materialized in tables on the server was recovered by the database recovery mechanisms. It then identifies the application's last completed request for each database connection and asks the server to re-send the result set if necessary; it can also resend any incomplete or interrupted SQL requests to the server. Once this step is complete, Phoenix/ODBC resumes normal processing of application requests. This creation of the new database session is masked from the application, giving the illusion of a single persistent database session.

4   Performance of Phoenix/ODBC

In this section we present early results from an ongoing performance evaluation of Phoenix/ODBC; complete results from this performance evaluation will be presented in a forthcoming paper. For this paper, our objectives were to (i) to measure the overhead of persisting session state on application performance, and (ii) measure the time required for Phoenix/ODBC to recover and reinstall a database session after server failure. For this evaluation we selected TPC-H, a current variant of the now obsolete TPC-D benchmark designed to test the performance of decision support queries in business environments. TPC-H defines queries and update functions that include a rich breadth of operators and selectivity constraints. The query suite, for example, ranges from a simple single-table query to a complex eight-way join query, while update functions carry out insert and delete. TPC-H also defines a benchmarking test, called the *power test*, suitable for measuring application performance.

TPC-H Power Test The TPC-H power test executes all queries and update functions defined in the benchmark one at a time in order and their running time is measured individually. This is intended to measure "raw query execution power". For this experiment we executed the power test fifty times for both native ODBC and Phoenix/ODBC and computed the average of these runs. The standard deviation of these runs is generally less than 1% of the mean.

Table 1 presents selected results from the TPC-H power test. Column one identifies the query and update function number, while the second column lists the number of tuples returned in the result or modified by an update. The third and fourth columns contain the running times using native ODBC and Phoenix/ODBC on the TPC-H database. For comparison purposes, the fifth column presents the difference between native ODBC and Phoenix/ODBC running times, while the final column displays the ratio of running times.

For query performance only (Total Query), the total run time of queries using Phoenix/ODBC is approximately one percent greater than when using native ODBC, which generates a temporary (volatile) result set. As we can see from measurements in Table 1, for these compute-intensive queries that produce a small result set this overhead is relatively small. We see an average overhead of just over one second for each query.

Table 1. Selected results from TPC-H Power Test using native ODBC and Phoenix/ODBC.

Query/ Update	Result Set/ Updates	Native ODBC seconds	Phoenix/ODBC seconds	Difference seconds	Ratio
Q01	4	106.297	107.706	1.4	1.013
Q02	100	4.775	5.262	.486	1.101
Q11	1048	16.372	17.967	1.594	1.097
Q16	18,000	18.868	18.034	-.834	.955
RF1	7,500	56.700	57.540	.84	1.015
RF2	7,500	335.600	336.970	1.37	1.004
Total Query		2277.556	2302.868	25.312	1.011
Total Updates		393.300	394.510	1.210	1.003

Refresh function RF1 inserts 1500 tuples into the ORDERS table and roughly 6000 tuples into the LINEITEM table to emulate the addition of new sales information, while refresh function RF2 deletes 1500 tuples from the ORDERS table and roughly 6000 tuples from the LINEITEM table to emulate the removal of stale or obsolete information. We decomposed each refresh function into two transactions, in which each receives one-half of the key range that is to be modified. The tuples corresponding to new orders and new lineitems were already loaded into the database, as were the keys corresponding to orders and lineitems to be deleted. Hence, the two transactions of refresh function RF1 submit a total of 4 insert requests to the server to insert tuples from these tables, while the two transactions of refresh function RF2 submit a total of 4 delete requests to the server to delete tuples that match these keys.

Phoenix/ODBC *wraps* insert and delete statement with a transaction, and within that transaction it records the number of tuples affected by the update in a Phoenix-managed table; this *status table* provides testable state for determining whether a statement completed. Thus, the primary overhead for data modification statements (insert, delete, update) is the creation of a transaction and a write to the status table to record statement completion. As we can see in Table 1, the Phoenix/ODBC overhead for data modification statements is negligible.

Recovering a Database Session   We also measured the time required for Phoenix/ODBC to recover a database session. To conduct this experiment we submit TPC-H query Q11 to the database and begin fetching tuples until we near the end of the result set, leaving a few tuples unread. Then we *"crash"* the server by terminating the database server. At this point the application is left waiting for the server to respond to its fetch request. We restart the server and measure the time required for Phoenix/ODBC to recover the session and respond to the outstanding fetch request.

Of interest in this experiment is: i) the time required to recover the virtual database session, and ii) the time required to recover the SQL state for active application requests. Together, these represent the time required for Phoenix/ODBC to recover an ODBC database session and continue application execution. Once Phoenix/ODBC is able to contact the server after a failure, it reconnects to the database, issues a series of ODBC function calls to reset connection options, and maps the new connections to the virtual database session. The time required to complete session recovery does not depend on the size of the result set, and in our client-server configuration this step required 0.37 seconds to complete for all experiments. Once the virtual session is reinstalled, Phoenix/ODBC then reinstalls SQL session state. It must first identify the client application's last outstanding request, in this case a fetch command, open the database table holding the result set and advance to the appropriate tuple.

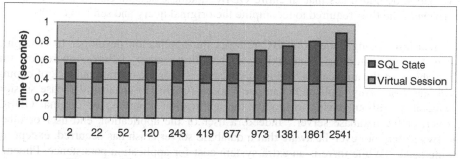

Figure 2. Elapsed time for session recovery over varying result sizes.

The results presented in Figure 2 are when Phoenix/ODBC re-positions the result set using a stored procedure that advances to a specified tuple, hence advancing through the result set on the server without passing tuples to the client. When the procedure completes, a table pointer is left in place and the next fetch request returns the desired tuple. Comparing Figure 2 with the total query Q11 response time plus the 10 seconds or so required to deliver the 2541 tuple results reveals that Phoenix/ODBC can recover an entire ODBC database session in less than a tenth of the time required to simply recompute query Q11.

5   Concluding Remarks

Status   Phoenix/ODBC provides persistent database sessions to client applications across server failures, without the application itself needing to take measures for its recoverability.   This offers improved application availability and reduces the application programming task of coping with system errors.   We leverage existing database system recovery mechanisms by wrapping ODBC to capture application interactions with the database and logging application state changes as tables on the database server.   We exploit the notion of a virtual database session in which an application interacts with a Phoenix/ODBC session that is in-turn mapped to ODBC and database sessions.   Our procedures detect database server failure and re-map the virtual session to a new database session into which we install the pre-crash session state once the server has recovered.   This integrates database server recovery *and* transparent session recovery.   The result is persistent client-server database sessions that survive a server crash without the client application being aware of the outage, except for possible timing considerations.   We implemented the Phoenix/ODBC prototype and have presented performance data on the costs to persist and recover ODBC database sessions, demonstrating the viability of the approach.

Initial results from our performance evaluation indicate the overhead to persist result sets for queries with a high degree of complexity, such as those found in the TPC-H benchmark, is modest.   For the TPC-H power test the difference is approximately 1%, while for the update functions the difference is less than 0.5%.   What is more, our evaluation demonstrates that an entire ODBC database session can be recovered in a fraction of the time required to recompute the original query and send its results.

Conclusion   Using Phoenix/ODBC relieves the application developer from coping with the programming complexity of handling server failures, increases the availability of the application, and in many cases avoids the operational task of coping with an error.   Any application can use Phoenix/ODBC to enhance database session availability without having to modify the application program, the original ODBC driver, or the database server.   Indeed, a user of the application, end user or other software, may not even be aware that a database server crash has occurred, except for some delay.   While there is an extra system cost for application persistence, Phoenix continues the trend of expending system resources to conserve more expensive and error-prone human resources.

References

[1] Bernstein, P., Goodman, N. and Hadzilacos, V. Recovery Algorithms for Database
    Systems. *IFIP World Computer Congress,* (September 1983) pp. 799-807.
[2] Kumar, V. and Hsu, M. (eds.) *Recovery Mechanisms in Database Systems.* Prentice Hall,
    NJ 1998
[3] Lomet, D.B. and Weikum, G. Efficient Transparent Application Recovery in Client-Server
    Information Systems. ACM SIGMOD 1998, Seattle, WA (June 1998) pp. 460-471.
[4] Lomet, D. Application Recovery Using Generalized Redo Recovery. *1998 Int'l. Conference
    on Data Engineering*, 154-163.

[5] Lomet, D. and Tuttle, M. Redo Recovery From System Crashes. 1995 *VLDB Conference,*
     Zurich, Switzerland, 457-468.
[6] Lomet, D. and Tuttle, M. A Formal Treatment of Redo Recovery with Pragmatic
     Implications. Available as Digital CRL Lab Technical Report.
[7] Transaction Processing Council. TPC Benchmark H. **http://www.tpc.org**, 1999.

Object View Hierarchies in DB2 UDB

Michael Carey[1], Serge Rielau[2], and Bennet Vance[1]

[1] IBM Almaden Research Center
[2] IBM Toronto Laboratory

Abstract In this paper, we describe the design and implementation of object views in IBM's DB2 Universal Database system. We first describe the object-oriented aspects of DB2's type system, their implications for views, and our design requirements. We then describe DB2's object view facility, showing its use to create object views of object data and of legacy relational data. We discuss key aspects of its implementation, explaining how the correctness of object view definitions is checked and how we ensure that queries against object views are translated into efficient queries against the underlying stored database. We close by discussing the current status of object views in DB2.

1 Introduction

The success of the relational data model [7] is largely due to the high level of data independence it provides, and to the resultant application programmer productivity gains [13]. Relational database systems achieve data independence in part by separating the logical database schema (base tables) from the underlying physical schema (file and index structures for table storage), and in part by providing a high-level *view* facility. Views enable database designers to define virtual tables to be included in the external schema (tables shown to users) that are defined by simply writing declarative SQL queries. Views are used to provide a consistent external schema to application programs when changes are made to base tables; they are also used to provide tailored views of a database to different users/groups, with access control permitting access to only those tables/views that they need [13].

While the relational model has been tremendously successful, the world continues to place ever-increasing demands on database technology. One source of these demands is the emergence of applications wishing to manage new data types (e.g., XML, text, image, audio, video, and spatial data) in large quantities. A second source is the contrast between the complexity of today's enterprises and the simplicity of the relational model: enterprises have entities and relationships (versus tables), variations within a given kind of entity (versus homogeneous tables), and both single- and multi-valued attributes (versus "flat" tables). A third source of the demands is the commercial growth of applications that use database systems to manage large quantities of complex interrelated data objects, such as CAD/CAM systems, e-commerce web servers, and digital libraries. These demands have led the database research community to work

C. Zaniolo et al. (Eds.): EDBT 2000, LNCS 1777, pp. 478–492, 2000.
© Springer-Verlag Berlin Heidelberg 2000

on integrating object technology with database technology for the past 10–15 years [3]. Perhaps the most significant outcome of this research is the fact that virtually all commercial relational database systems are currently evolving into *object-relational* database systems that provide extensible type systems, inheritance, support for complex objects, and rule (i.e., trigger) support [15].

The aforementioned evolution is taking place, as proposed in several "manifestos" [16,12], through the addition of object-oriented (O-O) constructs to the relational model and its SQL query language [8]. IBM's DB2 Universal Database system (UDB) has been making this transition since the debut of DB2 Version 2 for Common Servers (for Unix and Windows-based platforms) in 1995, which provided user-defined "distinct" types (UDTs), user-defined functions (UDFs), and triggers. Version 5, released in late 1997, extended these features to parallel platforms. In the fall of 1998, Version 5.2 of DB2 UDB added a number of new object-relational (O-R) features to the DB2 product, including user-defined structured types with inheritance, tables and subtables of these types, object ids and references, and path expressions. Of course, supporting objects, references, and inheritance only for stored data is not sufficient; they must be supported for views as well [12]. Version 5.2 provided initial object view support, and Version 6.1 extended it in late 1999.

This paper describes the design and implementation of object views in DB2 UDB. We start by reviewing DB2's structured types and table hierarchies. We then describe our object extensions to its view definition facilities; we motivate them in terms of our up-front design requirements as well as the requirements implied by DB2's O-R features for stored tables. Our focus then turns to some salient aspects of our implementation of object views and the issues that led to our implementation. Finally, we briefly discuss how DB2's object view facility compares with those of other systems and papers as well as with the SQL99 standard. We close by describing the current status of object views in DB2.

2   O-R Extensions in DB2 SQL

To appreciate the issues related to designing an object view facility for DB2, it is important to understand some of the details of the O-R extensions supported by DB2's dialect of SQL. In this section we give an overview of DB2's O-R SQL extensions using a simple university database example; this section is in effect a compressed version of the first half of [4], which provides far more detail. For the purpose of this simple example, university people will come in two basic flavors, students and employees, with professors being a more specific kind of employee. In addition to modeling university people, the example will also model the departments for their work or studies. Figure 1 gives the DB2 SQL syntax for creating the applicable *structured types*; Fig. 2 gives the syntax for creating *typed tables* in which to store instances of these types.

The things to notice in Fig. 1 are the creation of user-defined structured types, the use of inheritance, the presence of reference types, and the **ref using** clause. The types Person_t, Emp_t, Prof_t, and Student_t form a type hierarchy

```
create type Person_t as (
    name Varchar(40), birthyear Integer) ref using Integer mode db2sql;
create type Emp_t under Person_t as (salary Integer) mode db2sql;
create type Prof_t under Emp_t as (
    rank Varchar(10), specialty Varchar(20)) mode db2sql;
create type Student_t under Person_t as (
    major Varchar(20), gpa Decimal(5,2)) mode db2sql;
create type Dept_t as (name Varchar(20), budget Integer,
    headcount Integer, mgr Ref(Emp_t)) ref using Integer mode db2sql;
alter type Emp_t add attribute dept Ref(Dept_t);
```

Fig. 1. DDL for creating a type hierarchy

```
create table person  of Person_t   (ref is oid user generated);
create table emp      of Emp_t      under person inherit select privileges;
create table prof     of Prof_t     under emp    inherit select privileges;
create table student  of Student_t  under person inherit select privileges;
create table dept     of Dept_t     (ref is oid user generated,
                                        mgr with options scope emp);

alter table emp alter column dept add scope dept;
```

Fig. 2. DDL for creating a table hierarchy

for modeling the kinds of people in the example; a subtype inherits all the attributes of its parent type. The mgr attribute of Dept_t is a reference attribute that can refer to an instance of Emp_t; the dept attribute of Emp_t is also a reference. Types must exist before a SQL statement may refer to them, which is why the dept attribute is added to Emp_t only after the type Dept_t has been created. Finally, the optional clause "**ref using** Integer" tells DB2 to use integers as its internal representation for references to objects of these types and their subtypes.[1]

DB2 and SQL99 separate the notions of type and extent. Like rows in the relational world, typed objects reside in tables – typed tables, in this case. The first statement in Fig. 2 creates a typed table named person to hold Person_t objects. This table will have three columns, an *object id* column, named "oid" via the **ref is** clause, plus one column for each Person_t attribute (i.e., name and birthyear). The phrase **user generated** tells DB2 that the object ids for person objects will be provided by users when persons are inserted into the table or its subtables. The next three statements create subtables of the person table; emp and student are immediate subtables of person, and prof is a subtable of emp. The person table and its subtables together form the person *table hierarchy*. A good mental model for a table hierarchy is that its root table (person) is a

---

[1] The keywords **mode db2sql** are required for historical reasons related to SQL99.

heterogeneous collection of objects of its declared type and subtypes. Figure 2 also creates a typed table named dept to hold Dept_t objects.

Physically, the object ids in a DB2 table hierarchy are values of the **ref using** type (integers, in this example) that are required to be unique within the table hierarchy (i.e., across all of its tables/subtables). An object id value is assigned to an object when it is first created (by an insert statement), at which time its uniqueness is verified; once inserted, object ids are immutable. A reference value contains the object id of the referenced object, and an important property of a reference column in a typed table is its *scope*. The statement that creates the table dept in Fig. 2 includes the scope clause "mgr **with options scope** emp", telling DB2 that the objects referred to by mgr values in the table dept can be found in the table emp (or a subtable of emp).

So far we have spoken only of DDL extensions. SQL's DML statements – **insert, select, update,** and **delete** – have also been extended to deal with typed table hierarchies, and path expression support is provided to enable the convenient traversal of object references. The **insert** statement creates a new object in the specified table or subtable. The **select, update,** and **delete** statements each operate on the specified table or subtable and its subtables – that is, subtable rows are considered *substitutable* for supertable rows. The examples below illustrate the DML extensions. (Again, see [4] for further details.)

1. *Create a new CS department employee with oid 100 of type* **Ref(Emp_t)**, *name 'John Smith', birth year 1968, and salary $65,000:*

   insert into emp (oid, name, birthyear, salary, dept)
       values (Emp_t(100), 'John Smith', 1968, 65000,
           (**select** oid **from** dept **where** name – 'CS'));

2. *Select the oid, name, birth year, salary, and department of employees (including professors) born after 1970 whose salary exceeds $50,000:*

   select ∗ **from** emp **where** birthyear > 1970 **and** salary > 50000;

3. *Change the birth year for the person (who could be a "regular" person, an employee, a professor, or a student) whose oid is 200 to be the year 1969:*

   update person **set** birthyear = 1969 **where** oid = Emp_t(200);

4. *Delete the employees (including professors) who earn too much:*

   delete from emp **where** salary > 500000;

5. *Find the name, salary, and department name of employees who work in departments with budgets exceeding $150,000 per person:*

   select name, salary, dept−>name   **from** emp
   where dept−>budget > 150000 ∗ dept−>headcount;

6. *Find the names of people with a salary greater than $100,000 per year or a grade point average greater than 3.9:*[2]

   select name **from outer**(person) **where** salary > 100000 **or** gpa > 3.9;

7. *Give the names of students, as well as "regular" persons, born before 1965:*

   select name   **from** person
   where birthyear < 1965 **and deref**(oid) **is of** (Student_t, **only** Person_t);

---

[2] The **outer** construct exposes all the columns of person *and* of its subtables [4].

3 Object View Considerations/Requirements

The design of DB2 UDB's object view facility was guided by two forces. The first force was a set of desiderata for object views that came in part from the literature and in part from past experiments with object view facilities that we were directly involved in [5,6]. The second force was the nature of DB2's O-R extensions, since an acceptable object view system design for DB2 must offer a virtual alternative to the relevant O-R base table extensions.

The first force led us to the following list of desirable view facility properties:

1. The facility must support virtual databases containing interconnected object views (i.e., a "closed" set of object views that reference one another [10]).
2. Such sets of object views must be able to have mutually recursive references (e.g., virtual employees referencing virtual departments and vice versa).
3. Object views must have long-lived and unique object ids for use in referring to the objects that they contain, just as objects in typed tables do.
4. Structured types for object views should be potentially independent of the types of the objects that they are used to view, with users (not the system) deciding if/how the type of a view object should be related to the types of stored objects within the database's type hierarchies.
5. Similarly, the methods[3] available for use on view objects should not be dictated by the methods associated with the stored objects; it should be possible to have methods on view objects that do not exist on stored objects.
6. A given type should be usable as the type of a stored table *or* as the type of an object view, i.e., view types shouldn't be a special kind of type.

In the object view literature, one finds a number of papers in which the authors try to answer questions such as how to infer view types from object queries, how to place view types into the type hierarchy, and how to infer which methods should be automatically inherited by view types. From a pragmatic perspective, we felt that such approaches did not focus on most users' needs, and that one could arrive at a simpler yet useful object view facility through a different factoring of the problem; we will discuss this issue further as we proceed.

The second force, the nature of DB2's O-R extensions and their likely usage, led us to the following list of required view facility properties:

1. There should be a clean separation of type and extent in the model provided for defining object views.
2. Since stored objects live in table hierarchies, the object view system must provide a virtual equivalent of table hierarchies.
3. It must be possible to define object views over table hierarchies, and these views must be updatable.
4. It must also be possible to define object views over legacy (i.e., "flat") relational databases.

---

[3] Structured types in SQL99 can have methods as well as attributes. Although DB2 does not support methods today, we expect that it will in the not-too-distant future.

The first two of these required properties are direct consequences of DB2's O-R features for stored data. The next property came out of discussions with a potential customer, who pointed out that they rely heavily on SQL's use of views for authorization. Their planned use of our object extensions was to create base table hierarchies for storing CAD/CAM data, but then to allow access to the data only through appropriately restrictive view hierarchies. The last property on the above list came from thinking about what users of IBM's DataJoiner product, a heterogeneous database product that offers a single-DB2-database view of multiple back-end relational databases, would likely want to do with object views when they become available in DataJoiner.

4   Object View Hierarchies for SQL

Guided by the desiderata of the previous section, we extended DB2 with an O-R variant of the **create view** statement that is similar to the typed **create table** statement. Thus, DB2 supports the creation of typed object views, and they can either be root views or subviews of other object views. A root view and its subviews form a *view hierarchy* that is the virtual counterpart of a table hierarchy. The type used in an object view definition is a structured type, just as in a typed table definition, and there is nothing special about view types – a DB2 structured type can be used to define a typed table, a typed view, or both. The body of an object view definition is a SQL query, as for regular views, but its select list must be type-compatible with the view's declared type. Like typed tables, instances of object views have object ids whose column name is specified in the view definition; these ids must be unique within their object view hierarchy, and uniqueness is checked at view definition time. Just like base tables, object views may contain references, which must be scoped if they are to be dereferenced. The scope of a reference can be either an object view or a base table. Finally, the body of each view or subview in an object view hierarchy specifies how the objects in that view or subview are to be obtained; that is, each view/subview body tells DB2 how to compute the contents of one virtual table within the overall hierarchy.

4.1   Object Views of Object Tables

Suppose we wished to construct a set of interrelated object views more suitable for a certain group of users than the base tables and subtables defined in Sect. 2. Say these users should see only the non-academic employees and the well-funded departments (e.g., those whose budget exceeds $1M). Figure 3 gives DB2 type definitions appropriate to this group's view of the university database.

Note that these types are similar to our previous type definitions, but shorter; their intended use as view types doesn't make them special. Note also that these types are interrelated – dept in VEmp_t has type **Ref**(VDept_t), and conversely mgr in VDept_t has type **Ref**(VEmp_t). Such reference attributes let us create

> **create type** VDept_t **as** (name Varchar(20)) **ref using** Integer **mode db2sql**;
> **create type** VPerson_t **as** (name Varchar(40)) **ref using** Integer **mode db2sql**;
> **create type** VEmp_t **under** VPerson_t **as** (dept **Ref**(VDept_t)) **mode db2sql**;
> **alter type** VDept_t **add attribute** mgr **Ref**(VEmp_t);

Fig. 3. DDL statements for creating view types

view schemas that support path queries. Using the types of Fig. 3, our target users can work in blissful ignorance of the underlying schema of Sect. 2.

Given these types, Fig. 4 shows statements to create the desired object view hierarchy; notice their similarity to the **create table** statements of Sect. 2. The first statement creates an object view vdept of type VDept_t with an object id column named oid. The view body is a SQL query that tells DB2 how to derive the extent of the view (including the object id values for the view objects); here it selects the oid, name, and mgr columns from the dept base table, taking only those rows of the dept table that have a budget value greater than \$1M. The object ids for vdept objects are derived by calling the automatically generated function VDept_t to cast the corresponding dept object id to be of type **Ref**(VDept_t) instead of **Ref**(Dept_t). An intermediate cast to Integer is required because DB2 (and SQL99) references are strongly typed, and a reference of one type cannot be cast to be a reference to an unrelated type. Similarly, the mgr references for vdept objects are computed by typecasting the underlying dept object's mgr reference, and their meaning in path expressions is specified by telling DB2 (later in Fig. 4) that the scope of vdept's mgr field is the view vemp.

> **create view** vdept **of** VDept_t (**ref is** oid **user generated**)
>   **as select** VDept_t(Integer(oid)), name, VEmp_t(Integer(mgr))
>   **from** dept   **where** budget > 1000000;
> **create view** vperson **of** VPerson_t (**ref is** oid **user generated**)
>   **as select** VPerson_t(Integer(oid)), name **from only** (person);
> **create view** vemp **of** VEmp_t **under** vperson **inherit select privileges**
>   (dept **with options scope** vdept)
>   **as select** VEmp_t(Integer(oid)), name, VDept_t(Integer(dept))
>   **from   only** (emp);
> **alter view** vdept **alter column** mgr **add scope** vemp;

Fig. 4. Creating object views over object tables

The next two statements in Fig. 4 create the vperson view hierarchy. The second **create view** statement creates the object view vperson, of type VPerson_t, which is similar to the vdept view definition just discussed. The only noteworthy difference is the use of the keyword **only** in the **from** clause of the body of the new view. The **only** keyword, which can be used in most any DB2 SQL query, instructs DB2 to exclude subtable rows; vperson will thus contain rows derived only from the person base table, and not from emp, prof, or student rows. The third **create view** statement creates a subview vemp. Its query selects the same first two columns as its parent view, subtyping the object id appropriately, plus the additional attribute, dept, that VEmp_t instances have. The dept reference attribute is declared to have scope vdept. The keyword **only** is used in defining vemp to exclude academic employees.

Since DB2 requires the object ids of objects in object views to be unique within their view hierarchy, in this example DB2 must check (i) that the oid column of vperson is duplicate-free, (ii) that the oid column of vemp is duplicate-free, and (iii) that oids are still unique across these views when considered together. Later we will say more about how this is checked, but in this case it suffices for DB2 to observe that (i) the vperson oid values are derived from person object ids, which are known to be unique, (ii) the vemp oid values are derived from emp object ids, which are known to be unique, and (iii) person and emp rows live in the same table hierarchy (person), so no person oid value can possibly be the same as any emp oid value.

Once defined, object views can be used in queries, including path queries, and they can even be updated if the defining **select** statements are of an updatable nature (as they are here). The following query finds the employee and department names of view employees who work in a view department whose name starts with 'D'; since departments with small budgets are filtered out by the vdept view, references to such departments will behave like dangling references and will return nulls in the context of the query's path expressions [4]:

select name, dept−>name **from** vemp **where** dept−>name **like** 'D%';

4.2   Object Views of Regular Tables

DB2's object view facilities can also be used to create object views and view hierarchies out of existing relational (i.e., non-object) tables. This provides a migration path for users who have legacy relational data but wish to exploit object-relational modeling in new applications. Suppose we have an existing university database containing a pair of relational tables, emp and dept. Suppose further that the structure of these tables is emp(eno, name, salary, deptno) and dept(dno, name, mgrno), where the columns eno and dno are integer keys and the columns mgrno and deptno are corresponding foreign keys. Figure 5 shows how we can create the same object views as in Fig. 4 but using the legacy database as the stored data this time. In defining the vperson hierarchy, we assume that emp rows with null salary values are regular people, while emp rows with non-null salaries under $100K are the employees to be shown in the vemp view.

Notice that in Fig. 5, the view object ids are derived from the primary keys of the legacy tables, and their foreign keys are converted into scoped references. These uses of the legacy keys are made possible by the **ref using** clause (see

```
create view vdept of VDept_t (ref is oid user generated)
    as select VDept_t(dno), name, VEmp_t(mgrno) from dept;
create view vperson of VPerson_t (ref is oid user generated)
    as select VPerson_t(eno), name from emp where salary is null;
create view vemp of VEmp_t under vperson inherit select privileges
    (dept with options scope vdept)
    as select  VEmp_t(eno), name, VDept_t(deptno)
        from  emp    where salary < 100000;
alter view vdept alter column mgr add scope vemp;
```

Fig. 5. Creating object views over a legacy database

Fig. 1), which allows the representation type for references to be chosen to match the data type of a given legacy table's primary key column. Once these DDL statements have been executed, the resulting vdept and vperson view hierarchies will have the same behavior in queries as the object views that we created previously.

5 Implementation of Object View Hierarchies

Implementing object view hierarchies in DB2 turned out to be an interesting exercise. In this section we discuss our basic approach as well as some of the main issues that arose and how we addressed them.

5.1 Basic Implementation Approach

Storage management for table hierarchies in DB2 is based on the use of *hierarchy tables* (or *H-tables* for short). Inside the DB2 storage engine, all of the rows for a given table hierarchy live together in one physical table; this internal table, the H-table, includes the columns of all subtables in the hierarchy. The H-table for Sect. 2's person table hierarchy would thus contain a type id column (to distinguish among the rows of different subtables), an object id column, the name and birthyear columns for person rows, the additional salary and dept columns for emp rows, the rank and specialty columns for prof rows, and the major and gpa columns for student rows. A given row in this H-table has a type id to indicate whether it is a Person_t, Emp_t, Prof_t, or Student_t row, and the columns that do not apply for the row in question will simply contain null values. The H-table approach made for an expedient implementation that provided good overall query performance (e.g., avoiding expensive unions/joins for complex queries involving tables and subtables) as well as flexibility in terms of supporting indexes and various constraints over table hierarchies [4].

DB2's object view hierarchies are managed in much the same way as table hierarchies. Internally, the rows of all views/subviews of a given hierarchy "reside" together in a single *hierarchy view* (or *H-view*). Though not materialized as a physical entity, logically the H-view behaves no differently from an H-table. This approach allowed most of the DB2 query compiler code for object-table queries to be reused (i.e., to "just work") for object-view queries as well; moreover, the performance of queries involving multiple views in a hierarchy benefits as the computation of the H-view is shared among all views built on it.

When a user queries a view in the vperson hierarchy of Fig. 5, DB2 translates the user's query into operations involving the temporary internal views depicted in Fig. 6.[4] The first view in Fig. 6, emp_with_type_ids, prepends an extra column, type_id, to rows of the legacy table emp upon which the vperson hierarchy was defined (Fig. 5). This type id distinguishes among legacy emp rows based on whether they belong in vperson, vemp, or neither. The **case** expression that computes this type id inside emp_with_type_ids returns VPerson_t_id[5] when the employee's salary is null, thereby classifying an emp row as belonging to the object view of type VPerson_t (i.e., the vperson view) if it satisfies the predicate provided in the user's view definition for vperson. Similarly, the second predicate in the **case** expression is drawn from the view vemp, and associates VEmp_t's type id with those emp rows that satisfy the vemp predicate. If neither arm of the **case** expression is satisfied, the resulting type id will be null; this is appropriate, as rows that satisfy neither predicate should appear in neither of the hierarchy's object views (and a null type id will disqualify such rows from both).

> **internal view** emp_with_type_ids(type_id, eno, name, salary, deptno)
>   **as select** **case when** salary **is null**   **then** VPerson_t_id
>   **when** salary < 100000 **then** VEmp_t_id
>   end, eno, name, salary, deptno
>   **from**   emp;
> **internal view** vperson_hview(type_id, oid, name, dept)
>   **as select** type_id, eno, name,
>   **case when** type_id **in** (VEmp_t_id) **then** VDept_t(deptno) **end**
>   **from**   emp_with_type_ids;

Fig. 6. Hidden temporary views used internally for a view hierarchy

The second view in Fig. 6, vperson_hview, is the H-view itself, which serves as a representation of all rows (and all columns) of the vperson view and its subviews. Root-level columns of vperson_hview are selected directly from the view emp_with_type_ids, while subview columns (in this case, just the dept column of vemp) must be null for rows outside the subview (i.e., for superview rows and – in general – for rows of "sibling" views). Thus, after simply selecting the type_id and the root-level columns eno and name, vperson_hview uses a **case** expression to compute non-null dept values only for vemp rows. (In fact, DB2

---

[4] The syntax shown in Figs. 6 and 7 is not actual DB2 SQL syntax, and should not be taken too literally; it is simply intended to convey internal DB2 mechanisms.

[5] VPerson_t_id and VEmp_t_id are mnemonics for internal integer-constant type ids.

allows a subview's expression for computing a column value to override its parent view's expression for the column. When that occurs, the **case** expression not only discriminates between null and non-null cases, but also among the different expressions for different subviews.)

Given vperson_hview, Fig. 7 shows two of the internal views that DB2 uses to expand object views in users' queries. A reference to the view vemp behaves as if it were a reference to vemp_qtarget; the same virtual table is obtained, but vemp_qtarget derives this virtual table from the H-view, filtering rows via the computed type id rather than via the predicate in vemp's body. A reference to **outer**(person) behaves as if it were a reference to vperson_outer_qtarget (the internal view vperson_qtarget would be similar, but would omit the dept column). Our implementation examples have used an object view hierarchy over a legacy database, but all the central points in both Figs. 6 and 7 would be the same for object views on object tables (or on other object views, for that matter).

> **internal view** vemp_qtarget(oid, name, dept)
>   **as select** VEmp_t(oid), name, dept
>   **from** vperson_hview   **where** type_id **in** (VEmp_t_id);
> **internal view** vperson_outer_qtarget(oid, name, dept)
>   **as select** VPerson_t(oid), name, dept
>   **from** vperson_hview   **where** type_id **in** (VPerson_t_id, VEmp_t_id);

Fig. 7. Internal realization of two possible object view query targets

5.2   Disjointness of Views within a Hierarchy

DB2's object view facility requires uniqueness of object ids within a view hierarchy. When an object view is defined, local uniqueness of its object id is ensured by verifying that the view body mentions only one table (or view) in its **from** clause and selects as the view's object id a unique key (possibly with a type cast) of that table. Global uniqueness across a hierarchy is checked through a conservative static analysis of the predicates in the user's view definitions each time a **create view** statement is issued to create a new subview; by verifying *disjointness* of these predicates, this analysis seeks to guarantee that the newly created view can never contain rows with the same object id as any existing view in the hierarchy. The **create view** statement is rejected with an error report if the analysis fails to obtain such a guarantee.

For example, when the view vemp is created in Fig. 5, the system verifies that its predicate "salary < 100000" is disjoint from the vperson predicate "salary **is null**". Since both predicates refer to the same column (salary), and since a null value cannot satisfy a range predicate, disjointness is assured. It follows that the object id in any given emp row cannot be selected in both the vemp and vperson view bodies. If we defined a new subview vexec that applied the predicate "salary

>= 100000", this predicate would be recognized as disjoint from the other two. The checking algorithm can also cope with predicates involving ranges of values from multiple columns. For example, given numeric columns x and y, the system would recognize "x > 20 **or** y > 8" as disjoint from "x < 20 **and** y < 6", and would identify the subtly different predicate pair "x > 20 **or** y > 8" and "x < 20 **or** y < 6" as potentially overlapping. The checking algorithm is conservative in that its reasoning abilities are limited; e.g., it would not recognize "x < 20 **and** y < 6" and "x + y > 26" as disjoint, even though they are.

5.3   Rewrite Rules for Object View Queries

An important goal in the implementation of object views was that queries against object views be able to take advantage of the same optimizations as queries against base tables. Two new query rewrite rules that cooperate with DB2's preexisting rewrite rules help achieve the desired optimizations.

Figure 8 illustrates how these rewrites work. In the user query of Fig. 8a, the predicate "VDept_t(99) = dept" is potentially highly selective; if there is an index on the deptno column of the underlying emp table, we would like to use it. However, the dept column of **outer**(vperson), rather than mapping directly to the deptno column of emp, is computed by a **case** expression (Fig. 6). DB2 must therefore perform several rewrites before it can use an index on the deptno column.

Figure 8b shows the initial user query after expansion of the internal view vperson_outer_qtarget of Fig. 7. The expanded query incorporates the predicate from vperson_outer_qtarget, and now selects from vperson_hview. In Fig. 8c we expand vperson_hview, replacing Fig. 8b's reference to dept with the **case** expression from the body of vperson_hview (Fig. 6). We now refer to the rewrite rules in Fig. 9, which were introduced to ensure access to indexes for queries over object views. The first rule (Fig. 9a) rewrites a comparison against a **case** expression into a disjunction of conjunctions.[6] Application of this rule to Fig. 8c yields Fig. 8d, which has *two* predicates on the type id – one introduced by rewriting the **case** expression, and one carried over from Fig. 8c. In Fig. 8e, existing DB2 rewrites combine these two predicates and eliminate the cast function VDept_t, yielding the indexable predicate "99 = deptno".

In Fig. 8f we expand the internal view emp_with_type_ids, replacing the reference to type_id with the **case** expression from the body of emp_with_type_ids (Fig. 6). We are now ready to apply our second **case**-simplification rule from Fig. 9b, which turns an **in**-predicate on a **case** expression into a simple disjunction. The final query resulting from this simplification, shown in Fig. 8g,[7] has *two* indexable predicates on the underlying emp table – one on the deptno column, and one on the salary column.

---

[6] The first rule actually holds for an arbitrary relational operator (e.g., $\leq$, $\neq$, etc.) in place of the equal signs. In both rules, the predicates P_i must be disjoint, and special provisions must be made if any of the P_i are UNKNOWN (as can occur with three-valued logic), or if L or any of the V_i (which are assumed distinct) are null.

[7] No **or**'s appear, because this particular rewrite yielded only the single predicate P_2.

(a) **select** name **from outer**(vperson) **where** VDept_t(99) = dept

(b) **select** name   **from** vperson_hview
     where VDept_t(99) = dept **and** type_id **in** (VPerson_t_id, VEmp_t_id)

(c) **select** name   **from** emp_with_type_ids
     where VDept_t(99) =
                case when type_id **in** (VEmp_t_id) **then** VDept_t(deptno)
                end
            and type_id **in** (VPerson_t_id, VEmp_t_id)

(d) **select** name   **from** emp_with_type_ids
     where VDept_t(99) = VDept_t(deptno) **and** type_id **in** (VEmp_t_id)
            and type_id **in** (VPerson_t_id, VEmp_t_id)

(e) **select** name   **from** emp_with_type_ids
     where 99 = deptno **and** type_id **in** (VEmp_t_id)

(f) **select** name   **from** emp
     where 99 = deptno **and case when** salary **is null**   **then** VPerson_t_id
                         when salary < 100000 **then** VEmp_t_id
                         end in (VEmp_t_id)

(g) **select** name   **from** emp
     where 99 = deptno **and** salary < 100000

Fig. 8. Query rewrite steps for deriving an indexable predicate

(a) $L = \begin{pmatrix} \textbf{case when } P_1 \textbf{ then } V_1 \\ \textbf{when } P_2 \textbf{ then } V_2 \\ \vdots \\ \textbf{when } P_n \textbf{ then } V_n \\ \textbf{end} \end{pmatrix} \implies \begin{array}{l} (L = V_1 \textbf{ and } P_1) \textbf{ or} \\ (L = V_2 \textbf{ and } P_2) \textbf{ or} \\ \vdots \\ (L = V_n \textbf{ and } P_n) \end{array}$

(b) $\begin{pmatrix} \textbf{case when } P_1 \textbf{ then } V_1 \\ \textbf{when } P_2 \textbf{ then } V_2 \\ \vdots \\ \textbf{when } P_n \textbf{ then } V_n \\ \textbf{end} \end{pmatrix} \textbf{ in } (V_{i_1}, V_{i_2}, \ldots, V_{i_m}) \implies \begin{pmatrix} P_{i_1} \textbf{ or} \\ P_{i_2} \textbf{ or} \\ \vdots \\ P_{i_m} \end{pmatrix}$

Fig. 9. Case-simplification rules (for disjoint $\{P_i\}$, distinct $\{V_i\}$, and two-valued logic)

6   Relationship to Other Work and Systems

Among object-relational database products today, DB2 has arguably the most advanced object view support. The key alternative commercial systems with object-relational view support are Oracle 8i and Informix Universal Server. Oracle 8i supports object views over both object tables and legacy tables, and currently permits richer view bodies; however, it does not yet support inheritance, so one cannot have *hierarchies* of views (nor of tables). Informix Universal Server has table hierarchies and object views, but appears not to support view hierarchies. The early object-relational database product UniSQL [12] supported object views, but the notions of types and extents were not separated in that system, so its view facilities were rather different from those described here.

Space precludes a careful discussion of the extensive object-view research literature; we were most influenced by [10,1,14,11,2,5] – in particular, by the closure principle of Heiler and Zdonik [10], the object identity treatment of Kifer et al. [11], and the Garlic notion of object-centered views [5]. As mentioned earlier, we chose not to be influenced by work on inference of view types from view bodies, placement of view types into the type hierarchy, or inference of applicable view object methods from base object types.

Finally, DB2's object view support is closely related to (actually, a superset of) that of the SQL99 standard. SQL99 supports object view hierarchies, but has more restrictions on what is allowed in view bodies; in addition, DB2 offers several product extensions that are not included in the SQL99 standard.

7   Status and Future Plans

In this paper, we have described the design and implementation of object views and view hierarchies in IBM's DB2 Universal Database System. Object view support made its initial commercial debut in DB2 UDB Version 5.2, and support for view hierarchies over multiple underlying tables was added in Version 6.1. DB2's object view support provides a clear separation between types and extents (view types are just ordinary structured types); it also provides a clear separation between the types of views and their underlying objects' types. To our knowledge, the notion of view hierarchies is novel; it first appeared in DB2, and was subsequently carried to SQL99 in a standards proposal co-authored by IBM. Object views can be created both of object tables and legacy tables, and DB2's implementation ensures that standard optimizations on base tables are available for object views and object view hierarchies as well.

In the near future, we expect that DB2 will support methods on structured types [9]. It will then be possible for object views to have methods, since view types are just structured types. However, method delegation is an open issue that we need to address, as SQL99 has a value-based model of types that poses challenges for delegation. The other SQL99-related extension that we plan to make in the not-too-distant future is the addition of support for object ids whose values are derived from multiple object attributes.

Acknowledgments

The authors wish to thank Peter Schwarz, Ed Wimmers, Laura Haas, and Jerry Kiernan for many discussions that influenced DB2's object view design. Our thanks to Hamid Pirahesh, George Lapis, Cliff Leung, and Jason Sun for consulting on the implementation of object views and for implementing the query rewrite rules of Fig. 9. We thank Nelson Mattos for his help with the language design and for his key role in standardizing object view hierarchies in SQL99. Finally, we are indebted to Cheryl Greene for granting the second author time to make object views a reality in DB2.

References

1. S. Abiteboul and T. Bonner. Objects and views. In *Proceedings SIGMOD Conference, Denver, Colorado,* pages 238–247, 1991.
2. R. Agrawal and L. DeMichiel. Type derivation using the projection operation. In *Proceedings EDBT Conference, Cambridge, UK,* pages 7–14, 1994.
3. M. Carey and D. DeWitt. Of objects and databases: A decade of turmoil. In *Proceedings VLDB Conference, Mumbai (Bombay), India,* pages 3–14, 1996.
4. M. Carey et al. O-O, what have they done to DB2? In *Proceedings VLDB Conference, Edinburgh, Scotland,* 1999.
5. M. Carey, L. Haas, P. Schwarz, et al. Towards heterogeneous multimedia information systems: The Garlic approach. In *Proceedings IEEE RIDE–DOM Workshop, Taipei, Taiwan,* pages 124–131, 1995.
6. M. Carey and J. Kiernan. Extending SQL-92 for OODB access: Design and implementation experience. In *Proceedings ACM OOPSLA Conference, Austin, Texas,* pages 467–480, 1995.
7. E. Codd. A relational model of data for large shared data banks. *Commun. ACM,* 13(6):377–387, 1970.
8. A. Eisenberg and J. Melton. SQL:1999, formerly known as SQL3. *ACM SIGMOD Record,* 28(1):131–138, 1999.
9. Y. Fuh et al. Implementation of SQL3 structured types with inheritance and value substitutability. In *Proceedings VLDB Conference, Edinburgh, Scotland,* 1999.
10. S. Heiler and S. Zdonik. Object views: Extending the vision. In *Proceedings ICDE, Los Angeles, California,* pages 86–93, 1990.
11. M. Kifer, W. Kim, and S. Sagiv. Querying object-oriented databases. In *Proceedings SIGMOD Conference, San Diego, California,* pages 393–402, 1992.
12. W. Kim. Object-oriented database systems: Promises, reality, and future. In *Proceedings VLDB Conference, Dublin, Ireland,* pages 676–687, 1993.
13. R. Ramakrishnan. *Database Management Systems.* McGraw-Hill, 1997.
14. M. Scholl, C. Laasch, and M. Tresch. Updatable views in object-oriented databases. In *Proceedings DOOD-91 Conference, Munich, Germany,* pages 189–207, 1991.
15. M. Stonebraker and P. Brown. *Object-Relational DBMSs (2nd Edition).* Morgan Kaufmann, 1998.
16. M. Stonebraker et al. Third-generation database system manifesto. *ACM SIGMOD Record,* 19(3):31–44, 1990.

Query Systems

Plug&Join: An Easy-To-Use Generic Algorithm for Efficiently Processing Equi and Non-equi Joins

Jochen van den Bercken, Martin Schneider and Bernhard Seeger

Department of Mathematics and Computer Science
University of Marburg
Hans-Meerwein-Straße, 35032 Marburg, Germany
{bercken,maschn,seeger}@mathematik.uni-marburg.de

Abstract. This paper presents Plug&Join, a new generic algorithm for efficiently processing a broad class of different join types in extensible database systems. Depending on the join predicate Plug&Join is called with a suitable type of index structure as a parameter. If the inner relation fits in memory, the algorithm builds a memory resident index of the desired type on the inner relation and probes all tuples of the outer relation against the index. Otherwise, a memory resident index is created by sampling the inner relation. The index is then used as a partitioning function for both relations.

In order to demonstrate the flexibility of Plug&Join, we present how to implement equi joins, spatial joins and subset joins by using memory resident B+-trees, R-trees and S-trees, respectively. Moreover, results obtained from different experiments for the spatial join show that Plug&Join is competitive to special-purpose methods like the Partition Based Spatial-Merge Join algorithm.

1 Introduction

In order to cope with large sets of complex data, database management systems (DBMS) have to be equipped with new methods for processing queries. While query processing techniques for different application areas like spatial databases have already been integrated into commercial DBMS, there are also serious concerns about such special-purpose solutions. In particular, the complexity of current DBMS increases dramatically leading to all the well-known problems of software development and maintenance. While DBMS provide some advanced query processing techniques, most of the systems are still too inflexible since they are not intended for receiving new functionality from the user (or if so, this is too difficult). Although the idea of such an extensible system is well known in the database community since almost two decades, we still have the impression that there is a lack of basic generic query processing techniques.

In this paper, we reconsider the classical problem of join processing: For relations R and S and a predicate p the result set of a join $R\ p\ S$ consists of those tuples from the cartesian product of R and S which satisfy p. We are interested in *generic* and *efficient* methods for join processing which can be used in different application areas such as spatial databases (spatial join), temporal databases (temporal join), object-oriented databases (subset join) and others. Although the nested-loops join is an example of a

C. Zaniolo et al. (Eds.): EDBT 2000, LNCS 1777, pp. 495–509, 2000.
© Springer-Verlag Berlin Heidelberg 2000

generic method, it clearly fails to be efficient. Unfortunately, the methods proposed for equi joins (and which are implemented in todays commercial DBMS) cannot be used for supporting other types of joins.

In the following, we present a new generic join algorithm called Plug&Join which is applicable to a large number of joins including the ones mentioned above. Plug&Join is a generic algorithm that is parameterized by the type of an *index structure*. Note however that Plug&Join does *not* require a preexisting index on any of the relations. Depending on the specific index structure, Plug&Join is able to support different types of join predicates. We also show that it performs really fast. For spatial joins, we compare the performance of Plug&Join with the Partition Based Spatial-Merge Join (PBSM) [28] which is considered to be among the most efficient join methods to compute spatial joins. Plug&Join using R*-trees [6] is shown to be competitive to an improved version of PBSM [13] which runs considerably faster than the original version.

The remainder of this paper is organized as follows. First, we will give a review of previous work on join processing where our focus is put on generic algorithms. Section 2 introduces our model of the underlying index structure. Thereafter, we present our generic algorithm Plug&Join in more detail. In Section 3, we discuss several use-cases for Plug&Join. We start by explaining how to support equi joins and present thereafter the use-cases for spatial joins and subset joins. Section 4 presents an experimental comparison of Plug&Join and PBSM using non-artificial spatial data sets.

1.1 Review of Previous Work

Good surveys of algorithms for processing relational joins are provided in [30], [25] and [14]. There has been quite a lot of work on spatial joins recently ([27], [3], [5], [15], [22], [19], [23], [28], [24], [2], [26]). The spatial join combines two sets of spatial objects with respect to a spatial predicate. Most of the mentioned work has dealt with intersection as the join predicate, but there is also the need to support other predicates [29]. In temporal databases, so-called temporal joins are required ([31], [32]). A temporal join is basically a one-dimensional spatial join, but because of the high overlap of the data in temporal databases, most of the methods known from spatial joins perform poorly. In object-oriented databases, we need to support subset joins [18]. The join predicate of the subset join is defined on two set-valued attributes, say R.A and S.B, and all tuples of the cartesian product are retrieved where $R.A \supseteq S.B$. Most of these join algorithms have in common that they are designed to support one specific join operation and it is not evident how to extend their functionality to support other joins.

Generic frameworks for query processing techniques have attracted only little attention in the literature, so far. The GiST approach [17] consists of a framework for dynamic tree-based index structures which supports user-defined search predicates. Index structures like B+-trees, R-trees [16] and M-trees [10] can be derived from GiST. Actually, GiST is an ideal candidate for initializing Plug&Join as we'll explain in section 2.1. The Bulk Index Join [7] is a framework for join processing, but it assumes that a preexisting index has been created for one of the relations. In contrast, Plug&Join does not require a preexisting index for any of the relations.

Most related to Plug&Join is the Spatial Hash Join (SHJ) [23] of Lo and Ravishankar. The SHJ is primarily designed to support spatial joins, but the framework can easily be extended to support join predicates with a spatial relationship in a one- or multidimensional data space. The SHJ is a divide&conquer approach that partitions both of the relations into buckets. Lo and Ravishankar provide a classification according to the criteria whether the objects of the two input relations are assigned to one or multiple buckets. Plug&Join differs from SHJ for the following reasons: First, Plug&Join is more general since it can also be applied to join predicates like the subset predicate where the predicate is not related to a spatial domain. Second, our approach is more specialized since we do not allow data of one of the input relations to be assigned to multiple buckets. The main reason for this restriction is that otherwise duplicates may arise in the result set which lead to a substantial performance reduction when the join selectivity is high. Third, and most important, our generic algorithm is able to use index structures available in the DBMS to partition the data, whereas the partitioning function of SHJ still has to be implemented. We believe that the implementation is however too difficult and therefore, SHJ is not an adequate generic approach to an extensible DBMS.

2 Plug&Join

In this section we give a full description of Plug&Join. First, we discuss why we use index structures as a basis for our generic join algorithm. Thereafter, we give a detailed description of Plug&Join.

2.1 A Plea for Index Structures

Plug&Join partitions both join relations recursively until each partition of the inner relation fits in main memory. Therefore, the algorithm needs a partitioning function which has to be provided as a parameter. If an inner partition fits in memory, the algorithm has to join the inner partition with its corresponding outer partition. Thus, an appropriate main memory join algorithm has to be available.

By using a single type of index structure, we are in the position to cope with both requirements: First, a partitioning function can simply be created by inserting a sample of the inner relation into a memory resident index of the desired type. Each leaf of the index then corresponds to a pair of partitions of the join relations. Second, a simple but efficient main memory join algorithm can be obtained in a similar way: We build a memory resident index of the desired type on the inner partition and probe all tuples of the corresponding outer partition against that index.

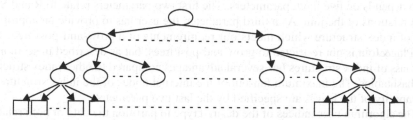

Fig. 1: Structure of a grow-and-post tree

In the following, we assume an index structure to be a *grow-and-post tree* [21]. We will give the reasons shortly after the description of grow-and-post trees.

Grow-and-post trees contain two types of nodes, see Figure 1: internal nodes and leaf nodes. Each of the internal nodes consists of a routing table with at most C entries referencing a subtree. A leaf node refers to a page on disk, i. e., there are at most B tuples stored in a leaf node.

As known for B+-trees, an insertion of a new tuple into a grow-and-post tree only requires the nodes from a single path of the tree. First, the tuple traverses the tree from the root to a leaf node in which the tuple is inserted into, i. e., the node *grows* in size. In case that a node overflows, it is split into two nodes, and a new entry has to be inserted into the parent node. This may again result in an overflow of the parent node, which is treated analogously. In terms of grow-and-post trees, index entries are *posted* in direction up to the root.

There are three reasons for choosing grow-and-post trees as the abstract index structure for Plug&Join:

First, in addition to B+-trees, many advanced index structures like the R-tree [16], S-tree [11], LSD-tree [20], M-tree [10] and the multiversion-B-tree [4] are grow-and-post trees. Some of them like B+-trees or R-trees are already implemented in DBMS or geographical information systems. These preimplemented index structures generally support a large set of different query types and therefore can also be used in combination with Plug&Join to support different types of joins. This does not hold in general for other kind of index structures like hashtables which are primarily designed to support exact match queries. Hashtables are therefore restricted to support equi joins only.

Second, frameworks like GiST allow to implement custom types of grow-and-post trees with little effort. Furthermore, it is even simpler in GiST to provide a new type of query for an index structure that has been implemented under GiST [1].

Third, grow-and-post trees are data-adaptive because of their ability to split full nodes. Therefore, an index created using a sample of a relation allows Plug&Join to partition the relation evenly with high probability. Note that grow-and-post trees have a kind of build-in adaption to data distributions, i. e. no specialized sampling technique has to be provided. It is however advantageous if the input arrives in random order. Consequently, Plug&Join using grow-and-post trees will generally alleviate the problem of data skew and reduce the overhead of repartitioning compared to using hashtables or other static index structures.

2.2 The Generic Algorithm

In this section, we give a detailed description of our algorithm Plug&Join. The algorithm depends on five input parameters. The first two parameters relate to R and S, the input relations of the join. As a third parameter, the user has to provide an appropriate type of index structure which meets our requirements of a grow-and-post tree. Note that Plug&Join is not restricted to grow-and-post trees, but as described in section 2.1, this class of index structures has several advantages compared to other index structures like hashtables. The maximum fan-out of the internal nodes of the index structure and the capacity of the leaves are specified by the last two parameters.

The algorithm uses indices of the desired type to partition the data of both relations where one pair of partitions corresponds to one leaf. In order to determine the maximum numbers of partitions (leaves), the function *getMaxLeaves* is called once for each invocation of Plug&Join. This function requires as input parameters the inner relation *R*, the type of the index structure *TreeType*, its fan-out and the capacity of its leaves. For a leaf *l*, we use the terminology *l.Rpart* and *l.Spart* to refer to the corresponding partitions that contain tuples from R and S, respectively.

```
Algorithm Plug&Join (R, S, TreeType, fanOut, leafCapacity)
   if (S is not empty)
      maxLeaves := getMaxLeaves(R, TreeType, fanOut, leafCapacity)
      index := createTree(TreeType, fanOut, leafCapacity)
      while R is not empty
         remove one tuple r from R
         if number of leaves of index <= maxLeaves
            insert r into the index
         else
            find the leaf into which r would have to be inserted
            if leaf overflows
               insert r into leaf.Rpart
            else
               insert r into leaf
      foreach leaf of index
         if leaf.Rpart is not empty
            move all tuples from leaf into leaf.Rpart
            flush leaf.Rpart to disk
      while S is not empty
         remove one tuple s from S and transform it into a query
         foreach leaf of index that is examined by the query
            if leaf is empty
               insert s into leaf.Spart
            else
               report all tuples in leaf that answer the query
      foreach leaf of index
         if leaf.Spart is not empty
            flush leaf.Spart to disk
      delete the index
      foreach pair (Rpart, Spart) produced before
         Plug&Join (Rpart, Spart, TreeType, fanOut, leafCapacity)
```

Plug&Join first creates a new index of the desired *TreeType*. Then, it reads from the inner relation R the tuples one by one and inserts them into the index. In order to support this step efficiently, the index is kept resident in main memory and therefore, no I/Os are performed.

First, let us discuss the case when all of the records of relation R fit in main memory. We therefore do not have to limit the number of leaves of the index to be created, thus the function *getMaxLeaves* will return ∞. After having built up the index in main memory, the tuples of the outer relation S are transformed into queries which are processed by the index immediately. The set of results obtained from all queries corresponds to the total result set of the join.

Second, let us consider the case when R does not fit in main memory. Then, we have to partition both relations R and S pairwise, see Figure 2. Each pair of partitions corre-

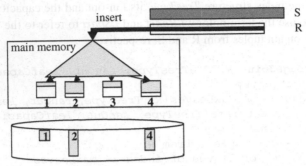

Fig. 2: Processing the inner relation *R*

sponds to one leaf of the index, so the function *getMaxLeaves* determines how many pairs of partitions to create. On the one hand, the number of pairs has to be big enough to minimize repartitioning. On the other hand, choosing the number too big increases random I/O, thus the performance degrades. As a first approach, we adopt the rule of PBSM, see section 4.1. Due to space limitations, we'll examine the problem in our future work. As long as the number of leaves of the index has not reached the threshold *maxLeaves*, the tuples of R are just inserted into the index. Recall that, by assumption, the index stores tuples in exactly one of its leaves, thus the tuples of relation R will not be replicated. As soon as the number of leaves of the index reaches the precomputed threshold, an overflow in one of the leaves does not result in a structural change anymore, but the tuple (which causes the overflow) is simply written into the associated Rpart. Each partition is implemented as a simple queue by a linked list of buckets on disk. The access to a queue is buffered in such a way that its last bucket is kept in main memory. In case that this bucket is also full, it is flushed to disk. The size of a bucket is given by the available main memory divided by the number of leaves.

After all tuples of R have been processed, we examine each leaf of the index. In case that its corresponding Rpart is not empty, we remove all tuples from that leaf, insert them into its Rpart and flush the Rpart to disk. Consider for example the situation illustrated in Figure 2 where a tree consists of four leaves. The leaves 1, 2 and 4 are written out to disk, whereas the tuples of leaf 3 remain in memory.

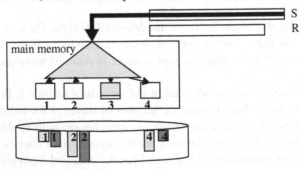

Fig. 3: Processing the outer relation *S*

Next, we process all tuples of S one by one, see Figure 3. We transform each tuple of S into a query which is directed by the index to each leaf or Rpart that may contain join partners. If a leaf is empty, that means its Rpart resides on disk, we add the query to its Spart. Note that depending on the type of the join, the tuples of S may be replicated here. If the leaf is not empty, we report those of its tuples which satisfy the query predicate.

When all queries are processed and the Sparts are written to disk, we have generated pairs of partitions on disk where the one partition belongs to relation R and the other to S. The memory resident index is deleted since it is not needed anymore. After that, we apply the same algorithm in a recursive fashion to each of these pairs of partitions.

3 Use-Cases of Plug&Join

In this section we describe in more detail how to apply our generic algorithm to specific use-cases. For sake of simplicity, we first start with the traditional equi join. Thereafter, we present the implementation of the spatial join and the subset join as special cases of Plug&Join. Most important in the following discussion is an appropriate choice of an index structure. Recall that Plug&Join uses the same type of index structure for partitioning the relations as well as for processing an in-memory index nested-loops join.

The GiST frameworks allows to implement with little effort all index structures that are discussed in this chapter, because all of them belong to the class of grow-and-post trees. As a consequence, implementing a specific index structure results in un implementation of a variety of join types that can be computed by Plug&Join using that index structure.

3.1 Equi Join

Let us assume that the join predicate is defined on attributes R.A and S.B of R and S, respectively. The equi join consists of the cartesian product of R and S where R.A = S.B. Plug&Join requires an index structure which efficiently supports insertions and exact match queries. These requirement is fulfilled by many different types of index structures including AVL-trees and red-black trees. We however expect that these main memory index structures are not available in current DBMS, and furthermore, they do not belong to the class of grow-and-post trees. Since B+-trees are the standard index structure in a DBMS for such a purpose, we also choose it to serve as the underlying index structure of Plug&Join.

Plug&Join creates only memory-resident indices. The index therefore has to be initialized such that the CPU-time of the relevant operations is minimized. As a general design goal, the maximum fan-out of the internal nodes and the capacity of the leaves of the index should be small enough: for B+-trees, small nodes will result in CPU-time savings when tuples of the inner relation R are inserted, whereas the processing of tuples of the outer relations S is not influenced by the size of the nodes because it is possible to use binary search in the nodes of a B+-tree.

While the tuples of an inner partition are inserted into the B+-tree, the tuples of the corresponding outer partition are transformed into queries. In case of processing equi joins, the tuples are interpreted as exact match queries which are processed on B+-trees. As a consequence, the tuples of the outer relation are assigned to at most one of the outer partitions.

The equi join is a symmetric join in that both relations may serve as the inner relation which serves as the source for creating the indices. This gives us the possibility to enhance our algorithm in the following way. For each invocation of our algorithm we declare the smaller partition to become the inner one. In general, this will reduce the number of recursive calls.

We previously emphasized that Plug&Join in combination with the same index structure can even support different types of joins, the following explains this more clearly. B+-tree supports primarily two types of queries: exact match query and range query. The so-called band join [12] is an example where the outer relation has to be transformed into range queries. This is however the only difference to the equi join when Plug&Join would be used to implement a band join.

3.2 Spatial Join

For the spatial join, the input relations R and S refer to a set of spatial objects. The result of the spatial join of R and S is defined to be the subset of the cartesian product of R and S where the spatial predicate is satisfied. In common with most work on spatial join processing, we assume here that the join predicate tests whether spatial objects overlap and that the spatial objects are rectilinear rectangles. In general, these rectangles refer to the minimum bounding boxes (MBB) of the actual objects. They can be used in a filter step [27] to prune the search space and to deliver a candidate set of the spatial join. An additional refinement step is required to identify the candidates which really satisfy the join predicate.

In order to use Plug&Join for spatial joins, an efficient index structure is required that supports insertions of objects (without clipping them) and window queries. The R*-tree [6], a variant of the R-tree [16], is among the most efficient index structures which fulfill these requirements. The R*-tree groups spatial objects hierarchically by their MBBs. The leaves of the R-tree contain the spatial objects (or references to them), whereas an entry of an internal node consists of the MBB of the spatial objects stored in its associated subtree. Due to the lack of ordering rectangles, the CPU-time consumption is generally higher than for a B+-tree. Splitting a node in the R*-tree requires $O(d*B \log B)$ time where B denotes the capacity of a node and d is the number of dimensions (here d=2). A window query also requires that all entries of a visited node have to be examined. It is therefore even more important than in case of B+-trees to use small values for the maximum fan-out and the capacity of the leaf nodes. Otherwise, the required CPU-time to insert and retrieve tuples is much too high leading to an inefficient implementation of the spatial join. We will show in our experiments in section 4.3 how to choose these two parameters.

For the spatial join supporting the overlap join predicate, the objects of the outer relation are transformed into window queries. In general, several leaves are required to answer window queries and therefore, objects of the outer relation are replicated by Plug&Join. However, the impact of replication on the performance is rather small for non-artificial data sets, because the volume of an object is small compared to the volume of the minimum bounding box of a partition. Moreover, the R*-tree has been designed to minimize the overlap of the bounding boxes stored in a node. This also results in a low replication of the outer relation.

Similar to the equi join, the spatial join is also a symmetric join such that both relations may serve as the inner relation. For each call of Plug&Join we always choose the smaller of both partitions to serve as the inner one.

3.3 Subset Join

In contrast to the pure relational data model, object-oriented models like the ODMG model [9] support set-valued attributes. As a consequence, it might be possible to specify joins based on set comparisons, for example whether the one set-value is a subset of the other. The subset join is of practical relevance because it implements a sort of a *forall*-predicate. As an example, consider relations *students* and *professors* where a set-valued attribute *courses* exists in both of the relations. For each professor, we might be interested in those students which attended all courses of this professor. The corresponding query can be expressed as a subset join.

In order to support subset joins, we need an index structure that support insertions and subset queries. Let R and S be relations with set-valued attributes R.A and S.B, respectively. The subset join computes the subset of the cartesian product of R and S where $R.A \supseteq S.B$ is satisfied. Among the most efficient index structures to support subset queries is the S-tree [11]. S-trees are grow-and-post trees which can be implemented under GiST. S-trees use signatures as a kind of approximation for a set-valued object where a signature is a bit vector of a predefined length. The leaves of the S-tree contain signatures of the objects, whereas an entry of an internal node of the S-tree consists of the signature which is computed by a bitwise OR on the bit vectors of all objects stored in the corresponding subtree. In our example, the bit vector of a student is computed by a bitwise OR on the bit vectors of the courses he/she attended.

A subset query is performed in the following way. First, the query is transformed into a bit vector. In our example, each professor corresponds to a single query, and the bit vector is obtained analogously to the one for students. Then, the query starts at the root of the S-tree and examines the bit vectors of each entry. If the bit vector of S is part of the bit vector of an entry, the corresponding subtree has to be examined recursively. Similar to the R-tree, the S-tree only provides candidates. Therefore, in a separate step the candidates must be tested whether they really fulfill the query condition. For the details of the search algorithm we refer the reader to [11].

Due to the overhead of splitting and searching nodes, we also suggest to choose the capacity of a leaf node and the fan-out of an internal node as small as possible. Moreover, a query generally proceeds to multiple leaves and therefore, replication occurs for the outer relation. In contrast to spatial joins and equi joins, the subset join is asymmetric, so that we are not able to swap the roles of the inner and outer partition on demand.

Despite the large amount of work in the area of join processing, we are not aware of a description of algorithms to process large subset joins. Note that [18] presented several proposals, but input relations are assumed to be small enough to process the entire join in main memory.

4 Experiments

In this section we present a few results from our experiments with Plug&Join. In particular, we show the results of a comparison of Plug&Join and a special-purpose method. In our experiments, we decided to examine the spatial join for the following reasons: First, the spatial join is the best-known non-equi join and many special-purpose algorithms have been proposed recently. Second, large real databases are available which can be used as data sources in our experiments. Among the different algorithms for spatial joins we choose the Partition Based Spatial-Merge Join (PBSM) [28] as the competitor of Plug&Join. PBSM has been shown in different experiments to be among the most efficient join methods ([24], [2], [13], [26]).

In the following we first give a detailed description of PBSM. In our experiments a modified version of PBSM [13] is used which runs considerably faster than the original algorithm. This is followed by an introduction of our computing model and a description of the spatial data sets. Thereafter, we first discuss some of the results which justify our claims previously made for Plug&Join. Finally, we present the results of our comparison of PBSM and Plug&Join.

4.1 PBSM

Partition Based Spatial-Merge Join (PBSM) [28] is a divide & conquer algorithm that breaks up the input relations R and S into partitions using an equidistant grid. Similar to Plug&Join, it is then sufficient to compute the join for pairs of partitions (where one belongs to R and the other belongs to S). We assume that the input relations refer to sets of key-pointer elements (KPE). A KPE consists of a pointer to a spatial object and its MBB.

PBSM as it was originally proposed in [28] performs in four phases which are described briefly in the following. In the first phase, the number of partitions p is computed such that the join of a pair of partitions can be processed in main memory (with high probability). For each of the input relations, p partitions are created by using an equidistant grid with NT cells, $NT \geq p$. A cell of the grid, also termed *tile*, is then assigned to one of the partitions. A KPE of a relation is inserted into a partition of the relation if its MBB intersects with one of the tiles that belong to the partition. This rule obviously results in replication of KPEs, i. e. a KPE can be stored in more than one partition. The advantage of assigning multiple tiles to a partition is that the KPEs are almost uniformly distributed among the partitions. Patel and DeWitt [28] recommend to use a hash function for mapping the tiles to partitions.

In the second phase, corresponding pairs of partitions of the input relations are treated which do not fit into main memory. For these pairs of partitions, repartitioning has to be performed in a recursive fashion. In the third phase, a corresponding pair of partitions is loaded into main memory and an in-memory join is performed using the plane-sweep method originally presented in [5]. Note that due to the replication of KPEs in different partitions the same result can be produced more than once. In order to eliminate these duplicates in the response set, the results obtained from the three phases are sorted in a final phase.

An important improvement of PBSM is presented in [13]. Instead of eliminating duplicates in a separate phase (which has a few serious disadvantages) an inexpensive on-line algorithm is proposed to decide whether a result of the first phase is a duplicate or not. Experiments in [13] have shown that the new method for duplicate elimination results in a substantial improvement over the original approach. Therefore, we also used PBSM with the new method for duplicate elimination in our experiments.

Important to PBSM is a good choice for p (number of partitions) and NT (number of tiles). Let M be the size of the available main memory and let sizeof(KPE) be the size of a KPE (36 bytes in our experiments). We suggest the following formula for computing p:

$$p = \left\lceil sf \times \frac{(\|R\| + \|S\|) \cdot sizeof(KPE)}{M} \right\rceil . \tag{1}$$

where $sf \geq 1$ is a scaling factor. We observed that for $sf = 1$, as it was proposed originally, the size of a pair of partitions is frequently larger than M and therefore, repartitioning has to be performed too often. In our experiments we found that $sf = 1.5$ is the best choice. The assignment of tiles to partitions is performed in a round-robin fashion (row by row). In order to avoid homogeneous assignment patterns, NT was chosen such that p is not a divisor of NT. The parameter NT was almost 60 times larger than p in our experiments.

4.2 The Computing Model

In our I/O model, data is transferred between main memory and secondary storage in pages of fixed size. The cost for reading a page consists of positioning the disk arm and transferring the page. Moreover, we also assume that a *contiguous* sequence of multiple pages can be read (written) with positioning the disk arm only once. Such a multi-page read is obviously less expensive than reading each of the pages separately. Our implementations were designed in such a way that multi-page I/Os are used whenever possible.

In the following, we investigate the performance of spatial join algorithms in different experiments using real data sets. The performance of the algorithms is simply measured by the total runtime (in seconds) of the corresponding C++ implementations on an Intel PC (with a Celeron 333 MHZ processor, 128 MB main memory and a 4 GB Micropolis disk) under Windows 95. Our current implementations do not support an overlapped processing of I/O and CPU. The join algorithms were allowed to use only a fraction of main memory, whereas the buffers of the operating system were turned off throughout our experiments.

Table 1: Datasets used in the experiments

data set	description	number of MBBs	coverage
CAL_RR	railways and rivers in California	625,640	0.21
CAL_ST	streets in California	1,888,012	0.12

In our experiments we used different real data sets derived from the TIGER files [8]. Due to space limitations we are only able to present the results of our largest spatial join in detail. We also performed other joins whose results are in agreement with the ones we present in this paper. The first data set CAL_RR contains the MBBs of the railways, rivers, administrative and hydrographic features from the state California, whereas the second data set CAL_ST contains the MBBs of the streets. The coverage of the data files (which is defined by the sum of the area of the MBBs divided by the area of the MBB of all MBBs) is rather small for these files. This is generally true for most of the real data sets. In Table 2 the output parameters of the spatial join are reported. The selectivity refers to the number of results divided by the product of the number of MBBs of the input relations.

Table 2: Spatial joins performed in our experiments

join	R	S	number of results	selectivity
J1	CAL_RR	CAL_ST	1,683,888	$1.43{\times}10^{-6}$

4.3 Plug&Join

In this section, we discuss how to choose the required parameters for Plug&Join. The generic algorithm requires appropriate values for the leaf capacity of the index and the fan-out of the internal nodes. In Figure 4, we present the execution time of spatial joins

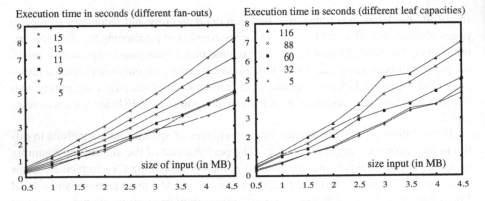

Fig. 4: Execution time as a function of the size of the input relations

for different settings of the parameters. Plug&Join employs the R*-tree in these experiments. In order to present the results as a function of the size of the partitions, we limit the join to the result set of window queries of different sizes which were performed on relations CAL_ST and CAL_RR. We examine in the following the case where the main memory is large enough to keep the input of the spatial join.

On the left-hand side of Figure 4, we plot the curves for different fan-outs of the internal pages of the index. The results show that small fan-outs are most promising. This result is not evident since a small fan-out reduces the quality of the partitioning of the R*-tree and therefore, it increases the cost of the window queries. This is because an insertion has fewer choices for proceeding from a node to one of its siblings. However, small fan-outs also reduce the cost of insertions. These performance gains are more relevant than the performance loss for the queries.

On the right-hand side of Figure 4, the execution time is plotted for different settings of the leaf capacity. The results show that the size of the leaves should be also small. There is no remarkable performance difference between a leaf capacity of 5 and 32. We choose in the following the larger value since the size of the index will be considerably lower for this value.

4.4 Comparison of PBSM and Plug&Join

In this section we present the execution time of PBSM and Plug&Join when the spatial join J1 is processed. Both algorithms are using formula 1 to compute the number of partitions built in each partitioning step. Plug&Join uses the R*-tree where the leaf capacity is 32 and the fan-out of the internal nodes is 5. In Figure 5, we plotted the exe-

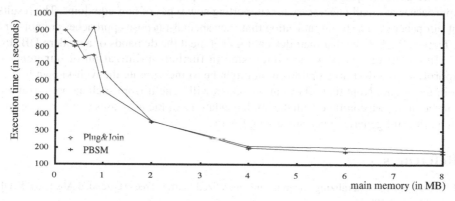

Fig. 5: Execution time as a function of the size of main memory for *Plug&Join* and *PBSM*

cution time of both join algorithms as a function of the available main memory. Plug&Join seems to be slightly superior for medium-sized memory, whereas PBSM performs slightly better for large main memories. Overall, these results basically show that both algorithms give similar performance.

5 Conclusions

This paper presents Plug&Join, a generic algorithm particularly suitable for processing non-equi joins in an extensible database system. Plug&Join requires an index structure satisfying the grow-and-post interface [21] for its initialization, but a preexisting index on any of the relations is not required. The index structure is used for two different problems: First, an in-memory index is built for partitioning both of the relations. Partitioning employs the ability of the index structure to support insertions and queries where the query predicate is directly derived from the join predicate. Second, temporarily built in-memory indices are used for processing joins on partitions that fit in memory.

The benefit of Plug&Join is that it can easily be customized to different types of joins. There are three possible approaches to customizing: First, the easiest would be when the required index structure is already available in the underlying system and the desired query predicate is supported. Second, the index structure might be implemented, but the query predicate has to be provided. Third, the index structure has to be implemented completely. Fortunately, generic toolboxes for implementing index structures like GiST [17] can be used to simplify the last two approaches. In this paper, we present different use-cases for processing equi joins, spatial joins and subset joins. The use-case for subset joins presents the first algorithm, we are aware of, that efficiently treats the subset predicate for large relations. For the spatial join, we present first results of a preliminary performance comparison of Plug&Join (using the R*-tree) with PBSM [28], one of the most efficient special-purpose algorithms. Overall, our results show that Plug&Join is competitive to PBSM.

The general question we address in this paper is whether special-purpose approaches are really necessary for supporting new types of non-equi joins. The results of our paper give a strong indication that such special-purpose approaches are not very effective. We believe that their design does not meet the demands of a modern DBMS.

In our future work we are interested in further optimization of our generic approach. One desirable optimization might be to incorporate the well-known hybrid join technique. Note that all of our use-cases will benefit from such an optimization. Furthermore, we continue with the implementations of the use-cases which will be part of a powerful generic query processing library.

References

1. Aoki, P. M.: Generalizing "Search" in Generalized Search Trees (Extended Abstract). ICDE 1998: 380-389
2. Arge, L.; Procopiuc, O.; Ramaswamy, S.; Suel, T.; Vitter, J. S.: Scalable Sweeping-Based Spatial Join. VLDB 1998: 570-581
3. Becker, L.; Finke, U.; Hinrichs, K.: A New Algorithm for Computing Joins with Grid Files. ICDE 1993: 190-197
4. Becker, B.; Gschwind, S.; Ohler, T.; Seeger, B.; Widmayer, P.: An Asymptotically Optimal Multiversion B-Tree. VLDB Journal 5(4): 264-275 (1996)
5. Brinkhoff, T.; Kriegel, H.-P.; Seeger, B.: Efficient Processing of Spatial Joins Using R-Trees. SIGMOD Conference 1993: 237-246
6. Beckmann, N.; Kriegel, H.-P.; Schneider, R.; Seeger, B.: The R*-Tree: An Efficient and Robust Access Method for Points and Rectangles. SIGMOD Conference 1990: 322-331
7. Van den Bercken, J.; Seeger, B.; Widmayer, P.: The Bulk Index Join: A Generic Approach to Processing Non-Equijoins. ICDE 1999: 257
8. Bureau of the Census: Tiger/Line Precensus Files: 1995 technical documentation. Bureau of the Census, Washington DC. 1996
9. Cattell, R. (editor): The Object Database Standard: ODMG-93, Release 1.2, Morgan Kaufmann, 1996
10. Ciaccia, P.; Patella, M.; Zezula, P.: M-tree: An Efficient Access Method for Similarity Search in Metric Spaces. VLDB 1997: 426-435

11. Deppisch, U.: S-tree: A Dynamic Balanced Signature Index for Office Retrieval. SIGIR 1986: 77-87
12. DeWitt, D. J.; Naughton, J. F.; Schneider, D. A.: An Evaluation of Non-Equijoin Algorithms. VLDB 1991: 443-452
13. Dittrich, J.; Seeger, B.: Data Redundancy and Duplicate Detection in Spatial Join Processing. ICDE 2000: to appear
14. Graefe, G.: Query Evaluation Techniques for Large Databases. Computing Surveys 25(2): 73-170 (1993)
15. Günther, O.: Efficient Computation of Spatial Joins. ICDE 1993: 50-59
16. Guttman, A.: R-Trees: A Dynamic Index Structure for Spatial Searching. SIGMOD Conference 1984: 47-57
17. Hellerstein, J. M.; Naughton, J. F.; Pfeffer, A.: Generalized Search Trees for Database Systems. VLDB 1995: 562-573
18. Helmer, S.; Moerkotte, G.: Evaluation of Main Memory Join Algorithms for Joins with Set Comparison Join Predicates. VLDB 1997: 386-395
19. Hoel, E. G.; Samet, H.: Benchmarking Spatial Join Operations with Spatial Output. VLDB 1995: 606-618
20. Henrich, A.; Six, H.-W.; Widmayer, P.: The LSD tree: Spatial Access to Multidimensional Point and Nonpoint Objects. VLDB 1989: 45-53
21. Lomet, D. B.: Grow and Post Index Trees: Roles, Techniques and Future Potential. SSD 1991: 183-206
22. Lo, M.-L.; Ravishankar, C. V.: Spatial Joins Using Seeded Trees. SIGMOD Conference 1994: 209-220
23. Lo, M.-L.; Ravishankar, C. V.: Spatial Hash-Joins. SIGMOD Conference 1996: 247-258
24. Koudas, N.; Sevcik, K. C: Size Separation Spatial Join. SIGMOD Conference 1997: 324-335
25. Mishra, P.; Eich, M. H.: Join Processing in Relational Databases. Computing Surveys 24(1): 63-113 (1992)
26. Mamoulis, N.; Papadias, D.: Integration of Spatial Join Algorithms for Processing Multiple Inputs. SIGMOD Conference 1999: 1-12
27. Orenstein, J.: Spatial Query Processing in an Object-Oriented Database System. SIGMOD Conference 1986: 326-336
28. Patel, J. M.; DeWitt, D. J.: Partition Based Spatial-Merge Join. SIGMOD Conference 1996: 259-270
29. Papadias, D.; Theodoridis, Y.; Sellis, T. K.; Egenhofer, M. J.: Topological Relations in the World of Minimum Bounding Rectangles: A Study with R-trees. SIGMOD Conference 1995: 92-103
30. Shapiro, L. D.: Join Processing in Database Systems with Large Main Memories. TODS 11(3): 239-264 (1986)
31. Soo, M. D.; Snodgrass, R. T.; Jensen, C. S.: Efficient Evaluation of the Valid-Time Natural Join. ICDE 1994: 282-292
32. Zurek, T.: Optimisation of Partitioned Temporal Joins. BNCOD 1997: 101-115

Querying Graph Databases[*]

Sergio Flesca and Sergio Greco

DEIS, Univ. della Calabria, 87030 Rende, Italy
{flesca,greco}@si.deis.unical.it

Abstract Graph data is an emerging model for representing a variety of database contexts ranging from object-oriented databases to hypertext data. Also many of the recursive queries that arise in relational databases are, in practice, graph traversals. In this paper we present a language for searching graph-like databases. The language permits us to express paths in a graph by means of extended regular expressions. The proposed extension is based on the introduction of constructs which permit us i) to define a partial order on the paths used to search the graph and, consequently, on the answers of queries, and ii) to cut off, nondeterministically, tuples with low priority. We present an algebra for partially ordered relations and an algorithm for the computation of path queries. Finally, we present applications to hypertext databases such as the Web.

1 Introduction

Graph data is an emerging model for representing a variety of database contexts ranging from object oriented databases to hypertext data [7,10,14,17]. Also many of the recursive queries that arise in relational databases are, in practice, graph traversals [21]. Recently, several languages and prototypes have been proposed for searching graph-like data such as the Web [1,4,5,6,8,12,16,18,19]. All these languages allow the user to express (declaratively) navigational queries, called path queries, by means of regular expressions denoting paths in the graph [11,17].

Path queries are of the form "find all objects reachable from a given node by paths whose labels form a word of the language defined by r" where r is a regular expression over an alphabet of labels. A drawback of path queries is the amount of data derived and the number of paths explored, which can be very large. Such cases can be solved by giving to the user the possibility to cut off, dynamically, data derived during the computation, for instance by specifying the size of the result. The elimination of tuples can be done nondeterministically, as proposed in [9] for relational databases, or on the basis of some criteria specified by the user. Moreover, it turns out that to manage preferences specified by users, tuples should be (partially) ordered. The elimination of tuples implies that the computation can be efficient since the whole graph does not need to be explored.

[*] Work partially supported by a MURST grant under the projects "Interdata", Telcal and Contact. The second author is also supported by ISI-CNR.

C. Zaniolo et al. (Eds.): EDBT 2000, LNCS 1777, pp. 510–524, 2000.
© Springer-Verlag Berlin Heidelberg 2000

To better capture the navigational aspects of graph-like data, we introduce the possibility of expressing preferences in regular expressions. For instance, the standard path query $\{x\}[a + b]$ denotes the set of nodes which are reachable from x by means of an arc labeled either a or b. In our approach the user has the possibility to give preference, for instance, to the nodes reached by means of an arc labeled a. This query can be defined as $\{x\}[a > b]$ and the result is a partially ordered set where the nodes reached from x by means of an arc labeled a are preferred to the nodes reached with an arc labeled b. We also allow the user to express preference on the length of paths and to cut off the domain of evaluation of queries. This is carried out by means of an operator $!_n$ (*cut*), which cuts off from relations tuples with low priority. For instance, a path query of the form $!_3(\{x\}[a > b])$ means that the answer must contain at most three nodes selected from those with higher priority. The nodes reached by means of arcs with label b are used only if there are less than three nodes reached from x with arcs labeled a. Observe that the operator *cut* is nondeterministic and it selects one element from the set of feasible subsets having the specified cardinality.

Thus, extended regular expressions capture the important aspect of navigational queries such as "search first the paths starting with the edge e_1 and next, in case the solution is not complete, those starting with the edge e_2". Hence, in this paper we introduce extended path queries and extend relational algebra for partially ordered relations. The resulting language, obtained from the combination of extended path queries and extended relational algebra, can be specialized to query a variety of databases such as graph databases, hypertext data, relational databases and object-oriented databases.

The rest of the paper is organized as follows. In Section 2 we recall basic concepts on regular expressions, database graphs and path queries. In Section 3 we introduce extended path queries. In Section 4 we present an algorithm for the computation of path queries. In Section 5 we introduce graph queries which combine an algebra for partially ordered relations, with path queries. In Section 6, we show how graph queries can be used to search the Web. Due to the limitation of space, the proofs of our results are omitted.

2   Database Graphs and Path Queries

In this section we recall basic definitions on regular expressions, database graphs and path queries [15,17].

Regular languages. A string over an alphabet Σ is a finite sequence of symbols from Σ; the empty string is denoted by ϵ. The concatenation of two strings x and y, written $x\,y$, is the string x followed by the string y. Any set of strings over an alphabet Σ — i.e. any subset of Σ^* — is called a language. Let Σ be a finite set of symbols and let L and L' be two languages over Σ^*. The concatenation of L and L', denoted $L\,L'$, is the set $\{xy | x \in L \wedge y \in L'\}$. Let $L^0 = \{\epsilon\}$ and let $L^i = LL^{i-1}$ for $i \geq 1$. The closure of L, denoted L^* is the set $\bigcup_{i=0}^{\infty} L^i$, i.e. L^* is the set of all strings obtained by concatenating zero or more strings from L. The (positive) closure of L, denoted L^+ is the set LL^* which is equal to $\bigcup_{i=1}^{\infty} L^i$.

Regular expressions over Σ and the sets that they denote are defined recursively as follows:

1. $\emptyset$ is a regular expression and denotes the empty language;
2. ϵ is a regular expression and denotes the language $\{\epsilon\}$;
3. For each $a \in \Sigma$, a is a regular expression and denotes the set $\{a\}$;
4. If r and s are regular expressions denoting the languages R and S, respectively, then a) $r + s$ denotes the language $R \cup S$, b) rs denotes the language RS, c) r^* denotes the language R^*.

Any language $\mathcal{L}(\alpha)$ denoted by a regular expression α is called regular.

Database graphs. A database graph $G = (N, E, \phi, \Sigma, \lambda)$ is a directed labeled graph, where N is a set of nodes, E is a set of edges, Σ is a finite set of symbols denoting labels for the arcs, ϕ is an incidence function mapping E to $N \times N$ and λ is an edge labeling function mapping from E to Σ. Let $G = (N, E, \phi, \Sigma, \lambda)$ be a database graph and let $p = (v_1, e_1, v_2, e_2, ..., v_n)$ where $v_i \in N$ and $e_j \in E$ be a path in G. The *label path* of p, denoted $\lambda(p)$, is a subset of Σ^* defined as $\lambda(e_1), ..., \lambda(e_{n-1})$ We say that a string w in Σ^* spells a path p in G if $w = \lambda(p)$ and we say that p satisfies a regular expression α if $\lambda(p) \in \mathcal{L}(\alpha)$.

Path queries. Given a database graph $G = (N, E, \phi, \Sigma, \lambda)$, a set of nodes $N_0 \subseteq N$ and a regular expression α over Σ, a path query $Q = N_0[\alpha]$ is defined as the set of nodes y such that there is a path from $x_0 \in N_0$ to y in G satisfying α.

Proposition 1. *Let $G = (N, E, \phi, \Sigma, \lambda)$ be a database graph, $N_0 \subseteq N$ a set of nodes, y a node in N and α a regular expression over Σ. The problem of checking if $y \in N_0[\alpha]$ is $\mathcal{NL}$-complete.* [1]   □

3 Partially Ordered Path Queries

Path queries permit us to express queries computing a complete set of nodes reachable from a source set. In applications where the number of nodes can be very large it is useful to cut the domain of evaluation by selecting subsets of the domain on the base of some criteria. Since the criteria define a (partial) order on the nodes, we use partially ordered languages.

3.1 Partially Ordered Languages

Definition 1. *A partially ordered relation is a pair $\langle R, >_R \rangle$ where R is a standard relation and $>_R$ is a partial order on the elements of R.*   □

---

[1] $\mathcal{NL} = NSPACE(log\, n)$ is the class of decision problems which can solved by means of a nondeterministic Turing machine using logarithm space.

Given two partially ordered sets $O_1 = \langle L_1, >_{L_1} \rangle$ and $O_2 = \langle L_2, >_{L_2} \rangle$, we say that O_2 is an instance of O_1, written $O_2 \vdash O_1$ if and only if $L_1 = L_2$ and $>_{L_1} \subseteq >_{L_2}$. A partially ordered set O_1 is linearly ordered if there is no partially ordered set O_2 different from O_1 such that $O_2 \vdash O_1$.

Before presenting the formal semantics of extended path queries we extend classical language operators to deal with partially ordered relations, i.e. languages whose strings are partially ordered. The semantics of the extended operators is given by defining the set of elements and the partial order of the result.

Union. The union of two partially ordered relations $O_1 = \langle S, >_S \rangle$ and $O_2 = \langle T, >_T \rangle$, denoted $O_1 \sqcup O_2$, is equal to $O_3 = \langle U, >_U \rangle$ where $U = S \cup T$ and $>_U$ is defined as follows:

1. if $a >_S b$ and $a >_T b$ then $a >_U b$;
2. if $a >_S b$ (resp. $a >_T b$) and $b \notin T$ (resp. $b \notin S$) then $a >_U b$.

Observe that if O_1 and O_2 are standard relations, i.e. $O_1 = \langle S, \emptyset \rangle$ and $O_2 = \langle T, \emptyset \rangle$, the operator $\sqcup$ coincides with the standard operator $\cup$. Observe also that, as the corresponding standard operator, the union operator is commutative, i.e. $O_1 \sqcup O_2 = O_2 \sqcup O_1$. We also introduce an operator which computes the union of two partially ordered relations by giving priority, in the resulting partial order, to the elements of the first relation.

Priorized Union. The priorized union of two partially ordered sets $O_1 = \langle S, >_S \rangle$ and $O_2 = \langle T, >_T \rangle$, denoted $O_1 \oplus O_2$, is equal to $O_3 = \langle U, >_U \rangle$ where $U = S \cup T$ and $>_U$ is defined as follows:

1. if $a >_S b$ then $a >_U b$;
2. If $a >_T b$ and $b \notin S$ then $a >_U b$;
3. if $a \in S$, $b \in T$ and $b \notin S$ then $a >_U b$.

Observe that if O_1 and O_2 are linearly ordered relations (lists), the operator $\oplus$ coincides with the union operator applied to O_1 and $(O_2 \setminus O_1)$ (the list derived from O_2 by deleting the elements in O_1). Observe also that the priorized union operator is not commutative ($S \oplus T$ may be different from $T \oplus S$).

Concatenation. The concatenation of two ordered languages $O_1 = \langle L_1, >_{L_1} \rangle$ and $O_2 = \langle L_2, >_{L_2} \rangle$, denoted $O_1 O_2$, is equal to $O_3 = \langle L_3, >_{L_3} \rangle$ where $L_3 = L_1 L_2$ and $>_{L_3}$ is defined as follows:

$x >_{L_3} y$ if for each $y_1 \in L_1$ and for each $y_2 \in L_2$ such that $y_1 y_2 = y$ there are $x_1 \in L_1$ and $x_2 \in L_2$ such that $x_1 x_2 = x$ and either i) $x_1 >_{L_1} y_1$ or ii) $x_1 = y_1$ and $x_2 >_{L_2} y_2$.

Thus, in the comparison of two strings x and y we search partitions x_1 and x_2 of x and y_1 and y_2 of y and then compare $x_1 x_2$ with $y_1 y_2$. In the comparison of $x_1 x_2$ and $y_1 y_2$ we first compare x_1 and y_1 and then, if $x_1 = y_1$, compare x_2 and y_2.

It is worth noting that the standard concatenation operator is distributive with respect to the standard union operator, i.e. $(L_1 \cup L_2) L_3 = L_1 L_3 \cup L_2 L_3$ and $L_1 (L_2 \cup L_3) = L_1 L_2 \cup L_1 L_3$. This, property is generally not true and we have the following results:

Proposition 2. *Let A, B and C be three partially ordered languages. Then*

1. $(A \sqcup B)\,C = AC \sqcup BC$, *and*
2. $(A \oplus B)\,C = AC \oplus BC$. □

However, $O_1\,(O_2 \sqcup O_3)$ (resp. $O_1\,(O_2 \oplus O_3)$) may be different from $O_1 O_2 \sqcup O_1 O_3$ (resp. $O_1 O_2 \oplus O_1 O_3$).

Example 1. Consider the languages $O_1 = \langle\{a, b\}, \{a > b\}\rangle$, $O_2 = \langle\{b\}, \emptyset\rangle$ and $O_3 = \langle\{a, b\}, \{b > a\}\rangle$.

1. $O_2 \sqcup O_3 = \langle\{a, b\}, \{b > a\}\rangle$ and $O_1(O_2 \sqcup O_3) = \langle\{aa, ab, ba, bb\}, \{ab > aa > bb > ba\}\rangle$.
   $O_1 O_2 = \langle\{ab, bb\}, \{ab > bb\}\rangle$ and $O_1 O_3 = \langle\{aa, ab, ba, bb\}, \{ab > aa > bb > ba\}\rangle$, $O_1 O_2 \sqcup O_1 O_3 = \langle\{aa, ab, ba, bb\}, \{ab > bb > ba, ab > aa > ba\}\rangle$.
   Therefore, $O_1\,(O_2 \sqcup O_3) \neq O_1 O_2 \sqcup O_1 O_3$.
2. $O_2 \oplus O_3 = \langle\{a, b\}, \{b > a\}\}$ and $O_1(O_2 \oplus O_3) = \langle\{aa, ab, ba, bb\}, \{ab > aa > bb > ba\}\rangle$.
   $O_1 O_2 \oplus O_1 O_3 = \langle\{aa, ab, ba, bb\}, \{ab > bb > aa > ba\rangle$.
   Therefore, $O_1\,(O_2 \oplus O_3) \neq O_1 O_2 \oplus O_1 O_3$. □

Closure. The (positive) closure of an ordered language O, denoted O^+, is defined as usual by using concatenation and union of ordered languages, i.e.

$$O^+ = \bigsqcup_{i=1}^{\infty} O^i$$

Priorized Closure. The (positive) priorized closure of an ordered language O, denoted $O^\triangleright$, is defined by using concatenation and priorized union of ordered languages. That is

$$O^\triangleright = \bigoplus_{i=1}^{\infty} O^i$$

Observe that we are considering only positive closures, i.e. the empty string ϵ is not in the closure of the language. Here regular languages are used to define paths in a graph starting from a given node and, since paths must have at least one arc, we only consider strings which are not empty.

The main difference between the closure operators $^+$ and $^\triangleright$ is that the operator $^\triangleright$ gives preference to shorter strings.

Example 2. Consider the partially ordered languages $P = \langle\{a, b\}, \{a > b\}\rangle$ and $Q = \langle\{b, c\}, \{b > c\}\rangle$. Then

1. $P \sqcup Q = \langle\{a, b, c\}, \{b > c\}\rangle$;
2. $P \oplus Q = \langle\{a, b, c\}, \{a > b > c\}\rangle$;
3. $P^2 = PP = \langle\{aa, ab, ba, bb\}, \{aa > ab > ba > bb\}\rangle$;
4. $P^1 \sqcup P^2 = \langle\{a, b, aa, ab, ba, bb\}, \{a > b, aa > ab > ba > bb\}\rangle$;
5. $P^1 \oplus P^2 = \langle\{a, b, aa, ab, ba, bb\}, \{a > b > aa > ab > ba > bb\}\rangle$; □

It is well known that, for standard regular languages, given a language L, $(L^+)^+ = L^+$ and $L^+L^+ = LL^+$. For partially ordered languages we have the following relations:

Proposition 3. *Given an alphabet Σ and letting O be a partially ordered language on Σ, then*

    1. $O^\triangleright O^\triangleright = O O^\triangleright$,
    2. $(O^\triangleright)^\triangleright = O^\triangleright$. $\square$

Let us now extend the definition of regular expression.

Definition 2. *Let Σ be an alphabet. The (extended) regular expressions over Σ and the sets that they denote are defined recursively as follows:*

    1. For each $a \in \Sigma$, a is a regular expression and denotes the language $\langle \{a\}, \emptyset \rangle$;
    2. If r and s are regular expressions denoting the languages R and S, respectively, then a) $r+s$ denotes the language $R \sqcup S$, b) $r > s$ denotes the language $R \oplus S$, c) rs denotes the language RS, d) r^+ denotes the language R^+ and e) $r^\triangleright$ denotes the language $R^\triangleright$. $\square$

Observe that an extended regular expression is associated to a partially ordered language where the partial order is implicit. Observe also that the expression ϵ is not an extended regular expression. The reason for not considering the empty string ϵ is that we use regular expressions to denote (non empty) paths in a given graph.

Definition 3. *Let G be a database graph. An* extended path query *is of the form $N[\alpha]$ where N is a set of nodes in G and α is an extended regular expression.* $\square$

A path query $Q = N[\alpha]$ defines a partially ordered set of nodes S such that $y \in S$ iff there is a path from $x \in N$ to y in G satisfying α. The partial order on the result S is defined as follows: given two nodes x and y in S, $x > y$ iff for each path p_1 from some $x_i \in N$ to y there is a path p_2 from some $x_j \in N$ to x such that $\lambda(p_2) > \lambda(p_1)$.

Let $Q = N[\alpha]$ be a path query. An answer to Q is any linearly ordered set X such that $X \vdash N[\alpha]$. Since Q may have one or more than one answer, we denote with $Ans(Q)$ the complete set of answers.

3.2 Computing Path Queries

We now discuss the problem of computing extended path queries. Before presenting our algorithm we introduce some notation. We shall use sets of nodes and lists of sets of nodes where each two sets of nodes are disjoint, i.e. the same node cannot belong to two different sets. A list containing the elements $S_1, S_2, ..., S_n$ will be denoted as $[S_1, S_2, ..., S_n]$ where S_1 is the head of the list and $[S_2, ..., S_n]$ is the tail. An empty list is denoted by $[\,]$. We shall also use the functions

1. *choice*, which receives as input two lists (containing sets of nodes) and selects nondeterministically one of them;
2. *append*, which receives as input two lists of disjoint sets of nodes, say $[S_1, ..., S_n]$ and $[T_1, ..., T_m]$ and returns the list $[S_1, ..., S_n, U_1, ..., U_m]$, where $U_i = T_i - (S_1 \cup ... \cup S_n)$, for $1 \le i \le m$.

Observe that the function *append* returns a list of disjoint sets if the input lists contain disjoint sets. Since the output of a query Q is an answer, we introduce a function which computes an instance of Q which can then be linearized to obtain one answer.

Our algorithm is implemented by means of the function *Query* reported in Figure 2. It receives as input a list of sets of nodes N_1, a regular expression α and returns a list of sets of nodes N_2. A list of sets of nodes $N = [S_1, ..., S_n]$ defines a partial order on the nodes contained in the sets; in particular $x > y$ holds if $x \in S_i$, $y \in S_j$ and $i < j$ (i.e. the set S_i precedes the set S_j in the list). Let N_2 be the list computed by the function *Query*, an answer is any linearly ordered set $N_3 \vdash N_2$. Every set of nodes appearing in the list computed by the function *Query* is reachable from a set of nodes in N_1 by means of paths spelling the same regular expression. Moreover, if a node is reachable by means of different paths, it is stored only once. Thus, our algorithm uses partially ordered sets represented by means of lists of sets of nodes. The following example shows how path queries are computed.

Example 3. Consider the path query $\{0\}[(a + b)(b > c)]$ and the database graph pictured in Figure 1

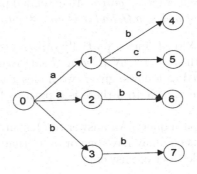

Fig. 1. Database graph.

The algorithm receives as input the list $L_0 = [\{0\}]$ and the regular expression $(a + b)(b > c)$. From the application of $a + b$ to L_0 we get either the list $L_1 = [\{1, 2\}, \{3\}]$ or the list $L_2 = [\{3\}, \{1, 2\}]$. Assuming we select the list L_1, from the application of $b > c$ to L_1 we get the list $L_3 = [\{4, 6\}, \{5\}, \{7\}]$. Thus, possible answers are $[4, 6, 5, 7]$ and $[6, 4, 5, 7]$. Alternatively, if we select the list L_2, from the application of $b > c$ to L_2 we get the list $L_4 = [\{7\}, \{4, 6\}, \{5\}]$ and possible *answers are* $[7, 4, 6, 5]$ *and* $[7, 6, 4, 5]$. *Indeed, the language associated with the regular expression is* $\langle \{ab, ac, bb, bc\}, \{ab > ac, bb > bc\} \rangle$.   □

Basically, the function *Query* checks the type of input regular expression α and if α is either of the form α_1^+ or of the form $\alpha_1^\flat$, it calls the function *Closure*, otherwise it calls for each set in the list, the function *Base*. The function *Base* receives asinput a set of nodes S and a regular expression α and returns a list of sets of nodes computed as follows:

1. if $\alpha = \alpha_1 + \alpha_2$ it calls recursively $Query([S], \alpha_1)$, $Query([S], \alpha_2)$ and, letting N_1 and N_2 be the results of the two calls, it returns either the result of $append(N_1, N_2)$ or the result of $append(N_2, N_1)$;
2. if $\alpha = \alpha_1 > \alpha_2$ it calls recursively $Query([S], \alpha_1)$, $Query([S], \alpha_2)$ and, letting N_1 and N_2 be the results of the two calls, it returns the result of $append(N_1, N_2)$;
3. if $\alpha = \alpha_1 \alpha_2$ it calls first $Query([S], \alpha_1)$, then letting N_1 be the result of the call, it calls recursively the function $Query(N_1, \alpha_2)$. The result given by the second call is returned.
4. if $\alpha = a$ it returns a list containing a unique set of nodes. The set contains all nodes reachable from a node in S by means of an arc labeled a.

The function *Closure* computes the closure of a regular expression α starting from a list of sets of nodes N. Basically, at each step it applies the regular expression α to a list of sets of nodes and *appends* the result to the current list. It stops when the application of the regular expression does not produce new nodes.

The output of the function *Query* is a partially ordered set of nodes. The following theorem states that our algorithm is correct.

Theorem 1. *Let G be a database graph and let $N[\alpha]$ be an extended path query. Let U be the result of the function* Query *applied to $[N]$ and α. Then, $U \vdash N[\alpha]$.*

For instance, the partially ordered set defined by the query $\{0\}[(a+b)(b > c)]$ reported in Example 3 is $\langle \{4, 5, 6, 7\}, \{4 > 5, 6 > 5\} \rangle$. Moreover, the partial order computed by the function *Query* may be $\langle \{4, 5, 6, 7\}, \{4 > 5, 6 > 5, 5 > 7\} \rangle$ or $\langle \{4, 5, 6, 7\}, \{7 > 4, 7 > 6, 4 > 5, 6 > 5\} \rangle$.

Theorem 2. *The function* Query *takes polynomial time in the size of the database graph.*   □

Corollary 1. *Let G be a database graph and let $N[\alpha]$ be a path query. Computing one answer of $N[\alpha]$ can be done in polynomial time.*   □

Function *Query(N:list of sets of nodes, α:Regular expression): list of sets of nodes;*
Output: N_1 *list of sets of nodes;*   *(answer of $N[\alpha]$)*
begin
    if $(\alpha = \alpha_1^+)$ **then return**   *Closure$(N, \alpha_1, +)$;*
    if $(\alpha = \alpha_1^\triangleright)$ **then return**   *Closure$(N, \alpha_1, \triangleright)$;*
    $N_1 := []$
    let $N = [S_1, ..., S_n]$;
    for $i := 1$ **to** n **do**
        $N_1 := append(N_1, Base(S_i, \alpha))$
    return N_1;
end;

Function *Base(S:set of nodes; α: Regular Expression): list of sets of nodes;*
Output: N_1 *list of sets of nodes;*   *(answer of $S[\alpha]$)*
begin
    if $(\alpha = \alpha_1 + \alpha_2)$ **then**
        return   *choice(append(Query([S], \alpha_1), Query([S], \alpha_2)),*
                                append(Query([S], \alpha_2), Query([S], \alpha_1)));
    if $(\alpha = \alpha_1 > \alpha_2)$ **then**
        return   *append(Query([S], \alpha_1), Query([S], \alpha_2));*
    if $(\alpha = \alpha_1 \alpha_2)$ **then return**   *Query(Query([S], \alpha_1), \alpha_2);*
    if $(\alpha = a)$ **then return** $[\{x : \exists s \in S \wedge \exists \ arc \ e \ in \ G \ s.t. \ \phi(e) = (s, x) \wedge \lambda(e) = a\}]$;
end;

Function *Closure(N:list of sets of nodes; α: Regular Expression, θ :operator): list of sets of nodes;*
Output: N_1 *list of sets of nodes; (answer of $N[\alpha^\theta]$)*
begin
    $N_1 := []$; $T = N$;
    repeat
        $T := Query(T, \alpha)$;
        if *all nodes in T appear in N_1* **then return** N_1;
        else if $\theta = +$ **then**
            $N_1 := choice(append(N_1, T), append(T, N_1))$;
            else $N_1 := append(N_1, T)$;
    forever;
end;

Fig. 2. *Extended path query evaluation*

4   Graph Queries

The limitation of database graphs, as presented in the previous sections, is that nodes do not have any associated information. Thus, we extend the definition of database graph by replacing nodes with tuples. More formally, given a domain D, a database graph on D, denoted by $G_{D^i} = (N, E, \phi, \Sigma, \lambda)$, is a directed labeled graph, where $N \subseteq D^i$ is a relation with arity i whereas E, ϕ, Σ and λ

denote domains and functions as defined in Section 2. A database graph can be queried by combining extended relational algebra with path queries.

The answer of an extended path query is a partially ordered set of nodes which are reachable from a source set by means of paths spelling a regular expression. Since a node also contains information, it could be useful to use, inside queries, information associated with nodes. Therefore, we introduce *graph queries* which combine path queries with relational algebra extended for partially ordered relations. Before presenting a formal definition of graph queries we refine the relational algebra operators not considered in Section 3.

Subtraction. The subtraction of two partially ordered relations $O_1 = \langle S, >_S \rangle$ and $O_2 = \langle T, >_T \rangle$, denoted $O_1 \backslash O_2$, is equal to $O_3 = \langle U, >_U \rangle$ where $U = S - T$ and $>_U$ is defined as follows: $a >_U b$ if and only if $a >_S b$ and $a, b \in U$.

Intersection. The intersection of two partially ordered relations $O_1 = \langle S, >_S \rangle$ and $O_2 = \langle T, >_T \rangle$, denoted $O_1 \sqcap O_2$, is equal to $O_3 = \langle U, >_U \rangle$ where $U = S \cap T$ and $>_U$ is defined as follows: $a >_U b$ if and only if $a >_S b$, $a >_T b$ and $a, b \in U$.

Observe that the intersection operator is commutative, i.e. $O_1 \sqcap O_2 = O_2 \sqcap O_1$ and that in the general case $O_1 \sqcap O_2$ may be different from $O_1 \backslash (O_1 \backslash O_2)$.

Cartesian product. The cartesian product of two partially ordered relations $O_1 = \langle S, >_S \rangle$ and $O_2 = \langle T, >_T \rangle$, denoted $O_1 \times O_2$, is equal to $O_3 = \langle U, >_U \rangle$ where $U = S \times T$ and $>_U$ is defined as follows: $(a, b) >_U (c, d)$ iff either 1) $a >_S c$ and $b >_T d$ or 2) $a >_S c$ and $b = d$ or 3) $a = c$ and $b >_T d$.

Selection. The selection of a partially ordered relation $O_1 = \langle S, >_S \rangle$ with condition C, denoted $\sigma_C(O_1)$ is equal to $O_3 = \langle U, >_U \rangle$ where $U = \sigma_C(S)$ and $>_U$ is defined as follows: $a >_U b$ if and only if $a >_S b$ and $a, b \in U$.

Projection. The projection of a partially ordered relation $O_1 = \langle S, >_S \rangle$ over a set of attributes A, denoted $\pi_A(O_1)$ is equal to $O_3 = \langle U, >_U \rangle$ where $U = \pi_A(S)$ and $>_U$ is defined as follows: $x >_U y$ iff $\forall b \in S$ s.t. $\pi_A(b) = y \; \exists a$ s.t. $\pi_A(a) = x$ and $a >_S b$.

The operator $\sqsubseteq$ extends the classical subset operator for standard sets to partially ordered sets. Given two partially ordered sets $O_1 = \langle S, >_S \rangle$ and $O_2 = \langle T, >_T \rangle$, then O_1 is a subset of O_2, denoted $O_1 \sqsubseteq O_2$, if $S \subseteq T$ and $>_S$ is the projection of $>_T$ on the elements of S, i.e. $a >_S b$ iff $a >_T b$ and $a, b \in S$. For standard relations the operator $\sqsubseteq$ coincides with the classical operator $\subseteq$.

Cut. Given a partially ordered relation $O_1 = \langle S, >_S \rangle$, then $!_n O_1$ selects nondeterministically from O_1 a set $O_2 = \langle T, >_T \rangle \sqsubseteq O_1$ with $|T| = min(n, |S|)$ such that there is no pair of elements $x >_S y$ with $y \in T$ and $x \notin T$.

Thus, the operator $!_n O_1$ selects nondeterministically from $O_1 = \langle S, >_S \rangle$ a subset with $min(n, |S|)$ elements. The elements are chosen on the basis of the partial order $>_S$.

We recall that nondeterministic constructs have been deeply investigated in deductive databases [2,13]. However, the *cut* operator proposed here differs significantly from both *witness* and *choice* operators proposed for Datalog. A construct similar to the cut is the "STOP AFTER" construct proposed for SQL [9].

Example 4. Consider the following three partially ordered relations: $P = \langle\{a,b\}, \{a > b\}\rangle$, $R = \langle\{b,c\}, \{b > c\}\rangle$, and $S = \langle\{(a,b),(c,d),(a,d)\}, \{(c,d) > (a,b), (a,d) > (a,b)\}\rangle$. Then

1. $P \sqcap R = \langle\{b\}, \emptyset\rangle$;
2. $P \times R = \langle\{(a,b),(a,c),(b,b),(b,c)\}, \{(a,b) > (b,b), (a,b) > (a,c), (a,c) > (b,c), (b,b) > (b,c)\}\rangle$;
3. $\pi_{\$1}(S) = \langle\{a,c\}, \emptyset\rangle$ and $\pi_{\$2}(S) = \langle\{b,d\}, \{d > b\}\rangle$ where $\$i$ denotes the $i-th$ attribute;
4. $R \backslash P = \langle\{c\}, \emptyset\rangle$;
5. $\sigma_{\$1=a}(S) = \langle\{(a,b),(a,d)\}, \{(a,d) > (a,b)\}\rangle$.
6. $!_1(P) = \langle\{a\}, \emptyset\rangle$, $!_2(S) = \langle\{(c,d),(a,d)\}, \emptyset\rangle$ whereas $!_1(S)$ can be either $\langle\{(c,d)\}, \emptyset\rangle$ or $\langle\{(a,d)\}, \emptyset\rangle$. □

Let us now introduce the formal definition of graph query.

Definition 4. *Let D be a domain and let $G_{D^i} = (N, E, \phi, \Sigma, \lambda)$ be a database graph. A graph query on G_{D^i} is an expression obtained by using path queries and extended relational algebra operators.* □

As for path queries, we define the concept of answer to a graph query. Let Q be a graph query, an answer to Q is any linearly ordered set $X \vdash Q$. $Ans(Q)$ denotes the complete set of answers.

The evaluation of graph queries can be done by combining extended relational operators with the function $Query$ which computes path queries. However, given a path query $N[\alpha]$, the function $Query$, applied to $[N]$ and α, returns a partially ordered set of nodes which is an instance of $N[\alpha]$. The following lemma guarantees that given a graph query Q which uses a path query Q', an instance of Q' (computed, for example, by means of the function $Query$) can be used to compute an instance of Q.

Lemma 1. *Let L_1, L_2, P_1 and P_2 be four partially ordered sets such that $P_1 \vdash L_1$ and $P_2 \vdash L_2$. Then*

1. *$(P_1 \ \theta \ P_2) \vdash (L_1 \ \theta \ L_2)$ with $\theta \in \{\sqcup, \oplus, \backslash, \sqcap, \times\}$;*
2. *$\sigma_C(P_1) \vdash \sigma_C(L_1)$ and $\pi_A(P_1) \vdash \pi_A(L_1)$.* □

Therefore, the evaluation of graph queries gives a partially ordered set which is an instance of the graph query.

Corollary 2. *Computing an instance of a graph query can be done in polynomial time.* □

Example 5. Let $G = (N, E, \phi, \Sigma, \lambda)$ be a database graph where N is a relation containing information about cities whereas arcs denote roads connecting cities and $\Sigma = \{interstate, highway\}$ denote types of road. N is a binary relation containing the name and the population of cities.

A query searching for a city with a population greater than one million which is reachable from Los Angeles by means of interstate roads can be expressed as

$$!_1(\sigma_{\$2>1000000} ((\sigma_{\$1='LosAngeles'} N) [interstate^+]))$$

Consider now the query searching for a city which is reachable from Los Angeles by means of interstate or highway roads with a preference for interstate roads. This query can be expressed as

$$!_1((\sigma_{\$1='LosAngeles'} N) [(interstate > highway)^+])$$

Finally, let us modify the above query to express a preference for cities reachable by paths with a shorter number of arcs. This query can be expressed as

$$!_1((\sigma_{\$1='LosAngeles'} N) [(interstate > highway)^\triangleright])$$

$\square$

5 Searching the Web

The World Wide Web is a large, distributed collection of documents connected by hyperlinks. This collection can be represented by means of a directed graph where nodes denote documents and arcs denote hyperlinks. Usually the Web is searched by navigating the graph. Navigational queries are expressed by means of regular expressions denoting paths in the graph. Standard regular expressions can be used to find all documents reached by paths satisfying a regular expression. Since the size of the graph is huge, the number of documents accessed can be enormous and, therefore, not useful. Partially ordered regular expressions can be used to introduce preferences in searching for documents in the Web.

In this section we show how extended regular expressions can be used to search the Web. We introduce an SQL-like language to express graph queries for the Web. Moreover, since the Web presents some peculiarities such as the possibility of finding documents by means of index servers, we first refine the definition of database graph.

The Web Data Model

The Web can be represented as a database graph $G = (N, E, \phi, \Sigma, \Gamma, \lambda, \psi)$ where N is a (virtual) relation containing documents and E is a (virtual) relation containing the set of arcs, Σ is a (possibly infinite) set of strings denoting labels, Γ is a (possibly infinite) set of strings denoting keywords, ϕ is the incidence function mapping E to $N \times N$, λ is an edge labeling function mapping E to Σ and ψ is a keyword search function mapping Γ to 2^N. A virtual relation is a relation whose elements can be accessed only by specifying a key attribute[19]. Thus, the relation N can be accessed only i) through selection operations of the form $\sigma_{\$1 = 'a'} N$, where $'a'$ is a constant string (denoting an URL) or ii) by calling the keyword search function which returns a set of URLs.

We follow the Web-SQL approach [18] where the schema of documents consists of the following attributes: Url, which is an identifier for the document, $Title, Data$, which denotes the data of the last update and $Text$. Thus, N is a virtual relation with four attributes where Url is a key attribute. Moreover, since hyperlinks have also associated information about the destination document, we assume that labels are pairs of the form $T : L$ where T denotes the type of hyperlink and L a string (label). More specifically, the type of hyperlinks we consider are local (denoted as L) and external (denoted as E). Local link means that the source and the destination documents are on the same host whereas external link means that the source and the destination document are on different hosts. Moreover, we assume that if the type of hyperlink is not specified, then it can be either local or external.

An SQL-Like Language

We now present an SQL-like language to search the Web. Although the syntax of the language resembles the language Web-SQL [18], the semantics is quite different. Indeed, we consider general paths and extended regular expressions whereas Web-SQL considers only simple paths and 'standard' path queries.

A Web query is of the form

> "SELECT" [$Number$ | "ALL"] $Attribute\text{-}List$
> "FROM" $Domain\text{-}List$
> "WHERE" $Condition$

where $Domain\text{-}List$ denotes a list of partially ordered sets of documents (called domains) which are identified by means of path queries. Each domain is denoted by a regular expression applied to a starting set of documents. The starting set of nodes can be either a set or a list of URLs. Moreover, a set of URLs can also be specified by using a predefined keyword search function, here called $Index$, which receives as input a string and gives a set of URLs.[2] A single domain term can be defined by using the following syntax:

$Domain\text{-}Term$ ::= $Starting\text{-}URLs$ "[" $Extended\text{-}Regular\text{-}Expr$ "]" "AS" Var
$Starting\text{-}URLs$ ::= $URL\text{-}Set$ | $URL\text{-}List$ |"Index" "(" $String$ ")"

In order to make the language more flexible in specifying paths, we use generalized path queries as defined in [4,18]. In particular, for labels we use the standard meta-symbols "%" and "_", used by SQL to denote, respectively, "any character string" and any "character". For instance, the regular expression

---

[2] Note that, index servers could also be modeled by a function returning a list of URLs.

$(L : ``\%")^+$ denotes paths containing only local links whereas $(E : ``dep\%")^+$ denotes paths containing only external links whose label starts with the string *"dep"*. We now present some examples of queries.

Example 6. The first query computes all documents reachable from the node with URL "www.unical.it" by navigating first a link with label "departments" or "faculties" and then navigating local links.

```
SELECT  ALL d.*
FROM    {"www.unical.it"} [ ("L : departments" + "L : faculties") (L : "%")+ ] AS d
```

The next query computes at most 10 documents reachable from the node with URL *"www.unical.it"* by navigating first a link with the label *"departments"* followed by any number of local links and next, if the solution is not complete, by navigating the link with the label *"faculties"* followed by any number of local links.

```
SELECT  10 d.*
FROM    {"www.unical.it"} [ ("L : departments" > "L : faculties") (L : "%")+ ] AS d
```

The last query computes at most 10 documents containing the string *"database"* which are reachable from the node with URL *'www.unical.it"* by first navigating local links and then, if the solution is not complete, by navigating links of any type.

```
SELECT 10 d.*
FROM   {"www.unical.it"} [ ((L: "%")+ > ("%")+)) ] AS d
WHERE  d.text LIKE "%database%"
```

☐

Observe that the first query is deterministic whereas the following two queries, which use extended path queries, asking for ten documents, may be nondeterministic.

Thus, the first query gives the complete list of documents reachable from "www.unical.it" by means of paths satisfying the regular expression whereas the second and third queries give a list of at most 10 documents.

Moreover, the list of documents computed by the queries also satisfies the partial order defined by the regular expressions. The next example presents a query which uses the function *Index*.

Example 7. The last query computes at most 10 documents containing the string "JDBC" which are reachable from nodes selected by querying the keyword search function with the string "Java Documentation" by navigating local links.

```
SELECT 10 d.*
FROM   Index("JavaDocumentation") [ "L: %"▷ ] AS d
WHERE  d.text LIKE "%JDBC%"
```

☐

References

1. Abiteboul S. Querying Semi-structured Data. In *Proc. Int. Conf. on Database Theory (ICDT)*, pages 1-18, 1997.
2. Abiteboul S., E. Simon, V. Vianu. Non-Deterministic Language to Express Deterministic Transformation. In *Proc. of the Ninth ACM Symposium on Principles of Database Systems (PODS)*, pages 215-229, 1990.
3. Abiteboul S., R. Hull, V. Vianu. *Foundations of Databases*. Addison-Wesley. 1994.
4. Abiteboul S., V. Vianu. Queries and Computation on the Web. In *Proc. Int. Conf. on Database Theory (ICDT)*, pages 262-275, 1997.
5. Abiteboul S., V. Vianu. Regular Path Queries with Constraints. In *Proc. Sixteenth Int. Symposium on Database Systems (PODS)*, pages 122-133, 1997.
6. Abiteboul S., D. Quass, J. McHugh, J. Widom, J. L. Wiener, The Lorel Query Language for Semistructured Data. in *Journal on Digital Libraries* 1(1), pages 68-88, 1997.
7. Beeri C, Y. Kornatzky, A logical query language for hypertext systems. In *Proc. European Conf. on Hypertexts*, pages 67-80, Cambridge University Press, 1990.
8. Buneman P., S. Davinson, G. Hillebrand, D. Suciu, A query language and optimization techniques for unstructured data. In *Proc. ACM SIGMOD Conf. on Management of Data*, pages 505-516, 1996.
9. Carey M., D. Kossmann, On Saying "Enough Already!" in SQL. In *Proc. ACM SIGMOD Conf.*, pages 219-230, 1997.
10. Consens M, Mendelzon A., GraphLog: a visual formalism for real life recursion. In *Proc. PODS Conf.*, pages 404-416, 1990.
11. Christophides,V., S. Cluet, G. Moerkotte, Evaluating Queries with Generalized Path Expressions, in *Proc. of the ACM SIGMOD Conf.*, pages 413-422, 1996.
12. Fernandez M.F., D. Florescu, J. Kang, A. Y. Levy, D. Suciu, STRUDEL: A Website Management System. in *Proc. ACM SIGMOD Conf.*, pages 549-552, 1997.
13. Greco S., D. Saccà, C. Zaniolo. Datalog with choice and stratified negation: from $\mathcal{P}$ to $\mathcal{D}^p$. In *Proc. 2nd Int. Conf. on Database Theory (ICDT)*, pages 82-96, 1995.
14. Gyssens, M., J. Paradaens, D. Van Gucht, A Graph-Oriented Object Database Model, in *Proc. of the Ninth Symposium on Principles of Database Systems*, pages 417-424, 1990.
15. Hopcroft J., J. Ullman. *Introduction to Automata Theory, Languages and Computation*. Addison Wesley, 1980.
16. Konopnicki, D., O. Shmueli, W3QS: A Query System for the World-Wide-Web, in *Proc. Int. Conf. on Very Large Data Bases (VLDB)*, pages 54-65, 1995.
17. Mendelzon A., P.T. Wood, Finding Regular Simple Path in Graph Databases, in *SIAM Journal on Computing*, 24(6), pages 1235-1258, 1995.
18. Mendelzon A., G. Mihaila, T. Milo, Querying the World Wide Web, in *Journal of Digital Libraries*, pages 54-67, 1997.
19. Mendelzon A., T. Milo, Formal models of web queries, in *Proc. on the Symp. on Principles of Database Systems (PODS)*, pages 134-143, 1997.
20. Van den Bussche J, G. Vossen. An extension of path expression to simplify navigation in objects. In *Proc. Int. Conf. on Deductive and Object-Oriented Databases (DOOD)*, pages 267-282, 1993.
21. Yannakakis M., Graph-theoretic methods in database theory, in *Proc. of the Ninth Symposium on Principles of Database Systems*, pages 230-242, 1990.

Hierarchical Declustering Schemes
for Range Queries

Randeep Bhatia[1], Rakesh K. Sinha[1], and Chung-Min Chen[2]

[1] Bell Laboratories, Murray Hill, NJ 07974, USA,
{randeep, rks1}@research.bell-labs.com
[2] Telcordia Technologies, Inc., Morristown, NJ 07960, USA,
chungmin@research.telcordia.com

Abstract Declustering schemes have been widely used to speed up access time of multi-device storage systems (e.g. disk arrays) in modern geospatial applications. A declustering scheme distributes data items among multiple devices, thus enabling parallel I/O access and speeding up query response time. To date, efficient declustering schemes are only known for small values of M, where M is the number of devices. For large values of M, the search overhead to find an efficient scheme is prohibitive. In this paper, we present an efficient hierarchical technique for building declustering schemes for large values of M based on declustering schemes for small values of M. Using this technique, one may easily construct efficient declustering schemes for large values of M using any known good declustering schemes for small values of M. We analyze the performance of the declustering schemes generated by our technique in 2-dimension, giving tight asymptotic bounds on their response time. For example we show, in 2 dimension, that using optimal declustering schemes for M_1 and M_2 devices we can construct a scheme for $M_1 M_2$ devices whose response time is at most seven more than the optimal response time. Our technique generalizes to any d dimension. We also present simulation results to evaluate the performance of our scheme in practice.

1   Introduction

The data appetite of modern scientific and business applications is increasing with the growth in the density and capacity of secondary storage devices. Consider, for example, the discipline of remote-sensing databases, where data sensed by earth-orbiting satellites, is collected and stored. It is estimated that by year 2000, satellites deployed by NASA of United States alone will be transmitting 1 terabytes of data to earth each day [14].

While accommodating terabytes of storage space is no longer out of reach, efficient retrieval of the data in response to user queries remains a technical challenge. This challenge is mostly due to the large gap in processing speed

---

C. Zaniolo et al. (Eds.): EDBT 2000, LNCS 1777, pp. 525–537, 2000.
© Springer-Verlag Berlin Heidelberg 2000

between the processor (and on-chip memory) and the disk in current computer systems. While the power of CPU has doubled almost every 18 months, the access time of hard disks has improved only marginally in recent years [15]. Slow disk access time results in idle CPU cycles and thus longer response time to user queries. Unfortunately, there are inherent mechanical limitations in the current storage technology that limit the rate of improvement in the disk *seek time*—the time for the disk read/write head to move from one track to another where the requested data resides.

Declustering is a common technique to get around the problem of large disk access time. The idea of declustering is to distribute data blocks among multiple disk devices, so they can be retrieved in parallel (i.e. in parallel disk seeks). Various declustering schemes have been proposed in the literature for two-dimensional or multidimensional data [10,12,16,11,9,18,19,6,20,21,17,7,13,4]. The basic intuition of all schemes is to place data blocks, that are most likely to be accessed together in a user query, on different disks. Consequently, the data blocks can be fetched from the disks in parallel, thereby reducing the response time of the query.

Range queries are a common class of queries in many applications including multidimensional database, image and GIS applications. An efficient declustering scheme is critical to fast response time of range queries. A "good" declustering scheme must ensure that the data blocks requested by a range query are distributed on different disks.

With the recent advances in computing and storage technologies, it is imperative to find efficient declustering schemes for large number of disk devices [15]. In this context, we are talking about tens to a few thousands of disks. Traditionally, the aggregate bandwidth that can be harnessed from the parallel disks is restricted by the I/O bus bandwidth—the speed at which the data can be moved from the disk drives to the memory. The practical use of massive parallel disks is further restricted by the main memory capacity and processor power. However, recent technological trends have made the use of massive parallel disks viable:

1. High-speed I/O buses or links: Storage manufacturers are offering faster buses or switch-based serial lines. For example, both Fast SCSI and Fibre Channel Arbitrated-Loop provide close to 100MB/sec bandwidth, as opposed to 20MB/sec of traditional SCSI. In additional, the development of switch-based Storage Area Network promises even a higher operation rate.
2. Economic provision of high-speed processor and large memory: With the continuing drop in cost and improvement in performance/capacity, high-end processors and large memory are more affordable than ever. A 300 MHz Intel Pentium II (500MIPS) is now priced less than $2000. A typical Sun Ultra Enterprise Server contains 512MG to 1GB of memory. This trend allows large amount of data to be loaded simultaneously from the disks to the memory and quickly processed.
3. High-scale cluster computing architecture: Cluster servers aggregate computing and I/O power by connecting multiple computing nodes. Each node

typically contains a number of processors, a memory module, and an array of disks. The nodes are connected through high-speed (Gb/sec) switch-based network. This architecture allows build-up of a distributed I/O subsystem with a large number of disks from smaller disk enclosures. A good example is the NCR WorldMark cluster [1], which is configured with 32 nodes, with each node containing four PentiumPro processors and 41 disks (a total of 1312 disks !).

We refer the reader to [15] for a detailed description of the above trends.

In this paper, we propose a new declustering scheme which is based on a hierarchical technique of efficiently constructing declustering schemes for large values of M, the number of disks, given declustering schemes for small values of M. We show that the "efficacy" of the declustering scheme for large values of M is directly proportional to the "efficacy" of the declustering scheme for small values of M: one may efficiently construct good declustering schemes for large values of M, using any known good declustering schemes for small values of M. We support our claims on the performance of the hierarchical declustering scheme by simulation as well by tight mathematical analysis on the performance of the scheme. Due to lack of space we omit all our proofs. These can be found in the full version of the paper [5]

2   Problem Definition and Related Work

Consider a dataset organized as a grid of $N_x \times N_y$ tiles (i.e., N_x columns and N_y rows). Given M disks, a declustering scheme, $s : N_x \times N_y \to M$, assigns tile (x, y) to the disk numbered $s(x, y)$. A **range query** is a query that retrieves a rectangular set of tiles contained within the grid. Let $tile_i(s, Q)$, $i = 0, 1, \ldots, M - 1$, represent the number of tiles in Q that get assigned to disk i under scheme s (we may omit parameter s when it is clear from the context). We define the (nominal) **response time** of query Q under scheme s to be $RT(s, Q) = max_{0 \le i < M}\ tile_i(s, Q)$. One may consider the unit of response time to be the average disk access time (including seek, rotational, and transfer time) to retrieve a data block. Thus, the notion of response time indicates the expected I/O delay for answering the query. The problem, therefore, is how to devise a declustering scheme that would minimize the query response time.

An ideal declustering scheme would achieve, for each query Q, the **optimal response time** $ORT(Q) = \lceil |Q|/M \rceil$, where $|Q|$ is the number of tiles in Q. It has been proved that such a scheme, historically referred to as the *Strictly Optimal* (SO) scheme, does not exist in general, except for a few stringent cases [2]. The SO scheme serves as a lower bound against which the performance of all other schemes is measured.

In the rest of the paper we would not make any distinction between data "tiles" and data "points". That is we would denote a data tile by a data point.

2.1   Related Work

One of the earliest proposed scheme for data declustering is the Disk Modulo (DM) [10] scheme, which assigns tile (x, y) to disk number $(x + y)$ mod M. The Field Exclusive-Or (FX) [16] scheme assigns tile (x, y) to disk number $dec(bi(x) \oplus bi(y))$ mod M. Here $bi(x)$ is the binary representation of x, $\oplus$ is the bitwise exclusive-or operation, and $dec(z)$ is the decimal number corresponding to the binary representation z.

The Hilbert Curve Allocation Method (HCAM) [11] scheme imposes a linear ordering on the tiles in the grid and assigns disk numbers $0, 1, \ldots M - 1$ to the tiles in a round robin fashion according to the linear ordering. It was shown in [11] that, in general, HCAM gives better performance than previously know schemes, including DM and FX.

It was shown in [20] that the family of Cyclic Declustering (CD) schemes— a simple generalization of the Disk Modulo scheme [10]—outperforms HCAM. Given M disks, the CD schemes assign tile (x, y) to disk numbered $(x + H \cdot y)$ mod M, where H, called the *skip value*, is a pre-determined parameter. To find a good skip value, two heuristics-based algorithms were proposed [20], both outperforming HCAM. One algorithm (GFIB) is based on Fibonacci numbers, and the other (EXH) is based on an exhaustive search of the best skip values. Additional heuristics for searching for good skip values are given in [17]. Extensions of GFIB and EXH for higher dimensions are given in [21]. It was shown in [20,21] that EXH has average performance close to the *Strictly Optimal scheme* and it outperforms GFIB. However, EXH requires substantial computational overhead than GFIB in determining the skip values because of the nearly brute force search effort, which makes EXH practically infeasible for large values of M or k. Recently a declustering scheme based on "Golden Ratio Sequences" (GRS) was proposed by the authors [4]. It was shown that the GRS scheme consistently outperforms the GFIB scheme and is competitive with the EXH scheme, without requiring any additional computational overhead. Very recently Atallah and Prabhakar [3] have proposed a new declustering scheme under the restriction that M is a power of 2. Their scheme has been our motivation for designing the hierarchical declustering scheme. Our scheme is a generalization of the scheme proposed in [3]. Whenever M is a power of 2 our scheme is identical to the scheme in [3].

Finally, there are graph-based schemes that transform the declustering problem into well-known graph theory problems [12,18,6]. These schemes bear high computing complexity and are more suited for non-uniform data grids.

2.2   Our Contribution

We propose a novel declustering scheme which is based on a hierarchical technique of efficiently constructing d dimensional declustering schemes for large values of M, the number of disks, given declustering schemes for small values of M. We present tight upper and lower bounds on the performance of the scheme for $d = 2$, thus establishing that the scheme has a good performance if the underlying schemes for small values of M have good performance. Specifically we establish in 2-dimension that given base schemes for M_i disks ($1 \leq i \leq k$), we can construct a hierarchical scheme for $M = M_1 M_2 \ldots M_k$ disks such that the response time of any query under the hierarchical declustering scheme is at most $(2kl + 4k - 1)$ more than its optimal response time (Theorem 1). Here l is the worst case difference between the response time and optimal response time for any of the base schemes. We establish a matching lower bound for the case when M is a power of 2 (Theorem 3) thus showing that our analysis is tight. We also present simulation results that support our theoretical results on the performance of the hierarchical declustering scheme. Due to lack of space we omit all our proofs. These can be found in the full version of the paper [5]

3   The 2-Dim Hierarchical Declustering Scheme

We start with declustering schemes D_i for M_i disks ($1 \leq i \leq k$). Our goal is to devise a declustering scheme D for M disks, where M is the product of $M_1, M_2, \ldots, M_k$.

We first define the base-$(M_1, M_2, \ldots, M_k)$ representation of any integer between zero and M.

Definition 1. *For any integer $0 \leq X < M$, base-$(M_1, M_2, \ldots, M_k)$ representation of X is defined to be $[x_1, x_2, \ldots x_k]$ such that*

1. *For all i, $0 \leq x_i < M_i$*
2. $X = (M_2 M_3 \cdots M_k) x_1 + (M_3 M_4 \cdots M_k) x_2 + \cdots + (M_k) x_{k-1} + x_k$

This definition is a generalization of the standard decimal or binary representation.

The (2-dimensional) hierarchical declustering scheme is described in Figure 1. On Line 1, we compute the base-$(M_1, M_2, \ldots, M_k)$ representation of X. On line 2, we compute the base-$(M_k, M_{k-1}, \ldots, M_1)$ representation of Y. This roughly has the effect of computing the base-$(M_1, M_2, \ldots, M_k)$ representation of Y and reversing the digit string. From the properties of base representation, we know that $0 \leq x_i, y_i < M_i$. We apply the declustering scheme for each M_i on the (x_i, y_i) pair and treat the resulting value as the i-th digit in base-$(M_1, M_2, \ldots, M_k)$ representation of $D(X, Y)$. The intuition behind this scheme is that we compose the most significant digits of X with the least significant digits of Y. This roughly has the following effect: if two points (X, Y) and (W, Z) are assigned to the same disk then the size of the range query containing these two points, $|X - W| \cdot |Y - Z|$, is large.

We can prove that if we start with near-optimal base schemes D_i's then the resulting hierarchical scheme is also very good. For example, if we start with strictly optimal base schemes then the difference in response time and optimal response time is bounded by a small constant.

All our results assume that the base schemes are *permutation* schemes.

Hierarchical-two-dim $D(X, Y)$

COMMENT: $M = M_1 M_2 \cdots M_k$. Given declustering scheme D_i for disk M_i.
1   $X = X \bmod M; Y = Y \bmod M$
2   $[x_1, x_2, \ldots, x_k] = BASE(M_1, M_2, \ldots, M_k, X)$
3   $[y_k, y_{k-1}, \ldots, y_1] = BASE(M_k, M_{k-1}, \ldots, M_1, Y)$
4   for $i = 1$ to k
5       $z_i = D_i(x_i, y_i)$
6   $D(X, Y) = [z_1, z_2, \ldots, z_k]$ in base-$(M_1, M_2, \ldots, M_k)$ representation.
        $= (M_2 M_3 \cdots M_k) z_1 + (M_3 M_4 \cdots M_k) z_2 + \cdots + (M_k) z_{k-1} + z_k$
7   return $D(X, Y)$

Fig. 1. Two-dim Hierarchical scheme for $M = M_1 M_2 \cdots M_k$ disks.

Definition 2. *A declustering scheme on M disks is a row (resp. column) permutation scheme if any row (resp. column) of length M is a permutation of $\{1, 2, \ldots, M\}$. An equivalent definition is: two points in any row (resp. column) receive the same disk assignment iff their distance is an exact multiple of M.*

A permutation scheme is both row and column permutation scheme.

Examples of permutation schemes include Disk Modulo [10], Cyclic declustering [20], and GRS [4].

Definition 3. *The additive error of any declustering scheme is defined as the maximum (over all queries) difference between response time and optimal response time.*

Theorem 1. *If we start with permutation schemes D_i for M_i $(1 \le i \le k)$ such that the additive error of base scheme D_i is l_i then the additive error of the hierarchical scheme D (for $M_1 M_2 \cdots M_k$ disks) is at most $2(l_1 + l_2 + \cdots + l_k) + 4k - 1$.*

When each M_i is equal to two (so that M is a power of two) we can prove a better bound.

Theorem 2. *If each M_i is equal to two (so that M is a power of two) and each D_i is bitwise exclusive-or then the resulting hierarchical scheme has additive error at most $2 \log M - 1$.*

We can also prove that this bound is asymptotically tight.

Theorem 3. *For any $i \ge 0$, If $M = 2^{6 \cdot 2^i}$ then there exists a query Q such that $RT(Q, M) - ORT(Q, M) \ge \frac{\log M}{6} + 1$.*

Suppose we start with near-optimal or optimal declustering schemes when number of disks is at most p, for some (small) integer p. Let P be the set of integers all of whose prime factors are at most p. Our technique enables us to construct a scheme for any $M \in P$. If M has a prime factor larger than p, one possibility is to use a declustering scheme for M' disks, where $M' < M$ and $M' \in P$. In this case Theorem 1 gives a bound on the additive error $RT(D, Q) - \left\lceil \frac{Q}{M'} \right\rceil$, whereas we want to bound $RT(D, Q) - \left\lceil \frac{Q}{M} \right\rceil$. This introduces an extra multiplicative error of $\left\lceil \frac{Q}{M'} \right\rceil / \left\lceil \frac{Q}{M} \right\rceil \approx \frac{M}{M'}$. The next theorem bounds this multiplicative error term.

Theorem 4. *(C. Pomerance) Let $p > 2$ and P be the set of integers all of whose prime factors are at most p. Then for all M, there exists an $M' \leq M$ such that $M' \in P$ and*

$$\frac{M}{M'} < 1 + \frac{1}{p}.$$

Discussion: Together Theorems 1, and 4 define the trade-off in choosing the appropriate p. Selecting a large p implies larger preprocessing cost for finding near-optimal "base" schemes, but the advantages are decreased multiplicative error (Theorem 4) and decreased additive error (Theorem 1).

4   The Multidimensional Hierarchical Declustering Scheme

Let us assume a d-dimensional space with d co-ordinates $X_1, X_2, X_3, \ldots, X_d$. We assume the existence of d-dimensional (permutation) base schemes D_i for M_i disks ($1 \leq i \leq k$). Figure 2. presents an algorithm for the multi-dimensional generalization of the hierarchical scheme.

Definition 4. *A permutation scheme in d dimension for M disks is a declustering scheme such that in every $M^{1/(d-1)} \times M^{1/(d-1)} \times \ldots M^{1/(d-1)}$ cube A there are M distinct disks and every $d - 1$-dim. hyperplane of A which is perpendicular to the other d dimension consist of distinct M disks. For example in 3 dimension permutation scheme there are M disks in every cube of side $M^{1/2}$ and whose every X, Y and Y, Z and Z, X plane consists of M distinct disks.*

Comparison to Atallah-Prabhakar's Scheme

Atallah and Prabhakar [3] proposed a declustering scheme when M is a power of two. They defined their scheme recursively in terms of "swaps" performed on smaller instances of the scheme. We can show that there scheme is special case of our scheme when all M_i's are equal to two. Thus our scheme is a generalization of their scheme.

Our generalization enables us to trade off preprocessing cost of finding good base schemes with substantially better performance of the hierarchical scheme. As we pointed out, in the discussion preceding Theorem 3, the benefits of starting with base schemes for many different disk numbers can be quite significant.

Hierarchical-multi-dim $D(X,Y)$

COMMENT: $M = M_1 M_2 \cdots M_k$. Given declustering scheme D_i for disk M_i.
The d co-ordinates are $X_1, X_2, X_3, \ldots, X_d$.

1 for $i = 1$ to d
2     $X_i = X_i \bmod M^{1/(d-1)}$
3 for $i = 1$ to $d - 1$
4     $[x_{i1}, x_{i2}, \ldots, x_{ik}] = BASE(M_1^{1/(d-1)}, M_2^{1/(d-1)}, \ldots, M_k^{1/(d-1)}, X_i)$
5 $[x_{d1}, x_{d2}, \ldots, x_{dk}] = BASE(M_k^{1/(d-1)}, M_{k-1}^{1/(d-1)}, \ldots, M_1^{1/(d-1)}, X_d)$
6 for $i = 1$ to k
7     $z_i = D_i(x_{1i}, x_{2i}, \ldots, x_{di})$
8 $D(X_1, X_2, \ldots, X_d) = [z_1, z_2, \ldots, z_k]$ in base-$(M_1, M_2, \ldots, M_k)$ representation
        $= (M_2 M_3 \cdots M_k) z_1 + (M_3 M_4 \cdots M_k) z_2 + \cdots + (M_k) z_{k-1} + z_k$
9 return $D(X_1, X_2, \ldots, X_d)$

Fig. 2. Multi-dim Hierarchical scheme for $M = M_1 M_2 \cdots M_k$ disks.

5 Geometric Intuition for the Schemes

In this section we will present a geometric intuition for the hierarchical permutation declustering scheme. Without loss of generality we will assume in this section that a declustering scheme D for M disks in 2-dim. is a $M \times M$ grid which represents the declustering scheme for points in the range $0 \le X < M$ and $0 \le Y < M$. In general, the point (X, Y) gets assigned to point $(X \bmod M, Y \bmod M)$ in this grid. Let $M = M_1 M_2$ and D_1, D_2 be permutation schemes for M_1, M_2 respectively. The hierarchical declustering scheme D for M has the following geometric interpretation. Let $c_1, c_2 \ldots c_{M_2}$ be M_2 copies of the scheme D_1 arranged in a vertical strip as shown in the figure below.

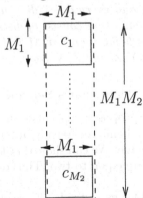

We view the disks in this vertical strip as meta-disks. Each meta-disk is replaced with a row of M_2 disks, resulting in an $M_1 M_2 \times M_1 M_2$ grid. Meta-disk $i, 0 \le i \le M_1 - 1$ is replaced with a permutation of disks $\{(i-1)M_2, (i-1)M_2 +$

$1, \ldots iM_2 - 1\}$. The disks within a meta-disk i in a particular copy c_j (of the scheme D_1) are arranged in a permutation which is determined as follows. Let R_j be the j-th row of the scheme D_2. We add $(i - 1)M_2$ to each component of R_j, thus yielding the permutation of the disks within meta-disk i, in copy c_j. Note that when we replace the meta-disks by their corresponding disks we get a permutation declustering scheme D for M. Let X, Y be a point in the grid for D. Note that this point is in a meta-disk which has coordinates $(X/M_2, Y \bmod M_1)$ in the D_1 scheme and this meta-disk is in the Y/M_1 copy of the scheme D_1 in the vertical strip. Finally this point is in the $X \bmod M_2$ component of the row of this meta-disk. Therefore we have:

$$D(X, Y) = D_1(X/M_2, Y \bmod M_1)M_2 + D_2(X \bmod M_2, Y/M_1).$$

Recall that for $M = m_1 m_2 \ldots m_k$, where each of the schemes D_i for m_i disks is a permutation scheme, the hierarchical scheme constructs the scheme D for M disks. Let us rewrite $M = M_1 M_2$, where $M_1 = m_1$ and $M_2 = m_2 \ldots m_k$. Then it is easily seen that the geometric construction above yields the hierarchical declustering scheme in a recursive representation.

The hierarchical scheme is generalized to higher dimensions as follows. Recall the definition of permutation scheme in higher dimensions (Definition 4). For ease of presentation in the following we will assume the number of disks $M = (M')^{d-1}$ and $M_i = (M_i')^{d-1}$. Let as before $M = M_1 M_2$ and D_1, D_2 be permutation schemes for M_1, M_2 respectively in d dimensions. The hierarchical declustering scheme D for M disks in d dimensions has the following geometric interpretation. Let $c_1, c_2 \ldots c_{M_2'}$ be M_2' copies of the scheme D_1 arranged in a vertical d dimensional tunnel as before. As before we view the disks in this vertical tunnel as meta-disks. Each meta-disk consists of $(M_2')^{d-1}$ disks arranged in a $d - 1$ dimensional hyperplane which is perpendicular to the Y axis. Meta-disk $i, 0 \le i \le (M_1')^{(d-1)} - 1$ consists of disks

$$(i - 1)(M_2')^{(d-1)}, (i - 1)(M_2')^{(d-1)} + 1, \ldots i(M_2')^{(d-1)} - 1.$$

The permutation of the disks within a meta-disk i in a particular copy c_j is determined as before by the $d-1$ dimensional hyperplane with coordinates $Y = j$, in the scheme D_2. Thus it can be shown that the d dimensional hierarchical declustering scheme (assuming that the d dimensions are $X, Y, Z_1, Z_2 \ldots Z_{d-2}$) can be represented recursively as follows.

$$\begin{aligned} D(X, Y, Z_1, Z_2 \ldots Z_{d-2}) = {} & D_1(X/M_2', Y \bmod M_1', Z_1/M_2', \ldots Z_{d-2}/M_2')(M_2')^{d-1} \\ & + D_2(X \bmod M_2', Y/M_1', Z_1 \bmod M_2', \ldots Z_{d-2} \bmod M_2'). \end{aligned}$$

Thus the d dimensional hierarchical declustering scheme can be mapped to a generalized 2 dimensional hierarchical scheme, where we define a $d - 1$ dimension vector (hyperplane) $X' = (X, Z_1, Z_2 \ldots Z_{d-2})$, such that $D(X', Y) = D_1(X'/M_2', Y \bmod M_1')(M_2')^{(d-1)} + D_2(X' \bmod M_2', Y/M_1')$.

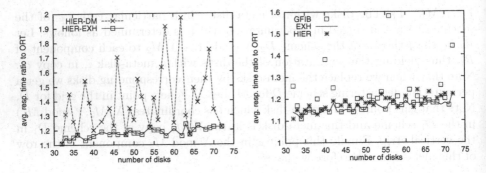

Fig. 3. HIER-DM vs. HIER-EXH   **Fig. 4.** HIER, GFIB and EXH. Grid size: 32×32.

6   Performance Evaluation

In [20,21], Prabhakar et al. used simulation involving various query loads to show that cyclic declustering schemes outperform previously known schemes (including HCAM, DM, and FX). For this reason and lack of space, we shall compare the hierarchical declustering scheme (HIER) only to cyclic declustering schemes in the presentation of our simulation results.

We use average response time ratio (to the optimum) as the major metric for performance comparison. There are slightly different ways to define "average response time ratio" [20,21,8]. However, our simulation results have shown that the relative performance among the schemes is not sensitive to the specific metric being used. Thus, we will only show the simulation results in the "average-by-all" cost metric. Given a scheme f and fixing the grid size and M, the "average-by-all" metric computes, for all query Q in the grid, the ratio $RT(f, Q)/ORT(Q)$, and then takes the average among the ratios. We have also excluded all queries with an area of 1 in the calculation, so the performance is not exaggerated due to the optimality of these trivial queries.

6.1   Two-Dimensional Data

First, we demonstrate the importance of choosing a good base scheme for HIER. Two versions of hierarchical schemes, HIER-DM and HIER-EXH, are tested: the former uses the disk modulo [10] as the base scheme; the latter uses EXH [20] as the base scheme. We construct hierarchical schemes for $M = 32 \ldots 72$, using base schemes for $M \leq 31$. Figure 3 shows the results for a 32×32 grid. As expected, HIER-DM gives poor performance in comparison to HIER-EXH because the former uses a poorer base scheme. In the following, the HIER scheme refers to HIER-EXH.

Figure 4 compares the performance of HIER, EXH, and the heuristic-based GFIB scheme [20] for a 32×32 grid. For evaluation purpose, we have also extended the search of EXH schemes to 72 disks. This allows us to validate

HIER's performance: its response time ratio is close to that of EXH, for M between 32 and 72. The performance of GFIB is less consistent, showing many peaks from the performance of EXH and HIER.

Figure 5 extends the comparison to 500 disks. Only GFIB and HIER are included in this experiment. The exhaustive search overhead of EXH has prohibited us from trying beyond 72 disks. For HIER, we take the EXH schemes for $M \leq 72$ as the building blocks. Thus, HIER is evaluated for every M between 32 and 500, except those that contain a prime factor greater than 72. It can be seen that while many of GFIB's data points (about 70%) cluster with the curve of HIER, there are also a remarkable number of points (about 30%) that deviates from the cluster. Overall, HIER provides a performance within 1.28 of the optimal response time, whereas GFIB may reach as high as 1.7. In addition, we have found that, for HIER, the worst deviation from the optimal response time is no greater than 3 and the average deviation is no greater than 0.46, for all values of M tested. The corresponding numbers are 5 (worst deviation) and 1.25 (average deviation) for GFIB. We have also tested with various grid sizes and the results are similar (see [5]).

6.2   Three-Dimensional Data

We started with base schemes for $M = 4, 9$, and 25, where each base scheme assigns M disks to a cube of side-length $\sqrt{M}$. It works as follows: Let $M' = \sqrt{M}$. Let $f(x, y, z)$, $0 \leq x, y, z \leq M' - 1$, denote the disk number assigned to point (x, y, z). First, assign all M distinct numbers to the horizontal plane $z = 0$. Then assign disks to plane $z = i$, where $i = 1, \ldots, M' - 1$ as $f(x, y, z) = f(x + h_1 \bmod M', y + h_2 \bmod M', z - 1)$, where h_1 and h_2 are some constants. That is, plane $z = i$ is a shift of plane $z = i - 1$ by a vector $(h_1, h_2, 0)$. We have set $(h_1, h_2) = (1, 1), (2, 1)$, and $(3, 2)$ for $M = 4, 9$ and 25, respectively. These base schemes are permutation schemes since in the cube every XY or YZ or ZX plane contains distinct disk numbers.

We experimented with 3D HIER schemes for $M \leq 1000$ that can be constructed based on the above three base schemes. Specifically, the values of M are: 16, 36, 64, 81, 100, 144, 225, 324, 400, 900 (note each of them can be expressed as x^2 where x is a product that contains only 2, 3, and 5 as factors).

For comparison purpose, we also include simulation results of 3D GFIB and EXH schemes [21] for these values of M. However, due to the search overhead for for 3D EXH schemes, we only have results for $M = 16, 36$ and 64.

Figure 6 shows the simulation results for a $32 \times 32 \times 32$ grid. To save time, we have computed the statistics based on a set of $32^3 = 32768$ randomly generated queries (as opposed to an enumeration of $(C_2^{33})^3$ queries!). For $M \leq 64$, all schemes have comparable performance: the difference is less than 0.3 from each other. As M increases beyond 64, GFIB's response time ratio increases sharply, whereas HIER's response time ratio increases at a much more moderate rate. For HIER, the worst and average deviation from the optimal response time are 15 and within 2.10, respectively; for GFIB the numbers are 42 and within 5.83.

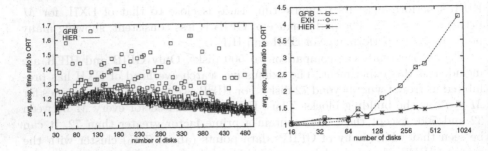

Fig. 5. HIER and GFIB. Grid size: 32×32.

Fig. 6. Performance of HIER, GFIB, and EXH. Cost metric: average-by-all. Grid size: $32 \times 32 \times 32$.

7   Conclusion

We propose a novel declustering scheme which is based on a hierarchical technique of efficiently constructing d dimensional declustering schemes for large values of M, the number of disks, given declustering schemes for small values of M. We present tight upper and lower bounds on the performance of the scheme in 2-dimension, thus establishing that the scheme has a good performance if the underlying schemes for small values of M have good performance. We also present extensive simulation results that support our theoretical results on the performance of the hierarchical declustering scheme.

Acknowledgements

We are grateful to Carl Pomerance and and Amin Shokrollahi for discussion. The proof of Theorem 4 is due to Carl Pomerance.

References

1. NCR WorldMark/Teradata 1 TB TPC-D Executive Summary. available from http://www.tpc.org/.
2. K. Abdel-Ghaffar and A. E. Abbadi. Optimal allocation of two-dimensional data. In *Proc. of 13th Int. Conf. on Database Theory*, 1997.
3. M.J. Atallah and S. Prabhakar. (Almost) optimal parallel block access for range queries. Manuscript. Dept. of Comp. Sci., Purdue University, May 1999.
4. R. Bhatia, R. K. Sinha, and C. M. Chen. Declustering using golden ratio sequences. Proc. 16th International Conference on Data Engineering (ICDE), 2000.
5. R. Bhatia and R. Sinha and C. Chen. Hierarchical declustering schemes for range queries. www.cs.umd.edu/~randeep/decluster-hier.ps. 1999 Manuscript.
6. C. Chang, B. Moon, A. Acharya, C. Shock, A. Sussman, and J. Saltz. Titan: a high-performance remote-sensing database. In *Proc. of 13th Int. Conf. on Data Engineering*, 1997.

7. C.M. Chen and R. Sinha. Raster-spatial data declustering revisited: an interactive navigation perspective. In *Proc. of 15th Int. Conf. on Data Engineering*, 1999.
8. C.Y. Chen and C.C. Chang. On GDM allocation method for partial range queries. *Information Systems*, 1992.
9. L.T. Chen and D. Rotem. Declustering objects for visualization. In *Proc. of 19th Int. Conf. on Very Large Data Bases*, 1993.
10. H.C. Du and J.S. Sobolewski. Disk allocation for cartesian product files on multiple disk systems. *ACM Trans. Database Systems*, pages 82–101, 1982.
11. C. Faloutsos and P. Bhagwat. Declustering using fractals. In *Proc. of 2nd Int. Conf. on Parallel and Distributed Information Systems*, 1993.
12. M.T. Fang, R.C.T. Lee, and C.C. Chang. The idea of declustering and its applications. In *Proc. of 12th Int. Conf. on Very Large Data Bases*, 1986.
13. H. Ferhatosmanoglu and D. Agrawal. Concentric hyperspaces and disk allocations for fast parallel range searching. In *Proc. of 15th Int. Conf. on Data Engineering*, 1999.
14. N.D. Gershon and C.G. Miller. Dealing with the data deluge. *IEEE Spectrum*, 1993.
15. K. Keeton, D.A. Patterson, and J.M. Hellerstein. A case for intelligent disks (idisks). *SIGMOD Record*, 27(3), 1998.
16. M.H. Kim and S. Pramanik. Optimal file distribution for partial match retrieval. In *Proc. of ACM Int. Conf. on Management of Data*, 1988.
17. S. Kou, M. Winslett, Y. Cho, and J. Lee. New GDM-based declustering methods for parallel range queries. In *Proc. of Int. Database Engineering and Applications Symposium*, 1999.
18. D.-R. Liu and S. Shekhar. A similarity graph-based approach to declustering problems and its applications towards parallelizing grid files. In *Proc. of 11th Int. Conf. on Data Engineering*, 1995.
19. B. Moon and A. Acharya and J. Saltz. Study of scalable declustering algorithms for parallel grid files. In *Proc. of 10th Int. Parallel Processing Symposium*, 1996.
20. S. Prabhakar, K. Abdel-Ghaffar, D. Agrawal, and A. E. Abbadi. Cyclic allocation of two-dimensional data. In *Proc. of 14th Int. Conf. on Data Engineering*, 1998.
21. S. Prabhakar, K. Abdel-Ghaffar, D. Agrawal, and A.E. Abbadi. Efficient retrieval of multidimensional datasets through parallel I/O. In *Proc. of 5th Int. Conf. on High Performance Computing*, 1998.

Author Index